IFIP Advances in Information and Communication Technology

628

Editor-in-Chief

Kai Rannenberg, Goethe University Frankfurt, Germany

Editorial Board Members

IFIP – The International Federation for Information Processing

IFIP was founded in 1960 under the auspices of UNESCO, following the first World Computer Congress held in Paris the previous year. A federation for societies working in information processing, IFIP's aim is two-fold: to support information processing in the countries of its members and to encourage technology transfer to developing nations. As its mission statement clearly states:

IFIP is the global non-profit federation of societies of ICT professionals that aims at achieving a worldwide professional and socially responsible development and application of information and communication technologies.

IFIP is a non-profit-making organization, run almost solely by 2500 volunteers. It operates through a number of technical committees and working groups, which organize events and publications. IFIP's events range from large international open conferences to working conferences and local seminars.

The flagship event is the IFIP World Computer Congress, at which both invited and contributed papers are presented. Contributed papers are rigorously refereed and the rejection rate is high.

As with the Congress, participation in the open conferences is open to all and papers may be invited or submitted. Again, submitted papers are stringently refereed.

The working conferences are structured differently. They are usually run by a working group and attendance is generally smaller and occasionally by invitation only. Their purpose is to create an atmosphere conducive to innovation and development. Refereeing is also rigorous and papers are subjected to extensive group discussion.

Publications arising from IFIP events vary. The papers presented at the IFIP World Computer Congress and at open conferences are published as conference proceedings, while the results of the working conferences are often published as collections of selected and edited papers.

IFIP distinguishes three types of institutional membership: Country Representative Members, Members at Large, and Associate Members. The type of organization that can apply for membership is a wide variety and includes national or international societies of individual computer scientists/ICT professionals, associations or federations of such societies, government institutions/government related organizations, national or international research institutes or consortia, universities, academies of sciences, companies, national or international associations or federations of companies.

More information about this series at http://www.springer.com/series/6102

Ilias Maglogiannis · John Macintyre ·
Lazaros Iliadis (Eds.)

Artificial Intelligence Applications and Innovations

AIAI 2021 IFIP WG 12.5
International Workshops

5G-PINE 2021, AI-BIO 2021, DAAI 2021,
DARE 2021, EEAI 2021, and MHDW 2021
Hersonissos, Crete, Greece, June 25–27, 2021
Proceedings

 Springer

Editors
Ilias Maglogiannis (iD)
University of Piraeus
Piraeus, Greece

John Macintyre
University of Sunderland
Sunderland, UK

Lazaros Iliadis (iD)
Democritus University of Thrace
Xanthi, Greece

ISSN 1868-4238   ISSN 1868-422X (electronic)
IFIP Advances in Information and Communication Technology
ISBN 978-3-030-79159-9   ISBN 978-3-030-79157-5 (eBook)
https://doi.org/10.1007/978-3-030-79157-5

This Springer imprint is published by the registered company Springer Nature Switzerland AG
The registered company address is: Gewerbestrasse 11, 6330 Cham, Switzerland

Preface

Artificial Intelligence (AI) continues to advance, following extreme development rhythms in the new era of the 21st century. It has already made its way into our daily lives in various forms. It is estimated that more than 80 billion USD have been invested by car industries for the design and development of autonomous self-driving vehicles. AI technologies like *Google Duplex* are accomplishing real-world conversations and arrangements with humans, using *Deep Neural Networks* (e.g., Google voice search, Wavenet). It is estimated by the International Data Corporation, a global provider of market intelligence, that investments in AI business globally will reach up to 110 billion USD by 2024. AI is a major part of the Fourth Industrial Revolution, together with other technologies like the *Internet of Things, Genetic Engineering, Quantum Computing*, and its impact in the evolution of our post-modern societies in various domains is huge and growing. On the other hand, there are major areas of ethical concern for our societies, namely privacy, surveillance, bias-discrimination, and elimination of entire job categories. Moreover, serious questions arise on the superiority and indispensability of human judgment on important aspect of life. In other words, "Can smart machines outthink our human judgment?".

The *17th International Conference on Artificial Intelligence Applications and Innovations* (AIAI 2021) offered insight into all timely challenges related to technical, legal, and ethical aspects of intelligent systems and their applications. New algorithms and potential prototypes employed in diverse domains were introduced.

AIAI is a mature international scientific conference series that has been held all over the world and it is well established in the scientific area of AI. Its history is long and very successful, following and propagating the evolution of intelligent systems.

The first event was organized in Toulouse, France, in 2004. Since then, it has had a continuous and dynamic presence as a major global, but mainly European, scientific event. It has been organized in China, Greece, Cyprus, Australia, and France. It has always been technically supported by the International Federation for Information Processing (IFIP) and more specifically by Working Group 12.5, which is interested in AI applications.

Following tradition, this Springer volume belongs to the IFIP AICT series. It contains the original research papers that were accepted, following a peer review process, for oral presentation at six (out of eight workshops) organized as satellite events under the framework of AIAI 2021:

- The 10th Mining Humanistic Data Workshop (MHDW)
- The 6th Workshop on 5G-Putting Intelligence to the Network Edge (5G-PINE 2021)
- The 1st Workshop on Defense Applications of AI (DAAI 2021)
- The 1st Workshop on Energy Efficiency and Artificial Intelligence (EEAI 2021)
- The 1st Workshop on Distributed AI for REsource-Constrained Platforms (DARE 2021)

- The 1st Workshop on Artificial Intelligence in Biomedical Engineering and Informatics (AI-BIO 2021)

In addition, this volume contains the abstracts of the presentations given by the invited speakers at the 1st Workshop on AI and Ethics (AIETH 2021), coordinated by Professor John Macintyre, University of Sunderland, UK.

The workshops were held during June 25–27, 2021, in Greece. The diverse nature of papers presented demonstrates the vitality of AI algorithms and approaches. It certainly proves the very wide range of AI applications and it promotes the timely advances in this area, in both theory and applications.

The response of the international scientific community to the AIAI 2021 workshops call for papers was more than satisfactory, with 72 papers initially submitted. All papers were peer reviewed by at least two independent academic referees. Where needed, a third referee was consulted to resolve any potential conflicts. A total of 35 papers (48.61% of the submitted manuscripts) were accepted to be published as full papers (12 pages long) in the proceedings. Owing to the high quality of the submissions, the Program Committees of the workshops decided that they should accept 5 more papers to be published as short papers (10 pages long).

June 2021

Ilias Maglogiannis
Lazaros Iliadis
John MacIntyre

Organization

Executive Committee

General Chairs

Ilias Maglogiannis	University of Piraeus, Greece
John Macintyre	University of Sunderland, UK

Program Co-chairs

Lazaros Iliadis	Democritus University of Thrace, Greece
Xiao-Jun Wu	Jiangnan University, China
Petia Koprinkova	Bulgarian Academy of Sciences, Bulgaria

Honorary Co-chairs

Plamen Angelov	Lancaster University, UK
Vera Kurkova	Czech Academy of Sciences, Czech Republic

Advisory Chairs

Pietro Lio	University of Cambridge, UK
Barbara Hammer	University of Bielefeld, Germany
Costas Iliopoulos	King's College London, UK

Publication and Publicity Chair

Antonis Papaleonidas	Democritus University of Thrace, Greece

Liaison Co-chairs

Ioannis Chochliouros	Hellenic Telecommunication Organization (OTE), Greece
Panagiotis Kikiras	European Defence Agency, Belgium

Special Sessions/Tutorials Co-chairs

Dimitrios Kalles	Hellenic Open University, Greece
Dimitrios Kosmopoulos	University of Patras, Greece
Kostantinos Delibasis	University of Thessaly, Greece

Steering Committee

Ilias Maglogiannis	University of Piraeus, Greece
Plamen Angelov	Lancaster University, UK
Lazaros Iliadis	Democritus University of Thrace, Greece

Workshops Co-chairs

Christos Makris	University of Patras, Greece
Katia Kermanidis	Ionian University, Greece
Phivos Mylonas	Ionian University, Greece
Spyros Sioutas	University of Patras, Greece

Program Committee

Georgios Alexandridis	University of the Aegean, Greece
Serafín Alonso Castro	University of Leon, Spain
Ioannis Anagnostopoulos	University of Thessaly, Greece
Costin Badica	University of Craiova, Romania
Giacomo Boracchi	Politecnico di Milano, Italy
Francisco Carvalho	Polytechnic Institute of Tomar, Portugal
Diego Casado-Mansilla	Polytechnic School of the University of Alcalá, Spain
Ioannis Chamodrakas	National and Kapodistrian University of Athens, Greece
Kostantinos Delibasis	University of Thessaly, Greece
Konstantinos Demertzis	Democritus University of Thrace, Greece
Georgios Drakopoulos	Ionian University, Greece
Mauro Gaggero	National Research Council of Italy, Italy
Eleonora Giunchiglia	University of Oxford, UK
Peter Hajek	University of Pardubice, Czech Republic
Giannis Haralabopoulos	University of Nottingham, UK
Lazaros Iliadis	Democritus University of Thrace, Greece
Andreas Kanavos	Ionian University, Greece
Nikos Karacapilidis	University of Patras, Greece
Petros Kefalas	CITY College, International Faculty of the University of Sheffield, Greece
Katia Kermanidis	Ionian University, Greece
Petia Koprinkova-Hristova	Bulgarian Academy of Sciences, Bulgaria
Stelios Krinidis	Centre for Research and Technology Hellas, Greece
Florin Leon	Technical University of Iasi, Romania
Aristidis Likas	University of Ioannina, Greece
Pietro Liò	University of Cambridge, UK
Ioannis Livieris	University of Patras, Greece
Doina Logofătu	Frankfurt University of Applied Sciences, Germany
Ilias Maglogiannis	University of Piraeus, Greece
Goerge Magoulas	Birkbeck, University of London, UK
Christos Makris	University of Patras, Greece
Mario Malcangi	University of Milan, Italy
Andreas Menychtas	University of Piraeus, Greece
Vangelis Metsis	Texas State University, USA
Nikolaos Mitianoudis	Democritus University of Thrace, Greece
Antonio Moran	University of Leon, Spain

Contents

10th Mining Humanistic Data Workshop (MHDW 2021)

6th Workshop on "5G – Putting Intelligence to the Network Edge" (5G-PINE 2021)

5G-PINE 2021 Workshop

The 6th Workshop on 5G-Putting Intelligence to the Network Edge (5G-PINE 2021) follows on the great success and the wider impact of its predecessors. The workshop was established and organized as a way to disseminate knowledge obtained from actual 5G EU-funded projects as well as from any other research activity in the wider thematic area of "5G Innovative Activities – Putting Intelligence to the Network Edge", and with the aim of focusing upon Artificial Intelligence (AI) in modern 5G-oriented telecommunications infrastructures.

Based on the selected research papers, we are confident that 5G-PINE 2021 will have had a strong impact on the broader context of AIAI 2021 (the conference which hosted the workshop). The preparatory work was mainly driven by the organizational effort and the dynamic coordination and supervision of Dr. Ioannis P. Chochliouros (Hellenic Telecommunications Organization (OTE), Greece), with the support of Dr. Latif Ladid (President of IPv6 Forum and researcher at the University of Luxembourg, Luxembourg), Dr. George Lyberopoulos (COSMOTE Mobile Telecommunications S. A., Greece), Mr. Daniele Porcu (ENEL Global Infrastructure and Networks S.r.l., Italy, and coordinator of the 5G-PPP project "Smart5Grid"), Professor Pavlos Lazaridis (University of Huddersfield, UK), Dr. Zaharias Zaharis (Aristotle University of Thessaloniki, Greece), Mr. Uwe Herzog (EURESCOM GmbH, Germany, and coordinator of the H2020 project "5G-DRIVE"), Dr. Tao Chen (VTT Technical Research Center of Finland, Finland), Dr. Slawomir Kukliński (Orange Polska and Warsaw University of Technology, Poland), Dr. Lechosław Tomaszewski (Orange Polska, Poland), Mr. Charalambos Mitsis (SmartNet S.A., Greece), Dr. Ioannis Neokosmidis (inCITES Consulting S.A., Luxembourg), Professor Nancy Alonistioti (National and Kapodistrian University of Athens, Greece), Dr. Monique Calisti (Martel Innovate GmbH, Switzerland), and Mrs. Kai Zhang (Martel Innovate GmbH, Switzerland).

Along with the above members of the Workshop Organizing Committee, the entire process has also been supported by more than 100 European experts, several of whom come from the relevant EU-funded H2020/5G-PPP projects "5G-DRIVE", "5G-VICTORI", and "Smart5Grid" as well as from the H2020-MCSA-ITN "MOTOR-5G" project. These projects have formed the "core" of the corresponding effort towards realizing a "joint" 5G-PINE workshop, which is purely 5G oriented. From the 24 papers originally submitted for consideration, 13 were finally accepted as full papers (an acceptance rate of 54%) due to the high quality of the works and, *most importantly*, due to their strong relevance to ongoing EU-funded research activities – especially the H2020/5G-PPP framework. The accepted papers promote important innovation aspects from current – and, in most cases, already validated and tested – 5G research activities, thus "harnessing" incentives for growth in the market sector.

This year's workshop promoted, *inter alia*, the context of modern 5G network infrastructures and of related innovative services in a complex and highly heterogeneous underlying Radio Access Network (RAN) ecosystem, strongly enhanced by the inclusion of cognitive capabilities and intelligence features, with the aim of improving network management. Furthermore, based upon the well-known Self-Organizing

Network (SON) functionalities, 5G-PINE 2021 promoted network planning and optimization processes through AI-based tools, which are able to smartly process input data from the environment and come up with knowledge that can be formalized in terms of models and/or structured metrics, in order to "depict" the network behavior at a satisfactory level. This allows us to gain in-depth and detailed knowledge about the whole underlying 5G ecosystem, understand hidden patterns, data structures and relationships, and, ultimately, use them for more efficient network management.

5G-PINE 2021 also supported delivery of intelligence directly to the network's edge, by exploiting the emerging paradigms of Network Functions Virtualisation (NFV), Software Defined Networking (SDN), Network Slicing, and Edge Cloud Computing. Moreover, it supported the promotion of rich virtualization and multi-tenant capabilities, optimally deployed close to the end-user. There was specific interest in the original scope of the H2020 **"5G-DRIVE"** project promoting cooperation between the EU and China, especially in terms of discussing the proposed V2X communications framework for the selected use cases dealing with Green Light Optimised Speed Advisory (GLOSA) and Intelligent Intersection, thus offering multiple opportunities for market growth. In addition, taking into account a "combined" conceptual approach in the automotive and the aviation sectors structured upon the same conceptual basis of the 5G System (5GS), various interactions and/or potential interdependencies between automotive, aviation, and 5G ecosystems were examined in a "joint" approach covering both the "5G-DRIVE" and the "5G!Drones" projects.

Moreover, the thematic context of the workshop covered the progress of the ongoing 5G-PPP/H2020 **"5G-VICTORI"** project, aiming at conducting large scale 5G network trials for advanced vertical use cases focusing on transportation, energy, media, and factories of the future, by leveraging and exploiting existing facilities. Mobile Edge Computing (MEC) has been identified as a cornerstone network capability for the delivery of the required performance for a significant number of vertical industries, indicatively, for the mission critical services of the railway industry, for the data-demanding services of modern Content Delivery Networks (CDNs), for the precision-critical services of the factories of the future, and many more. In this scope, three papers coming from the latest "5G-VICTORI" progressive effort were accepted: (i) a paper about future railway communications requirements "driving" 5G deployments, towards establishing Future Railway Mobile Communication System (FRMCS) services along with experimentation facilities for testing and evaluation; (ii) a paper proposing a prototype 5G/IoT implementation for transforming a legacy facility to a smart factory; and (iii) a paper describing an approach for optimizing media streaming services in mobile environments by utilizing 5G, including mmWave high speed data links, 5G Edge Computing, and relevant state-of-the-art media streaming standards (such as NBMP and MPEG SAND).

Another pillar of 5G-PINE 2021 was the innovative background of the ongoing 5G-PPP/H2020 **"Smart5Grid"** project, where emphasis has been put both on the description of the corresponding project objectives for the demonstration of 5G solutions to serve smart energy grids and on the description of four fundamental use cases coming from the energy vertical industry that may have a significant impact on the broader 5G market sector.

Last but not least, 5G-PINE 2021 also covered the framework promoted by the ongoing H2020-MCSA-ITN **"MOTOR-5G"** project, which focuses on embedding artificial intelligence into 5G communication systems for the smarter use of network-generated data, the automated enabling of network operators and service providers to adapt to changes in traffic patterns, security risks, and user behavior, thus paving the way towards safe and reliable next-generation wireless ecosystems.

The accepted papers focus upon several innovative findings coming directly from modern European research in the area, that is from nine 5G-PPP/H2020 projects coming from phases 2 and 3 ("5G-DRIVE", "5G-VICTORI", "Smart5Grid", "5G-PHOS", "MonB5G", "MARSAL", "5G!Drones", "5G-VINNI", and "Affordable5G") and three H2020 projects ("RESISTO", "FASTER" and "TYPHON"), also implicating for 5G beneficial uses, per case. All the above projects cover a wide variety of technical and business aspects and explicitly promote options for growth and development in the respective market(s). All accepted papers were fully aligned to the objectives of the 5G-PINE 2021 scope and purely introduced innovative features, able to "influence" a 5G effective deployment.

Organization

Workshop Co-chairs

Ioannis P. Chochliouros   Hellenic Telecommunications Organization (OTE), Greece

Latif Ladid   IPv6 Forum and University of Luxembourg, Luxembourg

George Lyberopoulos   COSMOTE Mobile Telecommunications S.A., Greece

Daniele Porcu   ENEL Global Infrastructure and Networks S.r.l., Italy

Pavlos Lazaridis   University of Huddersfield, UK

Zaharias Zaharis   Aristotle University of Thessaloniki, Greece

Uwe Herzog   EURESCOM GmbH, Germany

Tao Chen   VTT Technical Research Center of Finland, Finland

Slawomir Kukliński   Orange Polska and Warsaw University of Technology, Poland

Lechosław Tomaszewski   Orange Polska, Poland

Charalambos Mitsis   SmartNet S.A., Greece

Ioannis Neokosmidis   inCITES Consulting S.A., Luxembourg

Nancy Alonistioti   National and Kapodistrian University of Athens, Greece

Monique Calisti   Martel Innovate GmbH, Switzerland

Kai Zhang   Martel Innovate GmbH, Switzerland

5G Communications as "Enabler" for Smart Power Grids: The Case of the Smart5Grid Project

Daniele Porcu[1], Ioannis P. Chochliouros[2(✉)] (iD), Sonia Castro[3],
Giampaolo Fiorentino[4], Rui Costa[5], Dimitrios Nodaros[6], Vaios Koumaras[7],
Fabrizio Brasca[8], Nicola di Pietro[9], George Papaioannou[10], Irina Ciornei[11],
Antonios Sarigiannidis[12], Nikolay Palov[13], Teodor Bobochikov[14],
Charilaos Zarakovitis[15], and Anastasia S. Spiliopoulou[2]

[1] ENEL Global Infrastructure and Networks S.r.l., Rome, Italy
[2] Hellenic Telecommunications Organization (OTE) S.A., 99 Kifissias Avenue,
15124 Maroussi-Athens, Greece
ichochliouros@oteresearch.gr
[3] ATOS IT Solutions and Services Iberia SL, Madrid, Spain
[4] Engineering - Ingegneria Informatica SpA, Rome, Italy
[5] Ubiwhere Lda, Aveiro, Portugal
[6] Eight Bells Ltd., Nicosia, Cyprus
[7] Infolysis P.C., Athens, Greece
[8] Wind Tre SpA, Rome, Italy
[9] Athonet S.r.l., Bolzano, Italy
[10] Independent Power Transmission Operator S.A., Athens, Greece
[11] University of Cyprus, Nicosia, Cyprus
[12] Sidroco Holdings Ltd., Nicosia, Cyprus
[13] Software Company Ltd., Sofia, Bulgaria
[14] Entra Energy, Sofia, Bulgaria
[15] Axon Logic Ltd., Athens, Greece

Abstract. The fast 5G deployment at global level influences a variety of vertical sectors and offers many opportunities for growth and innovation, drastically affecting modern economies. Among the major sectors where significant benefits are expected is the case of smart grid, where the management of energy demand is expected to become more efficient, leading to less investments. 5G inclusion and adaptation in smart grid will allow easier balance of energy load and reduction of electricity peaks, together with savings of energy cost. In the present work we introduce the innovative scope proposed by the Smart5Grid research project, aiming to complement contemporary energy distribution grids with access to 5G network resources through an open experimentation 5G platform and innovative Network Applications (NetApps). Smart5Grid administers four meaningful use cases for the energy vertical ecosystem, in order to demonstrate efficiency, resilience and elasticity provided by the 5G networks. In particular, each one among these use cases is presented and assessed as of its expected benefits and proposed novelties, based on the corresponding demonstration actions.

I. Maglogiannis et al. (Eds.): AIAI 2021 Workshops, IFIP AICT 628, pp. 7–20, 2021.
https://doi.org/10.1007/978-3-030-79157-5_1

Keywords: 5G · Energy management · Energy vertical ecosystem · Grid fault detection · Inter-area oscillations · Latency · Network Applications (NetApps) · Power network remote inspection and maintenance · Smart-grid

1 Introduction

Today, the immense multiplicity of interconnected networks of power plants, energy transmission towers, substations, poles and wires that make up the power grid, can be considered as "the largest machine" in the world. This is not a surprise, considering that electricity is the most versatile controlled form of energy. What is more, to transfer electrical power efficiently nowadays, "smart grids" [1, 2] combine traditional grids with communication and information control technologies, targeting to achieve efficiency, cleanliness and security, in a way that will "reshape" the modern landscape in energy transportation [3–5].

The Fifth Generation (5G) networks [6–8] will be an important ingredient for the development of smart grid technologies, especially allowing the grid to adapt better to the dynamics of renewable energy and distributed generation. As renewable resources—such as solar and wind power—are gaining pace with dynamic trends to become prevalent in a few years from now [9, 10], the power grid will require integrated and more enhanced monitoring and control, as well as integration with substation automation in order to control differing power flows and to plan for stand-by capacity that supplements energy generation. Smart grid capabilities promise to control easier bi-directional power flows and to monitor, control and support distributed energy resources. This, in fact, implicates for more challenges as well as for more opportunities in the related market domain.

Furthermore, the 5G mobile networks will help to integrate previously unconnected devices to smart grids for accurate monitoring and improved forecasting of their energy needs [11, 12]. Consequently, the managing of energy demand will become more efficient and will implicate for less investments, as the smart grid will allow for easier balance of the energy loads, for reduction of electricity peaks and, ultimately, for reduction of energy costs [13]. In this modern scope, large cities will be able to plan their energy infrastructure based on collected data, spending less resources and reducing the "downtime". Likewise, from the perspective of power supply, 5G is expected to enable better efficiency, observability and controllability of the power system, especially at the distribution side [14]. Energy suppliers will be able to collect and store power grid related data at much faster rates, ensuring secure and stable power supply, while risk mitigation and fault management will become simpler and more straightforward.

Up-to-now, the power distribution grids have only seen very little application of mobile-network technology and, consequently, the coverage of the current communication networks remains practically low [15]. Most of the applied efforts practically focus on the three following pillars to achieve efficient communication at the power distribution level, that is: (i) Power Line Communications (PLC) that use the distribution lines and cables as a transmission channel; (ii) Wireless or Radio Communications (WLC) that use the radio technologies for transferring the information between two or more points, and; (iii) Fibre Optical Communications (FOC) that use pulses of light through an optical fibre for transmitting information. Utility companies may use communication networks based on a combination of two or more of these technologies for grid access, backhaul and backbone communications, based on specific applications. On the other hand, network operators have not participated actively and widely in providing communication services for the transmission and distribution grid operation, due to the variety of network technologies being used by the power grid operators [16]. Another important reason is that traditional 3G/4G public network is a large all-in-one channel/single shared network, where operators cannot provide different network slices to preferred customers. Lastly, using FOC to build communication networks on the distribution level has difficulties in the deployment due to the massive-connections and the wide areas where coverage is required [17]. Such concerns have resulted to a sort of "inactive" involvement of telecom operators in the highly demanding energy vertical.

Clearly, the "smart grid transformation" must rely on existing electrical infrastructures of the generation, transmission, distribution and consumption levels of a power grid and, as such, to connect energy metering and measuring devices through a communication network that enables real-time information flow and control among power devices. Because it consists of a unified network that fulfils all the key communication requirements of smart distribution grids (including flexibility, reliability, coverage throughput, latency and massive device support), 5G is the first communication technology expected to address the plethora of current and future challenges of the energy sector [18–20].

Our work is organised as follows: Sect. 1 serves as an introduction, identifying the important role that 5G is to perform in order to support the operation of power transmission and distribution grids. Section 2 briefly focuses on the specific context proposed by the ongoing Smart5Grid project which is among the few research initiatives for applying 5G in the energy vertical sector. Section 3 introduces four distinct use cases that are to be deployed during the project's life-time. Each one is presented and assessed, as of its intended beneficial use and in parallel with the corresponding demonstration scenario. Section 4 provides some concluding overview and remarks.

2 Smart5Grid: An Innovative Context for the Energy Ecosystem

Following to the above challenges and taking into account the enormous potential introduced by the intended 5G applicability in the market sector, the ongoing Smart5Grid project [21] aims to complement contemporary energy distribution grids with access to 5G network resources through an open experimentation 5G platform and innovative Network Applications (NetApps). Towards achieving this target, Smart5Grid administers four meaningful use cases for the energy vertical ecosystem, in order to demonstrate efficiency, resilience and elasticity provided by the 5G networks. On top, Smart5Grid provides an open environment to third parties for experimentation, which will be able to support development, testing and validation of 5G Network Applications specialised for the Energy Vertical [22].

The smart grid paradigm poses new challenges to communication networks requiring a flexible and orchestrated network, slicing and millisecond-level latency [23]. In order for today's power distribution grids to be transformed into "evolved" smart grids to enable efficient, fast and secure operation, power distribution companies need new tools allowing them to monitor/operate the distribution network and to maintain/increase reliability and Quality of Service (QoS). To efficiently deal with these issues, Smart5Grid's effort identifies the following high-level requirements for the communication network that will allow building innovative and high performance smart grids: (i) Very high device density for connecting thousands of energy metering and power electronic devices, in one location; (ii) very high bandwidth to allow massive data flows from multiple devices simultaneously, allowing remote maintenance and substation monitoring, and; (iii) ultra-low latency for fault detection, network isolation and operation of recovery devices within one power cycle (i.e. 20 ms for the 50 Hz frequency used in electric current).

Through the effective adoption of 5G networks and the expected assistance of the respective NetApps that will be developed and validated on real power grid facilities, Smart5Grid facilitates the current energy sector stakeholders (i.e. Distribution System Operators (DSOs) and Transmission System Operators (TSOs)) as well as future smart grid shareholders (i.e.: Smart Grid Operators, Independent System Operators, Energy Aggregators, Regional Distribution Organisations and Energy Service Providers (ESPs), etc.) to: (i) Easily and effectively create and offer advanced energy services; (ii) interact in a dynamic and efficient way, with their surrounding environment (by assessing and considering multiple options), and; (iii) automate and optimise the planning and operation of their power and energy services, thus enhancing their market activity. In this way, Smart5Grid envisages towards providing a more secure, reliable, efficient and real-time communication framework for the modern smart grids. In particular, Smart5Grid leverages on resilience and elasticity (i.e. network slicing [24]) provided by the 5G technology in order to contribute to an open and flexible platform for secure testing, validation and operation of NetApps, specifically targeting to the Renewable Energy Sources (RES) production and distribution of vertical ecosystem(s). The emerging 5G mobile cellular network, along with the celebrated new features introduced with it, (i.e., Ultra-reliable Low Latency Communication (URLLC), massive Machine Type Communications (mMTC) and enhanced Mobile Broadband (eMBB)) and the concept of MEC (Multi-Access Edge Computing) which extends the capabilities of cloud computing by bringing it to the edge of the network [25, 26], provides a competent environment for smart grids.

Notably, the Smart5Grid architectural framework aims to enable efficient and cost-effective distributed State Estimation (SE) algorithms based on more sophisticated optimisation techniques [27]. This will allow smart grid voltage and phase measurements to occur at a much greater frequency than it has been possible by using the legacy measurement infrastructure. SE is a key functionality of electric power grid's energy management systems and it aims to provide an estimate of the system state variables (i.e. voltage magnitude and angles) at all the buses of the electrical network from a set of remotely acquired measurements. Indeed, for URLLC, the generic radio interface latency target is about 0.5 ms, while reliability targets Packet Loss Rate of 10^{-5} for 32-byte packets and 1 ms latency [28]. The open testing platform built in the context of Smart5Grid will allow the implementation and experimentation with appropriate VNFs (Virtual Network Functions) [29] and NetApps, not only to Smart5Grid partners but also to third parties (i.e. entities outside the contractual Smart5Grid consortium). This will support and "give rise" to an experimental execution environment that increases reliability, availability and maintainability in smart grid energy networks, through application of specialised 5G solutions.

3 Smart5Grid Use Cases

The Smart5Grid project is focusing towards developing network applications specifically tailored to the requirements of existing real operational issues faced by the modern smart energy grids and, thereby, it will heavily contribute to the energy vertical ecosystem. NetApps will be consisted of appropriately chained VNFs that will be developed on the Smart5Grid platform and then tested and validated on real power grid infrastructures, under true operational conditions. Following to these actions, the successful and wide adoption of the Smart5Grid NetApps will allow the smooth penetration of (mobile) network operators, telecoms and ICT industries and SMEs (Small and Medium-sized Enterprises) into the energy sector for the provisioning of novel network services; in addition, it will offer automation and real-time inspection and control to the existing energy stakeholders. The real-life validation of the Smart5Grid NetApps has been planned to take place in four countries (Italy, Spain, Greece and Bulgaria). The intended, for demonstration, scenario and setup for each use case is described below.

3.1 Use Case 1: Automatic Power Distribution Grid Fault Detection

A fault in a distribution grid is an abnormal condition that can be caused by equipment (i.e. transformers and rotating machines) failure, human errors and/or various environmental conditions. Such an error consists of a stressful situation for the DSOs, since it can have a great impact on the supplied power quality; thus it can create equipment damages and, also, it may reduce the electrical system reliability and stability resulting to power interruptions. To maintain a reliable and high-quality power supply to consumers without any interruptions, smart grids and distribution networks require real-time self-healing (i.e. the identification and isolation of faults in the backbone network and automatic recovery in less than 1 s [30]). As manual outage handling in a control centre fails to achieve such short restoration time (manual switching takes on average 120 min [31]), automated fault detection solutions are widely used to restore the power supply within a few hundred milliseconds [32]. To do so, modern communication systems primarily use the international IEC 61850 standard [33] to support self-healing distributed functions, as it provides the required flexibility and interactivity for the implementation of such applications, while peer-to-peer communication via IEC 61850 Generic Object-Oriented Substation Event (GOOSE) messages provides analogue and binary data at low latency among the system components [34]. Typically, the controllers conduct self-healing of the distribution line in approximately 500 ms by isolating the fault, but the tremendous social and economic consequences of a potential fault have pushed the DSOs to constantly search for mobile communication network configurations that allow even shorter restoration times, with the ultimate challenge, the peer-to-peer, Layer-2, multicast IEC 61850 GOOSE communication to become less than 5 ms (i.e., less by two orders of magnitude) [15].

Smart5Grid Added Value: The inherent characteristics of the proposed MEC platform will contribute to the millisecond level precise discrimination of a line fault which is helpful to the immediate isolation and the rapid self-healing of the regional power supply. A dedicated monitoring feature will facilitate the communication troubleshooting at MEC level, discriminating if the eventual issue or quality degradation is either in RAN (radio access network) or IP network, increasing the system reliability. Coupling of the URLLC and mMTC 5G network services will allow the effective operation of grid control and protection devices, enabling the ultra-fast fault detection and isolation while, at the same time, the platform will support the big in number (thousands) of grid control and protection devices.

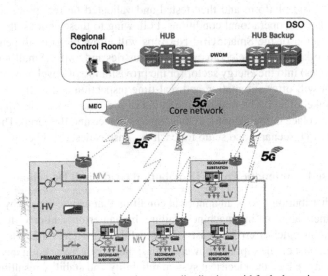

Fig. 1. Smart-grid automatic power distribution grid fault detection.

Scenario to be Demonstrated: Smart5Grid will demonstrate the capabilities of the developed NetApps to extract valuable information for the DSO by constantly monitoring the communication between the protection and fault detection devices on real power distribution infrastructures over a public 5G network, as illustrated in Fig. 1. As soon as a failure is detected and isolated in milliseconds using the Smart5Grid communication platform between the peripheral nodes, the central system and the communication among the Intelligent Electronic Devices (IEDs), the rest of the network shall continue its normal function whereas the goal of the demonstrated scenario will be the capability to minimise the SAIDI (System Average Interruption Duration Index) and CAIDI (Customer Average Interruption Duration Index), which are important indices for benchmarking by DSOs internationally [35].

3.2   Use Case 2: Remote Inspection of Automatically Delimited Working Areas at Distribution Level

Currently, DSOs are incurring high operational expenditures for inspecting and maintaining their infrastructures, as the inspection and the maintenance of the energy distribution grid assets is a very demanding and essential task [36]. Up-to-now, such actions are undertaken by human maintenance crews through visual examination. As a result, dedicated personnel are often exposed to dangerous working conditions, such as high heights for tower/pylon climbing inspections, difficult ground patrols and often exposures to electrical risks (e.g. electric arcs that can cause an electrocution) during substations' visits [37, 38]. For personnel safety precautions, planned power disruptions are scheduled during the inspection and maintenance procedures and so the capacity and availability of the distribution network is reduced periodically. Additionally, when maintenance works are performed in the vicinity of critical equipment of the distribution grid (e.g., transformers, circuit breakers, switchgears, etc.) the working areas are restricted and only authorised personnel can access them. As evident, it is critical for DSOs to obtain efficient and short-duration inspection and maintenance procedures from central offices to support the risk prevention and help field operators. This is done through the provision of advanced information/data, with remote inspection and maintenance procedures, without compromising quality.

Smart5Grid Added Value: The capabilities of the proposed Smart5Grid 5G platform will offer a solution for the improvement of working conditions for the power grid maintenance crews and inspection personnel, through remote inspection and control of the automatically delimited working areas. The 5G eMBB features will permit high-bandwidth communication between the power grid monitoring equipment (i.e. existing permanent and manual sensors and high-resolution cameras of various types) and the cloud-based inspection platform, in order to be processed with artificial intelligence (AI) and machine learning (ML) based algorithms and inference models; the latter will help to achieve automated evaluation of equipment condition and also automated delimitation of working areas at the period of their remote inspection. The Smart5Grid project aims to enable remote inspections in high risk areas and real time execution, by serving a variety of distribution network applications and by providing accurate results and information on the operational condition of the power grid assets through augmented reality. For maintenance works real-time control will be enabled, to assist the working procedures remotely and automatically without exposing the supervisor personnel to dangerous conditions.

Scenario to be Demonstrated: Smart5Grid will demonstrate the capabilities of the developed 5G platform and of the NetApp for the remote inspection of automatically delimited working areas at distribution level through the deployment of a private 5G network (see Fig. 2). The developed NetApp will: (i) Generate a detailed 3D volumetric model of the configuration of the power grid assets where the work will be carried out; (ii) automatically delimitate the working areas and the authorised personnel; (iii) permit the real-time communication of big data generated from the existing permanent and manual sensors and cameras within the working area; (iv) allow the real-time remote control of the work and capture the movements of the different operators (authorised

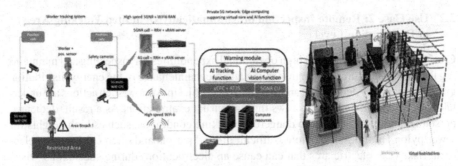

Fig. 2. 5G communication infrastructure in the substation (left) and 3D model of primary substation with open air busbars.

and non-authorised), and; (v) provide instant warning signals and alerts. It is expected that the developed 5G private network shall support peak data rate of 10 Gbps.

3.3   Use Case 3: Millisecond Level Precise Distribution Generation Control

Due to the climate change, the finite reservoirs of fossil fuels and the constantly reducing cost of RESs technologies, it is expected that by 2050 most of the worldwide electricity will be produced by renewable sources [10, 39]. This unprecedented high percentage creates new challenges for the power grid stability, as most of the RESs produce extremely volatile energy and have extreme power variations in short amounts of time. Additionally, the most widely used RESs (i.e., solar and wind energy) cannot reliably inject mechanical inertia into the local power grid, which creates reliability issues for keeping the frequency at the desirable level constant [40, 41]. As the RES deployment is essential, DSOs/TSOs need to deploy new techniques for keeping the power grid performance on high levels. Control of voltage and frequency in distribution and transmission grids are the key challenges of the future 100% renewable smart grids [10]. These new procedures are still under development, and they require many economic, legal, and technological changes (apart from the modifications in the electric grid). A major enabler is the interconnected communication systems and computing infrastructure, which interconnects control centres, substation automation units, energy storage systems and power plants of all sizes in a flexible, secure and consistent manner.

Today, the vast majority of the communication technologies used for the communication between the RES assets and the power grid are still wire-bound, including a variety of dedicated Industrial Ethernet and power line solutions, as there was no need for wireless connectivity in the past, due to the relatively static and long-lasting installation of the power grid equipment [42, 43]. With the advent of future Smart Grids and 5G, however, this will change fundamentally, since wireless connectivity can increase the degree of flexibility, mobility, versatility, and ergonomics required for the energy networks of the future. It is evident that the modern smart grid era will depend on devices that can monitor the various assets and manage big data, through ultrafast communications and cloud-based apps for efficient processing and decision-making [44, 45].

Smart5Grid Added Value: Smart5Grid will enable the connection of thousands of Medium Voltage (MV) and High Voltage (HV) level decentralised RESs units and their inverters, to a platform with installed 5G communication protocols, which will allow their aggregation and control by the DSOs/TSOs in millisecond rates. Through the developed platform, the electricity producers owning renewable generation assets can use fast real-time cloud-based tools to formulate optimal energy scheduling according to the power system needs. Additionally, they will be able to monitor and rebalance the network by managing the distributed flexibilities provided by their decentralised energy resources (i.e., Wind Plants, Hydro Plants, Storage and Dispatchable Loads), according to the incentives provided by the grid services markets and business models (e.g., aggregators, suppliers, storage owners). All exchanged messages will be secured (especially in terms of data integrity and authenticity) so that the probability of two consecutive packet errors to be negligible.

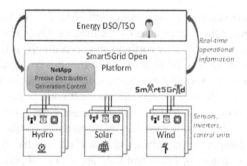

Fig. 3. Smart5Grid low latency distribution generation control of energy units.

Scenario to be Demonstrated: Various power electronic devices of grid-connected, decentralised renewable power plants will be used to demonstrate the capabilities of the developed monitoring platform on real operational conditions. The application will facilitate energy generation/consumption forecast for balancing purposes, enable energy cost optimising and visualisation of end-user behaviour, to optimally manage the energy profile, operational availability and flexibility services, through respective markets (intraday and balancing markets) in millisecond-level information exchange. The platform (cf. Fig. 3) will be designed for Hydro, Solar and Wind Power Plants, providing all the real-time operational information of the RES plants to the system operators and plant owners, allowing flexible plant management for procuring accurate and secure frequency and voltage control services by the DSOs/TSOs as well as visibility to plant owners for optimal plant management. Requirements on the communication service availability and reliability will be achieved by appropriate resilience and redundancy measures of the available generated power and accurate weather forecasts.

3.4 Use Case 4: Real-Time Wide Area Millisecond Level Precise Distribution Generation Control

Inter-area frequency oscillations represent one of the major challenges that face modern power systems, since their appearance is increasing due to the vast changes (i.e. increased penetration of renewable sources, growing energy demand, etc.) and constant expansion [46]. The appearance of inter-area oscillations creates many issues such as power quality degradation, limitation of transmission system capacity and, on several occasions, it can even lead to system instability. The detection and observation of inter-area oscillations is possible only with the use of synchronized measurements provided by the Phasor Measurement Units (PMUs) [47]. Exploiting PMU inputs for a robust, decentralised and real-time operational solution calls for novel communication infrastructure that will support the Wide Area Measurement Systems (WAMSs) of each smart grid, with aim to detect and counteract power grid disturbances in real time, while providing the observability needed.

Currently, the time-stamped phasor from each PMU is sent either through public Internet or serial cable to the Phasor Data Concentrator (PDC). The PDC receives data from all the PMU locations and, after sorting them accordingly, it transfers them to the WAMS [48]. For the WAMS to be able to obtain timely synchronized measurements from PMUs installed in all over the power system, the communication networks play an essential and crucial role. However, communication networks impose latency and errors, and these are the main obstacles towards the implementation of real-time applications. These are found to be the most known factors responsible for the degradation of the Wide Area Control damping capability which can even lead the system to instability, since the wide area controller is a near real-time application (operation rate of ~40 ms [49]).

Communication delays take place during data exchange between devices (e.g. PMUs and PDC) in a shared medium and they are mainly introduced by the long distance transportation of feedback signals, the medium type, the data buffering and the time required to send each bit. This kind of delay has the most variability mainly due to the conditions of the communication network (e.g. traffic, medium length, routers, switches, etc.). According to the IEEE Synchrophasor Standard C37.118.2-2011, typical delays from a PMU to the PDC are between 20–50 ms and each level above adds extra delays in the range of 30–80 ms [50], as illustrated in Fig. 4. Therefore, for a two-level communication infrastructure, the overall delays are in the range of 50–130 ms.

Smart5Grid Added Value: With the proposed network configuration and applications for the real-time communication of the time-stamped phasor from each PMU station to the developed virtual PDC (vPDC), Smart5Grid is expected to significantly minimise the communication and transfer delays of the current WAMSs. It is also expected that Smart5Grid communication platform will minimise the transfer delays of the PMU measurements and the feedback control signals, while it will also minimise the data dropouts—such events are experienced using the contemporary communication infrastructure that often compromise the WAMS operation. Message loss and corruption and interference with other, lower priority traffic will be avoided as much as possible. In this sense, Smart5Grid is envisioned to improve WAMS' reliability and performance, thus

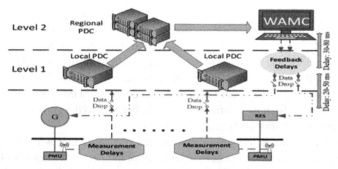

Fig. 4. Measurement infrastructure delays included for the data transfer between the PMUs, the local PDCs (Level 1) the regional PDC/WAMC (Level 2) and feedback delays from the WAMC to the local controllers.

contributing to the effective maintenance of the transmission and distribution power grid stability and reliability.

Scenario to be Demonstrated: Smart5Grid aims to demonstrate the 5G virtual PDC capabilities for serving the Wide Area Monitoring of end-to-end electricity networks, that is: from Distributed Energy Resources at Medium Voltage level operated by DSOs to High Voltage level operated by TSOs, as well as inter-TSO cross border Regional Security Coordination, aggregating the data from the PMU devices installed, enabling precise state measurements and processing to be made across grid segments. To do so, the four main functionalities of the developed Smart5Grid virtual 5G PDC NetApp will enable: (i) The comparison of different measured variables from various monitoring PMU devices for both real-time and historical data; (ii) the real-time monitoring of triggered events detected by PMU devices, as well as snapshots of the events in various levels of detail; (iii) the real-time displacement of the rate of change of frequency across the entire monitored network, and; (iv) configuration of the voltage magnitude and angle difference state measurements across the distribution and transmission grid segments in real-time. The developed 5G virtual PDC will be also applicable for TSO-DSO PMU configurations to maintain the stability of the overall power grid at national level.

4 Concluding Remarks

In the scope of the present work we have discussed the important role of modern 5G communications as a real "enabler" of the power grid domain, thus promoting significant opportunities for growth in the energy vertical sector. In particular, the deployment of 5G infrastructures and of all potential related facilities allows for the support of smart grid technologies within a fully converged environment, enhancing adaptation to the dynamics of renewable energy and distributed generation. 5G also contributes to the efficient integration of numerous devices to smart grids, allows handling of immense data sets and permits for exact monitoring and management of energy needs of various underlying systems, offering significant benefits in a variety of activities and services.

Smart5Grid is among the on-going research initiatives supporting transformation of the power distribution grids towards smarter entities via the beneficial incorporation of innovative 5G features. The project aims to identify high-level requirements for the communication network, allowing the structuring of innovative and high performance smart grids. Via the adoption of 5G network infrastructure and the effective inclusion of suitable Network Applications consisted of chained VNFs, an innovative platform shall be deployed. This will allow offering of multiple benefits to the corresponding market actors, coming from both energy and ICT sectors.

Smart5Grid has identified several operational use cases that will take place in 4 European countries. Each one has been assessed as of its specific framework of reference and about the expected positive impact. In particular, we have discussed options for the added value that shall be provided by the Smart5Grid intended approach and details about the scheduled demonstrations have also been presented. All use cases are about real scenarios of use and "face" direct challenges identified by the energy vertical sector, thus their further treatment is expected to be both innovative and purely beneficial.

Acknowledgments. This work has been performed in the scope of the *Smart5Grid* European Research Project and has been supported by the Commission of the European Communities */5G-PPP/H2020, Grant Agreement No. 101016912.*

References

1. Ekanayake, J., Liyanage, K., Wu, J., Yokoyama, A., Jenkins, N.: Smart Grid: Technology and Applications. Wiley, Chichester (2012)
2. Bakken, D.: Smart Grids: Cloud, Communications, Open Source, and Automation. CRC Press, New York (2014)
3. Mourshed, M., et al.: Smart grid futures: perspectives on the integration of energy and ICT services. Energy Procedia **75**, 1132–1137 (2015)
4. Panajotovic, B., Jankovic, M., Odadzic, B.: ICT and smart grid. In: Proceedings of the TELSIKS 2011, pp. 118–121. IEEE (2011)
5. Kuroda, K., Ichimura, T., Matsufuji, Y., Yokoyama, R.: Key ICT solutions for realizing smart grid. In: Proceedings of the SGE 2012, pp. 1–8. IEEE (2012)
6. Rost, P., Banchs, A., Berberana, I., Reitbach, M., Doll, M., et al.: Mobile network architecture evolution toward 5G. IEEE Commun. Mag. **54**(5), 84–91 (2016)
7. Andrews, J.G., et al.: What will 5G be? IEEE J. Sel. Areas Commun. **32**(6), 1065–1082 (2014). https://doi.org/10.1109/JSAC.2014.2328098
8. Chochliouros, I.P., et al.: Business and market perspectives in 5G networks. In: Proceedings of the Joint 13th CTTE and 10th CMI Conference 2017, pp. 1–6. IEEE (2017)
9. International Energy Agency (IEA): Empowering Variable Renewables: Options for Flexible Electricity Systems. IEA, Paris (2008)
10. International Renewable Energy Agency (IRENA): Global Energy Transformation: A Roadmap to 2050. Irena, Abu Dhabi (2019)
11. Matinkhah, S.M., Shafik, W.: Smart grid empowered by 5G technology. In: Proceedings of the 2019 SGC, pp. 1–6. IEEE (2019)
12. Kumari, A., Tanwar, S., Tyagi, S., Kumar, N., Obaidat, M.S., Rodrigues, J.J.P.C.: Fog computing for smart grid systems in the 5G environment: challenges and solutions. IEEE Wirel. Commun. **26**(3), 47–53 (2019)

13. Cosovic, M., Tsitsimelis, A., Vukobratovic, D., Matamoros, J., Anton-Haro, C.: 5G Mobile cellular networks: enabling distributed state estimation for smart grids. IEEE Commun. Mag. **55**(10), 62–69 (2017)
14. Li, W., Wu. Z., Zhang, P.: Research on 5G network slicing for digital power grid. In: Proceedings of the ICEICT 2020, pp. 679–682. IEEE (2020)
15. The 3rd Generation Partnership Project (3GPP): TS 22.261 V17.1.0: technical specification group services and system aspects; service requirements for the 5G system; Stage 1 (Release 17), December 2019
16. IHS Markit: 5G network slicing enabling smart grid: commercial feasibility analysis. Industry Report (2019). https://www-file.huawei.com/-/media/corporate/pdf/news/5g-network-slicing-enabling-smart-grid-commercial-feasibility-analysis-en.pdf?la=en
17. Global System for Mobile Communications Association (GSMA): Smart grid powered by 5G SA-based network slicing (2020). https://www.gsma.com/futurenetworks/wp-content/uploads/2020/03/2_Powered-by-SA_Smart-Grid-5G-Network-Slicing_China-Telecom_GSMA_v2.0.pdf
18. 5G-Infrastructure-Association (5G-IA): 5G and energy. Version 1.0. (5G-PPP White Paper on Energy Vertical sector), September 2015. https://5g-ppp.eu/wp-content/uploads/2014/02/5G-PPP-White_Paper-on-Energy-Vertical-Sector.pdf
19. Leligou, H.C., Zahariadis, T., Sarakis, L., Tsampasis, E., Voulkidis, A., Velivassaki, T.E.: Smart grid: a demanding use case for 5G technologies. In: Proceedings of PerCom 2018, pp. 215–220. IEEE (2018)
20. Tabassum, H., Salehi, M., Hossain, E.: Mobility-aware analysis of 5G and B5G cellular networks: a tutorial (2018). https://arxiv.org/abs/1805.02719
21. Smart5Grid Project (Grant Agreement No. 101016912). https://smart5grid.eu/
22. NRG5 Project: Deliverable 1.2: NRG-5 reference architecture and functional decomposition, March (2018). http://www.nrg5.eu/wp-content/uploads/2019/01/Deliverable-D1.2-compressed.pdf
23. Jha, A.V., Ghazali, A.N., Appasani, B., Mohanta, D.K.: Risk identification and risk assessment of communication networks in smart grid cyber-physical systems. In: Awad, A.I., Furnell, S., Paprzycki, M., Sharma, S.K. (eds.) Security in Cyber-Physical Systems. SSDC, vol. 339, pp. 217–253. Springer, Cham (2021). https://doi.org/10.1007/978-3-030-67361-1_8
24. Chochliouros, I.P., Spiliopoulou, A.S., Lazaridis, P., Dardamanis, A., Zaharis, Z., Kostopoulos, A.: Dynamic network slicing: challenges and opportunities. In: Maglogiannis, I., Iliadis, L., Pimenidis, E. (eds.) AIAI 2020. AICT, vol. 585, pp. 47–60. Springer, Cham (2020). https://doi.org/10.1007/978-3-030-49190-1_5
25. Chochliouros, I.P., et al.: Putting intelligence in the network edge through NFV and Cloud computing: the SESAME approach. In: Boracchi, G., Iliadis, L., Jayne, C., Likas, A. (eds.) EANN 2017. CCIS, vol. 744, pp. 704–715. Springer, Cham (2017). https://doi.org/10.1007/978-3-319-65172-9_59
26. Global System for Mobile Communications Alliance (GSMA): An introduction to 5G network slicing. GSMA, November 2017. https://www.gsma.com/futurenetworks/wp-content/uploads/2017/11/GSMA-An-Introduction-to-Network-Slicing.pdf
27. Guo, Y., Wu, W., Zhang, B., Sun, S.: A distributed state for power systems incorporating linear and non-linera models. Int. J. Electr. Power Energy Syst. **64**, 608–616 (2015)
28. The 3rd Generation Partnership Project (3GPP): 3GPP TR 22.804 V16.3.0: Technical specification group services and system aspects; study on communication for automation in vertical domains (CAV) (Release 16), July 2020. https://www.3gpp.org/ftp/Specs/archive/22_series/22.804/
29. European Telecommunications Standards Institute: ETSI GS NFV 002 V1.2.1 (2014-12): Network Functions Virtualisation (NFV); architectural framework, ETSI. https://www.etsi.org/deliver/etsi_gs/NFV/001_099/002/01.02.01_60/gs_nfv002v010201p.pdf

30. Madrigal, M., Uluski, R., Mensan Gaba, K.: Practical Guidance for Defining a Smart Grid Modernization Strategy. DC, World Bank, Washington (2017)
31. Brown, R.E.: Electric Power Distribution Reliability, 2nd edn. CRC Press, New York (2016)
32. Le, D.P., Bui, D.M., Ngo, C.C., Le, A.M.T.: FLISR approach for smart distribution networks using E-Terra Software - a case study. Energies 11(12), 3333 (2018)
33. International Electrotechnical Commission (IEC): IEC 61850 Standard: Communication networks and systems for power utility automation. IEC https://webstore.iec.ch/publication/6028
34. Kriger, C., Behardien, S., Retonda, J.: A detailed analysis of the GOOSE message structure in an IEC 61850 standard-based substation automation system. Int. J. Comput. Commun. Control 8(5), 708–721 (2013)
35. Council of European Energy Regulators (CEER): CEER Benchmarking Report 6.1 on the Continuity of Electricity and Gas Supply (2018). https://www.ceer.eu/documents/104400/-/-/963153e6-2f42-78eb-22a4-06f1552dd34c
36. Prettico, G., Flammini, M.G., Andreadou, N., Vitiello, S., Fulli, G., Masera, M.: Distribution system operators observatory 2018: overview of the electricity distribution system in Europe. European Commission, Joint Research Centre (2019)
37. Workers' Compensation Board: Working safely around electricity (2014). https://www.casa-acsa.ca/wp-content/uploads/2014-11_Working_Safely_Around_Electricity.pdf
38. Energy Safe Victoria: Electricity hazards safety guide - creating a safer state with electricity and gas: for emergency services workers (2018). https://esv.vic.gov.au/wp-content/uploads/2019/11/ElectricityHazardsSafetyGuide_LoRes.pdf
39. European Parliament: European policies on climate and energy towards 2020, 2030 and 2050 (2019). https://www.europarl.europa.eu/RegData/etudes/BRIE/2019/631047/IPOL_BRI(2019)631047_EN.pdf
40. Nguyen, N., Mitra, J.: An analysis of the effects and dependency of wind power penetration on system frequency regulation. IEEE Trans. Sustain. Energ. 7(1), 354–363 (2015)
41. Delille, G., François, B., Malarange, G.: Dynamic frequency control support by energy storage to reduce the impact of wind and solar generation on isolated power system's inertia. IEEE Trans. Sustain. Energ. 3(4), 931–939 (2012)
42. Kellner, T.: The network effect: the internet of electricity is coming and this little device is making it happen. Digital Grid (2019). https://www.ge.com/news/reports/the-network-effect-the-internet-of-electricity-is-coming-and-this-little-device-is-making-it-happen
43. European Union Agency for Cybersecurity (ENISA): Communication network interdependencies in smart grids (2016)
44. Akhavan-Hejazi, H., Mohsenian-Rad, H.: Power systems big data analytics: an assessment of paradigm shift barriers and prospects. Energ. Rep. 4, 91–100 (2018)
45. Ho, T.M., et al.: Next-generation wireless solutions for the smart factory, smart vehicles, the smart grid and smart cities (2019). https://arxiv.org/pdf/1907.10102.pdf
46. International Energy Agency (IEA): Status of power system transformation 2019. Technology Report, May 2019
47. Phadke, A.G., Bi, T.: Phasor measurement units, WAMS, and their applications in protection and control of power systems. J. Mod. Power Sys. Clean Energ. 6(4), 619–629 (2018)
48. Appasani, B., Mohanta, D.K.: A review on synchrophasor communication system: communication technologies, standards and applications. Prot. Control Mod. Power Sys. 3(1), 1–17 (2018)
49. Zacharia, L., Asprou, M., Kyriakides, E.: Design of a data delay compensation technique based on a linear predictor for wide-area measurements. In: Proceedings of the 2016 IEEE PES General Meeting (PESGM), pp. 1–5. IEEE (2016)
50. Zacharia, L., Asprou, M., Kyriakides, E.: Measurement errors and delays on wide-area control based on IEEE Std C37.118.1-2011: impact and compensation. IEEE Sys. J. 14(1), 422–432 (2020)

5G-VICTORI: Future Railway Communications Requirements Driving 5G Deployments in Railways

Ioanna Mesogiti[1]([✉]) [iD], Eleni Theodoropoulou[1], Fotini Setaki[1],
George Lyberopoulos[1], Anna Tzanakaki[2], Markos Anastassopoulos[2],
Christina Politi[3], Panagiotis Papaioannou[3], Christos Tranoris[3], Spyros Denazis[3],
Paris Flegkas[4], Nikos Makris[4], Nebojsa Maletic[5], Darko Cvetkovski[5],
Jesus Gutierrez Teran[5], Panteleimon Konstantinos Chartsias[6], Konstantinos Stamatis[6],
Marievi Xezonaki[6], Dimitrios Kritharidis[6], Alexandros Dalkalitsis[7],
Manfred Taferner[8], and Martin Piovarci[8]

[1] COSMOTE Mobile Telecommunications S.A., Athens, Greece
imesogiti@cosmote.gr
[2] National and Kapodistrian University of Athens, Athens, Greece
[3] University of Patras, Patras, Greece
[4] Department of Electrical and Computer Engineering, University of Thessaly, Volos, Greece
[5] IHP - Leibniz-Institut für Innovative Mikroelektronik, Frankfurt, Germany
[6] Intracom Telecom S.A., Athens, Greece
[7] TRAINOSE S.A., Athens, Greece
[8] Kontron Transportation Austria AG, Vienna, Austria

Abstract. The complete transformation of the ICT domain driven by 5G network principles and capabilities, will impact significantly the path towards digitalization of many vertical industries, with modern railway transportations being one of them. In this context, Future Railway Mobile Communication System (FRMCS) service requirements and system principles are very well mapped to 5G service and network concepts associated with network performance, technology neutrality at various levels as well as network planning and deployment options. However, the flexibility of 5G networks implies that concepts are pinned down to deployment paradigms so that afore assertions are proved. The 5G-PPP project 5G-VICTORI aims at delivering a complete 5G solution suitable for railway environments and FRMCS services, along with experimentation deployments for testing and evaluation in operational railway environments. This paper discusses the service Key Performance Indicators (KPIs) and technical requirements and provides an overview of the proposed experimental deployment in an operational railway environment in the area of Patras, Greece.

Keywords: 5G · Railway communications · FRMCS · Edge computing · Vertical services

© IFIP International Federation for Information Processing 2021
Published by Springer Nature Switzerland AG 2021
I. Maglogiannis et al. (Eds.): AIAI 2021 Workshops, IFIP AICT 628, pp. 21–30, 2021.
https://doi.org/10.1007/978-3-030-79157-5_2

1 Introduction

The explosive growth in the demand for broadband and mobile services is visible in all environments of human activity. In this landscape, modern railway transportation environments, present huge demand for network deployments to support a broad range of novel services addressing various end-user categories.

Existing telecommunications infrastructures deployed in the railway environment includes several flexible technologies and different public and private network deployments to serve the demand for versatile services from various end-users. However, rail service requirements are pushing existing networks deployed in the railway environment to their limits, making total coverage for all services along the extensive railway tracks very challenging. This effect is further emphasized when considering current sub-optimal utilization of resources and slow service deployment. The Future Railway Mobile Communication System (FRMCS) standard [10], succeeding GSM-R, aims to address these inefficiencies and meet future service requirements. FRMCS is considered as a key enabler for rail transport digitalization and reflects the technology neutrality and network services approach of 3GPP 4G/5G standards, tailored to the service specificities and deployment challenges of the railway environment. The FRMCS and 3GPP collaboration as defined in the specification series [1–4] fulfills the expectations of both worlds.

A number of projects and programmes (EU, national funded, equipment vendor supported, etc., e.g. [5, 14]) are focusing on the technical realization of the FRMCS concepts and principles, in delivering deployment paradigms and evaluating FRMCS services over these. In this landscape, the 5G-PPP 5G-VICTORI project [6] is extending existing 5G experimentation facilities towards adopting a novel 5G solution for FRMCS. The project focuses on delivering two implementation paradigms, available for experimentation at railway operational sites in Greece and Germany. This paper aims at providing an overview of the FRMCS services that drive the deployment and that will be demonstrated at a railway facility in Patras, Greece, as well as a discussion on the underlying challenges.

This paper is organized as follows: initially, the service and network deployment requirements and options are discussed on the basis of key railway vertical services. An overview of the 5G-VICTORI experimentation network deployment in Patras facilities—covering these requirements—is presented in the subsequent section. Following these, aspects related to the operational adoption of such solutions are discussed, while conclusions are drawn at the end.

2 Railway Vertical Services and Requirements in 5G-VICTORI

2.1 Vertical Services, Requirements and KPIs

In modern railway transportation facilities, there is a demand for a broad range of novel services addressing various end-users and rail related operational services. These, collectively denoted as FRMCS services are applications for passengers, critical services and emergency services for stakeholders engaged in train operation, as well as complementary services related to optimization of train operation. Detailed information on the railway environment requirements and vertical applications is provided in [3] and [16], along with their typical categorization into "Business", "Performance" and "Critical" services. The 5G-VICTORI project includes services that represent all FRMCS service types and aggregates their requirements.

In particular, "Business services" refer to communication and broadband connectivity services provided to passengers present at railway facilities, i.e. at the train stations/ platforms, on-board. These services include infotainment, digital mobility, travel information services etc. Indicatively wireless internet, infotainment services, Video on Demand (VoD) and linear TV services are used at Patras 5G-VICTORI facilities, imposing the following service requirements (aligned with [1]):

- Support for High-resolution Real-time Video Quality of video content/TV streaming channels, implying jitter limits below 40 ms, end-to-end latency below 100 ms and guaranteed datarates of 5-10 Mbps per stream.
- Low Channel/ Stream Switching time, corresponding to the time between the triggering of channel switching and the presentation of the new channel on screen; typically to be under the 1–2 s, corresponding to end-to-end network latency below 150 ms.
- Total Wagon Traffic Density accounting for 100–300 users per train (peak time) for this service, requiring in total 500 Mbps even 1 Gbps at large, highly congested trains.

The "Performance services" category includes non-critical services related to train operation, and can be sub-grouped into: i) passenger information services, ii) advisory services, iii) telemetry services and iv) infrastructure monitoring and maintenance services. Usually these services are deployed and consumed inside the railway facilities environment. In the context of 5G-VICTORI (at Patras facilities), CCTV services for supervision of the rail tracks quality and provision of maintenance when needed will be used as example. Cameras mounted on the train will be capturing images/video of the tracks, viewed in real time at an emulated Railway Operations/Monitoring Center. Such services pose requirements related to:

- High-resolution Real-time Video Quality of CCTV camera stream, implying jitter limits below 40 ms, end-to-end latency below 150 ms and guaranteed bit rate of 3–15 Mbps per stream depending on the required picture resolution.
- High availability and seamless service provisioning under speed high mobility for critical CCTV services related to real-time monitoring for next generation trains and railway facilities.
- In operational cases [1, 3] one can consider also asynchronous operation of CCTV/data monitoring/etc. for services based on post-processing of (video) captures, that further introduces the requirement for bulk transfer of infrastructure monitoring data (e.g. CCTV archives), collected over time. Depending on the scheduling of the transfer, and the coverage footprint of the network, this may impose a requirement of uploading several GB-TB of data (towards an Operations' center), introducing the need for network data rates exceeding 500 Mbps (500 Mbps–1 Gbps) at specific network coverage areas.

"Critical services" are related to train operation/movement, railway automation and operation control systems, trackside maintenance, emergency and safety services, etc., and involve information exchange between various users/stakeholders, e.g. railway infrastructure operators, train operators, railway staff, railway first responders, etc. Usually, these services are deployed and consumed inside the railway facilities environment. However, there is a critical requirement for service availability at any part of the facilities, including the extensive railway tracks. Mission-Critical Push-to-Talk (MCPTT) and Mission Critical Data (e.g. between the controller(s) at the train/operations center and the driver/on-board staff etc.) are used as indicative applications of this type in the context of 5G-VICTORI. Such services impose requirements (aligned with [1, 3]) related to:

- Intelligible Voice Quality of MCPTT session, that implies extensive network coverage with adequate signal quality to support it.
- Communication session Setup time, which given the criticality of the service, needs to be very fast, not exceeding 1 s.
- Low Session Loss Rate (SLR) (number of sessions released due to failure over a specific time window) which is practically impacted by network availability and reliability over the railway facilities. SLR of 10^{-2} sessions/h is the target for operational network deployments.
- High Service Reliability, which reflects general critical services reliability levels of 99,99% (up to 99,9999%), depending on the criticality of use of MCPTT, and relates to network availability and service reliability levels.

In addition, the following generic requirements have been identified commonly for all services of the railway transportations vertical. In particular,

- Service Availability on board the train, whenever it resides along the tracks (and at station platforms), for synchronous service operation is required, implying network coverage at the vertical premises. In the railway environment vertical premises include the extensive network of railway tracks and the railway stations/ platforms). The exact Service Availability levels (target values) depend on the nature of the services supported and vary between low levels for Business to very high for Critical services.
- Service Availability with significantly high network performance requirements at specific facility areas is required for asynchronous service operation.
- Seamless service provisioning to train wagons at high speeds is required, reflecting the vertical specific requirement for mobility at trains velocity (reaching 100 km/h and in cases 250 km/h), for all services provided on-board.

The key characteristic of the aggregate traffic patterns in this environment is that they are predictable; at access network level they are limited by the passenger capacity of one train, they follow a specific route along the tracks and they are restricted to the facilities of the railway.

2.2 Network Deployment Requirements and Options

To meet the FRMCS service requirements and KPIs, novel architectural solutions and network deployment options tailored to the railway environment need to be considered. The access network deployment (coverage) involves the application of common network planning principles, starting with the characterization of the area under study. In practice, area characteristics along the railway tracks may vary from remote, isolated areas, with challenging terrain for radio coverage (e.g. mountainous, with many curves, tunnels, etc.) to metropolitan areas (e.g. with high buildings, with many curves, tunnels etc.). Considering the access network capacity, as aforementioned aggregate data rates of at least 300 Mbps–1 Gbps are required at train level, and in cases that this is not possible, data rates of 1–1.5 Gbps are required at places where the train resides for some time, e.g. at platforms, train depots, etc. Apparently, there is no single solution to address such environment. In addition, considering the FRMCS principle of technology neutrality [16], solutions comprising different wireless access technologies shall be considered, both 3GPPP and non-3GPPP, not necessarily provisioned by a common 3GPP 5G core network (5GCN).

Consecutively, at the transport network layer, multiple solutions can be considered. 5G-PICTURE [5] proposed a converged Optical-Wireless solution. However, where fiber deployment is not possible or cost-effective, deployments with multiple wireless transport hops can provide an alternative solution [11]. Adhering to FRMCS technology neutrality principle, at transport network segments, solutions comprising different technologies and aggregating backhaul traffic from multiple technologies access network nodes can be considered.

Currently, private GSM-R networks serve part of the railway communication needs -the Rail-critical services part of FRMCS services- while public telecom networks serve another part. The fact that most FRMCS services are deployed and consumed in the railway facilities environment, makes this environment best suited to determine the end-to-end network architecture and deployment options. In practice, this means that private network deployments for FRMCS is a valid option as long as service continuity is ensured for "Business services" consumed across private and public networks. At this point, spectrum availability is a key factor that will impact the deployment models for railway communications. In case spectrum allocation policies for FRMCS follow the GSM-R ones—characterized by very short bandwidth allocations dedicated to Railway Operators, the available bandwidth may be sufficient to cover the needs of Rail Critical Services, but it might not be enough to serve additional "Business" or "Performance" services.

Other business factors may as well lead to public networks being extended to the railway facilities for FRMCS service provisioning. In these cases, a distributed core network deployment allowing service deployment and processing at edge compute resources, and traffic offloading at Mobile Edge Computing (MEC) components can serve well the purpose of meeting the performance requirements (especially for low latency), while optimizing public network utilization and performance. Moving one step further, for services that are consumed/ processed/ stored at train level, the inclusion of on-board edge resources in the distributed network and service deployment setup will be considered.

The performance requirements and the diversity of services included in the complete FRMCS service set as well as the need to support multiple tenants on top of a single infrastructure necessitates the adoption of the 5G concept of network slicing at service and tenant level. In general, FRMCS services can be well-mapped to the 3GPP distinction of services to uRLLC (ultra-Reliable Low Latency), and eMBB (enhanced Mobile Broadband), as basis for network layer slicing, over either a single private network deployment or a distributed public one.

3   5G-VICTORI Deployment for FRMCS

Considering the FRMCS services as well as the deployment requirements and challenges related to the railway environment, 5G-VICTORI has proposed a disaggregated, layered experimentation framework [11]. Based on 5G-VICTORI proposed approach, leveraging on the findings of [5], appropriately extending the 5G-VINNI experimentation facility in Patras, Greece [12] the project develops an FRMCS deployment in an operational rail environment in Patras presented in Fig. 1.

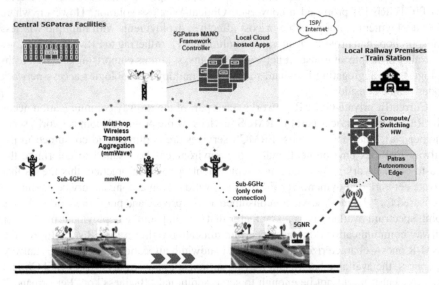

Fig. 1. Blueprint of 5G-VICTORI deployment for FRMCS in Patras

Last Mile Transport and Access Network: In this context, the deployment includes a multi-technology dense transport network providing transport coverage along a high-speed railway track in the area of Patras. In particular, to demonstrate multi-technology track-to-train (as last-mile transport network) communication, the proposed setup comprises both mmWave and Sub-6 track-side Access Points (APs) to be deployed along the track between two stations. The mmWave (V-Band, 60 GHz) APs feature beam steering capabilities for the train-to-track connectivity and are capable to provide up to 1 Gbps data rates. The Sub-6 APs allow for wider sector coverage, suitable for more challenging parts of the route.

Each trackside stanchion of the rail facility includes a pair of mmWave and/or Sub-6 APs, each one facing the each opposite directions of the track, since APs are quite highly directional to maximize performance. To ensure connectivity also as the train moves between the trackside APs, the proposed scheme suggests that antenna modules are installed at the front as well as at the rear part of the train rooftop. Seamless service and session continuity are ensured between the multi-technology APs by employing mobility-support functions, leveraging Software Defined Network (SDN) programmability for the established end-to-end flows.

An on-board train installation is foreseen to allow connectivity of various access network technologies (WiFi APs or gNBs) available to the end-users as well as to provide compute capabilities for applications' edge processing.

As aforementioned, there are areas where trackside network deployment is not feasible, hence certain asynchronous FRMCS services can rely on high speed access network connectivity at train stations' platforms. To experiment with such deployments, the 5G-VICTORI setup will include also a 3GPP 5G NR node at a train station in Patras' train facility. This complements the picture of multi-technology 3GPPP and non-3GPP access in the railway environment.

Transport Aggregation: The transport aggregation network part relies on state-of-the-art Point-to-Point Ethernet mmWave links at 70/80 GHz (E-Band) providing a total of up to 10 Gbps capacity towards the cloud/central facilities. The transport network nodes feature SDN capabilities providing support for network slicing.

Edge Computing: For the deployment of services, cloud compute resources are available at the central cloud infrastructure of the 5G Patras facility (University of Patras premises). However, to achieve high network performance and to optimize resource utilization, private network deployment and edge computing are considered in various ways apart from the central cloud option.

In particular, edge computing is considered at the on-board train installation, to provide the necessary storage and compute capabilities for asynchronous "business" and "performance" services. Virtualization of the edge resources allows the use for various applications/services, and the integration at various layers with the rest of the multi-technology, multi-layer network setup. In practice, virtualized edge resources can be integrated with the non-3GPP last-mile transport and WiFi access connectivity layer for hosting part of the synchronous applications. At the same time virtualized edge resources can be used for hosting components of the asynchronous services (e.g. storage of CCTV captures, storage/processing of measurements etc.) temporarily, during the periods that 5G access network coverage is unavailable.

At the 3GPP network layer, MEC is considered via the deployment of the complete 5GCN close to the vertical premises. The implementation is based on the Patras 5G Autonomous Edge, which is a portable "box", ideal for on-premise 5G deployments, containing everything from the 5G NR and 5GCN and Service Orchestrations on a Virtualized environment based on OpenStack. The Patras 5G Autonomous Edge is currently deployed in an indoor configuration, and it will be setup to provide the full stack of 5G

NR in a standalone configuration with 100 MHz bandwidth along with a single cell at the train station. All services are orchestrated via Openslice [8, 13] and monitoring is available through Grafana, Prometheus and Netdata.

Network Management, Orchestration and Slicing: Adhering to the 5G-VICTORI architecture, a network management and service orchestration layer operates on top of the aforesaid dense, multi-technology Patras 5G facility, to ensure that use cases and FRMCS services are delivered through multiple slices across the distributed compute resources in the railway environment. This layer is based on Open Source MANO (OSM) [9] and Openslice [8, 13], and it assumes automated deployment of end-to-end services and multiple customized-slices over the complete infrastructure (access, transport and core).

In particular, the Patras 5G facility service offering is based on Openslice which follows the Network Slice as a Service (NSaaS) paradigm. The Patras 5G facility service derives content from a 5G Service Catalogue of offerings—which advertises various 5G and generic NFV services to verticals/customers that can be included in their service order towards the facility. The service order of the vertical is then passed to the Openslice Service Orchestrator (SO) in the Patras 5G facility [15]. The SO then instantiates the network slice by subsequent calls to the respective network function virtualization orchestrator (NFVO). Moreover, the deployed software stack at the Patras 5G facility can be used to orchestrate services both at the central facility as well as the connected edge sites in the city.

In the context of 5G-VICTORI railway use case, compute and network resources are included in the orchestration domain Patras5G facility NFVO and Openslice instance. The FRMCS application components are managed as 3rd party virtual network functions (VNFs)/ Network Service Descriptors (NSDs) by the Patras5G facility NFVO, thus automated deployment of these services across the distributed compute resources is supported, along with creation of an end-to-end slice.

4   Further Challenges and Requirements

Different end-to-end network architecture designs and various deployment options (e.g. integration of public and private networks) are feasible for offering FRMCS services in the railway facilities environment. The fact that FRMCS services are deployed and consumed inside the railway facilities environment, can define the future end-to-end network architecture and deployment options. In some cases it is expected that FRMCS will be provided over distributed public networks as separate, virtualized network instances or simply as separate network service slices. In other cases, private 5G networks may be deployed to cover the service needs in the railway environment. Several business aspects underpin these decisions, and several business requirements revolve around them.

In all cases, the physical network infrastructure will be a critical investment aspect. In some cases, incumbents may undertake the physical network infrastructure deployment. However, in other cases, considering the spatial and temporal constraints character of these services established telecom operators may express low interest in getting involved in such infrastructure deployments. On the contrary, business-wise, exploiting the lack of high competition, stakeholders of the railway industry (e.g. railway operators and/or other engineering companies) are expected to have high interest in investing in private network infrastructures towards the digitalisation of their own business activities, leveraging on their existing experience in operating private networks. At the same time, ownership of facilities is a significant asset for railway operators considering the site acquisition costs necessary in any infrastructure deployment. An expansion of these activities, together with the exploitation of these investments by opening them up to passenger services and to other stakeholders (e.g. content providers, telecom operators) can generate new revenue streams. Such deployments can be considered as niche 5G provisioning systems, fostering the smaller telecom operator industry. As aforementioned, spectrum allocation policies is a key factor to enable the support of highly demanding Business and Performance services apart from Critical ones over a single network.

In such niche 5G networks deployed by the vertical at issue, additional challenges may arise, that need to be tackled. Indicatively, the deployment options to be followed at the access network layer, as well as the distribution and orchestration of multiple MEC resources in the extensive infrastructure of railway tracks entail significant network planning challenges. For services that are not locally restricted to railway facilities, it is needed to ensure continuity outside the boundaries of the niche 5G systems, which will involve the interconnection or even tighter interoperability with public ones (e.g. in the form of national roaming, or even in the form of service migration across networks). Last but not least, licensing aspects related to networks service provisioning to the public and access network deployment need also to be dealt with. At this point, a policies framework fostering the deployment and operation of small-scale networks is key.

5   Conclusions

This paper has provided an overview of the FRMCS service requirements and KPIs, on the basis of key applications spanning across all identified FRMCS service categories: "business", "performance", "critical". These applications have been used as a basis for the definition of system specifications of the 5G-VICTORI solution. Delivering a high-performance deployment for this demanding vertical entails detailed network coverage planning based on various technologies and on the placement of compute resources at the right proximity to the end user.

To this end, specifications have been nailed down to an experimentation deployment for testing and evaluation service performance in operational railway environment in the area of Patras, Greece. The latter entails a multi-technology environment, comprising various wireless technologies at last mile and aggregation transport segments, incorporating edge capabilities at various network parts, as well as 3GPP and non-3GPP access. On top of such infrastructure, designing, instantiating and orchestrating critical and non-critical services oven a multi-layer edge processing architecture, especially when various quality is required via slices is a key challenge that 5G-VICTORI will address in the next years.

Acknowledgements. The research leading to these results has received funding from the European Union's Framework Programme Horizon 2020 under grant agreements (1) No. 857201 and project name "5G-VICTORI: VertIcal demos over Common large scale field Trials fOr Rail, energy and media Industries".

References

1. 3GPP TS 22.289, Mobile communication system for railways; Stage 1, Rel. 17
2. 3GPP TR 22.989, Study on future railway mobile communication system, Rel 15
3. 3GPP TR 22.889, Study on future railway mobile communication system (FRMCS) Stage 1, Rel. 17
4. 3GPP TR 22.890, Study on supporting railway smart station services, Rel 17
5. 5G-PPP project 5G-picture. https://www.5g-picture-project.eu/. Accessed Mar 2020
6. 5G-PPP project 5G-victori. https://www.5g-victori-project.eu/. Accessed Mar 2020
7. 5G-victori project: deliverable D4.1, Field trials methodology and guidelines, September 2020
8. Tranoris, C.: OpenSlice: an opensource OSS for delivering network slice as a service, February 2021. https://arxiv.org/abs/2102.03290. Accessed Mar 2020
9. ETSI OpenSource MANO (OSM). https://osm.etsi.org/. Accessed Mar 2020
10. Future railway mobile communication system, UIC, international union of railways. https://uic.org/rail-system/frmcs/. Accessed Mar 2020
11. Zou, J., et al.: Europe's first 5G-ready railway trial utilizing integrated optical passive WDM access and broadband millimeter-wave to deliver multi-Gbit/s seamless connectivity. In: 2020 European Conference on Optical Communications (ECOC), Brussels, Belgium, pp. 1–3 (2020). https://doi.org/10.1109/ECOC48923.2020.9333361
12. Mahmood, K., et al.: Design of 5G end-to-end facility for performance evaluation and use case trials. In: 2019 IEEE 2nd 5G World Forum (5GWF), pp. 341–346 (2019). https://doi.org/10.1109/5GWF.2019.8911639
13. Openslice, open source, operations support system. http://openslice.io. Accessed Mar 2020
14. Shift2rail initiative. https://shift2rail.org/. Accessed Mar 2020
15. Tranoris, C., Denazis, S.: Patras 5G: an open source based end-to-end facility for 5G trials, ERCIM NEWS, Special Theme 5G, Number 117, April 2020
16. UIC, International Union of Railways: Future railway mobile communication system user requirements specification v5.0, February 2020. https://uic.org/IMG/pdf/frmcs_user_require ments_specification-fu_7100-v5.0.0.pdf. Accessed Mar 2020

5G-VICTORI: Optimizing Media Streaming in Mobile Environments Using mmWave, NBMP and 5G Edge Computing

Louay Bassbouss[1(✉)], Mehdi Ben Fadhel[1(✉)], Stefan Pham[1(✉)], Anita Chen[1(✉)], Stephan Steglich[1(✉)], Eric Troudt[1(✉)], Marc Emmelmann[1(✉)], Jesús Gutiérrez[2(✉)], Nebojsa Maletic[2(✉)], Eckhard Grass[2,5(✉)], Stefan Schinkel[3(✉)], Annette Wilson[4(✉)], Sven Glaser[4(✉)], and Christian Schlehuber[6(✉)]

[1] Fraunhofer FOKUS, Kaiserin-Augusta-Allee 31, 10589 Berlin, Germany
{louay.bassbouss,mehdi.ben.fadhel,stefan.pham,anita.chen,
stephan.steglich,eric.troudt,marc.emmelmann}@fokus.fraunhofer.de
[2] IHP - Leibniz-Institut für Innovative Mikroelektronik, Im Technologiepark 25,
15236 Frankfurt (Oder), Germany
{teran,maletic,grass}@ihp-microelectronics.com
[3] PaxLife Innovations GmbH, Große Weinmeisterstraße 2, 14469 Potsdam, Germany
stefan@paxlife.aero
[4] Rundfunk Berlin-Brandenburg, Marlene-Dietrich-Allee 20, 14482 Potsdam, Germany
{annette.wilson,sven.glaser}@rbb-online.de
[5] Humboldt-Universität zu Berlin, Institut für Informatik, Berlin, Germany
[6] Deutsche Bahn AG, An der Welle 3, 60322 Frankfurt am Main, Germany
Christian.Schlehuber@deutschebahn.com

Abstract. This paper describes an approach for optimizing media streaming services in mobile environments by utilizing the fifth-generation mobile network technology (5G), including millimeter Wave (*mmWave*) high speed data links, 5G Edge Computing and relevant state-of-the-art media streaming standards, such as *Network Based Media Processing (NBMP)* and *Server and Network Assisted DASH (MPEG SAND)*. Although the solution described in this paper can be applied to media streaming in various mobility scenarios, the focus of this work is on rail environments and allowing video-on-demand (VoD) catalogues (Mediatheks) to be made available to train passengers via regular VoD apps – even when trains are not connected to the Internet. To achieve this objective, we introduce caching nodes inside trains and their respective stations. The work presented in this paper will be trialed in a railway station in Berlin, as part of the EU-funded research project, 5G-VICTORI.

Keywords: 5G · mmWave · NBMP · Edge Computing · Data Shower · SAND · CDN

Published by Springer Nature Switzerland AG 2021
I. Maglogiannis et al. (Eds.): AIAI 2021 Workshops, IFIP AICT 628, pp. 31–38, 2021.
https://doi.org/10.1007/978-3-030-79157-5_3

1 Introduction

The aim of digital technologies in the framework of the Fourth Industrial Revolution is to influence a large variety of sectors, with an emphasis on vertical markets for ICT industries, such as transportation, energy, media, and factories of the future. A few examples stemming from this influence include the offering of connected goods, collaborative and automated processes within and across sectors, optimized processes (energy, transportation, logistics, etc.), and new and improved services concerning safety and security.

5G platforms play an essential role in bringing technology players, vendors, operators and vertical markets together. Their interactions are orchestrated in targeting new business models and opportunities for the ICT and vertical industries, and enabling cross-vertical collaborations and synergies in order to offer additional enhancements in value propositions.

There is a clear need to deploy 5G solutions for vertical industries. One of the first steps in the deployment process is the development of 5G infrastructures with flexible architectures in order to address a wide range of vertical applications. These infrastructures would offer converged services across heterogeneous technology domains and have a unified software deployment. In this context, the EU-funded research project, 5G-VICTORI [1], aims to conduct large-scale trials for advanced use case verification in commercially relevant 5G environments for transportation, energy, media and factories of the future, including specific use cases involving cross-vertical interaction. This objective is based on the work being developed within the 5G-PPP ICT-17 5G experimental platforms [2], 5G-VINNI [3], 5GENESIS [4], 5G-EVE [5] and 5GUK [6]. The Berlin cluster exploits the Berlin Platform, which is a 5G infrastructure that is currently being developed in the context of the ICT-17 5GENESIS Project. This cluster will run three use cases at the Berlin Central Station (*Berlin Hauptbahnhof*): 1) digital mobility 2) rail critical services and 3) CDN and media services in dense and mobile environments. This paper will focus on the work being developed within the third use case in order to optimize media streaming services in mobile environments enabled by 5G technologies, including mmWave [8], Edge Computing and media streaming standards such as NBMP [9] and MPEG SAND [10]. The details of this approach are described in the following sections.

2 Background and Concepts

This section presents the relevant components that play significant roles in optimizing media streaming with 5G: content delivery, monitoring and analytics, and media processing.

2.1 Data Shower and Multi-CDN

Streaming services usually deliver their content via content delivery networks (CDNs) [7], which are caches strategically placed at certain nodes of the Internet. These caches hold copies of content in order to optimize media delivery for end-users. CDNs enable a higher level of service reliability and can be designed to optimize the distribution of network load and transmission costs. This concept is extended with 'Multi-CDNs [15]', which connects multiple CDN providers into one large network and combines the power of each. The fastest and most reliable CDN in a region is then selected. In 5G-VICTORI, we follow the multi-CDN concept and extend the streaming service's CDN to trains by equipping them with caches. These caches are filled with content via mmWave high-speed links or so called "Data Shower" to ensure seamless connectivity. This approach allows the transfer of media content from the CDN cache at the train station into the train's cache with multi-Gbps data rates. Data showers are installed at selected locations along the train route—with a starting point at train stations. The Berlin Central Station, a facility of Deutsche Bahn, is used to validate this use case for real-life environments by using the video-on-demand (VoD) catalogue, Mediathek, offered by a German public broadcaster, Radio Berlin Brandenburg (RBB).

2.2 Streaming Monitoring and Analytics via MPEG-SAND

To ensure the reliability of the end-to-end streaming workflow (encoding, packaging, delivery, playback, etc.), it is important to make the right instruments available for monitoring the entire workflow. For this purpose, we use the MPEG-SAND standard, specified in ISO/IEC 23009-5 [11], which defines standardized message formats for communication between server, client and network elements involved in the streaming process of MPEG-DASH. SAND-capable components can exchange real-time information of network and servers, as well as player behaviour and performance data. The SAND Metric Reporting will be integrated into the core of the 5G Network and ARD player (used in the RBB Mediathek), supporting shared resource allocation of multiple streaming clients that compete for bandwidth within the same network.

2.3 Network-Based Media Processing – NBMP

Leveraging processing capabilities and resources in a network is a trending approach in order to accomplish complex media processing tasks, while efficiently utilizing available resources and ensuring the potential for scalability. Deploying such complex services on top of microservices that may run on different cloud services, on an edge, or on-premise, can be a very intricate and time-consuming task.

Network-Based Media Processing (NBMP) [9] provides the high flexibility that is necessary for deploying such complex workflows on top of microservices. NBMP defines interfaces, media, and metadata formats to address fragmentation issues and offer a unified way to perform media processing tasks on top of any cloud platform or IP network. For this reason, we considered the NBMP standard for the deployment of Data Shower and multi-CDN applications.

NBMP consists of three main network entities (see Fig. 1):

1. **Workflow-Manager:** the central entity that manages and configures NBMP workflows and relevant functions.

2. **Tasks:** implements one media processing function at a time. A *Function*, once loaded, becomes a *Task*, which is then configured by the Workflow Manager through the Task API and can begin to process incoming media.
3. **Function Repository:** offers APIs for function discovery and loading function description documents.

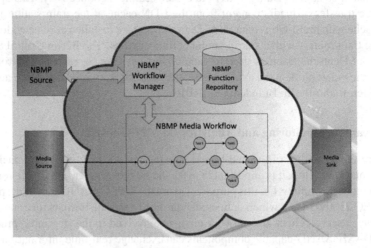

Fig. 1. NBMP Network entities overview [12]

NBMP allows the ability for easier deployments and service updates on distributed architectures, which opens the horizon for several use cases such as "network-assisted media quality enhancement" and "network-assisted media distribution".

3   Data Shower Architecture and Deployment

As mentioned in Sect. 2.1, the main approach followed in the 5G-VICTORI project (to optimize media distribution in mobile environments) is to extend the streaming service's CDN to train stations and trains by equipping them with caches. Media content is transferred from the station cache to the train cache via high-speed mmWave data links, during the time in which trains make their scheduled stops at each station. This installation is called a "Data Shower", which means that a large amount of data is transferred between two endpoints within a short amount of time. While connected to the train's onboard Wi-Fi, passengers can stream the content from the train cache to their personal mobile devices without any interruptions and/or worries of high mobile data plan usage. A high-level overview of this approach is depicted in Fig. 2. In this diagram, there are two users of the same ARD Player App: ARD Player (1) retrieves media content from the CDN cache via public Internet, while ARD Player (2) retrieves content from the train cache while connected to the onboard Wi-Fi in the train.

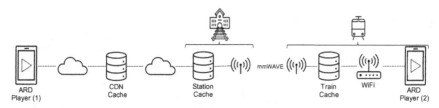

Fig. 2. High level overview

This approach has several advantages. First, content licenses that are already purchased by streaming services for conventional distribution via the Internet, are considered valid. It would be different if the streaming service offered its content via a portal of the train company. In this setup, the train company would become a third-party provider and thus, an additional entity in the exploitation chain. In our setup, the train company is merely the provider or host of the distribution infrastructure. The legal situation is therefore the same as with classic CDNs. A second advantage is that passengers can use the regular app of a streaming service (web or mobile) that is already installed on their personal device(s). Once connected to the train's onboard Wi-Fi, users will experience high-quality on-demand video without any strain on their mobile data budgets.

For cache nodes placed in trains, we rely on standard solutions that are mature in terms of performance and have proven themselves to be efficient in large-scale deployments, such as NGINX [14]. [14] To use NGINX as a for caching purposes, it is operated in a reverse proxy mode. Requests for which NGINX stores responses are then answered directly.

In most cases, not all content of a VoD service's catalogue will fit into the train's cache. High demands are placed on hardware installed in trains, for example, with regards to energy consumption, temperature development and reliability. Accordingly, the hardware is expensive. Content catalogues of large VoD services like ARD-Mediathek [13] have storage requirements of well over 100 TB. Storage spaces of this size are not bargainable, even in the consumer segment. At the latest time in which several VoD services want to offer their services in trains, storage space becomes scarcer and each service must be selective about the content that is made available. Our system currently allows for an editorial preselection of content based on certain criteria. It is conceivable that this provision will later be supplemented or replaced by an automatic selection system, which can foresee what passengers are keen to watch, such as recommendation engines.

The NBMP-enabled Data Shower architecture is depicted in Fig. 3. It describes the functional building blocks of the system that can be deployed on computing and storage nodes at train stations, in trains or in the cloud. Train station components are assumed to have a continuous Internet connection and are hosted on computing resources that are physically located close to the mmWave radio link equipment. This principal applies to components in trains as well, however, do not require a permanent Internet connection.

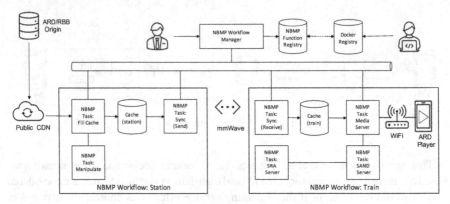

Fig. 3. NBMP Enabled data shower architecture

The station and train components are deployed as NBMP workflows. Each workflow component is an NBMP Task, which implements a specific function that can be easily integrated into the workflow and communicates with other tasks through unified APIs and messaging mechanisms. The workflows can easily be defined, configured and updated via the NBMP workflow manager that is running in the cloud. In a proof-of-concept implementation, each NBMP function is implemented as a Docker image that is available in a centralized Docker registry. The NBMP function registry provides all necessary information in order to deploy a function that becomes an NBMP task. In our case, the task is a Docker container. As such, newly developed features can easily be accessible via the registry and used in new or existing workflows. This functionality becomes more vital in scenarios where media functions are provided by different vendors.

The trial will support the testing of communication between the mmWave unit installed at the rolling stock (Deutsche Bahn train) and the mmWave unit attached to the infrastructure (railway station). In such mobile environments, the use of directional antennas (together with beamforming/beam steering capabilities) becomes necessary to ensure seamless connectivity.

Figure 4 sketches the scenario of the test trial at Berlin Central Station. As the train is approaching or departing the station, beam alignment mechanisms are required to avoid significant signal drops. However, frequent invocations of these mechanisms could lead to a deterioration in performance if the link is not continuously maintained.

The COTS mmWave devices used in the trial will operate at 60-GHz band (i.e., 57–66 GHz) in the four non-overlapping channels used in 802.11ad, where the center frequencies are 58.32, 60.48, 62.64, and 64.8 GHz. The channel bandwidth is 2.16 GHz and the maximal transmit power of approximately 23 dBm, allowing the device to reach a distance of 150 m. The devices allow for an achievable data rate of 2.5 Gbps.

The server installed on the train features two SFP+ connectors at 10 Gbps, which is connected to the mmWave unit attached to the upper part of the train. At the infrastructure level (platform), a simple ruggedized NUC with an IP68 rating is connected to the mmWave unit via a 10 Gbit Ethernet/SFP+.

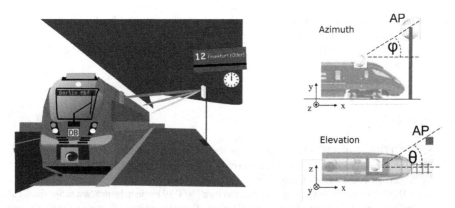

Fig. 4. a) Sketch of the track-to-train communication using mmWave pencil beams b) Azimuth and elevation requirements depending on the angles, COTS hardware used for the trial.

For ensuring seamless connectivity between the two mmWave units, an analysis of the azimuth (XY plane) and elevation (XZ plane) angles between the mmWave unit attached to the train and that of the infrastructure must be carried out. The goal of this analysis is to determine the optimal mounting spots and orientation of both mmWave units. The speed of the train and height at which the units are installed, along with the rate of change of the azimuth and elevation angles as the train moves along the track, will be key parameters that will allow for an evaluation of the beam/sector changes and adaptation time offered by the equipment. This analysis will be required to ensure a maximal data transfer whilst both units are in reach, therefore allowing the transfer of big chunks of media data from the infrastructure to the train.

4 Conclusion

Streaming videos to train passengers can be a frustrating experience, especially if the Internet connection along the train route is not reliable. To address this issue, the 5G-VICTORI project follows the approach of extending conventional CDNs into caches that are deployed in trains and their respective stations, thus improving the overall user experience. We propose that, unlike conventional CDNs, cache nodes in the train do not need to have a permanent connection to the Internet but can be filled with media content via a wireless (mmWave) high speed data connection equipment installed in train stations and in trains. This method occurs shortly before and after the train stops at each station. In this paper, we described the approach, architecture and how state-of-the-art media streaming technologies and standards (such as NBMP and MPEG-SAND) are utilized to achieve our objectives. A planned field trial at Berlin Central Station using the RBB video catalogue will assess the benefits of providing video streaming for train passengers as they reach the stations, and if this concept can be adopted in other locations and means of transportation.

Acknowledgements. The research leading to these results has received funding from the European Union's Framework Programme Horizon 2020 under grant agreements (1) No. 857201 and project name "5G-VICTORI: VertIcal demos over Common large-scale field Trials fOr Rail, energy and media Industries".

References

1. 5G-VICTORI H2020 5G-PPP Project. https://www.5g-victori-project.eu/
2. 5G PPP "The 5G Infrastructure Public Private Partnership" Infrastructure Projects. https://5g-ppp.eu/5g-ppp-phase-3-1-projects/
3. 5G-VINNI "5G Verticals Innovation Infrastructure" ICT-19 Project. https://www.5g-vinni.eu/
4. 5GENESIS "5th Generation End-to-end Network, Experimentation, System Integration, and Showcasing" ICT-17 Project. https://5genesis.eu/
5. 5G-EVE "5G European Validation platform for Extensive trials" ICT-17 Project. https://www.5g-eve.eu/
6. 5GUK Test Networks, University of Bristol 5GUK Test Network. http://www.bristol.ac.uk/engineering/research/smart/5guk/
7. Peng, G.: CDN: Content Distribution Network. CoRR cs.NI/0411069 (2004)
8. Niu, Y., Li, Y., Jin, D., et al.: A survey of millimeter wave communications (mmWave) for 5G: opportunities and challenges. Wireless Netw. **21**, 2657–2676 (2015). https://doi.org/10.1007/s11276-015-0942-z
9. Network-Based Media Processing (NBMP) vision paper. https://mpeg.chiariglione.org/standards/mpeg-i/network-based-media-processing/nbmp-vision-paper
10. DASH-IF position paper: server and network assisted DASH (SAND). https://dashif.org/docs/SAND-Whitepaper-Dec13-final.pdf
11. ISO/IEC 23009-5:2017 Information technology — Dynamic adaptive streaming over HTTP (DASH) — Part 5: Server and network assisted DASH (SAND). https://www.iso.org/standard/69079.html
12. ISO/IEC 23090-8:2020 Information technology — Coded representation of immersive media — Part 8: Network based media processing. https://www.iso.org/standard/77839.html
13. ARD Mediathek –RBB. https://www.ardmediathek.de/rbb/
14. NGINX | High Performance Load Balancer, Web Server, & Reverse Proxy. https://www.nginx.com/
15. Adhikari, V.K., et al.: Unreeling netflix: understanding and improving multi-CDN movie delivery. In: 2012 Proceedings IEEE INFOCOM, Orlando, FL, USA, pp. 1620–1628 (2012). https://doi.org/10.1109/INFCOM.2012.6195531

A Novel Architectural Approach for the Provision of Scalable and Automated Network Slice Management, in 5G and Beyond

Sławomir Kukliński[1,2], Lechosław Tomaszewski[1], Ioannis P. Chochliouros[3]([⊠]) [iD],
Christos Verikoukis[4], Robert Kołakowski[1,2], Anastasia S. Spiliopoulou[3],
and Alexandros Kostopoulos[3]

[1] Orange Polska, ul. Obrzeżna 7, 02-691 Warsaw, Poland
[2] Warsaw University of Technology, pl. Politechniki 1, 00-661 Warsaw, Poland
[3] Hellenic Telecommunications Organization (OTE) S.A., 99 Kifissias Avenue,
15124 Maroussi-Athens, Greece
ichochliouros@oteresearch.gr
[4] Centre Tecnologic de Telecomunicacions de Catalunya (CTTC), Avinguda Carl Friedrich
Gauss 7, 08860 Castelldefels Barcelona, Spain

Abstract. The paper discusses a novel architecture proposed within the scope of
the ongoing MonB5G EU-funded project. Considering a multiplicity of challenges
towards realizing an effective network slice management in modern 5G networks,
our work considers explicitly the context promoted by the Zero-touch network
and Service Management (ZSM) framework, assessed as an indispensable part
of next-generation management systems. MonB5G focuses upon the provision of
scalable and automated management and orchestration of high numbers of parallel
network slices, as envisioned in 5G and beyond. Within this scope, we propose a
detailed architecture composed of static and dynamically deployed components.
Altogether, they support operations related to slicing orchestration, fault management (self-healing), self-configuration, performance optimization (including
energy saving), and security-related operations of slices. In the paper, we identified
each separate architectural layer and explained all involved modules and interfaces.
The proposed framework is able to support the deployment of a massive number
of slices in different administrative and technological domains. Furthermore, the
potential extensions and/or enhancements of the architecture are also proposed
and assessed.

Keywords: 5G · Artificial Intelligence (AI) · Machine Learning (ML) ·
MANO · Network management · Network slicing · Orchestration · Virtual
Network Function (VNF) · Zero-touch network and Service Management (ZSM)

1 Introduction

As 5G technology is growing and very rapidly expanding in a great variety of applications
and/or related sectors [1–3], this radically transforms the underlying communications

I. Maglogiannis et al. (Eds.): AIAI 2021 Workshops, IFIP AICT 628, pp. 39–51, 2021.
https://doi.org/10.1007/978-3-030-79157-5_4

market and creates a multiplicity of advantages for the participating actors [4] in view of new pervasive mobile services of different vertical industries.

5G introduces the use of virtualization technology as a means to offer customized communication service capabilities over the same infrastructure by partitioning it into individualized slices [5]. In this way, it is possible to satisfy the service requirements of different vertical industries. The slices consist of a set of Virtual Network Functions (VNFs) that encapsulate specific sub-services that the slice needs to provide the service functionalities it was designed for [6]. VNFs are mapped to physical nodes of the infrastructure, while the virtual links of the slice are mapped to physical links. The future 5G networks are projected to support massive numbers of network slices with different performance requirements, functionality and timespans [7–9] working concurrently, which together with the already high complexity of the network slicing solution, makes the tasks related to management and orchestration problematic.

The network slice management differs from classical network management schemes as it requires administrating not a single but multiple network domains and the complexity of architectures and the number of managed objects scale up rapidly. The slice-based network management concept generates a set of challenges related to scalability, security, automation in the management of heterogeneous resources (e.g. communication, computational and storage), as well as to energy efficiency without sacrificing performance. The elevated requirements for coverage, bandwidth and latency, as well as inter-domain operation, further exacerbate the complexity of network management [10], making already devised, standard, human-centric managing solutions insufficient and ineffective. The currently widespread centralized approach to network management also negatively impacts the separation and security of network slices as well as the complexity of the central managing entity. Moreover, centralisation also increases the overhead related to slice management data that has to be sent to the management system during the slice operation.

2   Zero-Touch Management in the Scope of the MonB5G Project

The Zero-touch network and Service Management (ZSM) framework [11] is envisaged as a next-generation management system that aims to have all operational processes and tasks executed automatically, ideally fully autonomous. It is based on a variety of distinct principles, including modularity, extensibility, scalability, model-driven and open interfaces, closed-loop management automation, support for stateless management functions, resilience, separation of concerns in management, service composability, intent-based interfaces, functional abstraction, simplicity and automation. In this scope, Artificial Intelligence (AI) is envisioned as a "key enabler" of self-managing capabilities, resulting in lower operational costs, accelerated time-to-value and reduced risk of human error [12].

Zero-touch management is perceived as one of the "key concepts" that can contribute to and significantly simplify network slice management and orchestration tasks. With the extensive usage of AI-driven mechanisms, its goal is to provide self-managed networks with little to no human interaction [13]. With the aim of facing this challenge and within the scope of the ongoing EU-funded MonB5G project [14], an innovative architecture is proposed, capable of "addressing" the aforementioned issues by enabling distribution of functions and provision of strong separation of management of network slices' runtime and orchestration domains.

More specifically, MonB5G aims to provide a new model for the management and orchestration of high numbers of parallel network slices as envisioned in 5G and beyond. One of its core pillars is about promoting data-driven mechanisms, based on novel distributed machine learning algorithms, to enable self-management and self-configuration of network slices, towards reaching the principle of scalable zero-touch network management, where federated Machine Learning- (ML-) aided algorithms will enable a proactive, energy-efficient and secure resource management and slice creation [15]. The main goal of the MonB5G approach is to achieve scalable and automated management of multiple network slices.

The proposed architectural concept intends to facilitate self-managed slices composed of self-managed functions, further extended to slices that are created in multiple orchestration domains. In the related scope, the issue of management complexity is addressed by using AI at multiple levels to achieve specific management goals and to minimize interactions between architectural entities, e.g. by means of hierarchical closed-loop controls and aggregated Key Performance Indicators (KPIs). A heavy emphasis is also set on security [16], management programmability and energy efficiency [17] aspects of network slicing. Furthermore, the proposed concept is deeply rooted in the already devised network slicing management and orchestration solutions that have been developed by other EU-funded projects (in the 5G-PPP framework) or research and standardization bodies.

The MonB5G framework uses the management system decomposition that follows the ITU-T [18] and the MAPE (Monitor-Analyse-Plan-Execute) paradigm [19] as the basis. In our case, the MAPE concept is implemented in a distributed way by means of multiple AI-driven operations. Moreover, the runtime management of slices is distributed and programmable. Additionally, the MANO approach has been slightly enhanced by distributing some orchestration functions [20, 21].

3   Architectural Framework

The key features of the proposed MonB5G framework are the following: (i) a strong separation of concerns; (ii) distribution of management operations; (iii) hierarchical, end-to-end (E2E) slice orchestration; (iv) In-Slice Management (ISM) capability of driving the orchestrator; (v) scalable and programmable slice management; (vi) enhanced security of slices; (vii) support for Management as a Service (MaaS); and (viii) programmable, energy-aware infrastructure management. The abovementioned features are in line with several already established requirements of ETSI ZSM [22, 23].

The MonB5G architecture is composed of static and dynamically deployed components. Altogether, they support operations related to slicing orchestration, fault management (self-healing), self-configuration, performance optimization (including energy-saving), and security-related operations of slices. The overall MonB5G framework is presented in Fig. 1. The MonB5G framework is composed of three distinct layers:

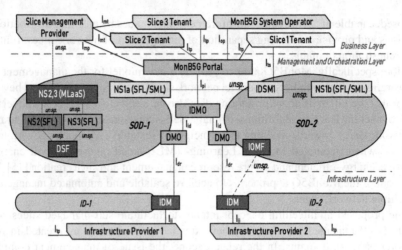

Fig. 1. MonB5G architectural framework.

- **Business Layer,** consisting of the business entities operating the framework, provides slice management services to slice tenants or own a slice (slice tenants).
- **Management and Orchestration Layer,** composed of the core functions of the framework responsible for management and orchestration of Network Slices (NSs), slice Life Cycle Management (LCM), and management interfaces' exposure to specific business entities.
- **Infrastructure Layer,** consisting of the infrastructure, infrastructure providers and functions enabling communication with Management and Orchestration Layer and enabling optimization of usage of infrastructural resources.

According to the architecture presented in Fig. 1, we can distinguish *static* and *dynamic components*. The **static components** are described and discussed in the following paragraphs. Slice Tenants use the MonB5G portal, Slice Management Providers and Infrastructure Providers to request operations regarding slice LCM (i.e. slice deployment, slice modification and slice termination). It also exposes the capabilities offered by the MonB5G framework (available slice templates, etc.) and partakes in negotiations related to the business dimension of the contract. The portal is also used to pass all the accounting and billing-related information and it implements three northbound web interfaces that expose the MonB5G framework capabilities to: MonB5G System Operator (I_{op}, allowing the operator to manage the whole MonB5G system), Slice Tenants (Slice Tenants and Infrastructure Providers use I_{tp} – the interface for slice LCM) and Slice Management Providers (I_{mp} – the interface that the Slice Management provider uses for the communication with Slice Tenants for runtime slice management). Slice Management Providers may use the MaaS platform, called MonB5G Layer as a Service (MLaaS), to offer management of multiple instances of slices based on the same template (as the slice runtime management is slice-specific). LCM of MLaaS is done via the I_{mp} interface. I_{mt} is a web interface used by Slice Management Provider for the runtime slice management communication with Slice Tenants

The *Inter-Domain Manager and Orchestrator (IDMO)* is at the heart of the system. This entity plays a crucial role in slice preparation and deployment phases by negotiation of deployment policy with a slice requester (Slice Tenants, Slice Management Providers or Infrastructure Providers). MonB5G Portal interacts with IDMO via the southbound I_{pi} interface to perform negotiations related to the business dimension of the contracts. The exchanged information concerns aspects like availability of resources, existing policies, the resource demand and other data that enables allocation of a certain amount of resources to the requester. After the successful establishment of the contract, the I_{pi} interface is used for LCM of negotiated slices. If the infrastructure has multiple owners, IDMO may decide how to split the end-to-end slice template dynamically to a new one, which supports inter-domain interaction of slice components located in different orchestration domains. The split may be shaped by various factors, e.g. price, performance or energy efficiency.

The *Domain Manager and Orchestrator (DMO)* is responsible for the orchestration and management of each of the Slice Orchestration Domain (SOD) slices. DMO can be seen as a combination of resource-oriented Operations Support Systems (OSS)/Business Support Systems (BSS) and an orchestrator (it can be either a MANO orchestrator or other). In a similar way to IDMO, all DMO operations are AI-driven. Therefore, the internal structure of DMO is also composed of Functional and MonB5G Layers. The operations related to resource management as well as the exchange of infrastructure-related data (e.g. about energy consumption) are done via the I_{dr} interface.

IDMO interacts with DMOs via the I_{id} interface by using domain handlers to deploy the end-to-end-slices based on the information obtained from DMOs. This interface can be seen as an extended MANO *Os-Ma-Nfvo* interface, it may provide LCM abstractions and provides IDMO data and management capabilities of DMO. It is responsible for modification of the end-to-end slice template before its deployment according to the negotiated contract, and it can be seen as an E2E orchestrator. IDMO may also interact with IDM (via DMO) in order to decide how to deploy slice instance, considering the price, performance or other important factors such as energy efficiency.

The proposed framework assumes that the Infrastructure may also need management. To that end, it is proposed a separate management entity called *Infrastructure Domain Manager (IDM)*. This provides the overall management of the Infrastructure. Its interface to DMO allows for allocating resources (Network Functions Virtualisation Infrastructure (NFVI) agent), exchanging the information related to the energy consumption of resources, and exchanging the information related to the cost of resources that can be used by IDMO for resource brokering. The framework enables programmable infrastructure management. DMO can dynamically deploy management functions that cooperate with IDM to achieve infrastructure management. IDM has an interface to the Infrastructure Provider, who can use the MonB5G portal to ask for the deployment of additional infrastructure management functions, called *Infrastructure Orchestrated Management Functions (IOMFs)*, which are specific for the virtualization technology used in the infrastructure and tools. IDMO can orchestrate the functions upon request of an Infrastructure Provider via the MonB5G Portal.

The **architecture's dynamic components** are slices that are defined in a different way than NGMN has defined them. In MonB5G, a slice is a set of functions that implement a specific goal (not necessarily a network), for example, network management, implementation of services or accelerators that support certain operations of multiple slices.

In MonB5G slice structure (cf. Fig. 2), two separate layers can be extinguished: the slice management part called *Slice MonB5G Layer (SML)* and slice main part called the *Slice Functional Layer (SFL)*. The former performs FCAPS (Fault, Configuration, Accounting, Performance, Security) at the slice-level and can be considered as an embedded slice-level OSS/BSS, with interfaces to the Element Managers (EMs) of the slice's Virtual Network Functions (VNFs)/Physical Network Functions (PNFs) or Cloud-Native Functions (CNFs) and to DMO. SML can be a part of the slice template or be deployed independently.

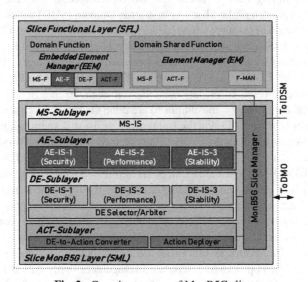

Fig. 2. Generic structure of MonB5G slice.

SFL contains a set of virtual functions that are dedicated solely to a slice and managed via the modified *Element Manager (EM)*, called *Embedded Element Manager (EEM)*, which contains components responsible for its VNF monitoring (MS-F), anomaly detection (AE-F), decision engine (DE-F) and actuating component (ACT-F). SFL can also use functions that are shared functions available in SOD. Such functions may be used by all or some slices. The functions are called *Domain Shared Functions (DSFs)*, which can be implemented as PNFs/VNFs or CNFs and can be reused by SFLs of multiple slices. The use of DSFs provides a reduced footprint of the deployed slices improving that way also slices' deployment time. DSFs are grouped for their management and are managed by the DMO.

SML is an implementation of the ISM [23] concept having in mind the AI-based MAPE management and it provides direct, intent-based management to the Slice Tenant. The SML-based slice management approach can also be used for end-to-end slice management [23] when slices are implemented across multiple domains (SODs). In such a case, the IDSM entity is responsible for the end-to-end slice management. It interacts with SMLs of all domain slices that compose the end-to-end slice. IDSM is a part of the slice template (a set of VNFs), and in some cases, it can be generated automatically by IDMO (if IDMO is responsible for slice template split between multiple SODs). When IDSM is in use, it provides to the Slice Tenant the management interface. IDSM is also responsible for the calculation of slice-related KPIs. I_{ts} is a web interface used by Slice Tenant for runtime slice management and interaction with IDSM or SML.

It is assumed that Monitoring System Sublayer provides generic, reusable monitoring that is consumed by AEs, DEs and other entities of SML, as presented in Fig. 3. MS (Monitoring System) should contain:

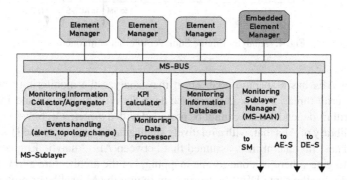

Fig. 3. Monitoring System Sublayer internal components.

- *Monitoring Information Collector/Aggregator* – an entity, which interacts with the *Embedded Element Managers (EEMs)*, i.e. MAPE-based Element Managers (presented in Fig. 2) of SML;
- *Monitoring Information Database* – a database in which collected monitoring data are stored in a raw and pre-processed format;
- *Monitoring Information Processor* – an entity that is responsible for filtering, interpolation and prediction of the monitoring data;
- *Slice KPI calculator* – an entity that is used for the calculation and prediction of slice specific KPIs
- *Monitoring Sublayer Manager* – an entity that allows remote configuration of MS sublayer operations.

The MS sublayer's output is accessible to other components of SML via a message bus (publish/subscribe paradigm in use). MS has to interact with EEMs that are VNF-specific, but most of the MS operations are generic. Therefore, many of the internal components of MS can be reused for multiple slice templates. The protocols for efficient communication between EEMs and MS and the adaptability of monitoring (adaptive sample rate or resolution, using gossiping protocols, etc.) are out of the scope of the paper, but such mechanisms are allowed by the MonB5G framework.

The *Analytic Engines Sublayer* includes a set of AEs (Analytic Engines) and the *AE Sublayer Manager* that is used to configure AEs remotely, as depicted in Fig. 4.

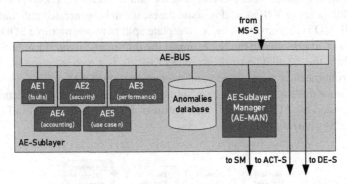

Fig. 4. Analytic Engine Sublayer internal components.

Each of AEs has a specific goal, i.e. it may analyze the monitoring traffic for a specific security threat, fault or performance degradation. The internal specification of AE is algorithm-dependent and cannot be provided with *a priori*; it is, however, possible to create a library of AEs that, with a relatively small adaptation, can be used for different slice templates. In general, it is assumed that between AE (Analytic Engine) and DE (Decision Engine), there is a one-to-one mapping, but the architecture allows to use of multiple AEs for the same DE. It is worth mentioning the MS sublayer provides some kind of abstraction of the monitored data that positively contributes to the reusability of AEs.

The *DE Sublayer* consists of the entities that are responsible for the reconfiguration of SFL or SML. It is assumed that the DE sublayer is composed of multiple DEs, as presented in Fig. 5. Each of them is trying to reach a specific goal regarding performance optimization according to KPIs, fault handling, security, or enforcing the slice's energy-efficient operations. The input to the DE sublayer is the output of AE and MS sublayers. Each of the FCAPS functions may require multiple DEs. The existence of multiple "selfish" DEs implies the need for their decisions arbitrage. For this problem, the *DE Selector/Arbiter* component is implemented in the DE sublayer. The component can be AI-driven as one of the implementation options is implementing several DEs that use different algorithms for the same goal. In such a case, the *Coordinator/Arbiter* is creating a ranking of DEs. As the feedback-loop-based management's stability can be an issue, a special entity called *Stability Observer* is introduced in the DE sublayer. It is used in order to avoid the chaotic behaviour of the system or the ping-pong effect. The *Stability Observer* uses *Reconfiguration History Database* to restore to the last stable configuration. This database stores recent reconfiguration decisions together with the input values that were used by DEs to take the decision reconfiguration. As other sublayers of SML, the DE sublayer has a *DE Sublayer Manager* that can be used for the change of the configuration of its components or their policies.

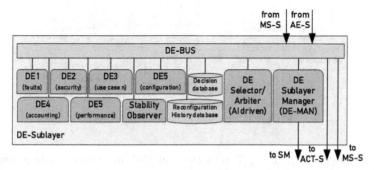

Fig. 5. DE Sublayer internal components.

The DE decision can be used for the reconfiguration of SFL or SML. In both cases, there are three possible reconfiguration operation types:

- Reconfiguration of functions/nodes of SFL/SML;
- Change of resource allocation to SFL/SML components (including transport). Dependent on the implementation, it can be done directly or by the interaction with DMO;
- Modification of SFL/SML by the upgrade of the slice template. In this case, the SML will interact with DMO requesting deployment or removing a specific function or a node.

It is noteworthy that the modification of resource allocation to SFL or SML by SML can be proactive instead of the MANO orchestration's reactive approach. Moreover, in the case of SFL, resource allocation can be driven by slice Quality of Experience. The modification of the SFL template, driven by SML, may be used for cloning some slice functions to optimize slice traffic or add additional components like DPIs (Deep Packet Inspections) or firewalls. The same mechanism can be used for the programmability of SML, providing that way programmability of the slice management plane. Using the mechanism during SML runtime, new components like AEs or DEs can be added. This feature is vital for the evaluation of different AE and DE algorithms, but the programmability is also important in real implementations.

The *Actuating Functions Sublayer* role is to convert high-level (intent) reconfiguration commands obtained from the DE sublayer into a set of atomic reconfiguration commands, as shown in Fig. 6.

Due to the existence of the ACT sublayer, the DEs do not have to deal with reconfiguration details. Therefore, they can be designed in a more generic way. The ACT sublayer can be seen as a set of device-specific (i.e. node/functions) drivers. ACT typically interacts with EMs/EEMs of SFL, but they may also interact with DMO requesting orchestration related action (adding or removing a VNF).

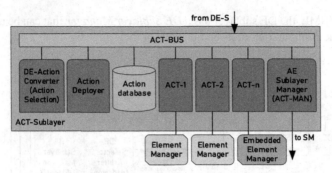

Fig. 6. ACT-Sublayer internal components.

Slice Manager (SM), cf. Fig. 7, is an entity of SML that provides interactions with DMO and IDSM; it can also be used for the manual management of SFL or to implement Policy-Based Management. It interacts with EEMs, MS, AEs and DEs. It is responsible for sending to DMO and, if applicable, to IDSM, slice-related synthetic information (KPIs). SML provides direct, intent-based management to the Slice Tenant. This is a perfect way of providing slices management isolation. For that purpose, the Slice Manager has a tenant portal and a set of tools that enable simple and comfortable slice management by slice tenant. A *conditio sine qua non* for such management is the management's embedded intelligence that is in our case provided by AI algorithms.

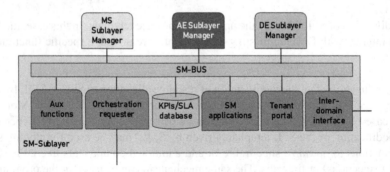

Fig. 7. Slice Manager internal components.

The management interface is created after slice deployment, and the slice tenant can use it for the lifetime of a slice. For accounting and historical reasons, the accounting data combined with slice resource consumptions and KPIs are transferred to the IDMO Accounting database before termination of the slice.

4   Assessment and Further Expectations

According to our best knowledge, the proposed preliminary concept is the first one that addresses the scalability and robustness of network slicing management and orchestration by using a distributed, AI-driven and programmable management architecture.

These features make the proposed approach effective, scalable and flexible, on a dynamic basis.

The ETSI ZSM requirements list contains over 170 different topics that makes impossible to recall all of them in the context of the current MonB5G approach. More specifically, some of the requirements concern procedures like testing or software upgrade; therefore, they are not related directly to the actual MonB5G architecture. The list is "flat" and without any grouping. For the purpose of our current approach, it has been decided to split them into several categories related to the specific aspects of autonomic service management. These categories all fully satisfied by the MonB5G context and include: (i) Monitoring and data analytics (which is about the requirements associated with collection of the performance data, their aggregation and ways of data usage to fuel analytic engines); (ii) management actions (which consist of requirements in terms of network maintenance, coordination of management, recovery actions, etc.); (iii) management operations (which relate to access to network slicing management services, LCM, management data policies, etc.); (iv) control loops (their operation, disabling in terms of faulty operation, etc.); and (v) several other important requirements not belonging to previous categories.

The use of distributed components with embedded intelligence has made it possible to use intent-based interfaces that also reduce the information exchange between management functions and subsystems. Moreover, we have used a multi-domain orchestration and separation of each slice's management from domain resource management. The use of the ISM concept can reduce the number of external slice interfaces and provides a perfect separation of the slice management plane that cannot be achieved in the 3GPP approach to network slicing management. The implementation of slice management as a part of a slice (i.e. a set of VNFs) provides higher scalability of slice performance and allows for the programmability of slice management services on-the-fly.

In addition, AI-enabled management operations can be adopted at different levels of the management hierarchy. In this scope, AI-driven slice management functionalities can be embedded as a part of a slice, providing, in that way, the higher elasticity in the creation and the deployment of diverse slice types. This framework also provides a strong separation of concerns which contributes significantly to complexity reduction and easier administration of slices, especially in multi-domain slices deployed over different infrastructure domains belonging to several owners. Altogether the abovementioned features enable making a significant step towards self-managed network slices.

Acknowledgments. This work has been performed in the scope of the *MonB5G* European Research Project and has been supported by the Commission of the European Communities *(H2020, Grant Agreement No. 871780).*

References

1. Global System for Mobile Communications Alliance (GSMA): An Introduction to 5G Network Slicing. GSMA (2017). https://www.gsma.com/futurenetworks/wp-content/uploads/2017/11/GSMA-An-Introduction-to-Network-Slicing.pdf

2. Rost, P., Banchs, A., Berberana, I., Reitbach, M., Doll, M., et al.: Mobile network architecture evolution toward 5G. IEEE Commun. Mag. **54**(5), 84–91 (2016)
3. Andrews, J.G., Buzzi, S., Choi, W., Hanly, S.V., et al.: What will 5G be. IEEE JSAC Spec. Issue 5G Wirel. Commun. Syst. **32**(6), 1065–1082 (2014)
4. Chochliouros, I.P., et al.: Business and market perspectives in 5G networks. In: Proceedings of the Joint 13th CTTE and 10th CMI Conference 2017, pp. 1–6. IEEE (2017)
5. Bosneag, A.M., Wang, M.X.: Intelligent network management mechanisms as a step towards SG. In: Proceedings of the NOF-2017 Conference, pp. 52–57 IEEE (2017)
6. European Telecommunications Standards Institute: ETSI GS NFV 002 V1.2.1: Network Functions Virtualisation (NFV); Architectural Framework, ETSI (2014). https://www.etsi.org/del iver/etsi_gs/NFV/001_099/002/01.02.01_60/gs_nfv002v010201p.pdf
7. Sharma, S., Miller, R., Francini, A.: A cloud-native approach to 5G network slicing. IEEE Commun. Mag. **55**(8), 120–127 (2017)
8. Elliott, J., Sharma, S.: Dynamic End-to-End Network Slicing unlocks 5G Possibilities. Nokia (2016). https://www.nokia.com/blog/dynamic-end-end-network-slicing-unlocks-5g-possibilities/
9. Chochliouros, I.P., Spiliopoulou, A.S., Lazaridis, P., Dardamanis, A., Zaharis, Z., Kostopoulos, A.: Dynamic network slicing: challenges and opportunities. In: Maglogiannis, I., Iliadis, L., Pimenidis, E. (eds.) AIAI 2020. AICT, vol. 585, pp. 47–60. Springer, Cham (2020). https://doi.org/10.1007/978-3-030-49190-1_5
10. Chochliouros, Ioannis P., et al.: Putting intelligence in the network edge through NFV and cloud computing: the SESAME approach. In: Boracchi, G., Iliadis, L., Jayne, C., Likas, A. (eds.) EANN 2017. CCIS, vol. 744, pp. 704–715. Springer, Cham (2017). https://doi.org/10.1007/978-3-319-65172-9_59
11. European Telecommunications Standards Institute: ETSI GS ZSM 002 V1.1.1: Zero-touch Network and Service Management (ZSM); Reference Architecture, ETSI (2019). https://www.etsi.org/deliver/etsi_gs/ZSM/001_099/002/01.01.01_60/gs_ZSM002v010101p.pdf
12. Benzaid, C., Taleb, T.: AI-driven zero touch network and service management in 5 g and beyond: challenges and research directions. IEEE Netw. **34**(2), 186–194 (2020)
13. Carrozzo, G., Shuaib Siddiqui, M., Betzler, A., Bonnet, J., et al.: AI-driven zero-touch operations, security and trust in multi-operator 5G networks: a conceptual architecture. In: Proceedings of EuCNC 2020, pp. 254–258. IEEE (2020)
14. H2020/5G-PPP MonB5G project: Distributed management of Network Slices in beyond 5G, Grant Agreement No.871780. https://www.monb5g.eu/
15. Jiang, C., Zhang, H., Ren, Y., Han, Z., et al.: Machine learning paradigms for next-generation wireless networks. IEEE Wirel. Commun. **24**(2), 98–105 (2017)
16. Benzaid, C., Taleb, T.: ZSM security: threat surface and best practices. IEEE Netw. Mag. **34**(3), 124–133 (2020)
17. Chen, X., Wu, J., Cai, Y., Zhang, H., et al.: Energy-efficiency oriented traffic offloading in wireless networks: a brief survey and a learning approach for heterogeneous cellular networks. IEEE J. Sel. Areas Commun. **33**(4), 627–640 (2015)
18. International Telecommunication Union – Telecommunication Standardization Sector (ITU-T): ITU-T Recommendation M.3000 (02/00): Overview of TMN Recommendations (2000)
19. IBM Corporation: An architectural blueprint for autonomic computing. Autonomic Computing White Paper, 4th edn. (2006)
20. European Telecommunications Standards Institute: ETSI GS NFV-MAN 001 V1.1.1: Network Functions Virtualisation (NFV); Management and Orchestration, ETSI (2014). https://www.etsi.org/deliver/etsi_gs/nfv-man/001_099/001/01.01.01_60/gs_nfv-man001v010101p.pdf

21. European Telecommunications Standards Institute: ETSI GR NFV-IFA 023 V3.1.1: Network Functions Virtualisation (NFV); Management and Orchestration; Report on Policy Management in MANO; Release 3, ETSI (2017). https://www.etsi.org/deliver/etsi_gr/NFV-IFA/001_099/023/03.01.01_60/gr_NFV-IFA023v030101p.pdf
22. European Telecommunications Standards Institute: ETSI GS ZSM 001 V1.1.1: Zero touch network and Service Management (ZSM); Requirements based on documented scenarios, ETSI (2019). https://www.etsi.org/deliver/etsi_gs/ZSM/001_099/001/01.01.01_60/gs_ZSM 001v010101p.pdf
23. Kukliński, S., Tomaszewski, L.: DASMO: A scalable approach to network slices management and orchestration. In: Proceedings of NOMS 2018 - 2018 IEEE/IFIP Network Operations and Management Symposium, pp. 1–6. IEEE (2018)

A Prototype 5G/IoT Implementation for Transforming a Legacy Facility to a Smart Factory

Panagiotis Papaioannou[1]([✉]), Nikolaos Tzanis[2], Christos Tranoris[1],
Spyros Denazis[1], and Alexios Birbas[1]

[1] Department of Electrical and Computer Engineering,
University of Patras, Patras, Greece
{papajohn,sdena,birbas}@upatras.gr, tranoris@ece.upatras.gr
[2] Department of Research, Technology and Development Independent Power
Transmission Operator (IPTO), Athens, Greece
n.tzanis@admie.gr

Abstract. A typical factory consists of several low functionality sensors. This work presents an architecture that can enhance the day-to-day operation of the site by combining modern IoT and legacy equipment and transforming the site for the 5G era. Operation and security of the site will benefit from the low latency the proposed Mobile Edge Computing architecture offers. Constant and uninterrupted monitoring makes preventive maintenance decisions even more accurate. Multitier architecture allows monitoring of each site to be performed locally without delays, while overall monitoring and control of remote sites is feasible as well.

Keywords: Smart factory · 5G · IoT

1 Introduction

A Smart Factory is defined as a smart and reconfigurable network of interconnected sensors, machines, and production systems, which collect, exchange and analyze data in a unified and automated way [1]. It is characterized by the ability to collect, store, and handle large amounts of data, originating from different types of sensors, and support different applications with diverse requirements. Actions in a Smart Factory can be divided into three broad categories: operation, security, and maintenance. Maintenance activities require support of low cost, energy efficient sensors, planted in a distributed and heterogeneous infrastructure. Security and operation services ask for low latency and high reliability

Supported by the H2020 European Projects 5G-VINNI (grant agreement No. 815279) and 5G-VICTORI (grant agreement No. 857201).

I. Maglogiannis et al. (Eds.): AIAI 2021 Workshops, IFIP AICT 628, pp. 52–61, 2021.
https://doi.org/10.1007/978-3-030-79157-5_5

communication and high bandwidth for CCTV. Modern trends in network architectures and virtualization technologies such as Multi-access Edge Computing (MEC) and Network Function Virtualization (NFV), inherently supported by 5G, will be major enablers for the development of such Factories. MEC is used to get processing power and storage capabilities as close to the edge of the mobile network as possible. No longer is there a simple base station or a cell tower but enough computing power to run services and applications near their source. These services can benefit greatly from the local processing by minimizing the transport delay to the core network.

NFV architecture separates network functions from the underlying infrastructure, providing optimized reconfiguration, easy integration of new services, and guaranteed isolation, through the concept of network slicing. Application and network functionalities are defined as Virtual Network Functions (VNFs) and orchestrated by an NFV Orchestrator (NFVO), responsible for the management of virtual resources across multiple data centers.

Through ICT-17 projects [2], 5G testbeds become available to verticals to test their applications and their benefit from the services provided by 5G. To this end, the 5G-VICTORI [3] project conducts large-scale trials for advanced vertical use case verification for Transportation, Energy, Media, and Factories of the Future related use cases.

For the Factories of the Future use case, the project's objective is to demonstrate how the concept of Smart Factory can be substantially improved by the services provided by an underlying 5G ICT infrastructure. Considering that traditional factories already use legacy infrastructure (sensors, networks, industrial protocols) for their operation, the smooth transition to a new, modern factory model must assure backward compatibility with the legacy equipment.

This paper describes the work related to the Factories of the Future use case, towards the transformation and modernization of the monitoring system of a traditional facility for the 5G era, by introducing the NFV and MEC architectures and incorporating the legacy equipment to the solution. The rest of the paper is organized as follows: In Sect. 2 the details of the use case trials are presented. Sect. 3 describes the proposed architecture while Sect. 4 details the infrastructure of the used testbed. In Sect. 5 two specific use scenarios for our architecture are presented. Finally, we conclude this work by presenting the results of our approach and our future directions.

2   Specific Use Case

The trial takes place at the Independent Power Transmission Operator (IPTO) facility located near the University of Patras, Greece. The facility consists of two different sites divided by sea and electrically interconnected via a High Voltage (HV) submarine cable and is ideal for demonstrating how applications of the three different classes (operation, maintenance, security) can be supported by a 5G enabled infrastructure.

Operation: The two sites serve as terminal points of the submarine cable and are equipped with several hard-wired sensors, measuring various quantities such as oil pressure level, battery level, etc. The sensors produce thousands of measurements every minute, but only at local level, and provide limited information through indication lights. A unified monitoring system, able to process data from both sites in real-time and generate alerts or auto trip signals in case of major problems, will lead to great improvement in power quality, and support fault prediction algorithms, minimizing the power network down-time. Since the legacy sensors are not network enabled, the first step is to enhance them with a network interface. In this sense, legacy sensors will be first connected to a Modbus TCP interface and then connected via ethernet to the rest of the network.

Preventive Maintenance: The overall infrastructure at both sites needs continuous monitoring, to schedule timely maintenance activities and prevent equipment degradation and failure. Currently, inspection of equipment, buildings, etc., is performed by personnel, and since the facilities are spread to remote and hard to reach locations, this is a demanding and costly task. Preventive maintenance applications collect measurements from sensors planted in key locations of the facilities, compare them with historical data and produce useful reports regarding the health of the infrastructure. For this reason, several wireless sensors will be planted to the facilities. Due to the enormous number of sensors that need to be used to cover every inch of the facilities and the difficulty to access many remote locations, low-cost and low-power devices must be used. This concept is directly related to the massive IoT (mMTC) concept, where small and infrequent data packets are transmitted from numerous standalone devices. The network technology providing connectivity to such devices must satisfy these requirements and support high capacity and low latency for some use cases.

Security: The two sites also serve as local warehouses for IPTO, where pieces of equipment such as copper cables and transformers are stored and maintained. ADMIE facilities have been the victim of copper cable theft and vandalism for several years. An advanced security system consisting of a set of FHD cameras and motion control sensors will be deployed in the facilities. The deployed equipment should be able to stream high quality data to be used complementary to the sensors generated data. An application will process the generated data, recognize unauthorized access to facilities and trigger corresponding alarms.

This particular use case can greatly benefit by using a MEC architecture. Operation and Security applications can meet their strict latency requirements, by leveraging the local processing capabilities of MEC architecture. Preventive maintenance activities also act on local level, so local storage and processing of the data produced by the various sensors, can lead to substantial reduction in cloud storage and communication bandwidth at the core network. Moreover, since a Smart Factory is a continuously evolving system, new services may be deployed in the future, especially in the areas of Industry 4.0 and 5G. In this sense, the proposed architecture, shown in Fig. 1, is easily reconfigurable and expandable with the minimum cost and effort.

3   High Level Architecture

In order to fulfill the requirement for local processing and storage at each site, while also being able to connect and remotely configure the two sites as a unified monitoring system, the end-to-end architecture depicted in Fig. 1 is considered. A multi-tier architecture will be implemented, where each site is able to perform local processing and storage activities, and information is forwarded to the core cloud only when necessary. At each site, except from the already installed sensors, new types of sensors based on a diverse set of different technologies (5G, NB-IoT etc.) will be deployed, as well as the required network elements that provide coverage to them.

Each site will have an Edge Cloud, consisting of a server with adequate computational capabilities to support the use case applications requirements. The server will host an Edge IoT Platform, responsible for the collection and storage of the measurements originating from the different sensors. Furthermore, the server will also host a set of Virtual Network Functions to facilitate our Use Case specifics.

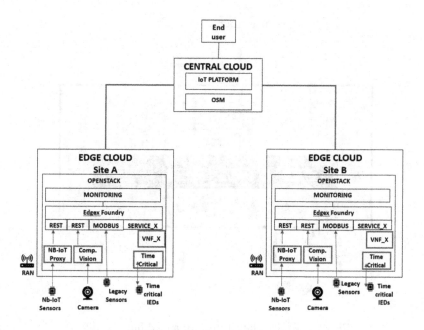

Fig. 1. Basic architecture

NB-IoT Proxy: To support the NB-IoT connectivity, a VNF is deployed to act as a gateway for the NB-IoT devices. Besides being responsible for the reception and initial handling of the data received by the NB-IoT devices it also forwards these to the Edge IoT Platform. Further functionality, like decision making or issuing commands to the NB-IoT devices can be added.

Optical Recognition: For other aspects of the use case, VNFs like optical recognition for the cameras is also planned to be deployed on the Edge cloud.

Time Critical Services: For the real-time operation case, a VNF checking the data received from specific Intelligent Electronic Devices (IEDs) and emitting control signals to them, in case of emergency, will be deployed.

Edge IoT Platform: The deployed IoT platform is EdgeX Foundry [4], an open-source, vendor-neutral, Edge IoT platform, developed under the Linux Foundation Edge umbrella. EdgeX Foundry acts as a middleware between the various sensors and devices, and the vertical applications that use the information provided by these devices. The platform's architecture is depicted in Fig. 2 and is organized as a set of different containerized microservices, each one belonging to one service family.

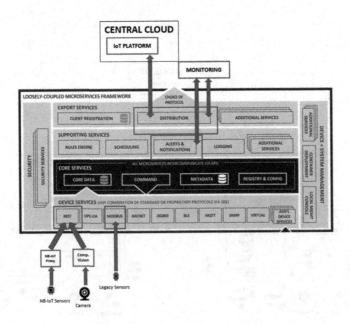

Fig. 2. EdgeX architecture with added functionality

The Device Services family provide a southbound API with the different devices, sensors, and actuators. It is a set of connectors, encapsulating the specific requirements of different open source or proprietary protocols, and providing a unified way for the interaction with the edge devices. These connectors are used to collect measurements from the edge devices and translate them into meaningful information or take commands from the vertical applications and transform them into protocol-specific messages understood by the edge devices. As implied by the name, the Core Services family performs the core functionality of the platform. Core data is a centralized database for data readings collected by devices and sensors, whereas core command enables the different microservices, applications, or external systems to interact with the end devices. The configuration and registry services are used to configure the specific deployment (e.g. add or remove a new sensor).

In our implementation, Modbus TCP and REST device services of EdgeX Foundry are used. Modbus device service is used for data collection and issuing of commands to the legacy Modbus sensors. The REST device service receives measurements from sensors using protocols not currently supported by an EdgeX device service. In this case, the NB-IoT-Proxy will be deployed as VNF, which receives the NB-IoT capable sensors' measurements, packets them in appropriate REST requests, and transmits them to the EdgeX REST device service.

Central Cloud: The two sites are interconnected through a core cloud infrastructure. The central cloud also hosts a set of Use case specific VNFs such as the IoT platform responsible for the collection, processing, and storage of the aggregated data from the two sites. It also gives remote access to the end user, and the ability to configure centrally the overall ICT infrastructure.

4 Infrastructure/Testbed

The infrastructure used for our experimentation is the Patras5G testbed infrastructure [5,6], which currently deploys one of the main 5G experimental facilities in 5G-VINNI [7], a European HORIZON 2020 project. This 5G facility is used to host verticals and applications (in the areas of Media, Gaming, Transportation and Energy) from two ICT 19 European HORIZON 2020 projects (5G-SOLUTIONS [8] and 5G-VICTORI [3]) .

The main cloud platform is located inside Patras University, and can host among others, 5G core network components and any NFV required for services oriented to the supported verticals. The cloud platform offers a total computing power of 212 CPUs and 768 Gigabytes of RAM and 30 TB of storage.

Furthermore, the facility can also deploy outdoor MEC units capable of supporting both cloud computing and 5G or other wireless connections. The main MEC unit of the facility is the "5G Autonomous Edge" [9], a mobile box, built for on-demand 5G deployments depending on the verticals' use case requirements. The Autonomous Edge (Fig. 3) is based on 3 INTEL Xeon based servers giving in total 16 cores, 128 Gigabytes of RAM and 1 TB of storage. Additionally, it is connected with a 5G Software Defined Radio interface. (Ettus USRP N310 [10])

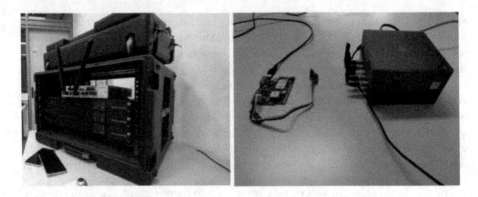

Fig. 3. Autonomous edge and NB-IoT setup

Software wise, both core platform and MEC platform support the ETSI NFV architecture. A basic element of this architecture is the Management and orchestration (MANO), which is the framework that coordinates the network resources and the management of VNFs. Open Source MANO (OSM) [11] is the MANO used, while the virtualized environment is based on Openstack [12].

ETSI OSM is an ETSI initiative to create an Open Source NFV-MANO framework aligned with its reference architecture and standards. ETSI OSM provides an end-to-end network service orchestration functionality through the interaction of the core components of its architecture. The module Resource Orchestrator (RO) of OSM, plays a fundamental role since it is the block in charge of managing the allocation of computational resources (i.e., the compute, network, and storage). This accommodates the execution over an NFVI of various virtual network functionalities included in a network service. For this purpose, the RO supports the interactivity with a large variety of VIM solutions such as Openstack.

On top of the core platform and any number of deployed MEC devices, the Patras5G testbed infrastructure hosts an Operations Support System (OSS), called Openslice [13]. It supports VNFD/NSD onboarding to OSM and Network Service (NS) deployment management, which allows control of what applications and services can be run and deployed on our experimentation infrastructure.

Regarding 5G connectivity, the facility can support 4G/5G core services along with the required radio using SDR based solutions. Both open source and commercial implementations can be used and deployed as required. 5G capable UEs include mobile phones and CPEs acting as gateways to legacy devices. Furthermore, NBIoT is also supported by the facility both in deploying such a network and providing NB-IoT enabled devices such as the Sara R410 NB-IoT developer boards [14]. These devices connect through a deployed NB-IoT network and can transmit information such as location, humidity, temperature etc.

For further support of the services provided by the Patras5G also provides monitoring solutions if required that allow the gathering of various metrics (system or network related) from the deployed services and deliver them to the

interested parties. The solution used is Netdata [15] an open-source, performance and health monitoring system for systems and applications which can be
configured to gather metrics from various sources.

For more persistent storage and centric oriented monitoring, an IoT platform
is deployed to gather data from each of the IPTO sites. Furthermore, VPN
services are also available for secure and isolated services among the users of the
infrastructure.

5   Scenarios

Towards a realization of the proposed architecture, in this section, two different
operational scenarios are presented. In scenario 1, the services collect, store, and
visualize a set of measurements from an NB-IoT gateway, whereas in scenario
2, the NB-IoT gateway and the EDGEX foundry are reconfigured by issuing
specific commands to them.

Scenario 1: Figure 4 illustrates the complete flow for a set of measurements,
originating from a Sodaq Sara R410 NB-IoT [14] gateway, to the end user.

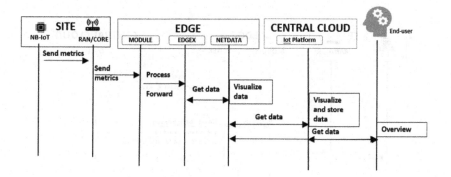

Fig. 4. Sequence diagram of NB-IoT data path

The NB-IoT device is connected to the NB-IoT cellular network, deployed
by the Limenet Mini [16], and periodically sends the sensor's readings (temperature, humidity and location), via a custom-made UDP client. The gateway is
configured to send a new set of measurements every 1 sec. The other end of the
connection is the NB-IoT proxy deployed as VNF.

At the NB-IoT proxy, a UDP server receives the UDP packet and extracts the
needed information. For each reading, a different HTTP request is constructed
and sent to the corresponding REST device of the EdgeX Foundry REST device
service. In this scenario, three REST devices named Sara_temp1, Sara_hum1 and
Sara_loc1 are added in the configuration service of EdgeX.

When the HTTP request for a reading is received by the assigned REST device, the device service translates the request and stores the reading at the EdgeX database via the Core Service functionality. From there, every vertical application can access the data via HTTP GET requests. MEC approach allows for the readings to be locally stored and further processed on site.

For real-time monitoring of the facility at a local level, a Netdata instance can also be deployed at the MEC whenever requested. This is achieved by instantiating a NS which deploys a VNF that automatically installs and configures Netdata. This VNF can communicate with EdgeX Foundry through periodic HTTP GET requests to collect and visualize the stored measurements. By accessing Netdata the site health status can be monitored locally. For a holistic monitoring of the IPTO sites, and for applications that require synchronized measurements from both sites, each MEC can also connect to an IoT platform on the core network allowing the monitoring of all sites on central IPTO site.

Scenario 2: Besides getting measurements from the deployed devices, the architecture also allows for on-the-fly configuration changes on the deployed services. This can be performed by using the day-2 configuration capabilities of the OSM, which allows us to send appropriate commands to the Network Functions to implement our services. This scenario can be seen in Fig. 5.

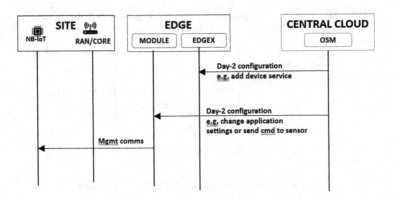

Fig. 5. Sequence diagram of control path

In this scenario two changes are performed to the previous setup. First, OSM's day-2 configuration capabilities can be used to add a new device entry at the EdgeX foundry Core service. As a second change, a modification of the reporting period of the UDP client in the NB-IoT gateway is required. This time OSM issues a command to the NB-IoT endpoint with the new reporting period value. The NB-IoT endpoint then translates the command and forwards it to the respected NB-IoT gateway through their communication path. Instead of altering the reporting period, the command could refer to other configuration allowed by the software running on those devices, providing a rudimentary over-the-air update of those devices.

6 Conclusions and Future Work

This work presents current prototype results of the transformation process of a legacy facility to a Smart Factory, adopting a cloud-edge architecture and modern 5G/IoT solutions able to support sufficiently the different services deployed in a Smart Factory (operation, security, maintenance). By leveraging the concepts of NFV and MEC, and a set of open-source applications (EdgeX, Net Data, OSM), the IoT platform and related monitoring solution is centrally reconfigured in a flexible and cost effective manner, in order to support new services, especially in the areas of Industry 4.0 and 5G. Towards this realization, two different services are presented, for data collection and for on-the-fly reconfiguration.

Our next steps will be to enhance the solution with new functionality for the support of different industrial communication protocols, and new types of sensors. We will contribute to the open source community by extending the capabilities of the EdgeX platform. Furthermore, we will take advantage of the local processing capabilities provided by the architecture to achieve improved real-time equipment awareness and develop smarter control techniques.

References

1. Smart Factory of Industry 4.0: Key Technologies, Application Case, and Challenges. https://ieeexplore.ieee.org/stamp/stamp.jsp?arnumber=8207346
2. Information and Communication Technologies (H2020-ICT-2018-20) Call. https://ec.europa.eu/info/funding-tenders/opportunities/portal/screen/opportunities/topic-details/ict-17-2018
3. 5G VICTORI Homepage. https://www.5g-victori-project.eu/
4. EdgeX Foundry Homepage. https://www.edgexfoundry.org/
5. Tranoris, C., Denazis, S.G.: Patras 5G: An open Source based End-to-End facility for 5G trial. In: ERCIM News, vol. 2019, Issue 117 (2019)
6. Patras 5G homepage. https://wiki.patras5g.eu/
7. Horizon 2020 homepage. https://www.5g-vinni.eu/
8. 5G Solutions project homepage. https://www.5gsolutionsproject.eu/
9. Autonomous edge Homepage. https://wiki.patras5g.eu/5g-autonomous-edge
10. Ettus Homepage. https://www.ettus.com/all-products/usrp-n310/
11. OSM Homepage. https://osm.etsi.org
12. Openstack Homepage. http://www.openstack.org/
13. Openslice Homepage. https://openslice.readthedocs.io/en/stable/
14. Sodaq Homepage. https://support.sodaq.com/Boards/Sara_AFF/
15. NetData Homepage. https://www.netdata.cloud/
16. LimeNetMini Homepage. https://limemicro.com/products/systems/limenet-mini/

Advanced First Responders' Services by Using FASTER Project Architectural Solution

Christina C. Lessi[1]([✉]), Ioannis P. Chochliouros[1], Panagiotis Trakadas[2], and Panagiotis Karkazis[2]

[1] Hellenic Telecommunications Organization (OTE) S.A., 99 Kifissias Avenue, 15124 Maroussi, Athens, Greece
`clessi@oteresearch.gr`

[2] Synelixis Solutions S.A., 157 Perissou and Chalkidos, 14343 Athens, Greece

Abstract. As the 5G technologies start to become a reality in telecommunication networks, more services and applications are designed to take advantage of the new features that 5G technology is offering. Additionally, several vertical sectors are using advanced applications in order to improve their performances. One important vertical is the Mission Critical Services (MCS) sector, which could significantly exploit 5G networks. When an emergency event occurs, such as a strong earthquake or a flood, the network traffic is proved to be rapidly increased. At the same time, the first responders need all the available resources in order to offer their services efficiently. In a situation like the one described which is extremely demanding and the available resources should be used as a priority by the first responders, the existing 4G network does not seem to be sufficient. It must be ensured that the first responders could be interconnected in a reliable network, which will provide a low latency and ultra-high throughput transmission being able to support all the advanced equipment and devices (UAVs, robots, AMRs, augmented reality and virtual reality glasses, etc.) that the first responders need. These requirements are satisfied by 5G networks. The 5G network architecture has been designed and implemented based on a new approach. The 5G network architecture that was designed and implemented for the needs of FASTER project and the advantages that this architecture offers to the first responders is presented in this paper.

Keywords: 5G · First responders · Network Functions Virtualization (NFV) · Network portability · Network softwarisation · Non-standalone 5G architecture · Small cell (SC) · Virtual network function (VNF)

1 Introduction

In the event of an emergency, the first responder is the one who will immediately offer assistance at the scene. FASTER project [1] is focusing on providing solutions to protect first responders in hazardous environments and enhance their capabilities in terms of situational awareness and communication. For that reason, augmented reality technology equipment, drones and wearables are proposed as part of this innovative toolbox.

I. Maglogiannis et al. (Eds.): AIAI 2021 Workshops, IFIP AICT 628, pp. 62–70, 2021.
https://doi.org/10.1007/978-3-030-79157-5_6

However, this equipment in order to be useful should be interconnected through a reliable network. As it is presented in Fig. 1, the throughput demand is rapidly increased few minutes after the emergency event and when the first responders start offering their services.

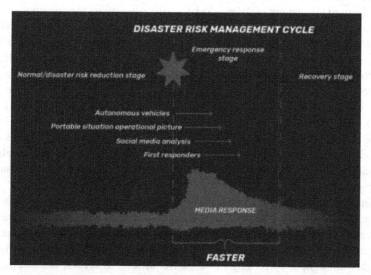

Fig. 1. Throughput requirements in a disaster risk management cycle [1].

Apart from the requirement of increased throughput [2, 3], the increased reliability [4] and coverage [5, 6] as well as the very low latency [7, 8] are also critical requirements for the network in order to support efficiently the needs of first responders. Although a 4G network includes features that are remarkable and it is quite efficient, the advanced requirements that are needed are so demanding and thus it is difficult for a 4G network to efficiently support them. On the contrary, a 5G network supports all the desired features to realize such cases. For example, the 4G network throughput is 50 Mbps, while the corresponding one for 5G could be more than 1 Gbps; but the most innovative advantages of a 5G network over a 4G network are the low latency, the reliability and the location accuracy.

The low latency is one of the most important parameters of the network, since the first responders will use real time applications. In 4G networks the latency is 200 ms, while in 5G networks it could be even below than 5 ms. That difference could be crucial not only because it will improve the services offered by first responders, since they will use real-time data such as 8 K video streams [9, 10], and virtual reality (VR)/augmented reality (AR) enhanced features [11], but also the low latency could play an important role in the safety of the first responders allowing high location accuracy because the exact location of first responders could be detected instantly.

Finally, high reliability is a network requirement which is crucial for the services offered by the FASTER project. The first responders will be connected to a control centre and to each other, by using wearables or smart phones. This connectivity must be uninterrupted. Any interruption of communication could be dangerous, given the conditions under which first responders offer their services. The way 5G network ensures the high reliability is by boosting higher traffic capacity and by supporting the slicing feature. The network is divided into slices, each of which may have specific requirements. For example, in a case where an earthquake occurs it is proven that network users rapidly increase the used throughput of the network since they are trying to communicate to each other. That phenomenon could lead to a significant reduction of the available throughput of a legacy network, causing interruptions or connection inability. The slicing feature could resolve such sort of problem in a situation like this, by offering a unique slice to be used by the first responders. Therefore, the necessary network resources are secured and first responders are served according to MCS stringent requirements. There are 3 main slices specified by 3GPP (3rd Generation Partnership Project) Release 15 [12]: Ultra-reliable low-latency communication (URLLC), enhanced Mobile Broadband (eMBB) and massive Machine Type Communications (mMTC). The URLLC applications require network capabilities that are also required in the FASTER framework, such as reliability (target value 99.999%), low latency (target value 1 ms), location accuracy and high throughput.

It is important to be mentioned that reliability and low latency could also be achieved by the outdoor small cell architecture. The original macro cell could be divided into smaller cells. These smaller cells are using short-range and low-power base stations to ensure connectivity to the network [13]. The advantage of this architecture is that it can offer higher throughput by reusing the same frequencies in several small cells, taking full advantage of available spectrum.

2   FASTER 5G-Enabling Network

For the purposes of the FASTER project, the Non-Standalone architecture is adopted. The Non-Standalone (NSA) architecture is designed to take advantage of the 4G network equipment, offering 5G services. On the contrary, the Standalone (SA) architecture is solely using 5G equipment. Taking into consideration the large number of new hardware that must be deployed in a SA network architecture, the NSA architecture is preferred by operators in the first stage of the 5G deployment.

The FASTER network architecture is based on URLLC applications as it is presented in Fig. 2 [14]. This figure depicts the 5G New Radio access network (5 gNR), which is

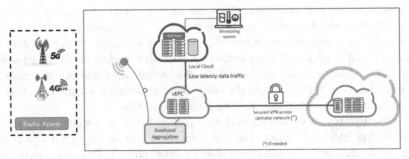

Fig. 2. Network architecture for an industrial enterprise URLLC application.

connected to the virtual Evolved Packet Core (vEPC). The vEPC is finally connected with the Open Source MANO (OSM).

In Fig. 3, the architecture that is used in the FASTER project is presented in more details. It is shown that it is separated into three distinct parts:

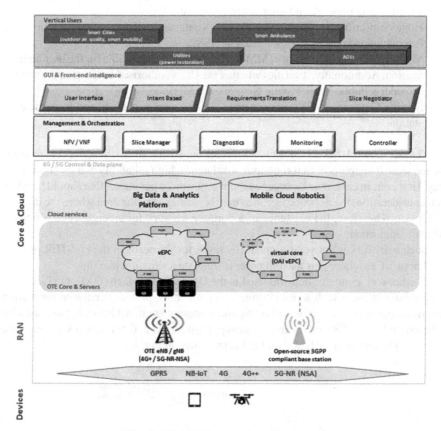

Fig. 3. High-level network architecture.

- The User Equipment (UE) is the part of the network which includes all the equipment that can be connected to the network, such as wearables, smart phones, drones and AR equipment.
- The UE layer is connected wirelessly with Radio Access Network (RAN), which in the FASTER case is the 5 gNR. A RAN is separated into the hardware (baseband node and radio units) and the software (components needed to operate the 3GPP wireless system including LTE and 5G) part.
- The Core Network (CN) is the third part of the FASTER 5G NSA architecture, which is based on a virtual EPC (vEPC). The vEPC is composed of the following network elements:

- Packet Data Network Gateway (P-GW), which is responsible for ensuring the network quality-of-service (QoS). Additionally, it collects charging information.
- Baseband unit (BBU), which is responsible to ensure the communication through the physical interface.
- Policy and Charging Rules Function (PCRF) which determines policy rules in a multimedia network and operates in real-time.
- Home Subscriber Server (HSS) is the user's database. All the user subscription data (username and password) are hosted in HSS.
- Mobility Management Entity (MME): The MME is responsible for the user authentication. Additionally, it verifies whether the UE is authorised to camp on the service provider's Public Land Mobile Network (PLMN).
- Serving Gateway (S-GW) is a gateway which routes packets to and from the base station.

The 5G network has the ability to meet all the advanced first responders' requirements, since it supports high throughput, low latency, high reliability and location accuracy. However, in case of an emergency there is one more parameter that should be taken into consideration: the network facilities may be damaged in the area where the disaster took place. Therefore, the existence of a portable network for emergency situations is critically important.

Such a network is not yet designed. However, for the needs of the FASTER project, a 5G network emulator was used in order to emulate a situation like this.

The network emulator that was used is the Open Air Interface (OAI). OAI includes several built-in tools such as monitoring and error tools, protocol analyser, simulation functions, performance profile and configurable login system. Additionally, its hardware is based on Ettus USRP cards and it can support both 4G and 5G network architecture [15, 16]. The architecture based on OAI is presented in Fig. 4.

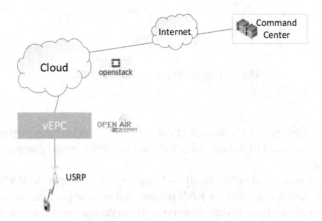

Fig. 4. 5G testbed based on Open Air Interface platform.

The advantages of the use of OAI are significant. Taking into consideration its technical characteristics, it can provide an Internet connection, since it is an actual network, and not a simulated one [17]. Additionally, it could offer flexibility in design and upgrade, since is based on software defined elements.

The main advantage of OAI is that it could be used in a rear case scenario where portability is needed. For example, in a case of a strong earthquake there are many cases where the local network elements could not operate appropriately. In that case network portability could be a very crucial feature. OAI could play the role of the portable network in the FASTER project trials and simulate this scenario even though it is not developed for this purpose.

3   FASTER QoS Monitoring Framework

The ability to deploy and monitor the performance of the network elements and services on cloud computing environments is one of the advanced features of 5G technologies that the FASTER platform will take advantage of. This feature will offer high flexibility and dynamicity to the operational characteristics of first responders.

In this respect, in the context of the FASTER project, services and tools for the monitoring of the cloud infrastructure and the services running on it, are designed and implemented, as it is presented in Fig. 5.

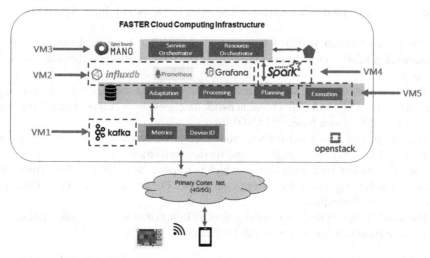

Fig. 5. Services and tools running on FASTER cloud resources.

Creating an architecture that will be based on the innovative and emerging principles of cloud-native computing, 5G networking and Machine Learning (ML) is not straightforward, given the requirements posed by the First Responder (FR) operations in the field, as expressed in the FASTER use cases. The architecture shown in Fig. 5 specifies the QoS provisioning, through the monitoring of specific and relevant metrics, such as latency, bandwidth, computation efficiency, etc., collected not only from the infrastructure but also from the running services deployed in virtual machines (VMs) – as shown in

Fig. 5 – or containers. Special attention has been paid in order to include the monitoring of cross-layer interactions between network and application related metrics.

One of the main innovations of the FASTER architecture is the optimized management of the network service (NS)/virtual network functions (VNFs) lifecycle, especially under the prism of the interchangeable utilization of different environments (edge/fog/internet) that would be able to provide resilience on the communication infrastructure. In order to cope with such requirements, FASTER QoS Monitoring Framework system consists of two main components that collaborate to achieve optimization of the service quality and processing, namely, the Monitoring Analysis Planning Execution (MAPE) framework and the Management and Orchestration (MANO) platform. In this perspective, the framework will allow for the timely reaction of the service with respect to scaling and/or placement of the service (or functions), in order to optimize the performance of the service and thus satisfy the user requirements during runtime.

With respect to the MAPE components, their realization is based on VMs and docker containers running on them. This approach is quite suitable for the development of the FASTER ecosystem because it provides two advantages: first, the deployment of services on VMs leads to easy scalability that might be needed in future requirements; and, second, the containers are easy to manage and the containerized services provide fast instantiation times. The VMs are provided and managed by an OpenStack environment consisting of one controller node and two compute nodes. The MAPE component introduces five internal services with distinct corresponding roles and responsibilities. Specifically:

- The Message broker (kafka) where metrics from different types of sources (NFVI (network functions virtualisation infrastructure), VMs, containers, applications, etc.) are collected.
- The Adaptation service which correlates the collected metrics with the running instances of VNFs and CNFs (core network functions) by incorporating information from the OSM (Open Source MANO).
- The Analysis services which prepares and executes ML algorithms to forecast resource demand, future network conditions and service performance,
- The Planning and Execution service which is responsible to enforce the recommendations and configuration directives to the Service Orchestrator of the OSM (through its northbound interface).
- The Monitoring service which consisting of an InfluxDB database, Prometheus server and a Grafana server connected with Prometheus.

With respect to the Management and Orchestration platform, the overall assessment [18, 19] showed that all MANOs have their own strengths and weaknesses. In particular, the ETSI supported architectural approaches, as presented by OSM and SONATA [20], make them the most prominent candidates under the considered criteria and given the resources and use cases of FASTER. Taking also into consideration the sustainability issue OSM has been selected as the most suitable platform for the resource management and orchestration (MANO) in FASTER. The OSM instance runs on VM and it is connected with the same OpenStack environment but it uses different tenant with admin privileges. This set up can guarantee isolation between the FASTER services and the user NS which are initiated via the OSM.

4 Conclusion

In this paper, the 5G network solution proposed by the FASTER project was presented. The network is designed in a way to meet two main needs of first responders, that is: their safety and the offering of advanced means to optimize their services' ability.

The safety of the first responders can be ensured by using several wearables which will inform the control center and the other first responders about the situation of each first responder. Additionally, in order to optimize their services, the first responders will use advanced equipment such as smart phones, smart bracelets and other wearables. This equipment should be connected to the network, which must satisfy several requirements such as high throughput, low latency, high reliability and coverage.

These requirements could be satisfied by a 5G network. Therefore, the 5G network solution that is proposed for the needs of first responders was presented. This architecture is separated into 3 layers: the access and the core layer and the cloud. Additionally, the importance of network virtualization was presented as well as the solution that is adopted by the FASTER project. Finally, the use of OAI as a tool to support both network requirements and the ability of portability was explained and the architecture was presented.

Acknowledgments. This work has been performed in the scope of the *FASTER* European Research Project and has been supported by the Commission of the European Communities (*Grant Agreement No.833507*).

References

1. FASTER Project (Grant Agreement No.833507). https://www.faster-project.eu
2. Zafeiropoulos, A., Fotopoulou, E., Peuster, M., Schneider, S., et al.: Benchmarking and profiling 5G verticals' applications: an industrial IoT use case. In: Proceedings of the 6th IEEE Conference on Network Softwarization (NetSoft), pp. 310–318. IEEE (2020)
3. Pol, A., Roman, A., Trakadas, P., Karkazis, P., Kapassa, E., Touloupou, M., et al.: Advanced NFV features applied to multimedia real-time communications use case. In: Proceedings of the 2nd IEEE 5G World Forum (5GWF), pp. 323–328. IEEE (2019)
4. Michailidis, E.T., Nomikos, N., Trakadas, P., Kanatas, A.G.: Three-dimensional modeling of mmWave doubly massive MIMO aerial fading channels. IEEE Trans. Veh. Technol. **69**(2), 1190–1202 (2019)
5. Trakadas, P., et al.: Hybrid clouds for data-Intensive, 5G-Enabled IoT applications: an overview, key issues and relevant architecture. Sensors **19**(16), 3591 (2019)
6. Nomikos, N., et al.: A UAV-based moving 5G RAN for massive connectivity of mobile users and IoT devices. Veh. Commun. **25**(9), 1–18 (2020)
7. Nomikos, N., Michailidis, E.T., Trakadas, P., Vouyioukas, D., Zahariadis, T., Krikidis, I.: Flex-NOMA: exploiting buffer-aided relay selection for massive connectivity in the 5G uplink. IEEE Access **7**, 88743–88755 (2019)
8. Nomikos, N., Trakadas, P., Hatziefremidis, A., Voliotis, S.: Full-duplex NOMA transmission with single-antenna buffer-aided relays. Electronics (MDPI) **8**(12), 1482 (2019)
9. Alvarez, F., et al.: An edge-to-cloud virtualized multimedia service platform for 5G networks. IEEE Trans. Broadcast. **65**(2), 369–380 (2019)

10. Alemany P., Soenen, T., de la Cruz, J.L., et al.: Network slicing over a packet/optical network for vertical applications applied to multimedia real-time communications. In: Proceedings of the 2019 IEEE Conference on Network Function Virtualization and Software Defined Networks (NFV-SDN), Dallas, TX, USA, pp. 1–2. IEEE (2019)
11. Shekhawat, Y., Piesk, J., Sprengel, H., Domínguez Gómez, I., Vicens, F., et al.: orchestrating live immersive media services over cloud native edge infrastructure. In: Proceedings of the 2nd IEEE 5G World Forum (5GWF), pp. 316–322. IEEE (2019)
12. The 5G Infrastructure Public Private Partnership (5G-PPP): 5G PPP Platforms Cartography. https://5g-ppp.eu/5g-ppp-platforms-cartography/
13. Global5G Project: Deliverable D3.4: White paper on Small Cells (2019). https://global5g.org/sites/default/files/BookletA4_5gCells.pdf
14. 5G-EVE project: Deliverable D2.1: Initial detailed architectural and functional site facilities description (2018). https://zenodo.org/record/3540439#.Xv2OK8fVKUk
15. https://www.openairinterface.org/?page_id=864
16. https://gitlab.eurecom.fr/oai/openairinterface5g/-/wikis/home
17. Gkonis, P.K., Trakadas, P.T., Kaklamani, D.I.: A comprehensive study on simulation techniques for 5G networks: state of the art. Anal. Future Challenges. Electron. (MDPI) 9(3), 468 (2020)
18. Trakadas, P., et al.: Comparison of management and orchestration solutions for the 5G era. J. Sens. Actuator Netw. 9(1), 4 (2020)
19. Peuster, M., et al.: Introducing automated verification and validation for virtualized network functions and services. IEEE Commun. Mag. 57(5), 96–102 (2019)
20. SONATA Project (Grant Agreement No.671517). https://www.sonata-nfv.eu/

High Mobility 5G Services for Vertical Industries – Network Operator's View

Lechosław Tomaszewski[1(✉)], Ioannis P. Chochliouros[2],
Robert Kołakowski[1,3], Sławomir Kukliński[1,3], and Michail-Alexandros Kourtis[4]

[1] Orange Polska S.A., ul. Obrzeżna 7, 02-691 Warszawa, Poland
lechoslaw.tomaszewski@orange.com
[2] Hellenic Telecommunications Organization (OTE) S.A., 99 Kifissias Avenue,
15124 Maroussi-Athens, Greece
[3] Warsaw University of Technology, ul. Nowowiejska 15/19, 00-665 Warszawa, Poland
[4] Orion Innovations P.C., Ameinokleous 43, 11744 Athens, Greece

Abstract. The 5G System (5GS) is regarded as a multi-faceted, universal communication platform that could address the increasingly stringent requirements of both modern industries and network end users. Several proposed mechanisms, such as network slicing or its control exposure, aimed to facilitate access to the network for the external stakeholders, enable the creation of one common ecosystem that could be exploited according to the specific service needs. With the recent advancements in the automotive and aviation sectors, the significant increase of interest regarding the current state of preparedness of the 5GS and its capabilities to support those services is observed. The paper presents the analysis of the 5G technology readiness in the context of high mobility vehicular scenarios, including automotive and unmanned aviation use cases. The significant features and key gaps and challenges have been outlined with the emphasis on the dynamics of business processes and interactions between automotive, aviation and 5G ecosystems.

Keywords: 5G System · MEC · Vertical services · V2X · UAV · UTM · RAN · Slicing · Management · Provisioning · Architecture

1 Introduction

Since the early visions, the 5G System (5GS) has been presented as a versatile platform, able to build individualized communication solutions responding to the needs of very diverse and demanding use cases. The well known IMT-2020 triangle of fundamental use profiles at the vertices: enhanced Mobile Broadband (eMBB), Ultra Reliable Low Latency Communications (URLLC), and massive

Supported by the Horizon 2020 projects: EU-China 5G-DRIVE (Grant Agreement No. 814956) and EU 5G!Drones (Grant Agreement No. 857031).

© IFIP International Federation for Information Processing 2021
Published by Springer Nature Switzerland AG 2021
I. Maglogiannis et al. (Eds.): AIAI 2021 Workshops, IFIP AICT 628, pp. 71–84, 2021.
https://doi.org/10.1007/978-3-030-79157-5_7

Machine Type Communications (mMTC) constitutes a map of various use cases, which shows conceptually their relation to these profiles [1]. Furthermore, the Key Performance Indicators (KPIs) characterising the "promised" 5GS in comparison to the previous generation show serious gaps to be filled (30–50× in E2E latency, 100× in individual connection data rate and served terminals per area unit, 1.5× in terminal velocity). Today, after 5 years and with more than 100 commercial implementations of 5GS all over the world, the first reality check can be performed to validate the 5G technology maturity vs. the excited expectations. A very important aspect, which goes beyond the internal features of 5GS, is the ability to be adopted operationally by the network operator and by the business processes of the wider ecosystem in which it will be embedded.

One of the flagship applications of 5G networks in vertical industries are automotive and unmanned aviation use cases, which are highly demanding in terms of data rate, latency, reliability and mobility as well as subject to strict regulations. In addition, the ongoing COVID-19 pandemic has exposed their socio-economic importance to be much greater than previously expected. For these use cases, 5GS should not only be a static, focused only on itself, element of the overall landscape, but it must actively participate in various multilateral business processes. Thanks to the EU trial projects 5G-DRIVE and 5G!Drones, it was possible to recognize the broad context and needs of these industries, which challenge the 5G network and its operator.

2 Overview of the Vertical Industries in Focus

2.1 Automotive Sector

The automotive sector is rapidly gaining popularity on the market with the projected annual growth of 44.2% and is expected to expand from the market value of 689 million USD in 2020 to 12,859 million USD in 2028 [2]. Currently, the automotive market is built atop two communication technologies: WLAN-based Dedicated Short-Range Communications and cellular (LTE, 5G). Mobile communication systems are considered as the main drive of acceleration of Vehicle-to-everything (V2X) ecosystem development, due to better performance in terms of cybersecurity and handling large numbers of messages in congested traffic environments – the features being inline with core motivations of V2X, i.e. improving road safety, traffic efficiency and energy saving. These motivations are planned to be achieved by building the extensive Intelligent Transport System (ITS) allowing road users to acquire, share and use the information to support individual actions, and optimizing the road traffic flows.

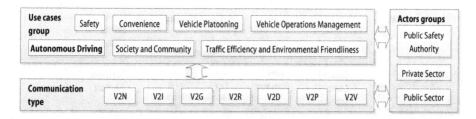

Fig. 1. V2X ecosystem

The V2X ecosystem (cf. Fig. 1) involves interactions of vehicles with other objects: network (V2N), infrastructure (V2I), grids (V2G), road-side units (V2R), devices (V2D), pedestrians (V2P) and other vehicles (V2V), each being a part of the ITS ecosystem. Typically, the V2X use cases are categorized as it follows [3]: (i) *Safety:* mechanisms for safety improvement (emergency braking, collision warning, lane change assistance, etc.); (ii) *Society and Community:* use cases of interest to the society and public (vulnerable road user protection, traffic light priority, crash reporting, etc.); (iii) *Convenience:* facilitation for drivers (infotainment, assisted and cooperative navigation, autonomous smart parking); (iv) *Autonomous Driving:* semi-, fully-automated and remote; (v) *Vehicle Platooning:* creating dynamic groups of vehicles to exchange information and coordinate operations (e.g. maintenance of inter-vehicle distance); (vi) *Traffic Efficiency and Environmental Friendliness:* enhancements for traffic optimization (e.g. green light optimal speed advisory, traffic jam information, Smart routing); (vii) *Vehicle Operations Management:* operational and management use cases benefiting vehicle manufacturers (sensors monitoring, remote support, etc.). Demand for handling diverse service data with different Quality of Service (QoS) requirements causes 5GS to be projected as a leading communication technology for V2X systems. In addition to connectivity, 5GS can facilitate automotive services by hosting these systems on the Mobile Network Operator's (MNO) infrastructure as an integrated part of the 5GS, especially close to the edge of the network.

2.2 Unmanned Aviation Sector

The vast expansion of Unmanned Aerial Vehicles (UAV) services' market is commonly expected in all regions of the world (15.5% annual market value growth between 2019 and 2025, from 19.3 to 45.8 billion USD) [4]) due to the huge variety of UAV use cases in multiple economic areas. Further market acceleration can be achieved by overcoming the "Visual Line of Sight" flights barrier with an omnipresent communication platform, optionally with aid of "First Person View" (FPV) – real time 360° video for pilot. Hence, the 5G services supporting UAV operations are potentially a huge business opportunity for MNOs.

The unmanned aviation is a highly regulated sector, primarily due to safety, in terms of flight and airspace management. It is commonly accepted that the

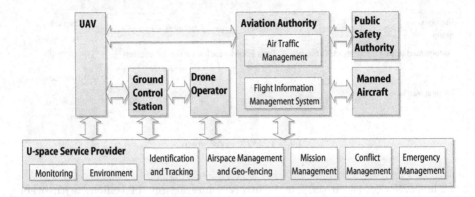

Fig. 2. U-space ecosystem

UAV ecosystem will be built around the UAV Traffic Management (UTM) system [5], which in EU will be developed as U-space, i.e. a framework of services and procedures for management of massive UAV traffic in a common EU airspace, to be implemented in 4 phases (U1-U4), gradually introducing new obligatory services within a common EU regulation (U1 in force since January 1st, 2021).

The U-space ecosystem [6] (cf. Fig. 2) – composed of multiple actors and entities – is founded on the U-space Service Provider (USP), i.e. an operator of a UTM system. To induce competition, there may exist more than one USP in a specific area. The USP's role is to provide services essential for coordinated flight planning, execution and control, which may be categorized as: (i) *Identification and Tracking:* registration, e-identification, position reporting and surveillance; (ii) *Airspace Management and Geofencing:* automated airspace areas access control; (iii) *Mission Management:* operation plan preparation, optimisation and processing, risk analysis assistance and dynamic management of airspace capacity; (iv) *Conflict Management:* pre-/in-flight conflict resolution; (v) *Emergency Management:* incident, accident and violations reporting; (vi) *Monitoring:* infrastructure monitoring, traffic control and lawful recording of all U-space inputs; (vii) *Environment:* weather, geo-spatial positioning, electromagnetic interference, navigation and communication coverage, and population density. 5GS functionalities can actively contribute to various USP services, so 5GS can be perceived as a part of USP, and its services and capabilities as "added-value" U-space resources. To enable support of massive UAV traffic, deep integration of both aviation and 5G ecosystems, including business processes, is advisable.

Last but not least, the role of 5GS is to provide the connectivity between U-space entities and actors, especially the communication links both for non-payload (flight-related, i.e. for UAV control and traffic management) and payload exchange (use case-specific, e.g. real-time video, still photos, sensoric data, etc.), meeting the QoS requirements. Additionally, the UAV actors' systems can be distributed and hosted by the MNO's infrastructure (especially at the edge).

3   3GPP 5GS Support of Vertical Industries in Focus

3.1   Approach to the Requirements

V2X/UAV service requirements for 5GS are defined in [7]/[8], respectively. QoS KPI targets have been specified for various communication links necessary for both vehicle classes. In case of V2X, there is a non-payload communication only, compared to payload/non-payload context differentiation used for UAV. The top targets are more challenging in case of V2X by one order of magnitude (e.g. latency of 3 ms for emergency alignment of car trajectory vs. 10 ms for approaching autonomous navigation infrastructure by a drone; data rate of 1 Gbps for low-distance V2V sensor information sharing vs. 120 Mbps for airborne 4 × 4K Artificial Intelligence (AI) surveillance; reliability of 99.999% for remote car driving control vs. 99.99% for FPV aid for pilot). Such approach is motivated by much higher proximity of automotive vehicles and their higher maximum speed (250 km/h vs. 160 km/h). Merely, the required horizontal positioning accuracy is comparable (0.1 m); for UAV it is specified only for payload.

Apart from the above requirements related to the quality properties of communication links, both sectors impose added-value functional requirements:

Group Communication: it is required to enable communication between V2X objects in proximity, which expose V2X applications to others, including their discovery, either directly or via 5GS, with integrity and confidentiality kept, also between different Public Land Mobile Networks (PLMNs). In case of UAVs, this feature addresses broadcasting of drone's presence (identifier, location, flight azimuth and velocity) for collision avoidance in a small radius (600 m).

Connectivity Sharing: enabled by detection of other V2X User Equipment (UE); the on-board UE may obtain network access via another V2X UE, when unable to connect to the network directly, with necessary confidentiality and integrity protection. While the feature is not demanded for UAVs, it might be used for sustaining the connectivity in the areas of poor coverage.

Service Assurance and Provisioning: both sectors request the 3rd party (V2X application, UTM system, etc.) ability to receive service monitoring information on per-UE basis, including early notification about possible QoS fluctuations or potential connectivity stopping. It is also required that the 5GS shall expose the information about service status (availability, estimated QoS) in a certain geographical area at a certain time, which is of premium importance for remote driving planning as well as for legally required UAV flight plan approval procedures. Additionally, in case of V2X sector, the support of negotiation of spatial/temporal connectivity QoS between the 3rd party and 5GS is required. This feature might be also useful in case of necessary flight plan alterations for on-going flights.

User Plane (UP) Data Augmenting: requested for UAV services; here, UP data packets sent to UTM are demanded to be additionally "certified" by PLMN with e.g. UE/subscriber identifier or UE location.

Joint Authorization: UTM (generally: 3rd party) can be involved in UAV UE authorization to operate, i.e. admission to the specific communication network.
UE Capability Validation and Problems Detection: 5GS is required to identify and validate if UE has the UAV-specific capabilities, especially supports interactions of UAV with UTM. Additionally, 5GS shall support detection, identification and reporting of problematic UAV system components with on-board UE to UTM, including their abnormal behavior, e.g. flight area violation.
Control Take-Over: there is a requirement of the 5GS ability to enable UTM (or other lawfully authorized entity) to take over the communication used for UAV control. This requirement is related to the public safety issue; a problematic UAV may be forced to land or steered to a safe crash area.
Identity Handling: the approach to this issue is extremely different. While in the V2X sector the privacy protection is fundamental [9] to avoid vehicle tracking by its UE identity (pseudonymization required), the continuous aircraft identification and tracking is fundamental in the aviation.

The area of possible synergy of both sectors' high-level requirements is large. Apart from that, there are disjoint requirements, which may contribute as added value to the complementary sector, however. Only the last issue is contradictory. Hence, shared components should be expected, for architectural and operational reasons (reusability and common know-how for operation/maintenance).

3.2 Implementation of Requirements – Architecture and Mechanisms

The generic vision of the 5GS architectural framework [10] envisions functionalities and mechanisms to support basic V2X/UAV requirements, i.e. related to providing communication links with specific QoS targets. Moreover, its inherent functional upgradeability provides means for implementation of "added-value" requirements. The features of 5GS, fundamental for the V2X/UAV support, are:
Control and User Plane Separation (CUPS), i.e. Control Plane (CP) functions may be independently placed in a centralized location, while UP can be implemented at the closest possible location to the user or UP-supported application (e.g. for latency minimization), which further enables independent scaling of both planes, more flexible design, deployment and dimensioning of the network, and dynamic optimization of UP traffic distribution.
CP programmability, additionally boosted by its **Service-Based Architecture** (SBA), where 5GS-native Network Functions (NFs) and specific Application Functions (AFs) expose services as their Producers or discover/consume them as Consumers, within the RESTful framework (API) based on JSON (serialization), HTTP/2 (application layer), and TCP (transport).
UP programmability, i.e. UP Function (UPF) flexibly composed as a chain of atomic functions to process the UP traffic (e.g. firewall, Deep Packet Inspection, selective marking or altering, encapsulation, classification, forwarding or redirection of user traffic, anti-virus protection, parental control, etc.).

Network slicing (NS), i.e. split of handling of various communication services with mutually conflicting requirements among separated specialized sub-networks (to be built on flexibly shared common resources), which are customized according to service specificity. Efficient customization of these sub-networks is further enhanced by CUPS and SBA. Slice-specific CP functions may be flexibly integrated with 5GS CP, using separation mechanisms of the CP communication bus. Slice-specific UP data processing chain – as a service-customized UPF. As UE may use applications demanding various communication services, the UE multi-slice attachment ability has to be supported.

Embedded analytics is included as Network Data and Management Data Analytics Functions (NWDAF in CP and MDAF [11] in the management layer, respectively), which expose analytics services to other functions. Their functionality include NFs data collection, processing, analysis and metadata exposure, including notifications of data-driven events (e.g. threshold- or condition-based).

Location Services (LCS) [12] framework, as the 5GS CP extension, enables providing target UE location information (geographic location, velocity, or civic location), considering the security aspects. To enable privacy control, several mechanisms have been introduced, including aliases for UE anonymity maintenance, restricted access by codewords, LCS clients whitelisting, etc. The LCS framework supports both UE-assisted and network-based (upgraded RAN nodes) location.

Network control/management capabilities exposure for external systems integration is based on Network Exposure Function (NEF) located in CP and Exposure Governance Management Function (EGMF) [11] located in the management layer. For standardization of supported integration mechanisms at the 5GS North Bound Interface (NBI), additional Common Application Programming Intertface Framework (CAPIF) [13] and Service Enabler Architecture Layer for Verticals (SEAL) [14] have been defined.

4   Key Gaps and Challenges

The 5GS readiness to handle the services for high mobility applications is currently limited in many aspects, discussed below. Due to the 3GPP standardization timeline, the majority of them is still under development (either from scratch or being enhanced as a part of the Release 17 scope (further indicated as [R17]). Therefore, vendors' solutions will be available well after the half of 2022 when the freeze of the 3GPP Release 17 is scheduled.

4.1   Network Slicing

NS is a fundamental enabler of majority of 5G services for the high mobility applications. It concerns especially the UAV sector, where multiple non-payload and payload communications links with drastically different characteristics may be required. However, there are currently two factors to detain implementation of NS: the migration policy adopted by MNOs and the current status of the

3GPP standardization[R17]. In Europe, all MNOs have chosen to implement 5GS according to the Non-Stand Alone architecture, with at least the overwhelming majority of the Option 3/3a/3x (cf. [15,16]), so NS is not supported there, inherently. This approach accelerated the 5G technology implementation in Radio Access Network (RAN), especially as in some countries new 5G bands are still unavailable. However, it may have further negative effect by delaying the implementation of 5G Stand Alone architecture. Until then, 5G networks in Europe will remain "boosted LTE networks" (with just higher data rates) without full 5G functionality and services support.

4.2   RAN Mechanisms

5GS is expected to bring several RAN solutions to address diverse and elevated transmission requirements implored by robustness of served communication types. Several mechanisms have already been introduced to the New Radio (NR) both at physical and procedural level. The intensive work on development of NR features is a major part of the 3GPP Release 17 and subject to its timeline.

RAN Slicing[R17]: a fundamental NR mechanism to ensure QoS levels of Protocol Data Unit sessions and their isolation, by means of L1/L2 scheduling and per-slice Radio Resource Management (RRM) policies [17]. Its support is only in scope of the 3GPP Release 17.

Proximity Services (ProSe)[R17]: a basis for direct UE-UE communication. So far, the preliminary studies have been published, outlining i.a. the key issues as discovery of UEs, relay support and charging aspects [18]. The essentials of the ProSe core element, i.e. Sidelink (PC5 interface), have already been defined [17].

Minimization of Drive Tests[R17]: a mechanism of acquisition of radio measurement data, which are inherently taken by UEs. These data might be further used for 3D network coverage optimization or be exposed to the vertical industry.

Beam Management: essential mechanisms for interference mitigation. Some of them (beamforming, beam sweeping, etc.) have been described for NR in [19], but the technology is still not mature enough to support URLLC use cases [20].

Radio Resource Allocation Mechanisms: grant-free access for the uplink and preemptive punctured scheduling for the downlink [17], which enable skipping resource allocation negotiation procedures and mitigation of the related delay, critical for URLLC transmission. Other mechanisms may be added during the studies on URLLC enhancements for Industrial Internet of Things[R17].

Applications Impact on RAN: the O-RAN concept that introduces RAN programmability is of premium importance for V2X and UAV services, due to enabling of external applications impact on RAN mechanisms. The example use cases include: context-based (e.g. velocity, path) dynamic handover management for V2X, flight path-based on-demand dynamic resource allocation for UAV or radio resource allocation for UAV applications on per UE-basis [21].

4.3   Specific Architectural Support of V2X/UAV Use Cases

In addition to generic 5GS mechanisms, 3GPP addresses some aspects of service support for high mobility use cases to specialized architectural and application-layer solutions, individually defined for each of the vertical sectors in focus.

The specific support of V2X services is partially standardized within the 3GPP Release 16 and covers SEAL-based application layer issues (dynamic grouping; group communication – via PC5 or mobile network; file and application message distribution; and cross-PLMN PC5 communication) [22] and relevant 5GS architecture-level mechanisms (V2X communication, including its authorization, provisioning and QoS; V2X application server discovery and subscription) [23]. Further enhancements are in progress[R17] and the studies both for layers of application (extended QoS specific for V2X use case category – cf. Sect. 2.1 – and automation level; tele-operated driving; network slicing and multi-PLMN support; connection relaying; enhancements of group communication and management; vehicle tracking, multi-V2X service provider support) [24] and 5GS architecture (QoS-aware power efficiency of PC5 for pedestrian UEs) [25] have recently been finalized.

The UAV-specific support has not been provided within 5GS, yet. Its first standardization is currently underway[R17]. The study reports on UAV connectivity, identification and tracking (UAV and its controller identification, authorization for operation and connectivity to UTM – commonly with UTM, pairing and tracking) [26] and SEAL-based application layer support for the UAV ecosystem (mechanisms of direct and on-network broadcast communication; network capability exposure and management related to QoS provisioning, UAV real-time monitoring/locating/trajectory deviation tracking, UAV command and control communication modes switching, real-time media session monitoring; UAV systems pairing and identification; and alignment of UAV and edge enabler layers) [27] have recently been closed.

Although the solutions of finalized studies in both vertical sectors are only proposals for further selection and validation during the normative documents development, there is a fundamental difference in the architectural approach. It is assumed that V2X Application Servers will be integrated with 5GS individually via NEF as V2X-specific AFs to interact separately with 5G CP. In case of UAV sector, it is proposed to implement specialized shared function(s) to expose 5GS CP services to the UAV environment actors: drone operator, UTM or third party authorized entities. Such approach follows the idea of a UAV ecosystem gateway function [28], which is not only a mediator to expose generalized UAV-related mechanisms through an API commonly used by these actors. Its role is also to coordinate all their interactions with 5GS CP, to exploit functional similarities in various interactions and contexts for simplification of the overall architecture and to avoid excessive signaling exchange caused by same, multiplied requests (e.g. continuous, real-time UAV tracking for reporting to UTM and drone operator, for position broadcasting, for mechanism of early warning about possible connection loss and for autonomic trajectory deviation detection). However, from a global point of view, the defined solution proposals in both sectors do not fully use the capabilities of the 5GS architecture – due to the use of a uniformized approach for both 4G and 5G networks. It also seems that the opportunities for architectural synergy of both sectors will not be exploited.

While the LCS framework is not dedicated exclusively to the automotive and aviation sectors, some significant features tightly associated with UAV/V2X applications, including LCS continuity aspect, low latency and high accuracy positioning, positioning service areas, etc., are still under development[R17].

4.4 Multi-Access Edge Computing

The UAV/V2X Application Plane is expected to operate at the edge of the network, therefore usage of ETSI Multi-Access Edge Computing (MEC) framework [29] capabilities is deemed as an enabler for latency reduction and transport network offloading. Whilst the latter is an indisputable advantage, the foremost is questionable due to properties of virtualization technologies. Studies [30,31] show that each Virtual Machine (VM) or container impose significant latency overhead due to sharing of physical resources and extra processing layers for virtualization ($\sim$150–300 µs for working alone and even a few ms in heavily loaded clusters by concurrent bandwidth-demanding VMs). Moreover, the paradigm of high modularization and distribution multiplies the effect above and in turn nullifies the time gain on infrastructure placement close to RAN (each 6 µs of delay is the equivalent of $\sim$1 km of fiber). Hence, MEC can be treated as a way to compensate the losses caused by virtualization. The 3GPP standardization of 5GS and MEC integration has been recently started[R17], but there are still unsolved concerns about the overall integrated architecture [32].

4.5 Agile Management and Provisioning Architecture

Considering high mobility and latency-critical UAV/V2X services, the need for efficient mechanisms of management and orchestration becomes a fundamental issue, especially when responsiveness to service and traffic demand changes introduces safety risks. While NS enabled by softwarization and virtualization is a widely adopted vision, the dynamic slicing [33] – i.e. the dynamic and continuous metamorphoses of the network, following the needs in a timescale of seconds – still remains an open challenge, thus the need for extensive research.

3GPP adopts the ETSI Management and Orchestration (MANO) framework [34] and designs the vision of the 5GS management as complementary to MANO. Its centralized operation fundamentally increases the overhead related to slice modification such as resource reallocation, and also raises significant concerns in terms of scalability and efficiency. In the case of multi-domain hierarchical and recursive orchestration, reconfiguration of stitched sub-slices would incrementally intensify the issue. In [35], the results of time needed for slice instantiation and scaling-out (which is only the final, actuating step of the entire process of adaptive network transformation) have been presented. In case of small slices, the first process consumed from around 15 s–50 s depending on the slice size (number of VNFs). The latter proved to be executable in approximately 15 s, which may not be sufficiently fast to satisfy the soaring UAV/V2X requirements.

The initial step of the network adaptation process requires the appropriate mechanisms for obtaining relevant input data from CP. While the generic SBA-based 5GS CP architecture allows for the potential implementation of any analytical functions as AFs, the "turnkey" mechanisms to support V2X/UAV use cases are of premium importance for carrier-grade implementation. The recently finalized study [36] proposes new 5GS automation enablers (as new services or capabilities of NWDAF) for e.g. optimized radio access technology/frequency selection, anomaly detection and aiding its cause analysis, UE dispersion analytics, UE movement patterns and traffic analytics, predictive mobility management, and real-time data collection and analytics. Further mechanisms for so called "context awareness" will need to be developed in the future. The research on AI-driven management algorithms is also only at the beginning of the way (several initiated EU research projects). Automation and autonomization of network management ("self-managing networks") in the 5G era is becoming an inevitable necessity. MNOs are under constant pressure to reduce operating costs, so the increase in the number of managed communication networks (in particular as a result of slicing) must take place with the same staff.

Finally, it should be noted that the scope of the 3GPP vision of network management, and therefore also of the 5GS integration with the ecosystems of vertical industries, is very limited compared to the comprehensive vision of the telecommunications operator's processes and related information systems map by TMF [37]. The integration of telecommunications and vertical industry sectors must also include the integration at the level of operational processes. For example, flight feasibility check request cannot be comprehensively answered based only on some momentary status of 5GS, read out from CP or real-time management system. Other support systems have to be involved, e.g. configuration management, change management, planning management, etc. In case of emergency flight route replanning, the dynamics of the end-to-end interaction (from changed route feasibility check request through answer validation and provisioning request to report of successful completion of network reconfiguration) will be extremely high and the timescale of tens of second may be demanded. Therefore, a comprehensive reference architecture for integrating the cooperating ecosystems must be thoroughly thought out.

5   Conclusions

The participation of telecommunications operators in European projects has resulted in the understanding of the broad context of the needs of industrial sectors that are addressed to the telecommunications network. This is all the more important as the wide adoption of network virtualization and slicing will bring serious market disruption in the long term. Therefore, operators must give a proactive response to these changes, looking for new business opportunities in ground and airborne vehicular vertical industries.

This paper presents the current progress of 5GS development in the context of offered support for the vertical industries in focus. The preparedness of the network to meet the expectations has been evaluated on the basis of mechanisms that could facilitate vehicular use cases and with respect to the requirements established by the 3GPP in preceding standardization activities. From the operator's point of view, the 3GPP support for UAV/V2X services is still very limited mostly due to lack of implementation of NS as well as mechanisms that enable addressing the requirements for URLLC transmission (RRM, adaptive coverage improvement, etc.). Considering characteristics and dynamics of vehicular services, a substantial gap exists with relation to mechanisms for direct UE-UE communication. The opportunities for architectural synergy and reusability of solutions for both sectors will not be exploited, probably. Moreover, the approach to deployments of latency-critical services at the edge of the network needs redefinition to enable mitigation of the delay overhead induced by virtualization process.

The aforementioned standardization limitations will probably be overcome by 3GPP in the next 1.5 years. However, a significant challenge beyond the scope of 3GPP interests are the mechanisms necessary for highly dynamic automated 5G network management and orchestration, as well as, in particular, full integration of operational processes through the integration of a broader spectrum of information systems of both sectors in focus than in the 3GPP vision.

The 5G technology was invented and defined to enable the implementation of new services (in particular, to meet the full requirements of the V2X and UAV sectors) – it is a paradox that it does not currently support them. This means that there is still a lot of work to be done to make the carrier-grade implementation of these services feasible.

References

1. ITU-R: IMT Vision - Framework and overall objectives of the future development of IMT for 2020 and beyond (M.2083, Feb 2015)
2. Markets and Markets: Automotive V2X Market. https://www.marketsandmarkets.com/Market-Reports/automotive-vehicle-to-everything-v2x-market-90013236.html. Accessed on 7 June 2021
3. 5GAA: C-V2X Use Cases Methodology, Examples and Service Level Requirements. https://5gaa.org/wp-content/uploads/2019/07/5GAA_191906_WP_CV2X_UCs_v1-3-1.pdf. Accessed on 7 June 2021
4. Markets and Markets: Unmanned Aerial Vehicle (UAV) Market. https://www.marketsandmarkets.com/Market-Reports/unmanned-aerial-vehicles-uav-market-662.html. Accessed on 7 June 2021
5. Global UTM Association: UAS Traffic Management Architecture. www.gutma.org/docs/Global_UTM_Architecture_V1.pdf. Accessed on 7 June 2021
6. GOF USPACE Project: SESAR 2020 GOF USPACE Summary, FIMS, Design and Architecture. https://www.sesarju.eu/node/3203. Accessed on 7 June 2021
7. 3GPP: Service requirements for enhanced V2X scenarios (TS 22.186 V16.2.0, June 2019)
8. 3GPP: Unmanned Aerial System (UAS) support in 3GPP scenarios (TS 22.125 V17.3.0, April 2021)
9. 3GPP: Service requirements for V2X services (TS 22.185 V16.0.0, July 2020)

10. 3GPP: System architecture for the 5G System (TS 23.501 V17.0.0, Mar 2021)
11. 3GPP: Management and orchestration; Architecture framework (TS 28.533 V16.7.0, April 2021)
12. 3GPP: 5G System (5GS) Location Services (LCS); Stage 2 (TS 23.273 V17.0.0, Mar 2021)
13. 3GPP: Common API Framework for 3GPP Northbound APIs (TS 23.222 V17.4.0, April 2021)
14. 3GPP: Service Enabler Architecture Layer for Verticals (SEAL); Functional architecture and information flows (TS 23.434 V17.1.0, April 2021)
15. 3GPP: Architecture configuration options for NR (RP-161249, June 2016)
16. 3GPP: Study on new radio access technology: Radio access architecture and interfaces (TR 38.801 V14.0.0, April 2017)
17. 3GPP: NR and NG-RAN Overall description; Stage-2 (TS 38.300 V16.5.0, Mar 2021)
18. 3GPP: Study on system enhancement for Proximity based Services (ProSe) in the 5G System (5GS) (TR 23.752 V17.0.0, Mar 2021)
19. 3GPP: NR; Medium Access Control (MAC) protocol specification, (TS 38.321 V16.4.0, Mar 2021)
20. Li, Y.R., Gao, B., Zhang, X., Huang, K.: Beam management in millimeter-wave communications for 5G and beyond. IEEE Access 8, 13282–13293 (2020). https://doi.org/10.1109/ACCESS.2019.2963514
21. O-RAN Alliance: O-RAN: Towards an Open and Smart RAN (White Paper, Oct 2018)
22. 3GPP: Application layer support for Vehicle-to-Everything (V2X) services; Functional architecture and information flows (TS 23.286 V17.1.0, April 2021)
23. 3GPP: Architecture enhancements for 5G System (5GS) to support Vehicle-to-Everything (V2X) services (TS 23.287 V16.5.0, Dec 2020)
24. 3GPP: Study on enhancements to application layer support for V2X services (TR 23.764 V17.1.0, Dec 2020)
25. 3GPP: Study on architecture enhancements for 3GPP support of advanced Vehicle-to-Everything (V2X) services; Phase 2 (TR 23.776 V17.0.0, Mar 2021)
26. 3GPP: Study on supporting Unmanned Aerial Systems (UAS) connectivity, Identification and tracking (TR 23.754 V17.1.0, Mar 2021)
27. 3GPP: Study on application layer support for Unmanned Aerial Systems (UAS) (TR 23.755 V17.0.0, April 2021)
28. Tomaszewski, L., Kołakowski, R., Kukliński, S.: Integration of U-space and 5GS for UAV services. 2020 IFIP Networking Conference, pp. 767–772 (2020)
29. ETSI: Multi-access Edge Computing (MEC); Framework and Reference Architecture (GS MEC 003 V2.2.1, Dec 2020)
30. Oljira, D. B., Brunstrom, A., Taheri, J., Grinnemo, K.: Analysis of Network Latency in Virtualized Environments. In: 2016 IEEE Global Communications Conference (GLOBECOM), pp. 1–6. https://doi.org/10.1109/GLOCOM.2016.7841603
31. Sollfrank, M., Loch, F., Denteneer, S., Vogel-Heuser, B.: Evaluating docker for lightweight virtualization of distributed and time-sensitive applications in industrial automation. IEEE Trans. Industr. Inf. 17(5), 3566–3576 (2021). https://doi.org/10.1109/TII.2020.3022843
32. Tomaszewski L., Kukliński S., Kołakowski R.: A new approach to 5G and MEC integration. In: Maglogiannis I., Iliadis L., Pimenidis E. (eds.) Artificial Intelligence Applications and Innovations. AIAI 2020 IFIP WG 12.5 International Workshops. AIAI 2020. IFIP Advances in Information and Communication Technology, vol. 585. Springer, Cham (2020). https://doi.org/10.1007/978-3-030-49190-1_2

33. Chochliouros I. P., Spiliopoulou A. S., Lazaridis P., Dardamanis A., Zaharis Z., Kostopoulos A.: Dynamic network slicing: challenges and opportunities. In: Maglogiannis I., Iliadis L., Pimenidis E. (eds.) Artificial Intelligence Applications and Innovations. AIAI 2020 IFIP WG 12.5 International Workshops. AIAI 2020. IFIP Advances in Information and Communication Technology, vol. 585. Springer, Cham (2020). https://doi.org/10.1007/978-3-030-49190-1_5

34. ETSI: Management and Orchestration (ETSI NFV MAN 001 V1.1.1, Dec 2014)

35. Trakadas, P., et al.: Comparison of management and orchestration solutions for the 5G era. J. Sens. Actuator Netw. **9**(1), 4 (2020). https://doi.org/10.3390/jsan9010004

36. 3GPP: Study on enablers for network automation for the 5G System (5GS); Phase 2 (TR 23.700-91, V17.0.0, Dec 2020)

37. TMF Homepage. https://www.tmforum.org/opendigitalframework. Accessed on 7 June 2021

Machine Learning-Based, Networking and Computing Infrastructure Resource Management

Ioannis P. Chochliouros[1], Alexandros Kostopoulos[1(✉)], Miquel Payaró[2], Christos Verikoukis[2], Sabrina De Capitani di Vimercati[3], Evgenii Vinogradov[4], Vida Ranjbar[4], John Vardakas[5], Md Arifur Rahman[6], Polyzois Soumplis[7], and Emmanuel Varvarigos[7]

[1] Hellenic Telecommunications Organization (OTE) S.A., 99 Kifissias Avenue, 15124 Maroussi, Athens, Greece
alexkosto@oteresearch.gr
[2] Centre Tecnològic de Telecomunicacions de Catalunya (CTTC/CERCA), Barcelona, Spain
[3] Universita degli Studi di Milano, Milan, Italy
[4] Katholieke Universiteit Leuven, Leuven, Belgium
[5] Iquadrat Informatica SL, Barcelona, Spain
[6] IS-Wireless, Warsaw, Poland
[7] Institute of Communications and Computer Systems (ICCS), Athens, Greece

Abstract. 5G mobile networks will be soon available to handle all types of applications and to provide service to massive numbers of users. In this complex and dynamic network ecosystem, end-to-end performance analysis and optimization will be key features in order to effectively manage the diverse requirements imposed by multiple vertical industries over the same shared infrastructure. To enable such a vision, the MARSAL project [1] targets the development and evaluation of a complete framework for the management and orchestration of network resources in 5G and beyond by utilizing a converged optical-wireless network infrastructure in the access and fronthaul/midhaul segments. At the network design domain, MARSAL targets the development of novel cell-free-based solutions. Namely, scalable and cost-efficient wireless access points deployment will be achieved by exploiting the distributed cell-free concept combined with wireless and wired serial fronthaul approaches. We will target the inclusion of these innovative functionalities in the O-RAN project. In parallel, in the fronthaul/midhaul segments MARSAL aims to radically increase the flexibility of optical access architectures for Beyond-5G cell site connectivity via different levels of fixed-mobile convergence. In the network and service management domain, the design philosophy of MARSAL is to provide a comprehensive framework for the management of the entire set of communication and computational network resources by exploiting novel ML-based algorithms of both edge and midhaul data centers, by incorporating the Virtual Elastic Data Centers/Infrastructures paradigm. Finally, at the network security domain, MARSAL aims to introduce mechanisms that provide privacy and security to application workload and data, targeting to allow applications and users to maintain control over their data when relying on

© IFIP International Federation for Information Processing 2021
Published by Springer Nature Switzerland AG 2021
I. Maglogiannis et al. (Eds.): AIAI 2021 Workshops, IFIP AICT 628, pp. 85–94, 2021.
https://doi.org/10.1007/978-3-030-79157-5_8

the deployed shared infrastructures, while AI and Blockchain technologies will be developed in order to guarantee a secured multi-tenant slicing environment.

Keywords: Cell-free · Distributed cloud · Network automation · Machine learning · Secure multi-tenancy

1 Introduction

The number of people living in megacities, (i.e., cities with a population greater than 10 million) has increased from 69.5 million in 1975 to a staggering 472.8 million in 2015 [2]. In parallel, the percentage of network traffic originating and terminating in a city is increasing [3] through the use of popular online services and smart city applications. It is expected that Smart Megacities will become the primary source of data, characterized by massive data growth and processing requirements. Today these requirements are served by a variety of optical and wireless networking and edge/fog/cloud computing technologies and infrastructures deployed in the cities and belonging to different providers, while smaller business owners (e.g., stadium operators) are also deploying their own infrastructures. In such an environment, 5G networks are set to address the demands of a fully connected and mobile society, enabling a wide variety of applications over the same infrastructure [3], while carrying 45% of the total mobile traffic and serving up to 65% of the world's population [4]. These numbers are expected to increase due to the urbanization of global population and the increase of the size and volume of megacities [2, 5].

5G changes the landscape of mobile networks profoundly, with an evolved architecture supporting unprecedented capacity, spectral efficiency, and increased flexibility. Moreover, 5G adopts Edge computing as a key paradigm, evolving from centralized architectures (e.g., based on Cloud-RAN (C-RAN)) towards multiple tiers of Edge nodes and a virtualized RAN (vRAN). Open RAN initiatives such as O-RAN have a key role in this evolution, complementing the 3GPP 5G standards with a foundation of vRAN network elements. However, these technologies have been in large developed in isolation between them, making difficult to fully exploit their capabilities in an integrated, end-to-end and secure manner. Algorithms do not only run in the cloud, and optical and wireless links cannot be abstracted in the same way. When going to cell-free networking concepts, more nodes and links will be interconnected, serving local and global secure applications. Thus, it is essential to rethink the architecture and algorithms running elastically at the scale of a city or building level.

In general, application traffic flows from and towards end-users and end-devices, served by multiple levels of storage and computing entities from the edge to the cloud, while utilizing a diverse set of wireless and optical technologies in the fronthaul, midhaul and backhaul network segments. These infrastructure resources belong to different administrative domains, operate in parallel in the same network areas and are usually shared between competing flows, computations and data in static and/or statically multiplexed manner. Thus, it is clear that targeted innovation activities need to take place to fully exploit key technological developments, towards a disaggregated infrastructure model, where technological infrastructure blocks can be transparently and flexibly replaced by others, while offering similar networking and/or computing offerings and control and monitoring capabilities. Specifically, key advances are required both in the network design and network/service orchestration levels:

- The network infrastructure should be able to support multiple distributed edge nodes and a huge number of Access Points (APs), which are coordinated and orchestrated by entities in a low-cost and near-zero latency manner;
- A unified and hierarchical infrastructure is essential to provide intelligent management of communication, computation and storage resources, which can be further enhanced by incorporating efficient Machine-Learning (ML) algorithms;
- The support of multiple tenants should be followed by the application of mechanisms that are able to guarantee data and information security and integrity especially in multi-tenant environments, which would play a vital role in enabling various use-cases and industry verticals targeted in 5G and Beyond (B5G) systems.

This is where MARSAL steps in, proposing a new paradigm of elastic virtual infrastructures that integrate in a transparent manner a variety of novel radio access, networking, management and security technologies, which will be developed under the MARSAL framework in order to deliver end-to-end transfer, processing and storage services in an efficient and secured way.

To this end, MARSAL focuses on three pillars to enable a new generation of ultra-dense, cost-efficient, flexible and secure networks: (i) network design pillar; (ii) virtual elastic infrastructure pillar, and; (iii) network security pillar. For the network design pillar, MARSAL pushes cell-free networking towards the distributed processing cell-free concept. This will enable wireless mmWave fronthaul solutions, which will be implemented and integrated with existing vRAN elements while being in-line with the O-RAN Alliance. In parallel, MARSAL's second pillar is built based on the Elastic Edge Computing notion, targeting to optimize the functionality of the Multiple Access Edge Computing (MEC) and the network slicing management systems via a hierarchy of analytic and decision engines. Finally, under its third pillar, MARSAL will develop novel ML-based mechanisms that guarantee privacy and security in multi-tenancy environments, targeting both end users and tenants.

In this paper, we focus on a wide range of experimental scenarios that MARSAL will consider. The first domain includes a set of use cases focused on cell-free networking in dense and ultra-dense hotspot areas (Sect. 2). The second domain includes use cases related to cognitive assistance, as well as security and privacy implications in 5G and beyond (Sect. 3). We conclude our remarks in Sect. 4.

2 Cell-Free Networking in Dense and Ultra-Dense Hotspot Areas

During high-popularity events, both indoors (e.g., music concerts) and outdoors (e.g., a fair), a large number of users tend to stream high volumes of content from multiple handheld devices, thus creating a heavy burden to the network infrastructure both in the uplink and in the downlink direction.

The current state-of-the-art (SoTA) solution is network densification that involves small cells with Massive MIMO (Multiple-Input, Multiple-Output) capabilities (i.e., a large number of transmitting and receiving antennas with beamforming and precoding techniques). In this case, users are bounded to the service area of a single cell. This solution is limited by inter-cell interference, with a performance at the cell edges being a particular concern. This makes cell-free networking [6], an emerging B5G technology, highly suitable to hotspot areas. Cell free concept can offer seemingly infinite capacity and it fully mitigates the cell edge challenges as the users are served by multiple rather than just one access point. Also, a massive number of distributed antennas exploit spatial diversity to mitigate the counter effect of large-scale fading, and consequently, the users will enjoy a higher quality of service [6–8].

Two deployment scenarios of MARSAL cell-free NG-RAN (Next Generation RAN) will be explored as the project proofs-of-concept (PoCs): That is, we will accommodate dense traffic via: (i) Hybrid MIMO fronthaul [9, 10] in an outdoor scenario, and; (ii) Serial Fronthaul [11, 12] in an indoor setting. The indoors scenario showcases MARSAL's Fixed-Mobile Convergence (FMC) solution, supporting integrated connectivity of mobile and fixed clients, that share the same Midhaul and Edge infrastructure (e.g., MEC hosts).

2.1 Dense User-Generated Content Distribution with mmWave Fronthauling

This scenario's main objective is to demonstrate and evaluate MARSAL's distributed cell-free NG-RAN in terms of increased capacity and spectral efficiency gains and the adaptivity of dynamic clustering and RRM (Radio Resource Management) mechanisms in managing connectivity resources in a dynamic environment with varying hotspots areas. Furthermore, we aim at evaluating the Hybrid MIMO Fronthaul in terms of its ability to offer a dynamic AP topology.

During outdoors events, such as fairs or festivals, it is common for dense user-generated content to be streamed by spectators via their handheld devices, and consumed locally in real-time. This puts very high stress on the radio interfaces. In this scenario, MARSAL's cell-free NG-RAN will be evaluated while supporting dense video traffic at the uplink and downlink direction. The cell-free vRAN components on dense user-generated content distribution with mmWave fronthauling experimental scenario will be consisting of the following layers: RLC, MAC, RRC, PDCP, SDAP. The layers are apportioned into two virtualized components, i.e., the distributed unit (vO-DU) and centralized unit (vO-CU). The vO-CU can be further splitted into vO-CU_UP (user plane) and vO-CU_CP (control plane). Even though each communication layer the components within the layer can be a separate as a software component for the purpose of this use case vO-DU and vO-CU can be treated as three monolithic, virtualized applications (so called Virtualized Network Functions-VNFs).

Specifically, APs from KU Leuven [13] will be interconnected with Radio Edge nodes, which host MARSAL's vRAN elements, while the Near-RT (Near Real-Time) RIC (RAN intelligent Controller) and vCU_CP VNF (Virtual Network Function) will be deployed at a Regional Edge node (REN). To deploy cell-free vRAN components on the RENs, we will consider higher and lower layers split options according to the specification of 3GPP, O-RAN and small cell forum. The choice of how to split RAN functions depends on factors related to radio network deployment scenarios, constraints and intended supported services, e.g., support of specific QoS per offered services (e.g., low latency, high throughput), support of specific user density and load demand per given geographical area, availability of transport networks with different performance levels, from ideal to non-ideal, and application type e.g., real-time or Non-Real Time, respectively. Furthermore, MARSAL's Hybrid MIMO fronthaul solution will be leveraged for the interconnection of RUs (Remote Units) and Radio Edge nodes, while point-to-point mmWave links will be established between neighbouring Radio Edge nodes, facilitating DU (Distributed Unit) cooperation without capacity constraints from the Midhaul and Fronthaul interfaces. The performance of the cell-free NG-RAN will be evaluated via pre-recorded video content that will be uploaded and downloaded by User Equipment (UE) to/from a video streaming MEC app deployed at the Regional Edge node, to emulate Dense User-Generated Content streaming both in the uplink and in the downlink direction. This scenario will demonstrate and evaluate the following sub-scenarios, showcasing numerous MARSAL innovations related to cell-free networking and Hybrid MIMO fronthauling:

- Demonstrate MARSAL's data-driven approaches for AP cluster formation and RRM, that consider per-user rate and estimated CSI (Channel State Information) as well as computational and fronthaul constraints. Evaluate their effect on channel capacity and spectral efficiency at the uplink and downlink, showcasing how they react to changes in hotspot areas.
- Demonstrate MARSAL's dynamic adaptability algorithms, showcasing their capabilities in selecting the optimal AP-DU and inter-DU cooperation levels and how these are affected by fronthaul capacity constraints, and evaluate the effect of the point-to-point (PtP) Xn-line interface in inter-DU cooperation.
- Demonstrate dynamic adaptability of the AP topology via beam-steering and beam-sharing, offered by the new Hybrid MIMO interface, and showcase optimized cluster formation leveraging on the adaptive topology.

2.2 Ultra-Dense Video Traffic Delivery in a Converged Fixed-Mobile Network

This scenario will showcase MARSAL's solution towards Fixed-Mobile Convergence in an ultra-dense indoors scenario. Mobile clients served by a distributed Cell-Free RAN will be sharing the Optical Midhaul with third party FTTH (Fiber-to-the-Home) clients. The spectral efficiency and channel capacity gains of the distributed Cell-Free RAN in a Serial Fronthaul topology, and the load balancing and end-to-end slice reconfiguration mechanisms of the converged infrastructure will be demonstrated and evaluated.

In large concert venues, visual content which supplements the live event can be captured locally (e.g., from multiple fixed 4k cameras, as well as unmanned aerial vehicles (UAVs)), and distributed to a high number of spectators in real time, generating ultra-high-density video traffic. MARSAL's distributed cell-free RAN in a Serial Fronthaul topology will be deployed in this scenario. The Serial Fronthaul allows a large number of cell-free APs to be interconnected in a bus topology, significantly increasing spectral efficiency but with minimal cabling requirements; hence Serial Fronthauling is considered an ideal solution for indoors venues. Moreover, in this scenario, Radio Edge nodes, that host the vRAN elements, are interconnected via PtP and PtMP (Point-to-Multi-Point) Midhaul links with the Regional Edge. The Regional Edge nodes, interconnected in a WDM (Wavelength Division Multiplexing) ring topology, will host the Near-RT RIC and vCU_CP VNFs. The SDTN (Software-Defined Transport Network) controller and Near-RT RIC SDN (Software-Defined Network) function will also be deployed at the Regional Edge nodes. The performance of this scenario will be evaluated via pre-recorded 4k/HDR (High Dynamic Range) video that will be uploaded and downloaded by UEs to/from a video streaming MEC application deployed at the Regional Edge node. Fixed clients will be included as well in this scenario that will be served by the same infrastructure via PtMP links sharing capacity with the Radio Edge node. In this scenario, a number of MARSAL innovations will be showcased and evaluated:

- Demonstrate load balancing between fixed and mobile traffic through the coordination of the two SDN controllers, leveraging unused capacity from the PtMP link to serve traffic from the mobile clients of the cell-free RAN. Evaluate the distributed control plane's capability to adapt to workload variations in near-real time.
- Demonstrate adaptive cooperation between multiple cell-free serial fronthaul, leveraging on the Midhaul links for information sharing. Showcase the effect of Midhaul capacity limitations on the levels of cooperation and achieved Spectral Efficiency.
- Evaluate the energy savings that can be achieved via traffic aggregation on a limited number of wavelengths and shutdown of unused SFP+ (enhanced small form-factor pluggable) modules in light load conditions, under the control of the SDTN controller.

3   Cognitive Assistance and Its Security and Privacy Implications in 5G and Beyond

Future generations of 5G will bring support for hyper-connectivity, offering seemingly unlimited bandwidth and zero perceived latency, and facilitating disruptive PoCs that are not currently technically feasible. These include real-time, interactive Next-Generation Internet (NGI) applications that support human-centered interaction via novel interfaces (e.g., vision and haptics). One such application is Cognitive Assistance, which takes the concept of Augmented Reality (AR) one step further, relying on real-time video and scene analytics and activity recognition to provide personalized feedback for activities the user might be performing (e.g., recreational activities, furniture assembling, sightseeing, etc.). One of the main challenges is ensuring zero perceived latency to guarantee a satisfactory user experience, and also to send timely feedback, especially for time sensitive activities. Furthermore, the high computational load and massive data sets required for scene analysis and activity recognition makes on-device execution infeasible. This PoC will also address the many security and privacy implications inherent in applications that process personal data and Personally Identifiable Information (PII) as per the GDRP (General Data Protection Regulation) provisions [14]. Challenges related to multi-tenant infrastructures, such as policy-driven sharing of operational data and blockchain-based Network Slicing as a Service (NSaaS) will also be addressed.

3.1 Cognitive Assistance and Smart Connectivity for Next-Generation Sightseeing

The main objective of this scenario is to demonstrate and evaluate MARSAL's Virtual Elastic Infrastructure, showcasing its ability to ensure high reliability and quality of experience for Next-Generation human-centred applications with new terminal types, while sharing resources with high-priority 5G NFs (Network Functions).

In this scenario, two real-time and interactive Cloud-Native applications for outdoors sightseeing, supporting human-centered interaction via 3D cameras, will be deployed at MARSAL's multi-tenant Elastic Edge Infrastructure. The latter will include a MEC platform which will be deployed at Regional Edge and Radio Edge Data Centres (DCs) and Centralized orchestrators (i.e., the MEO (Mobile Edge Orchestrator) and NFVO (Network Functions Virtualization Orchestrator)) which will be deployed at a Core-tier Data Centre. It must be noted that the Edge and Core Data Centres will also host the 5G NFs (e.g., the 5G Core VNFs) while resource sharing will be accomplished via MARSAL's innovative MEO. In the targeted scenario an enhanced strolling experience with overlaid information relevant to their surroundings and activities (e.g., restaurant ratings, nearest ATMs (automated teller machines) or bus-stations, touristic information, etc.) is offered to users equipped with untethered, 5G-enabled AR glasses. Specifically, an AR sightseeing application will apply real-time video analytics on the user's field-of-view to detect user intent or activity and offer visual guidance in the form of relevant information that is optically super-imposed. Furthermore, at certain attraction points, IoT (Internet of Things) nodes equipped with novel interfaces (i.e., 3D cameras) and 5G connectivity will be deployed to facilitate interaction with the user. A Cognitive Assistance application will encourage the user to manipulate in real-time the virtual representation of an artefact, projected at their AR glasses. Gesture recognition will be implemented via real-time analysis of the 3D camera stream, while the application offers cognitive visual guidance, superimposing information at the users' field of view explaining how the exhibit (or artefact) is used in real time. Both applications will rely on MARSAL's Virtual Elastic Infrastructure to optimize and disaggregate their AR, scene analysis and activity recognition application functions in multiple tiers (i.e., Regional Edge, Radio Edge, on-device). The following MARSAL innovations will be demonstrated and evaluated:

- Demonstrate and evaluate the capabilities of the MEO to derive the optimal placement of the (containerized) application functions at the Radio Edge or Regional Edge DCs, achieving optimized distribution of latency budgets. The computational requirements and latency constraints of application functions will be derived from at the applications' manifest files. This will result in imperceptible latency of the untethered AR applications, comparable to tethered AR, which will be validated by user tests.
- Demonstrate the collaborative interaction of the MEC system with the 5G UPF for real-time inter-DC traffic steering for load balancing purposes, evaluating the effect on resource utilization. Unbalanced demand will be emulated in the coverage area of certain Regional Edge nodes, and the ability of the MEC system to uniformly re-direct traffic will be showcased.

- Demonstrate the Analytic and Decision engines of MARSAL's Self-Driven infrastructure, and evaluate their ability derive accurate context representations and successfully drive the NFVO and MEO. Evaluate their effectiveness in achieving a set of objectives, related to SLA (Service Level Agreement) requirements (e.g., which of the two AR applications to prioritize) and cost considerations (e.g., related to OPEX, energy costs, etc.).

3.2   Data Security and Privacy in Multi-tenant Infrastructures

This scenario will demonstrate and evaluate MARSAL's privacy and security mechanisms that guarantee the isolation of slices and ensure collaboration of participants in multi-tenant 5G and Beyond infrastructures without assuming trust. These mechanisms will also be evaluated in terms of their ability to mitigate the increased privacy risks of NGI applications that process Personally Identifiable Information (PII).

This scenario assumes a multi-tenant infrastructure with one MNO (Mobile Network Operator) and two MVNOs (Mobile Virtual Network Operators), each serving an OTT (Over-The-Top) application provider, while MARSAL's Threat Detection and Threat Analysis engines are leveraged to ensure the isolation of slices and prevent cross-slice attacks. The OTT applications that will be deployed in separate slices, process sensitive PII related to outdoors sightseeing, including video streams with users' field of view and tracked location. This information is stored for further processing at a multi-tenant Distributed Cloud Solution (or DCS) with Storage Nodes provided by multiple infrastructure owners. MARSAL's AONT (all or nothing transform) mechanism and NFS (Network File System) gateway, coupled with policy-driven storage resource allocation and anonymization will guarantee data security, and facilitate distributed computation on massive data sets (e.g., applying data analytics to build a user profile) while offering integrity guarantees. Furthermore, this scenario will demonstrate the ability of MVNOs to cooperate in a decentralized, blockchain-assisted scenario, leveraging smart contracts to negotiate slice resources and MARSAL's privacy-preserving representation learning algorithms to protect their sensitive operational data. More specifically, the following security and privacy MARSAL innovations will be demonstrated and evaluated:

- Demonstrate the ability of MARSAL to guarantee end-to-end slice security and isolation of OTT applications, even in the presence of compromised sub-slices in the shared infrastructure. Cross-slice attacks will be emulated based on real-world cyber-attack datasets and the ability of the Threat Detection and Threat analysis engines to detect malicious flows will be evaluated.
- Demonstrate decentralized cooperation of NVNOs via smart contracts. Significant cost reductions will be demonstrated when MVNOs face peak demand at different times, and hence can share slice resources when they are not used. MVNOs further cooperate via sharing operational data regarding traffic profiles. Joint training of the NSaaS (Network Slicing as a Service) traffic prediction models without exposing sensitive information will also be showcased via MARSAL's privacy-preserving representation learning algorithms.

- Evaluate MARSAL's perpetual data security guarantees in terms of the minimum number of nodes required to reconstruct a resource, assuming a varying number of compromised Storage Node providers, and applying different fragmentation and data allocation strategies. Demonstrate assurance of data protection and privacy requirements of all stakeholders (i.e., infrastructure owners, OTT application providers, and end users).
- Demonstrate Distributed Computation (e.g., to derive the user profile via data analytics) on data sets containing PII which are stored at the DCS by multiple tenants. The policy-driven NFS gateway and MARSAL's probabilistic integrity mechanisms will be evaluated in terms of their ability to offer privacy and integrity guarantees expressed in MARSAL's policy language.

4 Discussion

5G mobile networks will be soon available to handle all types of applications and to provide services to massive numbers of users. In this complex and dynamic network ecosystem, an end-to-end performance analysis and optimization will be key features, in order to effectively manage the diverse requirements imposed by multiple vertical industries over the same shared infrastructure.

To enable such a vision, the MARSAL project targets the development and evaluation of a complete framework for the management and orchestration of network resources in 5G and beyond, by utilizing a converged optical-wireless network infrastructure in the access and fronthaul/midhaul segments.

At the network design domain, MARSAL targets the development of novel cell-free based solutions that allows the significant scaling up of the wireless APs in a cost-effective manner by exploiting the application of the distributed cell-free concept and of the serial fronthaul approach, while contributing innovative functionalities to the O-RAN project. In parallel, in the fronthaul/midhaul segments MARSAL aims to radically increase the flexibility of optical access architectures for Beyond-5G Cell Site connectivity via different levels of fixed-mobile convergence.

At the network and service management domain, the design philosophy of MARSAL is to provide a comprehensive framework for the management of the entire set of communication and computational network resources by exploiting novel ML-based algorithms of both edge and midhaul DCs, by incorporating the Virtual Elastic Data Centers/Infrastructures paradigm.

Finally, at the network security domain, MARSAL aims to introduce mechanisms that provide privacy and security to application workload and data, targeting to allow applications and users to maintain control over their data when relying on the deployed shared infrastructures, while AI (Artificial Intelligence) and Blockchain technologies will be developed in order to guarantee a secured multi-tenant slicing environment.

Acknowledgments. The paper has been based on the context of the *"MARSAL"* (*"Machine Learning-Based, Networking and Computing Infrastructure Resource Management of 5G and Beyond Intelligent Networks"*) Project, funded by the EC under the Grant Agreement (GA) No. 101017171.

References

1. MARSAL ("Machine Learning-based Networking and Computing Infrastructure Resource Management of 5G and Beyond Intelligent Networks") 5G-PPP/H2020 project, Grant Agreement No. 101017171. https://www.marsalproject.eu/
2. Szmigiera, M.: Megacities - Statistics & Facts, April 2021. Statista https://www.statista.com/topics/4841/megacities/
3. Cisco: Cisco Visual Networking Index: Forecast and Trends, 2017–2022 White Paper, Cisco (2019). https://davidellis.ca/wp-content/uploads/2019/05/cisco-vni-feb2019.pdf
4. Ericsson: Ericsson Mobility Report 2019. Ericsson (2019). https://www.ericsson.com/en/mobility-report/reports
5. United Nations (UN): 2018 Revision of World Urbanization Prospects. UN, Department of Economic and Social Affairs (2018). https://www.un.org/development/desa/publications/2018-revision-of-world-urbanization-prospects.html
6. Ngo, H.Q., Ashikhmin, A., Yang, H., Larsson, E.G., Marzetta, T.L.: Cell-free massive MIMO versus small cells. IEEE Trans. Wirel. Commun. **16**(3), 1834–1850 (2017)
7. Björnson, E., Sanguinetti, L.: Making cell-free massive MIMO competitive with MMSE processing and centralized implementation. IEEE Trans. Wirel. Commun. **19**(1), 77–90 (2020)
8. Björnson, E., Sanguinetti, L.: Scalable cell-free massive MIMO systems. IEEE Trans. Commun. **68**(7), 4247–4261(2020)
9. Colpaert, A., Vinogradov, E., Pollin, S.: Fixed mmWave multi-user MIMO: performance analysis and proof-of-concept architecture. In: Proceedings of the 2020 IEEE 91st Vehicular Technology Conference (VTC2020-Spring), pp. 1–5. IEEE (2020)
10. Blandino, S., Mangraviti, G., Desset, C., Bourdoux, A., Wambacq P., Pollin, S.: Multi-user hybrid MIMO at 60 GHZ using 16-antenna transmitters. IEEE Trans. Circ. Syst. I Reg. Papers **66**(2), 848–858 (2019)
11. Shaik, Z.H., Björnson, E., Larsson, E.G.: Cell-free massive MIMO with radio stripes and sequential uplink processing. In: Proceedings of the 2020 IEEE International Conference on Communications Workshops (ICC Workshops), pp. 1–6. IEEE (2020)
12. Van der Perre, L., Larsson, E.G., Tufvesson, F., De Strycker, L., Björnson, E., Edfors, O.: RadioWeaves for efficient connectivity: analysis and impact of constraints in actual deployments. In: Proceedings of the 2019 53rd Asilomar Conference on Signals, Systems, and Computers, pp. 15–22. IEEE (2019)
13. Chen, C.-M., Volski, V., Van der Perre, L., Vandenbosch, G.A.E., Pollin, S.: Finite large antenna arrays for massive MIMO: characterization and system impact. IEEE Trans. Antennas Propag. **65**(12), 6712–6720 (2017)
14. European Union (EU): Regulation (EU) 2016/679 of the European Parliament and of the Council of 27 April 2016, on the protection of natural persons with regard to the processing of personal data and on the free movement of such data, and repealing Directive 95/46/EC (General Data Protection Regulation). Off. J. Eur. Union, **L119**, 1–88 (2016). https://eur-lex.europa.eu/legal-content/EN/TXT/PDF/?uri=CELEX:32016R0679&from=EL

Power Control in 5G Heterogeneous Cells Considering User Demands Using Deep Reinforcement Learning

Anastasios Giannopoulos[⊠], Sotirios Spantideas, Christos Tsinos, and Panagiotis Trakadas

National and Kapodistrian University of Athens, 34400 Psachna, Evia, Greece
{angianno,sospanti,ptrakadas}@uoa.gr

Abstract. Heterogeneous cells have been emerged as the dominant design approach for the deployment of 5G wireless networks . In this context, inter-cell interferences are expected to drastically affect the 5G targets, especially in terms of throughput experienced by the mobile users. This work proposes a novel Deep Reinforcement Learning (DRL) scheme, targeting at minimizing the difference between the allocated and requested user throughput through power regulation . The developed algorithm is employed in heterogeneous cells that are controlled in a centralized manner and validated for 5G-compliant channel models. First, the proposed learning framework of the DRL method is presented, mainly including the stabilization of the learning-related hyperparameters. Then, the DRL method is evaluated for several simulation scenarios and compared to well-established optimization methods for power allocation, namely the Water-filling and Weighted Minimum Mean Squared Error (WMMSE) algorithms, as well as a fixed power control scheme. The evaluation outcomes demonstrate the ability of the DRL framework in accurately approaching the user requirements, whereas the Water-filling and WMMSE solutions present large deviations from the user demands since they aim at the total network-wide throughput maximization.

Keywords: 5G · Heterogeneous Cell · Power Control · Deep Q-Learning · Reinforcement Learning · Radio Resource Management

1 Introduction

Next-generation broadband wireless networks are characterized by an ever-growing need for high-volume investments targeting at the delivery of rich-content and low-latency services [1–3]. In the 5G era, the configuration of the wireless networks has become an increasingly important issue, since it is strongly related to the 5G network design specifications. In order to cope with these demanding specifications, the design requirements of 5G networks inherently involve self-configuration and optimization capabilities of the network parameters [4], enabling autonomous decision-making processes. Thus, there is an ever-increasing need for the deployment of intelligent, adaptive and scalable

© IFIP International Federation for Information Processing 2021
Published by Springer Nature Switzerland AG 2021
I. Maglogiannis et al. (Eds.): AIAI 2021 Workshops, IFIP AICT 628, pp. 95–105, 2021.
https://doi.org/10.1007/978-3-030-79157-5_9

optimization algorithms with respect to the radio resource management (RRM). In this context, increased network densification has been introduced in 5G-enabled systems to maximize the total network-wide throughput, embracing the concept of Ultra Dense Networks (UDNs) [5]. Nevertheless, the dense deployment of the network elements, along with the large number of mobile users lead to a significant increase in the complexity of the wireless environment, which, in turn, has a significant impact on the degradation of the network performance and reduction of the experienced Quality of Service (QoS) [5].

In 5G wireless networks, the RRM usually involves the solution of non-convex optimization problems. For purposes of finding optimal or sub-optimal solutions to these problems, deterministic, as well as stochastic methods have been established [5–7]. Although these algorithms perform well for small-scale cellular systems, they fail to provide adequate solutions when high-dimensional wireless environments are considered. To this end, the rapid progress in machine learning (ML), and specifically reinforcement learning (RL), has led to intelligent and automatic approaches towards the solution of complex optimization problems [8, 9]. Several CCO techniques employing ML methods have been proposed [10–12]. One of the major challenges arising in UDNs is the power allocation [11, 13]. Since multiple Radio Units (RUs) operate simultaneously in the same coverage network area, the inter- and intra-cell interference should be carefully regulated. Several joint optimization schemes have been proposed, including the channel/power allocation and power and user association approaches [11–18]. In particular, a multi-agent DRL framework was proposed in [13] for dynamic power allocation based on cross-cell channel state information (CSI). Finally, a fair power control scheme for UDNs employing RL was proposed in [16], whereas a joint consideration of power/user association was investigated in [18], targeting to optimize the long-term total network utility in heterogeneous networks, using DRL.

In this paper, a DRL algorithm for power allocation in heterogeneous cells is proposed on 5G-compliant network configurations. The need for interference mitigation involves not only the inter-microcell interference control, but also the power regulation of the respective macrocell, which is responsible to cover the white spaces of the macro-area and complement the cell coverage. This two-fold power control framework is addressed in the present work, along with simultaneous consideration of the user demands, aiming to the optimal satisfaction of the user requests through power adjustment of the RUs. The main contributions of this paper are identified as: (i) The proposed scheme follows a demand-driven approach, by incorporating the difference between the requested and the allocated throughput in the rewarding system (ii) As opposed to deep learning models [9], this approach does not require training data or any prior knowledge of the telecommunication environment, providing robustness against the dynamic nature of the wireless systems (iii) The proposed algorithm is tested in a realistic 5G-compliant wireless environment in a generic manner that can be easily modified to incorporate different network settings (number of RUs, number of available resource blocks, etc.) and (iv) An alternative state space modeling of the telecommunication environment is determined, including a three-fold information for each user inside the network area: associated RU, the associated resource block (RB) and whether the user is satisfied or not. The values of these three parameters are acknowledged to the DRL agent, offering the flexibility to train for different user association realizations.

2 System Model and Algorithm Description

2.1 System Model

A heterogeneous network area that includes a macrocell (MaC) and M microcells (MiC, $m = 1, 2, \ldots, M$) is considered. The available number of RBs at each RU is F ($f = 1, 2, \ldots, F$), depending on the both the operational 5G frequency band and the employed 5G numerology scheme. It is assumed that the total bandwidth is equally distributed amongst the F RBs, resulting in a single-RB bandwidth of $B_1 = B_2 = \cdots = B$. Each RU n ($n = 1, 2, \ldots, M + 1$; $n = 1$ is the MaC ID, while $n = 2, 3, \ldots, M + 1$ is the MiC IDs) transmits over RB f with a specific power $P_{n,f}$. A minimum power level P_{min} is defined for each RB specific transmission to indicate signaling processes. A sum power constraint is also established for each RU, separately for MaC (P_{max}^{MaC}) and MiC (P_{max}^{MiC}), for power budget purposes, i.e. $\sum_{f=1}^{F} P_{1,f} \leq P_{max}^{MaC}$, for the MaC and $\sum_{f=1}^{F} P_{n,f} \leq P_{max}^{MiC}$, $\forall n > 1$ for the MiCs.

The mobile user $u \in \{1, 2, \ldots, U\}$ (i.e. U is the total number of users) located inside the network area can occupy a single RB f of a particular RU n, whereas multiple users can be associated with a specific RU. An allocation matrix A (with elements $a_{n,f,u} \leftarrow 1$) is additionally defined to denote whether user u is connected to the RB f of RU n (or 0 otherwise). Moreover, each user u requests a service s from a set of available service classes S, corresponding to realistic throughput requirements in order to ensure adequate QoS. Thus, a demand vector D_u ($D_1, D_2, \ldots, D_U$) is introduced to designate the requested service class of user u, expressed in terms of throughput. Importantly, a capacity overflow in a particular MiC occurs when all of its available RBs have been occupied by F mobile users.

As already mentioned, the dense wireless environment is related with the superposition of multiple interference signals both from the operating RU of the MaC and the operating RUs of the MiCs that are located in close proximity. The signal-to-interference-plus-noise ratio (SINR) received by a user u that is linked to RB f of RU n is given by:

$$SINR_u^{n,f} = \frac{P_{n,f} \cdot G_{n,f,u}}{(\sum_{n' \neq n}^{M+1} P_{n,f} \cdot G_{n',f,u}) + N_0}, \tag{1}$$

where $P_{n,f}$ stands for the operating power of the RU n over RB f, $G_{n,f,u}$ stands for the channel gain from RU n to user u and N_0' denotes the noise power density at the receiver. The channel gain reflects the propagation losses of the wireless environment (e.g. urban, rural, etc.) and also depends on the distance between the RU and the user [21]. The channels models are according to the 5G specifications detailed in [21] and different models for path loss are employed for the MaC (UMa channel model) and MiC (UMi channel model) depending on the user association, but also on the respective distance

98 A. Giannopoulos et al.

between the user u and RU n. Finally, the downlink user data rate can be expressed by ($\beta = 1$, a Bit Error Rate (BER) threshold of $BER = 10^{-6}$ is assumed):

$$R_u^{n,f} = B \cdot log\left(1 + \beta \cdot SINR_u^{n,f}\right), \tag{2}$$

2.2 Problem Formulation

The algorithm aims at minimizing the difference between the allocated and the requested throughput (Eq. 4) for each individual user by regulating appropriately the power levels of each RB of the $M + 1$ RUs, thus ensuring that the user requirements are fulfilled. Formally, the non-convex *optimization problem (P)* may be defined as:

$$(P) \qquad \min \sum_{u=1}^{U} \left(D_u - R_u^{n,f}\right) \tag{3}$$

s.t.:

$$(C1) \qquad \sum_{n=1}^{M+1} \sum_{f=1}^{F} a_{n,f,u} \leq 1, \forall u = 1, \ldots, U \tag{4}$$

$$(C2) \qquad \sum_{f=1}^{F} P_{1,f} \leq P_{max}^{MaC}, \sum_{f=1}^{F} P_{n,f} \leq P_{max}^{MiC}, \forall n = 2, \ldots, M+1 \tag{5}$$

$$(C3) \qquad P_{n,f} \geq P_{min}, \forall n = 1, \ldots, M+1; f = 1, \ldots, F \tag{6}$$

$$(C4) \qquad \sum_{f=1}^{F} a_{n,f,u} \leq F, \forall n = 1, \ldots, M+1 \tag{7}$$

$$(C5) \qquad R_u^{n,f} \leftarrow min\left\{D_u, R_u^{n,f}\right\}, \forall u = 1, \ldots, U \tag{8}$$

The optimization problem constraints can be described as follows: (C1) guarantees that each user can only be associated to one RB of a single RU (either MaC or MiC), (C2) ensures that the power limitations are satisfied for the MaC and MiC RUs respectively, (C3) secures a minimum power level for each RB intended for transmission of signaling processes (sleep mode), (C4) designates that a user cannot establish any connection link due to channel capacity restrictions (in case that all RBs of an RU are occupied by other mobile users) and, finally, (C5) ensures that the allocated throughput is upper bounded by the user demands.

The conventional approaches to solve problems similar to P involve either their non-convexity relaxation [19], which results in traditional solutions for convex optimization problems, or finding sub-optimal solutions in an iterative manner due to their NP-hard nature [20]. However, these methods suffer from significant challenges in large-scale optimization, computational complexity and time required for convergence. On the other hand, DRL exhibits the following advantages [12, 14, 15]: (i) the optimal policies can be captured without requiring analytical environment description, (ii) the algorithm can perform well even when large state/action spaces are considered, (iii) the training phase does not require previously gathered samples; instead, the knowledge is extracted in a trial-and-error basis through interaction with the wireless environment and (iv) pre-trained RL agents can be inferred in near-real time without requiring extensive re-programming.

2.3 Deep Q-Learning Framework and Algorithm Outline

In the presented DRL framework (see Fig. 1), a central network entity observes the telecommunication environment and regulates the power of the RBs of all RUs in the network area in order to minimize the difference between the allocated and the requested throughput (optimization problem P). Initially, the controller has no prior knowledge of the environment and regulates the power levels randomly (performs random actions during the exploration phase). Then, the controller evaluates the impact of the performed actions through positive (e.g. increase in sum-rate of users) or negative feedback (e.g. interference increase) from the environment. As the proposed scheme unfolds, the agent/controller begins to utilize its past experience and gradually exploits the actions that have beneficial outcomes. The Q-values are estimated by using a neural network attached in the agent's side. In principle, a DRL scheme involves the following:

State Space The wireless environment is effectively acknowledged to the agent via 3 parameters for each mobile user: (i) the number of the associated RU, (ii) the number of the RB that the user currently occupies and (iii) a binary value v specifying whether the user requirements are satisfied or not. The state transition sequence is expressed by $S = \{S_1, \ldots, S_t, \ldots, S_T\}$, where the system state at a given time t is given by $S_t = [(RU_1, RB_1, v_1), \ldots, (RU_U, RB_U, v_U)]$. The user u is associated with the RU/RB that provides the best-quality signal (maximum throughput association).

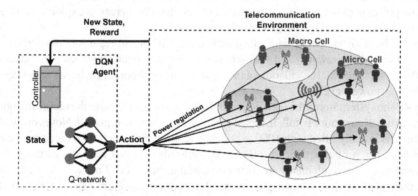

Fig. 1. The interaction cycle between the DQN agent and telecommunication environment.

Action Space The DQL agent performs a sequence of actions $\{A_1, \ldots, A_t, \ldots, A_T\}$. At a specific time instance t, the agent selects a single RB of each RU and then regulates its power, i.e. $A_t = [(f_1, a_1), \ldots, (f_{M+1}, a_{M+1})]$ and the adjustment value of the power on the f-th RB of the n-th RU is expressed by $a_n \in \{P_S, 0, -P_S\}$, where the power step P_S is a constant value. Thus, the agent selects an RB from each RU and then applies either a power step increase or a power incremental decrease or keeps the power fixed for this RB.

Reward System Once the agent performs an action, a new network system state is triggered, leading to different user RB/RU association configuration and throughput allocation. The response of the wireless environment may be expressed as:

$$
r_t = \begin{cases}
I = \sum_{u=1}^{U} min\left\{D_u, R_u^{n,f}\right\}_t - \sum_{u=1}^{U} min\left\{D_u, R_u^{n,f}\right\}_{t-1}, & if I > 0 \\
\sum_{u=1}^{U} \{D_u\}_t, & if \left\{R_u^{n,f}\right\}_t \geq \{D_u\}_t, \quad \forall u \\
0, & otherwise
\end{cases}
\tag{9}
$$

Intuitively, this rewarding system definition (*Case 1*) reflects the main objective of the proposed algorithm; it is beneficial to allocate a throughput vector uniformly to all users that is as close as possible to their demand vectors, rather than aiming at the total network throughput maximization. Furthermore, the high-valued positive reward (*Case 2*) implies that the agent will prefer actions that lead to complete fulfillment of all users (when possible). The progression of the DRL algorithm can be described in the following steps:

Step 1: The cognitive controller associates each user with a specific RU/RB pair based on the maximum throughput criterion. Each RU/RB is initialized to transmit with random power level before the agent starts to explore the environment.
Step 2: An RB is selected for each RU and its power is regulated depending on the operational mode of the algorithm: in exploration phase, an RB is randomly selected and its power is either increased, decreased or kept fixed, whereas in exploitation phase the action is estimated by the Q-network.
Step 3: The environment provides feedback to the DRL agent regarding the performed action (immediate reward) and the next state. This procedure involves the update of RU/RB association and calculation of the allocated throughput for each user with respect to the new power levels.
Step 4: The system stores the experience tuple $(s_t, a_t, r_{t+1}, s_{t+1})$ into the replay memory. In case that the memory is full, the least recently used tuple is replaced. Noteworthy, the memory is initially filled with 1000 experience tuples corresponding to random actions.
Step 5: A batch of experience tuples N_B is randomly selected from the memory. The current state s_t batch elements are forward-passed through the Q-network to predict the Q-values of all actions. The weights of the Q-network neurons are adjusted through the back-propagation method (Stochastic Gradient Descent).
Step 6: Every N_u steps, the weights of the Q-network model are cloned to the *target* Q-network model.

Step 7: The agent reduces the value of ε (linear decay) to get closer to the exploitation mode and repeats steps 1–6 until convergence.

3   Simulation Results

In this section, simulation results regarding the stabilization of the proposed DRL method's hyperparameters are provided. The algorithm was implemented in Python 3.8 (Keras and Tensorflow 2.0 for the DQN). To this end, the proposed DRL scheme is tested by considering a 5G-compliant network that includes a single MaC containing 4 MiCs, operating at 3.5 GHz. Moreover, two separate maximum power limitations were established for MaC (80 W) and MiCs (25 W) respectively, while the minimum power level per RB is set to 0.1 W. Moreover, 5G numerology 4 was considered in all simulation scenarios, resulting in 6 available RBs per MaC/MiC cell (the total bandwidth of each RU is 20 MHz). For this reason, 7 users are randomly placed within the radius of each MiC (100 m), thus ensuring that at least one residual user will be associated with the MaC. The interference mitigation challenge in this configuration setup lies in the fact that the MaC inevitably causes serious interferences in all MiCs, as an attempt to cover the residual (out of MiC capacity) user demands.

The optimization of the DQN hyperparameters included simultaneous consideration of the learning rate (a), the discount factor (γ) and the power step (P_S). Towards this direction, several values of these parameters were tested in terms of the accumulated average reward. The learning curves of the DQN agent are sequentially illustrated in Figs. 2, 3 and 4. Evidently, the values of the hyperparameter triplet (a, γ, P_S) were stabilized at (10^{-3}, 0.7, 1) as the optimal values of throughput increment convergence.

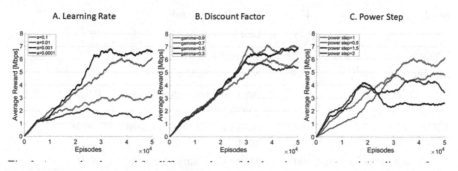

Fig. 2. Accumulated reward for different values of the learning rate α (panel A), discount factor γ (panel B) and power step P_S (panel C).

Furthermore, the performance of the DRL algorithm was tested in three validation scenarios and compared to three baseline power allocation methodologies, namely the Water-filling algorithm [6], the Weighted Minimum Mean Squared Error (WMMSE) method [7] and the fixed average power allocation. According to the latter method, all RUs transmit with the median power level, equally distributed amongst their RBs, as a trade-off between maximization of the coverage radius and minimization of the harmful interference.

The validation scenarios include: (i) all users request service class 2 (1 Mbps), (ii) all users request a random service class uniformly selected from service set S and (iii) all users request the most demanding service class 3 (2.5 Mbps). All evaluation scenarios were conducted by employing the DRL learning hyperparameters and network simulation parameters, summarized in Table 1.

The DRL algorithm was tested by inferring $N_i = 1000$ exploitative solutions (Monte-Carlo simulations), where in each realization, the users are randomly placed inside the network area. For each compared methodology, the Average (across N_i simulations) Variation from Demands (AVD) is defined as:

$$AVD = \frac{\sum_{i=1}^{N_i} \sum_{u=1}^{U} |R_u^i - D_u^i|}{N_i}, \tag{10}$$

where R_u^i and D_u^i are the allocated and requested throughput of user u, respectively, in the i-th simulation setup. AVD reflects the average residual throughput relative to the total user demands.

Table 1. Simulation setup parameters.

Parameter	Value	Parameter	Value
Central Frequency f_c	3.5 GHz	Memory size	5000
Bandwidth B	20 MHz	Batch size N_B	64
Number of RBs F	6	Loss function	Huber loss
5G numerology	4	Service class S	{0.1, 1, 2.5} Mbps
Number of RUs M	4	Noise Power Density	−174 dBm/Hz
Power step P_S	1 W	Learning rate α	10^{-3}
Maximum power P_{max}^{MaC}	80 W	Discount factor γ	0.7
Maximum power P_{max}^{MiC}	25 W	Number of hidden layers	3
Minimum power P_{min}	0.1 W	Activation function of input and hidden layers	ReLu
MiC radius	100 m	Activation function of output layer	Linear
Update target frequency N_u	100	Monte-Carlo simulations N_i	1000

The resulting evaluation metrics are depicted in Fig. 5 for all the validation scenarios. As expected, Water-filling and WMMSE algorithms outperform both DRL and Fixed Average methods in terms of total network-wide utility. This is attributed to the inherent optimization objective of these algorithms, which involves the direct maximization of the sum-rate at the cost of unbalanced throughput allocation amongst the users, presumably resulting in over- and under- satisfaction of several users' requirements. For instance, both Water-filling and WMMSE algorithms attempt to benefit from good channel conditions, producing power configurations with enhanced power levels in the favorable (in terms of SINR level) channels. On the contrary, *AVD* results (lower plane of Fig. 5) illustrate the demands-driven approach, followed by the proposed DRL framework.

In this context, the proposed DRL scheme aims at satisfying the user requirements regardless of their channel condition, thus ensuring minimization between the requested and the allocated throughput. The proposed method achieves a total network throughput solution comparable to the Fixed Average scheme, also allocating approximately 80% total network throughput with respect to the WMMSE algorithm (about 270 Mpbs). However, concerning the user satisfaction (*AVD* performance metric), the proposed DRL method outperforms all the other baselines, achieving significantly lower values (*AVD* = 0.6, 1.6 and 4.3 for validation scenarios i, ii and iii, respectively), as depicted in the lower panel of Fig. 5. Evidently, as the user requirements increase in terms of the requested throughput, the difference between their demands and allocated throughput becomes more noticeable.

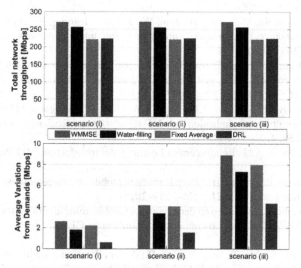

Fig. 3. Comparison amongst methods: DRL performance against *Waterfilling, WMMSE* and *Fixed Average* methods for the different validations scenarios in terms of total network throughput (up) and *AVD* (down) across 1000 network realizations.

4   Conclusion

In this work, a DRL framework for power regulation in heterogeneous cells is proposed and applied in 5G-compliant simulation scenarios. The objective of the proposed algorithm is the minimization of the difference between allocated and requested throughput of the mobile users through appropriate adjustment of both MaC and MiC transmit power. The assessment results clearly indicate that the presented DRL method effectively minimizes the variation between the user demands and the allocated throughput as compared to the Water-filling and WMMSE algorithms, as well as a fixed average power allocation scheme.

Acknowledgment. This work has been partially supported by the Affordable5G project, funded by the European Commission under Grant Agreement H2020-ICT-2020–1, number 957317 through the Horizon 2020 and 5G-PPP programs (www.affordable5g.eu/).

References

1. Andrews, J.G., et al.: What will 5G be? IEEE J. Sel. Areas Commun. **32**, 1065–1082 (2014)
2. Trakadas, P., et al.: Hybrid clouds for data-intensive, 5G-enabled iot applications: an overview, key issues and relevant architecture. Sensors **19**, 3591 (2019)
3. Trakadas, P., et al.: Comparison of management and orchestration solutions for the 5G era. J. Sens. Actuator Netw. **9**, 4 (2020)
4. Calabrese, F.D., Wang, L., Ghadimi, E., Peters, G., Hanzo, L., Soldati, P.: Learning radio resource management in RANs: framework, opportunities, and challenges. IEEE Commun. Mag. **56**, 138–145 (2018)
5. Morocho-Cayamcela, M.E., Lee, H., Lim, W.: Machine learning for 5G/B5G mobile and wireless communications: potential, limitations, and future directions. IEEE Access **7**, 137184–137206 (2019)
6. Qi, Q., Minturn, A., Yang, Y.: An efficient water-filling algorithm for power allocation in OFDM-based cognitive radio systems. In: 2012 International Conference on Systems and Informatics, ICSAI 2012, pp. 2069–2073 (2012)
7. Shi, Q., Razaviyayn, M., Luo, Z.Q., He, C.: An iteratively weighted MMSE approach to distributed sum-utility maximization for a MIMO interfering broadcast channel. IEEE Trans. Sig. Process. **59**, 4331–4340 (2011)
8. Sutton, R.S., Barto, A.G.: Reinforcement Learning: An Introduction. MIT Press, Cambridge (2018)
9. Zhang, C., Patras, P., Haddadi, H.: Deep learning in mobile and wireless networking: a survey. IEEE Commun. Surv. Tutor. **21**, 2224–2287 (2019)
10. Balevi, E., Andrews, J.G.: A novel deep reinforcement learning algorithm for online antenna tuning. In: 2019 IEEE Global Communications Conference, GLOBECOM 2019 - Proceedings (2019)
11. Zhang, Y., Kang, C., Ma, T., Teng, Y., Guo, D.: Power allocation in multi-cell networks using deep reinforcement learning. In: IEEE Vehicular Technology Conference (2018)
12. Zhao, N., Liang, Y.C., Niyato, D., Pei, Y., Wu, M., Jiang, Y.: Deep reinforcement learning for user association and resource allocation in heterogeneous cellular networks. IEEE Trans. Wirel. Commun. 5141–5152 (2019)
13. Nasir, Y.S., Guo, D.: Multi-agent deep reinforcement learning for dynamic power allocation in wireless networks. IEEE J. Sel. Areas Commun. **37**, 2239–2250 (2019)
14. Lei, L., Yuan, D., Ho, C.K., Sun, S.: Joint optimization of power and channel allocation with non-orthogonal multiple access for 5G cellular systems (2016)
15. Xu, Z., Wang, Y., Tang, J., Wang, J., Gursoy, M.C.: A deep reinforcement learning based framework for power-efficient resource allocation in cloud RANs. In: IEEE International Conference on Communications (2017)
16. Amiri, R., Mehrpouyan, H., Fridman, L., Mallik, R.K., Nallanathan, A., Matolak, D.: A machine learning approach for power allocation in HetNets considering QoS. In: IEEE International Conference on Communications (2018)
17. Zhang, M., Chen, M.: Power allocation in multi-cell system using distributed deep neural network algorithm. In: International Conference on Wireless and Mobile Computing, Networking and Communications. IEEE Computer Society (2019)

18. Zhao, G., Li, Y., Xu, C., Han, Z., Xing, Y., Yu, S.: Joint power control and channel allocation for interference mitigation based on reinforcement learning. IEEE Access **7**, 177254–177265 (2019)
19. Palomar, D.P., Chiang, M.: Alternative distributed algorithms for network utility maximization: framework and applications. IEEE Trans. Automat. Contr. **52**, 2254–2269 (2007)
20. Tang, M., Long, C., Guan, X.: Nonconvex optimization for power control in wireless CDMA networks. Wirel. Pers. Commun. **58**, 851–865 (2011)
21. 3GPP: Study on channel model for frequencies from 0.5 to 100 GHz. Technical report (TR) 38.901, 3rd Generation Partnership Project (2017)

The Challenge of Security Breaches in the Era of 5G Networking

Maria Belesioti[1], Jorge Carapinha[2], Rodoula Makri[3],
and Ioannis P. Chochliouros[1(✉)] (iD)

[1] Hellenic Telecommunications Organization (OTE) S.A., 99 Kifissias Avenue,
15124 Maroussi-Athens, Greece
{mbelesioti,ichochliouros}@oteresearch.gr
[2] Altice Labs, Aveiro, Portugal
[3] Institute of Communication and Computer Systems (ICCS), Athens, Greece

Abstract. Communications play a fundamental role in the economic and social well-being of the citizens and on operations of most of the Critical Infrastructures (CIs). 5G networks and future communications technologies radically transform the way we communicate, by introducing a vast array of new connections, capabilities and services in a multiplicity of sectors. In this scope, network function virtualization and end-to-end network slicing are two promising technologies empowering 5G networks for efficient and dynamic network/service deployment and management. Resilience of critical infrastructure systems and especially in telecommunication networks can be considered as "key factor" that can reduce vulnerability, minimize the consequences of threats as well as their cascade effects, accelerate mitigation and facilitate re-adaptation to a disruptive event. In this context, comprehensive knowledge of the complete surrounding environment and of the most important factors that affect and/or determine resilience, can evolve at a fundamental aspect concerning the case resilience of critical telecommunication. Based on this idea, the RESISTO project provides a holistic situation awareness for telecommunication infrastructures and simultaneously enhances resilience, while acting as an on top safety net boosting the faster and more reliable management enabling the digital transformation of our society and a variety of business processes. In this paper we specifically discuss the impact of the RESISTO platform when a security breach occurs in a 5G mobile network.

Keywords: 5G · Critical Infrastructure (CI) · Machine learning · Resilience · Security · Threats · SDN · SDS · Network virtualization

1 Introduction

5G is a global network and services (r-)evolution that affects drastically a multiplicity of sectors in our modern societies and economies [1, 2]. Through its main technological enablers (such as cloud computing, Mobile Edge Computing (MEC), Software Defined Networking (SDN) and Network Function Virtualization (NFV)), 5G is expected to

© IFIP International Federation for Information Processing 2021
Published by Springer Nature Switzerland AG 2021
I. Maglogiannis et al. (Eds.): AIAI 2021 Workshops, IFIP AICT 628, pp. 106–117, 2021.
https://doi.org/10.1007/978-3-030-79157-5_10

offer novel opportunities for growth and modify the features and capabilities of modern networking [3]. Among the actual challenges [4] are also those related to network and service security [5] where 5G is anticipated to change the landscape, especially as far as security of Critical Infrastructures (CIs) is concerned. To this respect, the ongoing EU-funded RESISTO [6] project will help Communications Infrastructures Operators, especially in the 5G era, to take the best countermeasures and reactive actions exploiting the combined use of risk and resilience preparatory analyses, detection and reaction technologies, applications and processes in the physical and cyber domain.

Many socioeconomic activities (such as health domain, transport, telecommunications, electric energy, finance) that are considered as "vital" for the proper functioning of the society and for public safety are supported by many physical and cyber assets and systems, one of which is telecommunication services. Serious disruptions of these services could cause as cascade effect, disruption in other dependent infrastructure causing major impact and discomfort in the continuity of everyday life of the society [7]. Critical Infrastructure Protection (CIP) means all activities aimed at ensuring the functionality, continuity and integrity of CIs in order to deter, mitigate and neutralize a threat, risk or vulnerability [8, 9]. For this reason, an attack, either cyber or physical, in telecommunication systems may cause dangerous consequences in the physical world. Hence, resilience – together with security and reliability – are assessed as fundamental properties of both physical and cyber infrastructure aiming to ensure safety of people, of the environment and of the controlled physical processes [10]. In particular, with the actual exponential growth in wireless data traffic and demand for faster networks, network resilience is assessed as a critically important factor in emerging 5G networks [11, 12]. The issue of network resilience is strongly linked to the 5G network architecture as well. In general, a convenient 5G network architecture will enable the creation of mobile networks upon virtualization platforms, by utilizing the cloud and will offer corresponding services.

Telecom operators have SOCs (Security Operation Centres) for the logical protection of their infrastructure and different systems (such as CCTV, access control, intrusion detection, biometrics, etc.) for the physical security management and, in some cases, a PSIM (Physical Security Information Management) which is a category of software platform for single monitoring, increased control, improved situation awareness and management reporting through one comprehensive user interface. In each domain the systems or platforms for the protection include specific modules for the correlation of information.

However, modern 5G architectures are designed to close security gaps from previous iterations of cellular networks [13]. The SDN architecture with its separation of data and control plane from network devices drastically simplifies configuration and management of security policies, with significant reduction of security risks associated to policy inconsistency. The key concept that underpins SDN is the logical centralization of network control functions by decoupling the control and packet forwarding functionality of the network. NFV complements this vision through the virtualization of these functionalities based on recent advances in general server and enterprise IT virtualization. Considering the maturity of the technologies that 5G can leverage on, SDN is the one that is moving faster from development to production [14]. NFV and SDN along with network slicing [3, 15, 16] offer mobile network providers the ability to support several 5G requirements and provide related services. In fact, 5G is claimed to satisfy the dramatically growing need of users and things for the imminent 2020 horizon and beyond. More specifically, in the 5G scope we identify (Fig. 1) three major groups of use cases, namely [17]: (i) enhanced mobile broadband (eMBB) focusing on services with high requirements for bandwidth, such as streaming high definition (HD) videos, Virtual Reality (VR) and Augmented Reality (AR); (ii) ultra Reliable and Low-Latency Communications (uRLLC) aiming to support multiple advanced services for latency-sensitive connected devices (such as factory automation, autonomous driving and the PPDR (Public Protection and Disaster Relief) use cases or robotic synergies), and, finally; (iii) massive Machine-Type Communications (mMTC) are about services that include high requirements related to connectivity provision in huge numbers of devices (such as sensors that typically transmit and receive only small amount of data sporadically); an mMTC network is designed to support of up to 1 million devices per square km, which is 10 times the maximum amount currently possible with 4G LTE.

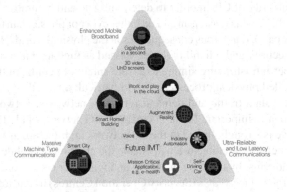

Fig. 1. 5G services and opportunities [18].

Each virtualized network slice consists of a number of Virtual Network Functions (VNFs) each one providing predefined services in its slice and all the VNFs of a slice collectively provide wireless network access to the Users' Equipment (UEs) attached to that slice. However, although SDN and virtualization bring significant innovation in the communication networks by expanding their services offering, they also open a wide window to new source of attacks [19, 20]. At the same time, physical security continues to be an open challenge when it comes to the protection of the physical infrastructure's integrity as a whole, due to the increased complexity of the networks architecture further extended with pervasive use of IoT (Internet of Things).

Section 1 serves as an introduction to 5G opportunities, in parallel with the intended support of CIs; in particular we identify the importance of network resilience and security in modern network infrastructures such as those promoted by the 5G enabling technologies. Section 2 discusses the fundamental architecture proposed by the RESISTO project and further assesses the roles of the main entities composing the essential RESISTO platform. Section 3 attempts to briefly introduce several aspects originating from the modern 5G threat landscape under a more generalized context, by focusing on a selected use case about network response to a security breach. The work summarizes with some concluding remarks.

2 Main Entities of the RESISTO Platform

A critical issue in service delivery in a 5G network is its resilience [21, 22]. 5G provides preventative measures to limit the impact to known threats, but the adoption of new network technologies introduces potential new threats that telecom operators need to face [23]. In 5G, "build first and secure later" typical paradigm should be replaced by "security and resiliency by design" and "security and resiliency by operation". Thus 5G networks should be designed in such a way that security and resilience are taken into account as a cornerstone feature in both design and operation stages [24]. The RESISTO concept [6] has been envisioned from the assumption that by combining physical and cyber security assessment and (up to real time) management within interacting operating tools, improved business and asset continuity can be further protected. RESISTO develops a cooperation framework that allows different parts of the overall Communication CI security personnel to exchange data and signals, to recognize complex attack patterns coming from different sources at different levels and, based on real time simulation of attack propagation within the CI and across interconnected CIs, to select and implement the best response and, in case of failure, the optimal mitigation strategy [25].

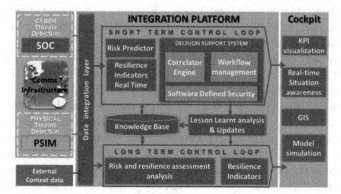

Fig. 2. RESISTO high level architecture.

The RESISTO project has thus developed an innovative architecture (as depicted in Fig. 2) aiming to "face" the challenges posed by recent 5G advances [26–28]. The main element of this architecture is the RESISTO Cockpit which acts as the main user-interface providing the users real-time situation awareness of potential threats and alarms and related data, along with indicators to assess the resilience of the infrastructure. An additional important element is the model simulation for interdependency analysis that allowing to simulate the impact of the identified threats on the modelled infrastructure and to evaluate potential cascading effects. We also have the Geo-referenced data representation on a map, derived from sensors warning about critical events and data processed from the integrated systems to enhance real-time knowledge of potential critical situation.

The Long-Term Control Loop is in charge of defining the configuration of the system, according to the security assessment and updating it on a periodic basis or when specific events take place (new threats or discovery of previously undetected vulnerabilities). It mainly consists of: (i) the "Risk and resilience assessment analysis" that identifies the context, analyzes the interdependencies (physical, cyber, logical and geographic) and risks, assesses these risks and suggests the risk treatment, and; (ii) "Resilience Indicators" as summing up the resilience of CI communication in its operational phase.

Besides, RESISTO's Short-term Loop is another element of high importance into the related architecture. It is in charge of promptly responding to attacks and threats that may "impact" the operational life of the system. This element is essentially based on the following components:

- The "Risk Predictor" that evaluates the impacts of exploitations and countermeasures. In particular, this component gathers data on anomalies and security attacks from the physical domain (PSIM-C), the cyber domain (SOC), and the Correlator Engine, while it predicts the effects of countermeasures on the CI, accounting for interdependencies among virtual and physical domains. Moreover, it models the interdependencies of CI elements, with the simulation of the short-term effects of failure, both in terms of faults propagation and with respect to performance degradation.
- The "Resilience Indicators in Real-Time", which are a real-time set of indicators that measure the risk and resilience of the communication infrastructure derived as output of the "Risk and resilience assessment analysis".
- The "Decision Support System" which consists of several distinct parts. One of them, the "Correlator Engine", is maybe the most important part of the Short-Term Control Loop. This is a rule-based engine customized to detect threats, alarms, critical events defined by the "Risk and resilience assessment analysis" and the "Interdependency analysis" able to detect critical situations to manage. The correlator engine consists of two components namely: (i) an event stream processing module in order to identify threats and dangerous situations through the analysis of heterogeneous data sources in real-time by using several event correlation techniques, such as temporal correlation (based on event time) and logical – or causal – ones, and; (ii) the machine learning (ML) algorithms module in order to analyze the behavior of the RESISTO platform and the phenomena affecting the system, so that to make decisions, accordingly. The results of the application of ML algorithms can enhance the way the RESISTO platform detects dangerous situations by means of the correlation and definition of new rules and thresholds which trigger alarms. This module is also able to build intelligent defense models to prevent damages created by cyber-attacks. In this regard, the use of classification algorithms (e.g. Artificial Neural Networks) for analyzing the network traffic, inspecting the system logs and correlating these data with the monitoring of resource utilization of the systems, can lead to significant improvements in detecting anomalies and attacks, occurring over the communications network. The Correlator is a logically centralized entity. However, it can take advantage of the NFV and SDN of the underlying communication network to enable seamless distribution of detection

and analysis functions among several geographical dispersed points of presence (such as data centers), creating the means to implement fog/-computing topologies.

The Correlator also triggers the Workflow Management software engine in charge to guide the operator during the reaction phase. On the basis of the alarm type, the most appropriate workflow is selected and executed. A workflow is a conditional sequence of steps and each separate step can specify a procedural action, drive a physical actuator, carry out a complex action on the communication network, isolate a faulty or attacked component, reconfigure a part of the network, disable a 5G slice, etc.

Another important part is the Software Defined Security (SDS), which is a sort of a reaction/resilience mechanism that performs a dynamic, flexible reconfiguration of security/resilience mechanisms and relocation (virtualization) of security functions, in a way similar to what currently done in SDN. SDS integrates mitigation and resiliency functionalities into a unique framework able to dynamically and proactively react to the evolving threats by enforcing the most appropriate security policies in each CI node. Such framework is fed by an appropriate Decision Support System (DSS) taking the data stored into the Knowledge Base as valuable input parameters.

Based on an Integrated Risk and Resilience analysis management and improvement process [29, 30] availing all resilience cycle phases (prepare, prevent, detect, absorb, etc.) and technical resilience capabilities (sense, model, infer, act, adopt), RESISTO implements an innovative DSS to protect communication infrastructures from combined cyber-physical threats exploiting the SDS model on a suite of state-of-the-art cyber/physical security components (i.e.: blockchain, machine learning, IoT security, airborne threat detection, holistic audio-video analytics) and services (Responsible Disclosure Framework) for detection and reaction in presence of attacks or natural disasters. The involvement of communications operators in the RESISTO framework will allow the implementation of a set of mitigation actions and countermeasures that significantly reduce the impact of negative events in terms of performance losses, social consequences and cascading effects, in particular by bouncing efficiently back to original and forward to operational states of functioning.

3   The 5G Threat Landscape

The 5G era has already arrived, bringing faster speeds and lower latency thus enabling a complete new business sector and also offering innovative applications. Although the 5th generation of communications is more robust than its predecessors, when it comes to security the high complexity of 5G infrastructures as well as the overarching nature of 5G, make it not easy to manage [31, 32]. The lack of information since existing deployments are still evolving and the large number of potential stakeholders involved makes the assessment of cyber threats a hard task. On the other hand, the involvement of several stakeholders which play different roles in the 5G ecosystem, will foster the effort for security assurance of the network at different levels and separate layers [24, 33].

According to the 5G-PPP White Paper on the 5G architecture [34], the list of stakeholder roles in the 5G ecosystem is the following: (i) Service customers (SCs); (ii)

Service Providers (SPs); (iii) Mobile Network Operators (MNOs) also known as Network Operators (NOPs); (iv) Virtualization Infrastructure Service Providers (VISPs), and; (v) Data Centre Providers (DCPs). Complementary to stakeholders, 5G spans in many vectors through which adversaries can attack. One of the most important concerns regarding threats is posed by telecommunication operators as critical infrastructure operators, which are evolving their networks using 5G technology for critical services. 5G will utilize more ICT components and services while, at the same time, people, companies and organizations will "build" their everyday activities on 5G services potentially increasing network vulnerabilities. In addition, it is a fact that as 5G will be expanded based upon 3G and 4G LTE already deployed mobile networks, and deployment actions are carrying part of legacy vulnerabilities in terms of security [33, 35, 36].

3.1 5G Network Response to a Security Breach

The complexity added by 5G requires traditional (i.e. preconfigured) security solutions to be supplemented and reinforced with dynamic mechanisms, instantiated and deployed by AI-based systems [37]. Thus, early and integrated threat detection is a key requirement and strongly affects both 5G network deployment and behaviour. Complex mechanisms based on a combination of big data and ML can be used to identify threats not spotted by conventional solutions supported by basic filters.

In addition, prompt reaction is also a key requirement. 5G provides a number of tools to avoid or mitigate the effects of security and resilience threats, which are mainly related to the capability to detach network functions from the infrastructure and flexibly control the lifecycle of network services. The independence between network and infrastructure, which strictly speaking is not enabled by 5G, but rather the virtualization of network resources, paves the way to the definition of innovative security use cases [32, 33]. Network slicing is the main enabler and catalyst to properly deliver those use cases. The combination of AI-based detection tools with network slicing provides new possibilities to prevent or mitigate many of the security and resilience threats in telco infrastructures, especially for 5G, and is likely to represent a relevant research topics in the next few years [21, 24]. The use case described in this section hopefully illustrates the synergies that can be obtained through the combination of these two technological trends.

The proposed use case [38] aims to showcase the vulnerabilities of 5G Communication Networks considered as Critical Infrastructures and how the RESISTO platform aims to deal with these challenges. The increasing complexity of the 5G architecture and the extensive use of programmable platforms are the key elements of high concern, in the proposed scope.

Network slicing is an important tool to provide isolated networks, each optimized for specific types of traffic characteristics. One such characteristic could be related to security and safety requirements – by means of slicing, it will be possible to dynamically confine the impact of security requirements to single slices, rather than the whole network. In addition, new recovery mechanisms are enabled by network slicing, especially the capability to establish network resources on-demand. This use case [38] comprises a mission-critical (MC) scenario based on a 5G telecommunication mobile network in which the probability of an ongoing cyber/physical attack or equipment failure is assessed by continuous analysis of specific parameters (e.g. temperature) or abnormal behaviour, making use of machine learning techniques. The use case definition is based on the execution of different actions depending on the perceived probability of equipment failure.

We consider a SP that builds and operates a network slice based on own resources – core network, core DC (hosting the majority of the 5G Core components), coloured black in Fig. 3, as well as resources leased from an independent Network Slice Subnet Provider (NSSP A) – C-RAN (Cloud Radio Access Network) and edge components, coloured green in Fig. 3. For the purposes of the use case, a second NSSP (NSSP-B) having a business relationship with the SP, is also able to provide C-RAN and edge components if/when needed (e.g. for reasons of malfunction or quick traffic growth), but not active by default.

Phase 1 (preparation): The use case is triggered when the probability of service loss affecting resources run by NSSP-A goes above a certain threshold, e.g. 35% (possible cause – temperature rising in Edge Point-of-Presence (PoP)). The event may be accidental, caused by a natural event or by a malicious action. At this stage, the risk is classified as low to medium. The preparation of a smooth transition from NSSP-A to NSSP-B is started through the creation of a slice subnet (C-RAN, Edge, x-haul) dimensioned according to the number of users. Recovery mechanisms (e.g. equipment restart) if available and feasible, are attempted. The SP requests NSSP-B to instantiate an edge slice subnet, in case a relocation of resources from NSSP-A proves to be necessary as a result of the identified issue.

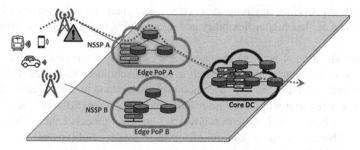

Fig. 3. 5G Network response to a security breach – activation phase.

Phase 2 (activation): When the service loss probability goes above a second threshold (e.g. 50%), the risk is classified as high. The slice subnet that had been instantiated in the previous step is activated at this point (colored blue in Fig. 3). This includes the activation of all Virtual Machines (VMs)/containers, as well as the virtual links. At the same time, non-essential resources are shutdown.

Phase 3 (migration): When a third service loss probability threshold (e.g. 65%) is exceeded, then actuation/mitigation is triggered. The affected C-RAN and edge components are relocated from NSSP A to NSSP B; however, the service interruption should not be noticed from the customers. This is illustrated in Fig. 4, below.

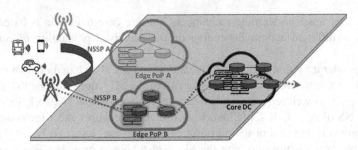

Fig. 4. 5G Network response to a security breach – mitigation phase.

In a 5G environment, the actuation phase takes advantage of network slicing and the capability to deploy network services on demand. In this case, the affected resources (i.e. those provided by NSSP A) should be deactivated and replaced by different resources in such a way that service continuity can be guaranteed.

In this use case, the assets affected are the NSSPs and, as a consequence, the SP. The SP has a key role and provides communication services to end-users, supported by network slices. The SP is also supposed to provision of the network, thus it is also able to perform the role of Network Slice Provider (NSP). A network slice can be composed of multiple network slice subnets (e.g. core, edge). Each slice subnet may be owned and operated by the SP, or by an independent NSSP. The security threat vectors in 5G will be multi-dimensional, as 5G networks will connect infrastructures, interconnect societies and industries, providing anything-as-a-service, and integrate new models of service delivery. Since 5G has higher flexibility and agility, NFV and SDN play a vital role in 5G [39].

The virtualization of network resources, and especially network slicing, enable the definition of new business models based on new stakeholders and roles. In this context, the definition of any 5G use case should be understood under a specific business ecosystem, where different players are responsible for playing different roles [40]. The use case described above is based on novel 5G business models enabled by Network as a Service (NaaS) and the separation of service providers and (virtual) infrastructure providers. In addition, the possibility of sharing mobile access/edge network resources among competitor operators under certain circumstances (e.g. natural events such as forest fires affecting the availability of the mobile network in a certain zone) has been suggested for possible implementation as a way to avoid loss of communication, which is often a cause for aggravation of the related effects.

The discussed use case demonstrates how the RESISTO platform can be used to mitigate the following risks, including among others: (i) Service delivery failure in a geographical area, as a result of intentional malicious actions (e.g. cyber-physical attacks, motivated either by terrorism and economic sabotage), equipment malfunctions or natural events (e.g. forest fire, potentially endangering significant components of the network infrastructure physically located on that zone); (ii) financial losses, both to operators (loss of income, customer churn) and end users (especially businesses for which communication is a critical requirement); (iii) damages caused by network disruptions, especially in emergency scenarios, potentially exposing human lives to risk. The most significant contribution of RESISTO is on the decision-making process.

The innovations of the use case are mainly related to the combined use of two types of tools for security threat detection and mitigation, respectively: (i) Artificial Intelligence (AI)/ML-based detection mechanisms for early detection of security threats, and; (ii) network automation and programmability, enabled by 5G cornerstones such as network virtualization, software defined networking and network slicing. This use case is expected to evaluate and demonstrate the preparedness of the RESISTO platform to handle the specific challenges of 5G and the ability to exploit the 5G features mentioned above in scenarios of cyber-physical attacks or natural events.

4   Discussion

5G will provide super-high data rates, better quality of service and very low latency through dense base station deployments. Communities will rely on 5G far more than ever compared to previous communications systems. Factories, businesses and critical infrastructure will all rely on 5G data connectivity, and this technology will transform business. The diffusion of Software Defined Network (SDN), slicing and virtualization techniques, and the use of programmable platforms will become pervasive. However, although SDN brings significant innovation in terms of adaptability, new source of attacks appear in the horizon. At the same time, physical security represents an open challenge when it comes to protection of physical infrastructure integrity as a whole, due to the increased complexity of the 5G architecture.

The management of security and resilience of critical infrastructures based on 5G will constitute one of the most important challenges of the years to come, as both of these network features can strongly influence design and operation of the corresponding infrastructure. In particular, the dynamicity and the softwarized environment in which the future infrastructure will be deployed will need intelligent prevention and mitigation strategies that RESISTO platform can sufficiently offer on top of telco operators' security systems. This platform also fits for the support of 5G modern deployments and behaviour as explained for a selected use case of 5G network response to a security breach.

Acknowledgments. The paper has been based on the context of the *"RESISTO" ("RESIlience enhancement and risk control platform for communication infrastructure Operators")* Project, funded by the EC under the Grant Agreement (GA) No. 786409.

References

1. Rost, P., Banchs, A., Berberana, I., Reitbach, M., Doll, M., et al.: Mobile network architecture evolution toward 5G. IEEE Commun. Mag. **54**(5), 84–91 (2016)
2. Agiwal, M., Roy, A., et al.: Next generation 5G wireless networks: a comprehensive survey. IEEE Commun. Surv. Tutor. **18**(3), 1617–1655 (2016)
3. Chochliouros, I.P., et al.: Enhancing network management via NFV, MEC, cloud computing and cognitive features: the "5G ESSENCE" modern architectural approach. In: Iliadis, L., Maglogiannis, I., Plagianakos, V. (eds.) AIAI 2018. AICT, vol. 520, pp. 50–61. Springer, Cham (2018). https://doi.org/10.1007/978-3-319-92016-0_5

4. Next Generation Mobile Networks (NGMN) Alliance: NGMN 5G White Paper, NGMN Alliance (2015)
5. Ahmad, I., Kumar, T., Liyanage, M., Okwuibe, J., et al.: 5G: security analysis of threats and solutions. In: Proceedings of CSCN-2017, pp. 193–199. IEEE (2017)
6. RESISTO ("RESIlience enhancement and risk control platform for communication infraS-Tructure Operators") H2020 Project (Grant Agreement No. 786409). http://www.resistoproje ct.eu/
7. Setola, R., Luiijf, E., Theocharidou, M.: Critical infrastructures, protection and resilience. In: Setola, R., Rosato, V., Kyriakides, E., Rome, E. (eds.) Managing the Complexity of Critical Infrastructures. SSDC, vol. 90, pp. 1–18. Springer, Cham (2016). https://doi.org/10.1007/978-3-319-51043-9_1
8. European Commission: Commission Staff Working Document on a new approach to the European Programme for Critical Infrastructure Protection Making European Critical Infras-tructures more secure, SWD (2013) 318 final, 28 August 2013. http://ec.europa.eu/transpare ncy/regdoc/rep/10102/2013/EN/10102-2013-318-EN-F1-1.PDF
9. Council of the European Union: Council Directive 2008/114/EC of 8 December 2008 on the identification and designation of European critical infrastructures and the assessment of the need to improve their protection. Off. J. **L345**, 75–82 (2008)
10. Aziz, F.M., et al.: Resilience of LTE networks against smart jamming attacks: wideband model. In: Proceedings of the IEEE PIMRC 2015, pp. 1344–1348. IEEE (2015)
11. Abhishek, R., Tipper, D., Medhi, D.: Network virtualization and survivability of 5G net-works: framework, optimization model, and performance. In: Proceedings of the 2018 IEEE Globecom Workshops (GC Wkshps), pp. 1–6. IEEE (2018)
12. Abhishek, R.: Resilience and survivability of 5G networks. Ph.D. thesis, University of Missouri-Kansas City, USA. Proquest LLC, May 2020
13. 5GAmericas: Security Considerations for the 5G Era - A 5GAmericas' White Paper, July 2020
14. European Union Agency for Cybersecurity (ENISA): Threat Landscape for 5G Networks. ENISA, December 2020
15. Nguyen, V.-G., Brunstrom, A., Grinnemo, K.-J., Taheri, J.: SDN/NFV-based mobile packet core network architectures: a survey. IEEE Commun. Surv. Tutor. **19**(3), 1567–1602 (2017)
16. Olimid, R.F., Nencioni, G.: 5G network slicing: a security overview. IEEE Access **8**, 99999–100009 (2020)
17. International Telecommunication Union – Radiocommunications Sector (ITU-R): Recom-mendation ITU-R M.2083-0 (09-2015): *"IMT Vision – Framework and overall objectives of the future development of IMT for 2020 and beyond"*. ITU-R (2015)
18. Geller, M., Nair, P.: 5G Security Innovation with Cisco – White paper (2018)
19. GSM Association (GSMA): Migration from Physical to Virtual Network Functions – Best Practices and Lessons Learned Version 0.1. GSMA, October 2018
20. The 3rd Generation Partnership Project: 3GPP TR 33.848 V0.5.0 (2019-11): Technical report 3rd Generation Partnership Project; Technical Specification Group Services and System Aspects; Security Aspects; Study on Security Impacts of Virtualisation (Release 16). 3GPP (2019)
21. Taleb, T., Ksentini, A., et al.: On service resilience in cloud-native 5G mobile systems. IEEE J. Sel. Areas Commun. (JSAC) **34**(3), 483–496 (2016)
22. Sterbenz, J.P.G., Çetinkaya, E.K., Hameed, M.A., Jabbar, A., et al.: Evaluation of network resilience survivability and disruption tolerance: analysis topology generation simulation and experimentation. Telecommun. Syst. **52**, 705–736 (2013)
23. Xie, L., et al.: Network survivability under disaster propagation: modeling and analysis. In: Proceedings of the IEEE WCNC-2013, pp. 473–475. IEEE (2013)

24. Arfaoui, G., et al.: Security and resilience in 5G: current challenges and future directions. In: 2017 IEEE Trustcom/BigDataSE/ICESS, pp. 1–8. IEEE (2017)
25. Yusta, J.M., Correa, G.J., Lacal-Arantegui, R.: Methodologies and applications for critical infrastructure protection: state-of-the-art. Energy Policy **39**(10), 6100–6119 (2011)
26. Belesioti, M., Chochliouros, I.P., et al.: Enhancing critical infrastructure protection: the RESISTO concept. In: Proceedings of EuCNC 2018, pp. 591–592. IEEE (2018)
27. Belesioti, M., Makri, R., Fehling-Kaschek, M., Carli, et al.: A new security approach in telecom infrastructures: the RESISTO concept. In: Proceedings of the DCOSS-2019/SecRIoT-2019 Workshop, pp. 212–218. IEEE Computer Society (2019)
28. RESISTO Project: Deliverable 2.7: "RESISTO Platform and Tools Reference Architecture-final", December 2019
29. Häring, I., et al.: Towards a generic resilience management, quantification and development process: general definitions, requirements, methods, techniques and measures, and case studies. In: Linkov, I., Palma-Oliveira, J.M. (eds.) Resilience and Risk. NSPSSCES, pp. 21–80. Springer, Dordrecht (2017). https://doi.org/10.1007/978-94-024-1123-2_2
30. Bellini, E., Ferreira, P.: Managing interdependencies in critical infrastructures - a cornerstone for system resilience. In: Haugen, S., Barros, A., et al. (eds.) Safety and Reliability – Safe Societies in a Changing World, pp. 2687–2692. CRC Press, Boca Raton (2018)
31. Dutta, A., Hammad, E.: 5G security challenges and opportunities: a system approach. In: Proceedings of the 2020 IEEE 3rd 5G World Forum (5GWF), pp. 109–-114. IEEE (2020)
32. Fang, D., Qian, Y., Hu, R.Q.: Security for 5G mobile wireless networks. IEEE Access **6**, 4850–4874 (2017)
33. Cao, J., Ma, M., Li, H., Ma, R., Sun, Y., et al.: A survey on security aspects for 3GPP 5G networks. IEEE Commun. Surv. Tutor. **22**(1), 170–195 (2020)
34. 5G Public Private Partnership (5G-PPP): View on 5G Architecture – White Paper, Version 3.0. 5G-PPP, June 2019
35. Khan, R., Kumar, P., Jayakody, D.N.K., Liyanage, M.: A survey on security and privacy of 5G technologies: potential solutions, recent advancements, and future directions. IEEE Commun. Surv. Tutor. **22**(1), 196–248 (2019)
36. Ahmad, I., Kumar, T., Liyanage, M., Okwuibe, J., et al.: Overview of 5G security challenges and solutions. IEEE Commun. Stand. Mag. **2**(1), 36–43 (2018)
37. 5GAmericas: The Evolution of Security in 5G - White Paper, July 2019
38. RESISTO Project: Deliverable 2.8: "Table-Top Read Teaming Results of RESISTO Architecture, Scenarios and Use Cases Tabular Report", January 2020
39. Liyanage, M., Ahmad, I. Bux Abro, A., Gurtov, A., and Ylianttila, M.: Comprehensive Guide to 5G Security. Wiley (2018)
40. The 3rd Generation Partnership Project: 3GPP TR 28.801 v15.1.0: "Technical report Technical Specification Group Services and System Aspects; Telecommunication management; Study on management and orchestration of network slicing for next generation network (Release 15)". 3GPP (2018)

Top Challenges in 5G Densification

Eleni Theodoropoulou[1]($\boxtimes$) (iD), Ioanna Mesogiti[1], Fotini Setaki[1], Konstantinos Filis[1],
George Lyberopoulos[1], Agapi Mesodiakaki[2], Marios Gatzianas[2], Christos Vagionas[2],
George Kalfas[2], Mauro Agus[3], and Annachiara Pagano[3]

[1] COSMOTE Mobile Telecommunications S.A., 99 Kifissias Avenue,
15124 Maroussi, Athens, Greece
etheodorop@cosmote.gr
[2] Aristotle University of Thessaloniki, Thessaloniki, Greece
[3] Telecom Italia, Turin, Italy

Abstract. The current report attempts to explore the top challenges that the MNOs
need to overcome during 5G deployment in highly dense populated areas. Indicatively, the MNOs are warned about site acquisition challenges and electrifica-
tion/energy related needs for a huge number of sites that shall be installed discretely
at street level, the demand for rigorous testing and measurements to ensure full network coverage and always-on operation so that even mission critical applications
(such as automotive and e-health apps) are enabled, accompanied by associated
cost factors. Provided that at the time of writing (beg/2021) little is the worldwide
experience from operating 5G networks, potential actions are suggested towards a
smooth and efficient short time-to-market 5G deployment. In addition, indicative
5G densification related figures (e.g. amount of h/w nodes and distances among
them), are calculated based on a specific FiWi PtMP network solution aiming at
supporting the ultra-broadband 5G NR fronthaul bandwidth, while alleviating the
need to install fiber terminations at every Base Station site.

Keywords: 5G densification · MNOs · Challenges · Network dimensioning
tool · Traffic estimation tool · 5G-PHOS use cases · Distance between 5G-PHOS
elements

1 Introduction

The 5G technology requires significant transformations of the legacy networks towards
service-driven and highly dense network deployments bringing along various challenges
for the Mobile Network Operators (MNOs), not only technical but also business and
cost related ones. Since 5G nationwide networks will be gradually deployed, the MNOs
shall consider all types of geographical areas, in conjunction with the traffic demand, the
service requirements of the 5G services (eMBB, mMTC/mIoT, URLLC) and the network
operation services that shall be supported. In particular, in urban, dense urban and hotspot
environments, high traffic density and capacity needs are expected, either under normal
daily conditions or occasionally/periodically, during crowded events or with seasonality

I. Maglogiannis et al. (Eds.): AIAI 2021 Workshops, IFIP AICT 628, pp. 118–127, 2021.
https://doi.org/10.1007/978-3-030-79157-5_11

based activity (e.g., touristic areas). The 5G network densification, that is, the deployment of the 5G access nodes in very short distances among them, constitutes a big challenge for the telecom operators. The densification of the 5G network will be realized with very low-powered (operating in licensed and unlicensed spectrum) radio access nodes and tiny antennas, compared to those of the previous mobile technology generations, and much smaller cells of few meter range, to satisfy the traffic demand and the stringent QoS requirements. The 5G small cells will be deployed at street level, attached to bus stops, outdoor advertising, traffic lights, information kiosks billboards, utility poles, the sides of buildings, etc. How many 5G access nodes are required to support the multitude of the 5G innovative application and services in a residential or a business area of a big European city, or in case of a stadium during a crowded athletic event or a concert? How close to each other do these nodes have to be installed? What about the suitability of their location in terms of power supply and the total energy needs? The above are only indicative problems that the MNOs will face, and they certainly depend on the traffic demand and the technology solutions to be adopted, while currently, little experience from actual dense 5G deployment can be shared. Inspired by the 5G-PHOS project [1], a Phase-2 5G-PPP project that deals with 5G densification issues, the current report attempts to investigate the top challenges[1] that the MNOs need to overcome during 5G deployment in dense urban/hotspot areas efficiently.

The paper is organized as follows: After the introduction, a list of the currently most predominant challenges for the telecom operators concerning the 5G network densification is presented and discussed, followed by potential hints and mitigation activities to be considered proactively. The next section provides an overview of the 5G-PHOS solution followed by indicative 5G-PHOS specific 5G densification figures, for various scenarios in dense, ultra-dense and hotspot environments and for three future timeslots. Finally, conclusions are drawn at the end.

2 Telecom Operators' Challenges Associated with 5G Densification

2.1 Site Acquisition at Street Level (Including Power Supply and Transport Capabilities) and Licensing

The acquisition of a huge number of 5G sites -ideally power enabled and/or with fiber connectivity- is critical for the competitiveness of the MNOs, since it implies high rental costs and can affect the time-to-market and the offered QoS/QoE.

Site acquisition is a time-consuming, complex and resource-intensive task. MNOs could accelerate 5G network rollout by establishing new frame agreements with site owners, e.g. municipalities, transport, energy/grid and road operators and individuals incl. incentives (if possible) while achieving rental costs reduction and resolving power and transport issues. In this content, the 5G deployment in densely populated areas, can be facilitated by the Art.57 of the European Electronic Communications Code [24],

---

[1] Challenges related to network technologies and operation (network orchestration, slicing, NFV/SDN, synchronization issues, beam verification, service continuity/handovers, security, etc.), and service provisioning QoS/QoE (latency, bitrates, etc.), are considered beyond the scope of this study since they will be addressed by the technology itself.

with administrative charges only. For example, in 2017 TIM and the Municipality of Turin signed a 3-year Memorandum of Understanding to cooperate for making Turin a leading 5G enabled Smart City, to promote the joint development of digital solutions and the deployment of innovative applications. In any case, the MNOs shall (i) capitalize on own or rent assets (2G/3G/4G sites, xDSL/NGA cabinets, buildings, shops); thus, fixed telephony service providers being favored, and (ii) pursue frame agreements with other MNOs on infrastructure sharing (on street-level furniture, rooftop RRHs, fiber infrastructure, power/energy, fronthaul/ backhaul, etc.) [5]. In case of fiber connectivity, the Dense WDM equipment (either mounted behind the radio unit or in a hole under the site) shall be considered [4].

2.2 Aesthetic Impact and Other Social/public Issues

Especially when it comes to highly dense deployment, the visual impact of the new equipment should be minimal in order to appease environmental and public concerns, while at the same time the equipment must be compact and flexible to support a wide variety of innovative but demanding services (smart city and V2X applications, mobile connectivity everywhere, etc.), without compromising performance and efficiency.

Sleek size factors may also mitigate construction works to speed up the 5G installation in highly dense areas. In addition, small and light weight equipment could be integrated in existing constructions, such as lighting poles, traffic lights or underground sites, like the Ericsson's "zero sites", "street furniture sites" and "vault sites" solutions [10]. Such solutions could prove attractive for site owners or utilities so as to proceed with the desired frame agreements with mutual benefits for the involved parties (e.g., a municipality could improve the lighting of an area), while preventing vandalism activities by efficient and not provocative camouflage. To further avoid such incidents and behaviors attributed to health concerns about EM radiation and COVID-19 due to public misinformation [25, 26], as well as to address the reluctance of a number of cities to allow dense network deployment, the MNOs must be prepared, leverage previous experience and proactively raise awareness of the public through campaigns (YouTube videos, advertisements, posts at social media, etc.), on: (a) the 5G benefits and (b) the highly strict and extremely low EM limits set by the Intern'l Commission on Non-Ionizing Radiation Protection (ICNIRP); in practice, 10 to 50 times lower than the emission levels where health effects may start. Noted here that an updated version of ICNIRP indications has been published; to be considered in Council Recommendation 1999/519/EC [23, 24].

2.3 Energy Consumption Demand (and Energy Optimization)

The energy consumption in 5G networks, strongly associated with the traffic demand rise, significantly exceeds that of the LTE networks by 2–5 or 3 ½ times [11, 12] and is indeed a major issue in the few real 5G deployments [13]. It is critical that the energy does not follow the traffic rise [9], especially in highly dense areas where exponential 5G traffic increase is expected, while one of the 5G-PPP key targets is saving up to 90% of energy per service provided [14]. Recent studies show that 5G networks are up to 90% more energy efficient per traffic unit than any previous wireless technology generation, but the overall network energy will rise dramatically [16, 17], although not identifiable yet. Besides the traffic explosion, the power usage increase in the overall 5G network is mostly attributed to the RAN due to: denser deployments, new power-hungry components, including microwave or mm-wave transceivers, faster data converters, high-power/low-noise amplifiers, field-programmable gate arrays (FPGAs) or Application-Specific Integrated Circuits (ASICs), MIMO antennas, as well as edge compute facilities for local processing to support low-latency applications and IoT [13].

The goal of decreasing energy consumption in the telecommunications sector has led the researchers and the industry to focus on energy-saving features in the radio base station and network levels, such as peak shaving, voltage boosting, energy storage, artificial intelligence (AI) and machine learning (ML) techniques, as well as new 5G architectures and protocols. Additionally, practices that are up to the MNOs to adopt include: (i) Selecting low power access network solutions, green powered (by solar panels, batteries, etc.) and supporting energy-saving features [19]; (ii) network intelligence, e.g. power-off gNBs when no traffic is available; (iii) capitalization on existing assets/sites; (iv) infrastructure sharing among MNOs (at gNB/fronthaul/backhaul level); (v) exploration of optimal energy consumption deployments [15, 18] through area specific studies and network measurements.

2.4 Service Continuity Related to Power Issues

Another great challenge for the MNOs is to ensure electrification (e.g. access to different sources/means) and seamless power supply (incl. redundancy) of the 5G dense/ultra-dense network deployments so that 24×7 service continuity (at street level) is enabled to support specific, critical services, e.g. automotive related ones.

To ensure always-on connectivity, batteries/generators (super-capacitor to cover micro interruptions and lithium batteries to cover long blackouts) seem to be mandatory. In cases of local powering solutions, in addition to the AC connection cost per site, cost and efficiency must be carefully considered since a huge number of solar panels, AC/DC converters and batteries will be required. Remote powering also exhibits advantages, such as the centralized connection to AC grid, redundancy concepts realization, centralized backup and associated cost reduction, introduction of power line duplication or power rings. For example, in cases of fiber connectivity availability, the utilization of Low Voltage DC (LVDC) technology (up to 400VDC for TLC/ICT applications) in the primary distribution segment and the usage of Safety Extra Low Voltage (SELV) DC to feed directly the equipment could be an option [6–8]. Obviously, a monitoring/management system shall enable awareness of the power network status in real-time and performing appropriate maintenance activity.

Integration/maximization of renewable energy apart from greening the cellular networks and leading to OPEX reduction, it will also limit the peak on-grid energy consumption, ensuring service continuity in case of grid failure. Extra accumulated energy managed by a smart controller, without however compromising service continuity, could feed the grid.

2.5   Increased Network Planning, Deployment and Optimization Complexity

The extremely low electromagnetic limits in conjunction with the high density of low-powered gNB/access nodes, the introduction of mm-wave technologies, the frequency chunks' availability, the refarming, the technology alternatives for fronthaul and backhaul, the intensively variable radio environment, make access network planning and deployment very challenging or even impossible in some cases [15, 16], while interference and total spatial electromagnetic power must be kept at minimum, which becomes even harder, if the acquisition of the optimal locations as indicated by the planning tools may not be possible.

To overcome all these planning/deployment complexity factors and guarantee 5G offerings at the desired high QoS/QoE especially in dense 5G deployments, continuous network and traffic monitoring is required, more accurate planning tools shall be used, while huge optimization effort for long(er) periods of testing (coverage, interference, throughput, latency, handovers, dropped calls, etc.) and fine tuning/troubleshooting activities must be conducted by the MNOs. Regarding the transport network, various converging technologies shall be selected capable of supporting deployment flexibility and scalability, by taking into account various factors such as area specifics, technologies' deployment feasibility, traffic/usage forecasts, long-term services roadmaps, as well as the implicated costs.

2.6   Spectrum Related Issues

5G utilizes different parts of the radio spectrum to deliver performance, capacity and coverage [22]. Spectrum resources allocation and management constitute a primary challenge. Despite the advancements in access network (e.g., massive MIMO, scheduling and signal processing techniques) which contribute to the efficient usage of spectrum resources, large chunks of spectrum will still be needed (see 66–71 GHz and 40.5–43.5 GHz allocations) for dense small cell networks. At the same time, to satisfy the coverage and capacity requirements for wide areas, low frequency bands currently allocated for nationwide mobile network deployments will be needed; thus rendering refarming (and related investment on new frequency license acquisition) a huge challenge for MNOs.

2.7   Huge CAPEX and OPEX

The deployment of 5G networks will require CAPEX and OPEX investments on 5G (frequency) license, new equipment/hardware, site rental, energy, backhaul and civil works, network equipment operation and maintenance, sophisticated monitoring and optimization tools, as well as trained and skillful engineers [2, 3]. To pursue reduction of the costs especially related to the increasingly complicated, distributed, ultra-dense 5G network deployments, without compromising the offered QoS/QoE, the MNOs shall: (i) conduct realistic techno-economic studies (with different deployment scenarios, critical radio parameters, alternative technologies, etc.); (ii) spend huge effort on network optimization; (iii) select flexible, energy/cost efficient, future proof solutions, (iv) shutdown previous generation networks (e.g., 3G); (v) adopt best site acquisition and energy strategy (see (a), (c), etc.). Concerning the electricity cost, it is expected to rise dramatically accounting for 15–20% of the total OPEX [13]. Indicatively, China Mobile, one of the leading 5G mobile operators is seeking subsidies from the Chinese government to be able to afford it.

3   5G-PHOS Solution Overview

5G-PHOS, a Phase-2 5G-PPP project attempts to address, in a flexible and efficient way, the challenging 5G densification framework to support the demanding coverage and capacity requirements of urban, dense urban and hotspot environments at any time and under any circumstances, along with the wide variety of 5G services. In this context, the 5G-PHOS project proposes an ultra-broadband converged FiWi PtMP fronthaul network, capable of supporting the required 5G NR fronthaul bandwidth, and exhibiting a wide range of benefits [27], including alleviating the need to install fiber terminations at every MNO site, offering fast roll-out and short time-to-market, by replacing or complementing fixed/fiber based solutions. 5G-PHOS solution builds upon the prevalent enhanced eCPRI standard and creates the necessary infrastructure to interconnect eCPRI-capable equipment in a PtMP way, including (Fig. 1): the Master and the Slave Flexbox Units, the Rooftop Remote Radio Head (R-RRH) (incl. PCBs), the Secondary Lamppost RRH (SL-RRH) [27].

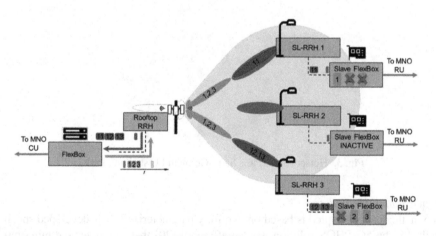

Fig. 1. The 5G-PHOS architecture

4   5G-PHOS Densification Figures

The aim of this section is to provide indicative deployment configuration instances (amount and inter-distance of H/W components) of the 5G-PHOS solution in three Use Cases envisioned by the 5G-PHOS project and in three "timeslots" (i.e., 2022, 2027, 2032), so that the expected rise in 5G services usage and 5G subscribers can be supported. The Use Cases under study [20] refer to:

1. A Dense area located at the District 15 of Paris (Fig. 2), covering a total area of 2,359,800 m² (2280 m × 1035 m).
2. An Ultra Dense area located in the vicinity of the Eiffel Tower (Fig. 2) covering a total area of 283,812 m² (804 m × 353 m).
3. A Hotspot area corresponding to the seats area (18,467 m²) of the Paris Saint-Germain (PSG) FC stadium[2] (Fig. 3).

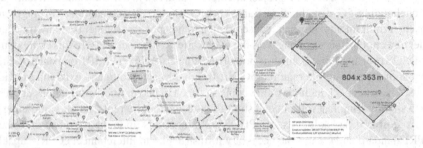

Fig. 2. Dense area (District 15, Paris) and ultra-dense area (greater area of the Eiffel Tower, Paris)

Fig. 3. Hotspot area (Paris Saint-Germain FC stadium, Paris)

Dimensioning Methodology

The methodology adopted is based on two fully parameterized tools developed specifically for the 5G-PHOS solution: (i) A traffic tool [20] that calculates the min, max, average and peak offered traffic for a set of input parameters (subscribers, concurrent services usage, service and tenants' requirements, etc.); (ii) A dimensioning tool [21] that models the 5G-PHOS architecture, incorporates dimensioning rules and area/UC specific deployment aspects/restrictions and taking into account the offered traffic demand, calculates automatically the (optimal) configuration(s) of 5G-PHOS network deployment (number and inter-distance of R-RRHs, SL-RRHs, PCBs, master and slave Flexbox units) for the (9) cases under study (3 use case scenarios for each of the 3 years).

List of Assumptions

---

[2] http://www.stadiumguide.com/parcdesprinces/.

- Worst case (offered) total traffic scenarios per UC [20]: Busy Hour for the Dense UC; a big event, e.g. a concert for the Ultra-Dense and a football match for the Hotspot UCs, for different 5G subscribers' penetration rates and 5G coverage area percentages for the three (3) time periods.
- Dimensioning related/element: R-RRH range/PCB azimuth, PCB throughput, #channels/PCB, #PCBs/Master Flexbox, Master Flexbox throughput, etc.
- Radio related: Max bitrate/SL-RRH, overheads vs. FS (Functional Split), SL-RRH range, etc.
- Number of 5G MNOs: 3 for Dense and Ultra-Dense, 1 for the Hotspot UC.
- Traffic offloading over fiber connected SL-RRHs: 30/20/12% for Y-2022/2027/2032 (in Dense UC), 30% (in Ultra Dense and Hotspot UCs) for all years.
- Area characteristics: perimeter, Km^2, population density, etc.
- Restrictions: #SL-RRHs that can be connected to a (R-RRH) PCB based on #channels and coverage area, #MNO-RRHs/SL-RRH, etc.

5G-PHOS Densification Figures
See Table 1

Table 1. 5G-PHOS network dimensioning/configuration per UC.

Use Case	Dense			Ultra-Dense			Hotspot		
Year	2022	2027	2032	2022	2027	2032	2022	2027	2032
Traffic (Gb/s)	35	400	2000	45	200	600	50	180	350
5G area coverage	10%	17%	23%	10%	15%	23%	100%	100%	100%
#R-RRHs	3	5	7	4	4	4	10	11	21
#PCBs (Tx+Rx)	46	76	106	32	32	32	20	22	42
#SL-RRHs	23	38	104	10	16	32	20	63	123
#Slave Flexbox	23	38	104	10	16	32	20	63	123
#Master Flexbox	2	3	4	1	1	1	1	1	2
Ave dist. (m) btw SL-RRHs	194	115	82	60	58	51	34	20	14
Ave dist. (m) btw R-RRHs	323	325	325	95	116	145	65	59	31

Evaluation of Results and Generic Remarks
The dimensioning tool calculates (automatically) all valid configurations, taking into account both network coverage and capacity requirements. Although it is 5G-PHOS specific, given its parameterized, expandable and customizable structure, it could support any 5G solution and any scenario could be potentially investigated. The results are indicative of the order of magnitude for both the amount of the H/W elements and the short distances between them, as well as for the network evolution path. They can also be used as a reference for comparison with other 5G solutions or as input for the investigation of the energy/power consumption of the related network segments. They could be also utilized for 5G-PHOS techno-economic studies, to provide insights for

the MNOs' deployment strategy and risks mitigation. Future technology evolution may improve the current densification figures, but nonetheless the initial figures presented here can be employed as a roadmap for estimating costs and initial planning. For more accurate results, a planning tool is considered as more appropriate.

5   Summary

In this paper the MNOs are warned on significant challenges, they have to cope with, related the 5G densification in densely populated areas (e.g., site acquisition, H/W and environmental footprint impacting on the public opinion, energy consumption expected increase, the demand for service continuity, the increased complexity in network planning, deployment, optimization and spectrum allocation, the related cost factors). Hints and recommendations are discussed to support MNOs' competitiveness efficiency and sustainability. In addition, a study on 5G densification is conducted, based on fully parametrized traffic and dimension tools. Although indicative and 5G solution specific, the outcomes provide the order of magnitude of 5G densification figures in dense and hotspot areas over the years, and could further assist MNOs in their deployment strategy, cost and energy savings.

Acknowledgements. The research leading to these results has received funding from the European Union's Framework Programme Horizon 2020 under grant agreement No. 761989 and project name "5G-PHOS: 5G integrated Fiber-Wireless networks exploiting existing photonic technologies for high-density SDN programmable network architectures".

References

1. 5G-PHOS project. http://5g-phos.eu/
2. From Standards to Service - the European Way to 5G, IEEE 5G Tech Focus, vol. 1, no. 4, December 2017. https://futurenetworks.ieee.org/tech-focus/december-2017/from-standards-to-service-the-european-way
3. Mobile Operator 5G Capex Forecasts: 2018–2023. http://www.heavyreading.com/details.asp?sku_id=3568&skuitem_itemid=1789
4. Lessons learned. https://www.ericsson.com/en/blog/6/2020/lessons-from-the-first-wave-of-5g-deployments-why-transport-is-critical-to-5g-rollout
5. White paper. https://www.ftthcouncil.eu/documents/Reports/Technical%20Converg ence_V17_FINAL_7march2019_Bis.pdf
6. Posca, P., Marone, B.: Powering future network architectures. In: Intelec 2018. https://doi.org/10.1109/INTLEC.2018.8612371
7. ITU-T, L.1210 (12/2019). https://www.itu.int/rec/dologin_pub.asp?lang=f&id=T-REC-L.1210-201912-I!!PDF-E&type=items
8. 5G Italy, The Global mtg. in Rome, 3-5/12/199. https://www.5gitaly.eu/2019/wp-content/upl oads/2019/12/libro5G_2019_online.pdf
9. 5G networks up to 90% more energy efficient than 4G. https://www.information-age.com/5g-networks-found-90-more-energy-efficient-than-4g-123492972/
10. Invisible sites. https://www.ericsson.com/en/networks/offerings/urban-wireless/invisible-sites

11. 5G Power. https://www.huawei.com/en/publications/communicate/89/5g-power-green-grid-slashes-costs-emissions-energy-use
12. Starting to face up to 5G power cost. https://www.lightreading.com/asia-pacific/operators-starting-to-face-up-to-5g-power-cost-/d/d-id/755255
13. Mobile operator strategies to cut power cost. https://www.telecomlead.com/5g/5g-mobile-operator-strategies-to-cut-their-huge-power-cost-94645
14. MTN Consulting. https://www.fiercewireless.com/tech/5g-base-stations-use-a-lot-more-energy-than-4g-base-stations-says-mtn
15. Ericsson. https://www.ericsson.com/en/blog/2019/9/energy-consumption-5g-nr
16. Nokia confirms 5G as 90% more energy efficient. https://www.marketwatch.com/press-release/nokia-confirms-5g-as-90-percent-more-energy-efficient-2020-12-02
17. Nokia talks up 5G energy efficiency. https://telecoms.com/507709/nokia-talks-up-5g-energy-efficiency-but-power-consumption-is-only-going-one-way/
18. How renewable energy will power 5G. https://na.panasonic.com/us/trends/how-renewable-energy-will-power-5g-mobile-service
19. 5G-PHOS, Deliverable D2.1: Initial Report on Use Cases, System Requirements, KPIs and Network Architecture. http://5g-phos.eu/pdf/5G-PHOS_D2.1_Final.pdf
20. 5G-PHOS, Deliverable D2.4: Final Report on Use Cases, System Requirements, KPIs and Network Architecture. http://www.5g-phos.eu/pdf/5G-PHOS_D2.4_FINAL.pdf
21. Why complex to deploy? https://digis2.com/5g-why-is-it-so-complex-to-deploy/
22. Publications Office of the EU. https://op.europa.eu/en/publication-detail/-/publication/9509b04f-1df0-4221-bfa2-c7af77975556/language-en
23. Directive (EU) 2018/1972. https://www.technologyslegaledge.com/2018/12/the-new-european-electronic-communications-code-updated/
24. Article 57. https://www.legislation.gov.uk/eudr/2018/1972/article/57
25. Cell towers vandalized. https://www.pcmag.com/news/over-50-cell-towers-vandalised-in-uk-due-to-5g-coronavirus-conspiracy-theories
26. 5G coronavirus conspiracy. https://www.cnet.com/health/5g-coronavirus-conspiracy-theory-sees-77-mobile-towers-burned-report-says/
27. Theodoropoulou, E., et al.: A framework to support the 5G densification. In: Maglogiannis, I., Iliadis, L., Pimenidis, E. (eds.) AIAI 2020. IAICT, vol. 585, pp. 3–14. Springer, Cham (2020). https://doi.org/10.1007/978-3-030-49190-1_1

TYPHON: Hybrid Data Lakes for Real-Time Big Data Analytics – An Evaluation Framework in the Telecom Industry

Antonis Misargopoulos[1]([✉]) [iD], George Papavassiliou[2] [iD], Christos A. Gizelis[1] [iD], and Filippos Nikolopoulos-Gkamatsis[1] [iD]

[1] Hellenic Telecommunications Organization S.A. (OTE), Marousi, Attiki, Greece
{amisargopo,cgkizelis,fnikolop}@ote.gr
[2] Avlos LLC, Cambridge, MA 02139, USA
george@avlos.ai

Abstract. In this paper we aim to present outcomes from the evaluation and deployment of the TYPHON H2020 project (The TYPHON project receives funding under the European Unions Horizon 2020 Research and Innovation Programme under grant agreement No. 780251) in a container-based production ecosystem supported by Hellenic Telecommunications Organization S.A. (OTE). The main objective is to implement a successful production-ready deployment following best practices in terms of infrastructure, monitoring and high availability while achieving analysis in real-time of massive streams of data. Moreover, our intent is to evaluate the TYPHON architecture when integrated by a Telecom Industry user and present the benefits of its adaptation by IT Units for predictive maintenance purposes.

Keywords: Hybrid persistence architectures · Big data analytics · Evaluation framework and measures · Adaptation to telecom industry

1 Introduction

The Hellenic Telecommunications Organization S.A. (OTE) [1] as the largest telecommunications provider in Southeast Europe provides its customers with a wide variety of ICT services addressing a large customer base. OTE owns repositories of big data sets from a variety of sources such as call centers, billing, mobility, traffic data, etc., and concentrates huge amounts of both operational by means its infrastructure as well as consumer-related data through its customers in daily basis. In collaboration with Avlos [2], a technology company providing custom and innovative technology solutions to enterprises worked together in order to evaluate the TYPHON [3] driven approach and methodology towards its adaptation by Telecom industries.

© IFIP International Federation for Information Processing 2021
Published by Springer Nature Switzerland AG 2021
I. Maglogiannis et al. (Eds.): AIAI 2021 Workshops, IFIP AICT 628, pp. 128–137, 2021.
https://doi.org/10.1007/978-3-030-79157-5_12

2   Related Work and Current Status

Predictive maintenance is the art of anticipation of equipment failures to allow for in advance scheduling of corrective actions, thereby preventing unexpected downtime and improving the customer service quality. The main goal of predictive maintenance is to enable proactive scheduling of corrective work and thus, prevent unanticipated failures. Predictive maintenance requires insights into the running conditions of equipment and software. In a corporate environment, there is a diversity of computing systems and software, which are utilized by employees given their diversity of tasks.

Nowadays, the use of logs to estimate system level-failures with a high-confidence poses many challenges. As logs are mainly used for debugging purposes, the following challenges emerge:

- they rarely contain explicit information on failure prediction unless structured properly
- they contain heterogeneous data including symbolic sequences, numeric time-series, categorical variables, unstructured text; and
- they produce massive amounts of data, posing computational challenges.

To make use of log data, we first had to interpret them, filter out a large amount of noise (i.e. data irrelevant to our goal), and extract predictive features. Next, we had to collect known failure cases for learning/evaluating models, transform the problem into an appropriate learning scenario and determine performance indicators that reflect real-world needs. The effort and cost of modern database architectures assisting the above process are often discouraging, given that the volume, variety, veracity, and complexity of the logs, lead to heterogeneous data sets that are very hard to even be queried.

In this context the TYPHON project offers a concrete methodology to interact with a number of relational and non-relational databases and perform modeling activities on both open and closed data sets. Using TYPHON capabilities OTE is given the opportunity to overcome the following limitations:

- handle large volumes of data that come from different database sources
- analyze large amounts of diversely structured data
- run analytics (i.e. statistical algorithms) measures on massive amounts of data in near real-time to extract insights.

For OTE, the TYPHON architecture offers an environment to interact with a diversity of data sources, minimizing the effort and time required to analyze such complex data sets. The following sections present how TYPHON capabilities can be exploited as well as the evaluation framework implemented to assess the level of adaption efficiency with respect to the challenges emerge in a Telecom business environment like OTE.

3   TYPHON and OTS Solutions at OTE

TYPHON platform offers solid framework for managing big volume of data stored in heterogeneous persistent back-ends to calculate advanced KPIs in near to real-time basis; i.e.:

- Technologies for designing hybrid *polystores* [4] are agnostic of the structure of the data, the availability, partitioning, and consistency requirements of different subsets of the data, and the available deployment resources
- Novel algorithms offer hybrid polystore design models transformation into pre-configured optimized virtual machines which can be deployed on cloud infrastructure
- An extensible high-level language for querying and modifying data stored in hybrid polystores is available, as well as capabilities for translating high-level queries into efficient native queries
- A high-performance framework for publishing and processing data access and updating events to facilitate real-time monitoring and predictive analytics
- Technologies for evolving the organization and distribution of data in hybrid polystores, along with tools for monitoring use of polystores for enhanced evolution

Besides the interest of the academic community, an open source innovative solution like TYPHON could inspire companies/organizations of diverse large-scale industry areas to gain from. The adoption though, by an industry environment where business need is fulfilled by an off-the-self (OTS) solution/product is out of discussion a great challenge. In particular, at OTE a problem like this can be described as follows:

- The Dynatrace monitoring tool [5], at the moment running in-house, analyses streams of logs from CRM services and evaluates in real-time the user experience of its CRM services. The software utilized, requires a data store and ETL pipelines to be set in place; and its cost as well as deployment burdens the Operations department.
- A time-consuming process is followed to amend data on already stored records.
- At the moment the user experience of CRM services can hardly be predicted. Data is spread across data stores without any point of communication; moreover, performing any statistical analyses techniques on top of this multitude and diverse set of data stores is hard.

In the next section it is described the experience in deploying and utilising each of the TYPHON components within the context of OTE, the degree to which OTE requirements have been satisfied, the level of efficiency on how TYPHON technologies can cover all business related measures, and finally what benefits TYPHON as solution can bring to OTE in terms of service quality, time or cost.

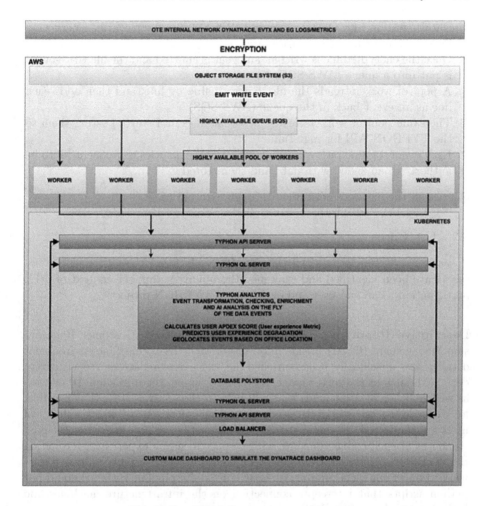

Fig. 1. Our E2E infrastructure architecture

4   Our Evaluation Framework

In this section we present our approach for the assessment of TYPHON solution within OTE organization. I.e., the end-to-end (E2E) infrastructure architecture we deployed to run the evaluation, and the use cases and measurement scenarios themselves.

4.1   Deployment Architecture

Figure 1 depicts the E2E infrastructure architecture we deployed that is based on following steps:

1. Data ingestion into Object Storage (AWS S3) [6] after Security Encryption Pass; i.e., anonymization[1] procedure
2. Once the encrypted file is written, an event is emitted and the file write-event is put into a queue (AWS SQS) [7]
3. A pool of workers reads the file, parses it line by line, and then adds each line as an event back in the queue (AWS SQS)
4. The same pool of workers reads the event lines and starts posting them to the TYPHON API for ingestion
5. Each event log line passes through TYPHON Analytics component [8] to be authorized, amended with data and then stored

Queries on the data are performed through external tools.

4.2   Use Cases

To validate the functionality of the TYPHON platform, the following two use cases have been identified and examined thoroughly within the context of OTE participation as an end user and evaluator at TYPHON project:

Descriptive Reporting. OTE IT Department injected Customer Relationship Management (CRM) session information with virtual machine environment details. More specifically, it has enriched the user's session data source with extra data fields such as the server name, server farm name, the user's real IP address as well as other relevant fields that will help in the analysis. It is thus possible, for example, to run statistical analyses and classifications of which subsets of users are connected via the virtualized infrastructure or not; and what the consequences of such connections are with respect to user's experience. Exploiting the TYPHON Analytics Component capabilities, OTE used a unified framework to inject the data running an Apache Flink [9] pipeline rather than ad-hoc python scripts that intercepts connection on the infrastructure machines and later store it in the TYPHON Polystore.

Predictive Maintenance for Improved Quality of Service (QoS). In this use case as a first step data is gathered and enriched in massive amounts within the TYPHON polystore, and as a second step large queries run across all underlying databases where the data is modeled to generate enriched data that will serve as the basis of a prediction model capable of forecasting a service degradation based on faults and errors counts in the back-end infrastructure that supports the CRM system. This type of prediction modeling and forecasting had lead to proactive, and even automated, measures to be taken by the IT Department for maintenance tasks and will, as a result, improve the quality of the provided service.

---

[1] A type of information sanitization for privacy protection by removing personally identifiable information from a data set.

4.3   Scenarios

User Experience Apdex Scoring and Threshold Determination. Application Performance Index (Apdex[2]) [10] is an open standard for measuring performance of software applications in computing. It converts measurements into insights about user satisfaction, by specifying a uniform way to analyze and report on the degree to which measured performance meets user expectations. The Apdex method converts many measurements into one number on a uniform scale of 0 to 1 (0 = no users satisfied, 1 = all users satisfied). The resulting Apdex score is a numerical measure of user satisfaction with the performance of enterprise applications. The Apdex formula is the number of satisfied samples plus half of the tolerating samples plus none of the frustrated samples, divided by all the samples:

$$
\text{Apdex}_t = \frac{\text{SatisfiedCnt} + (\text{ToleratingCnt} * 0.5) + (\text{FrustratedCnt} * 0)}{\text{TotalSamplesCnt}}, \quad (1)
$$

where the sub-script t is the target time, and the tolerable time is assumed to be 4 times the target time.

The Dynatrace system at OTE calculates Apdex scoring to determine whether a user of the application is satisfied with their experience. We used the Analytics component of the TYPHON to produce the same or similar metric. Note that scoring for the user experience of our application is highly influenced by the underlying hardware they connect with. Using Apache Flink to process buckets of data in real time and determining the Apdex for a user session within a certain time window, we derive a similar Apdex scoring pattern as that which the Dynatrace platform currently provides for the internal operations team.

Importing Java Statistics functions into Apache Flink for calculating probabilities and quantiles for the gamma distribution [11,12], which defines an Erlang distribution [13,14] when the shape value is positive, OTE used TYPHON itself to identify the appropriate thresholds to establish whether the user experience is "satisfying", "tolerable", "intolerable". In the end we should have an Apdex metric timeseries that represents the user experience per connected machine cluster. By doing this, we can infer the discrepancies in response time and session duration between users that connect directly to the application and those that are connected through a virtualized server middle ware cluster. The reporting performed inside the TYPHON Platform will be compared and evaluated with respect to the one reporting, which is currently performed outside TYPHON.

Data Preparation and Annotation as a Platform. Using the TYPHON Platform's Analytics and its APIs we are able to amend and filter data appropriately, similar to the data injection that is happening currently by the Internal Operations Unit. This will happen instantly as the data comes into TYPHON and with the appropriate tables in the Data Model used, metadata will be added

---

[2] https://www.apdex.org/.

to the current data streams entering the databases. In detail, a table is going to be created in the TYPHON polystore with a bijection of IP addresses to retail shop locations which will be used by the Analytics Component. The Apache Flink consumer will analyse the IP address of the incoming data point and then query this internal table. In case that the IP exists in the table, it will resolve and amend the geolocation of the retail shop in the data point; otherwise the record will be rejected.

Using TYPHON as a Data Lake to Extract Massive Amounts of Data for Machine Learning (ML) Training. By directly accessing data components through the TYPHON Query Language component (TyphonQL) API [15], we evaluated the querying of massive amounts of data to use as the training set of a ML Prediction Model. In this scenario the ultimate objective was to conclude how TYPHON can assist in the training of ML Models. To do this, the TyphonQL and TYPHON Analytics components would be utilized to hook various ML frameworks into the platform and perform the training. Thus, the platform succeeded with respect to its performance when tasked with running oversized data queries as well as being able to process these queries in a paginated manner.

5   Evaluation Measurements Insights

In this section it is presented the evaluation KPIs and the full prototype test measurements for the TYPHON capabilities within the scope of OTE as Use Case of Telecom industry.

Support of Highly Available Data Stores. TYPHON uses technologies underneath that have been battle tested in production for years, i.e., MongoDB [16], MariaDB [17] etc. It has thus managed to expose their highly available/clustered versions for a fail safe deployment of stateful services (i.e. databases) in a cloud native environment (Kubernetes [18]).

Support for a Wide Variety of Data Stores. Given the current support for a variety of data stores (MariaDB, MongoDB, Cassandra [19], ArangoDB [20]) the platform provides us with the versatility not only to use currently existing databases but also to extend the data sources to others not previously thought of or considered.

Accuracy of Apdex Scoring. The TYPHON Analytics component is based on a streaming database solution (Kafka [21]) which is also highly available and has been run in production systems for years by a multitude of organizations. Using the TYPHON Analytics Component we were able to reproduce the mathematical calculations that extract meaningful statistical data from TYPHON with 100% accuracy, in fact we can implement any mathematical function operating within a time window of data. Dynatrace has its own proprietary algorithm for calculating Apdex and as expected, our results are not identical since we used one of the open formulas of the Apdex equations. We essentially managed to prove though that we are able to develop any mathematical/statistical function in the TYPHON Analytics API to reproduce any statistically significant result or measure we are interested in.

Cost of Maintenance. We have observed that running TYPHON on Kubernetes gives a significant cost reduction on the operations and maintenance of the platform. Not only we were able to switch between cloud providers or on-premise deployments, but we had also observed a significant cost reduction running the platform in this cloud native manner compared to other systems. This is a direct result of its open source nature, containerized and cloud native deployments and the cost of ownership.

Deprecation of Currently Running Systems. Assuming that TYPHON can be used both as a real time analytics solution as well as a data lake (polystore) system, the platform is able to replace a number of systems that are running internally. For example, it could replace the variety of proprietary and costly stores used to gather multidimensional data; i.e. aggregators and analyzers like Dynatrace and Vertica [22], as well as internally provided bulky Data lake systems like Hadoop.

6   New Capabilities Adopting TYPHON Technologies

6.1   Benefits for Users/Customers

The aforementioned measures provide a very promising scenario for using TYPHON in a diversity of areas within the organization to optimize the analysis of data with our own customer base as well as internal operations. For example, using TYPHON platform OTE can gather information from a variety of sources, generate insights and act on maintenance of machines within our stores proactively, even automatically, to replace parts, machines, software, before they malfunction.

There are areas though, that we have not yet explored; i.e., using TYPHON as a data lake of numerous stores running underneath it, we should be able to connect data sources that we had not yet thought of and improve the User Experience (UX) of our customers in our digital stores or generate customer behavior analysis and optimisation metrics. The experience and technical knowledge gained from an H2020 project like TYPHON could be used in our industrial environment for exploiting Big Data Analytics or ML capabilities, i.e., alerting notification based on KPI threshold violations or proactive warning upon potential service degradation based on past measures.

6.2   Benefits for OTE

For internal operations, the realm of possibilities widens even more. Most significantly in the areas of cost of ownership, operational resilience and staff productivity.

Cost of Ownership. Based on the measures extracted above the cost of ownership on an open source solution like TYPHON significantly decreases in various contexts. Given the amount of different solutions already running internally that it can replace, by acting both as a real time analytics solution as well as a hybrid data lake without the need to change the underlying data sources, we have found a cost reduction in significant scale. Additionally, operating the solution on Kubernetes provides significant cost and agility benefits. Not only there is no need by Operation Engineers to retrain on a different platform as they are already familiar with the Kubernetes framework, but the deployment platform itself also enables us to migrate quickly from one cloud solution to another; it can even be moved on premises if its deployed in the cloud and vice versa.

Operational Resilience. The significant power that the deployment of TYPHON on a cloud native solution like Kubernetes provides is that of resilience. That is, the highly available nature of a platform like Kubernetes allows the TYPHON platform to provide fail safe guarantees for a seamless deployment and run-time configuration as well as blue-green deploy scenarios. By using the highly available versions of the underlying data stores we can be assured of significant uptimes because:

- restoring and roll-back at any stage when a failure happens at run time or during deployments remains seamless, quick and safe
- the clustered version of the databases and their replication allow for a node to fail without data loss.

Staff Productivity. Since the deployment and operational overhead is reduced dramatically, data engineers' productivity increases significantly with respect to the business case at hand. Instead of worrying about the operations and the performance of their queries since the deployment is taken cared by a scheduler like Kubernetes, the data engineers are now able to focus solely on analysing the business problem at hand and mining the data needed with ease to derive the appropriate insights that will finally help them resolve any issue or incident comes to front.

7   Conclusion

Summarizing the evaluation parameters presented in the previous section, it is now clear that TYPHON architecture and components follow an open source-like methodology which is the demand of the IT Unit within a Telecom Organization. Such an industry owns, handles and processes an extremely large diversity of data stored in various and heterogeneous databases and systems. Open source solutions generally speaking follow a more cost-effective approach than a proprietary one. Moreover, it is favored for industry players, since it utilizes open standards in order to reduce the cost of ownership of systems or delay system obsolescence.

TYPHON Polyglot system managed to meet and fully satisfy the requirements of OTE with respect to the ability to handle a wide variety of data stores with high availability. This is crucial for a company with a large size of several hundreds of retail stores and millions of customers/subscribers. In this context the need for a solution that will contribute to time efficiency and cost reduction will always be of high priority. The flexibility that TYPHON architecture offers in terms of easiness in integration as well as the wide diversity of supported heterogeneous persistence back-ends optimize resource allocation and improve staff productivity to handle human-expert tasks more efficiently.

References

1. OTE Group of Companies, Research & Innovation. https://www.cosmote.gr/cs/otegroup/en/ereuna_kai_kainotomia.html/
2. Avlos.ai. https://avlos.ai/
3. TYPHON Project, Polyglot and Hybrid Persistence Architectures for Big Data Analytics. https://www.typhon-project.org/
4. Fink, J., Gobert, M., Cleve, A.: Adapting queries to database schema changes in hybrid polystores. In Proceedings of IEEE International Workshop on Source Code Analysis and Manipulation (2020)
5. The Dynatrace software intelligence platform. https://www.dynatrace.com/platform/
6. Amazon Simple Storage Service S3. https://docs.aws.amazon.com/s3/index.html/
7. Amazon Simple Queue Service SQS. https://docs.aws.amazon.com/AWSSimpleQueueService/latest/SQSDeveloperGuide/welcome.html/
8. Zolotas, A., Barmpis, K., Medhat, F., Neubauer, P., Kolovos, D., Paige, R.F.: An architecture for the development of distributed analytics based on polystore events. In: Gadepally, V., et al. (eds.) DMAH/Poly -2020. LNCS, vol. 12633, pp. 54–65. Springer, Cham (2021). https://doi.org/10.1007/978-3-030-71055-2_5
9. Apache Flink. https://flink.apache.org/
10. Apdex (Application Performance Index). https://en.wikipedia.org/wiki/Apdex
11. Gamma distribution. https://mathworld.wolfram.com/GammaDistribution.html
12. Gamma distribution. https://en.wikipedia.org/wiki/Gamma_distribution
13. Erlang distribution. https://mathworld.wolfram.com/ErlangDistribution.html
14. Erlang distribution. https://en.wikipedia.org/wiki/Erlang_distribution
15. TyphonQL Compilers and Interpeters, Centrum Wiskunde & Informatica (CWI) and SWAT.engineering, TYPHON Project D4.5 Final deliverable, Public distribution. https://4d97e142-6f1b-4bbd-9bbb-577958797a89.filesusr.com/ugd/d3bb5c_4349c798cf42409d93a4d588ab1f4162.pdf
16. MongoDB, A source-available cross-platform document-oriented database. https://www.mongodb.com/
17. MariaDB Relational Database. https://mariadb.org/
18. Kubernetes K8s, An open-source system for automating deployment, scaling, and management of containerized applications. https://kubernetes.io/
19. Apache Cassandra, An open-source, distributed, wide-column store, NoSQL database management system. https://cassandra.apache.org/
20. ArangoDB, An open-source multi-model database for graph and beyond. https://www.arangodb.com/
21. Apache Kafka Connector. https://ci.apache.org/projects/flink/flink-docs-stable/dev/connectors/kafka.html
22. Vertica, A unified advanced analytics database. https://www.vertica.com/v9/

V2X Communications for the Support of GLOSA and Intelligent Intersection Applications

Ioannis P. Chochliouros[1]([✉]) [iD], Anastasia S. Spiliopoulou[1], Pavlos Lazaridis[2], Zaharias Zaharis[3], Michail-Alexandros Kourtis[4], Slawomir Kuklinski[5,6], Lechosław Tomaszewski[5], Dimitrios Arvanitozisis[1], and Alexandros Kostopoulos[1]

[1] Hellenic Telecommunications Organization (OTE) S.A., 99 Kifissias Avenue, 15124 Maroussi-Athens, Greece
ichochliouros@oteresearch.gr
[2] The University of Huddersfield, Queensgate, Huddersfield HD13DH, UK
[3] Aristotle University of Thessaloniki, 54124 Thessaloniki, Greece
[4] ORION Innovations Private Company, Athens, Greece
[5] Orange Polska, Warsaw, Poland
[6] Warsaw University of Technology, Warsaw, Poland

Abstract. The rapid development of 5G provides opportunities for growth for a great variety of services, also including cooperative Intelligent Transport Services (C-ITS). In this framework, of high importance are Vehicle-to-Everything (V2X) applications that can contribute towards improving driving safety, efficiency and comfort, together with the inclusion of automation processes. Based on the broader context for promoting innovative features and by assessing various opportunities appearing for the benefit of the market sector, our work specifically focuses on the scope of the 5G-DRIVE project, supporting cellular V2X trials between the EU and China. In particular, we explain the benefits for the two selected cases of use about Green Light Optimised Speed Advisory and Intelligent Intersection. Both can be examined in a joint form of architectural implementation, as in our approach. These use cases support the realization of an enhanced traffic management in urban areas, contribute to road safety and reduce fuel consumption.

Keywords: 5G · Autonomous driving · Cellular V2X (C-V2X) · Connected and automated mobility (CAM) · Cooperative ITS (C-ITS) · GLOSA · Intelligent transportation systems (ITS) · Latency · Reliability · Road safety · Vehicle-to-Network (V2N) communications · Vehicle-to-Vehicle (V2V) communications

1 Introduction

Advances in wireless communications and, in particular vehicular communications, have led to the advent of cooperative Intelligent Transportation Systems (ITS) [1]. These

© IFIP International Federation for Information Processing 2021
Published by Springer Nature Switzerland AG 2021
I. Maglogiannis et al. (Eds.): AIAI 2021 Workshops, IFIP AICT 628, pp. 138–152, 2021.
https://doi.org/10.1007/978-3-030-79157-5_13

systems are a global phenomenon and have been among the priorities for many "actors" of the market sectors such as the automotive industry, network and service operators and policy makers. ITS imply for the effective inclusion of ICT and electronics so that to deal with a series of actual critical challenges affecting modern societies, such as traffic congestion, transport efficiency, environmental conservation and enhanced security. In fact, ITS' main objective is to provide an improved system by informing users about traffic situations and by making transportation safer, more efficient and more environmentally sustainable.

In recent years, ITS have been widely applied along with the development of IT technologies such as robotics, signal and image processing, computing, sensing, and communications. ITS vary in the technologies they apply, from basic management systems such as car navigation, traffic signal control systems, container management systems, variable message signs, enforcement systems for monitoring applications (security closed circuit TV systems), through to more advanced applications that integrate live data and incorporate feedback from other sources, such as parking guidance and information systems or weather information. Furthermore, ITS can apply to the vast transportation infrastructure of highways and streets as well as to a growing number of vehicles and can also apply to all transport modes thus facilitating their interlinking or multimodality. Regarding the European framework, the ITS Directive 2010/40/EU [2] adopted since August 2010 and its subsequent already adopted Delegated Regulations, for instance on road safety, real-time-traffic and multimodal travel information, provide the necessary legal and technical framework to steer and ensure the interoperability of deployed ITS services [3, 4].

A typical example of an anticipated evolution strategy towards the beneficial use and inclusion of the fifth generation of mobile communications (5G) is the case of the "connected vehicles" application. In Europe, Basic System Profiles (BSPs) have been developed by the Car-to-Car Communication Consortium (C2C-CC) [5] and the EU funded C-Roads Platform project [6], assuming ITS-G5 with IEEE specifications as radio access technology for Vehicle-to-Vehicle (V2V) and Vehicle-to-Infrastructure (V2I) communication. However, during the latest years, research in the area of intelligent vehicles has been focused upon Cooperative ITS (C-ITS) which is a case of vehicle communications with each other and/or with the underlying infrastructure [7]. C-ITS offer benefits such as improvement of the quality and the reliability of information that is exchanged between vehicles, traffic signals, road environment as well as with other road users [8]. They also improve existing services and support the offering of new ones which, in turn, results to social and economic benefits; this also leads to greater efficiency of the road transport and increases safety with various sorts of alerts generated from the increased information available.

Modern vehicles are becoming safer, cleaner and more intelligent, mainly due to the fact that they can incorporate a variety of sensors together with assistant systems, enabling them to better monitoring their surrounding environments. Exchanging of information between vehicles and/or the roadside infrastructure allows vehicles to be conceived from autonomous systems to cooperative systems. The development of C-ITS is primarily driven by applications for active road safety and traffic efficiency, which help drivers to be aware of other vehicles, disseminate warnings about road hazards, and provide real-time information about traffic conditions for speed management and navigation. Such applications rely on always-on connectivity among the vehicles in the vicinity – including the roadside infrastructure – and frequent data exchange. Additionally, Internet access and location-based services, such as for point-of-presence and road access control, improve the driving convenience.

Our work is organised as follows: Sect. 1 serves as an introduction, explaining current trends and challenges rising from modern C-ITS. Section 2 briefly focuses on the specific context of V2X communications, especially within the 5G framework of reference. Section 3 discusses the V2X approach proposed in the 5G-DRIVE framework, which promotes corporative research and joint trials for 5G deployment and testing between the EU and China. Section 4 discusses the concept of the two selected use cases being about GLOSA and intelligent intersection. Our work summarises with an overview of our approach.

2   V2X Communications in the 5G Era

In order to reduce the number of road accidents and improve road safety, vehicles should be able to detect what is happening around them, predict what will happen next and take protective actions, *accordingly*. The case of "V2X" ("Vehicle-to-Everything", where "X" stands for "Vehicle" (V2V), "Network" (V2N), "Infrastructure" (V2I), "Cloud" (V2C), "Pedestrian" (V2P), "Road Side Unit (RSU)" (V2R) and "Sensors"(V2S)) is a sort of solution which can be assessed as a wireless sensor system allowing vehicles to share information (between them or with other (network) entities) via a dedicated communication channel [9]. Compared with standard sensors (such as radar, light detection and ranging (LIDAR), lasers, ultrasonic detectors, etc.) the use of a V2X communication system can allow reception of information out of sight and test of hidden threats, thus increasing driver's perception. Consequently, this improves driving safety, efficiency and comfort and results to an enhanced driving automation process [10]. This also contributes to the minimization of pollutant emissions and, in a more generalized concept, serves several "key" objectives of the EU transport policy. Automation, in the above framework, is assessed as "automated and autonomous driving applications" actively interacting with the intelligent surrounding environment.

5G-based Connected and Automated Mobility services along roads implicates for a wide variety of digital services in and around vehicles, including safety-related, transport efficiency-related and other commercial services offered, to become available or supported by 5G multi-service networks [11]. The growth of the next generation of mobile technologies (5G) is expected to become a critical "game changer" for most of the applications offered, as it allows for an extended range of connectivity performances including gigabit speeds and mission critical reliability, *among others*. The immense opportunities provided to all involved market actors, also including the so-called "vertical industries", further widen all potential options for innovation and economic growth, via the offering of new services/applications able to revolutionize our every-day experiences [12, 13].

The V2X technology becomes the next "big feature" to evolve further the automotive and transportation industry [14]. In particular, the V2X concept uses the latest generation of information and communication technology to realize omnidirectional

V2V, V2I, V2P and V2N/V2C network connection [15] and, consequently, the above types of V2X applications can use "co-operative awareness" to provide more intelligent services for the involved end-users. This means that entities, such as vehicles, road-side infrastructure, application server and pedestrians, can collect knowledge of their local environment (e.g., information received from other vehicles or sensor equipment in proximity) to process and share that knowledge in order to provide more intelligent services, such as cooperative collision warning or autonomous driving [9]. The basic categories of V2X services have originally been described in [16] and can be grouped into the following main categories based on ITS definition of basic set of services: (i) Road Safety Requirements (e.g., queue warning use case related requirements); (ii) Mutual Vehicle Awareness – Information only (e.g. forward collision warning requirements), and; (iii) Vehicle Related Application Requirements (e.g. automated parking system requirement). The related service requirements can be categorised as follows:

- *Latency Requirements:* This implicates for the maximum tolerable elapsed time from the instant a data packet is generated at the source application to the instant it is received by the destination application. Low Latency values are provided to support services in the case of mutual awareness of vehicle or to send warning messages as defined in some use cases in [16].
- *Reliability Requirements:* This implicates for the maximum tolerable packet loss rate at the application layer; a packet is considered lost if it is not received by the destination application within the maximum tolerable end-to-end latency for that application.
- *Message Size Requirements:* Messages sizes are important when multicast or broadcast messages are being sent to vehicles within range to either warn them for collision prevention or when an event occurs to inform other vehicle about an accident.
- *Frequency Requirements:* This implicates for the minimum required bit rate for the application, to function correctly. The sending rates, that is the frequency of messages, is a relatively important context, especially for critical vehicular safety application.
- *Range Requirements*: This is the maximum distance between source and destination(s) of a radio transmission, within which the application should achieve the specified reliability.
- *Speed Requirements:* It is the maximum relative and absolute speed under which the specified reliability should be achieved.

It is predicted that by 2022, there will be more than 125 million vehicles connected by various V2X technologies [17], being able to offer unprecedented safety, novel transportation services as well as other novelties [18].

3   5G-DRIVE's Implementation of V2X Communications

The consideration of V2X communications in various potential scenarios, implicates for a variety of concerns to be taken into account, as these strongly affect the applicability of modern solutions such as intelligent transportation and automated driving [19]. Each one among the potential solutions sets different requests about latency, reliability, throughput, user density, and safety of the corresponding V2X framework [16]. In recent years, different regions in the world have conducted intensively V2X trials. There are two V2X technical paths followed by the global automotive industry. One is the ETSI ITS-G5 [20], being an extension of the original IEEE 802.11p standard, modified and optimized for operation in a dynamic automotive environment; this sort of technology includes data exchange between high-speed vehicles and between the vehicles and the roadside infras- tructure in the licensed ITS band of 5.9 GHz (5.85–5.925 GHz). The other is the 3GPP LTE-V2X rooted from the 3GPP standards [21, 22]. The LTE-V2X is a wireless commu- nication technology for V2X with high data rate and controlled QoS [23] which is based on the evolution of LTE mobile communication technology defined by 3GPP, including two kinds of working modes of cellular communication (Uu) and direct communica- tion (PC5) [24]. The Uu mode uses the existing LTE cellular network to implement V2V communication by forwarding and the PC5 mode is similar to the dedicated short range communications (DSRC), enabling direct communication between vehicles [18]. Additionally, the PC5 interface has been enhanced in many aspects to accommodate exchanges of rapidly changing dynamic information (position, speed, driving direction, etc.) and future advanced V2X services (automatic driving, vehicle platooning, sensor sharing, etc.) [25]. 3GPP Releases 15 and 16 [26, 27] have defined both a traditional Base Station-User Equipment (BS-UE) Uu interface and a peer-to-peer PC5 interface for V2X communication. Those 5G systems are designed to support 10 ms end-to-end (E2E) latency, 1 ms physical (PHY) layer latency and 99.999% reliability.

Different regions show their own preference on the technologies. For example, China selects C-V2X (LTE-V2X) as the national standard while in Europe the debate is ongo- ing on how to adopt these technologies. The Cellular in association with V2X (C-V2X) is a communicating base that offers enhanced road safety and autonomous driving [28]. It uses a transmission mode called direct C-V2X, which provides longer communication range and higher reliability to connect "vehicles", "things" and "humans". The 5G Auto- motive Association (5GAA), the international association with the mission to promote C-V2X technologies, expects that the first commercial deployments of V2X will occur in China and Europe, while deployments in the US and other parts of Asia will follow closely. Considering that the life cycle of road infrastructure is normally 30 years, and the life cycle of a car is 10–15 years, the selection the V2X technology will be critical for the future evolution of technologies. For compatibility reasons, it is crucial that the various regions cooperate to ensure harmonization of technologies. Under this consid- eration, Europe and China have established a way of cooperation on C-V2X technology validation through joint research and trials.

The 5G-DRIVE EU-funded project [29] is one of the projects that work on C-V2X trials with China. One of the two fundamental aims of the project is to compare the performance in selected V2X use cases and identify any potential interoperability prob- lems, for the synchronization of the effective use of 5G technologies and for handling challenging spectrum issues before the expected wide roll-out of 5G. Towards this direc- tion, the 5G-DRIVE context focuses upon LTE-V2X communications using the 5.9 GHz band for Vehicle-to-Vehicle and the 3.5 GHz band for Vehicle-to-Network applications, by realizing demonstrations in real-life setups. The 5G-DRIVE scope supports collabo- rative actions between solid research competence, commercial grade test-beds and some of the stakeholders (who will eventually become major customers of the 5G systems and the proposed applications).

As previously mentioned, in Europe the V2X deployment is underpinned by the European Commission's C-ITS Framework Directive [2]. The related EU standardization efforts are driven by: (i) the European Car-2-Car Communication Consortium [5], an industry consortium of automobile manufacturers, suppliers and research organizations; (ii) ERTICO, a European organization of stakeholders with public and private partners, and; (iii) the ETSI's Centre for Testing and Interoperability (CTI). The C-ITS standards follow a general architecture, specified in [30] and [31], with the ITS station as the core element, representing vehicle, personal (mobile personal devices), roadside (infrastructure), and central (backend systems and traffic management centres) subsystems. For C-ITS, the ISO OSI reference model was adapted to cover horizontal layers for access technologies, networking and transport, facilities and applications, and vertical entities for management and security. In November 2016, the European Commission approved the C-ITS strategy for the EU, providing a legal framework to facilitate the convergence of investments and regulatory frameworks across the EU. In the EU, C-ITS services are implemented in phases, based on their priority [32]. There are two priority groups called *Day 1* and *Day 1.5* services [33]. The former have been deployed, starting from 2019; these services are used for hazardous location notifications and signage and include road works warning, weather conditions, emergency break light, etc. The later include in-vehicle signage, green light optimal speed advisory (GLOSA), traffic signal priority request, etc.; these services include vulnerable road user (VRU) protection, on/off street parking information, traffic information, etc.

In China, the V2X development is regulated by the Ministry of Industry and Information Technology (MIIT), the Ministry of Public Security (MPS) and the Ministry of Transport (MOT). The MIIT specifies the spectrum for V2V and V2I operation, and coordinates the C-V2X trial activities in China. The MPS takes charge of the standard revision on traffic light and regulations on traffic information access. The MOT is responsible for regulating the road infrastructure for V2X services. The three ministries have so identified the V2X test specification. So far, the LTE-V2X trials have been done in Wuxi, Shanghai, and other pilot areas. The V2X services defined, "match" the Day-1 C-ITS services defined by Europe. However, in China some Day-1.5 services (like VRU protection) have also been tested. C-V2X has initially been standardized by 3GPP in Release 14. Both Europe and China have adopted 5.9 GHz spectrum for the V2V, V2I, and V2P services. In addition, Qualcomm, Huawei, and Datang have released LTE-V2X chipsets and modules. The C-V2X standard continued in 3GPP release 15 for performance improvement. The 5G V2X, known as NR-V2X has been within the scope of 3GPP Release 16 and introduces the 5G New Radio features and low latency services into C-V2X.

A primary goal of C-ITS is to ensure users of the same service can interoperate with each other, to maximize the safety effect [34]. However, automotive and transport ecosystems involve different stakeholders such as car original equipment manufacturers (OEMs), regional roads and transport authorities as well as third-party service providers, who may adopt different implementation solutions when offering the same services. This makes interoperability of C-ITS services a real challenge. Even both Europe and China have considered C-V2X technologies, when comparing the different flavours of V2X standards, there are differences in terms of both message types and available functional capabilities. For example, while China uses Basic Safety Message (BSM) for both status information and event notifications, Europe has split these into Cooperative Awareness Message (CAM) and Decentralised Environmental Notification Message (DENM) [35]. The CAM protocol conveys critical vehicle state information in support of safety and traffic efficiency application, with which receiving vehicles can track other vehicles' positions and movement. The DENM protocol disseminates event-driven safety information in a geographical region. EU-China collaborative projects such as the case of 5G-DRIVE, investigate these inter-operability problems.

The purpose of the V2X trial collaboration between EU and China is to evaluate similar use cases and identify potential interoperability problems. 5G-DRIVE [29] is an EU H2020 project working under EU-China collaboration agreement and cooperates with a *5G Large-scale Trial project* led by China Mobile. One of its main objectives is to develop "key" 5G technologies at pre-commercial test-beds, test V2X services and then demonstrate IoV (Internet of Vehicles) services by using V2I and V2V communications. The project develops two dedicated use cases, that is the GLOSA (Green Light Optimised Speed Advisory) and intelligent intersection, while special attention is paid for automated driving challenges. Thus, 5G-DRIVE's framework promotes research and innovation cooperation on 5G and V2X through joint trials and dedicated research activities [36, 37]. The project incorporates 17 partners from 10 European countries and works on trials in V2N, V2V and V2I scenarios. The V2N scenario tests the performance of cellular network to support V2N services, in which DENM, In-Vehicle Information (IVI), Signal Phase and Timing (SPAT) and MAP messages [38] are evaluated. The multi-access edge computing (MEC) server is deployed in the 5G network to process vehicle sensing data. The V2V and V2I scenarios are realised by using LTE-V2X modules.

5G-DRIVE has two V2X trial sites in Espoo and in Ispra. The Espoo trial site is located in Karaportti area at Espoo, Finland, which is equipped with 3.5 GHz base-stations, LTE-V2X equipment and mobile traffic light. The length of the roads available in site is about 2.6 km including intersections and parking areas. The trial use cases in the Espoo trial site include GLOSA and intersection safety. The JRC site at Ispra, Italy, features 36 km of internal roads under real-life driving conditions and 9 vehicle emissions laboratories for calibration and electromagnetic compatibility and interference testing, *among others*. The JRC Ispra site also evaluates GLOSA and tests the co-existence of LTE-V2X and ITS-G5 in the 5.9 GHz band.

4 GLOSA and Intelligent Intersection V2X Use Cases

Since vehicles usually spend most of their time moving at high speed, this may have serious consequences when an accident happens and even threaten the safety of the driver and passengers. Safety always has the highest priority, so how to ensure vehicle safety has always been a serious topic.

A method to reduce extreme stop-and-go driving on urban streets is to optimize signal timings. Historically, signal timing optimization tools were developed to reduce delays and stops experienced by urban drivers. More recently, new methods in traffic signal optimization have incorporated changes in drivers' behaviour to achieve optimum performance at signalised intersections. In this framework, traffic lights control – as one of the traffic management methods – becomes an important and effective way to improve urban road capacity, ease traffic congestion and reduce vehicle delay time [39]. Traffic light forecast is a service that improves safety and convenience for drivers by assisting them at intersections. This includes services like Time-To-Green (TTG), which provides real time information about the traffic light cycles and Green Light Optimised Speed Advisory (GLOSA), which calculates the optimum approach speed to get a green light at the upcoming intersection [40]. These services that act as "cooperative" green light functions, implicate for several benefits as they: save fuel and reduce pollution; "bring" comfort to drivers; increase throughput, and; enhance safety as relaxed drivers can behave in a more secure way [41].

The GLOSA systems are an interesting "first-step" in advanced driver-assistance systems (ADAS) based on V2X communication with infrastructure, before the use of information by autonomous vehicles to handle intersections. A GLOSA-based business model aims to provide car drivers an optimized driving experience through real-time optimized speed advice; in this scope, a participating service provider will offer a software application (or an on-board unit) to the car drivers, thus enabling them to track their speed and location. Through integrating user/traffic data, the service provider will offer real-time advice with regards to the (expected) state of upcoming traffic lights, allowing the car drivers to alter their speed, accordingly.

A GLOSA system uses timely and accurate information about traffic signal timing and traffic signal locations to guide drivers (through infrastructure-to-vehicle communication) with speed advice for a more uniform commute with less stopping time through traffic signals [42]. A potential implementation can be evaluated for two types of traffic signal timing: predictable fixed-time signal timing and unpredictable actuated-coordinated signal timing. The objective of GLOSA systems is to provide to the driver the optimal speed to cross the next intersection with a green phase [43, 44]. GLOSA systems improve traffic efficiency by: (i) reducing stop times; (ii) bettering the fluidity of the traffic; (iii) giving anticipating data which improve the safety; and (iv) reducing CO_2 emissions, fuel consumption and reducing waiting time and travel time. This system can ensure a continuous flow of vehicles if several traffic lights are coordinated; moreover it is also useful for emergency vehicles to request a right of way if traffic lights are able to communicate. GLOSA systems have been shown to reduce significantly both CO_2 emissions and fuel consumption by giving drivers speed recommendations when approaching a traffic light [45, 46].

In a GLOSA use case, an RSU co-located with a traffic light (and having access to its internal finite state machine), broadcasts timing information about the traffic light's "red", "amber" and "green" status via SPAT messages. Neighbouring vehicles can receive these messages and process them locally along with their own positioning, speed and direction data. By doing so, on-board V2X modules can notify drivers about the optimal speed to reach an upcoming traffic light in green status or, alternatively, to be aware that the traffic light will nevertheless transition to red imminently. The dynamic information is disseminated using the SPAT V2X I2V message and contains the traffic lights' time to change and speed advice information that apply to group of ingressing lanes [47]. The MAP and SPAT messages are already standardized and profiled [48]. However, the interpretation of their content at the receiving side (cooperative vehicles) and the relation between this content and the actual current status of the traffic light controller can still lead to confusion. Knowing how to interpret the SPAT content at the receiving side is particularly critical in the case of Connected Automated Vehicles (CAVs) [49].

For the purpose of conducting the GLOSA trial, the JRC has deployed a commercial C-ITS roadside unit covering a section of its internal road infrastructure. The RSU sits at the junction of two suburban-type roads of 420 m and 220 m, respectively, at a height of approximately 10 m. In addition, the RSU is connected to the internal JRC network infrastructure to allow remote configuration, management and traffic monitoring. The commercial RSU runs an Automotive Grade Linux operating system, thus allowing the execution of custom user space applications (such as a virtual traffic light for the GLOSA service).

Intersections are hazardous places. The intersection plays an important role in the traffic network, but it is also one of the main causes of traffic accidents. Based on statistical data, more than 50% of the combined total of fatal and injury crashes in the U.S. in 2018 occurred at or near intersections [50]. Crashes near intersections might also lead to serious traffic jams on multiple roads, which apparently waste time and money of drivers and also cause unnecessary air pollution. It is also reported that about 94% of the intersection-related crashes had critical reasons attributed to drivers, such as inadequate surveillance, false assumption of other's action and turned with obstructed view [51]. Usual relevant threats arise from interactions among pedestrians, bicycles and vehicles, more complicated vehicle trajectories in the absence of lane markings, phases that prevent knowing who has the right of way, invisible vehicle approaches, vehicle obstructions and also illegal movements. Accidents can also occur because drivers, bicyclists and pedestrians do not have the information they need to avoid wrong decisions [52]. In these cases, the missing information can be calculated and communicated by an intelligent intersection [53, 54] so that to significantly enhance security [55]. A proper set of information may be about providing the current full signal phase, an estimate of the time when the phase will change, the occupancy of the blind spots of the driver or autonomous vehicle, and detection of red-light violators, *among others*. Following to the above concerns, the intersection management becomes one of the most challenging problems within the transport system for keeping traffic safety and smoothing traffic flow [56, 57]. Traffic light-based methods have been efficient but are not able to deal with the growing mobility and social challenges. On the other hand, the advancements of automation and communications have enabled cooperative intersection management [58, 59], where road users, infrastructure, and traffic control centres are able to communicate and coordinate the traffic safely and efficiently. Examples of intelligent management systems include machine learning methods, fuzzy systems, and multi agents, as well as enhancing V2I connectivity as in GLOSA systems. In all cases the objective is to ensure that the intersection operates well and serves the public [60].

By using V2V, V2I, and I2V communication and Autonomous Vehicle (AV) technologies, a sort of autonomous intersection management can improve the efficiency of existing intersections [61]. An intelligent intersection can broadcast two crucial information messages. A SPAT I2V message that the SAE has standardized [48], gives the full signal phase (not just the partial view of the signal that a user or AV has) and an estimate of the time when the signal phase will change. Together with what road users and AV sensors can see, SPAT eliminates most possible conflicts. The second message informs an AV [59] what its blind spots are and which of them (if any) is occupied by another user. Computation of the SPAT message requires real time access to the intersection phase. Calculation of blind spot occupancy requires real time sensing of well-defined regions of the intersection. These two messages can resolve all conflicts within the intersection. Active monitoring of intersections provides the driver and/or intelligent vehicle system a very important time advantage to take action, even before a problem would have otherwise become visible. This means the technology potentially allows drivers to take preventative action and avoid critical situations. The 5G-DRIVE intelligent intersection use case deals with safety on intersections, by focusing on infrastructure detection situations that are difficult to perceive by vehicles themselves. A good example is the situation where a vehicle wants to make a right turn while parallel VRUs also have a green phase and right of way (permissive green for motorized traffic), as depicted in Fig. 1(a).

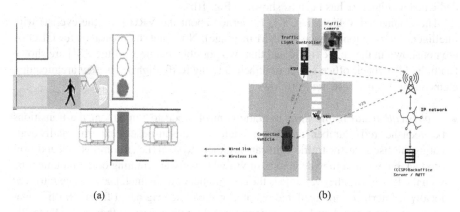

(a)   (b)

Fig. 1. (a) Intelligent intersection; (b) proposed joint architecture for both uses cases.

When a pedestrian is detected on the crosswalk (as in the grey area of Fig. 1(a)) a Decentralised Environmental Notification Message (DENM) should be broadcasted by the RSU. (A DENM is structured as a code for a specific warning event together with a small map of the relevance area and the approach towards it and the approach is similar to the principle of the MAP, so that vehicles should check whether they are close to the approach and driving in the same direction). When the DENM message is transmitted, the back-office should geocast this to all vehicles in the vicinity. This is to warn vehicles further upstream that a potential conflict may occur in the future and to prevent future hard braking. In the yellow areas of Fig. 1(a), given a movement direction of the pedestrian towards the intersection, the infrastructure should send out Collective Perception Messages (CPM) [62]. This is to warn vehicles further upstream that a potential conflict may occur in the future and to prevent future hard braking. This use case deals with safety on intersections, focusing on infrastructure detection of situations that are difficult to perceive by vehicles themselves. The example of the collision avoidance is shown in Fig. 1(a). In this example, a vehicle wants to make a right turn, while parallel VRUs also have a green phase and right of way (permissive green for motorized traffic). Other DENMs can also be tested within the 5G-DRIVE, as the DENM message supports various warnings. Depending on the complexity of the warning, the message can have a different length, which can result in different results with regards to communication performance. It should be noted that the focus of the use case is not on the human-machine interface, but on the V2X performance and that situations on the test tracks are mostly emulated not to put real pedestrians at risk and ease requirements on timing the approach of the vehicle.

The intelligent intersection use case development has been done in parallel with the GLOSA use case. GLOSA is dedicated for sending CAM messages but intelligent intersection is dedicated for using SPAT messages to improve vehicle situation awareness. Currently, the vehicle and interfaces exist in the software level and first implementation exists but with ITS G5. Now the communication devices are changed to C-V2X but this should not influence to messages minimally. A joint set-up supporting both use cases has been proposed in the trials taking place at the site in Finland. For this purpose, a dedicated architecture has been as shown in Fig. 1(b).

The Connected Vehicle 1 (CV1) is warned about the VRU (i.e., the cyclist) with intelligent intersection service (DENM message). Note that the messages for GLOSA are not shown in the above figure and that two possible locations of the RSU are shown (with the MEC/back-office server or attached to the traffic light). The key architectural elements of this use case are as follows:

- A *physical/virtual traffic light* in static control mode to implement the transitions between the "red", "amber" and "green" states. For the purpose of experimentally evaluating this use case, the traffic light can be either physical (i.e., a commercial, end-user product, but without loop detectors) or virtual (a software running on/communicating with the RSU). Another variable is the communication channel. Data can be retrieved locally if interfaces are available on-site, or it can be originated from a traffic management centre and distributed to communicate with agents in the field. The traffic light is only required for the GLOSA use case and the content of the SPAT message has to be retrieved from it.
- An *LTE-V2X RSU* as well as a *ITS-G5 RSU,* both co-located with the traffic light (if physical) or running/communicating with the traffic light implementation (if virtual). When a VRU is detected in the zebra crossing of Fig. 1(b), a DENM should be broadcasted by the RSU, while the back-office should geocast this to all vehicles in the vicinity. In the yellow areas, given a movement direction of the VRU towards the intersection, the infrastructure should send out CPM. For GLOSA it should broadcast both MAP and SPAT messages.
- At least *two (on-board units) OBUs* (one ITS-G5, one LTE-V2X) deployed in the test vehicles. The OBUs receive and process the MAP, SPAT, DENM and CPM messages locally to show GLOSA information or compute the potential conflicts with the VRUs on the zebra crossing and also warn vehicles further upstream that a potential conflict may occur in the future and to prevent future hard braking.

- An *automated vehicle with sensors* to fill CPM messages with real sensor data in V2V scenarios.
- A *traffic camera* detecting and tracking vulnerable road users (VRUs).
- A *traffic camera server* can provide connectivity between the RSUs and various supporting services/servers running in the respective testing data centre. When a pedestrian is detected in the zebra crossing, a DENM should be broadcasted by the RSU, while the RSU back-office server should geocast this to all vehicles in the vicinity (Connected vehicle 1, Connected vehicle 2). In the yellow areas, given a movement direction of the VRU towards the intersection, the infrastructure should send out CPM. The length of the yellow area is the same as the length of the zebra area. For more controlled testing it should also be possible to generate messages based on emulated VRU movements.
- *RSU back-office server* in the data centre running all needed supporting services.

5   Concluding Remarks

In the scope of the present work we have discussed the important role of V2X communications for the promotion of modern 5G features, especially within the area of C-ITS and automated driving, towards enhancing traffic management in urban environments and also enhancing road safety. The way of realising any possible solution, also implicates for different demands as of latency, reliability, throughput, user density and safety. More specifically, our approach has been around the scope of the innovative research performed by the 5G-DRIVE project, which is a synergetic collaborative effort between EU and China that promotes testing LTE-V2X communications using the 5.9 GHz band for V2V applications and the 3.5 GHz band for V2N applications. Our main focus has been about the discussion of the two 5G-DRIVE selected uses cases, that is GLOSA and intelligent intersection. Both can offer a multiplicity of advantages for the participating users at various domains ranging from enhanced road safety and comfort to the reduction of fuel consumption and emissions.

For the 5G-DRIVE project, GLOSA is an attractive V2X use case to improve the traffic flow. It provides drivers an optimal speed advice when they approach to a signalized intersection and they are instructed to maintain actual speed, slow down, or adapt a specific speed. On the other hand, intelligent intersections have been assessed as "indispensable" parts of modern road infrastructures, especially with the aim or proving the necessary information preventing from accidents and allowing for better security of both drivers and VRUs, while on-the-move. Both use cases have been discussed and assessed as of their respective technological background, especially via the use of dedicated, per case, messages serving informative purposes. In addition, on the basis of the 5G-DRIVE trials, we have proposed a sort of joint architectural approach able to serve both use cases. Future trials will provide more detailed results on the potential applicability and the novelties provided by our approach.

Acknowledgments. This work has been performed in the scope of the *5G-DRIVE* European Research Project and has been supported by the Commission of the European Communities/H2020, Grant Agreement No. 814956.

References

1. European Telecommunications Standards Institute (ETSI): TR 102 638 V1.1.1 (2009-06): Intelligent Transport Systems; Vehicular Communications; Basic set of Applications; Definitions (2009)
2. European Parliament and Council: Directive 2010/40/EU of the European Parliament and of the Council of 7 July 2010 on the framework for the deployment of Intelligent Transport Systems in the field of road transport and for interfaces with other modes of transport. Official Journal (OJ) L207, 06 August 2010, pp. 1–13 (2010)
3. European Commission: Communication on A European Strategy on Cooperative Intelligent Transport Systems, a milestone towards cooperative, connected and automated mobility. [COM(2016) 766 final] (2016)
4. European Telecommunications Standards Institute (ETSI): ETSI TS 103 723 V1.2.1: Intelligent Transport Systems (ITS); Profile for LTE-V2X Direct Communication (2020)
5. Car-to-Car Communication Consortium: Basic System Profile, Release 1.5.0. (2020)
6. C-Roads Platform. https://www.c-roads.eu
7. Festag, A.: Cooperative intelligent transport systems in Europe. IEEE Commun. Mag. 53(12), 64–70 (2015)
8. Lu, M., Blokpoel, R.J.: A sophisticated intelligent urban road-transport network and cooperative systems infrastructure for highly automated vehicles. In: Proceedings of the 2016 World Congress on Intelligent Transport Systems, pp. 1–8 (2016)
9. Storck, C.R., Duarte-Figueiredo, F.: A survey of 5G technology evolution, standards, and infrastructure associated with vehicle-to-everything communications by internet of vehicles. IEEE Access 8, 117593–117614 (2020)
10. Next Generation Mobile Networks (NGMN) Alliance Ltd.: V2X White Paper – V1.0 (2018). https://www.ngmn.org/wp-content/uploads/V2X_white_paper_v1_0-1.pdf
11. 5G Public Private Partnership (5G-PPP):2020): 5G Strategic Deployment Agenda for Connected and Automated Mobility in Europe (2020)
12. Andrews, J.G., Buzzi, S., Choi, W., et al.: What Will 5G Be? IEEE JSAC 32(6), 1065–1082 (2014). Special Issue on 5G Wireless Communications Systems
13. Malandrino, F., Chiasserini, C.F.: Present-day verticals and where to find them: a data-driven study on the transition to 5G. In: Proceedings of the 2018 14th Annual Conference on Wireless On-demand Network Systems and Services (WONS), pp. 1–5 (2018)
14. Global System for Mobile Communications Association (GSMA): Connecting Vehicles – Today and In the 5G Era with C-V2X – White Paper (2019)
15. 5G Americas: Cellular V2X Communications Towards 5G – White Paper (2018)
16. The 3rd Generation Partnership Project (3GPP): 3GPP TR 22.885 V14.0.0: Study on LTE Support for Vehicle to Everything (V2X) Services Architecture Enhancements for V2X Services (Release 14) (2015)
17. Counterpoint: Global Connected Car Tracker 2018, Market Research Report (2018)
18. Chen, S., Hu, J., et al.: Vehicle-to-everything (V2X) services supported by LTE-based systems and 5G. IEEE Commun. Stand. Mag. 1(2), 70–76 (2017)
19. Rebbeck, T., Steward, J., Lacour, H.A., Killeen, A., et al.: Final Report for 5GAA Socio-Economic Benefits of Cellular V2X. 5G Automotive Association (5GAA) (2017)
20. Eckhoff, D., Sofra, N., German, R.: A performance study of cooperative awareness in ETSI ITS G5 and IEEE WAVE. In: Proceedings of the 2013 10th Annual Conference on Wireless On-demand Network Systems and Services (WONS), pp. 1–5 (2013)
21. Roux, P., Sesia, S., Mannoni, V., Perraud, E.: System level analysis for ITS-G5 and LTE-V2X performance comparison. In: Proceedings of the 2019 IEEE 16th International Conference on Mobile Ad Hoc and Sensor Systems (MASS-2019), pp. 1–9. IEEE (2019)

22. Molina-Masegosa, R., Gozalvez, J., Sepulcre, M.: Comparison of IEEE 802.11p and LTE-V2X: an evaluation with periodic and aperiodic messages of constant and variable size. IEEE Access **8**, 121526–121548 (2020)

23. Araniti, G., Campolo, C., Condoluci, M., Iera, A., Molinaro, A.: LTE for vehicular networking: a survey. IEEE Commun. Mag. **51**(5), 148–157 (2013)

24. The 3rd Generation Partnership Project (3GPP): 3GPP TS 23.285 V14.9.0: Architecture Enhancements for V2X Services (Release 14) (2019)

25. 5G Automotive Association (5GAA): An Assessment of LTE-V2X (PC5) and 802.11p Direct Communications Technologies for Improved Road Safety in the EU (2017)

26. The Third Generation Partnership Project (3GPP): TR 21.915 V15.0.0: Release 15 Description; Summary of Rel-15 Work Items (Release 15) (2019)

27. The Third Generation Partnership Project (3GPP): TR 21.916 V1.0.0: Release 16 description; Summary of Rel-16 Work Items (Release 16) (2020)

28. Kutila, M., Pyykonen, P., Huang, O., Deng, W., Lei, W., Pollakis, E.: C-V2X supported automated driving. In: Proceedings of the IEEE 2019 International Conference on Communications, Workshops (ICC Workshops 2019), pp. 1–5. IEEE (2019)

29. 5G-DRIVE Project (Grant Agreement No. 814956). https://5g-drive.eu/

30. European Telecommunications Standards Institute (ETSI): EN 302 665 V1.1.1: Intelligent Transport Systems (ITS); Communication Architecture (2010)

31. International Organization for Standardization (ISO): ISO 21217:2014 (Intelligent transport systems - Communications access for land mobiles (CALM) – Architecture (2014)

32. European Commission: C-ITS platform, Technical report (2016)

33. Mellegård, N., Reichenberg, F.: The day 1 C-ITS application green light optimised speed advisory - a mapping study. Elsevier Transp. Res. Procedia **49**, 170–182 (2020)

34. Lu, M., Türetken, O., Adali, O.E., Castells, J., Blokpoel, R., Grefen, P.: C-ITS (Cooperative Intelligent Transport Systems) deployment in Europe - challenges and key findings. In: Proceedings of the 25th ITS World Congress, pp. 1–10 (2018)

35. European Telecommunications Standards Institute (ETSI): ETSI EN 302 637-3 V1.2.2: ITS Vehicular Communications: Basic Set of Applications; Part 3: Specification of Decentralized Environmental Notification Basic Service (2014)

36. Kostopoulos, A., Chochliouros, I.P., et al.: 5G trial cooperation between EU and China. In: Proceedings of the IEEE 2019 International Conference on Communications, Workshops (ICC Workshops 2019), pp. 1–6. IEEE (2019)

37. Chochliouros, I.P., et al.: Testbeds for the implementation of 5G in the European Union: the innovative case of the 5G-DRIVE project. In: MacIntyre, J., Maglogiannis, I., Iliadis, L., Pimenidis, E. (eds.) AIAI 2019. AICT, vol. 560, pp. 78–92. Springer, Cham (2019). https://doi.org/10.1007/978-3-030-19909-8_7

38. Amelink, M.: Signal phase and time (SPAT) and map data (MAP). Amsterdam Group (2015)

39. Yang, K., Guler, S.I., Menendez, M.: Isolated intersection control for various levels of vehicle technology: conventional, connected, and automated vehicles. Transp. Res. Part C: Emerg. Technol. **72**, 109–129 (2016)

40. Stevanovic, A., Stevanovic, J., Kergaye, C.: Green light optimized speed advisory systems: impact of signal phasing information accuracy. J. Transp. Res. Board **2390**(1), 53–59 (2013)

41. Radivojevic, D., Stevanovic, J., Stevanovic, A.: Impact of green light optimized speed advisory on unsignalized side-street traffic. J. Transp. Res. Board **2557**(1), 24–32 (2016)

42. Katsaros, K., Kernchen, R., Dianati, M., and Rieck, D.: Performance study of a green light optimized speed advisory (GLOSA) application using an integrated cooperative ITS simulation platform. In: Proceedings of the 7th International Wireless Communications and Mobile Computing Conference (IWCMC), pp. 918–923 (2011)

43. Lebre, M.A., Le Mouël, F., Ménard, E., Garnault, A., et al.: Real scenario and simulations on GLOSA traffic light system for reduced CO_2 emissions, waiting time and travel time. In: Proceedings of the 22nd ITS World Congress, pp. 1–12 (2015)
44. Wan, N., Luckow, A., Vahidi, A.: Optimal speed advisory for connected vehicles in arterial roads and the impact on mixed traffic. Transp. Res. Part C: Emerg. Technologies **69**, 548–563 (2016)
45. Bradaï, B., Garnault, A., Picron, V., Gougeon, P.: A green light optimal speed advisor for reduced CO_2 emissions. In: Langheim, J. (ed.) Energy Consumption and Autonomous Driving. LNM, pp. 141–151. Springer, Cham (2016). https://doi.org/10.1007/978-3-319-19818-7_15
46. Bodenheimer, R., et al.: Enabling GLOSA for adaptive traffic lights. In: Proceedings of the IEEE 2014 Vehicular Networking Conference (VNC), pp. 167–174. IEEE (2014)
47. MAVEN Project: Deliverable 4.1 Cooperative adaptive traffic light with automated vehicles (Initial version) (2018)
48. Society of Automotive Engineers (SAE): SAE J2735_201603, Dedicated Short Range Communications (DSRC) Message Set Dictionary (2016)
49. Englund, C., Chen, L., Ploeg, J., et al.: The grand cooperative driving challenge 2016: boosting the introduction of cooperative automated vehicles. IEEE Wirel. Commun. **23**(4), 146–152 (2016)
50. U.S. Department of Transportation, Federal Highway Administration: Safety Evaluation of Multiple Strategies at Signalized Intersections (Publication No. FHWA-HRT-17-062) (2018). https://www.fhwa.dot.gov/publications/research/safety/17062/17062.pdf
51. General Motors. GM self-driving safety report (2018)
52. Ahn, H., Del Vecchio, D.: Safety verification and control for collision avoidance at road intersections. IEEE Trans. Autom. Control Syst. **63**(3), 630–642 (2018)
53. Grembek, O., Kurzhanskiy, A., et al.: Making intersections safer with I2V communication. Transp. Res. Part C Emerg. Technol. **102**, 396–410 (2019)
54. Guler, S.I., et al.: Using connected vehicle technology to improve the efficiency of intersections. Transp. Res. Part C: Emerg. Technologies **46**, 121–131 (2014)
55. Kurzhanskiy, A., Varaiya, P.: Safety and Sustainability with Intelligent Intersections. University of California, Berkeley (2019)
56. Chen, L., Englund, C.: Cooperative intersection management: a survey. IEEE Trans. Intell. Transp. Syst. **17**(2), 570–586 (2016)
57. Rios-Torres, J., Malikopoulos, A.A.: A survey on the coordination of connected and automated vehicles at intersections and merging at highway on-ramps. IEEE Trans. Intell. Transp. Syst. **18**(5), 1066–1077 (2016)
58. Chouhan, A.P., Banda, G.: Autonomous intersection management: a heuristic approach. IEEE Access **6**, 53287–53295 (2018)
59. Namazi, F., et al.: Intelligent intersection management systems considering autonomous vehicles: a systematic literature review. IEEE Access **7**, 91946–91965 (2019)
60. Muralidharan, A., Coogan, S., et al.: Management of intersections with multi-modal high-resolution data. Transp. Res. Part C **68**, 101–112 (2016)
61. Wuthishuwong, C., Traechtler, A.: Consensus-based local information coordination for the networked control of the autonomous intersection management. Complex Intell. Syst. **3**(1), 17–32 (2017)
62. European Telecommunications Standards Institute (ETSI): ETSI TR 103 562 V0.0.15: Intelligent Transport System (ITS); Vehicular Communications; Basic Set of Applications; Analysis of the Collective -Perception Service (CPS) (2019)

Artificial Intelligence in Biomedical Engineering and Informatics Workshop (AI-BIO 2021)

AI-BIOMED 2021 Workshop

Artificial Intelligence (AI) is gradually changing the routine of medical practice and the level of acceptance by medical personnel is constantly increasing. Recent progress in digital medical data acquisition through advanced biosignal and medical imaging devices, machine learning, and high-performance cloud computing infrastructures, push health-related AI applications into areas that were previously thought to be only the province of human experts. Such applications employ a variety of methodologies including fuzzy logic, evolutionary calculations, neural networks, or deep learning. Advanced image processing and artificial intelligence methods can support medical diagnostics, follow-up monitoring, preventive medicine, assessment of therapy, and many other domains. These areas have been in recent years the subject of many research papers and research grants. Consequently, this workshop is devoted to the subject of artificial intelligence, in its broadest sense, in biomedical engineering and health informatics.

The workshop aims to support research and innovation on Artificial Intelligence in Biomedical Engineering and Informatics (AI-BIOMED) and especially in:

- Wearable Systems
- Medical and Sensor Data Processing
- Machine Learning in eHealth
- Medical Image Analysis and Radiomics
- Robotics in Biomedical Engineering
- Quantified Self Technologies and Applications
- Intelligent Data Processing and Predictive Algorithms in eHealth
- Smart Homes and Assistive Environments
- Data Mining of Health Data on the Cloud
- Security, Safety, and Privacy in Intelligent eHealth Applications

Organization

Workshop Chairs

Ilias Maglogiannis   University of Piraeus, Greece
Ioanna Chouvarda   Aristotle University of Thessaloniki, Greece
Spyretta Golemati   National and Kapodistrian University
                                   of Athens, Greece
Michail Sarafidis   National Technical University of Athens,
                                   Greece

A Machine Learning Approach for Recognition of Elders' Activities Using Passive Sensors

Anastasios Panagiotis Psathas$^{(\boxtimes)}$ ⓘ, Antonios Papaleonidas$^{(\boxtimes)}$ ⓘ, and Lazaros Iliadis ⓘ

Department of Civil Engineering, Democritus University of Thrace, 67100 Xanthi, Greece
{anpsatha,papaleon,liliadis}@civil.duth.gr

Abstract. The increasing ageing population around the world, is calling for technological innovations that can improve the lives of elderly people. Real time monitoring their activities is imperative in order to mitigate the detrimental occurrences and dangerous events like falls. The aim of this research is to develop and test a Machine Learning model, capable to determine the activity performed by the elderly in their everyday environment. Data for this research was acquired by setting up two fully monitored rooms, equipped with *Radio Frequency Identification* (RFID) antennas, while subjects who participated in the experiment were wearing a *Wearable Wireless Identification* and *Sensing Platform* (W^{2}ISP) tag. The dataset consisted of 14 healthy elders, who would perform four activities namely: sitting on the bed, sitting on a chair, lying in bed and ambulating. Nine independent variables were used, eight of which were obtained by the sensors as raw data vectors and the ninth is the gender. The final data set includes 75,128 records. Totally, 25 Classification Algorithms were used in an effort to determine the more efficient model. The best performance has been achieved by employing the *Bagged Trees* algorithm. A combination of *10-fold Cross validation* and *Grid Search* was used in order to tune the values of the hyperparameters and to avoid any form of overfitting or underfitting. The accuracy and the generalization ability of the optimal model, have been proved by the high values of all performance indices, with a very small deviation for the case of the fourth activity. Thus, this approach can be reliably used (with low cost) by caregivers, hospital staff or anyone else in charge, to watch for potentially dangerous situations for the elders.

Keywords: Elders' activity recognition · Machine Learning · Bagged Trees · Human activity recognition · RFID · W^{2}ISP

1 Introduction

Rapid development of microelectronics and computer systems over the last decade, led to the implementation of sensors and wearable devices with unprecedented features [22]. High computing power, small size and low cost of sensors and computing devises allow people to interact with appliances in their daily lives [41]. Monitoring and classifying human activities using body-sensors is emerging as an important research area

© IFIP International Federation for Information Processing 2021
Published by Springer Nature Switzerland AG 2021
I. Maglogiannis et al. (Eds.): AIAI 2021 Workshops, IFIP AICT 628, pp. 157–170, 2021.
https://doi.org/10.1007/978-3-030-79157-5_14

in Machine Learning (ML) [26]. The use of wearable sensors, such as gyroscopes and accelerometers, for activity recognition, is becoming increasingly popular in relation to computer vision and video analysis [11]. Computer vision and video analysis are limited by the computational resources of mobile and ubiquitous systems, as well as by the diversified, dynamic environment in which such systems need to operate [16].

Sensor-based activity recognition has many potential applications, including health monitoring [12], assisted living [20] and sports coaching [35]. The aim of such efforts is mitigation of activities for the elderly at high risk of falling, especially in hospitals or in age care facilities. It is interesting that such accidents often occur in the bedroom [2]. The rapid increase in the number of old people in our post-modern societies during the recent decades, has called for ways to make their lives easier. Many of these people live alone and in most of the cases they do not have someone to take care of them all the time. Fourth industrial revolution can offer a solution towards this major humanistic and social problem. A correct recognition of such high risk events can lead to an intervention to mitigate an event that can potentially cause further physical injury and mental distress [21]. Accurate recognition of real time activities is imperative as most falls occur during moving in the house i.e. changes of static activities or locations namely: sit to stand, stand to sit or ambulating [29].

The development of models for *Human Activity Recognition* (HAR) is a growing field of study, with many potential applications [37]. In 2006, Pirttikangas et al. [23] tested a Multilayer Perceptron and k-Nearest Neighbor (k-NN) model for HAR of 17 activities, achieving an overall recognition accuracy of 90.61%. In 2011, Casale et al. [9], used the *Random Forest* algorithm, in order to model *walking, climbing stairs, talking with a person, staying standing, and working at compute*r. They achieved an overall accuracy around 90%. In 2013, Ahmed and Loutfi [1] performed HAR by using *Case Based Reasoning, Support Vector Machines* (SVM) and *Neural Networks* (NN), achieving overall accuracy equal to 0.86, 0.62 and 0.59 respectively for 3 categories of activities (*breathing, walk or run, sitting and relaxing*). In 2018, Brophy et al. [7], proposed a hybrid *Convolutional NN-SVM* model with an overall HAR accuracy equal to 92.3% for 4 activities (*walking and running on a treadmill, low and high resistance bike exercise*). A more recent research was made by Mehdi et al. (2019) [4], where a *Deep NN* was developed for 5 activities (*Standing, Walking, Jogging, Jumping and Sitting*). The model had an F1-score equal to 0.86. In 2020, Psathas et al. [24], applied a combination of *Fast Fourier Transform* (FFT) and *Bagged Trees* for HAR of 15 subjects who performed 8 different activities, achieving an overall accuracy of 92.8%.

Most of the sensors used in the above researches are bulky, battery powered, strapped or attached to various parts of participant bodies. The use of these sensors for monitoring particularly elders, is unsuitable as reported by user's acceptability studies [14]. Furthermore, these types of sensors also require maintenance such as regular recharging or replacement of batteries during their operational life. In contrast, a new generation of passive (battery less) sensors, such as sensor-enabled RFID tags [17] are offering exciting new prospects for wearable sensor-based applications. Passive sensors are lightweight and small, hence they can be used for discreet/unobtrusive monitoring. Furthermore passive sensors are maintenance free, as they require no battery while at the same time they can be easily embedded into garments, turning removal of the monitoring device, especially by cognitively impaired patients, not an easy task [19].

Recent studies show that passive devices can be really efficient for HAR performance. In 2014 Wang et al. [40], introduced a wearable system using passive tags for subjects which achieved an accuracy of 93.6% on HAR. In 2016, Li et al. [23] described an Activity Recognition System (ARS) for dynamic and complex medical setting, using passive RFID technology, achieving an accuracy of 96% and 0.74 F-Score for 10 medical activities. In 2018, Ryoo et al. [30], proposed a *Backscattering Activity Recognition Network of Tags* (BARNET) which comprises of a network of passive Radio Frequency (RF) tags, capable to recognize human daily activities with an average error of 6%. In 2016, Shinmoto et al. [34], developed a RFID system with W^2ISP tags for generating bed and chair exit alerts for elders achieving an overall accuracy equal to 94%.

In this paper, the authors have chosen to use the publicly available dataset *Activity recognition with healthy elders, using a battery-less wearable sensor* [39]. The aim of this research is the activity recognition of 14 healthy elders (*siting on bed, siting on chair, lying on bed and ambulating*) in specially designed rooms to simulate hospital conditions using a RFID system with W^2ISP tags.

The innovation of this research effort is the extensive use of Machine Learning (ML) algorithms and the exhaustive search for the determination of the optimal model using the employment of 10-fold Cross Validation with Grid Search. Data from passive sensors are usually characterized by sparsity and noise [42]. Thus, HAR modeling is a challenging task.

The rest of the paper is organized as follows. Section 2 describes the dataset and its features. Section 3 provides the architecture of the proposed model. Section 4 presents the experimental results and the evaluation of the model. Finally, Sect. 5 concludes the research.

2 Dataset

As it has already been said, the data set chosen for this study is the publicly available *Activity recognition with healthy elders using a battery-less wearable sensor* [39]. It was developed by *Roberto Luis Shinmoto Torres, Damith Ranasinghe and Renuka Visvanathan* of the *University of Adelaide* [38]. It contains 75,128 records of sequential motion data from 14 healthy elders aged 66 to 86 years old, while performing 4 different activities wearing passive and battery-less sensors, in two clinic rooms. The records for each activity and each room are presented in the following Table 1.

Table 1. Total Record for each activity and each room

	Sitting on bed	Lying on bed	Ambulating	Sitting on chair	Total
Room 1	15162 (25.89%)	30983 (59.04%)	1956 (3.73%)	4381 (8.35%)	52,482
Room 2	1253 (5.53%)	20529 (90.65%)	334 (1.47%)	530 (2.34%)	22,646

The authors' previous effort [24] performed HAR of fifteen subjects aged between 21–55 years old, regarding eight activities (e.g. *ascending/descending stairs, cycling*) using *Photoplethysmography* (PPG) and *Electrocardiogram* (ECG) Sensors. Thus, the selection of this data set is ideal, as it extends the research effort to a different age group, with different activities (more static), using passive sensors that have sparsity and noise in their sampling [42].

2.1 The Sensor Platform – Hardware Description

The sensing platform used in this study consists of:

- W^2ISP compatible passive sensor, enabling RFID tag [32].
- RFID infrastructure consisting of a commercial-off-the-shelf *Ultra high frequency* (UHF) RFID reader (Impinj IPJ-REV-R420-GX11M operating in the frequency range 920–926 MHz) and circularly polarized antennas (Laird S9028PCLJ) [27].

The W^2ISP RFID tag contains a triaxial accelerometer (ADXL330) with a flexible antenna for wearability [17] and a microprocessor (MSP430F2132) [34]. W^2ISP devices are small, battery free, can be read approximately from a distance of 4 m when worn by a human, weighs approximately 3 g and the mass production cost per tag is estimated to be about \$3 [8]. When a W^2ISP tag is adequately powered, a data stream with an upper bound of 40 Hz sampling rate can be obtained. The W^2ISP tag is powered by the energy collected from the electromagnetic field created by the RFID antennas [27].

The RFID infrastructure is also used to collect data from the W^2ISP tag where the communication is governed by the air interface protocol ISO 18000-6C [36]. A single RFID compatible sensor platform can communicate with multiple tags and individual W^2ISP tags can be identified using the unique electronic identifier communicated by the W^2ISP tag along with the sensor data.

The triaxial accelerometer embedded in W^2ISP tag measures the acceleration resulting from a participant's motion and the component of gravity along the accelerometer's axes: *frontal* (a_f), *vertical* (a_v), and *lateral* (a_l). The RFID reader provides tag activation and measures the strength of the wireless signal, backscattered from the W^2ISP tag, where this information is correlated with the distance between an RFID reader antenna and the W^2ISP tag. The power of the radio signal of an observation sent by the tag and received by a specific antenna and measured by an RFID reader is referred to as the received signal strength indicator (RSSI) [27]. It is recorded with the antenna identifier (aID) that captures a given observation from the W^2ISP tag. Thus, a single sensor observation can be represented as the five feature vector [a_f, a_v, a_l, RSSI, aID]. The W^2ISP tag is attached to silver fabric and the subjects ware it at chest height.

2.2 Rooms Setting

Most falls of the elderly occur around the bed and the chair area, both in residential houses and clinics [42]. Thus, the developers of the data set, decided that sampling should be done in areas that simulate hospital rooms. These two rooms were framed with RFID antennas. In room 1, 4 reading antennas were used (one at ceiling level and three at the wall), while in rooms 2, 3 antennas were used (two at ceiling level and one at the wall) [38]. The antennas were strategically placed so as to cover the maximum space inside the room. Each subject was asked to perform a series of broadly scripted activity routines that were an alternation between activities (1) *sitting on bed*, (2) *lying on bed,* (3) *sitting on chair* and (4) *walking from A to B*, where A, B are the bed, chair or door [41]. Totally, 10 subjects were recorded for the first room 1, and five for the 2nd. One subject participated in both rooms.

2.3 Dataset Features

The data set consists of nine features, eight of which are generated by the W^2ISP sensor and by the RFID reader and one is the gender of the subject. The features resulting from the sensor and the reader are presented in Table 2.

Table 2. Features from W^2ISP Sensor and RFID reader

Feature	Abbreviation
Record time	tID
Antenna identification	aID
Acceleration on X axis	a_v
Acceleration on Y axis	a_l
Acceleration on Z axis	a_f
Frequency channel	fCH
Phase	φ
Received signal strength indicator	RSSI

The three axes X, Y and Z are relative to the sensor; where vertical (v), lateral (l) and frontal (f) axes are relative to the subject. The tID refers to time (in seconds) of each record. The features RSSI, fCH, a_v, a_l, a_f and aID were described in Sect. 2.1. Phase refers to the magnitude that expresses the removal of an oscillating body from its equilibrium position at a given point in time. In radio waves, the phase refers to how far the sensor is from the antenna that recorded the measurement.

The activities performed by the subjects, were observed and recorded along with the label of each activity by a researcher. Thus, alongside the features of the dataset, the label of each activity (Table 3) is included. More information about the dataset can be found in [34, 38, 39, 41, 42].

Table 3. Activity with the corresponding label

Activity	Sitting on bed	Sitting on chair	Lying on bed	Ambulating
Activity label	1	2	3	4

2.4 Dataset Pre-processing

The dataset provides 60 *.csv files for room 2 and 28 *.csv files for room 2. Each *.csv file includes the eight features from the W^2ISP sensor and the RFID reader and the label for each record. The feature *Gender* of the participant is included in the last character *.csv name. Matlab Platform was chosen, in order to perform the pre-processing of the dataset. Data handling has been achieved by writing code from scratch. The following Algorithm 1 is presenting in a natural language form, the Matlab Script reading people data (Table 4).

Algorithm 1. The Read_Patiences.m Matlab Script

Script: *Read_Patiences.m*
Inputs: The 87 *.csv files
    Step 1: For i = 1, 2, ..., 87:
        a. Read the ith *.csv file and convert it in *Matlab_Table_i* (x_i rows and 9 columns)
        b. Read the title of the ith *.csv file. If the letter M (Male) is included add a column to *Matlab_Table_i* with x_i rows and the value 1. Else, if the letter F (Female) is included add a column to *Matlab_Table_i* with x_i rows and the value 2.
    Step 2: Append the 87 in one *Matlab_Table* ($x_1 + x_2 + ... + x_{87}$ = 75,128 rows and 10 columns)
    Step 3: Shuffle the rows of the *Matlab_Table* (to eliminate any pattern on the original data)
    Step 4: Apply Principal Component Analysis (PCA) [43] at the 9 columns of the table (except label column)
    Step 5: Discard the columns that PCA indicates (tID feature was selected based on the correlation matrix of PCA, see Table 4) and form the *Final_Table* (75,128 x 9).
    Step 6: Split the *Final_Table* (75,128 x 9) into 2 tables: (1) **Train Data** (70% of *Final_Table*), (2) **Test Data** (30% of *Final_Table*).
Outputs: (1) **Train Data** (52,724 x 9), (2) **Test Data** (22,576 x 9)

Table 4. Correlation matrix for features

Correlation	Gender	tID	α_v	α_l	α_f	aID	RSSI	φ	fCH
Gender	1	−0,14	0,25	−0,08	0,02	−0,11	−0,1	0,04	0,01
tID	−0,14	1	**−0,73**	**−0,63**	**−0,77**	0,09	0,06	**0,82**	−0,03
α_v	0,25	**−0,73**	1	−0,06	0,39	0,16	−0,13	0,05	0,06
α_l	−0,08	**−0,63**	−0,06	1	−0,13	−0,28	0,03	−0,02	−0,03
α_f	0,02	**−0,77**	0,39	−0,13	1	−0,04	−0,16	0,06	0,1
aID	−0,11	0,09	0,16	−0,28	−0,04	1	−0,2	0,02	0,05
RSSI	−0,1	0,06	−0,13	0,03	−0,16	−0,2	1	0,01	−0,19
φ	0,04	**0,82**	0,05	−0,02	0,06	0,02	0,01	1	−0,05
fCH	0,01	−0,03	0,06	−0,03	0,1	0,05	−0,19	−0,05	1

3   Classification Model

A total of 25 classification algorithms have been employed namely: *Fine Tree, Medium Tree, Coarse Tree, Linear Discriminant, Quadratic Discriminant, Linear SVM, Quadratic SVM, Cubic SVM, Fine Gaussian SVM, Medium Gaussian SVM, Coarse Gaussian SVM, Cosine KNN, Coarse KNN, Cubic KNN, Weighted KNN, Fine KNN, Medium KNN, Gaussian Naive Bayes, Kernel Naïve Bayes, Boosted Trees, **Bagged Trees**, Subspace Discriminant, Subspace KNN, RUSBoost Trees, Ensemble Adaptive Boosting.* However only the *Bagged Trees* algorithm that achieved the highest performance is described in the following chapter.

3.1   Bagged Trees

Bagging is a ML method of combining multiple predictors. It is a model's averaging approach. Bagging is a technique generating multiple training sets by sampling with replacement from the available training data. [6] This method was introduced by Leo Breiman, in 1996 and it is the acronym for **Bootstrap AGGregatING**. [5]. *Bootstrap aggregating* improves classification and regression models in terms of stability and accuracy. It also reduces variance and helps to avoid overfitting. It can be applied to any type of classifiers. Bagging is a popular method in estimating bias, standard errors and constructing confidence intervals for parameters. In the case of binary classification, the algorithm creates a classifier H: D $\rightarrow$ {-1, 1} on the base of a training set of example descriptions (in our case played by a document collection) D. The bagging method creates a sequence of classifiers H_m m = 1, ..., M in respect to the modifications of the training set. These classifiers are combined into a compound model, whose prediction is given as a weighted combination of particular classifier predictions according to the following function 1:

$$H(d_i, c_j) = sign\left(\sum_{m=1}^{M} a_m H_m(d_i, c_j)\right) \tag{1}$$

The meaning of the above given function can be interpreted as a voting procedure. The research effort [33] describes the theory of *classifier voting*. Parameters α_m, m = 1, ..., M are determined in such a way that more precise classifiers have stronger influence on the final prediction than less precise classifiers. The precision of base classifiers H_m can be only a little bit higher than the precision of a random classification. That is why these models Hm are called weak classifiers. *Bagged Trees* use the Breiman's '*Random Forest*' (RF) algorithm.

A RF consists of a collection of tree-structured classifiers {$T(\mathbf{x}, \Theta_b)$, $b = 1, \ldots$} where {Θ_b} are independent identically distributed random vectors and each tree casts a unit vote for the most popular class at input $\mathbf{X}$ [28]. The Bagged Trees Algorithm is described in the form of *Natural Language* in Algorithm 2. The total Number of Trees is denoted as B. The default value of m in the classification is $\sqrt{p}$ the minimum number of nodes is 1 and the default value of m in regression is $\frac{p}{3}$ where the minimum number of nodes is 5.

Algorithm 2. Bagged Trees Algorithm

Inputs: *Train Data*

  Step 1: *For b = 1 to B:*
  - *Create a bootstrap sample C with size N from the training set.*
  - *Build a random tree T_b in the bootstrap sample by following the following steps at each terminal node of the tree until the minimum number of nodes n_{min} reached:*
    - *Select m variables from p randomly*
    - *Select the optimal separation variables from m*
    - *Divide the node into two others*

  Step 2: *Give the set of Trees* $\left\{ T_\beta \right\}_1^B$

To predict a new point x:

$$\text{Regression: } f^B(x) = \frac{1}{B}\sum_{b=1}^{B} T_b(x) \tag{2}$$

$$\text{Classification: } G_{rf}^{B}(x) = \text{majority vote}\left\{ C_b(x) \right\}_1^B \tag{3}$$

3.2 Tuning of Hyperpatameters

It has already been said that we have chosen the combination of *n-fold Cross Validation and Grid Search*. As it is indicated in existing literature [15], this is one of the most widely strategies used in ML [3]. More specifically, the employed procedure is the following:

a) The range and the step (unit of transition to the next value) of the values of the hyperparameters that are examined, is initially defined.
b) Considering all possible values combinations, the best combination of hyperparameters is found. For each combination, its classification accuracy (i.e. the average in 10-folds) is calculated, and the one with the greatest accuracy is optimal
c) After finding the best combination of hyperparameters, step a. is applied with other range and step. New range and new step is defined around the hitherto optimal hyperparameters. Step b is performed, in order to reach in a higher value of classification accuracy. [13].

The process is repeated, shrinking the range and the hyperparameter step even further, until the optimal classification accuracy is achieved.

3.3 Evaluation of the Proposed Algorithm

Given the fact that this is a multiclass classification problem the *"One Versus All"* Strategy was used for the determination of the evaluation indices. Although, accuracy is the overall evaluation index of the developed ML models, it may be misleading. Thus, four more indices have been used to estimate the efficiency of the algorithms [25]. The calculated validation indices are presented in the following Table 5.

Table 5. Calculated indices for the evaluation of the multi-class classification approach

Index	Abbreviation	Calculation
Sensitivity (also known as true positive rate or recall)	SNS, REC, TPR	SNS = TP/(TP + FN)
Specificity, (also known as true negative rate)	SPC, TNR	SPC = TN/(TN + FP)
Accuracy	ACC	ACC = (TP + TN)/(TP + FP + FN + TN)
F1 score	F1	$F1 = 2 \cdot TP/(2 \cdot TP + FP + FN)$
Precision (also known as positive predictive value)	PREC	PREC = TP/(TP + FP)

The indices TP, TN, FP and FN refer to the True Positive, True Negative, False Positive, False Negative indices respectively. SNS is the measure of the correctly identified positive cases from all the actual positive cases. It is important when the cost of False Negatives is high. In contrast, PREC is the measure of the correctly identified positive cases from all the predicted positive cases. Thus, it is useful when the cost of False Positives is high. SPC is the true negative rate or the proportion of negatives that are correctly identified. The *F1* score can be interpreted as the harmonic mean (weighted average) of the Precision and Recall. As it is known from the literature, Accuracy can be seriously considered when the class distribution is balanced while F1 score is a better metric when there are imbalanced classes as in the above case [31].

4 Experimental Results

The optimal number of grid divisions for the Grid Search was equal to 10, and we have chosen to employ the typical *10-fold Cross Validation*. The hyperparameters that were tuned by the bagged trees algorithm, are the *number of trees, the maximum number of branches, and learning rate.* Table 6 presents the name of each hyperparameter, the acceptable range of the optimal value (defined for the specific case), and its optimal value.

Table 6. Hyperparameter's name, range of search and optimal value

Hyperparameter	Range	Optimal value
Number of trees	10–500	71
Maximum number of branches	1–75319	4547
Learning rate	0,001–0,1	0,056

Table 7 presents the *Confusion Matrix for the Training process*. A total of 52,159 observations out of 52,724 have been classified correctly, a percentage of 98.93%. The algorithm erroneously classified only a small particle of the observations. However, these cases are negligible as in total they are 565. The incorrect classifications with significant weight in this *Confusion Matrix* are those mentioned in cells (4, 1) = 251 and (4, 2) = 58 for which the older person seems to be lying down while actually moving around the room. This means that if an accident occurs at that time, the consequences will be unpleasant as it will not have been properly predicted. But the algorithm works extremely well predicting almost all cases (Table 8).

Table 7. Confusion matrix for the training data

Predicted class					
Actual class	Label	1	2	3	4
	1	**11199**	49	49	51
	2	51	**3330**	0	27
	3	25	1	**36335**	0
	4	**251**	**58**	3	**1295**

Table 8. Evaluation indices for the training data

Index	1	2	3	4
SNS	0.987	0.9777	0.999	**0.806**
SPC	0.992	0.998	0.997	0.998
ACC	0.990	0.996	0.999	0.992
F1	0.979	0.973	0.999	**0.869**
PREC	0.97	0.969	0.999	0.943

In order to confirm the effectiveness of the Bagged Trees Algorithm that was developed during the elaboration of this dissertation, it was necessary to test the algorithm on first time seen data. Table 9 presents the Confusion Matrix of the Bagged Trees Algorithm for the Testing data. The algorithm predicts with great accuracy the activity that elders undertake. The correct observations were 22,336 in relation to the total 22,596 contained in the testing data. This means that only 260 cases were wrongly classified with the percentage once again at 98.85%. However, most of the observations that were classified incorrectly are those of the fourth class.

Table 9. Confusion matrix for the testing data

Predicted class					
Actual class	Label	1	2	3	4
	1	**4808**	21	22	22
	2	29	**1415**	0	17
	3	9	0	**15569**	2
	4	**117**	**20**	1	**544**

The very reliable performance has been verified by the indices presented in Table 10. The indicators are very good for almost all classes. The case of class 4 seems to have slightly reduced performance although the SNS and F1-Score are high. The algorithm is still efficient and can predict the activities performed by elders with relatively high accuracy. Once again, it is clear from the indices, mainly from the SNS and F1-Score, that there is very efficient classification performance with a slightly reduced accuracy in the case of class 4, i.e. the activities of elders that are walking.

Table 10. Evaluation indices for testing data

Index	1	2	3	4
SNS	0.987	0.969	0.999	**0.801**
SPC	0.991	0.998	0.997	0.998
ACC	0.990	0.996	0.998	0.992
F1	0.978	0.970	0.999	**0.861**
PREC	0.969	0.972	0.999	0.931

This is mainly due to the fact that there is less data in this class and the data set is not completely balanced. The number of instances recorded for class 4 was the smallest compared to the other 3 cases. Nevertheless, the performance is excellent and the accuracy indicators have very high values.

5   Conclusion and Future Work

A publicly available dataset was used in this research [32]. The data set includes 14 healthy elders who perform the activities (1) *sitting on bed*, (2) *sitting on chair*, (3) *lying on bed* and (4) *ambulating*, wearing passive and battery-less sensors, in two clinic rooms. After processing the data, the tID variable was removed.

Overall, twenty five classification algorithms were employed. The *Bagged Trees* algorithm has achieved the optimal performance.

The accuracy rate was high, showing a success rate of 98.93% on Train Data. The performance of the model is sealed by the evaluation indicators which have values very close to one.

Regarding the class 4, "ambulating" it is worth saying that some indicators are slightly lower (SNS = 0.806 and F1-Score 0.869) though still high. This is mainly due to the fact that the data set is not perfectly balanced. The number of records recorded for class 4 was the smallest compared to the other three classes. Furthermore, class 4 is the only one that contains movement of the subject. Thus, it is possible for this movement to affect the performance of the model. Nevertheless, even for this class, the performance of the algorithms is sufficiently satisfactory. The robustness and the generalization ability of the developed model, is confirmed in the testing phase.

Consequently, the model can be adopted by caregivers and hospital staff, in order to monitor the activity of the elderly and adjust the alarms for dangerous situations.

Further extension of this paper could be done in order to optimize the research. A first thought is to develop additional data vectors for the minority class 4, with the well-known and Mathematically Documented, *Synthetic Minority Over-sampling Technique* (SMOTE) [10]. Finally, future research could include the development of Deep Learning models after looking for more parameters that could potentially affect the problem.

References

1. Ahmed, M.U., Loutfi, A.: Physical activity identification using supervised machine learning and based on pulse rate. Int. J. Adv. Comput. Sci. Appl. **4**(7), 210–217 (2013)
2. Becker, C., Rapp, K.: Fall prevention in nursing homes. Clin. Geriatr. Med. **26**(4), 693–704 (2010)
3. Bergstra, J., Bengio, Y.: Random search for hyper-parameter optimization. J. Mach. Learn. Res. **13**(1), 281–305 (2012)
4. Boukhechba, M., Cai, L., Wu, C., Barnes, L.E.: ActiPPG: Using deep neural networks for activity recognition from wrist-worn photoplethysmography (PPG) sensors. Smart Health **14**, (2019)
5. Breiman, L.: Arcing the edge. Technical report 486, Statistics Department, University of California at Berkeley (1997)
6. Breiman, L.: Bagging predictors. Technical report 421, Department of Statistics, University of California at Berkeley (1994)
7. Brophy, E., Veiga, J.J.D., Wang, Z., Smeaton, A. F., Ward, T.E.: An interpretable machine vision approach to human activity recognition using photoplethysmograph sensor data. arXiv preprint arXiv:1812.00668
8. Buettner, M., Greenstein, B., Sample, A., Smith, J. R., Wetherall, D.: Revisiting smart dust with RFID sensor networks. In: Proceedings of the 7th ACM Workshop on Hot Topics in Networks (HotNets-VII) (2008)
9. Casale, P., Pujol, O., Radeva, P.: Human activity recognition from accelerometer data using a wearable device. In: Vitrià, J., Sanches, J.M., Hernández, M. (eds.) IbPRIA 2011. LNCS, vol. 6669, pp. 289–296. Springer, Heidelberg (2011). https://doi.org/10.1007/978-3-642-21257-4_36
10. Chawla, N.V., Bowyer, K.W., Hall, L.O., Kegelmeyer, W.P.: SMOTE: synthetic minority over-sampling technique. J. Artif. Intell. Res. **16**, 321–357 (2002)
11. Chen, L., Wei, H., Ferryman, J.: A survey of human motion analysis using depth imagery. Pattern Recogn. Lett. **34**(15), 1995–2006 (2013)

12. Chen, W., Wei, D., Zhu, X., Uchida, M., Ding, S., Cohen, M.: A mobile phone-based wearable vital signs monitoring system. In The Fifth International Conference on Computer and Information Technology (CIT 2005), pp. 950–955. IEEE (2005)
13. Eitrich, T., Lang, B.: Efficient optimization of support vector machine learn-ing parameters for unbalanced datasets. J. Comput. Appl. Math. **196**(2), 425–436 (2006)
14. Gövercin, M., et al.: Defining the user requirements for wearable and optical fall prediction and fall detection devices for home use. Inform. Health Soc. Care **35**(3–4), 177–187 (2010)
15. Hsu, C.W., Chang, C.C., Lin, C.J.: A practical guide to support vector classification (2003)
16. Junker, H., Amft, O., Lukowicz, P., Tröster, G.: Gesture spotting with body-worn inertial sensors to detect user activities. Pattern Recogn. **41**(6), 2010–2024 (2008)
17. Kaufmann, T., Ranasinghe, D.C., Zhou, M., Fumeaux, C.: Wearable quarter-wave folded microstrip antenna for passive UHF RFID applications. Int. J. Antennas and Propag. (2013)
18. Li, X., et al.: Activity recognition for medical teamwork based on passive RFID. In: 2016 IEEE International Conference on RFID (RFID), pp. 1–9. IEEE (2016)
19. Miskelly, F.: A novel system of electronic tagging in patients with dementia and wandering. Age Ageing **33**(3), 304–306 (2004)
20. Nehmer, J., Becker, M., Karshmer, A., Lamm, R.: Living assistance systems: an ambient intelligence approach. In: Proceedings of the 28th International Conference on Software Engineering, pp. 43–50 (2006)
21. Oliver, D.: Prevention of falls in hospital inpatients. Agendas for research and practice. Age Ageing **33**, 328–330 (2004)
22. Pantelopoulos, A., Bourbakis, N.G.: A survey on wearable sensor-based systems for health monitoring and prognosis. IEEE Trans. Syst. Man Cybern. Part C (Appl. Rev.) **40**(1), 1–12 (2009)
23. Pirttikangas, S., Fujinami, K., Nakajima, T.: Feature selection and activity recognition from wearable sensors. In: Youn, H.Y., Kim, M., Morikawa, H. (eds.) UCS 2006. LNCS, vol. 4239, pp. 516–527. Springer, Heidelberg (2006). https://doi.org/10.1007/11890348_39
24. Psathas, A.P., Papaleonidas, A., Iliadis, L.: Machine learning modeling of human activity using PPG signals. In: Nguyen, N.T., Hoang, B.H., Huynh, C.P., Hwang, D., Trawiński, B., Vossen, G. (eds.) ICCCI 2020. LNCS (LNAI), vol. 12496, pp. 543–557. Springer, Cham (2020). https://doi.org/10.1007/978-3-030-63007-2_42
25. Psathas, A.P., Papaleonidas, A., Papathanassiou, G., Valkaniotis, S., Iliadis, L.: Classification of coseismic landslides using fuzzy and machine learning techniques. In: Iliadis, L., Angelov, P.P., Jayne, C., Pimenidis, E. (eds.) EANN 2020. PINNS, vol. 2, pp. 15–31. Springer, Cham (2020). https://doi.org/10.1007/978-3-030-48791-1_2
26. Ramasamy Ramamurthy, S., Roy, N.: Recent trends in machine learning for human activity recognition—a survey. Wiley Interdiscip. Rev.: Data Min. Knowl. Discov. **8**(4), (2018)
27. Ranasinghe, D.C., Sheng, M., Zeadally, S.: Unique radio innovation for the 21st Century: building scalable and global RFID networks. Springer, Heidelberg (2010). https://doi.org/10.1007/978-3-642-03462-6
28. Rifkin, R., Klautau, A.: In defense of one-vs-all classification. J. Mach. Learn. Res. **5**(Jan), 101–141 (2004)
29. Robinovitch, S.N., et al.: Video capture of the circumstances of falls in elderly people residing in long-term care: an observational study. Lancet **381**(9860), 47–54 (2013)
30. Ryoo, J., Karimi, Y., Athalye, A., Stanaćević, M., Das, S. R., Djurić, P.: Barnet: towards activity recognition using passive backscattering tag-to-tag network. In: Proceedings of the 16th Annual International Conference on Mobile Systems, Applications, and Services, pp. 414–427 (2018)
31. Sammut, C., Webb, G.I.: Encyclopedia of Machine Learning and Data Mining. Springer, Boston (2017). https://doi.org/10.1007/978-1-4899-7687-1

32. Sample, A.P., Yeager, D.J., Powledge, P.S., Mamishev, A.V., Smith, J.R.: Design of an RFID-based battery-free programmable sensing platform. IEEE Trans. Instrum. Meas. **57**(11), 2608–2615 (2008)

33. Schapire, R.E., Freund, Y., Bartlett, P., Lee, W.S.: Boosting the margin: a new explanation for the effectiveness of voting methods. Ann. Stat. **26**(5), 1651–1686 (1998)

34. Shinmoto Torres, R.L., Visvanathan, R., Hoskins, S., Van den Hengel, A., Ranasinghe, D.C.: Effectiveness of a batteryless and wireless wearable sensor system for identifying bed and chair exits in healthy elders. Sensors **16**(4), 546 (2016)

35. Smith, R.E., Zane, N.W., Smoll, F.L.: Behavioral assessment in youth sports: coaching. Med. Sci. Sports Exerc. **15**(3), 208–214 (1983)

36. Su, Y., Wickramasinghe, A., Ranasinghe, D.C.: Investigating sensor data retrieval schemes for multi-sensor passive RFID tags. In: 2015 IEEE International Conference on RFID (RFID), pp. 158–165. IEEE (2015)

37. Shinmoto Torres, R.L., Ranasinghe, Damith C., Shi, Q.: Evaluation of wearable sensor tag data segmentation approaches for real time activity classification in elderly. In: Stojmenovic, I., Cheng, Z., Guo, S. (eds.) MindCare 2014. LNICST, vol. 131, pp. 384–395. Springer, Cham (2014). https://doi.org/10.1007/978-3-319-11569-6_30

38. Torres, R.L.S., Ranasinghe, D.C., Shi, Q., Sample, A.P.: Sensor enabled wearable RFID technology for mitigating the risk of falls near beds. In 2013 IEEE International Conference on RFID (RFID), pp. 191–198. IEEE (2013)

39. UCI Machine Learning Repository. https://archive.ics.uci.edu/ml/datasets/Activity+recognition+with+healthy+older+people+using+a+batteryless+wearable+sensor. Accessed 21 Mar 2021

40. Wang, L., Gu, T., Xie, H., Tao, X., Lu, J., Huang, Yu.: A wearable RFID system for real-time activity recognition using radio patterns. In: Stojmenovic, I., Cheng, Z., Guo, S. (eds.) MindCare 2014. LNICST, vol. 131, pp. 370–383. Springer, Cham (2014). https://doi.org/10.1007/978-3-319-11569-6_29

41. Wickramasinghe, A., Ranasinghe, D.C.: Recognising activities in real time using body worn passive sensors with sparse data streams: to interpolate or not to interpolate? In: proceedings of the 12th EAI International Conference on Mobile and Ubiquitous Systems: Computing, Networking and Services on 12th EAI International Conference on Mobile and Ubiquitous Systems: Computing, Networking and Services, pp. 21–30 (2016)

42. Wickramasinghe, A., Ranasinghe, D.C., Fumeaux, C., Hill, K.D., Visvanathan, R.: Sequence learning with passive RFID sensors for real-time bed-egress recognition in elders. IEEE J. Biomed. Health Inform. **21**(4), 917–929 (2016)

43. Wold, S., Esbensen, K., Geladi, P.: Principal component analysis. Chemometr. Intell. Lab. Syst. **2**(1–3), 37–52 (1987)

Analyzing Collective Knowledge Towards Public Health Policy Making

Spyridon Kleftakis, Konstantinos Mavrogiorgos, Nikolaos Zafeiropoulos,
Argyro Mavrogiorgou(✉), Athanasios Kiourtis, Ilias Maglogiannis,
and Dimosthenis Kyriazis

University of Piraeus, Piraeus, Greece
{spiroskleft,komav,nikolaszaf,margy,kiourtis,imaglo,
dimos}@unipi.gr

Abstract. Nowadays there exists a plethora of diverse data sources producing tons of healthcare data, augmenting the size of data that finally is stored both in Electronic Health Records (EHRs) and in Personal Health Records (PHRs). Thus, the great challenge that emerges is not only to gather all this data in an efficient and effective manner, but also to extract knowledge out of it. The latter is the key factor that enables healthcare professionals to take serious clinical decisions both on individual and on collective level, finally forming representative public health policies. Towards this direction, the current paper proposes a system that supports a new paradigm of EHRs, the eXtended Health Records (XHRs), which include the majority of the health determinants. XHRs are then transformed into XHRs Networks that capture the clinical, social and human context of diverse population segmentations, producing the corresponding collective knowledge. By exploiting this knowledge, the proposed system is finally able to create multi-modal policies, addressing various facts and evolving risks that arise from diverse population segmentations.

Keywords: EHRs · PHRs · Collective knowledge · Data analysis · Public health policies

1 Introduction

Nowadays there is a tremendous amount of data that is generated from various sources. Those sources belong to many different domains such as health, business, governance, finance, insurance, etc. [1]. The great challenge that has emerged is not only to gather this data in an efficient and effective manner, but also to extract knowledge from this. Especially when it comes to the healthcare domain, dealing with the aforementioned challenge becomes of vital importance because of the nature of health data and the knowledge that this data is able to offer if manipulated correctly. Based on a recent research [2], 92% of healthcare providers have already begun to address this challenge by promoting the use of digitalization in healthcare facilities. This digitalization includes the introduction of storing, previously paper-based, health data in digital formats. By

I. Maglogiannis et al. (Eds.): AIAI 2021 Workshops, IFIP AICT 628, pp. 171–181, 2021.
https://doi.org/10.1007/978-3-030-79157-5_15

doing so, it becomes feasible to perform computational tasks upon this data, extracting useful knowledge and information. Characteristic examples of such initiatives represent both the Electronic Health Records (EHRs), where healthcare professionals are able to store patients' data, and the Personal Health Records (PHRs), where patients are able to store their personal healthcare data by themselves. Based on [3], there has been continuous growth in the adoption of national electronic health record (EHR) systems over the past 15 years, while the 46% of this growth took place in the past 5 years.

However, those initiatives do not currently offer the opportunity to perform more complex computational tasks on healthcare data, such as big data analytics, in order to generate collective knowledge [4]. Even though there have been put various research efforts for combining the diverse and heterogeneous data coming from EHRs and PHRs, and thus generating collective knowledge, none of these has reached a fully mature level of functionality. This fact relies mainly on the lack of the usage of a universal standard that would enable the interoperability of such diverse healthcare data, regardless of its origin, nature, and format. Collective knowledge is the key factor that enables healthcare professionals to take serious clinical decisions not only on an individual, but also on a collective level [5]. Especially the collective level plays a major role, where a specific type of healthcare professionals, namely policy makers, are responsible for creating protocols, interventions and policies for the well-being of the general population. It is quite obvious that finding a way to combine EHRs and PHRs data and analyzing it would have a tremendous constructive impact on public health [5].

In order to contribute to the aforementioned area, this paper proposes a system that supports a new kind of EHRs and PHRs, namely eXtended Health Records (XHRs), which are able to integrate different kinds of healthcare data coming from both EHRs and PHRs. As soon as the system successfully constructs these XHRs, it exploits them in order to build discrete XHRs' networks based on common characteristics that the XHRs may have. The XHRs networks are then analyzed using top-notch algorithms finally assisting policy makers in creating protocols, interventions and policies for the public health. To achieve that, the system follows a two-phases process, where in the first phase it develops the proposed XHRs, whilst in the second phase it proceeds with the formulation of the XHRs networks, and the generation of collective knowledge.

This paper is organized as follows. Section 2 thoroughly analyzes the related work regarding the general concepts of EHRs, PHRs, as well as public health policies, outlining the innovations that the proposed system provides towards these directions, highlighting its importance for solving known issues that healthcare information systems currently have. Section 3 describes the general architecture of the proposed system, as well as its supported functionalities. Finally, Sect. 4 summarizes our overall work and provides insights regarding the following steps.

2 Literature Review

2.1 Electronic Health Records and Personal Health Records

The usage of Electronic Health Records (EHRs) and Personal Health Records (PHRs) in the healthcare domain is indisputable. Whereas an EHR is a computer record that originates with and is controlled by health professionals, including diverse kinds of clinical tests (e.g., hematological, imaging, biochemical), a PHR can be generated by physicians, patients, hospitals, pharmacies, and other sources, being controlled by the patient, containing information such as nutrition, sport activity, as well as user-generated biosignals [6]. Finding correlations between those two (2) types of records promotes disease prevention, risk management, and rational resource allocation, whilst favors the development of strategies for their efficient management [7]. Their unified form can be stored in cloud computing infrastructures for their rapid and efficient exploitation, while it can be regularly updated with new flows in order to capture the changes of the environment regarding new health data and new characteristics of the populations of interest. Updating this data provides the possibility of improving the quality of the exported knowledge, while maintaining the performance of the prediction tools at high levels.

In the literature there is often the tendency to consolidate health data of different types in order to exploit it in two (2) main pillars of development, Personalized Medicine and Population Health [8]. Personalized Medicine is related to the provision of personalized care to patients in the form of targeted recommendations and suggestions [9], which are based on standards derived from specific genetic traits, as well as diseases and allergies of the patient, in contrast with traditional methods that extract knowledge about the average patient [10]. On the other hand, Population Health refers to the provision of generalized care in the form of recommendations and predictions based on knowledge extracted from population data. This data is used to find population, environmental and social factors that affect the health of the masses and aim at the efficient management of resources and large-scale risk [11].

In addition to the value of healthcare data (primary and secondary) that is stored by health professionals for the acquisition of collective knowledge, in recent years the importance of collecting and utilizing health data generated by the user through mobile phones and mobile devices (wearables) is highlighted [12]. That is why Information Technology (IT) business giants such as Apple, Microsoft, and Samsung are taking advantage of the knowledge generated by this data in order to create applications that will guide users towards self-improvement of their health. Applications such as Runtastic [13], Runkeeper [14], Fitbit [15], Garmin Connect Mobile [16], Strava running and cycling [17], MisFit [18], and devices such as Withings [19] and iHealth [20] extend their functionality to health data collection by investing in the storage of PHRs to extract useful knowledge. Consequently, the aggregation of large volumes of data in combination with the technological developments of recent years in software and hardware has made great strides in the transformation of heterogeneously produced information into usable knowledge.

In this context, heterogeneity of data is necessary in order to be able to codify and interpret the mechanisms, as well as to predict the effects of pathogens, which are not affected by isolated factors, but their patchwork. In this patchwork of factors, connections and interactions are identified, the understanding of which is the key for further analyzing the data and extracting useful knowledge. At the same time, the simultaneous identification of specific characteristics of the data for a particular record may signal an event of medical interest, while the correlation of data between the records may be linked to the disclosure of empirical medical knowledge. Identifying facts, experience, and correlations between health records is critical for extracting usable knowledge [21–26].

However, data diversity also raises challenges regarding the high degree of curse of dimensionality, which inevitably leads to sparse data, lack of records and noise content [27]. The above elements are a major obstacle to the efforts of prediction tools to extract standards with effective resolution that can be generalized to different data. In order for an information system to gain in-depth knowledge of the data subsets within EHRs and PHRs, which are responsible for revealing medical empirical knowledge, interactions and events, the creation of EHRs and PHRs networks is a prerequisite. The extraction of solid representations or phenotypes from heterogeneous features contained in the underlying EHRs and PHRs, can be achieved by using clustering techniques such as K-Means [28], Hierarchical [29], and Spectral Clustering [30], as it is proposed in the literature in order to create similar networks. The main purpose of these networks is to create multidisciplinary cooperation, taking as sectors the different sources of data, in order to identify new factors of influence, facts and empirical knowledge across the sectors. Initiatives such as the Hitech and Patient Protection and Affordable Care Act (PPACA) are moving towards similar links that form networks of EHRs and PHRs [31]. Based on the same logic for creating networks of EHRs and PHRs, Electronic Medical Records and Genomics and Scalable Precision Medicine Oriented Knowledge Engine initiatives discover internal knowledge structures between EHR and DNA data [32, 33].

2.2 Public Health Policies

Public health is defined in several different ways [34], [35] all of them agreeing to the general concept that public health is the science and art of preventing disease, promoting health and prolonging life through an organized effort of society. Moreover, in the modern literature there is a reference to the term "new public health", which stems from the need to consider the health issues of the population as a problem that is not solved only by medical care. In this light, primary health care has been recognized as a key factor in achieving improved health of the population [36].

Based on that, every modern state must ensure that the health system provides every citizen with the highest possible level of physical, mental and social health and well-being [37]. Achieving this goal requires structured planning of public health policies, which have to be constantly updated and evaluated, based on the ever-changing needs of the population. The current era is characterized by the existence of a wealth of data that relates to various areas of public health, such as data coming from official organizations, public and private hospitals, primary healthcare providers, research data related to risk factors and health problems of populations (either as a whole or specific groups), electronic prescription data, as well as data from wearable devices that more and more people use and provide information about their state of health. The value of this enormous amount of health data is limited by their fragmentary nature and non-interconnectedness, resulting in their difficult, incomplete and fragmentary utilization to identify the main health problems of the populations and the consequent design of public health policies.

In order to properly form such public health policies, the key point lies in the utilization of health data in its electronic form in order to improve the relevant policies. The whole process from finding the sources of electronic health data, to integrating them into the system, analyzing and evaluating them in order to formulate public health policies, should be based on a specific methodology, which will focus on the basic principles of Epidemiology and Public Health. In short, the starting point for investigating and prioritizing the health problems of a population is the study of routine statistical series. Regular statistical series contain data of epidemiological and medical-social interest which are collected for other purposes (legal, economic, demographic) but can be used to study health issues [38]. Finding the health problems of the population from various sources, would lead to the second step, which is the prioritization of these problems as well as the risk factors, in order to design appropriate health policies and interventions. This process presupposes the existence of criteria for the evaluation of these problems (e.g., based on the incidence, mortality, burden of disease and finally the cost of health coverage). Prioritization is particularly important at this stage, as the problems that need to be addressed are multiple and at many different levels, and their prioritization is done according to the possibilities and the special needs of each time period. Finally, in the third step, the public health researcher, having identified the required data and having focused on the specific problem she wants to address, should look for past and existing public health programs, on the specific subject.

2.3   Advancements of Proposed System

To go beyond the aforementioned aspects, being capable of forming public health policies based on collective knowledge, the proposed system allows the recording and differentiation of similar health-related information from different sources. Therefore, it is able to collect data from healthcare providers and patients, from medical monitoring devices, mobile devices, wearables, etc. To achieve that, it is based on a scalable model of information integration, the XHRs, which is able to be enriched with new entities regarding health information that is also included in EHRs and PHRs. XHRs are designed and implemented based on the HL7 FHIR standard [39], which is widely used and easily implemented. In addition, the proposed system isolates the logic of information exchange from the logic of information storage and data analysis.

As for the XHRs networks, existing information systems for extracting knowledge from EHRs and PHRs do not take full advantage of all the heterogeneous data being processed. This is because they handle health records in isolation and independently. This approach ignores the existence of hidden connections and interrelationships. It therefore leads to the creation of independent and fragmented services, to the limited exploitation of data and, ultimately, to the export of knowledge of limited value, which is reflected in spasmodic health strategies and ineffective provision of personalized medical care. In contrast to this approach, the proposed system seeks to exploit all the heterogeneous data that reside inside the diverse EHRs and PHRs, by searching for clusters with important health interactions among them, penetrating the different domains of the data source. Taking advantage of advanced clustering and classification techniques, it identifies empirical knowledge and correlations as well as noise and sparse data layout.

With regards to health policies, as stated in the literature review, in order to properly form public health policies, the key point lies in the utilization of health data in its electronic form in order to improve the relevant policies. Thus, the whole process from finding the sources of electronic health data, to integrating them into the system, analyzing and evaluating them in order to formulate public health policies, is based on a specific methodology, which adopts the basic principles of Epidemiology and Public Health. Towards this direction, the proposed system is able to integrate data from different sources so that the available information is in a detailed and editable format, in order to take a holistic approach to health data and draw conclusions. An important problem is that the above data, although available for study and processing, is fragmentary, comes from many different sources, expresses different populations and requires great care in processing and comparing. As a first step, the proposed system provides a centralized repository where the researchers can enter and locate information about the most important data concerning the health of a population. At the same time, the system always ensures that the data is updated from the abovementioned sources, since they are updated on a regular basis. The ability to search for older files within the system is also legitimate, in case long-term comparisons are desired. In case that the data from the existing regular statistical series are not sufficient for the purposes of the respective research activity, the public health researcher is able to seek data from specific epidemiological surveys.

3   Proposed System

3.1   System Architecture

The proposed system, aims at the development of innovative mechanisms and services for achieving integrated health data management and successful formulation of public health policies. The methodology that is followed in the system improves the possibilities of utilizing health data through the integration of technologies that allow its holistic analysis, based on knowledge and experience from similar databases, and their continuous evolution through integration of data. This system can add value to health policymaking by shaping populations with similar characteristics. To achieve that, it applies a three (3) phases process of data collection and management that directly or indirectly relates to the health of the citizen-patient, as depicted in Fig. 1. In short, the suggested system consists of three (3) separate pillars. In the first pillar, XHRs, the required information is derived from the data sources' exploration, in order to correlate and interpret heterogeneous data sources and environmental information of the individuals. In the second pillar, XHRs Networks, diverse groups of XHRs are created, so as to create opportunities for personalized health, disease prevention and health promotion. Finally, the third pillar, offers all the means for achieving both creation and co-creation of multi-modal policies, by incorporating mechanisms for risk analysis, as well as for compilation of predictions, addressing various evolving risks that are realized from diverse population segmentations.

In deeper detail, the first pillar (i.e., XHRs) refers to the development of the XHRs, which include all health determinants, in order to form a complete picture of the individuals. Towards this direction, each dataset that is fed into the XHRs must contain fully cleaned, reliable and interoperable data. To achieve that, the system includes (i) the Data Reliability component, which is responsible for identifying and removing possible errors and inconsistencies of the data, and (ii) the Data Interoperability component that

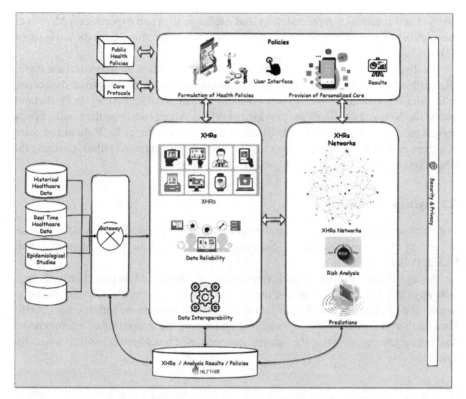

Fig. 1. Proposed system architecture

is responsible for the reception of different types of data that may use diverse international standards and convert it to the most commonly used HL7 FHIR standard. Hence, XHRs include cleaned, reliable and interoperable data related to the health of individuals/patients, incorporating not only prevention (e.g., vaccinations, diet and lifestyle) and care data (primary and secondary), but also additional data identified as determinants of health (e.g., social security data, environmental data, data from social networks). Thus, an XHR contains four categories (4) of data: (i) health and social data recorded by the patient and her environment, (ii) social care data collected by social actors, (iii) objective data in which clinical signs recorded and transmitted in the form of biomarkers by medical devices connected to the individual and/or patient (such as activity trackers, smartwatches, wearables, etc.), and (iv) health and care data (primary and secondary) including data stored by health professionals.

The second pillar (i.e., XHRs Networks) refers to the export of knowledge from the XHRs networks. To this context, the system creates interconnected XHRs, which are created based on the previously constructed XHRs. Thus, the latter include features such as identifying and disseminating events that affect the individual and/or patient, disseminating knowledge and experience, and establishing relationships through interaction and interoperability with other XHRs. This means that XHRs are able to create fully interoperable ecosystems in an automated way based on various criteria related to lifestyle and potential symptomatology and exchange data and experiences. Moreover, the system offers machine learning mechanisms for predictions and risk analysis on XHRs.

Finally, in the third pillar (i.e., Policies), the system offers its web interface that is responsible for presenting all the produced analytical results, coming from the second pillar. More specifically, a user is able to visualize the results of Risk Analysis, Predictions and XHRs Networks, through the provided interface. After processing the results, policy makers are able to model and evaluate their policies through this pillar. It should be noted that there exists an extra component outside of the abovementioned pillars, covering the whole system, namely the Security and Privacy component.

3.2 System Functionalities

The proposed system provides several mechanisms with specific functionalities in order to support the creation of XHRs, Networks of XHRs and the formulation of Public Health Policies.

As depicted in Fig. 2, the system offers certain capabilities. More particularly, through Gateways and Information Sources, the system is able to support various diverse information sources that generate health data of different formats. In the same context, XHRs Data Exchange Gateways are responsible for managing the integration of heterogeneous health data sources, allowing the efficient connection of heterogeneous sources with the system.

Fig. 2. Supported system functionalities

Regarding Data Cleaning, all the collected data are evaluated in terms of their quality, being processed by a series of mechanisms, in order to be successfully corrected and verified. On top of that, a sequence of actions are performed for ensuring the reliability of all the cleaned data. Hence, a key functionality of the system is the Data Reliability, which is performed based on the compliance rules that the system's data should follow. As for the Data Interoperability functionality, this refers to the ability of the system to create appropriate mechanisms that are able to encode all the collected information from one structure to another through appropriate rules and transformations, trying to give a more indicative design step of the HL7 FHIR standard. In order to manage all this data, the system exploits the Big Data Management functionality, by using a non-relational database (i.e., MongoDB). Thus, the system is able to receive a large amount of data and manage it properly.

With regards to the XHRs Networks, those are generated by utilizing advanced clustering and classification techniques, through which the system aims at identifying empirical knowledge and interrelationships among the different XHRs that have been constructed and stored into the system. Those networks are supported by two (2) additional functionalities, namely the Data Analysis for Risks and Predictions and Data Analysis for Personalized Care. The first one has to do with the appliance of appropriate feature extraction or feature selection techniques, as well as state of the art machine learning algorithms. The second one refers to the ability of providing personalized care by analyzing healthcare data on an individual level.

Concerning the Public Health Policies, the system provides the policy makers with the suitable tools for designing, creating and evaluating them. Thus, the information is made available in the most possible explanatory form, leading the healthcare professionals to safely draw conclusions. Last but not least, the Privacy and Security of data is essential. As a result, one of the main priorities of the system is to accomplish real-time anonymization of XHRs in order to ensure the anonymity of the patients during the operational processes of analysis and management of big data. Moreover, it is also crucial to protect the system's resources and that is why an access control-based system has been developed for verifying the role of each user entering the system.

4   Conclusions

Today, at a time when data is being produced in huge quantities and their exploitation is considered priceless, it is imperative that health information systems manage this data effectively. Healthcare systems currently in use, have several loopholes in managing different data from different sources. They also experience performance issues when handling big data. The system proposed in this paper offers a solution for the productive handling of diverse health datasets towards the extraction of collective knowledge out of it, and the formulation of effective public health policies. Specific processes take place in each pillar of the system in order to make the best possible use of this data.

The proposed system is still a work in progress and many design iterations have to be done, taking into consideration the evolving challenges in the field of big data in the healthcare domain. It should be also noted that the main functionality of each component has already been implemented and we are currently working on a first evaluation and testing of the proposed system architecture, utilizing healthcare data from different data sources. Based on the results we have recorded so far, it is within our future goals to add new data sources to the system. We also want to improve the design of XHRs to include more attributes and types of healthcare data. In addition, we aim to enrich the data reliability component by using state-of-the-art algorithms to clean up primary data from different sources, as well as upgrade the techniques used by XHRs networks. Finally, we aim to use all the appropriate machine learning and deep learning algorithms in order to achieve top results in defining and evaluating health policies.

Acknowledgement. The research has been co-financed by the European Union and Greek national funds through the Operational Program Competitiveness, Entrepreneurship and Innovation, under the call RESEARCH – CREATE – INNOVATE (project code: BeHEALTHIER - T2EDK-04207).

References

1. Top 10 Challenges Healthcare Companies Face Today. https://www.finoit.com/blog/top-10-healthcare-challenges/. Accessed April 2021
2. The State of Healthcare Industry – Statistics for 2021. https://policyadvice.net/insurance/ins ights/healthcare-statistics/. Accessed April 2021
3. WHO: Analysis of third global survey on eHealth based on the reported data by countries (2016). https://www.who.int/gho/goe/electronic_health_records/en/. April 2021
4. Menachemi, N., Collum, T.H.: Benefits and drawbacks of electronic health record systems. Risk Manag. Healthc. Policy **4**, 47 (2011)
5. Bate, L., Hutchinson, A., Underhill, J., Maskrey, N.: How clinical decisions are made. Br. J. Clin. Pharmacol. **74**(4), 614–620 (2012)
6. Kahn, J.S., Aulakh, V., Bosworth, A.: What it takes: characteristics of the ideal personal health record. Health Aff. **28**(2), 369–376 (2012)
7. Cyganek, B., et al.: A survey of big data issues in electronic health record analysis. Appl. Artif. Intell. **30**(6), 497–520 (2016)
8. Boccia, S.: Why is personalized medicine relevant to public health? Eur. J. Public Health **24**, 349–350 (2014)
9. Swati, B.B., Jayashree, R.P.: Machine learning approach to revolutionize use of holistic health records for personalized healthcare. Int. J. Adv. Sci. Technol. **29**(05), 313–321 (2020)
10. Benson, T.: Principles of Health Interoperability HL7 and SNOMED. Springer, London (2012). https://doi.org/10.1007/978-1-4471-2801-4
11. Kruse, C., Stein, A., Thomas, H., Kaur, H.: The use of electronic health records to support population health: a systematic review of the literature. J. Med. Syst. **42** (2018). https://doi.org/10.1007/s10916-018-1075-6
12. Asimakopoulos, S., Asimakopoulos, G., Spillers, F.: Motivation and user engagement in fitness tracking: Heuristics for mobile healthcare wearables. Informatics **4**(1), 5 (2017). Multidisciplinary Digital Publishing Institute
13. Runtastic. Runtasitc: Running, Cycling and Fitness GPS Tracker. https://www.runtastic.com. Accessed April 2021
14. Runkeeper. Runkeeper - Track your runs, walks and more with your iPhone or Android phone. https://runkeeper.com. Accessed April 2021
15. FitBit. Fitbit Official Site for Activity Trackers & More. https://www.fitbit.com. Accessed April 2021
16. Garmin. Garmin Connect. https://connect.garmin.com. Accessed April 2021
17. Strava. Strava| Run and Cycling Tracking on the Social Network for Athletes. https://www.strava.com. Accessed April 2021
18. Misfit. Smartwatches, Fitness Trackers & Wearable Technology – Misfit. https://misfit.com. Accessed April 2021
19. Nokia. Nokia Health (Withings)| Connected health devices for the whole family: scales, activity & HR monitors, thermometer, camera…. https://health.nokia.com. Accessed April 2021
20. iHealth. iHealth Labs Europe - Connected Health. https://ihealthlabs.eu. Accessed April 2021
21. Noura, S.A.-H., Eimear, E.K.: Personalized medicine and the power of electronic health records. Cell **177**(1), 58–69 (2019)
22. Bennett, C.C.: Utilizing RxNorm to support practical computing applications: capturing medication history in live electronic health records. J. Biomed. Inform. **45**(4), 634–641 (2012)
23. Dorda, W., Duftschmid, G., Gerhold, L., Gall, W., Gambal, J.: Introducing the Electronic Health Record in Austria. Studies in Health Technology and Informatics, vol. 116. IOS Press, Amsterdam (2005)

24. Haveman, H., Flim, C.: eHealth Strategy and Implementation Activities in the Netherlands. eHalth ERA Project (2007)
25. Xu, J., Gao, X., Sorwar, G., Crol, I.P.: Implementation of e-health record systems in Australia. Int. Technol. Manag. Rev. **3**(2), 92–104 (2013)
26. Chiaravalloti, M.T., Ciampi, M., Pasceri, E., Sicuranza, M., De Pietro, G., Guarasci, R.: A model for realizing interoperable EHR systems in Italy. In: Proceedings of the 15th International HL7 Interoperability Conference (2015)
27. Jensen, P.B., Jensen, L.J., Brunak, S.: Mining electronic health records: towards better research applications and clinical care. Nat. Rev. Genet. **13**(6), 395–405 (2012)
28. Chousiadas, D., Menychtas, A., Tsanakas, P., Maglogiannis, I.: Advancing quantified-self applications utilizing visual data analytics and the Internet of Things. In: Iliadis, L., Maglogiannis, I., Plagianakos, V. (eds.) AIAI 2018. IAICT, vol. 520, pp. 263–274. Springer, Cham (2018). https://doi.org/10.1007/978-3-319-92016-0_24
29. Cohen, M.J., et al.: Identification of complex metabolic states in critically injured patients using bioinformatic cluster analysis. Crit. Care **14**(1), 1–11 (2010)
30. Huang, G.T., Cunningham, K.I., Benos, P.V., Chennubhotla, C.S.: Spectral clustering strategies for heterogeneous disease expression data. In: Pacific Symposium on Biocomputing. NIH Public Access, pp. 212 (2013)
31. Pew research Centre. Internet Project survey of US citizens, pewinternet.org 2012. www.pewinternet.org. Accessed April 2021
32. Kho, A.N., et al.: Electronic medical records for genetic research: results of the eMERGE consortium. Sci. Transl. Med. **3**, 79re1 (2011)
33. Nelson, C.A., Butte, A.J., Baranzini, S.E.: Integrating biomedical research and electronic health records to create knowledge-based biologically meaningful machine-readable embeddings. Nat. Commun. **10**, 3045 (2019)
34. Winslow, C.E.A.: The Evolution and Significance of the Modern Public Health Campaign. Yale University Press, New York (1923)
35. Turnock, B.: Public Health. Jones & Bartlett Publishers, Burlington (2012)
36. Kremastinou-Kourea, J.: Public Health: Theory, Action, Policies. Publications Technogramma, Athens (2007)
37. National Action Plan for Public Health 2008 – 2012, Ministry of Health & Social Solidarity, Athens 2008. https://www.moh.gov.gr/articles/health/domes-kai-draseis-gia-thn-ygeia/ethnika-sxedia-drashs/95-ethnika-sxedia-drashs. Accessed April 2021
38. National Action Plan for Public Health 2019 – 2022, Ministry of Health, National Council for Public Health, Athens 2019. https://www.moh.gov.gr/articles/health/domes-kai-draseis-gia-thn-ygeia/ethnika-sxedia-drashs/6237-ethniko-sxedio-drashs-gia-thn-dhmosia-ygeia. Accessed April 2021
39. Kiourtis, A., Mavrogiorgou, A., Menychtas, A., Maglogiannis, I., Kyriazis, D.: Structurally mapping healthcare data to HL7 FHIR through ontology alignment. J. Med. Syst. **43**(3), 62 (2019)

Evaluating Mental Patients Utilizing Video Analysis of Facial Expressions

M. Tziomaka[1] , A. Kallipolitis[1(✉)] , P. Tsanakas[2], and I. Maglogiannis[1]

[1] Department of Digital Systems, University of Piraeus, Piraeus, Greece
{tziomakamel,nasskall,imaglo}@unipi.gr
[2] National Technical University of Athens, Athens, Greece
panag@cs.ntua.gr

Abstract. The objective of this work is to put in numbers the degree of symptoms severity based on the social behavior and cognitive functioning of mental patients when conducting a routine conversation with their attending doctor. Examination of patient's facial expression manifestations can be a key indicator towards the quantization of cognitive impairment in respect to receiving external emotion expressions. Recent advancements in computer vision machine and deep learning techniques allow the evaluation and recognition of temporal emotional status through facial expressions. In this context, the paper studies the application of these techniques for the automated recognition of Positive and Negative Syndrome Scale (PANSS) indicators by means of extracting features from patients' facial expressions during video teleconferences. The paper discusses the technical details of the implementations of a video classification methodology for the prediction of schizophrenia symptoms' severity, introduces a novel approach for the interpretation of video classification results and presents initial results where it is demonstrated that the proposed automated techniques can classify to a certain extend specific PANSS indicators.

Keywords: Schizophrenia · Facial emotion recognition · Speeded up Robust Features · Efficient Net · Bag of visual words · Interpretability · PANSS

1 Introduction

Schizophrenia is a severe, complex, heterogenous psychiatric disorder that, apart from the negative effects influencing the life of the patients and its kinsfolk, may have devasting side effects in the financial of balance of a country, accounting for generating large expenditures concerning unemployment, social and health care [1]. It has been estimated that it affects 20 million people worldwide [2], who are 2 or 3 times more likely to die than the general population [3]. Even though the disorder is treatable, a significant percentage of patients fail to receive appropriate care [4], while others fail to be recognized as patients due to important challenges that haunt the respective diagnosis process. Equally challenging remains the understanding of causes and inner mechanisms

© IFIP International Federation for Information Processing 2021
Published by Springer Nature Switzerland AG 2021
I. Maglogiannis et al. (Eds.): AIAI 2021 Workshops, IFIP AICT 628, pp. 182–193, 2021.
https://doi.org/10.1007/978-3-030-79157-5_16

that lead to the specific disorder. Except for the diagnosis of a patient with schizophrenia, the effort of clinicians lies as well on the assessment of symptoms' severity when referring to already diagnosed schizophrenic patients due to its importance in effectively treating the disorder. One of the most dominant and well-established procedures in the assessment of symptoms severity as the Positive and Negative Syndrome Scale (PANSS) interview [5]. As its name states, the interview focuses on the evaluation of two types of symptoms, the positive ones that refer to the excessive occurrence of normal functions and the negative ones which correspond to limited occurrence of normal functions. Overall, 30 symptoms are rated on a scale from 1 to 7, resulting to a maximum score of 210 points. The symptoms are divided in three main categories: positive, negative, and general psychopathology symptoms. The main idea that connects facial emotion recognition to schizophrenia and PANSS is hidden in the cognitive impairment of patients to perceive emotional material [6]. This deficiency to decode human emotion leads to the generation of the patient's facial expressions that can be informative of the symptoms' scale. Schizophrenic patients demonstrate discomfort when having to deal with the interpretation of neutral or negative facial expressions. Since this discomfort is evident on their own facial expressions [14], their quantification can discover new knowledge concerning the cognitive impairment on different stages of the disorder.

Driven by the latest advancements in the field of Emotion Artificial Intelligence (EAI) [7] and in a wide range of technological areas, namely Healthcare [11], Augmented Reality [12], Internet of Things [13], Business Analytics [10], Advanced Driver Assistance [9] and Gaming [8] the quantification of facial emotion recognition (FER) has become the heart of many human-centered applications and it is gaining the industry as well due to its overwhelming results. In many cases, these applications utilize the universally recognized basic emotions as defined by Ekman in [15] as a standardized procedure to classify facial expression.

Taking under considerations the achievements in EAI and the need for the quantification of patients' facial expression in order to predict and discover meaningful correlations with PANSS indicators, we are focusing only on certain symptoms that can be directly induced by the facial expression manifestations. The corresponding PANNS items have been dictated by specialized personnel. Therefore, in this paper, we describe the design and implementation of a machine learning methodology, based on hand-crafted and learned features, extracted from video teleconferences for the prediction of schizophrenic syndrome's severity that has been assessed through PANSS questionnaires. Our main contribution lies on the effective prediction of specific questionnaire indicators and the introduction of a novel approach for video classification results. The results for some PANSS indicators are encouraging and suggest that automated facial expression recognition can be utilized for the prediction of symptoms severity.

The remainder of this paper is structured in 6 sections, as follows: Sect. 2 presents the related research works, while Sect. 3 describes the proposed methodology workflow. Section 4 reports the experiments conducted and the corresponding results. Section 5 explains the integrated interpretability scheme. Finally, Sect. 6 concludes the paper.

2 Related Work

As stated earlier, the basic hypothesis behind the effort to discover hidden associations and knowledge lies on the difficulty that schizophrenic patients face when trying to recognize stimuli, mostly negative, [16, 17] on other humans' facial expressions as it is directly connected to their cognitive deficiency. In most research works, an attempt has been witnessed to directly measure this difficulty by scoring the patients' answers a) as proposed by the automated tool Emotion Recognition Index (ERI) [18] analysis to find associations with symptoms' severity, functionality and cognitive impairment [19], and b) following the emotion recognition assessment described in [16] to discover impairments in patients at clinical high-risk for schizophrenia before the full expression of psychotic illness [21].

Non-verbal behavior of schizophrenic patients and its relation to symptoms' severity is examined as well in the literature, as it accounts for the expression of 60–65% of social communication [20]. In [22], non-verbal behavior, following the modified version of the Ethological Coding System for Interviews (ESCI), and symptoms' severity, based on three established scales [PANSS, (Clinical Assessment Interview for Negative Symptoms) CAINS and the Calgary scale], were separately evaluated by different specialized personnel to reach the fruitful conclusion that association between negative symptoms and a limited engaging non-verbal behavior truly exists. A different non -verbal approach is proposed in [23] by means of a joystick tracking task to assess the visual motor processing of schizophrenic patients.

Contrary to the basic trend that manually assess the verbal or non-verbal responses of schizophrenic patients to exterior stimuli and driven by the achievements of deep convolution neural networks (DCNN) in the field of Computer Vision, the research work in [24] proposed an automatic methodology for the analysis of patients' facial expressions to estimate symptoms of schizophrenia. The human pose estimation is the starting point through which the face is detected by means of a designated neural network for face detection. The extraction of low-level features in terms of action units in faces with a separate VGG-16 net is followed by the extraction of high-level features concerning each video. The results are promising and verify the automated detection of correlations between patients' facial expression and the corresponding symptoms. Towards the same path of facial expression automated analysis by means of machine learning and deep learning techniques are directed the efforts in [25, 26]. The video samples, through which the automated analysis of facial expressions is performed, are taken during the professional-patient interview for the assessment of symptoms severity and are in certain cases captured in a multiple camera setting or by utilizing special equipment (i.e., depth cameras).

Inspired by the abovementioned research work, we propose a simple, yet efficient architecture for the prediction of symptoms severity based on low-level (frame) and high-level (video) representations extracted from video teleconferences between clinicians and schizophrenic patients. The successful realization of an automated facial expression analysis system for the prediction of schizophrenia symptoms will discharge the psychiatrists from the burden of manually annotating recorded videos, enhance objectivity and reliability at the procedure of symptoms' severity estimation and make the assessment accessible to more patients through better allocation of freed resources and telemedicine.

3 Methodology

3.1 Overview

To classify the videos into the subscales of PANSS, the utilized techniques in this work follow a methodology scheme, which consists of four consecutive stages: Data Preprocessing, Frame Representation, Video Representation and Classification (Fig. 1).

3.2 Data Processing

Initially, each input video is converted into a sequence of RGB frames, with a sampling rate of one frame per second. After the frame extraction, the face region in each frame is detected by utilizing the Multiple Task Cascaded Neural Network (MTCNN) deep learning model [24] and cropping is performed to the dimensions of the detected face. As a result, we obtain a segmented region from each frame, to which the frame is cropped.

3.3 Frame Representation

For the representation of each frame, experiments with two different feature extraction techniques were conducted: the method of bag of visual words (BOVW) and the method of transfer learning, by utilizing a pre-trained convolutional neural network (CNN) as feature extractor.

In the case of utilizing the technique of BOVW, the first step is to detect the interest points of each frame, by utilizing the Speeded Up Robust Features (SURF) algorithm feature detector. The SURF algorithm [26] automatically detects by means of a fast Hessian detector n interest points, where n is the interest points of an image, and describes each one of them by assigning a 64-dimensional vector. After the detection and description of all interest points from all images in the dataset, a collection of 64-dimensional vectors is formed, which is in turn clustered into k groups, where k is a hyperparameter, utilizing the k-means algorithm. The centroid of each cluster represents a visual word, resulting in the formation of a visual vocabulary of k visual words. Lastly, the interest points of each image are assigned to a visual word, and the frequency of each word in an image is computed, thus forming a histogram of k values for each frame.

On the second approach, the pre-trained CNN that works as a feature extractor for the frame representation is the base model of the EfficientNet family of networks, the EfficientNet-B0 [25]. The network's architecture emerged by utilizing the method of multi-object neural architecture search on the ImageNet dataset to optimize accuracy and FLOPS, making it a high quality, yet compact model. Its main building block is the mobile inverted bottleneck convolution (MB Conv), with the depth-wise separable convolution.

Unlike the traditional convolution operation, which applies a 2-D depth filter to directly convolve the input in depth as well, depth-wise separable convolution uses each filter channel only at one input channel. Precisely, it breaks the filter and image into three different channels and applies the corresponding filter to the corresponding channel. Finally, it combines the output by applying a pointwise convolution. The MB Conv Block flips the classic wide – narrow – wide approach, in which skip connections

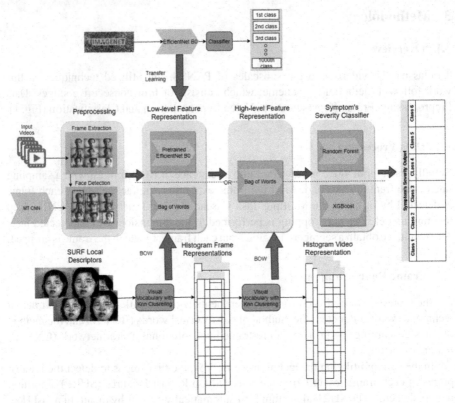

Fig. 1. Overview of the proposed methodology workflow with alternative scenarios.

exist between wide parts of the network, to a narrow– wide – narrow approach with skip connections between narrow parts of the network. The first step is a 1x1 convolution, which increases the depth, then follows a depth-wise convolution, and lastly another 1x1 convolution squeezes the network in order to match the initial number of channels for the skip connection. The EfficientNet-B0 not only provides better accuracy, as compared to other state-of-the-art models, but also improves the efficiency of the model by reducing the number of parameters. To leverage the power of the model, the method of transfer learning is employed, with weights pretrained on ImageNet. The pretrained model's last layers for classification are excluded and the layer that is used as a feature extractor, is the last convolutional layer that extracts richer features compared to the lower layers. Lastly, the output of the convolutional layer is flattened to create a single long 1,280-dimensional feature vector. To prepare the images before passing them through the network, all frames were resized according to EfficientNet-B0's input dimensions and normalized by subtracting the mean and dividing by the standard deviation RGB values of the ImageNet dataset, that were used to pretrain the model.

3.4 Video Representation

After the frame representation, the outcome from both approaches is a matrix of m x n for each video, where m is the number of frames in the video and n is the dimension of the feature-extracted vectors (n = k from the BOVW method or n = 1,280 from the transfer learning method). In turn, to represent each video with a vector, the method of BOVW was reapplied to the collection of all n-dimensional vectors of all videos. This collection of all frame representations is standardized and clustered into k' groups, with k' being an additional hyperparameter, as in this step the centroid of each of these clusters represents a visual word for the frame representations. Subsequently, the frame representations of each video are assigned to a visual word, to form a histogram of k' values for each video, which corresponds to a k'-dimensional vector.

3.5 Classification

To classify the video representations by means of the BOVW approach, we utilized three state-of-the-art machine learning models: XGBoost, Random Forest and Support Vector Machines (SVM) with radial basis function (RBF) kernel.

4 Experimental Results

The verification of the proposed methodology's performance on the task of predicting symptoms' severity on schizophrenic patients was done using a dataset that was organized and manually curated from video-teleconferences between professionals and patients obtained within the framework of the e-prevention project [30]. Patients are diagnosed with the disorder and have already suffered one serious episode. The ground truth concerning the symptoms severity was provided by PANSS questionnaires that were conducted by specialized personnel of the Eginition Hospital. At the time the tests were conducted, the number of videos is 167, corresponding to 22 patients. The videos are captured to two weeks or closer to the PANSS evaluation interview, which is a rather challenging requirement, given that previous work directly evaluates the video from the PANSS evaluation interview. Furthermore, they were captured in variating lighting and distance conditions and their duration spans from to 30 to 1141 s. During the video-teleconferences common everyday questions are asked to form a routine conversation between the individuals.

Regarding to the PANSS items that serve the cause of ground truth for the predictive model, ten were selected due to their correlation with the facial expressions, namely: excitement, hostility (positive items) anxiety, poor impulse, motor retardation, depression, tension (general items), blunted affect, poor rapport, lack of spontaneity, flow of conversation (negative items). For clarification, positive, negative, and general items are the three main scales of PANSS questionnaire. The values in the respective items that correspond to the symptoms' severity can take values from one to six according to Fig. 2. For the training of the various configurations of the predictive models a correspondence between videos and PANSS questionnaires was created by matching each video to the most recent questionnaire in a timeframe of two weeks, meaning that the video was captured at most two weeks before the questionnaire. The dataset was split into two subsets, training (70%) and testing (30%). The above-mentioned setting was utilized in different machine learning and deep learning techniques for the prediction of a specific PANSS item at a time.

As already mentioned in the methodology the various combinations of workflows follow the same guideline of a) initially transforming the input videos into cropped images of facial expressions, b) forming low-level representations from frames (facial expressions) and c) forming high-level representations from videos. In this context, we tested the following configurations: BOVW2, Bag of Visual Words (BOVW) for low-level representation and BOVW for high-level representation and EfficientNet to BOVW, EfficientNet for low-level representation and BOVW for high-level representation. For the determination of the number of clusters that would represent the visual vocabularies, we conducted exhaustive grid search resulting in different number of clusters for each case, for which we are presenting in Table 1 the best performing configurations. The performance is measured in terms of balanced accuracy and top-2 accuracy metrics. As far as the balanced accuracy metric is concerned, predictions of tension, hostility and poor impulse control's severities show the most promising results, whereas both configurations fail to predict anxiety and poor rapport. Against our expectations lies the fact that the pretrained Efficient Net extracted features show inferior performance than the SURF features. In some cases, such as the poor impulse control, poor rapport, tension, and excitement items top-2 accuracy supersedes the barrier of 80% and demonstrate big divergence from the balanced accuracy results.

5   Interpretability

Thanks to the simplicity of the proposed methodology, the direct association between the classification results and visual patterns in the video frames can be unveiled. The connection between cause and result is of major importance when developing a machine learning predictive model, since it provides useful insight concerning the reasoning of misclassifications, enhance trust and transparency towards the users and can lead to the discovery on newly breed knowledge through the dictation of patterns previously unknown to humans. Therefore, the build-in explainability properties in high-stake predictive models (i.e., health-care computer aided diagnosis systems) should be an important prerequisite [27]. In our proposed methodology (BOVW^2 configuration), the frame representation, video representation and classification stage are by design equipped with interpretable properties that can be seamlessly fused to provide measurements concerning the degree of visual patterns' influence to the result. As explained earlier, these measurements are the combination of a three-fold scheme. Firstly, the classifier provides a feature importance mechanism based on the individual inner workings that directly maps the output to those inputs that were mostly influential. By acquiring this feature importance map in the video representation stage, the information of the most important visual words is stored in a k' vector equal to the number of clusters corresponding to the clustering of all frame representations. Since, each frame is already assigned to a cluster, the importance of each frame can be calculated as follows:

$$I_{fr} = \frac{W_{vw}}{D_{fr}}, \tag{1}$$

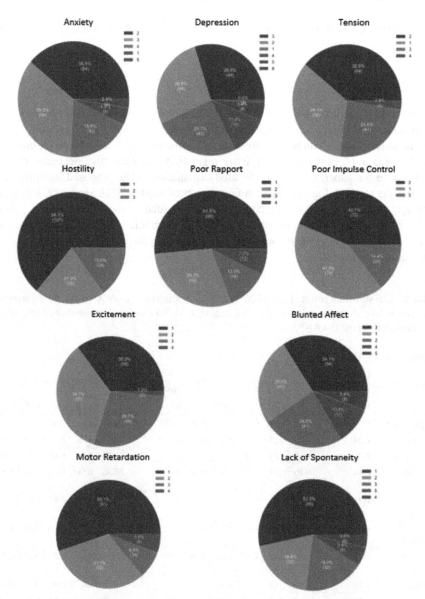

Fig. 2. Ground truth values according to selected PANSS items.

where I_{fr} is the importance of each frame, W_{fw} is the weight of the video visual word provided by the feature importance mechanism of the classifier and D_{fr} the distance of the frame representation from the assigned cluster in the frame representation clustering. In the same manner, the importance of each SURF keypoint in the cropped frame can be calculated to highlight the visual patterns in the patient's face that lead to the formation of a certain prediction, as described in Eq. (2):

$$I_k = \frac{I_{fr}}{D_k},$$
(2)

where I_k is the importance of each keypoint whose coordinates are known and D_k the distance of the frame representation from the assigned cluster in the keypoints representation clustering. I_k can be visually observed in the form of a heatmap on the cropped facial expression, but due to data privacy regulations the respective heatmaps cannot be shown in the paper. For a more detailed explanation of the proposed interpretation scheme, the methodology is based in the work presented in [28]. However, a general paradigm of the heatmap on a facial expression provided by the JAFFE dataset [29] is shown in Fig. 3. By utilizing the proposed interpretation scheme, useful knowledge can be extracted concerning the most significant frames and the most significant keypoints to the classification result.

Table 1. Classification results for $BOVW^2$ (left) and Efficient to BOVW (right) configurations based on balanced accuracy (left) and top-2 accuracy (right) metrics. The number of respective classes is shown next to PANSS items.

PANSS items	Configuration											
	$BOVW^2$						EfficientNet to BOVW					
	Balanced accuracy						Top-2 accuracy					
	RF		XFG		SVC		RF		XGB		SVC	
Depression (6c)	0.49	0.82	**0.6**	0.85	0.3	0.68	0.47	0.64	0.53	0.64	0.3	0.75
Anxiety (5c)	**0.44**	0.65	0.37	0.69	0.33	0.84	0.26	0.77	0.36	0.77	0.29	0.85
Tension (4c)	**0.7**	0.89	0.68	0.85	0.56	0.62	0.54	0.77	0.61	0.85	0.46	0.81
Poor rapport (4c)	0.44	0.86	0.49	0.9	0.34	0.68	0.41	0.86	**0.55**	0.82	0.34	0.57
Poor impulse control (3c)	**0.72**	1	0.71	0.79	0.39	1	0.43	0.96	0.66	0.82	0.37	0.96
Motor retardation (4c)	0.4	0.75	**0.6**	0.82	0.36	0.75	0.41	0.82	0.4	0.79	0.32	0.79
Excitement (4c)	0.58	0.78	**0.61**	0.82	0.42	0.78	0.49	0.85	0.47	0.85	0.41	0.67
Hostility (3c)	**0.72**	0.96	0.68	0.93	0.42	0.78	0.42	1	0.6	0.89	0.49	0.79
Blunted affect (5c)	**0.58**	0.68	0.55	0.64	0.34	0.64	0.34	0.64	0.47	0.68	0.3	0.64
Lack of spontaneity(5c)	0.49	0.64	**0.65**	0.79	0.4	0.75	0.49	0.64	0.26	0.68	0.43	0.75

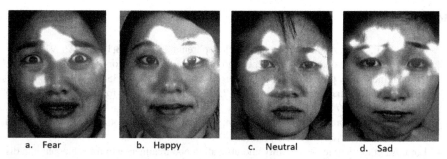

a. Fear   b. Happy   c. Neutral   d. Sad

Fig. 3. Keypoint importance heatmaps generated by the proposed methodology on facial expressions depicting four emotions from left to right: a. Fear, b. Happy, c. Neutral, d. Sad.

6 Conclusion

In this paper a video classification methodology for the prediction of schizophrenia symptoms' severity based on video-teleconferences between doctors and patients was presented. While the ground truth is provided by PANSS that are conducted in a two-weeks period before the videos, the predictive model manages to discover important correlations between facial expressions and specific PANSS items that evaluate symptoms' severity. The classification results show good performance in some cases. Although results are promising, further testing with the utilization of an anticipated larger dataset should be performed to enhance confidence in the presented results. The big divergence between the balanced and top-2 accuracy metrics can be strongly related with the subjectivity of PANSS questionnaire scoring. Future work will be focused on the utilization of transformers that are intended to extract knowledge from large sequences such as videos, the analysis and qualitive results of the interpretation scheme and towards the prediction of potential relapses of the disorder in diagnosed patients. Should public datasets be available, the testing for the generalization properties of our methodology will be conducted. To sum up, the PANSS questionnaire evaluation is a demanding task that requires time and excessive training and on-site presence. Automated estimation of PANSS items can assist clinician in this arduous process, make it more accessible to patients and provide objectivity and reliability.

Acknowledgment. This research has been co-financed by the European Regional Development Fund of the European Union and Greek national funds through the Operational Program Competitiveness, Entrepreneurship, and Innovation, under the call RESEARCH – CREATE – INNOVATE (project code: T1EDK-02890).

References

1. Owen, M.J., Sawa, A., Mortensen, P.B.: Schizophrenia. Lancet **388**(10039), 86–97 (2016)
2. GBD 2017 Disease and Injury Incidence and Prevalence Collaborators. Global, regional, and national incidence, prevalence, and years lived with disability for 354 diseases and injuries for 195 countries and territories, 1990–2017: a systematic analysis for the Global Burden of Disease Study 2017. The Lancet (2018)
3. Laursen, T.M., Nordentoft, M., Mortensen, P.B.: Excess early mortality in schizophrenia. Ann. Rev. Clin. Psychol. **10**, 425–438 (2014)
4. Lora, A., et al.: Service availability and utilization and treatment gap for schizophrenic disorders: a survey in 50 low- and middle-income countries. Bull. World Health Organ. **90**(1), 47–54 (2012)
5. Opler, M., Yavorsky, C., Daniel, D.G.: Positive and Negative Syndrome Scale (PANSS) training: challenges, solutions, and future directions. Innov. Clin. Neurosci. **14**(11–12), 77–81 (2017)
6. Kohler, C.G., Walker, J.B., Martin, E.A., Healey, K.M., Moberg, P.J.: Facial emotion perception in schizophrenia: a meta-analytic review. Schizophr Bull. **36**, 1009–1019 (2010)
7. Schuller, D., Schuller, B.W.: The age of artificial emotional intelligence. Computer **51**(9), 38–46 (2018)
8. McStay, A., Rosner, G.: Emotional artificial intelligence in children's toys and devices: ethics, governance, and practical remedies. Big Data Soc. **8**(1), 205395172199487 (2021)
9. Wilhelm, T.: Towards facial expression analysis in a driver assistance system. In: 14th IEEE International Conference on Automatic Face & Gesture Recognition (FG 2019), Lille, France, pp. 1–4 (2019)
10. Subhashini, R., Niveditha, P.R.: Analyzing and detecting employee's emotion for amelioration of organizations. Proc. Comput. Sci. **48**, 530–536 (2015)
11. Alhussein, M.: Automatic facial emotion recognition using weber local descriptor for e-Healthcare system. Clust. Comput. **19**(1), 99–108 (2016). https://doi.org/10.1007/s10586-016-0535-3
12. Chen, C.H., Lee, I.J., Lin, L.Y.: Augmented reality-based self-facial modeling to promote the emotional expression and social skills of adolescents with autism spectrum disorders. Res. Dev. **36**, 396–403 (2015)
13. Xi, Z., Niu, Y., Chen, J., Kan, X., Liu, H.: Facial expression recognition of industrial internet of things by parallel neural networks combining texture features. IEEE Trans. Ind. Inf. **17**(4), 2784–2793 (2021)
14. Tse, W.S., Lu, Y., Bond, A.J., Chan, R.C., Tam, D.W.: Facial emotion linked cooperation in patients with paranoid schizophrenia: a test on the interpersonal communication model. Int. J. Soc. Psychiatry **57**(5), 509–517 (2011)
15. Ekman, P.: Facial expression and emotion. Am. Psychol. **48**(4), 384 (1993)
16. Edwards, J., Jackson, H.J., Pattison, P.E.: Emotion recognition via facial expression and affective prosody in schizophrenia: a methodological review. Clin. Psychol. Rev. **22**, 789–832 (2002)
17. Adolphs, R., Tranel, D.: Impaired judgments of sadness but not happiness following bilateral amygdala damage. J. Cogn. Neurosci. **16**, 453–462 (2004)
18. Suárez-Salazar, J.V., Fresán-Orellana, A., Saracco-Álvarez, R.A.: Facial emotion recognition and its association with symptom severity, functionality, and cognitive impairment in schizophrenia: preliminary results. Salud Mental **43**(3), 105–112 (2020)
19. Burgoon, J.K., Guerrero, L.K., Floyd, K.: Nonverbal Communication, 1st (edn.). Allyn & Bacon, Boston (2010)

20. Amminger, G.P., et al.: Emotion recognition in individuals at clinical high-risk for schizophrenia. Schizophr. Bull. **38**(5), 1030–1039 (2012)
21. Worswick, E., Dimic, S., Wildgrube, C., Priebe, S.: Negative symptoms and avoidance of social interaction: a study of non-verbal behaviour. Psychopathology **51**(1), 1–9 (2018)
22. Lu, P.Y., Huang, Y.L., Huang, P.C., et al.: Association of visual motor processing and social cognition in schizophrenia. NPJ Schizophr **7**, 21 (2021)
23. Bishay, M., Palasek, P., Priebe, S., Patras, I.: SchiNet: automatic estimation of symptoms of schizophrenia from facial behaviour analysis. ArXiv http://arxiv.org/abs/1808.02531 (2018)
24. Zhang, K., Zhang, Z., Li, Z., Qiao, Y.: Joint Face detection and alignment using multitask cascaded convolutional networks. IEEE Signal Process. Lett. **23**, 1499–1503 (2016)
25. Tan, M., Le, Q.V.: EfficientNet: rethinking model scaling for convolutional neural networks. ArXiv http://arxiv.org/abs/1905.11946 (2019)
26. Bay, H., Tuytelaars, T., Gool, V.G.: Speeded up robust features. Comput. Vis. Image Underst. **110**(3), 346–359 (2008)
27. Rudin, C.: Stop explaining black box machine learning models for high stakes decisions and use interpretable models instead. Nat. Mach. Intell. **1**, 206–215 (2019)
28. Kallipolitis, A., Stratigos, A., Zarras, A., Maglogiannis, I.: Explainable fully connected visual words for the classification of skin cancer confocal images: interpreting the influence of visual words in classifying benign vs malignant pattern. In: 11th Hellenic Conference on Artificial Intelligence (2020)
29. Lyons, M., Akamatsu, S., Kamachi, M., Gyoba, J.: Coding facial expressions with Gabor wavelets. In Proceedings of the Third IEEE International Conference on Automatic Face and Gesture Recognition, pp. 200–205. IEEE Computer Society, Nara (1998)
30. Maglogiannis, I., et al.: Correction to: An Intelligent Cloud-Based Platform for Effective Monitoring of Patients with Psychotic Disorders. In: Maglogiannis, I., Iliadis, L., Pimenidis, E. (eds.) AIAI 2020. IAICT, vol. 584, pp. 293–307. Springer, Cham (2020). https://doi.org/10.1007/978-3-030-49186-4_38

An Inception-Based Architecture for Haemodialysis Time Series Classification

Giorgio Leonardi, Stefania Montani[✉], and Manuel Striani

DISIT, Computer Science Institute, Università del Piemonte Orientale,
Alessandria, Italy
stefania.montani@uniupo.it

Abstract. Classifying haemodialysis sessions, on the basis of the evolution of specific clinical variables over time, allows the physician to identify patients that are being treated inefficiently, and that may need additional monitoring or corrective interventions. In this paper, we propose a deep learning approach to clinical time series classification, in the haemodialysis domain. Specifically, grounding on our previous experience in adopting convolutional neural networks on haemodialysis time series, we have defined an inception-based architecture, able to exploit kernels of different sizes in parallel. The proposed architecture has outperformed the results obtained by resorting both to a more standard convolutional neural network, and to the state of the art approach ROCKET, since we reached higher accuracy values, coupled with a good Matthews Correlation Coefficient.

1 Introduction

End Stage Renal Disease (ESRD) is a severe chronic condition, which requires haemodialysis treatment. The efficacy of haemodialysis can be assessed on the basis of a few monitoring variables [2], regularly sampled during the treatment sessions (and thus recorded as time series). Among them, the behavior of the Haematic Volume (HV) is particularly important, because of its correlation to the water reduction rate and to the presence of cardiovascular alterations [10,17]. Classifying haemodialysis sessions on the basis of HV evolution over time allows the physician to identify patients that are being treated inefficiently, and/or that may need additional monitoring or corrective intervention because they are experiencing problems.

In the past [8,14], we proposed to afford this issue resorting to deep learning [13]. Specifically, we tested classical convolutional architectures, which are particularly suitable for time series data, due to their ability to model local dependencies that may exist between adjacent data points.

In this paper, we propose a more advanced convolutional solution, based on the exploitation of multiple instances of the so-called *inception* module [16].

© IFIP International Federation for Information Processing 2021
Published by Springer Nature Switzerland AG 2021
I. Maglogiannis et al. (Eds.): AIAI 2021 Workshops, IFIP AICT 628, pp. 194–203, 2021.
https://doi.org/10.1007/978-3-030-79157-5_17

In the following, we illustrate the network details and showcase our experiments, where the inception solution has outperformed both a standard convolutional neural network, and the state of the art tool ROCKET [4]: indeed, our approach has reached higher accuracy values, coupled with a good Matthews Correlation Coefficient.

The paper is organized as follows: in Sect. 2 we present background and related work; Sect. 3 illustrates the proposed deep learning architecture; Sect. 4 provides experimental results. Section 5 is devoted to discussion and conclusions.

2   Background and Related Work

Deep learning architectures are able to stack multiple layers of operations, in order to create a hierarchy of increasingly more abstract *deep* features [13]. These techniques have achieved a great success in computer vision, and also their adoption for time series data classification is gaining increasing attention in several domains [11,18,20], including health care (see, e.g., [6,8,15]).

In the following, we will introduce some background information about different deep learning architectures, as well as some related works dealing with their application to time series classification.

2.1   Convolutional Neural Networks

Convolutional Neural Networks (CNNs) operate by exploiting multiple convolution operators. A convolution is an operation which takes a filter and multiplies it over the entire area of the input. Convolution layers are followed by pooling layers, meant to further reduce dimensionality.

The convolution+pooling modules can be stacked in the network, providing progressively deeper architectures. The output of the final pooling layer is then typically flattened, and provided as an input to a fully connected network, outputting the class.

Composed of sparse connections with tied weights, CNNs have significantly fewer parameters than a fully connected network of similar size [1].

One-dimensional CNNs are particularly suitable for time series data, due to their ability to model local dependencies that may exist between adjacent data points [19], and to capture how the input evolves over time [12].

CNNs for time series classification have been proposed, e.g., in [3,5,15], and are the most popular deep learning approach in physiological signals classification, as testified in a recent survey [6]. We also obtained encouraging results in medical time series classification resorting to CNN in our previous work [8,14].

2.2   Inception Networks

The inception module, proposed in [16] as a building block for the GoogLeNet architecture, uses kernels of varied size in a convolution layer to capture features at different levels of abstraction. Since salient parts in images and sequences can have extremely large variation in size, choosing the right kernel for the convolution operation becomes difficult: large kernels are suited for globally distributed information, while small kernels work well with locally distributed information.

The inception module processes information at different scales, by exploiting branches with different kernels in parallel, and then aggregates them to efficiently extract relevant features. The network essentially gets a bit wider rather than deeper. Inception mitigates the problem of correctly setting the kernel size, since it simultaneously applies many convolutions with different kernel sizes to the same input.

This approach has been succesfully applied to the time series domain by the tool InceptionTime [7]. InceptionTime is however computationally expensive; as a further evolution, therefore, the tool ROCKET [4] has been proposed, which uses random convolutional kernels, and achieves satisfactory accuracy results while reducing computation time.

3   Inception-Based Classification

Our implementation of inception-based classification, depicted in Fig. 1, exploits a basic module (see the blue box in the figure) presenting three convolutions with kernels of sizes 1, 3, and 5, respectively, in parallel also to a 3 max-pooling path. The outputs of the parallel branches are then concatenated.

Three basic inception modules built as explained above are then cascaded in our proposed architecture, and passed through a final sigmoid layer for classification. Every convolution branch is composed by 16 kernels and is activated by the Rectified Linear Unit function. Parameters were set experimentally.

We have also implemented a simpler architecture for comparison. This architecture, depicted in Fig. 2, is a more standard CNN with 3 one-dimensional convolution layers, with a kernel size of 1, 3 and 5 respectively, Rectified Linear Unit activation function, and 16, 32 and 64 kernels respectively. Each convolution layer is followed by a max pooling layer with a pool size of 2. The output of the last pooling layer is provided to a layer using the sigmoid activation function to output a final node, representing the predicted class. The parameters values were set experimentally in this case as well.

4   Results

Our input HV time series were recordings of 240 samples on average, with a sampling time of 1 min. We truncated longer series, and added zeros to extend shorter series. We worked with a dataset of 5914 time series, belonging to 75 different patients (72 series per patient on average, varying from 1 to 280).

Our classification was a binary one, where positive cases represent time series whose plot suggests an insufficient reduction of water and metabolites from the patient's blood, while negative cases are related to non-problematic haemodialysis sessions. Examples of a positive and negative case are shown in Fig. 3.

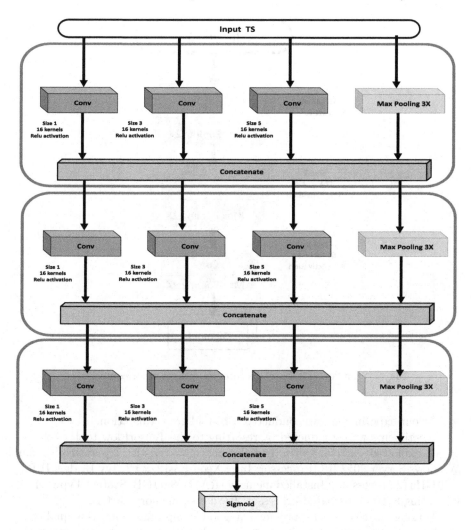

Fig. 1. Inception-based classification architecture (Color figure online)

We performed the labeling process in two steps: first, each time series was de-noised through wavelet transform and its gradient was calculated over time to apply a first temporary label; then, the labeled time series were validated by medical experts to confirm or to correct the automatically assigned labels on the basis of domain knowledge. At the end of the process, 4048 negative cases and 1866 positive cases were made available.

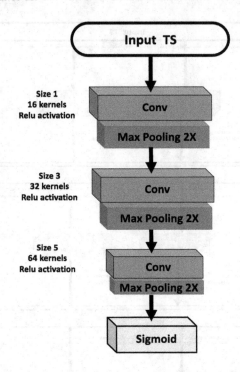

Fig. 2. Standard CNN architecture, implemented for comparison

For our experiments, we conducted a 10-fold cross validation.

Experiments were conducted by resorting to the TensorFlow tool[1].

We exploited a machine with the following characteristics: Operating System: Windows Server 2012 R2; Processor: Intel Xeon E3-12xx v2 (Ivy Bridge, IBRS) 2.70 GHz (2 processors); Installed memory (RAM): 8.00 GB; System Type: 64-bit Operating System, 64-based processor; Hard disk memory: 40 GB.

Working at 100 epochs provided a good compromise between quality of results and computation time, as shown in Figs. 4 and 5, which compare the evolution of the loss values over the number of epochs for the standard CNN and for the inception-based architecture, respectively.

The CNN approach provided an average accuracy of 76%. The complete results are shown in Table 1, which also reports on precision, recall, F1-score, Matthews Correlation Coefficient (MCC, a parameter which is particularly suitable to assess the quality of classification when dealing with unbalanced classes, and should be ideally close to 1), and K-statistics. The validation results are provided for each class and as the weighted average by class cardinality, according to the unbalanced distribution of positive and negative cases. Class 0 refers to the positive cases, while class 1 refers to the negative ones. MCC, K-statistics and accuracy are not related to a single class, therefore we provide them only as overall results.

---

[1] https://www.tensorflow.org/.

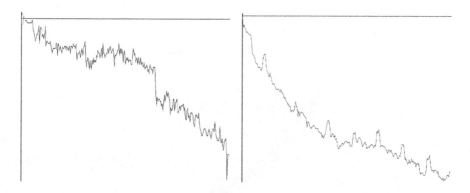

Fig. 3. Example of a positive case (left) and of a negative case (right)

Table 1. Results obtained by the CNN-based classifier

Class	Precision	Recall	F1-score	MCC	K-Stat	Acc.
0 (positive)	0.65	0.52	0.58			
1 (negative)	0.79	0.87	0.83			
Weighted ave.	0.74	0.76	0.74	0.42	0.41	0.76

Inception-based classification (Fig. 1) performed very well, as shown in Table 2. In particular, accuracy reached 88%, coupled with a MCC of 0.73, much higher than the 0.42 obtained by the standard CNN architecture.

Table 2. Results obtained by the inception-based classifier

Class	Precision	Recall	F1-score	MCC	K-Stat	Acc.
0 (positive)	0.84	0.78	0.81			
1 (negative)	0.90	0.93	0.91			
Weighted ave.	0.88	0.88	0.88	0.73	0.62	0.88

We also made a comparison to the state of the art literature approach ROCKET [4], presented in Sect. 2.2[2]. As shown in Table 3, ROCKET results were better then the ones of the basic CNN classifier, but poorer then the ones of our inception-based architecture.

---

[2] We exploited the implementation provided at https://github.com/angus924/rocket (last accessed on March 23rd 2021). Note that in this case the number of epochs cannot be set.

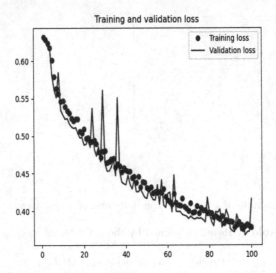

Fig. 4. Evolution of the loss values over the number of epochs for the standard CNN architecture

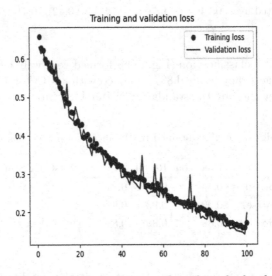

Fig. 5. Evolution of the loss values over the number of epochs for the inception-based architecture

Table 3. Results obtained by the ROCKET classifier

Class	Precision	Recall	F1-score	MCC	K-Stat	Acc.
0 (positive)	0.60	0.73	0.66			
1 (negative)	0.90	0.83	0.86			
Weighted ave.	0.80	0.80	0.80	0.53	0.53	0.80

As a final experiment, we tested a patient-based cross-validation (leave-one-patient-out). Each one of the three models tested above (namely, CNN-based architecture, inception-based architecture and ROCKET) was learned on all records from all patients except one, and tested on records from that single patient, and this procedure was repeated for all patients. This technique rules out overly optimistic results, that may be obtained when the dataset contains many records from a single patient, and the test is executed on some record of the same patient. The approach also allows one to mitigate the risk of overfitting [9].

The results obtained by the inception-based architecture (Table 4) and by ROCKET (Table 5) were (not surprisingly) worse than the corresponding ones already presented in Table 2 and Table 3, respectively, but still encouraging. Analogous considerations hold for the results of the CNN-based architecture (not reported due to lack of space).

Moreover, our proposed inception-based architecture outperformed the other tools in this experiment as well.

These findings support the hypothesis that our proposed architecture is actually performing well, and that high accuracy values should not be interpreted in the light of overfitting problems.

Table 4. Results obtained by the inception-based classifier with a leave-one-patient-out cross validation

Class	Precision	Recall	F1-score	MCC	K-Stat	Accuracy
0 (positive)	0.66	0.68	0.67			
1 (negative)	0.86	0.85	0.85			
Weighted average	0.79	0.79	0.79	0.52	0.52	0.79

Table 5. Results obtained by the ROCKET classifier with a leave-one-patient-out cross validatio

Class	Precision	Recall	F1-score	MCC	K-Stat	Accuracy
0 (positive)	0.50	0.70	0.58			
1 (negative)	0.90	0.80	0.85			
Weighted average	0.77	0.77	0.76	0.44	0.43	0.77

5   Conclusions

HV time series classification can help physicians in identifying haemodialysis treatment inefficiency, allowing for early interventions that can lead to an overall optimization of patient care.

In this paper, we have proposed a deep learning approach for HV classification, based on the exploitation of multiple inception modules, defining the architecture illustrated in Fig. 1. This solution reached an 88% accuracy in cross validation, coupled with a high MCC (0.73), outperforming the more standard CNN architecture we implemented for comparison, and even the state of the art tool ROCKET [4].

In the future, we plan to conduct additional experiments, by considering other haemodialysis time series variables as well.

Moreover, since deep learning methods operate as black boxes, and it can be difficult to justify misclassification, we will also consider the issue of explainability. To this end, we will investigate whether it is possible to adapt a knowledge-based strategy, along the lines we already tracked in [14].

References

1. Alom, M.Z., et al.: A state-of-the-art survey on deep learning theory and architectures. Electronics **8**(3), 292 (2019)
2. Bellazzi, R., Larizza, C., Magni, P., Bellazzi, R.: Temporal data mining for the quality assessment of a hemodialysis service. Artif. Intell. Med. **34**, 25–39 (2005)
3. Cui, Z., Chen, W., Chen, Y.: Multi-scale convolutional neural networks for time series classification. CoRR abs/1603.06995 (2016)
4. Dempster, A., Petitjean, F., Webb, G.I.: Rocket: Exceptionally fast and accurate time series classification using random convolutional kernels. Data Min. Knowl. Discov. **34**(5), 1454–1495 (2019)
5. Fan, X., Yao, Q., Cai, Y., Miao, F., Sun, F., Li, Y.: Multiscaled fusion of deep convolutional neural networks for screening atrial fibrillation from single lead short ECG recordings. IEEE J. Biomed. Health Inform. **22**(6), 1744–1753 (2018)
6. Faust, O., Hagiwara, Y., Hong, T.J., Lih, O.S., Acharya, U.R.: Deep learning for healthcare applications based on physiological signals: a review. Comput. Methods Programs Biomed. **161**, 1–13 (2018)
7. Fawaz, H.I., et al.: Inceptiontime finding: alexnet for time series classification. Data Min. Knowl. Discov. **34**(6), 1936–1962 (2019)
8. Leonardi, G., Montani, S., Striani, M.: Deep learning for haemodialysis time series classification. In: Marcos, M., et al. (eds.) KR4HC/TEAAM -2019. LNCS (LNAI), vol. 11979, pp. 50–64. Springer, Cham (2019). https://doi.org/10.1007/978-3-030-37446-4_5
9. Gao, Y., Zhang, X., Wang, S., Zoub, G.: Model averaging based on leave-subject-out cross-validation. J. Econometrics **192**, 139–151 (2016)
10. Krepel, H.P., Nette, R.W., Akcahuseyin, E., Weimar, W., Zietse, R.: Variability of relative blood volume during hemodialysis. Nephrol. Dial. Transplant. **15**, 673–679 (2000). https://doi.org/10.1093/ndt/15.5.673
11. Längkvist, M., Karlsson, L., Loutfi, A.: A review of unsupervised feature learning and deep learning for time-series modeling. Pattern Recogn. Lett. **42**, 11–24 (2014)
12. Lea, C., Vidal, R., Reiter, A., Hager, G.D.: Temporal convolutional networks: a unified approach to action segmentation. In: Hua, G., Jégou, H. (eds.) ECCV 2016. LNCS, vol. 9915, pp. 47–54. Springer, Cham (2016). https://doi.org/10.1007/978-3-319-49409-8_7

13. LeCun, Y., Bengio, Y., Hinton, G.E.: Deep learning. Nature **521**(7553), 436–444 (2015)
14. Leonardi, G., Montani, S., Striani, M.: Deep feature extraction for representing and classifying time series cases: towards an interpretable approach in haemodialysis. In: Proceedings of the 33rd International Florida Artificial Intelligence Research Society Conference, FLAIRS 2020, Miami, Florida. AAAI Press (2020)
15. Sani, S., Wiratunga, N., Massie, S., Cooper, K.: kNN sampling for personalised human activity recognition. In: Aha, D.W., Lieber, J. (eds.) ICCBR 2017. LNCS (LNAI), vol. 10339, pp. 330–344. Springer, Cham (2017). https://doi.org/10.1007/978-3-319-61030-6_23
16. Szegedy, C., et al.: Going deeper with convolutions. In: IEEE Conference on Computer Vision and Pattern Recognition, CVPR 2015, Boston, MA, USA, 7–12 June 2015, pp. 1–9. IEEE Computer Society (2015)
17. Titapiccolo, J.I., et al.: Relative blood volume monitoring during hemodialysis in end stage renal disease patients. In: Conference Proceedings: Annual International Conference of the IEEE Engineering in Medicine and Biology Society. IEEE Engineering in Medicine and Biology Society. Conference 2010, pp. 5282–5285, August 2010. https://doi.org/10.1109/IEMBS.2010.5626307
18. Wang, H., Sun, W., Liu, P.X.: Adaptive intelligent control of nonaffine nonlinear time-delay systems with dynamic uncertainties. IEEE Trans. Systems Man Cybern.: Syst. **47**(7), 1474–1485 (2017)
19. Wang, Z., Yan, W., Oates, T.: Time series classification from scratch with deep neural networks: a strong baseline. In: 2017 International Joint Conference on Neural Networks, IJCNN 2017, Anchorage, AK, USA, 14–19 May 2017, pp. 1578–1585. IEEE (2017)
20. Zhao, X., Shi, P., Zheng, X., Zhang, J.: Intelligent tracking control for a class of uncertain high-order nonlinear systems. IEEE Trans. Neural Netw. Learn. Syst. **27**(9), 1976–1982 (2016)

Workshop on Defense Applications in AI (DAAI 2021)

The 1st Workshop on Defense Applications of AI – (DAAI 2021)

This workshop was organized by the European Defense Agency (EDA) a European Union (EU) Organization. Defense and Security systems are becoming more and more complicated and at the same time equipped with a plethora of sensing devices which collect an enormous amount of information both from their operating environment as well as from their own functioning. Considering the accelerating technology advancements of AI, it is likely that it will have a profound impact on practically every segment of daily life, from the labor market to doing business and providing services.

The security and defense sectors will not remain idle or unaffected by this technological evolution. On the contrary, AI is expected to transform the nature of future defence and security domains, because by definition defense and security forces are highly dependent on (accurate) data and (reliable) information. The first Defense Applications of Artificial Intelligence (DAAI) Workshop aims at presenting recent evolutions in artificial intelligence applicable to defense and security applications.

Organization

Committee

Panagiotis Kikiras (Program Chair)   European Defence Agency
Evangelos Ouzounis   European Union Agency for Cybersecurity
Sergio Albani   European Union Satellite Centre
Fabrizzio Berizi   European Defence Agency.
Antonio Manzalini   Telecom Italia Mobile (TIM)
Massimiliano Nolich   Universita' degli studi di Trieste
Konstantinos Demertzis   .

Topics of Interest

1. Applications of AI in Security and Defence focusing on (machine learning, natural language processing, data management aspects, intelligent agents & robotics, computer vision, knowledge representation & reasoning, human-machine decision making)
2. Responsible and trusted AI applications and algorithms
3. Security and resilience of AI enabled systems
4. Cyber risk of AI based systems.

Keynote Speakers under the
DAAI 2021 Workshop

Artificial Intelligence Cybersecurity Challenges

Evangelos Ouzounis

European Union Agency for Cybersecurity

Bio: Dr. Evangelos OUZOUNIS is a senior expert at ENISA, the European Network Information Security Agency. He is responsible for the security policy section of the Technical Department of the Agency. The section contributes to the multi thematic program one, Resilience of public e-Communication Networks and develops position papers on emerging technical issues like mobile eIDs, social networking, virtual worlds and privacy issues of mobile eID cards. Dr. Ouzounis' personal contribution is on policy and regulatory issues related to the resilience of public e-Communication Networks. Recently, he published the analysis and stock taking of 25EEA countries' national policy and regulatory environments. His work will continue with development of good practice guides incident reporting management, information sharing, and exercises. Prior to his position at ENISA, Dr. Ouzounis worked several years as a project officer at the European Commission, DG Information Society and Media(DG INFSO). He significantly contributed to the development of DG INFSO's strategy and policy related to secure application provision (e.g. eGovernment, eBusiness and eHealth), eIds, and secure software development. Dr. Ouzounis was co-founder of Electronic Commerce Centre of Competence (ECCO) at Fraunhofer Institute for Open Communication Systems (FhG-FOKUS, Berlin, Germany). He led and managed more than 20 pan European and International R&D projects in the areas of virtual organizations, secure distributed middleware, intelligent agents and web services. He was a lecturer at Technical University of Berlin, wrote 2 books and more than 20 peer reviewed academic papers and chaired several international conferences. Dr. Ouzounis holds a Ph.D from the Technical University of Berlin and a master from the Technical University of Patras in computer engineering and informatics.

Application of AI for GEOINT Services in the Space and Security Domain

Sergio Albani

European Union Satellite Centre

The scope of the presentation will be to present the state of the art of GEOINT services for the security and defense applications and to demonstrate the benefit and impact of AI algorithms to these services.

Bio: Sergio Albani is the Head of Research, Technology Development and Innovation (RTDI) Unit at the European Union Satellite Centre. He is in charge of implementing new operational solutions in the Space and Security domain looking at the whole EO and collateral data lifecycle; this is performed by exploiting new data acquisition systems, secure satellite communications, emerging technologies and innovative EO based solutions. He is responsible for several H2020 projects as well as ESA Point of Contact and GEO Principal Alternate. Mr. Albani holds a Master's degree in Physics (Astrophysics and Space Physics branch) and a 2nd Level Specializing Master's Degree in journalism and Scientific & Institutional Communication.

A Lipschitz - Shapley Explainable Defense Methodology Against Adversarial Attacks

Konstantinos Demertzis[1,2]([⊠]), Lazaros Iliadis[1], and Panagiotis Kikiras[3]

[1] School of Civil Engineering, Democritus University of Thrace, Kimmeria, Xanthi, Greece
kdemertz@fmenr.duth.gr, liliadis@civil.duth.gr
[2] Department of Physics, International Hellenic University, St. Loukas, 65404 Kavala, Greece
[3] Department of Computer Science, University of Thessaly, 35100 Lamia, PC, Greece
kikirasp@uth.gr

Abstract. Every learning algorithm, has a specific bias. This may be due to the choice of its hyperparameters, to the characteristics of its classification methodology, or even to the representation approach of the considered information. As a result, Machine Learning modeling algorithms are vulnerable to specialized attacks. Moreover, the training datasets are not always an accurate image of the real world. Their selection process and the assumption that they have the same distribution as all the unknown cases, introduce another level of bias. Global and Local Interpretability (GLI) is a very important process that allows the determination of the right architectures to solve Adversarial Attacks (ADA). It contributes towards a holistic view of the Intelligent Model, through which we can determine the most important features, we can understand the way the decisions are made and the interactions between the involved features. This research paper, introduces the innovative hybrid Lipschitz - Shapley approach for Explainable Defence Against Adversarial Attacks. The introduced methodology, employs the Lipschitz constant and it determines its evolution during the training process of the intelligent model. The use of the Shapley Values, offers clear explanations for the specific decisions made by the model.

Keywords: Explainable AI · AI defense · Adversarial Attacks · Global interpretability · Shapley values · Lipschitz constraint

1 Introduction

Machine learning models typically accept input data and they lead to problem solving, such as pattern recognition by implementing a series of specific transformations. Most of these transformations prove to be very sensitive to small changes in their input [1]. Utilization of this sensitivity, can, under certain conditions, lead to a modification of the learning algorithm's behavior. The term *Adversarial Attack* [2, 3] is used to describe the design of specific input (not easily perceivable by human observers) which can lead the learning algorithm to erroneous results. This is a major problem in the reliability and security of computational intelligence methods. The problem arises from the fact that

© IFIP International Federation for Information Processing 2021
Published by Springer Nature Switzerland AG 2021
I. Maglogiannis et al. (Eds.): AIAI 2021 Workshops, IFIP AICT 628, pp. 211–227, 2021.
https://doi.org/10.1007/978-3-030-79157-5_18

learning techniques are designed for stable environments, in which training and testing data are considered to be generated from the same (possibly unknown) distribution [4]. For example, a trained neural network represents a large decision limit, corresponding to a common class. A properly designed and implemented attack corresponding to a modified input, may come from a slightly differentiated data set and it can lead the algorithm to make a wrong classification decision. For example, the basic structure of a simple neural network consists of two levels of perceptrons, where the former receives the input vector as input and the latter receives the output of the first layer and produces the final output of the network. A classifier that is implemented with the above architecture, accepts as input the vector of the graded characteristics $x_1, x_2, ..., x_D$ and produces the output y_k as follows [5]:

$$y_k = \sigma \left(\sum_{j=0}^{M} w_{kj}^{(2)} \sigma \left(\sum_{i=0}^{D} w_{ji}^{(1)} x_i \right) \right) k = 1, 2, ..., K \tag{1}$$

where k is the total number of the network's output, M is the number of the perceptrons, σ is the activation function and $w_{ji}^{(p)}$ the weights that should be trained.

Such classifiers require the input of a feature vector, which can serve as a good representation of the input model. This architecture is based on the direct promotion of the input, from a lower level to a higher one. A group of successive levels that accept input x, produces an output $F(x)$. The final result is equal to $F(x) + x$.

Let us assume a process that attempts *Adversarial Attacks* on a trained network, which classifies input x (of the input space I) as a member of class $F(x) = L, L \in \{1, ..., k\}$. Then the ADA is achieved by minimizing $\|r\|_2$ such as [6]:

$$F(x + r) = L_2 \neq L = F(x) \text{ και } x + r = I \tag{2}$$

In the above modeling, it is considered that two inputs are identical when the L_2 norm of their difference is small. This is a simplification of the problem as the aim is the maximization of the similarity that an observer perceives when he/she sees the two input values. Thus, the measure of similarity of two inputs is an important parameter of the problem, which also affects the approximate solutions that are usually developed. More generally, the detection of *Adversarial Attacks* for a distance $d(x, y)$ different than the L_2 norm of the difference between x, y, is estimated as [7]:

$$\underset{y}{argmin} d(x, y) : F(x) \neq L_2 \text{ and } d(x, y) < \tau \tag{3}$$

It should be specified that τ is the threshold for which if two images x, y have a distance $(x, y) < \tau$, then they are considered as similar by a human observer. For example, let us consider that we are developing an *Adversarial Attack*, by employing the *Fast Gradient Signed Method* (FGSM) [8]:

$$adv_x = x + \epsilon * sign(\nabla_x J(\theta, x, y)) \tag{4}$$

where adv_x is the *Adversarial Image*, x is the original input image, y is the original input label, ϵ is a multiplier to ensure that the perturbations are small, θ is a parameter of the

Fig. 1. Tank 92.55% confidence by VGG-16 Network Architecture

model and J is the loss. If we apply this specific procedure and the *VGG-16 Convolutional Neural Network* (as analytically described in the third chapter) we are performing an initial classification of the following image with 92.55% confidence (Fig. 1).

Then we develop perturbations which will be used for the development of the adversarial attacks [3, 9] (Fig. 2).

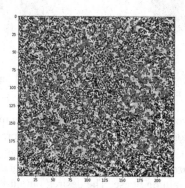

Fig. 2. Perturbations

After applying the FGSM methodology and developing the above perturbations, we obtain adversarial examples, which are given to the network for classification. The results are displayed in the images below (Figs. 3 and 4).

Adversarial Attacks, have been recorded against *anti-spam* filtering, where the system was misled based on the spelling of the keywords. Also, ADA have been used in *cyber-attacks*, by exploiting fake network packets, in deceptively detecting virus signatures and also in biometric identification attacks, where fake biometric features have been used. ADA Defense Strategies (ADA_DS) are based either on modifying the classifier's parameters in order to make it more robust, or on detecting attacks, by using a classifier that can generate *Aggressive Patterns*. Following this approach, ADA_DS recognize these patterns, by introducing them to their own training set. For example, during the

Fig. 3. Tank 80.95% (epsilon 0.15) and 64.62% (epsilon 0.17) confidence

Fig. 4. Tank 29.02% (epsilon 0.19) and Park bench 21.92% (epsilon 0.21) confidence

training of a Neural Network, it learns to successfully identify samples that belong to the training data distribution (DADI). At the same time, it produces large changes in its output, for samples that are in a close distance from the training DADI. Neural networks learn to recognize *Adversarial Attacks* by introducing a linear combination of the patterns of the original set, in the training phase. The desired output is the corresponding linear combination of the original desired outputs. The desired output is the corresponding linear combination of the desired outputs of the original models. More specifically, if $\lambda \in [0, 1]$ and x_i, x_j are two cases of the training set, then the values x_{new} and $f(x_{new})$ are given by the following Eqs. 5 and 6 [2, 7]:

$$x_{new} = \lambda x_i + (1 - \lambda)x_j \tag{5}$$

$$f(x_{new}) = \lambda f(x_i) + (1 - \lambda)f(x_j) \tag{6}$$

Thus, the training set acquires a more generalized distribution, and the network reaches a better generalization. It does not have large deviation for points of the input space located outside the distribution of the initial training set. The method succeeds in improving network's performance, even for the cases of datasets in which we would expect the classification function to display significant nonlinearities. Respectively, an effective method of defense is based on the observation that the aggressive cases do not belong to the manifold of the real input data. At the same time, they are closer to the sub-manifold to which the cases of their real category belong. Specifically, let us consider that Y_c is the set of vectors of the training data that belong to a class c, and y is the vector of the input features. Then the $\hat{f}_c(y)$ which is the density distribution of the actual characteristics of category c at point y is estimated as follows [7, 10]:

$$\hat{f}_c(y) = \frac{1}{|Y_c|} \sum_{y_i \in Y_c} exp\left(\frac{-\|y - y_i\|_2^2}{\sigma^2}\right) \tag{7}$$

Where $|Y_c|$ is the number of the elements of the set Y_c. According to this method, an aggressive input corresponding to a real class c_1, can be identified as class c_2, when $\hat{f}_{c_1}(x) > \hat{f}_{c_2}(x)$.

Extending this view, can be used to extract *Bayesian* uncertainty from a neural network (NN), which has been trained using the dropout method. In this case, an input x takes the output $y_1, y_2, \ldots, y_T$ for T different sets of the network's parameters. The network's uncertainty $U(x)$ in point x is estimated by the following relation [6, 8, 10]:

$$U(x) = \frac{1}{T} \sum_{i=1}^{T} y_i^T y_i - \left(\frac{1}{T} \sum_{i=1}^{T} y_i\right)^T \left(\frac{1}{T} \sum_{i=1}^{T} y_i\right) \tag{8}$$

Assuming that aggressive inputs occur in areas of the network where there is high uncertainty, U (x) is a useful metric for determining whether an input x is aggressive or not. Thus the combination of the above two metrics is an appropriate solution for detecting *Adversarial Attacks*.

2   Proposed Method

An innovative, hybrid *Lipschitz-Shapley* methodology for *Explainable Defense against Adversarial Attacks* was developed, aiming to offer a cybersecurity environment with robust solutions capable of recognizing specialized attacks. The proposed methodology, explores the evolution of the *Lipschitz* constant during the training of the intelligent model, while the *Shapley* Values produce clear explanations as to why the model made a particular decision. Specifically using the *Lipschitz* constant we can study the behavior of the *Scattering transform* when introducing *Aggressive Inputs*. This transformation, can approach the operation of a simple Neural Network's architecture, by allowing the study of the way NN succeed in solving difficult problems that require multistage extraction of features.

At the same time, the properties of this transformation explain how a Neural Network can achieve invariability in the displacement of the input, as well as in small deformations of the input, as in cases of elastic deformation. More specifically, the *Aggressive Inputs* are produced when in the input h we add a very small change p. Thus, we obtain the new input $h + p$, which is classified with a properly chosen input function p, in a different way than the initial input such as [4, 11, 12]:

$$\|S[m](h + p) - S[m](h)\| \leq \|p\| \tag{9}$$

So, it turns out that the output for an aggressive image is no different from the original input, more than $\|p\|$. Thus, the transformation follows the constraints of the *Scattering* transformation based on the following [13, 14]:

$$\sum_{i=1}^{N} \left| \widehat{\psi}_{(i,j)(\omega)} \right|^2 \leq \frac{C^2}{N}, \left| \widehat{\varphi}_{(\omega)} \right|^2 \leq C^2 \tag{10}$$

For a value C:

$$\|S[m](h+p) - S[m](h)\| \leq C^{m+1} \|p\| \tag{11}$$

This means that the constant C is a factor that determines how vulnerable the transformation is to the potential changes of the input against p.

In this research we attempt to detect the evolution of the *Lipschitz* constant [15], during the training of a neural network when we use defense methods. In particular, suppose that the input of a Convolutional Neural Network (CNN) is in the form of a vector. Let $f(x_{in}, c)$ be the output of the network for the class c when the input vector is x_{in}. Let y_{in}, h_{in} be two different input vectors, with respective output $f(y_{in}, c), f(h_{in}, c)$ where y_{ik}, h_{ik} are the outputs of the kth layer in channel i for each one of the 2 inputs. The CNN comprises of convolutional layers, pooling layers and ReLU activation functions. For each of the three types of layers we have:

1) Layer k is a convolution layer. As the images are expressed as one dimensional vectors, the convolution with a two dimensional core ψ_{ijk}, which connects the i output channel with the j input channel, is developed by multiplying the input vector with the table A_{ijk} that is produced by the initial core as follows [7, 11, 16, 17]:

$$x_{ik} = \sum_{j=1}^{N_k} A_{ijk} x_{j(k-1)} i = 1, 2, \ldots, M_k \tag{12}$$

where N_k is the number of the input channels and M_k is the number of the output channels of the convolutional layer k.

$$\|y_{ik} - h_{ik}\|_2 = \left\| \sum_{j=1}^{N_k} A_{ijk} y_{j(k-1)} - \sum_{j=1}^{N_k} A_{ijk} h_{j(k-1)} \right\|_2$$

$$= \left\| \sum_{j=1}^{N_k} A_{ijk} \left(y_{j(k-1)} - h_{j(k-1)} \right) \right\|_2$$

$$\leq \sum_{j=1}^{N_k} \left\| A_{ijk} \left(y_{j(k-1)} - h_{j(k-1)} \right) \right\|_2$$

$$\leq \sum_{j=1}^{N_k} \|A_{ijk}\|_2 \|y_{j(k-1)} - h_{j(k-1)}\|_2 \tag{13}$$

$$\Rightarrow \|y_{ik} - h_{ik}\|_2 \leq \sum_{j=1}^{N_k} \|A_{ijk}\|_2 \|y_{j(k-1)} - h_{j(k-1)}\|_2 \tag{14}$$

2) Let k be the Pooling layer where we do not have any overlapping areas, such as:

$$\|y_{ik} - h_{ik}\|_2 \leq \|y_{j(k-1)} - h_{j(k-1)}\|_2 \tag{15}$$

3) If the ReLU function is applied, then the output vector has the following form:

$$x_{ik} = \begin{bmatrix} x_{ik}(1) \\ x_{ik}(2) \\ \vdots \\ x_{ik}(m) \end{bmatrix} \tag{16}$$

The output $x_{ik}(t)$ is estimated as follows:

$$x_{ik}(t) = max(0, x_{i(k-1)}(t)) \tag{17}$$

$$\|y_{ik} - h_{ik}\|_2^2 = \sum_{t=1}^{m} |max(0, y_{i(k-1)}(t)) - max(0, h_{i(k-1)}(t))|^2$$

$$\leq \sum_{t=1}^{m} |y_{j(k-1)}(t) - h_{j(k-1)}(t)|^2 = \|y_{j(k-1)} - h_{j(k-1)}\|_2^2$$

$$\Rightarrow \|y_{jk} - h_{jk}\|_2 \leq \|y_{j(k-1)} - h_{j(k-1)}\|_2 \tag{18}$$

where $|max(0, \alpha) - max(0, \beta)| \leq |\alpha - \beta|$.

Based on the Eqs. 13, 14 και 17, we can estimate a constant L_{ik} for which:

$$\|y_{jk} - h_{jk}\|_2 \leq L_{ik} \|y_{10} - h_{10}\|_2 \tag{19}$$

The constant $L_{ik} = 1$, is defined recursively, and for any type of layer it is estimated as follows:

$$L_{ik} = \sum_{j=1}^{N_k} \|A_{ijk}\|_2 L_{j(k-1)} \tag{20}$$

1) Pooling layer and ReLU function:

$$L_{ik} = L_{i(k-1)} \tag{21}$$

If the network has p layers, we can find the *Lipschitz* constant that satisfies the following relation:

$$\|f(y_{in}, c) - f(h_{in}, c)\|_2 \leq L_{cp} \|y_{in} - h_{in}\|_2 \tag{22}$$

Having developed the method for finding a *Lipschitz constant* for the network, we study how it evolves during the training of a *Convolutional Neural Network*. To get a holistic picture of the network, we need to understand how it makes decisions, as well as its most important features and the interactions between them.

The use of global and Local Interpretability methodology, offers a more thorough approach. *Global interpretability*, provides an overview of the model. *Local interpretability*, focuses on explanations coming from a small data area where a single example is analyzed and it is explained why the model made a specific decision [18]. In small areas of data, the predictions may depend only linearly or monotonously on certain features, instead of having a more complex interdependence between them. *Shapley* values are a very effective way to generate explanations on the way a model works [19, 20]. Its mathematical background comes from the *Cooperative/Coalitional Game Theory*, where the "Payoff/Gain" of the players of a cooperative game is given by a real function that gives values to sets of players [19, 20]. The *Shapley* value is the only payoff function that satisfies the following four key properties [21, 22]:

1. Anonymity: the axiom of anonymity states that the order of the players does not affect the amount allocated to them by the *Shapley*. The consequence of the "*Axiom of Anonymity*" is the "*Axiom of Symmetry*", which states that the *Shapley* values of two symmetric players 1 and 3 are equal.
2. Efficiency: this axiom determines that the distribution of social wealth according to the *Shapley value* is collectively rational.
3. Zero-Useless: this axiom determines that if a player has zero contribution to social wealth, then his/her *Shapley* value equals 0.
4. Additionality: this axiom specifies that the *Shapley* value of the "*Sum Game*" is the sum of the *Shapley* values.

The connection of *Shapley* values to the problem of explaining the architectural structures of a network is done in the following manner: We consider the problem of architectural structures, as a "*Cooperative Game*" whose players are the characteristics of the data set. The "*Gain Function*" is the neural network's model under consideration and the model's predictions are the "*Corresponding Gains*". In this content, the *Strapley* values show the contribution of each feature and therefore the overall explanation why the model made a specific decision. In conclusion, the *Shapley* value for a characteristic i of a neural network's model f, is given by the following relation [21, 23]:

$$\varphi_i = \sum_{S \in F \backslash \{i\}} \frac{|S|!(M - |S| - 1)!}{M!} \left[f_{S \cup \{i\}}\left(x_{S \cup \{i\}}\right) - f_S(x_S) \right] \tag{23}$$

where F is the set of characteristics, S is a subset of F and $M = |F|$ is the size of F.

This relationship measures the weight of each attribute by calculating and adding its contribution when it is present in the forecast, whereas it subtracts it when it is absent.

More specifically [19, 24]:

1. $f_{S \cup \{i\}}\left(x_{S \cup \{i\}}\right)$: is the output when the i^∞ characteristic is present.
2. $f_S(x_S)$: is the output when the i^∞ characteristic is absent.

3. $\sum_{S \in F \setminus \{i\}} \frac{|S|!(M-|S|-1)!}{M!}$: is the weighted average of all possible subsets of S in F.

The *SHapley Additive exPlanations* method (SHAP) explains the models' decisions using *Shapley* values. An innovation of SHAP is that it functions as a linear model and more specifically as a method that estimates the additional contribution of each feature, so that an explanation is a local linear approach of the model's behavior. In particular, while the model can be very complex as an integrated entity, it is easy to approach it around a specific presence or absence of a variable. For this reason, the following step is the calculation of the degree of linear correlation, between the independent and the dependent variables of the set, with dispersion σ_X^2 and σ_Y^2 respectively. The next step is the calculation of the covariance $\sigma_{XY} = Cov(X, Y) = E(X, Y) - E(X)E(Y)$, which is calculated by the *Pearson Correlation Matrix R* as follows [1]:

$$R = \frac{\sigma_{XY}}{\sigma_X \sigma_Y} \tag{24}$$

The proposed architecture initially took into account the inability of the above method to detect nonlinear correlations such as *sinus wave, quadratic* curve, or to explore the relationships between categorical variables. The Predictive Power Score (PPS) technique was selected and used in this study, to summarize the prognostic relationships between the available data [25]. The PPS, unlike the correlation matrix, can work with non-linear relationships with categorical data, and also with asymmetric relationships, explaining that variable A informs variable B more than variable B informs variable A. Technically, scoring in the interval [0, 1] is a measure of the model's success in predicting a variable target, using a non-sample variable prediction. This fact, practically means that this method can enhance hidden patterns' discovery and can contribute towards the selection of suitable prediction variables.

The use of the PPS method, focuses on the fact that a *local explanation* must be obtained for the models that are ultimately capable of operating without training. However, the sensitivity of the *SHAP* method requires the implementation of feature selection before its application. This will enhance its ability to explain the models as long as the hyper-parameters' values are concerned, and it will increase the general ability to deal with the high dimensionality of data. The complexity of the problem becomes even higher, as it is combined with the large number of explanations that must be given for the produced predictions. Thus the distinction between relevant and irrelevant features as well as the distances between data points cannot be fully captured. Taking this observation seriously, feature selection was performed to optimally select a subset of the existing features. This was done without transformation, in order to reduce their number and preserve the most important and most useful of them. This step is crucial because if features with low resolution capacity are selected, the resulting system will not be able to perform satisfactorily, whereas if features that provide useful information are selected, the system will be simple and efficient.

In general, the goal was to select those characteristics that lead to long distances between classes and small variation between the instances of the same class. The process of feature selection was performed with the PPS technique. The metric of Mean Absolute Error (MAE) was used for the calculation of PPS in numerical variables. MAE is related to the average of the differences between the predicted and the observed values (Eq. 26) [1].

$$MAE = \frac{1}{n} \sum_{i=1}^{n} |f_i - y_i| = \frac{1}{n} \sum_{i=1}^{n} |e_i| \qquad (25)$$

where f_i is the estimated value and y_i is the actual. The average of the absolute value of the quotient of these values is defined as the absolute error of their relation $|e_i| = |f_i - y_i|$.

Respectively, the F-Score is the Harmonic Mean of Recall and Precision. It is used to overall assess classification efforts. The higher the F-Score, the higher the more accurate the classification. It is calculated from the following Eq. 27 [1]:

$$
\begin{aligned}
F_{Score} &= \frac{2 \times recall \times precision}{recall + precision} \\
&= \frac{2 TruePositives}{2 TruePositives + FalsePositives + FalseNegatives}
\end{aligned}
\qquad (26)
$$

3   Experiments

Having developed the method for finding a *Lipschitz* constant for the network, we study how it evolves during the training of the VGG-16 Network for a 224 × 3224 × 3 image data set [26]. This network is characterized by its simplicity, as it uses only 3 × 3 convolutional layers that are stacked one after the other, in scalable depth. The reduction in volume size is addressed with *Max Pooling*, while the architecture is completed by two fully interconnected levels each with 4,096 nodes, which are followed by a *Softmax* classifier.

The architecture of the VGG-16 is described in more detail as follows:

1. The input is an image of dimensions 224 × 224 × 3.
2. The first two layers have 64 channels of 3 × 3 filter size and same padding. Then after a max pool layer of stride 2 × 2, two layers have convolution layers of 256 filter size and filter size 3 × 3.
3. This followed by a max-pooling layer of stride 2 × 2 which is same as the previous layer. Then there are 2 convolution layers of filter size 3 × 3 and 256 filter.
4. After that, there are 2 sets of 3 convolution layer and a max pool layer. Each has 512 filters of 3 × 3 size with the same padding.
5. This image is then passed to the stack of two convolution layers.
6. In these convolution and max-pooling layers, the filters we use are of the size 3 × 3 instead. In some of the layers, it also uses 1 × 1 pixel which is used to manipulate the number of input channels. There is a padding of 1-pixel done after each convolution layer to prevent the spatial feature of the image.
7. After the stack of convolution and max-pooling layer, we got a 7 × 7 × 512 feature map. We flatten this output to make it a 1 × 25088 feature vector.

8. Finally, there are three fully connected layers. The first receives input from the last feature vector and outputs a $1 \times 4{,}096$ vector. The second layer also outputs a vector of size $1 \times 4{,}096$. The third layer outputs 1,000 channels for 1,000 classes. The output of the 3rd fully connected layer is passed to the *softmax* layer in order to normalize the classification vector (Fig. 5).

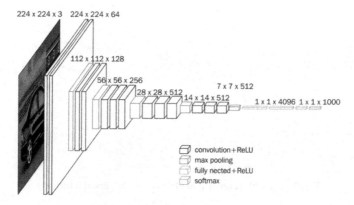

Fig. 5. VGG-16 Convolutional Network's Architecture

The network (as shown in Fig. 6) consists of 16 layers, where the last one has 1,000 different outputs, one for each image class (ILSVRC challenge).

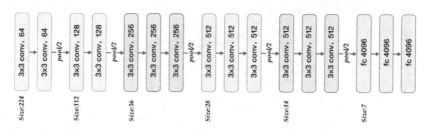

Fig. 6. VGG-16 Layers

So we record the average value of the constants L_{i16} which is symbolized as L_{out}:

$$L_{out} = \frac{1}{1000} \sum_{\iota=1}^{1000} L_{i16}$$

For the experimental validation of the proposed method, we trained the network using a mixture of real and aggressive inputs with the method of adversarial examples. On the other hand, we also trained the network with normal image patterns. At the end of each epoch, we recorded the constant L_{out} and studied how it evolves during network training. The results are presented in Fig. 7 below, where the *Adversarial* examples are introduced in the 10th season of training.

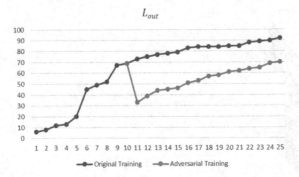

Fig. 7. Lipschitz constant in Original vs Adversarial training

The following Fig. 8 presents the evolution of the training error for both methods.

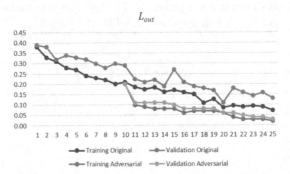

Fig. 8. Lipschitz constant in Original vs Adversarial training and validation

It is obvious that training with aggressive images leads to a neural network with smaller constant L_{out}. This confirms the assumption that networks with smaller *Lipschitz* constants behave better against aggressive images. It is worth noting that the constant we calculate is not a lower barrier to the *Lipschitz* network constant, but continues to exhibit the behavior we expect. Also if we observe the evolution of the error in the validation set, we see that the network that has been trained with aggressive images and presents smaller L_{out} constant, achieves smaller error and generalizes better. The *Shapley* values are then used as a way to generate *clear explanations of how the neural network works,* and *why the model made a particular decision.*

It should be emphasized that the explanations of a prediction in terms of the original input are more difficult than the explanations of predictions in terms of the convolutional layers (because the higher convolutional layers are closer to the output). In the following example we explain how the 7th intermediate level of the VGG-16 model affects the output probabilities for a particular input. Specifically, red pixels represent positive Shapley values, which increase the probability of a class, while green pixels represent negative values that reduce the probability of a class. We should emphasize that two explanatory classification variables (rank_outputs = 2) were used to simplify the process. This means that we explain only the two most likely classes for each entry, freeing the process from the explanation of all 1,000 classes that are part of the VGG-16 network. With this technique, it is possible to understand how the model makes decisions and what interactions take place between the used characteristics in order to achieve correct or incorrect categorization. It also offers the ability to manage, control and explain, how to handle multiple intermediate representations, as well as more advanced features that may be related to the hierarchical organization of the architecture in successive layers. Thus it reflects the structure of the dynamics of the developed system. The progressive classification and investigation of the intermediate relations of the input data along the levels of the hierarchical architecture, creates clear indications - evidence of how the final decision is made. This is achieved even if all the layers share the same weight values. Furthermore, the *Lipschitz-Shapley* combination clearly captures the transient states of the internal representations of the input signals, even for problems that require long internal memory intervals.

4 Conclusions

The idea of standardizing the proposed methodology, emerged based on the application of a single, universal method of explaining how to make decisions in intelligent systems. This approach should meet all the requirements for the case of the *Adversarial Attacks*. Trying to detect how the *Lipschitz* constant is evolving in the training of an intelligent model and using the *Shapley Values*, we manage to obtain clear explanations of the reasons that have led to a particular decision. This can enhance the development of modern information systems' security applications, resolving issues-queries such as:

1. How many neurons should each hidden level contain?
2. Which activation function works best in each hidden layer?
3. Does the addition of a new layer increase the performance of the architecture or not?
4. What is the function of the final layer, as well as which loss function can optimize the process?
5. Is there a need for normalization before the linear levels are added?
6. How many hidden layers need to be used?

When evaluating the proposed architecture as a whole, a significant advantage is focused on its ability to clearly display the information that has been modeled. This can lead to trusted models, which are based on detailed mathematical and physical frameworks of system's behavior. This is in contrast to the corresponding "black box"

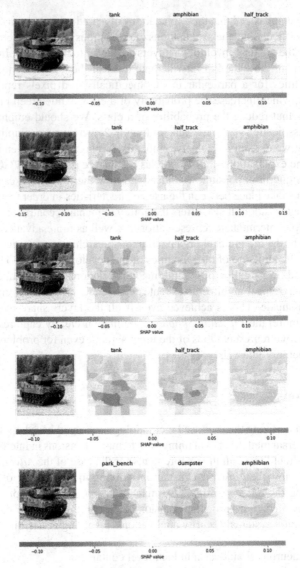

Fig. 9. Shapley values for Original photo and Adversarial examples

approach, which lacks explanations. Another important contribution of the proposed methodology, is related to the assessment of the uncertainty which is an inherent property of digital security problems (DSP). It is a fact that DSP do not follow specific distributions and they are often linearly unrelated. Finally, an important contribution of this method is that generalization is ensured experimentally, with unquestionable statistical validation techniques, even in the case of data use that contains a significant percentage of noise (Fig. 9).

Although the evaluation of the proposed methods was done by applying to particularly painful scenarios and data sets that emerged after exhaustive literature and experimental research procedures, an important limitation that should be noted is that in general intelligent methods are sensitive to data quality. Most of the small transformations related to the slightest changes in the input layer, were analyzed and proved to be of major importance. The utilization of this sensitivity can lead under certain conditions to the modification of the behavior of the learning algorithm. Designing an appropriate strategy to deal with Adversarial Attacks is a specialized and time consuming process. Such a process can be simplified by the proposed methodology, but it still remains a serious issue. Its automation and self-adaptation by machine learning models based on corresponding procedures, requires further investigation.

Proposals for the development and future improvements of the methodology, should focus on the automated optimization of the appropriate parameters, so that an even more efficient, accurate and faster explanation process is achieved, in a simple and unequivocal way. It would also be important to study the expansion of this system by implementing methods of self-improvement that would redefine the hyperparameters of the intelligent system automatically. This could lead to a more efficient system that would resist Adversarial Attacks very effectively.

References

1. Understanding Machine Learning, Pattern recognition and machine learning. Cambridge University Press. https://www.cambridge.org/il/academic/subjects/computer-science/pattern-recognition-and-machine-learning/understanding-machine-learning-theory-algorithms. Accessed 16 Feb 2021

2. Tygar, J.D.: Adversarial machine learning. IEEE Internet Comput. **15**(5), 4–6 (2011). https://doi.org/10.1109/MIC.2011.112

3. Zhu, Z., Lu, Y., Chiang, C.: Generating adversarial examples by makeup attacks on face recognition. In: 2019 IEEE International Conference on Image Processing (ICIP), pp. 2516–2520 (2019). https://doi.org/10.1109/ICIP.2019.8803269

4. Guo, H., Peng, L., Zhang, J., Qi, F., Duan, L.: Fooling AI with AI: an accelerator for adversarial attacks on deep learning visual classification. In: 2019 IEEE 30th International Conference on Application-specific Systems, Architectures and Processors (ASAP), vol. 2160–052X, pp. 136–136 (2019). https://doi.org/10.1109/ASAP.2019.00-16

5. Demertzis, K., Tziritas, N., Kikiras, P., Sanchez, S.L., Iliadis, L.: The next generation cognitive security operations center: adaptive analytic lambda architecture for efficient defense against adversarial attacks. Big Data Cogn. Comput. **3**(1), 6 (2019). https://doi.org/10.3390/bdcc3010006

6. Jing, H., Meng, C., He, X., Wei, W.: Black box explanation guided decision-based adversarial attacks. In: 2019 IEEE 5th International Conference on Computer and Communications (ICCC), pp. 1592–1596 (2019). https://doi.org/10.1109/ICCC47050.2019.9064243

7. Yu, P., Song, K., Lu, J.: Generating adversarial examples with conditional generative adversarial net. In: 2018 24th International Conference on Pattern Recognition (ICPR), pp. 676–681 (2018). https://doi.org/10.1109/ICPR.2018.8545152

8. Liu, Y., Mao, S., Mei, X., Yang, T., Zhao, X.: Sensitivity of adversarial perturbation in fast gradient sign method. In: 2019 IEEE Symposium Series on Computational Intelligence (SSCI), pp. 433–436 (2019). https://doi.org/10.1109/SSCI44817.2019.9002856

9. Li, H., Zhou, S., Yuan, W., Li, J., Leung, H.: Adversarial-example attacks toward android malware detection system. IEEE Syst. J. **14**(1), 653–656 (2020). https://doi.org/10.1109/JSYST.2019.2906120

10. Yuan, J., He, Z.: Adversarial dual network learning with randomized image transform for restoring attacked images. IEEE Access **8**, 22617–22624 (2020). https://doi.org/10.1109/ACCESS.2020.2969288

11. Chen, J., Lin, X., Shi, Z., Liu, Y.: Link prediction adversarial attack via iterative gradient attack. IEEE Trans. Comput. Soc. Syst. **7**(4), 1081–1094 (2020). https://doi.org/10.1109/TCSS.2020.3004059

12. Chauhan, R., Heydari, S.S.: Polymorphic adversarial DDoS attack on IDS using GAN. In: 2020 International Symposium on Networks, Computers and Communications (ISNCC), pp. 1–6 (2020). https://doi.org/10.1109/ISNCC49221.2020.9297264

13. He, X., Tong, G., Gao, W., Mi, X., Gao, P., Zhang, Y.: The method of adaptive gaussian decomposition based recognition and extraction of scattering mechanisms. In: 2018 12th International Symposium on Antennas, Propagation and EM Theory (ISAPE), pp. 1–4 (2018). https://doi.org/10.1109/ISAPE.2018.8634155

14. Zhao, X., Huang, M., Zhu, Q.: Analysis of hyperspectral scattering image using wavelet transformation for assessing internal qualities of apple fruit. In: 2012 24th Chinese Control and Decision Conference (CCDC), pp. 2445–2448 (2012). https://doi.org/10.1109/CCDC.2012.6244390

15. Loeb, I.: Lipschitz functions in constructive reverse mathematics. Log. J. IGPL **21**(1), 28–43 (2013). https://doi.org/10.1093/jigpal/jzs020

16. Hu, G.: Observers for one-sided Lipschitz non-linear systems. IMA J. Math. Control Inf. **23**(4), 395–401 (2006). https://doi.org/10.1093/imamci/dni068

17. Calliess, J.: Lipschitz optimisation for Lipschitz Interpolation. In: 2017 American Control Conference (ACC), pp. 3141–3146 (2017). https://doi.org/10.23919/ACC.2017.7963430

18. Demertzis, K., Tsiknas, K., Takezis, D., Skianis, C., Iliadis, L.: Darknet traffic big-data analysis and network management for real-time automating of the malicious intent detection process by a weight agnostic neural networks framework. Electronics **10**(7) (2021). https://doi.org/10.3390/electronics10070781. Art. no. 7

19. Cheng-Guo, E., Quan-Lin, L., Li, S.: The Shapley value of cooperative game with stochastic payoffs. In: The 26th Chinese Control and Decision Conference (2014 CCDC), pp. 1717–1722 (2014). https://doi.org/10.1109/CCDC.2014.6852446

20. Huafeng, X., Qiuhong, L.: The game theory analysis of risk share for PPP project based on Shapley value. In: 2010 2nd IEEE International Conference on Information Management and Engineering, pp. 112–115 (2010). https://doi.org/10.1109/ICIME.2010.5477813

21. Leon, F.: Optimizing neural network topology using Shapley value. In: 2014 18th International Conference on System Theory, Control and Computing (ICSTCC), pp. 862–867 (2014). https://doi.org/10.1109/ICSTCC.2014.6982527

22. Bao, X., Li, X.: Cost allocation of integrated supply based on Shapley value method. In: 2010 International Conference on Intelligent Computation Technology and Automation, vol. 1, pp. 1054–1057 (2010). https://doi.org/10.1109/ICICTA.2010.406

23. Zhang, L., Gao, Z.: The Shapley value of convex compound stochastic cooperative game. In: 2011 2nd International Conference on Artificial Intelligence, Management Science and Electronic Commerce (AIMSEC), pp. 1608–1611 (2011). https://doi.org/10.1109/AIMSEC.2011.6010580

24. Messalas, A., Kanellopoulos, Y., Makris, C.: Model-agnostic interpretability with shapley values. In: 2019 10th International Conference on Information, Intelligence, Systems and Applications (IISA), pp. 1–7 (2019). https://doi.org/10.1109/IISA.2019.8900669

25. Are Correlations any Guide to Predictive Value? on JSTOR. https://www.jstor.org/stable/298 5494?seq=1#metadata_info_tab_contents. Accessed 18 Apr 2021
26. Alippi, C., Disabato, S., Roveri, M.: Moving convolutional neural networks to embedded systems: the AlexNet and VGG-16 Case. In: 2018 17th ACM/IEEE International Conference on Information Processing in Sensor Networks (IPSN), pp. 212–223 (2018). https://doi.org/ 10.1109/IPSN.2018.00049

A Multimodal AI-Leveraged Counter-UAV Framework for Diverse Environments

Eleni Diamantidou⬤, Antonios Lalas$^{(\boxtimes)}$⬤, Konstaninos Votis⬤,
and Dimitrios Tzovaras⬤

Centre for Research and Technology - Hellas (CERTH), Information Technologies
Institute, 6th km Harilaou - Thermi, 57001 Thessaloniki, Greece
{ediamantidou,lalas,kvotis,dimitrios.tzovaras}@iti.gr

Abstract. Unmanned Aerial Vehicles (UAVs) have become a major part of everyday life, as well as an emerging research field, by establishing their versatility in a variety of applications. Nevertheless, this rapid spread of UAVs reputation has provoked serious security issues that can probably affect homeland security. Defence communities have started to investigate large field-of-view sensor-based methods to enable various civil protection applications, including the detection and localisation of flying threat objects. Counter-UAV (c-UAV) detection challenges may be granted from a fusion of sensors to enhance the confidence of flying threats identification. The real-time monitoring of the environment is absolutely rigorous and demands accurate methods to detect promptly the occurrence of harmful conditions. Deep learning (DL) based techniques are capable of tackling the challenges that are associated with generic objects detection and explicitly UAV identification. In this paper, we present a novel multimodal DL methodology that combines data from individual unimodal approaches that are associated with UAV detection. Specifically, this work aims to identify and classify potential targets of UAVs based on fusion methods in two different cases of operational environments, i.e. rural and urban scenarios. A dedicated architecture is designed based on the development of deep neural networks (DNNs) frameworks that has been trained and validated employing real UAV flights scenarios. The proposed approach has achieved prominent detection accuracies over different background environments, exhibiting potential employment even in major defence applications.

Keywords: Unmanned Aerial Vehicles (UAVs) · Multimodal deep learning · UAV detection

This work was supported by the European Union's Horizon 2020 Research and Innovation Programme Advanced holistic Adverse Drone Detection, Identification and Neutralisation (ALADDIN) under Grant Agreement No. 740859.

I. Maglogiannis et al. (Eds.): AIAI 2021 Workshops, IFIP AICT 628, pp. 228–239, 2021.
https://doi.org/10.1007/978-3-030-79157-5_19

1   Introduction

Unmanned Aerial Vehicles (UAVs) have gained a considerable part in several technological applications. In recent years, many industries have involved UAVs to produce solutions that improve time and resources consuming demands. Additionally, there has been a significant increase in UAVs training and practice, which has made the UAVs a friendly solution for the open public. A major part of applications that employ UAVs is associated with environment tracing such as vehicle tracking, natural disasters detection, reconnaissance of suspicious actions or cargo transportation [21]. However, there are a lot of restrictions regarding UAV flight plans and flight approvals. In addition, there is a possibility that a UAV may not have an authorised and appropriate flight plan [23]. According to many European countries authorities, UAVs should not fly over people, prisons, hospitals, government, military facilities, other sensitive areas or airports. Following that, counter-UAV (c-UAV) systems have introduced a new research field concerning national safety, since this novel technology is capable of causing security threats and harm civil protection. Due to their lightweight and small size, low vibration, low thermal cost and high power to weight ratio, the UAVs can conveniently fly at any environment including both urban and rural areas with the minimum level of intrusiveness on the environment [13]. Thus, finding an effective solution to accomplish accurate UAV detection is deemed necessary for security purposes, acquiring at the same time great attention from the research community. A variety of c-UAV solutions involve, among other, multi-sensory methods including vision, radar, acoustic or radio-frequency sensors.

A high-interest challenge relies on how efficiently a deep learning (DL) fusion model that utilises vision and radar schemes can identify the presence of UAVs near cities or in regions located in the outer parts of the cities. Since the different performance of the model may be critical for security purposes, the knowledge about the effects of the surrounding environment to the overall detection capabilities may pose a significant factor for the effectiveness of the final c-UAVs system. In this work, a multimodal DL based method is presented that employs thermal and 2D radar data, to adequately tackle aerial vehicle detection problems in cases where a flying threat is approaching an essential urban or rural infrastructure without permission. For this purpose, dedicated data captures have been conducted in different environments allowing for the training and comparison of topology-oriented models for accurate detection. Explicitly, this work aims to efficiently introduce a multimodal neural network-based algorithm for the UAV detection task in diverse environments, taking into account the different conditions that may be applied, and assess their impact in the final performance of the holistic system.

The rest of the paper is organised as follows. Section 2 provides an overview of recent studies regarding DL sensing methods for UAV detection systems. Section 3 is devoted to the detailed description of the UAV flights environments, together with the sensing modalities that can be utilised to address the UAV detection task. Also in this context, the recommended DL classification activities regarding the UAV detection task are proposed in Sect. 4. The experimental process as well as the corresponding evaluation procedure and results are provided in Sect. 5. Finally, Sect. 6 summarises the conclusions of this work.

2 Literature Review

Many novel multimodal techniques that employ multiple sensors and data fusion have been proposed in an attempt to increase accuracy of detection. An indicative example is associated with DL technology which established very promising approaches concerning sensing topologies and vehicle detection. In the context of c-UAV applications, bearing-only and radar sensors had been fused to detect and localise UAVs [7]. The employment of these sensors resulted in false alarm (FA) discrimination. In addition, the track extraction time was reduced, which corresponds to the necessary time that the system requires to output decisions. Another interesting work [3] proposed a methodology of radar and vision fusion, aiming to improve vehicle detection and identification reliability. The authors presented a high-level fusion of radar and vision fusion targets. This system utilised a video system to validate the radar detections and enhance the overall accuracy. The evaluation of this method was performed in urban environments achieving great results. Vision and radar systems remain among the well-known approaches to detect, identify and localise flying threats. Each sensor exhibits advantages and disadvantages in different scenarios, which affect the final detection decisions owning that the field of view varies depending on the background of the associated sensor that tracks a target [19]. Moreover, sensors have limitations that are related to the environment such as weather conditions and external noise. A principal task is to join different sensing modalities to overcome or compensate for possible detection weaknesses. Multi-sensor information methodologies indicate their applicability on UAV detection since they are capable of providing considerable advantages over single-sensor information [6]. Explicitly, this work, even though limited to a specific environment only, has efficiently introduced a neural network-based algorithm for the UAV detection task, formulating a general information fusion framework that merges extracted features from multiple modalities.

3 Description of the Environment and Sensing Methodologies

In recent years, UAVs have shown immediate growth in everyday life, generating many security issues. The commercial usage of UAVs has been extended to a variety of areas, where UAVs can regularly fly at different backgrounds without being noticed. Taking into account that UAVs have also a small size and they move quickly, the detection challenge within diverse environment has been made intensively complicated.

3.1 Multi-sensory Technology

Many available sensors can identify and localise flying threats. The majority of them refer to vision and radar systems. In our work, we take advantage of thermal imaging and 2D radar sensing capabilities. Both the 2D radar sensor and the panoramic thermal camera capture the predefined area over a long range in a 360 degrees point of view. This allows the sensors to perceive all the states of the environment. The 2D radar sensor functionality is based on the emission of radio waves to determine the range, the azimuth or the velocity of targets. As many targets as possible exist, there will also be many 2D radar reflections [20]. However, since UAVs are small and tend to fly close to the ground, even the more specialised radar sensors can face difficulties to identify and classify them as UAV threats. Regarding the thermal sensors, they illustrate great potential for UAV detection by detecting their heat signature. Thermal cameras detect flying targets at specific azimuths and elevations by recognising different levels of infrared radiation [24]. According to this, these sensors have a great sensitivity to weather conditions such as high temperature and humidity. Subsequently, each sensor imposes its advantages and disadvantages in several scenarios making the single-sensor UAV detection a demanding task. Nevertheless, it is tolerable to obtain an effective solution, especially assuming that supplemental technologies are incorporated to ensure maximum coverage in any possible gaps.

3.2 UAV Flight Regions

As mentioned above, UAVs can effortlessly fly over individual areas without drawing attention. As a result, it is essential to implement dedicated algorithms that have the ability to learn to identify UAV threats in several environments. Intending to appropriately address this research challenge, it appears a necessity to gather plenty of UAV detection data that correspond in different environments. Besides, the majority of algorithms that involve predictive capabilities are associated with DL techniques, which certainly demand considerable amounts of data [18], to discover patterns between the potential targets [18]. For these reasons, various data collection sessions were fulfilled during the European project ALADDIN [1] to capture UAV flights under different circumstances. The varying backgrounds and the several types of aerial vehicles produced an explicit and valuable dataset for DL research activities. The first data gathering session took place in a rural area at the Air Traffic Laboratory for Advanced unmanned Systems (ATLAS) in Villacarrillo, Spain. The remaining data gathering sessions occurred at an urban area on Markopoulo premises in Athens, Greece. ATLAS, that Fig. 1[a] represents, refers to a test flight centre located in an open field location, surrounded by trees. On the other hand, the Markopoulo Training Facility, presented in Fig. 1[b] is settled just outside the city of Athens. The aforementioned regions were selected to accurately gather data regarding UAV flights at both rural and urban environments, thus enabling comparison of the environment variability.

[a]   [b]

Fig. 1. UAV Test Flights. [a] The flight plan captured at ATLAS, was designed to simulate the intrusion of a protected area from the dark side of the hangars. [b] The flight plan captured at Markopoulo involved incoming drones from the dark side of the buildings of the protected area.

To further elaborate on the environment analysis of the UAV flight recordings, there are some variations of major importance between a rural and an urban area. The most notable difference between a rural and an urban scene is associated to the external environmental noise. UAV tracking in regions near cities can be affected by FAs similar to car traffic or by buildings that can cover possible threats. On the other hand, countryside areas involve less FAs. Despite that, the UAVs can still hide, for instance at trees, during a flight operation, making the identification between UAVs and FAs a really difficult task. Our DL fusion model has the virtue to tackle the above challenges. The main goal is to achieve a reliable UAV detection at both rural and urban environments with maximum accuracy.

4   Deep Learning Technology for UAV Detection

Various sensor-based methods utilise tracking trajectory techniques for flying vehicles to recognise their flight signature and decide if the vehicles are possible threats [5, 14, 16]. DL based methodologies have gained great attention in a wide range of vehicle detection over the past few years since they have shown successful results [12]. In a general sense, DL attempts to learn significant features from data, understand patterns and relations between them to obtain predictive power in new unseen data [9]. The Deep Neural Networks (DNNs) have the ability to learn high-level representations from data and recognise relations among them and the target variable to predict. The concepts of DL may undoubtedly further apply their findings in problem cases where the data are coming from multiple resources [15]. In the majority of world problems, the data arrive from multiple sources. The most interesting challenge in DL data fusion is to perform a joint representation of multimodal data [2]. A fundamental point is related to the way a DNN can detect patterns and associations between these data. Multimodal DL has to discover associations that link different modalities and join them. The predictive behaviour of a DL neural network derives from multi-layered and sometimes complicated structures [11]. Taking this into account, the findings of a Multi-layer Perceptron classifier are adopted [17].

4.1 Training Data

The proper formulation of a multi-input neural network architecture requires a joint data representation. A solution to this problem could be derived by the construction of a shared representation. As already noted, DNNs can learn significant relations and features from the input data [25]. Consequently, DNNs can be valuable feature extractors producing high-level representations from data. These high-level representations are in the form of large numerical feature maps that have been output from single DL feature extractors [8]. In the UAV detection problem, the input samples belong to two training classes: the UAV class and the FA class. Diving into the content of each training class, the FA class is characterised as a highly generic class, since FAs in a real-world scenario can be birds, trees, some clouds, sensor noise or even humans and cars referring to an urban environment. On the other hand, the UAV class is very precise, since it is only associated with several types of UAVs targets.

To efficiently combine thermal and 2D radar data to accomplish the task of UAV detection, two unimodal DNNs were utilised to generate a common representation at both input streams. The thermal camera and the 2D radar have a diverse perception of identifying targets in between them. The thermal camera features result in a three-dimensional signal considering that the information is extracted from images, whereas the 2D radar generates a two-dimensional signal. Therefore, each sensor ends with a unique type of detection. Following that, it is essential to discover an effective way to join multimodal information despite the different data meaning, shapes and types. In addition to that, handling data captured from different sensors leads to a necessity of data alignment. The input data refer to different capturing sessions and recordings using various types of UAVs under different time frames, spatial ranges, weather conditions, etc. allowing a wide diversity in the dataset. In addition, multimodal data require a matching process to properly align them in at least the temporal domain. Accordingly, an alignment method based on temporal adjustment was implemented. This process uses timestamps provided from each capture of each modality accordingly.

4.2 UAV Detection Algorithm Architecture

The aim of the proposed fusion algorithm is related to the task of classification and identification to enhance the UAV detection accuracy as data from two sources are combined. Our DL fusion neural network attempts to identify the presence of flying targets in two major scenarios. The first scenario is assigned to

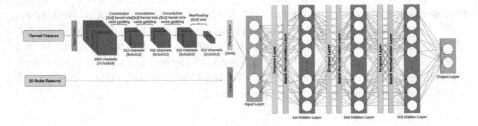

Fig. 2. Proposed architecture of fusion neural network for UAV classification. The neural network has two input streams that correspond to 2D radar data and thermal imaging data.

UAVs that fly in the countryside. The second scenario refers to UAV flights that are operated near urban areas. Figure 2 represents the concept and the design of the recommended architecture of the DL data fusion framework.

The neural network architecture has been designed utilising two input streams: high-level representations from thermal images and 2D radar signatures. Combining different modalities for enhancing the detection accuracy seems an intuitively appealing task [6]. Since the thermal and the 2D radar features belong in different dimensional space, they will have a different impact on the prediction output. The thermal data enable feature maps of $7 \times 7 \times 1024$ dimension, while the 2D radar data outputs feature maps of 1664 dimension. It is noted that the thermal input is considerably larger than the 2D radar input which seemingly results in a possible misleading learning process. To overcome dimensionality diversities and avoid displeasing learning issues, a further process of thermal data was implemented. The main solution concept relates to convolutions. Employing convolutions aims to shrink the multidimensional input without losing possible meaningful information [10]. The implementation of the proposed methodology includes a concatenation layer to combine the two input streams. Each stream is related to a different input tensor. The output of the concatenation layer returns a single tensor that contains the concatenation of all inputs. Several additional parameters can affect the training procedure. Among the major neural network initialisation parameters are the number of hidden units, the number of hidden layers and the optimisation method that the algorithm will update and adjust itself. In particular, the number of hidden units depends on the size of the dataset. Very few hidden units may produce generalisation errors due to underfitting effects. Too many hidden units may result in low training errors, but will make the training unnecessarily slow, and will lead in poor generalisation. Concerning the training process, the weights are initialised randomly, which means that the neural network is training without using weights of other pre-trained models. The Adam optimiser was adopted to adjust the DNN weights, while the learning rate was initialised equal to 0.001. Regarding the two-input streams neural network, it consists of one input layer that contains the joined thermal and 2D radar features, three fully connected hidden layers (dense layers) and one output layer. The input of the data fusion neural network is the concatenation of multiple unimodal features, as mentioned earlier. However, the output of the data fusion neural network is a binary problem classification result. Specifically, the output of our DNN is a probability according to the training classes: UAVs or FAs. Dropout layers have been employed to prevent overfitting during neural network learning [22]. Correspondingly, batch normalisation layers have been also employed to normalise input data [4] since they are coming from multiple resources and processes.

5   Experimental Process and Results

The data fusion concepts support two main purposes. The first purpose relates to detection accuracy enhancement while adding multiple modalities. The second and most meaningful purpose is relevant to missing modalities completion. Aiming to focus on a comprehensive examination about the fusion input data, two major experiments were conducted. According to this, the experiments utilised large amounts of data that represent individual cases of the problem to gain significant predictive power. These experiments aimed to identify which environmental setups have the merit of fusion concepts. For this reason, our neural network model architecture was trained on two diverse datasets to produce robust models that can identify UAVs in rural and urban areas. The two datasets involved high-level representations of thermal and 2D radar UAV detections recorded from the ATLAS flight centre and Markopoulo, referring to a rural and urban environment respectively.

The investigation on the classification behaviour and the evaluation performance of a proposed architecture using data with background diversities is certainly appealing. Powerful DL models need a suitable selection of the data that the neural network would train on and likewise the test data. The training set contains a known output and the model learns on this data to be generalised to other data later on. Assuming that, the train and validation processes would be applied to specific data during the learning process. In our experimental processes, both the fusion model with UAV detections recorded in the rural area and the fusion model related to the UAV flights near cities, employed training and validation samples involving an equal number of instances at both training classes. To verify the performance of our algorithms, the evaluation of the fusion models included UAV recordings with clear flight plans. Besides, to ensure the quality of the results, the UAV recordings that were selected for evaluation purposes, had as much as possible, similar flight plans. As a result, to properly test the fusion models and measure evaluation performance, two UAV recordings that follow the same notions of a flight plan were selected in both cases of the environmental setup. The main evaluation scenario refers to a UAV threat coming from far away. While the UAV is approaching the region of interest, it is hiding at protected areas and moving without being easily noticed. Both evaluation recordings were captured at daytime and the UAVs flew approaching a maximum 700 m distance from the sensors. Figure 1[a] demonstrates the flight plan of a UAV in a rural environment. In the same way, Fig. 1[b] involves the flight plan of a UAV in an urban environment.

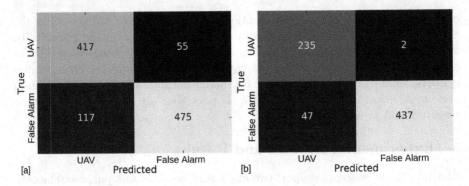

Fig. 3. Confusion matrices provide information about the validation performance of the multi-sensory model on target data points. Specifically, confusion matrix regarding the evaluation of the fusion model trained on data points recorded in [a] rural areas, and [b] urban areas.

For the evaluation process, the neural network was initialised with a set for evaluation samples to monitor the classification output based on ground truth labels, which in our case refers to the presence of a UAV. As a result, confusion matrices were utilised for examination of fusion model performance. A confusion matrix is an excellent performance measurement for classification problems. Each row of the confusion matrix represents the instances in a predicted class, while each column represents the instances in an actual class. It is necessary to remark that test flights correspond to real UAV flights scenarios. Accordingly, possible differences in the number of detection in each class are expected. Regarding the validation of the fusion model associated with rural area UAV flights, the confusion matrix in Fig. 3[a] describes that from the 472 positive samples that represent UAV detections, 417 samples were correctly classified as UAV, and only 55 samples were classified mistakenly as FAs. Likewise, among 592 negative samples, 475 samples were correctly classified as FAs, and 117 samples were classified wrongly as UAVs. In the same notions, the fusion model validation associated with urban area UAV flights is performed in Fig. 3[b]. The test flight captured in an urban environment involved 237 positive samples, where the largest part of detections was classified perfectly and only 2 samples were falsely classified as negatives. However, among 484 FA detections, 437 data points were accurately classified as FAs, and only 47 negative samples were inaccurately classified as UAV detections.

Accomplishing the task of fusion model evaluation, it is expected that the fusion model will succeed in the challenge of distinguishing UAVs from FAs in several cases. For quality estimation and efficient comparison between the two cases of the experiment, the precision, recall and the F1 score metrics were utilised since they are of the most prominent measures on a classification problem. As it was assumed, the two fusion models achieved exceptional performance at both the distinct environment training experiments. The evaluation metrics concerning the rural test flight feature samples are encouraging. Likewise, the

Table 1. Experimental results that present the performance of UAV classification task at rural environments

	Precision	Recall	F1 score
UAV	0.7808	0.8834	0.8290
False alarm	0.8962	0.8023	0.8467

Table 2. Experimental results that present the performance of UAV classification task at urban environments

	Precision	Recall	F1 score
UAV	0.8333	0.9915	0.9055
False alarm	0.9954	0.9028	0.9469

results that are referring to the urban test flight sample have shown even more exceptional performance as described in Table 1 and Table 2.

Many deductions may be derived during the examination of the outcomes that associate to the above mentioned experiments. At a first though, it may be expected that the performance of the fusion model that was trained by handling samples recorded in the rural environment should be higher than the related fusion model performance that used UAV detections captured in an urban environment. In a rural area, the UAVs are an easily recognisable target since the background is clear free of additional environmental noise. Considering this, the evaluation metrics of the rural area fusion model are expected to be improved compared to the evaluation metrics of the urban area fusion model. However, a different result arises, where the urban case exhibits better evaluation metrics. The principal explanation to this result relies on that the dataset that indicates the UAV flights in the countryside includes FAs which consist of fully generic detections. Namely, there are few FAs in the countryside, which could describe small parts of clouds, trees or birds. Moreover, in some cases, FAs may have been introduced by capturing sensor noise. In a public region, however, there is an increased number of well-defined false warnings. In this particular case, FAs can refer to buildings, public transport, aeroplanes or any other external noise. A classification problem requires training classes that consist of explicit data that precisely represent the desirable target. According to this, our experiment has shown that the same multimodal neural network architecture can classify more convenient UAV detections in an urban environment compared to a rural environment. This is mainly explained due to the well-defined nature of the false warnings in urban cases in comparison to the rural environment, where the cause of FAs is more obscure. Bearing in mind that the UAV, as well as the FA detections, were expressed equally in both cases of experimentation, our fusion model achieved higher evaluation performance at UAV detection data that are associated with regions near cities.

6 Discussion and Recommendations

This research aims to understand in an enhanced way, the learning behaviour of UAV high-level representation detections in two different backgrounds. In this context, complex experiments with individual input vectors were conducted to identify cases where the fusion model exhibited the merits of the multimodal learning concepts. The involved 2D radar and thermal sensors allowed for a global field of view which did not result in homogeneous data. Thus, the amount of all single-sensor feature maps varies, based on the limitations of each sensor. To overcome these boundaries, our proposed model architecture was based on robust DL architectures. As a result, we have successfully demonstrated the effectiveness of the multimodal data learning and appropriately established our efficient fusion model, which is suitable for efficient UAV detection in several environments. Moreover, an enhanced behaviour is observed when the fusion model is employed to urban scenarios, mainly due to clearly defined sources of FAs. The proposed approach is expected to set the basis for further enhancement of data fusion mechanisms for homeland security and defence applications of c-UAV technology, taking into account at the same time the attributes of diverse environments through increased adaptability.

References

1. **A**dvanced ho**L**istic **A**dverse **D**rone **D**etection, **I**dentification and Neutralization, ALADDIN 2020 Project. https://aladdin2020.eu/. Accessed 30 Mar 2021
2. Baltrušaitis, T., Ahuja, C., Morency, L.P.: Multimodal machine learning: a survey and taxonomy. IEEE Trans. Pattern Anal. Mach. Intell. **41**(2), 423–443 (2018)
3. Bombini, L., Cerri, P., Medici, P., Alessandretti, G.: Radar-vision fusion for vehicle detection. In: Proceedings of International Workshop on Intelligent Transportation, vol. 65, p. 70 (2006)
4. Chang, J.R., Chen, Y.S.: Batch-normalized maxout network in network (2015). arXiv preprint arXiv:1511.02583
5. Christnacher, F., et al.: Optical and acoustical UAV detection. In: Electro-Optical Remote Sensing X. vol. 9988, p. 99880B. International Society for Optics and Photonics (2016)
6. Diamantidou, E., Lalas, A., Votis, K., Tzovaras, D.: Multimodal deep learning framework for enhanced accuracy of UAV detection. In: Tzovaras, D., Giakoumis, D., Vincze, M., Argyros, A. (eds.) ICVS 2019. LNCS, vol. 11754, pp. 768–777. Springer, Cham (2019). https://doi.org/10.1007/978-3-030-34995-0_70
7. Jovanoska, S., Brötje, M., Koch, W.: Multisensor data fusion for UAV detection and tracking. In: 2018 19th International Radar Symposium (IRS), pp. 1–10. IEEE (2018)
8. Kavukcuoglu, K., Sermanet, P., Boureau, Y.L., Gregor, K., Mathieu, M., Cun, Y.L.: Learning convolutional feature hierarchies for visual recognition. In: Advances in Neural Information Processing Systems, pp. 1090–1098 (2010)
9. LeCun, Y., Bengio, Y., Hinton, G.: Deep learning. Nature **521**(7553), 436–444 (2015)
10. LeCun, Y., et al.: Lenet-5. Convolutional Neural Netw. **20**(5), 14 (2015). http://yann.lecun.com/exdb/lenet

11. Liu, W., Wang, Z., Liu, X., Zeng, N., Liu, Y., Alsaadi, F.E.: A survey of deep neural network architectures and their applications. Neurocomputing **234**, 11–26 (2017)
12. Manana, M., Tu, C., Owolawi, P.A.: A survey on vehicle detection based on convolution neural networks. In: 2017 3rd IEEE International Conference on Computer and Communications (ICCC), pp. 1751–1755. IEEE (2017)
13. Mészarós, J.: Aerial surveying UAV based on open-source hardware and software. International archives of the photogrammetry, remote sensing and spatial information sciences **37**(1), 555 (2011)
14. Moses, A., Rutherford, M.J., Valavanis, K.P.: Radar-based detection and identification for miniature air vehicles. In: 2011 IEEE International Conference on Control Applications (CCA), pp. 933–940. IEEE (2011)
15. Ngiam, J., Khosla, A., Kim, M., Nam, J., Lee, H., Ng, A.Y.: Multimodal deep learning. In: ICML (2011)
16. Opromolla, R., Fasano, G., Accardo, D.: A vision-based approach to UAV detection and tracking in cooperative applications. Sensors **18**(10), 3391 (2018)
17. Pal, S.K., Mitra, S.: Multilayer perceptron, fuzzy sets, classifiaction. IEEE Trans. Neural Netw. **3**, 683–697 (1992)
18. Papernot, N., McDaniel, P., Jha, S., Fredrikson, M., Celik, Z.B., Swami, A.: The limitations of deep learning in adversarial settings. In: 2016 IEEE European Symposium on Security and Privacy (EuroS&P), pp. 372–387. IEEE (2016)
19. Samaras, S., Diamantidou, E., Ataloglou, D., Sakellariou, N., Vafeiadis, A., Magoulianitis, V., Lalas, A., Dimou, A., Zarpalas, D., Votis, K., et al.: Deep learning on multi sensor data for counter UAV applications-a systematic review. Sensors **19**(22), 4837 (2019)
20. Samaras, S., Magoulianitis, V., Dimou, A., Zarpalas, D., Daras, P.: UAV classification with deep learning using surveillance radar data. In: Tzovaras, D., Giakoumis, D., Vincze, M., Argyros, A. (eds.) ICVS 2019. LNCS, vol. 11754, pp. 744–753. Springer, Cham (2019). https://doi.org/10.1007/978-3-030-34995-0_68
21. Shakhatreh, H., et al.: Unmanned aerial vehicles (UAVs): a survey on civil applications and key research challenges. IEEE Access **7**, 48572–48634 (2019)
22. Srivastava, N., Hinton, G., Krizhevsky, A., Sutskever, I., Salakhutdinov, R.: Dropout: a simple way to prevent neural networks from overfitting. J. Mach. Learn. Res. **15**(1), 1929–1958 (2014)
23. Stöcker, C., Bennett, R., Nex, F., Gerke, M., Zevenbergen, J.: Review of the current state of UAV regulations. Remote Sens. **9**(5), 459 (2017)
24. Thomas, A., Leboucher, V., Cotinat, A., Finet, P., Gilbert, M.: UAV localization using panoramic thermal cameras. In: Tzovaras, D., Giakoumis, D., Vincze, M., Argyros, A. (eds.) ICVS 2019. LNCS, vol. 11754, pp. 754–767. Springer, Cham (2019). https://doi.org/10.1007/978-3-030-34995-0_69
25. Wiatowski, T., Bölcskei, H.: A mathematical theory of deep convolutional neural networks for feature extraction. IEEE Trans. Inf. Theory **64**(3), 1845–1866 (2017)

Cyber Attack Detection and Trust Management Toolkit for Defence-Related Microgrids

Medentzidis Charalampos-Rafail[1], Kotsiopoulos Thanasis[1,2(✉)],
Vellikis Vasileios[1], Ioannidis Dimosthenis[1], Tzovaras Dimitrios[1],
and Sarigiannidis Panagiotis[2]

[1] Centre for Research and Technology Hellas,
Information Technologies Institute, 57001 Thermi, Greece
`kotsiopoulos@iti.gr`
[2] Department of Electrical and Computer Engineering,
University of Western Macedonia, Karamanli and Ligeris Street,
50100 Kozani, Greece

Abstract. The rise of microgrids in defence applications, as a greener, more economical and efficient source of energy and the consequential softwarization of networks, has led to the emerge of various cyber-threats. The danger of cyber-attacks in defence microgrid facilities cannot be neglected nor undermined, due to the severe consequences that they can cause. To this end, this paper presents a cyberattack detection and cyber attack severity calculation toolkit, with the aim to provide an end-to-end solution to the cyberattack detection in defense IoT/microgrid systems. Concretely, in this paper are presented and evaluated the SPEAR Visual Analytics AI Engine and the SPEAR Grid Trusted Module (GTM) of the SPEAR H2020 project. The aim of the Visual Analytics AI Engine is to detect malicious action that intend to harm the microgrid and to assist the security engineer of an infrastructure to easily detect abnormalities and submit security events accordingly, while the GTM is responsible to calculate the severity of each security event and to assigns trust values to the affected assets of the system. The accurate detection of cyber-attacks and the efficient reputation management, are assessed with data from a real smart home infrastructure with an installed nanogrid, after applying a 3-stage attack against the MODBUS/TCP protocol used by some of the core nanogrid devices.

Keywords: Microgrids · Artificial intelligence · Fuzzy logic · Cyber-attack detection

1 Introduction

The usage of renewable energy resources instead of the traditional coal-based energy generation systems is gaining more and more popularity in defence applications among other domains. There are numerous reasons for the adoption of

I. Maglogiannis et al. (Eds.): AIAI 2021 Workshops, IFIP AICT 628, pp. 240–251, 2021.
https://doi.org/10.1007/978-3-030-79157-5_20

renewable energy in this domain, such as the extremely dangerous and costly usage and transportation of fossil fuel in remote regions of military operations that could jeopardize the security of military personnel [15]. Also, the severe environmental footprint of coal usage as the basic means of energy production is another reason. Finally, relocatable temporary camps usually depend on oversized generators to meet peak loads, even if these loads are very rare, which is both costly and inefficient [10].

Thus, it is understandable that more efficient and secure ways of energy production are needed. One of the basic means of green energy production towards that purpose, is based on microgrid technology. A microgrid is a small-scale local energy cyber-physical system with a controllable group of interconnected loads and distributed energy resources (DERs) that can operate independently both when connected and isolated from the main grid [21], which is one of the main reasons of its usefulness in military applications. In such cyber-physical systems, the physical part is strongly influenced by the integrity of the cyber part [12].

On the one hand, the monitoring and control of flexible assets within a microgrid by means of information and communication technologies enhances the resilience of the system, but on the other hand also incurs the risk of security breaches. The more complex the microgrid is, the more is the reliance on distributed, active control of the network, increasing the potential impact of an attack. In order to minimize that risk, AI technology can be leveraged to train algorithms that can capture patterns of data flows in such systems, that indicate malfunctions or specific cyber-attacks. Secure and Private Smart Grid (SPEAR) H2020 project [1], offers a holistic solution for the protection of Smart Grid infrastructures, including microgrids. The technology developed within SPEAR has been tested and evaluated in a Smart Home infrastructure with an installed nanogrid among other systems. To this end, the contribution of this paper can be summarized in the following points:

- A deep-learning methodology for anomaly detection, combining unsupervised learning to capture the 'normal' operation patterns and an ensemble hard voting to classify a sample as normal/anomaly.
- Visualization of the detected anomalies through the visual analytics dashboard, with the possibility to submit a security event.
- A fuzzy-logic methodology for severity quantification of a security event and consequentially the calculation and assignment of a representative trust value to the affected microgrid asset.
- The evaluation of the proposed solution is implemented in a real nanogrid testbed of a Smart Home.

2   Related Works

Many studies have been investigated regarding the security of microgrid systems in terms of attack detection, node trust assessment or both. In [9] a methodology is proposed based on time-frequency information using the parametric time-frequency logic (PTFL). This technique does not require the modeling knowledge of the microgrid, but the anomalous electricity measurements, called traces are required for anomaly detection related to false data injection (FDI) and denial of service attacks (DoS), as well as physical faults of a microgrid. The same anomalies are detected by a framework that does not require system knowledge, by monitoring the outputs of inverters/converters against operational bounds, using metric temporal logic (MLT) [8].

An FDI attack detection and mitigation mechanism for the distributed secondary control of AC microgrids is proposed by the authors of [21]. Kullbback-Liebler (KL) divergence is applied to measure the difference between the Gaussian distributions of actual and expected measurements. Trust for individual DERs is represented by the entropy of a DER's own and its neighbour's trustworthiness information on a communication graph. Another deception attack (replay, spoofing, FDI, stealth) detection approach, this time for DC microgrids, is presented in [23], where an analytical consistency-based anomaly detection mechanism is utilized, which manipulates primal and dual variables associated with the proposed distributed algorithm.

In [20] an online monitoring system models the state of the Cyber Physical System (CPS), as a function of its relationships between constituent components, using a combination of model-based and data-driven strategies. The state estimation is done by using the KASE (Kalman Autoregressive State Estimation with Latent Factors and Exogenous Inputs) Invariant Algorithm. The system is periodically retrained using historical data while also updating the CPS state estimation using new data instances. The illiad system has also a front-end section and warns the user in case of anomalies.

The authors in [18] proposed a framework for distributed frequency control and intrusion detection in isolated microgrids. By casting it as a consensus optimization problem, the partial primal-dual algorithm is adopted. For the intrusion problem, two types of malicious network attacks are studied. As a mitigation mechanism, model-based anomaly detection and localization strategies are developed by exploring dual variable-related metrics.

In [16] an intelligent anomaly detection method based on prediction intervals (PIs) is introduced to distinguish malicious attacks with different severities during a secured operation. The proposed anomaly detection method is constructed based on the lower and upper bound estimation method (LUBE) and a modified symbiotic organisms search (SOS) algorithm to provide optimal feasible PIs over the smart meter readings.

The rest of the paper is organized as follows: Sect. 3 describes the system architecture by presenting its constituent components and the methodologies supporting their functionality. Section 4 discusses the evaluation by presenting the experiments that where conducted to assess the anomaly detection capabilities and the the trust management efficiency. Finally, Sect. 5 includes the conclusions of this paper and the future steps regarding the foreseen extensions of the toolkit.

3   System Architecture

Our toolkit consists of two main components. The Anomaly Detection Module and the Grid Trusted Module (GTM) engine. The Anomaly Detection Module is part of the SPEAR Visual Analytics component and is responsible to provide visual-based anomaly detection techniques to the security engineer, allowing also to submit security events in the format defined by [2]. GTM engine is responsible to correlate the security events with the impact that a cyberattack can deliver to each asset of the microgrid. Both of the modules are part of the SPEAR SIEM [13].

3.1 Anomaly Detection Module

The purpose of the Anomaly Detection Module is to identify anomalies in the network packets. The network packets are captured via the SPEAR sensor [13] using the wireshark tool [6]. The features used from the wireshark filtering in order to perform the anomaly detection are: packet length, tcp window size, modbus tcp length, modbus tcp prot. id, modbus tcp trans. id, modbus tcp unit id, modbus function code, modbus reference number (8 in total). A brief description of each feature can be found in [5]. The data preprocessing includes the selection of the best features and the resolve of NaN values. The best features are selected by calculating the correlation matrix, we select high correlated features i.e. correlation threshold 0.75. There is a problem arising with NaN values as protocols are changing during time, this problem is resolved by setting $1e-10$ to NaN values.

AI Engine. An Ensemble hard voting method has been implemented as the core of the AI engine. Ensemble learning fuses the outcome of multiple models and provides prediction with increased accuracy [22]. The ensemble method consists of a seq2seqLSTM autoencoder and three classifiers. The Random Forest classifier, the Logistic Regression classifier and the Gaussian Naive Bayes classifier of the scikit-learn package [4].

First of all, for each feature of the network packets, a seq2seqLSTM autoencoder is created. Figure 1 depicts the seq2seqLSTM autoencoder architecture. The input data is converted to sequences using the sliding window technique. The target data is the input data but offset by one in the future, a process called teacher forcing [17]. The network packet fields from normal conditions are used

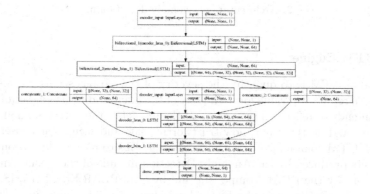

Fig. 1. Seq2SeqLSTM Model

for training the seq2seq autoencoder, to learn the patterns. The data records used during the prediction phase are unlabeled.

Afterwards, the mean absolute error is calculated between the predicted values and the unlabeled data which was not used for training. The mean absolute error is used as an anomaly score. This technique is common and can be found also in [11,25]. The seq2seqLSTM autoencoder is built using the Tensorflow library [7] with the Adam optimizer and the mean absolute error as loss function. The anomaly scores for each data source and the ground truth label are then passed as input to the Voting Ensemble Classifier. Each classifier estimates the probability for each sample to belong either to class normal or class anomalous. After each prediction, the output of the hard voting Ensemble method is the label for each sample representing the normal or anomalous category. Figure 2 illustrates the architecture of the Ensemble method.

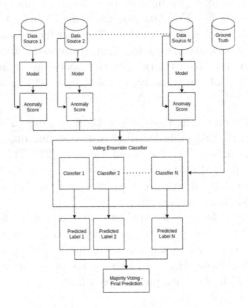

Fig. 2. Architecture of anomaly detection module

3.2   GTM Engine

The goal of GTM is to quantify the severity of the various security events and calculate a reputation value for each asset of the microgrid. This kind of quantification intends to reflect on the one hand the impact of the detected anomaly for each asset and on the other, how trustworthy, safe and secure each asset is. To this end, GTM communicates with the Message Bus to receive the various security events produced by the Anomaly Detection module of the Visual Analytics component, by the BDAC component and by the SPEAR SIEM BASIS. GTM is built using Python and the Fuzzy Logic library called scikit-fuzzy [3]. The utilized fuzzy logic systems described below are based on the Mamdani fuzzy inference approach [19]. The defuzzification of each crisp value is implemented with the centroid method.

Figure 3 depicts the GTM engine architecture. GTM is a backend component and SPEAR VIDS is utilised for the visualization of its outcomes and its configuration, defining a specific threshold value for each asset. If an asset's reputation value or the first derivative of the reputation value drops below the particular thresholds, then a GTM alert is generated for the specific asset(s). All the security events received from the Message Bus, are undertaken by the GTM Fuzzy Logic Core and the GTM Fuzzy Reputation Reduction System, to calculate a reputation value for each asset. These reputation values are sent to the VIDS to visualize them. Finally, the reputation values of GTM are stored into the GTM database as historical data.

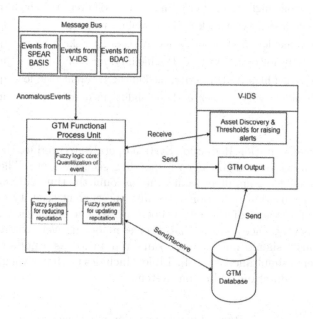

Fig. 3. Architecture of the GTM engine

The core of the GTM engine is the GTM Functional Process Unit, which consists of three elements: (a) the Fuzzy Logic Core, (b) the Fuzzy Reputation Reduction System and (c) the Fuzzy Reputation Recovery System.

The Fuzzy Logic Core quantifies the incoming anomalous incidents using Fuzzy Logic and by taking into consideration first of all the subcategory of the event (Cyber Attack or Anomaly) and the following security event fields: asset value, the event risk, the priority and the reliability. These specific fields are defined by the SPEAR OSSIM [13] which is an extension of [2]. The Fuzzy Logic Core utilises the fuzzy theory to map the value of each aforementioned variable into a quantified value without specifying rules in a strict manner. Table 1 illustrates indicative fuzzy logic rules used by the Fuzzy Logic Core. The rules are derived by forming the fuzzy universe and they are in total 161. The fuzzy universe is unique and mandatory for each variable used to calculate the quantified value of the security event.

Table 1. Indicative rules of fuzzy logic core

No	Input	Output
Rule 1	asset value: high AND priority: high AND event risk: high AND subcategory: Attack AND reliability: high	quant. value: low
Rule 2	asset value: low AND priority: low AND event risk: low AND subcategory: anomaly AND reliability: low	quant. value: high
Rule 3	asset value: high AND priority: medium AND event risk: high AND subcategory: Attack AND reliability: medium	quant. value: low
Rule 16	asset value: low AND priority: low AND event risk: low AND subcategory: Attack AND reliability: medium	quant. value: medium
Rule 20	asset value: high AND priority: medium AND event risk: low AND subcategory: Attack AND reliability: medium	quant. value: medium

The Fuzzy Reputation Reduction System operates to produce the reputation value of any asset related to the corresponding security event. The reputation value of each asset is computed, taking into account the time difference between the previous reputation reduction value and the current security event as well as the quantified value of the Fuzzy Logic Core. The reputation reduction is applied in this way, since an asset that receives malicious events occasionally and not continuously should not have the same reputation as a node that receives malicious events simultaneously [14]. Table 2 includes the 9 fuzzy logic rules used by the Fuzzy Reputation Reduction System.

Table 2. Rules of fuzzy reputation reduction system

No	Input	Output
Rule 1	time: low AND quant. value: low	reput. value: low
Rule 2	time: low AND quant. value: medium	reput. value: low
Rule 3	time: low AND quant. value: high	reput. value: medium
Rule 4	time: medium AND quant. value: low	reput. value: low
Rule 5	time: medium AND quant. value: medium	reput. value: medium
Rule 6	time: medium AND quant. value: high	reput. value: high
Rule 7	time: high AND quant. value: low	reput. value: medium
Rule 8	time: high AND quant. value: medium	reput. value: high
Rule 9	time: high AND quant. value: high	reput. value: high

Last but not least, the Fuzzy Reputation Recovery System undertakes to increase the reputation value based on the time difference between the last reduction of an asset's reputation value and the current time. The Fuzzy System for reputation recovery works in parallel with the Fuzzy Logic Core and the Fuzzy System for reputation reduction. A time interval threshold is also applied in order to start calculating reputation update for each asset. The threshold is configurable by the user and is based on his/her desire. The functionality of the Fuzzy Reputation Recovery System is also based on fuzzy rules. Table 3 visualizes the Reputation Recovery System fuzzy rules.

Table 3. Rules of fuzzy reputation update system

No	Input	Output
Rule 1	time: low AND quant. value: low	reput. value: medium
Rule 2	time: low AND quant. value: medium	reput. value: medium
Rule 3	time: low AND quant. value: high	reput. value: high
Rule 4	time: medium AND quant. value: low	reput. value: medium
Rule 5	time: medium AND quant. value: medium	reput. value: medium
Rule 6	time: medium AND quant. value: high	reput. value: high
Rule 7	time: high AND quant. value: low	reput. value: medium
Rule 8	time: high AND quant. value: medium	reput. value: high
Rule 9	time: high AND quant. value: high	reput. value: high

4 Evaluation

The evaluation of the toolkit that was described in the previous section, was performed in the Smart Home test bed of CERTH/ITI, where a nanogrid is deployed as described in [24]. The PV inverter and the battery energy storage system inverters/chargers of the nanogrid, support monitoring and control through MODBUS/TCP protocol. An attack to their communication channels could have severe consequences, as it could not only lead to the nanogrid system corruption, but also to possibly irreversible equipment damage. Due to the importance of preserving the security of those channels, the evaluation was based on a 3-stage cyber-attack against the MODBUS/TCP protocol. The attack was performed against a deployed production honeypot imitating the PV inverter of the Smart Home, so that no real equipment would be endangered. The 3-stage cyber-attack consists of the following steps:

- Uid Brute Force : As a first step a scan of the supported IDs of all the MODBUS clients, is performed.
- Function Enumeration : The second step of the attack enumerates the supported function codes of the target MODBUS device.
- WriteAllRegisters: As a final step, a DoS attempt is performed by arbitrarily writing values in the registers of the target MODBUS device.

After performing the attacks, the toolkit was evaluated by creating a test set with both normal packet fields and packet fields from network traffic related to the aforementioned attack. The classification results of our methodology illustrated in Table 4, showed quite satisfactory performance, indicating the appropriateness of our methodology. The method was able to achieve 83% Accuracy, 80% Precision, 95% Recall and 87% F1 Score.

Table 4. Confusion Matrix of the test set results

		Actual class	
		Anomalous	Normal
Predicted class	Anomalous	312	15
	Normal	79	153

The dashboard of the visual analytics tool, assists the security engineer to identify security events by highlighting the detected anomalies in corresponding time series plots, where each time step corresponds to a different packet, as can be seen in Figure 4a . After further investigating the related data, the security engineer can come up with a conclusion about the nature of the security event and submits it by using the form in Fig. 4b.

The GTM engine was evaluated both in terms of reputation reduction behaviour and scalability. As more security events are produced for a microgrid's asset, the GTM engine reduces the reputation more rapidly as can be seen in Fig. 5 a. Specifically, 5 consecutive events were generated and after the second event, the GTM starts to decrease the reputation of the asset with higher rate.

In order to assess the scalability of GTM, we submitted several artificial security events to get the response time, which is depicted in Fig. 5 b. As can easily be observed from the figure, the response time follows a linear course and is not affected by the increasing number of submitted security events (10, 50, 100, 200 , 500, 1000 respectively).

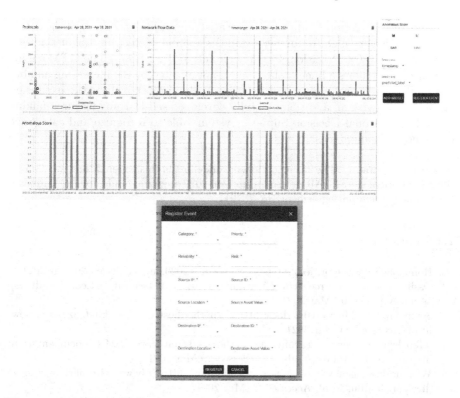

Fig. 4. a. (top) Visualization of the anomaly detection outcome, b. (bottom) Security event submission form

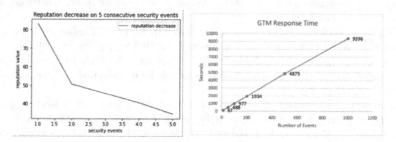

Fig. 5. a. Attacked asset reputation reduction after 5 consecutive events b. GTM response time

5   Conclusions

In this paper an anomaly detection and visualization system tool with trust management functionality was presented and evaluated in a real infrastructure. The AI algorithms used in the Anomaly Detection Module and the three main elements of GTM engine's core, were listed and described. Afterwards the evaluation of the toolkit and the 3-stage cyber attack were documented. The results for the Anomaly Detection Module are very satisfying and the accuracy of the detection system is very high. In further detail,the anomaly detection toolkit achieved 83% Accuracy, 80% Precision, 95% Recall and 87% F1 Score. The GTM engine response time follows a linear course and is not affected by the increasing number of submitted security events. Future steps of the project include the expansion of this toolkit with an addition of a fully developed self-learning feature, making it a fully functional Decision Support System, able to recognize and categorize the nanogrid's anomalies.

Acknowledgement. The aforementioned work effort in this paper is conducted under the framework of the SPEAR project, a Horizon 2020 program, funded by the European Union under the grant agreement No. 787011.

References

1. Home page - spear project: https://www.spear2020.eu/. Accessed 26 Mar 2021
2. Ossim: The open source siem, alienvault: https://cybersecurity.att.com/products/ossim. Accessed 04 Mar 2021
3. Scikit-fuzzy - skfuzzy v0.2 docs: https://pythonhosted.org/scikit-fuzzy/overview.html. Accessed 24 Mar 2021
4. scikit-learn: machine learning in python - scikit-learn 0.24.1 documentation: https://scikit-learn.org/stable/. Accessed 29 Mar 2021
5. Wireshark · display filter reference: Modbus: https://www.wireshark.org/docs/dfref/m/modbus.html. Accessed 29 Mar 2021
6. wireshark -google: https://www.wireshark.com. Accessed 29 Mar 2021
7. Abadi, M., Agarwal, A., Barham, P., et al.: TensorFlow: large-scale machine learning on heterogeneous systems (2015). https://www.tensorflow.org/. software available from tensorflow.org
8. Beg, O.A., Yadav, A.P., Johnson, T.T., Davoudi, A.: Formal online resiliency monitoring in microgrids. In: 2020 Resilience Week (RWS), pp. 99–105 (2020)
9. Beg, O.A., Nguyen, L.V., Johnson, T.T., Davoudi, A.: Cyber-physical anomaly detection in microgrids using time-frequency logic formalism. IEEE Access **9**, 20012–20021 (2021)
10. Berardi, U., Tomassoni, E., Khaled, K.: A smart hybrid energy system grid for energy efficiency in remote areas for the army. Energies **13**(9), 2279 (2020)
11. Borghesi, A., Bartolini, A., Lombardi, M., Milano, M., Benini, L.: Anomaly detection using autoencoders in high performance computing systems. Proc. AAAI Conf. Artif. Intell. **33**, 9428–9433 (2019)
12. Canaan, B., Colicchio, B., Ould Abdeslam, D.: Microgrid cyber-security: Review and challenges toward resilience. Appl. Sci. **10**(16), 5649 (2020)
13. Grammatikis, P.R., et al.: Secure and private smart grid: the spear architecture. In: 2020 6th IEEE Conference on Network Softwarization (NetSoft), pp. 450–456. IEEE (2020)
14. Hadjichristofi, G., Varveris, G.: Visualizing and aggregating behavior for trust evaluation. In: 2019 IEEE 24th International Workshop on Computer Aided Modeling and Design of Communication Links and Networks (CAMAD), pp. 1–6. IEEE (2019)

15. Kashem, S.B.A., De Souza, S., Iqbal, A., Ahmed, J.: Microgrid in military applications. In: 2018 IEEE 12th International Conference on Compatibility, Power Electronics and Power Engineering (CPE-POWERENG 2018), pp. 1–5. IEEE (2018)
16. Kavousi-Fard, A., Su, W., Jin, T.: A machine-learning-based cyber attack detection model for wireless sensor networks in microgrids. IEEE Trans. Industr. Inf. **17**(1), 650–658 (2020)
17. Lamb, A., Goyal, A., Zhang, Y., Zhang, S., Courville, A., Bengio, Y.: Professor forcing: a new algorithm for training recurrent networks (2016). arXiv preprint arXiv:1610.09038
18. Lu, L.Y., Liu, H.J., Zhu, H., Chu, C.C.: Intrusion detection in distributed frequency control of isolated microgrids. IEEE Trans. Smart Grid **10**(6), 6502–6515 (2019)
19. Mamdani, E.H., Assilian, S.: An experiment in linguistic synthesis with a fuzzy logic controller. Int. J. Man Mach. Stud. **7**(1), 1–13 (1975)
20. Muralidhar, N., Wang, C., Self, N., Momtazpour, M., Nakayama, K., Sharma, R., Ramakrishnan, N.: illiad: Intelligent invariant and anomaly detection in cyber-physical systems. ACM Trans. Intell. Syst. Technol. (TIST) **9**(3), 1–20 (2018)
21. Mustafa, A., Poudel, B., Bidram, A., Modares, H.: Detection and mitigation of data manipulation attacks in AC microgrids. IEEE Trans. Smart Grid **11**(3), 2588–2603 (2019)
22. Opitz, D., Maclin, R.: Popular ensemble methods: an empirical study. J. Artif. Intell. Res. **11**, 169–198 (1999)
23. Shi, D., Lin, P., Wang, Y., Chu, C.C., Xu, Y., Wang, P.: Deception attack detection of isolated DC microgrids under consensus-based distributed voltage control architecture. IEEE J. Emerg. Sel. Top. Circuits Syst. **11**(1), 155–167 (2021)
24. Tsolakis, A.C., et al.: Design and real-life deployment of a smart nanogrid: a greek case study. In: 2020 IEEE International Conference on Power and Energy (PECon), pp. 321–326 (2020)
25. Zimmerer, D., Kohl, S.A., Petersen, J., Isensee, F., Maier-Hein, K.H.: Context-encoding variational autoencoder for unsupervised anomaly detection (2018). arXiv preprint arXiv:1812.05941

On the Potential of SDN Enabled Network Deployment in Tactical Environments

George Lazaridis[1,2(✉)], Kostas Papachristou[1], Anastasios Drosou[1],
Dimosthenis Ioannidis[1], Periklis Chatzimisios[2], and Dimitrios Tzovaras[1]

[1] Centre for Research and Technology Hellas, Thessaloniki, Greece
{glazaridis,kostas.papachristou,drosou,djoannid,
dimitrios.tzovaras}@iti.gr
[2] International Hellenic University, Thessaloniki, Greece
{glazaridis,pchatzimisios}@ihu.gr

Abstract. Modern critical operations and defence applications require highly demanding information and communication systems, making ad hoc networks, which are mainly used nowadays in tactical zones, to be difficult to manage. The evolution of the Software Defined Networking (SDN) technology has brought new perspectives to security and defence applications, making them more reliable, more stable, more secure and more portable. This research paper proposes an SDN topology for secure communications in a tactical environment, overcoming several challenges that a conventional network faces. Moreover, an Artificial Intelligence (AI) methodology, exclusively used in SDN environments is presented, providing Quality of Service (QoS) features to the network, based on which rerouting paths can be calculated. Finally, our routing methodology is illustrated using representative evaluation scenarios.

Keywords: Software Defined Networking · Defense · Security · Artificial Intelligence · OpenFlow · Quality of Service

1 Introduction

Even though the field of Artificial Intelligence (AI) research emerged in 1956 at a workshop at Dartmouth College, it has made significant progress over the years, both in industry and academia [6]. The rapid development of AI has also brought about great changes in the field of defense and security systems, which combine a large number of Internet of Things (IoT) devices being capable of accumulating quantities of data, regarding the environment they are operating in, as well as information related to their own operation. Furthermore, safe communications

This work has been partially supported by the European Commission through project SDN-microSENSE funded by the European Union Horizon 2020 programme under Grant Agreement no 833955. The opinions expressed in this paper are those of the authors and do not necessarily reflect the views of the European Commission.

I. Maglogiannis et al. (Eds.): AIAI 2021 Workshops, IFIP AICT 628, pp. 252–263, 2021.
https://doi.org/10.1007/978-3-030-79157-5_21

in a tactical assembly area or in a military camp, is an aspect that should be seriously considered. In order to circulate trusted information through defense and security systems, reliable communication networks should be established, taking advantage of AI techniques. These types of communication networks face several challenges, due to the outdoor environment they operate in, compared to conventional networks. They should be distinguished by portability in order to be easily deployed in any environment and operate with low power consumption. Moreover, they should be able to cover a large area of interest and be easily extendable, depending on the needs of the network deployment. Communication networks are facing the challenge of sustainability in environments with high vegetation, ground irregularities, where Quality of Service (QoS) and the data transmission rates are poor. Tactical networks, should be able to adapt transmission paths and overcome any malfunction or destruction of routing hardware. All these challenges are bypassed, and the survivability of the communication network is achieved thanks to topology of the SDN network and the rerouting techniques that the AI algorithms offer.

Over the past decade, SDN has majorly evolved, leading to a new era in the area of networks. Major technology conglomerates, such as Facebook, Google or Amazon have introduced the SDN technology to their complex data centers. The innovative approach behind SDN is the introduction of dynamic and programming methods to automate network management processes [2]. Traditional networks' architecture, consist of intermediary devices, such as a routers or switches, each of which has its own control plane and takes decisions independently regarding the forwarding policy of each packet. On the other hand, SDN virtualizes the control plane by moving it to a central place, commonly called SDN controller. The major advantages of introducing the SDN technology to defense and security domain applications include the centralized view of the entire network, the low overall operating and equipment costs, the granular security, the ability to shape and control data traffic by implementing AI-based QoS provisioning algorithms and the offer of enhanced flexibility, scalability and efficiency compared to traditional networks. Current routing algorithms in non-SDN networks, such as Open Shortest Path First (OSPF) [13], can only support best-effort services. In other words, the network makes no commitment that data will be transmitted or that it will be of acceptable quality, especially in the presence of high network traffic [1]. With the rising need for internet services, it is more critical than ever for Internet Service Providers (ISPs) to guarantee QoS provisioning.

The following are the key contributions of this paper: (i) We introduce an AI-based QoS algorithm for rerouting in SDN environments used in defense and security applications (ii) we describe a low cost SDN testbed deployed in our research center's premises, built in order to be able to adequately test the proposed AI algorithm and promote the capabilities of such SDN architectures in tactical ad-hoc networks, ensuring portability, survivability and sustainability.

The rest of our paper is organized as follows: Sect. 2 presents some background information on SDN technology together with the related work. Section 3 outlines the proposed defense SDN enabled network, presenting both the SDN enabled topology to be used in security and defense applications and the developed AI QoS algorithm. Section 4 demonstrates two evaluation scenarios and finally Sect. 5 concludes the work done and propose potential future work.

2   Background and Related Work

Defence and security organizations implement advanced, integrated communication systems incorporating technologies that are cutting edge when used solely, but if these technologies are appropriately combined, they can achieve flexible and secure communications, capable of transmitting video, audio or data in tactical areas. OpenFlow is an SDN network protocol that enables the researchers to fully monitor the routing of packets in an SDN environment.

OpenFlow is an open protocol that can be used to program the data flows in SDN enabled switches and routers. Flow tables, secure channel and the OpenFlow protocol are the three elements, which make up OpenFlow. On the other hand, a SDN switch is a multi-port bridge, which allows any OpenFlow-compatible SDN controller to control its data plane. Multiple OpenFlow instances, known as datapaths, can run on a switch managed by OpenFlow. The key component of a SDN architecture and the brain of the system is the SDN controller, which is responsible for managing network flows and programming SDN enabled intermediary devices. An SDN controller uses a southbound interface, such as OpenFlow, in order to manage network elements (SDN enabled switches or routers), but it can also use a northbound interface, such as a REST API, in order to enable third-party applications to communicate with the SDN controller.

The area of SDN technology provides a wide range of research topics, therefore each of the following research papers covers a different aspect of SDN. Śliwa et al. [12] investigates how SDN techniques can promote survivability of military networks, on the strategic/operational and tactical levels. Furthermore, the SDN technology in combination with supporting techniques, will contribute in addressing the emerging complexities in military networks leading to challenging situations. Streit et al. [17] introduce in their work, a controller-equipped topology update process, which can be used in military communication applications using the SDN technology. This process was developed in order to provide a detailed and accurate description of the network topology and achieve QoS conform delivery rates, before the SDN controller begins the routing procedure. Gkioulos et al. [5] make available a comprehensive literature research of the application of the SDN technology in the wide fields of tactile networks, coalition networks, ad-hoc networks, tactical networks, and/or mission-critical infrastructures. Spencer et al. [15] conclude that even though SDN technology is still under research, and has been deployed only in high-bandwidth and highly secure data center ecosystems, it has a range of convincing advantages in tactical networks. However, a range of obstacles must be solved before the framework can be applied to tactical networks.

As already stated, SDN technology is evolving rapidly, leading to new kind of hybrid ad-hoc networks with SDN support, which can be used in a plethora of applications and fields. Yu et al. [19] presented in their work a practical implementation of a Wireless SDN mobile ad-hoc network which takes advantage of all of the benefits of Device-to-Device (D2D) data transmissions, while still having the stability of a SDN network. Poularakis et al. [14] researched thoroughly the SDN technology in order to be used in mobile ad-hoc networks to support connectivity and service requirements, the feasibility and the reliability of such proposed networks. Moreover, in a SDN enabled tactical ad hoc network, Liu et al. [11] investigated the controller deployment issue and recommended a SDN enabled mobile ad hoc network architecture. In their work the authors also modeled and customized the controllers' implementation in order to ensure latency and reduce energy consumption. Finally, the Reliable and Dynamic Routing Technique (RaDRT) solution is analyzed in Streit et al. [16], which uses a SDN approach to control traffic flow routing in ad-hoc environments.

3   Defense SDN Enabled Network

3.1   Proposed SDN Topology

This section describes the development and the implementation of an ad-hoc SDN enabled network, proposed for security and defense applications in tactical environments. This network is distinguished by reliability, portability, scalability, inter-connectivity, low deployment cost, easy network management, security, real-time information transfer with low latency and end-to-end encryption privacy. By its nature, a SDN network is capable of rerouting data paths programmatically, with the use of AI algorithms. The main components of SDN enabled networks are the SDN controller and a database, SDN enabled switches, a MQTT broker and different kinds of end devices, such as laptops, mobile phones, tablets, walkie-talkies, Global Positioning System (GPS) devices, which are capable of connecting to the SDN network through wireless Access Points (APs), Bluetooth gateways or direct Ethernet connections. All previously mentioned technologies are combined together in order to formulate a novel SDN topology, which can be used in a tactical environment. Figure 1 illustrates the topology of the proposed defense SDN enabled network.

SDN Controller: The SDN controller is the brain of the SDN enabled network, being able to programmably compose the flow's route. For our environment, the Open Network Operating System (ONOS) was selected to be the SDN controller. ONOS is the leading open source SDN controller for building next-generation SDN solutions and it is written in the Java programming language [8]. The controller is installed on an Ubuntu-based computer running on the control plane.

Database: An InfluxDB database was installed and configured on a computer running the Ubuntu operating system, in order to collect network data regarding the performance of the SDN enabled network and more precisely the network statistics coming from each SDN enabled switch. The collected data is either

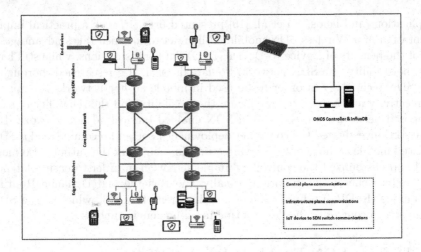

Fig. 1. Proposed defense SDN enabled network topology

used by our custom-built visualization tools in order to graphically represent network information to the administrator or forward this information to intrusion detection algorithms to further process it.

SDN Enabled Switches: Open vSwitch, also known as OVS, is a multilayer software switch that interconnects virtual devices in the same host or between different hosts, licensed under open-source Apache 2.0 license. OVS allows programmers to create forwarding functions in order to automate and control network traffic and supports standard management interfaces. The software-based Open vSwitch, which will be running on a Raspberry Pi 3B+ board, will form a SDN-Switch for the network. The SDN enabled switch includes a built-in Ethernet port and with the use of four USB-to-Ethernet adapters, it expands its network capabilities. The proposed SDN enabled network consists of nine SDN enabled switches. Five of them are part of the core network, where the system administrator is able to program different flow routes, while the remaining four are part of the edge network and allow different kind of devices to connect to the SDN network. The SDN switches are able to connect to each other either by taking advantage of their Ethernet interface or by using any wireless technology [7].

Wireless AP: An AP is a network device that establishes a Wireless Local Area Network (WLAN) in a desired environment. An AP uses an Ethernet cable to link to a wired router, switch, or hub and broadcasts a Wi-Fi signal to a specific location. In our case, a Raspberry Pi 3B+ board is configured to operate as AP, allowing devices to connect wirelessly to the SDN enabled network. The AP is connected via Ethernet cable to an edge SDN enabled switch, expanding the capabilities of a wired SDN network [4].

Bluetooth Gateway: A Bluetooth gateway is a physical device, which allows Bluetooth-based products to connect to other devices or hardware. In our SDN enabled network, Raspberry Pi 3B+ boards are reconfigured accordingly, by adding software, in order to transform them into Bluetooth gateways and expand the connectivity of devices used in SDN networks by adding direct connection of Bluetooth devices. These types of gateways allow Bluetooth devices, used in tactical areas or military camps to firstly connect, in a secure mode, to the SDN enabled network and then translate the Bluetooth packets into MQTT packets in order to be sent over the SDN network to a desired recipient. Such tactical devices, which are capable of connecting via Bluetooth to the SDN network, could be a Bluetooth-enabled smartphone, a Bluetooth-enabled laptop or a portable GPS device [10].

MQTT Broker: A Message Queuing Telemetry Transport (MQTT) broker is a server that accepts all messages from clients and forwards them to the correct destination clients. On the other hand, an MQTT client could be any system, which has installed an MQTT library and connects to an MQTT broker over a network. In the proposed SDN enabled topology, the MQTT broker is installed as an end device on a Raspberry Pi 3B+ board, using the Mosquitto MQTT Broker software. This MQTT broker is part of the Bluetooth gateway system, responsible for the transmission of Bluetooth packets translated into MQTT packets. The MQTT broker can be placed anywhere in the SDN enabled network [9].

End Devices: Practically any device that contains a Bluetooth, a Wi-Fi or an Ethernet interface, could be an end device capable of connecting to the SDN enabled network. Many different kinds of devices can be used in security and defense applications, namely laptops, smartphones, portable GPS devices, walkie-talkies, tablets. Regarding their operating system, they will be able to run a custom-built application, which will allow them to securely send different types of data through the SDN enabled network, such as text messages, video, audio or any type of file. Furthermore, this application offers a lightweight end-to-end encryption mechanism, allowing sensitive information to pass through the network in a secure way and inaccessible to unauthorized users. Finally, even though the devices are able to connect to the SDN enabled network in a first stage, the SDN controller is responsible for granting access to them or rejecting them. This way, even if we try to embrace a Bring Your Own Device (BYOD) logic, only certified devices will be allowed to access and distribute sensitive information.

3.2   AI Enabled SDN Routing

In this section, we present the SDN rerouting methodology that is able to estimate and enforce flow rules of the defense SDN network ensuring energy, QoS provisioning and security efficiency. More specifically, we collect real-time metrics from the network in order to calculate a number of routing objectives that concern energy, QoS and security information per SDN switch and link. By employing multi-objective optimization incorporating evolutionary algorithms, a set of the best solutions (i.e. flow rules) is identified. The set of new flow rules is then applied to the SDN system.

Network Monitoring: Our method collects various SDN traffic statistics and metrics in order to calculate security, QoS and energy consumption related objectives. First, QoS is a representative description of the overall performance of the network. Our approach utilizes the delays between switches and resource utilization statistics (i.e. CPU load and memory usage) to estimate a QoS metric for all the links and switches of the network. Since sensitive switches and links must be protected from attacks, each switch is characterized by a sensitivity level, which is estimated based on the amount of data serves each switch. Similarly, each link has a sensitivity level based on the amount of data being transmitted using this link. Every communication process between IoT devices consumes an amount of electrical energy, which could be translated into a financial cost. Therefore, the traffic in the network should be optimized in order to minimize the total energy consumption, and thus, have a lower operational cost. In our approach, the energy usage within a switch is estimated using the memory and disk metrics for each switch.

Concluding, the SDN topology of an IoT network is modeled as an undirected graph, $G = (N, E)$, where N indicates the set of the nodes (n) that represent the SDN switches and the E is the set of edges (e) that refer to the communication links between two switches. Each node n of the graph has the c_n, m_n and d_n attributes that correspond to the CPU, memory and disk metrics of the switch, while the total packets is represented by the p_n attribute. Finally, each edge e of the graph has the d_e and p_e attributes which are the delay of the communication and the total packets between two switches.

Routing Policies Formulation: A SDN flow rule (p) consists of a number of switches n and links e, while the set of all the alternative paths is devoted by P, where $p \in P$. The five flow routing objectives that must be followed and concern security, QoS and energy consumption information are listed below::

1. **Maximize the switch QoS**: The switch QoS is defined as

$$J_1(p) = \sum_{n \in p} c_n + m_n, \tag{1}$$

where c_n and m_n are the CPU load and memory usage metrics if the switch n belongs to the path p.

2. **Maximize the link QoS**: The link QoS is defined as

$$J_2(p) = \sum_{e \in p} d_e, \tag{2}$$

where d_e is the connection delay of the communication link e that belongs to the path p.

3. **Avoid sensitive switches**: The switch sensitivity is defined as

$$J_3(p) = \sum_{n \in p} p_n, \tag{3}$$

where p_n is the total number of packets served by the switch n that belongs to the path p.

4. **Avoid sensitive links**: The link sensitivity is defined as

$$J_4(p) = \sum_{e \in p} p_e, \tag{4}$$

where p_e is the total number of packets transmitted by using the link e belonging to the path p.

5. **Minimize energy consumption**: The energy objective is defined as

$$J_5(p) = \sum_{n \in p} d_n + m_n, \tag{5}$$

where d_n and m_n is the disk and memory metrics of the switch n that belongs to the path p.

Routing Optimization: The above presented objectives may be contradicting, i.e. optimizing the value of one objective may be negatively affecting the values of other objectives. In such cases, a multi-objective optimization approach is adopted that identifies a set of optimal solution, called Pareto optimal. In our case, the multi-objective optimization problem is formulated as follows:

$$\begin{aligned} \arg\min_{p} \quad & (J_1(p), J_2(p), J_3(p), J_4(p), J_5(p)) \\ \text{subject to} \quad & J_i^{min} \leq J_i(p) \leq J_i^{max}, \forall i \in [1,5], p \in P, \end{aligned} \tag{6}$$

where P is the possible set of solutions, $J_i, \forall i \in [1,5]$ are the objective functions (Eqs. (1), (2), (3), (4) and (5), respectively) that must be minimized simultaneously and $J_i^{min} \leq J_i(p) \leq J_i^{max}$ are optional constraints that the objectives might have.

Since the number of all the available paths can be very large, i.e. $O(n!)$, in the complete graph of order n, the estimation of Pareto front by calculating all the available paths is not feasible for realistic SDN networks where the number of forwarders may be up to some hundreds. In order to quickly estimate the Pareto optimal solution set, a multi-objective routing optimization based on evolutionary algorithms is incorporated in our methodology. Evolutionary algorithms belong to Computational Intelligence field and efficiently produce solutions in computationally problems using robust approximation models. Evolutionary algorithms iteratively optimize a set of possible solutions. A set of possible solutions is called population that is evolved by applying a number of genetic operators to produce a new population based on objective functions [3].

In our approach a possible solution is represented by a sequence of nodes of the graph representing the forwarders of the SDN network. Each valid possible solution (i.e. there is a communication link for each pair of the sequence) is characterized by five objectives using the objective Eqs. (1), (2), (3), (4) and (5). The population is evolved using the Multi Objective Evolutionary Algorithms by Decomposition (MOEA/D) [18]. MOEA/D finds optimal solutions for each objective and then evolves the initial population based on these solutions by applying operators. After the iteration is finished, the unique solutions of the final population comprise the Pareto optimal solution set.

Algorithm 1: Pseudo-code for multi-objective routing optimization using the Evolutionary approach

---

Input :
- a graph G where the nodes (n) and edges (e) indicate the forwarders and communication links of the SDN network
- the source node s and destination node d of a data flow
- the generation size ($gens$)

Output: the set of optimal routing paths (O)

1 Generate random population $P = p_1, p_2, \ldots$ between s and d ;
2 **for** *each p_i of P* **do**
3   check if p_i is valid;
4   calculate the fitness based on the objectives (1), (2), (3), (4) and (5);
5   evolve population using genetic operators;
6   update population with update solution;
7 **end**
8 **while** *iteration $\leq$ gens* **do**
9   repeat step 1;
10 **end**
11 find the unique solutions of the final population (Pareto optimal solution set Par);
12 **if** *the weights of each objective are known* **then**
13   compute the unique optimal solution (p_{opt}) by minimizing the equation (7);
14   let $O = p_{opt}$;
15 **else**
16   let $O = Par$;
17 **end**

The unique optimal solution can by found by minimizing the following objective function when the importance of each objective is available (e.g. provided by the network operator)

$$\arg \min_{p} \alpha \, J_1(p) + \beta \, J_2(p) + \gamma \, J_3(p) + \delta \, J_4(p) + \epsilon \, J_5(p), \qquad (7)$$

where $\alpha + \beta + \gamma + \delta + \epsilon = 1$. The values of $\alpha, \beta, \gamma, \delta, \epsilon$ define the user preference for each objective. The step-by-step outline of the proposed routing optimization is given in Algorithm 1.

4   Evaluation Scenarios

In this section, two evaluation scenarios are presented to illustrate the proposed SDN routing methodology and its effectiveness in tactical environment challenges. More specifically, we assume that there is a request for communication between two defense-related IoT devices, (i.e. between two mobile phones), while the data flow can be routed from a set of switches. In the first one, we assume that some links of the SDN network have significant transmission delays that would correspond to tactical environments with high vegetation and/or ground irregularities where the data transmission rates are poor. The second scenario examines the case where some SDN switches have a large volume of data for processing, meaning that such network areas may have been overloaded.

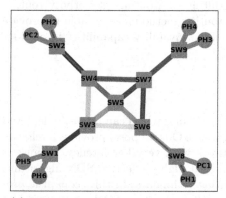 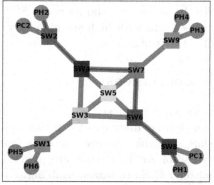

(a) The darker blue a communication link between switches appears, the less connection delays are experienced.

(b) The darker blue a node is colored, the less data packets are travelled from this node.

Fig. 2. The estimated flow rule corresponding to optimal link QoS and switch sensitivity (Color figure online)

Figure 2 depicts the path $SW8 \rightarrow SW6 \rightarrow SW7 \rightarrow SW4 \rightarrow SW2$, which is both QoS and sensitivity efficient, since it consists of links with low delays, while it avoids switches with a large data packet load, resulting in outdoor critical SDN network with high sustainability and survivability capabilities. In this example, PH, PC and SW nodes denote mobile phones, PCs and switches, respectively.

To demonstrate the two scenarios, we used a synthetic representative graph that represent a SDN network with IoT devices (e.g. mobile phones, PCs) that are inter-connected through SDN switches. For each switch and communication link, we randomly assigned values that correspond to network metrics, namely resource utilization (c_n, m_n, d_n) and traffic (p_n) metrics for each switch, connection delays (d_e) and total packets (p_e) between switches. Using these network metrics, our methodology computes the five objectives (i.e. Eqs. (1), (2), (3), (4) and (5)), respectively) for all the possible paths (i.e. flow rules) between

PH_1 and PH_2 (representing two mobile phones) and, then, the Pareto optimal solution set is calculated by Algorithm (1). The estimated optimal flow rules regarding the QoS and sensitivity efficiency are shown in Fig. 2. More specifically, the optimal flow rule is red highlighted (path $SW8 \rightarrow SW6 \rightarrow SW7 \rightarrow SW4 \rightarrow SW2$) in both cases, while the switch nodes and links are colored based on the packet load and link delay metrics, respectively. As already stated, the darker blue a communication link between switches appears, the less connection delays are experienced. On the other hand, the darker blue a node is colored, the less data packets have crossed this node.

Our methodology is able to estimate a QoS efficient routing path (i.e. $SW8 \rightarrow SW6 \rightarrow SW7 \rightarrow SW4 \rightarrow SW2$) consisting of links with low delays and avoiding some links (e.g. $SW3 \leftrightarrow SW4$, $SW3 \leftrightarrow SW6$) with significant transmission delays. In addition, the proposed path avoids switches (e.g., $SW3$, $SW5$) with a large data packet load resulting in a optimal sensitivity routing path. In conclusion, the proposed SDN routing methodology is able to provide routing paths with high sustainability and survivability capabilities in outdoor critical environments.

5   Conclusions

In this paper we presented a SDN enabled network, which can be easily deployed in outdoor environments for critical operations. Our proposal provides a reliable, secure, portable, private and stable network with very low latency, because it consists of low cost hardware, together with highly effective SDN algorithms that offer QoS strategies, enabling rerouting techniques. In this scope, the proposed AI algorithm was presented and evaluated in our SDN enabled testing environment, promoting QoS techniques, which were used in order to reroute the packets in the SDN network. Finally, we intend to extend the capabilities of our proposed AI algorithm, not only taking advantage of the network and resources metrics, but also taking into account the application requirements of the end device. This will significantly improve the survivability of the communication network. On the other hand, the SDN enabled network will be further researched in order to extend the privacy and encryption features of the sensitive communications over the proposed network. Furthermore, the extensibility of the network will be ensured, by introducing new technologies, such as 5G, which will operate collaboratively with the SDN network and will increase connectivity.

References

1. Azzouni, A., Boutaba, R., Pujolle, G.: Neuroute: predictive dynamic routing for software-defined networks (2017)
2. Dutra, D.L.C., Bagaa, M., Taleb, T., Samdanis, K.: Ensuring end-to-end QoS based on multi-paths routing using SDN technology. In: GLOBECOM 2017–2017 IEEE Global Communications Conference, pp. 1–6 (2017)
3. Emmerich, M.T., Deutz, A.H.: A tutorial on multiobjective optimization: fundamentals and evolutionary methods. Natural Comput. 17(3), 585–609 (2018)

4. Gilani, S.S.A., Qayyum, A., Rais, R.N.B., Bano, M.: SDNMESH: an SDN based routing architecture for wireless mesh networks. IEEE Access **8**, 136769–136781 (2020)
5. Gkioulos, V., Gunleifsen, H., Weldehawaryat, G.K.: A systematic literature review on military software defined networks. Future Internet **10**(9) (2018)
6. Haenlein, M., Kaplan, A.: A brief history of artificial intelligence: on the past, present, and future of artificial intelligence. California Management Review **61**, 000812561986492 (2019)
7. Hassan, M., Vien, Q.T., Aiash, M.: Software defined networking for wireless sensor networks: a survey. Adv. Wirel. Commun. Networks **3**, 10–22 (2017)
8. Iurian, C.M., Ivanciu, I.A., Marian, B.M., Zinca, D., Dobrota, V.: An SDN architecture for IoT networks using ONOS controller. In: 2020 19th RoEduNet Conference: Networking in Education and Research (RoEduNet), pp. 1–6 (2020)
9. Jutadhamakorn, P., Pillavas, T., Visoottiviseth, V., Takano, R., Haga, J., Kobayashi, D.: A scalable and low-cost MQTT broker clustering system. In: 2017 2nd International Conference on Information Technology (INCIT), pp. 1–5 (2017)
10. Khanchuea, K., Siripokarpirom, R.: A multi-protocol IoT gateway and wifi/ble sensor nodes for smart home and building automation: Design and implementation. In: 2019 10th International Conference of Information and Communication Technology for Embedded Systems (IC-ICTES), pp. 1–6 (2019)
11. Liu, W., Hu, X., Yan, X.: Controller deployments based on qos guarantees in SDN-enabled tactical ad hoc networks. In: 2020 12th International Conference on Communication Software and Networks (ICCSN), pp. 73–78 (2020)
12. Śliwa, J.: SDN and NVF in support for making military networks more survivable. In: 2019 International Conference on Military Communications and Information Systems (ICMCIS), pp. 1–6 (2019)
13. Manzoor, A., Hussain, M., Mehrban, S.: Performance analysis and route optimization: redistribution between EIGRP, OSPF & BGP routing protocols. Comput. Stand. Interf. **68**, 103391 (2020)
14. Poularakis, K., Qin, Q., Marcus, K.M., Chan, K.S., Leung, K.K., Tassiulas, L.: Hybrid SDN control in mobile ad hoc networks. In: 2019 IEEE International Conference on Smart Computing (SMARTCOMP), pp. 110–114 (2019)
15. Spencer, J., Willink, T.: SDN in coalition tactical networks. In: MILCOM 2016–2016 IEEE Military Communications Conference, pp. 1053–1058 (2016)
16. Streit, K., Schmitt, C., Giannelli, C.: SDN-based regulated flow routing in manets. In: 2020 IEEE International Conference on Smart Computing (SMARTCOMP), pp. 73–80 (2020)
17. Streit, K., Dreo Rodosek, G.: Cetup: controller-equipped topology update process for tactical ad-hoc networks. In: Proceedings of the 17th ACM Symposium on Performance Evaluation of Wireless Ad Hoc, Sensor & Ubiquitous Networks. PE-WASUN '20, New York, NY, USA, pp. 57–66. Association for Computing Machinery (2020)
18. Trivedi, A., Srinivasan, D., Sanyal, K., Ghosh, A.: A survey of multiobjective evolutionary algorithms based on decomposition. IEEE Trans. Evol. Comput. **21**(3), 440–462 (2016)
19. Yu, H.C., Quer, G., Rao, R.R.: Wireless SDN mobile ad hoc network: From theory to practice. In: 2017 IEEE International Conference on Communications (ICC), pp. 1–7 (2017)

Distributed AI for
Resource - Constrained Platforms
Workshop (DARE 2021)

DARE 2021 Workshop

The standard approach explored by IoT applications of leveraging cloud computing to address constraints at the level of end and edge nodes is no longer viable, especially for applications with hard real-time requirements and increasing AI usage. Managing the complexity and heterogeneity of IoT systems is a big challenge for the future of edge computing as data is collected and analyzed on a large network of different devices, and the setup may change at run-time. Only with an open and technology-agnostic approach can this challenge be addressed for a broad set of applications. In addition, an edge computing system can maintain its function without access to a centralized infrastructure. With application services and tasks deployed on local resources, network problems will become less critical. At the same time, as data become more valuable, security and privacy concerns will play an important role. In a networked IoT system, a single vulnerable device can be an entry point for cyberattacks.

The Distributed AI for REsource-Constrained Platforms (DARE) workshop focuses on AI and ML techniques, edge computing systems, and security and privacy in view of data sharing, to enable the smart and sustainable planning and operation of resource-constrained IoT and edge computing applications. This first edition of the workshop (DARE 2021) was organized within the scope of the ITEA3 MIRAI project (https://itea3.org/project/mirai.html) and welcomed innovative contributions, early results, and position papers on topics such as open and interoperable ad-hoc architectures for on-demand computation, scalable edge/fog computing IoT applications, run-time adaptation of edge/fog computing infrastructures, advanced AI algorithms and techniques for continual and evolving learning, distributed and composable ML models and techniques guaranteeing high-quality decision-making, security and privacy on the edge including secure data sharing between edge nodes, and industrial experiences on these topics. The aim of the workshop was to foster informal discussions and cross-fertilization on the convergence of AI and edge computing.

Five contributions were selected for presentation. An invited contribution by the MIRAI project consortium analyzes the shortcomings of current centralized AI approaches and the benefits that distributed AI approaches can bring to the different industrial use cases considered in the project. The four other contributions address a variety of pertinent and challenging topics within the scope of DARE: data filtering and privacy mechanisms for resource-constrained platforms, distributed learning architectures for cybersecurity of IoT devices, data compression using low-cost machine learning techniques, and a performance assessment of local ML computation and network usage for the task of object tracking in multi-camera scenarios. All contributions were peer reviewed by at least two independent members of the Program Committee.

Organization

Program Committee

Luis Almeida	CISTER/University of Porto, Portugal
Veselka Boeva	Blekinge Institute of Technology, Sweden
Emiliano Casalicchio	Blekinge Institute of Technology, Sweden
Nicolás González-Deleito	Sirris, Belgium
Anna Hristoskova	Sirris, Belgium
Pedro Santos	CISTER/Polytechnic of Porto, Portugal
Joana Sousa	NOS Inovação, Portugal
Barış Bulut	Enforma Bilişim A.Ş, Turkey

A First Sensitivity Study of Multi-object Multi-camera Tracking Performance

Miguel Ramos[1] , Carlos Pereira[2] , and Luis Almeida[1,3]([⊠])

[1] Faculty of Engineering, University of Porto, Porto, Portugal
{up201808904,lda}e.up.pt
[2] NOS Comunicações, Senhora da Hora, Portugal
dee12014@fe.up.pt
[3] CISTER Research Center on Real-Time & Embedded Computing Systems,
Porto, Portugal

Abstract. Computer Vision is becoming widely used for a myriad of purposes, e.g. people counting and tracking. To execute this application in real-time, a relatively complex algorithm processes intensive data streams to identify people in a visual scenario. Although such algorithms frequently run in powerful servers on the Cloud, it is also common that they have to run in local commodity computers with limited capacity. In this work we used the Multi-Camera Multi-Target algorithm of the recent OpenVINO^{TM} toolkit to detect and track people in small retail stores. We ran the algorithm in a common personal computer and analyzed the variation of its performance for a set of different relevant scenarios and algorithm configurations, providing insights into how these affect the algorithm performance and computational cost. In the tested scenarios, the most influential factor was the number of people in the scene. The average frame processing time observed varied around 200 ms.

Keywords: Computer Vision · Machine learning · Object detection · People counting and tracking

1 Introduction

Computer Vision (CV) became widely disseminated since the first decade of 2000 s with the inception of Deep Learning (DL) [14] and the capacity to execute it in computationally efficient ways. DL is a field within Machine Learning (ML) that consists on training computers so they can learn empirical models like humans do, with numerous applications, such as speech recognition, forecasts and image identification. DL uses Neural Networks (NN) with multiple intermediate layers of neurons [2] allowing representations of arbitrary complex data, much like the human brain works. Some of the most common model architectures used in DL are R-CNN [4], YOLO [15], SSD [13] and RetinaNet [12].

C. Pereira—This work was developed while this author was at NOS Comunicações.

I. Maglogiannis et al. (Eds.): AIAI 2021 Workshops, IFIP AICT 628, pp. 269–280, 2021.
https://doi.org/10.1007/978-3-030-79157-5_22

Nowadays, a common application of DL is object detection. Extending the detection of objects from a single frame to a set of consecutive frames enables tracking objects motion, too. Applied to people this is commonly called people counting and tracking.

Our specific motivation is to use security cameras already deployed in small retail spaces to obtain anonymized information from customers, namely their paths in real-time within the store, enabling new forms of on-the-fly market analysis. For this purpose, the video streams from the cameras have to be transported to a server for real-time processing. Using a server in the Cloud brings significant advantages in processing time, but also implies significant Internet communication with its overhead and exposure to the threat of access to private data. For this reason, this application requires processing in the premises of the store. In turn, this brings up the challenge of executing the counting and tracking algorithm in a local server, with limited resources.

In this paper we study the performance of people counting and tracking using multiple cameras with overlapping fields of view and an already trained DL system running on an ordinary personal computer. We selected the recent OpenVINO^{TM} toolkit [9] since it is currently the only open framework to offer a Multi-Camera Multi-Target algorithm. Then we carried out a sensitivity study to determine the parameters that impact the algorithm performance the most. We considered the number of people in the scenario, the speed of their movements, the level of overlap between the cameras and their frame-rate. The performance was assessed with the MOTA (Multi-Object Tracking Accuracy) metric and the average frame processing time. To the best of our knowledge, this is the first such study carried out on the Multi-Camera Multi-Target algorithm of OpenVINO^{TM}. The next section discusses related work, Sect. 3 presents the experimental setup while Sect. 4 discusses the results. The conclusion appears in Sect. 5.

2   Related Work

Object detection aims at determining the objects location in an image and assigning a semantic category to each one, together with an identifier. Tracking aims at assigning the same identifier to the same object as it moves around in the scene. Tracking can be rather challenging when there are objects' occlusions, significant changes in illumination and objects' posture, and when objects exit and reenter the scene [5].

These challenges are tackled by image object detectors, which can be split into two main groups: i) two-stage detectors and ii) one-stage detectors [11]. The former uses a region proposal generator to propose the presence of objects in the image, inserting them in a bounding box, then the features from the candidate boxes are extracted and, finally, the classification and regression procedures are executed for each of the candidates boxes. The most representative two-stage detector is the Faster R-CNN [4]. On the other hand, one-stage detectors propose the candidate boxes directly, without using a generator. The most well-known one-stage detectors are YOLO [15] and SSD [13]. The two-stage detectors provide an accurate localization and identification of the objects and the one-stage detectors can deliver high processing speed results. Faster R-CNN models, nevertheless, can be as fast as the others if specific configurations are made, but better accuracy can only be attained by sacrificing speed [6].

While a good detector is key for improving single-camera performance, good appearance features are crucial for multi-camera performance [17]. Moreover, specific algorithm configurations, e.g., threshold for occlusion detection, play an important part on the overall performance of the re-identification task. Throughout the last decade, several studies proposed custom algorithms and implementations to solve the multi-camera multi-target challenge, but limitations on flexibility and openness hinder reproducibility and improvements [16,19]. To circumvent this, open frameworks such as OpenCV and Caffe have been gaining adoption as they set a common ground for all developers and researchers [3,10]. Still, until the release of OpenVINO^{TM}, and to the best of our knowledge, no free open-source framework capable of addressing multi-camera multi-target tracking and counting was available. Additionally, the toolkit is tuned to take advantage of Intel hardware, yielding considerable performance improvements when comparing to either OpenCV or Caffe [7].

3   Experimental Setup

We organized the workflow of the target sensitivity study as follows. First, we chose an algorithm for people counting and tracking that is real-time capable. Second, we defined the variables' spaces to be explored and the performance metrics. Third, we carried out experiments to cover the variables space, assessing the defined performance metrics. From this step we could identify the variables that exert a stronger impact on people counting and tracking.

We ran the algorithm on a Thinkpad 580s laptop computer with Windows 10 Pro, featuring a 7th generation Intel®Core^{TM} i5-7300U processor (2.60 GHz, up to 3.50 GHz with Turbo Boost, 2 Cores, 4 Threads, 3 MB Cache), integrated Intel® HD Graphics 620 accelerator and 8 GB of DDR4 2133 MHz RAM.

3.1   OpenVINO^{TM} Toolkit

As we referred before, the OpenVINO^{TM} toolkit [9] is currently the only free and open framework to offer a Multi-Camera Multi-Target algorithm. It includes a comprehensive set of algorithms and tools to develop ML-based applications using state-of-the-art artificial neural networks, including convolutional, recurrent and attention-based networks, optimized for Intel® hardware to maximize performance. The toolkit also includes an extensive set of pre-trained models, the Open Model Zoo, and demo applications [8] that show how to use the toolkit Inference Engine in specific use-cases.

The Multi-Camera Multi-Target algorithm allows tracking a predefined class of objects in video streams captured by several cameras. It uses two models in the Intermediate Representation format, namely Object Detection and Object Re-Identification. The first one is responsible for identifying the target class of objects in the video frames, and the second one assures that each correctly detected object is assigned a unique identifier (ID). As input, the algorithm can receive paths to pre-recorded video files or indexes of cameras for real-time operation. The algorithm workflow consists on reading tuples of frames, one from each source, and for each frame in the tuple it runs the object detector and then, for each detected object, it extracts embeddings using the re-identification model. Then, all the extracted embeddings are passed to the tracker which assigns an ID to each object. Finally, the algorithm displays the resulting bounding boxes and unique object IDs assigned during the tracking process.

3.2 OpenVINO™ Models

Inside the OpenVINO™ group of pre-trained models there are multiple options for each specific task. To help deciding which one suits a specific purpose best, the toolkit provides a set of characteristics about each model. For object detection, we chose the ***person-detection-retail-0013*** [9] model given its superior Average Precision (AP) metric. This model is based on MobileNetV2-like backbone that includes depth-wise convolutions to reduce the amount of computation for the 3×3 convolution block [18]. Concerning the re-identification models, we chose ***person-reidentification-retail-0277*** [9] for the same reason as the object detection model. In this case, we observed the superior Rank@1 accuracy and mean AP metrics on the Market-1501 dataset. This is a person re-identification model for a general scenario. It uses a whole body image as input and outputs an embedding vector to match a pair of images by the cosine distance. The model is based on the OmniScaleNet backbone with Linear Context Transform blocks developed for fast inference.

3.3 Multi-object Tracking Metrics

To assess the algorithm performance we chose one well-known tracking metric, namely MOTA [1], together with the average frame processing time.

MOTA is defined in Eq. 1 where ϕ represents the number of fragmentations (number of times a tracking ID switches) and T is the overall number of detections. FP and FN are the sums of f_{p_t} (false positives) and f_{n_t} (false negatives) over all frames t from all cameras. False positives correspond to situations in which the tracker detects a target in a frame where there is none in the ground-truth. Conversely, false negatives are cases in which the tracker failed to detect targets that existed in the ground-truth.

$$\text{MOTA} = 1 - \frac{FN + FP + \phi}{T} \tag{1}$$

3.4 Variables Space

For the targeted sensitivity analysis we organize the variables to study in two groups, namely algorithm variables and video variables. Algorithm variables represent the 14 algorithm configuration parameters in OpenVINO. To reduce this number we carried out a few preliminary sensitivity tests (Table 1). We assigned three different values to each parameter covering the respective scales and assessed the variation of the MOTA metric. Then, we picked just the four that caused the strongest metric variation (column R in Table 1).

Table 1. Preliminary sensitivity tests to choose algorithm variables

Variables		Scale	MOTA (%)			R Average Interval (%)	Selected Parameters
			R1	R2	R3		
mct_config	time_window	[1, 20, 80]	93.5	93.3	93.3	0.1	
	global_match_tresh	[0.01, 0.2, 0.8]	61.0	93.3	71.7	27.0	x
sct_config	time_window	[0.5, 10, 80]	49.0	93.3	93.3	22.2	x
	continue_time_thresh	[10, 50, 90]	93.2	93.3	93.3	0.1	
	track_clear_thresh	[5, 30, 80]	72.2	93.3	93.6	10.7	
	match_threshold	[0.1, 0.375, 0.8]	93.3	93.3	93.3	0	
	merge_thresh	[0.05, 0.15, 0.8]	93.2	93.3	71.6	10.9	
	n_clusters	[1, 10, 20]	93.3	93.3	93.3	0	
	max_bbox_velocity	[0.05, 0.2, 0.8]	93.3	93.3	72.3	10.5	
	detection_occlusion_thresh	[0.1, 0.7, 0.9]	56.7	93.3	55.7	37.1	x
	track_detection_iou_thresh	[0.1, 0.5, 0.9]	77.2	93.3	59.7	24.9	x
	interpolate_time_thresh	[1, 10, 80]	93.2	93.3	93.6	0.2	
	detection_filter_speed	[0.1, 0.6, 0.9]	91.0	93.3	86.5	4.6	
	rectify_thresh	[0.1, 0.5, 0.9]	93.3	93.3	93.3	0	

Video variables are those related to the videos visual content, namely number of people in the store, the speed of their motion, the frame-rate of the cameras and the overlap of their fields of view. For convenience, both overlap and speed are classified in a few qualitative groups. For overlap we considered the case in which the cameras all point to the center of the room (maximum overlap) and when the side cameras point to the sides reducing the overlap to about 50% of the image (minimum overlap). The speed was considered the same for all people in the room and its value was consistent with usual motion inside small stores, with the maximum at about 1m/s. Overall, the values used for the video variables are shown in Table 2 and cover realistic scenarios in the target spaces. The table also contains the final values decided for the algorithm variables, tuned after the preliminary experiments reported in the Table 1.

Table 2. Variables excursion for the sensitivity study

Video configurations			
Number of people	People speed	Frame-rate (fps)	Overlap level
{1, 2, 3}	{Low, Medium, Fast}	{4, 8, 15, 25}	{Minimum, Maximum}
Algorithm Configurations			
global_match_thresh	time_window	detection_occlusion_thresh	track_detection_iou_thresh
{0.15, 0.5, 0.85}	{0, 40, 70}	{0.1, 0.5, 0.9}	{ 0.1, 0.5, 0.9 }

3.5   Video Samples and Results Collection

In our setup we use an indoors space representing a small retail store equipped
with three cameras (Fig. 1). In this setup we defined all needed operational
scenarios to carry out the sensitivity study. For this purpose, we expanded all
possible combinations of the Video variables values (Table 2) resulting in 72
different scenarios. For each of these scenarios we recorded a 20 s video clip with
the streams from the three cameras synchronized, for the sake of reproducibility.

Camera 1   Camera 2   Camera 3

Fig. 1. Cameras perspectives (maximum overlap case)

After collecting the 72 video samples we feed them to the Multi-Camera
Multi-Target algorithm, one at a time. For each video all algorithm configurations are tested. The outcome of each experiment is saved in a *detections* file,
saved in JSON format, containing all the information about the obtained detections. In this step we also observe the execution time of the algorithm.

In parallel with the algorithm execution we build a ground-truth file that
holds the correct detections for every experiment. This file is generated using
the CV Annotation Tool (CVAT) that allows uploading a video file and then
manually draw the bounding boxes around people in each frame with the respective assigned ID. After creating the ground-truth annotations with CVAT, we
export them in an XML file that will be used as reference. In each experiment,
once we have the detections and the annotations files, we feed them as input to
the *run_evaluate.py* script of OpenVINO™ that will compare their similarity
and output the MOTA metric. The whole process is shown in Fig. 2.

4   Results and Analysis

In this section we present and discuss the results achieved when going through
the whole variables space defined in Sect. 3.4. According to Table 2, we have 72
different combinations of video variables, each corresponding to a different scenario and recorded in a separate video clip. Then we have 81 different algorithm
configurations that are applied to each of the 72 scenarios. This results in a total
of 5832 experiments. In the following figures, we present the results in box-plots,
with each box representing one specific video configuration and the variations
incurred by the 81 algorithm configurations.

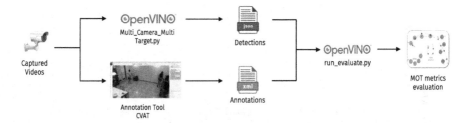

Fig. 2. Detection and evaluation process

4.1 Frames Processing Time

We measured the frames processing time so that all involved I/O overheads are included. Thus, we computed the total time lapsed from reading the first frame to the end of processing the last frame and then divided by the total number of frames in the video. This is a lump value, thus we carried out a simple experiment to observe the behavior of individual frame processing times considering possible interference from other software executing in the computer, e.g., Operating System (OS) services. We ran the tracking algorithm for a scenario of one person, moving at fast speed, with cameras capturing 25 fps and with maximum overlap. We collected three independent samples, each with 37989 measurements of the individual frame processing time. The results show a reasonable statistical consistency. The average frame processing time varied between 180 and 200 ms, the median varied between 184 and 194 ms and the quartiles varied between 177 and 184 ms for the 1st and 188 and 204 ms for the 3rd. Thus, when observing the average lump measurements we show next, we need to keep in mind that they are still affected by this level of variation.

4.2 Number of People and Speed Variation

The results for the impact of the number of people in the scene and their speed on the MOTA are shown in Fig. 3. The strongest variation is observed for the number of people in the scene. For the three speed scenarios, the median values of MOTA decrease approximately 3% for low speed and 5% for medium and high speeds, for each new person added to the scene (for all speed values together, we saw a MOTA median decrease of 4% per new person added to the scene). This inverse relationship between the number of people in the scene and the MOTA results can be explained by the fact that as we introduce new target elements in the video frames, the possibility of occurring occlusions, ID switches, motion blur and unpredictable behaviors also increases. These issues hamper the task of identifying and tracking people. The more elements in the video frames, the more complex the image analysis will be.

On the other hand, the variation with the speed of the targets in the scene is residual. Still, we can observe a subtle decrease in the MOTA results as the speed of the targets (people) in the frames increase. For each step in speed, we

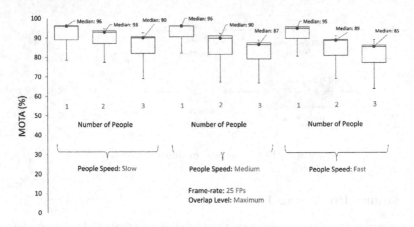

Fig. 3. MOTA results when varying the number of people in the scene and their speed

observe a decrease of the MOTA median value of approximately 1% for 1 person and 2% for 2 and 3 people (for all numbers of people together, we saw a MOTA median decrease of 2% per step in speed). Again, this inverse relationship is expected since a slower speed leads to smaller variations of the targets position between frames, leading to more consistent and accurate detections.

For the same scenarios, the measured average execution time per frame is shown in Fig. 4. Again, the impact of the number of people in the scene dominates the measurements, with a clear increase as more people are added. This is expected since more target elements (people) in the scene require more processing to analyze the video frames and output the correspondingly more detections and identifications. The figure shows an increase of approximately 34 ms from 1 person to 2 people and 50 ms from 2 to 3 people (across all speed classes).

In turn, the variation of the frame processing time with the speed of the targets in the scene is again residual, particularly between slow and medium speeds. Between medium and high speeds we can already observe a mild decrease of 10 ms in the execution time median (for all numbers of people). We believe this effect emerges from the same reason that causes a similar variation in MOTA results. Faster speeds imply larger changes between consecutive video frames, leading to lower accuracy, thus less detections and lower computational demand.

4.3 Overlap Level Variation

The impact of the level of overlap between the images captured by the three cameras revealed to be rather small on both MOTA and frame processing time, thus we do not show them here, due to space limitations. The MOTA median reduced approximately 3% when the overlap decreased from Maximum to Minimum. This variation can be due to the algorithm using the video frames from different cameras to support its decision about a specific ID assignment. If we have a high level of overlap, the frames from the different cameras will be more consistent,

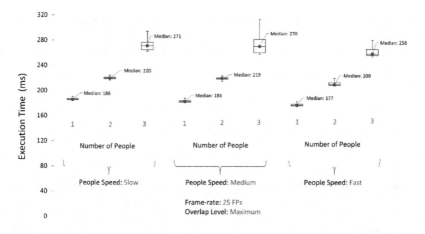

Fig. 4. Execution time results when varying number of people and their speed

facilitating identification assignment. Thus, detections will be more robust. The same happens with the average frame processing time, which decreases when the overlap decreases, again due to less accuracy of lower overlap that leads to less detections, thus less processing to do.

4.4 Frame-Rate Variation

The variation of the frame-rate of the cameras is one dimension that deserves special attention for two reasons. First, as referred in Sect. 4.1, the frame processing times are affected by interference, e.g., from the OS. Second, we are handling video clips off-line, processing their frames, one after the other, independently of the time it takes to process them. This is why we can process video clips that were acquired at any frame-rate. However, when processing in real-time, as desired in the target application scenario, this is clearly not possible. Altogether, we have observed frame processing times roughly in the range of 180 to 330 ms. This means that, with the computer we used in our experiments, the maximum frame-rate that can be sustained in real-time varies approximately between 3 and 6 fps. The results we show for higher frame-rates correspond to what would be achieved with sufficiently fast hardware.

Figure 5 shows the MOTA results for different frame-rates and number of people. The latter are consistent with those in Fig. 3 (fast scenario), showing a decreasing trend with more people, but with a stronger decrease from one person to two people than from two to three people. The variation with the frame-rate is significantly more pronounced. The values of MOTA increase sharply with low frame-rates and more softly with higher rates, seeming to reach a saturation around 95% for the single person scenario. Overall, for the three scenarios of number of people, MOTA increased approximately 26% from 4 to 8 fps, 19% from 8 to 15 fps and 8% from 15 to 25 fps. This type of variation is expected, too, since higher frame-rate means more frames collected by the source camera per video second, thus smoother variations between frames leading to more robust tracking. The striking observation, here, is that MOTA drops sharply for a frame-rate of 4 fps, which may compromise the use of OpenVINO in real-time with commodity hardware.

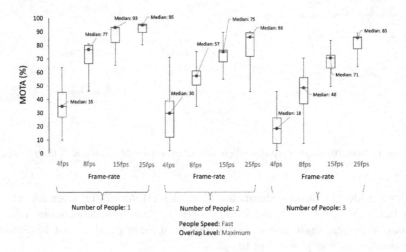

Fig. 5. MOTA results when varying frame-rate and number of people

The results for the frame processing time are shown in Fig. 6. In principle, this time should not vary with the frame-rate when processing the videos off-line, except for the interference referred in Sect. 4.1. The variations we observe within each scenario with a defined number of people prompt us to find an explanation. We believe this is due to extra cache delay incurred when reading the first frames. This would appear once during each experiment, as an offset in the lump measurements, thus being consistent with a higher impact for lower frame-rates, i.e., with less frames in the video file, the impact per frame is higher.

4.5   Other Variations

Finally, remember that the variations represented by the previous box plots arise from the 81 combinations of the algorithm variables. Curiously, whatever the algorithm configuration, the impact in MOTA is just moderate, frequently less than 10%, and even less in the frame processing time. In this case, there is a small but visible increase in this variation as the number of people in the scene increases.

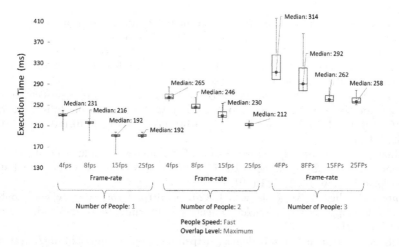

Fig. 6. Average frame processing time when varying frame-rate and number of people

5 Conclusion

In this paper we addressed the application of people counting and tracking in small retail stores using typical surveillance cameras and a common laptop computer. For counting and tracking we used the recent OpenVINO[TM] toolkit since it is open and optimized for execution on Intel-based computers. We used the Multi-Camera Multi-Target algorithm in the toolkit, which provides all the features needed for effective people counting and tracking, particularly re-identification. The core of the paper is a sensitivity study to assess the impact of video features and algorithm configurations on the quality of the counting and tracking and on the algorithm execution time. We defined a variables space reflecting realistic conditions, while being parsimonious in size. We found the number of people in the scene to be the most impactful variable. The average processing times indicate that real-time operation on the used hardware is limited to about 4 fps. This is still a challenge because such low value implies a significant degradation in the quality of the counting and tracking process. In the future, we plan to validate the approach in a real retail store in real-time operation and compare the MOTA metric with the usefulness of the results for the purpose of the application.

Acknowledgments. This work was financially supported by: Base Funding - UIDB/04234/2020 of the Research Centre in Real-Time and Embedded Computing Systems - CISTER - funded by national funds through the FCT/MCTES (PIDDAC).

References

1. Bernardin, K., Stiefelhagen, R.: Evaluating multiple object tracking performance: the CLEAR MOT metrics. EURASIP J. Image Video Process. **2008**(1), 1–10 (2008). https://doi.org/10.1155/2008/246309

2. Bezdan, T., Bacanin, N.: Convolutional neural network layers and architectures, pp. 445–451 (2019). https://doi.org/10.15308/Sinteza-2019-445-451
3. Bradski, G., Kaehler, A.: Opencv. Dr. Dobb's J. Softw. Tools **3** (2000)
4. Girshick, R., Donahue, J., Darrell, T., Malik, J.: Rich feature hierarchies for accurate object detection and semantic segmentation (2013)
5. Gong, S., Cristani, M., Loy, C.C., Hospedales, T.M.: The re-identification challenge. In: Gong, S., Cristani, M., Yan, S., Loy, C.C. (eds.) Person Re-Identification. ACVPR, pp. 1–20. Springer, London (2014). https://doi.org/10.1007/978-1-4471-6296-4_1
6. Huang, J., et al.: Speed/accuracy trade-offs for modern convolutional object detectors. In: Proceedings of the IEEE Conference on Computer Vision and Pattern Recognition, pp. 7310–7311 (2017)
7. Intel: Parallel universe issue 34 (2018). https://software.intel.com/content/dam/develop/external/us/en/documents/parallel-universe-issue-34.pdf. Accessed 10 Jan 2021
8. Intel® : Open model zoo demos. https://docs.openvinotoolkit.org/latest/omz_demos_README.html. Accessed 10 Nov 2020
9. Intel® : Openvino™ toolkit overview. https://docs.openvinotoolkit.org/latest/index.html. Accessed 2 Nov 2020
10. Jia, Y., et al.: Caffe: Convolutional architecture for fast feature embedding. In: Proceedings of the 22nd ACM international conference on Multimedia, pp. 675–678 (2014)
11. Jiao, L., et al.: A survey of deep learning-based object detection. IEEE Access **7**, 128837–128868 (2019)
12. Lin, T.Y., Goyal, P., Girshick, R., He, K., Dollár, P.: Focal loss for dense object detection (2017)
13. Liu, W., et al.: SSD: single shot MultiBox detector. In: Leibe, B., Matas, J., Sebe, N., Welling, M. (eds.) ECCV 2016. LNCS, vol. 9905, pp. 21–37. Springer, Cham (2016). https://doi.org/10.1007/978-3-319-46448-0_2
14. Pitts, W., McCulloch, W.S.: How we know universals the perception of auditory and visual forms. Bull. Math. Biophys. **9**(3), 127–147 (1947)
15. Redmon, J., Divvala, S., Girshick, R., Farhadi, A.: You only look once: unified, real-time object detection. In: 2016 IEEE Conference on Computer Vision and Pattern Recognition (CVPR), June 2016. https://doi.org/10.1109/cvpr.2016.91
16. Ristani, E., Solera, F., Zou, R., Cucchiara, R., Tomasi, C.: Performance measures and a data set for multi-target, multi-camera tracking. In: Hua, G., Jégou, H. (eds.) ECCV 2016. LNCS, vol. 9914, pp. 17–35. Springer, Cham (2016). https://doi.org/10.1007/978-3-319-48881-3_2
17. Ristani, E., Tomasi, C.: Features for multi-target multi-camera tracking and re-identification. In: Proceedings of the IEEE Conference on Computer Vision and Pattern Recognition, pp. 6036–6046 (2018)
18. Sandler, M., Howard, A., Zhu, M., Zhmoginov, A., Chen, L.C.: Mobilenetv 2: inverted residuals and linear bottlenecks. In: Proceedings of the IEEE Conference on Computer Vision and Pattern Recognition, pp. 4510–4520 (2018)
19. Xiong, F., Gou, M., Camps, O., Sznaier, M.: Person re-identification using kernel-based metric learning methods. In: Fleet, D., Pajdla, T., Schiele, B., Tuytelaars, T. (eds.) ECCV 2014. LNCS, vol. 8695, pp. 1–16. Springer, Cham (2014). https://doi.org/10.1007/978-3-319-10584-0_1

An Initial Analysis of the Shortcomings of Conventional AI and the Benefits of Distributed AI Approaches in Industrial Use Cases

Anna Hristoskova[1]([⊠]), Nicolás González-Deleito[1], Sarah Klein[1], Joana Sousa[2,3],
Nuno Martins[2,4], João Tagaio[2,5], João Serra[2], Carlos Silva[2], João Ferreira[2],
Pedro M. Santos[6,8], Ricardo Morla[7], Luís Almeida[7,8], Barış Bulut[9],
and Sencer Sultanoğlu[10]

[1] Sirris, Brussels, Belgium
anna.hristoskova@sirris.be
[2] NOS Inovação, Lisbon, Portugal
[3] Bold International, Lisbon, Portugal
[4] Caixa Mágica, Lisbon, Portugal
[5] KCSIT, Lisbon, Portugal
[6] Instituto Superior de Engenharia do Porto, Porto, Portugal
[7] Faculdade de Engenharia, Universidade do Porto, Porto, Portugal
[8] CISTER Research Center in Real-Time and Embedded Computing Systems, Porto, Portugal
[9] Enforma Bilişim, İstanbul, Turkey
[10] Eliar, İstanbul, Turkey

Abstract. The centralised approach of IoT (Internet of Things) applications lever-aging cloud infrastructures to address constraints at the level of end and edge nodes is no longer viable, especially for applications with hard real-time requirements and increasing AI (Artificial Intelligence) usage. This paper presents an initial analysis of the shortcomings of such centralised AI approaches applied to the five industrial use cases considered in the ITEA3 MIRAI project and discusses the expected benefits that distributed AI approaches will bring to these use cases, namely, to lift constraints such as computing power, bandwidth, latency, security and privacy.

Keywords: Artificial Intelligence (AI) · Distributed AI · Secure analytics · Access control · Privacy

1 Introduction

For the last two decades the usual approach for IoT applications has been to leverage on cloud infrastructures to address the computational and storage limitations and constraints at end and edge nodes. However, offloading processing capabilities to the cloud requires transferring data from edge devices to a backend cloud infrastructure, dealing with the

© IFIP International Federation for Information Processing 2021
Published by Springer Nature Switzerland AG 2021
I. Maglogiannis et al. (Eds.): AIAI 2021 Workshops, IFIP AICT 628, pp. 281–292, 2021.
https://doi.org/10.1007/978-3-030-79157-5_23

limitations imposed by the underlying communication channels, depending on the avail-ability constraints of both those communication channels and the cloud infrastructure, establishing proper mechanisms to secure data in transit and data at rest at the back-end (esp. when privacy-sensitive data is considered) [1], dealing with the costs incurred from the transmission of data and by the usage of the backend cloud infrastructure, etc. Depending on the application and underlying infrastructure, it might not be feasible to transmit all the data to the backend due to bandwidth limitations or cost constraints, resulting in only a fraction of the data being transferred, while the remaining data is discarded at a very early stage. In addition, the underlying communication channels' latency might be unacceptable for many industrial control application and applications with (hard) real-time constraints.

This has been changing in recent years. The advent of end and edge nodes with increased computational and storage capabilities makes it possible to perform a large range of increasingly resource-demanding computations (including AI-based tasks) locally at the edge, and only rely on a backend cloud for communicating results or performing computations requiring the combination and further processing of results from different edge devices or historical data sources. In addition, this increase in com-putation capabilities also enables neighbouring edge devices to perform tasks collabora-tively, leveraging on each other's available computational resources, before offloading computations to a cloud backend. These new possibilities pave the way for the (further) development of Distributed AI.

In this regard, existing local computation platforms for AI are typically based on high-performance hardware [2]. They contain expensive and power-hungry high-speed processors and AI accelerators. These platforms offer sufficient computational power and fulfil most needs even in industrial application scenarios, but they often come with prohibitively high investments and energy costs. In addition, they usually do not scale very well and represent a single point of failure.

A promising alternative technology approach are embedded computing devices in a massively parallel and distributed architecture, which may overcome most of the diffi-culties mentioned above. With this approach, the computation and storage can be located very near to the data source, making latency and bandwidth non-critical issues. Data col-lection, machine learning (ML) and inference tasks of AI applications can be distributed in a federated architecture. Tasks can be migrated in case of component failure and con-tinue their execution at other neighbouring devices, which offers robustness. Likewise, workloads can be shared among many different devices, which provides scalability.

However, suitable frameworks and building blocks for smart and sustainable plan-ning, deployment and operation of such distributed IoT and edge AI-computing appli-cations is still lacking. Here, smartness refers to a degree of autonomy (AI performed at the edge level), robustness (such as against connection cut-offs leading to insufficient data; external disturbances; single point of failure at the centre), ability to incorporate some of the global criteria and constraints in a centralised-like fashion even when most decisions are made at the edge, whereas the sustainability refers to a carefully-designed allocation of resources (such as computing, storage, and data transmission) as well as their expansion capability under increased demand. The ITEA3 industrial R&D project MIRAI, aims at building such a framework and corresponding building blocks through which IoT and edge computing applications can horizontally scale among edge devices, in addition to the vertical scaling to the cloud.

In this paper, we present each of the five use cases being considered in MIRAI, along with their needs at the level of AI and how distributed AI is expected to contribute to achieve their objectives. These use cases are provided by five different problem owner companies from three different countries (Belgium, Portugal and Turkey), and cover the following domains: renewable energy management, Internet provisioning for households, road traffic management, water consumption management, and dyeing for the textile industry. The paper concludes with a brief wrap up that presents the team's anticipations to move towards a common reference architecture model, MIRAI Framework Building Blocks (MFBB), indicating the types of models or standards whose logic or even parts of design could be recycled.

2 MIRAI Use Cases and Rationale for Distributed AI

This section presents the five use cases of the MIRAI project and discusses the shortcomings of conventional AI-based approaches and the needs for distributed AI for each of them.

2.1 Use Case 1: Distributed Renewable Energy Systems

With more and more distributed renewable energy assets such as solar panels and wind turbines installed, the electricity production becomes more fluctuating than with an old-fashioned coal-fired power plant. The grid needs to be increasingly capable of adapting to an ever-fluctuating residual load on different timescales, from seconds to months. Solar and wind assets, as well as storage, also need to cater for a better grid quality. At the same time, renewables worldwide are entering a "post-subsidy era", in which investors and asset owners need to secure bankable revenue streams. The combination of these two trends creates a need and opportunity for flexibility services, from switching off plants at negative energy prices, to charging and discharging battery systems to help stabilise the grid.

3E is a well-established Belgium-based company existing for already 20 years and counting about 100 employees. 3E provides consultancy and software solutions for monitoring and improving the performance of sustainable energy installations and for optimising energy consumption. More precisely, 3E's SynaptiQ Asset Operations[1] solution enables to manage solar and wind assets, monitor, report and improve their performance, and organise their maintenance. Thanks to MIRAI, 3E aims to provide optimised control of renewable energy plant assets and real-time status updates.

Current AI Shortcomings. The energy infrastructure is evolving from a hierarchical to a fully distributed architecture. Whereas in the past the lower-level nodes acted as pure consumers, an increasing number of nodes also produce energy and act therefore as producers, the so-called prosumers. This puts an additional stress level on the grid to guarantee stability and balance between electricity demand and supply (e.g. through

---

[1] https://3e.eu/solutions/digital-solutions/asset-operations.

energy storage systems). Nowadays, most solutions offer a centralised grid optimization service. This can though lead to exchange of information between competitors or to privacy violations, for example in case of single households [3, 4].

Currently, single assets can mainly be monitored via 3E's SynaptiQ Asset Operations platform but there is no knowledge shared between different assets. In case the energy market price becomes negative due to too high availability of energy in the electric grid, the only solution is to switch off the asset for a given time. So far, the assets provide a very basic forecast for negative energy prices only.

Distributed AI Expectations. 3E would like to execute (part of) the grid optimization service locally, on a prosumer's infrastructure. Being able to distribute the service in that way would enable a faster response to changes in the current status of the grid, as well as local energy production and consumption, and hence reduce latency. Further, it would enable to minimise the amount of actual data sent to the cloud for further processing in order to preserve prosumers' privacy.

Within MIRAI, single assets will be optimally controlled in real-time as the data will be used locally and with shared knowledge, without actually sharing data. One example is the case of negative energy market price: When the prices in the wholesale energy market are negative, in future, the assets shall not only be turned off to avoid losing revenue but by including flexible assets to shift energy, the produced electricity can be used in an optimal way. Hence, batteries can be charged during negative prices and this energy can be used to maximise self-consumption and/or to sell flexibility on short-term or balancing markets in order to increase revenue [5]. The decision on what to do and when to do it will be based on AI algorithms that forecast the energy production, consumption and market prices more precisely in a distributed way [6, 7]. This will lead to an optimised control of the single assets.

2.2 Use Case 2: Secure Internet Provisioning

DDoS (Distributed Denial of Service) attacks are one of the major issues related to availability and security when customers are using cloud-based applications. A DDoS attack tries to deplete the resources of an application, rendering it unavailable to its legitimate users. DDoS attacks may be driven to any final public access point through Internet. Through MIRAI, NOS, one of the main telecom companies in Portugal, aims at developing services for DDoS protection with focus on the home network, combining the best practice of application design with the availability of a set of features for DDoS mitigation. The solution will be focused on customers' premises and the protection will be smart and simple, taking into account the following points:

1. All customers' devices, such as gateways/routers, set-top boxes, IoT devices must be usable and safe regarding internal or external DoS.
2. No single or multiple device(s) can cause exhaustion of network resources preventing other devices on the network to have access to the Internet for an amount of time higher than an identified goal (% time, etc.).
3. Any device trying to deny access or denying access to others, by consuming all available bandwidth, sending too many requests/packets per second or any other form of denial, should be set into a quarantine mode.

4. Depending on the type of device and its characterization, an IoT device has some periodic communication in the network (such as check for updates, send updated statistics, or some more random based on Human interaction, etc.). Leveraging this knowledge, it is possible to know what is the normal (usual) and abnormal (unusual) traffic for it.

5. Support for device quarantine should send a notification to customer notifying him/her that the device is not acting/behaving correctly for "amount of time" and is blocked from all communication.

6. Device quarantine will only block temporarily access to the device with unexpected behaviour. All devices connected to the router will remain with Internet access with no impact of isolation done in affected devices.

Based on the aforementioned points, smart and faster AI models are needed in order to easily detect, identify and mitigate attacks in customers' premises. This is also specifically critical with the exponential growth of IoT, but also with 5G delivery, where speed and latency will play an important role. But most importantly the high density of communication implies a huge amount of connected "things" at home that may be vulnerable to cyberattacks.

On the perspective of AI, IoT devices present network traffic patterns that differ from other types of devices (e.g. personal devices such as laptops and smart phones). As many IoT devices are meant to provide sensing and actuation over some physical process (e.g. opening of a door), much of their network traffic is event-triggered and can be directly traced to physical actions by the customer [8]. IoT devices also transmit periodic packets for keep-alive or logging purposes. In turn, DDoS attacks involve that a large number of distributed devices request a service, simultaneously or in short succession, from the target node, thus disrupting the ability of the node to serve legitimate clients. Such attacks involve considerable amounts of traffic targeting a single or few nodes; in turn, nodes contributing to the attack may also generate uncommon traffic patterns, either at low or high rates. Thus, DDoS detection is typically handled in the literature as a problem of anomaly detection over the 'typical' network traffic patterns; in turn, typical patterns need to be learned given that the customer's IoT ecosystem may exhibit a wide variety of legitimate traffic profiles. ML methods are particularly suited to this task. A considerable number of works have explored the problem in the context of software-defined networking (SDN), as the paradigm enables a bird's-eye view of the traffic in a network [9]; but there are also works taking a closer look at anomaly detection in customer networks and considering the specific characteristics of IoT traffic patterns [10, 11].

Current AI Shortcomings. At the end of 2017, NOS launched a study in Portugal aiming at assessing attitudes and behaviours regarding Internet use and evaluating satisfaction with Internet Accesses Macro and Micro. 670 online interviews were carried out, targeting residents in the Portuguese territory, from 15 to 64 years old, Internet users, whether or not they have Internet access (fixed or mobile). The study was focused on the usage of WiFi access and the corresponding concerns on several areas such as: e-mail, social network access, information search, chats, home banking and online purchases. In all instances, security was in the top 3 of the users' concerns. There are several products and services for security targeting DDoS attacks; however, they are focused on enterprise environment. With the growth of IoT and the rise of 5G as well as WiFi6, there is a need to shift the paradigm of DDoS. It is critical to see the customer's home as an enterprise environment, where several devices are connected, huge amount of data is exchanged (personal and behavioural), and people have low cybersecurity literacy and, consequently, are vulnerable to attacks.

Distributed AI Expectations. MIRAI aims to develop services for DDoS protection with focus in the home network, combining the best practice of application design with the availability of a set of features for DDoS mitigation. The solution will be focused on customer's premises. The protection will be smart and simple. Thus, the service developed under the MIRAI framework will support features such as: active traffic monitoring & detection, automatic attack mitigations, availability guarantee, mitigation policies tuned to customers applications, metrics & alerts, mitigation flow logs and DDoS rapid response support. The DDoS mitigation should be always-on in terms of monitoring and analysis. This will be done through smart algorithms and filters before considering an anomaly. For that, data from traffic behaviour, consumed bandwidth per period and protocols normally used by the user will be analysed to classify the attack. This flow allows to reduce the false positives and negatives and to improve the efficiency of the mitigation actions. The development, implementation and scaling of an IoT framework based on smart auto-discover, smart interoperability and smart cybersecurity will be deployed.

2.3   Use Case 3: Traffic Management

Like many other aspects of our lives, cities and mobility are becoming smarter. Cameras, induction loops and smartphones, among others, monitor how we move and how road infrastructure is used, inform us about possible problems that we might encounter in our way, and route us through the most optimal path. Still, the safety of vulnerable road users (i.e. pedestrians and cyclists nearby railway crossings, in school streets and at complex intersections) remains an important problem with ample possibilities for improvement.

Macq, the provider of this use case, is a well-established Belgium-based family company existing for almost 100 years and counting more than 130 employees. Nowadays, most of Macq's solutions and research activities focus on smart mobility. In that area, Macq offers products ranging from sensor solutions for traffic monitoring, including advanced Smart Mobility cameras (able to operate on multiple lanes, distinguish between different types of vehicles, detect the number of passengers, estimate driving speed, etc.), to controllers for traffic light management at road intersections, and software packages for managing mobility-related data and extracting valuable insights to different types of decision makers (such as police and road authorities).

Through MIRAI, Macq mainly aims at extracting valuable road safety analytics at the edge (specifically from their Smart Mobility cameras) and at reacting quickly when a potentially dangerous situation is detected. This requires in turn being able to deal with bandwidth-intensive image data, to extract insights even in the presence of noise and missing data, and to rely on other operational devices in the immediate surroundings, while considering their processing capabilities, current load, and connection link to them.

Current AI Shortcomings. Especially for vulnerable road users, a given situation can look safe from a single point of view, but this risk assessment can easily change if additional aspects are considered. Imagine a child crossing a tram line with a tram in its back. One camera sees only the child and another one only the tram; both cameras have each a partial view of the situation and cannot detect an increased risk. Hence, several sensors and cameras are needed to provide a complete as possible view of complex road intersections, and an approach leveraging all the resulting information is needed, for which only little research has been conducted so far [12, 13].

While the most advanced of Macq's Smart Mobility cameras perform most of their computations locally, performing more advanced computations such as understanding a given situation (possibly based on information from several other nearby data sources) and to detect potentially dangerous situations when they occur, would require relying on a distributed infrastructure. On the one hand, the intrinsic nature of Macq's Smart Mobility camera data makes it challenging to merely transfer that data between other edge devices or to the cloud to perform the required computations. On the other hand, Macq's Smart Mobility cameras are deployed outdoors and are hence exposed to possibly harsh weather conditions. This results in incorrect readings, in communication problems, and, sometimes, in broken devices that need to be replaced.

Advanced ML and data mining approaches suitable for edge computing enable to leverage the computational power offered by edge devices. However, determining how to split tasks and perform computations between different neighbouring edge devices available and the cloud infrastructure remains a challenge to address ahead of fully exploiting the available edge and cloud infrastructure [14].

Distributed AI Expectations. The issues described above can only be overcome in case the information about a situation is shared between several devices and an AI algorithm judges from this collective knowledge. Within MIRAI, a collectively acting algorithm will be developed, additionally respecting every road user's privacy.

Being able to perform more advanced ML and data mining computations at the edge would enable a better exploitation of the computational edge capabilities, a more balanced usage of computational resources and faster response times, as bandwidth-intensive image data would not need to be transferred to the cloud. Additionally, the algorithms proposed will be able to operate even in the presence of noise and missing data to better ensure service continuity.

2.4 Use Case 4: Water Management

Water damages in buildings represent 31% of the operational costs of property & casualty insurance companies due to claims. In addition to reducing unnecessary water consumption and preserving drinking water resources, being able to detect water leakages as soon as they occur is crucial to prevent water damages in buildings.

Shayp is a young Belgium-based company providing solutions for the monitoring and management of water leakages for different types of buildings, ranging from small buildings such as individual homes to larger buildings such as schools, hospitals and office and administration buildings. Shayp collects water consumption information through a connected water metering device installed in those buildings. Measurements are collected every 6 min and are sent to the cloud through NB-IoT. From this data, Shayp extracts water consumption analytics and detects potential leakages present in a building.

Through MIRAI, Shayp aims at (i) reducing and optimising communication bandwidth, as it drains the most battery power; (ii) identifying anomalies already at the edge, enabling a faster detection of water leakages; and (iii) adding remote control features to its meters, enabling future updates and remote calibration.

Current AI Shortcomings. In the current setup, water consumption data is hosted in the cloud where it is processed and stored. This is where the leakage detection analysis is performed. The data is transferred via the NB-IoT communication protocol every 6 minutes. If the data is sent with a higher temporal granularity, the battery lifetime of the device decreases [15]. Currently, the leakage detection is based on statistical analysis and a high accuracy is reached within a time window of 3 h. In order to detect leakages earlier, the temporal resolution has to be higher. With the intention to keep the battery lifetime as long as possible, a trained ML model is planned to predict leakages on the device directly without the need of sending all data on a high temporal resolution.

Distributed AI Expectations. Within MIRAI, Shayp will take a first step from a purely statistical model to a distributed ML model in order to improve and speed up leakage detection [16], improve building classification [17, 18] and increase battery lifetime. This model will run locally on the edge devices and send water consumption to the cloud only if necessary. With an unsupervised approach on the edge, the leakage detection time will be reduced from 3 to 1 h with an at least stable if not increased battery lifetime.

2.5   Use Case 5: Continuous Auto Configuration of Industrial Controllers at Edge

The main challenge in this use case is to auto-tune PID (Proportional-Integral-Derivative) controllers at the edge level in a textiles production site, using data streamed from different edge devices, using ML algorithms. This use case is constructed by Enforma (a data analytics company) and Eliar (an industrial electronics hardware and service company), which have access to numerous pilot sites among Eliar's installation base in Turkey and more in EU & other countries.

The textile dyeing process is a batch process which takes 5–12 h depending on various process parameters such as fabric to be dyed, desired colour, chemicals and dye. Eliar produces textile machine process control devices and PLCs (Programmable Logic Controllers) which control the machines according to the desired recipe and process steps. In the textile dyeing process, one of the important criteria that will ensure "right first time" is the correct temperature control of the machine. Currently, PID parameters are tuned by technicians according to their personal experience during installation of the dyeing machine. This may cause inconsistency in the process control and sustainability issues due to inefficient use of resources such as energy, steam, water, chemical, dye, and time.

Through MIRAI, the goal is to tune PID parameters adaptively with the output of the AI algorithm working on the process controllers and PLCs, which are IoT devices operating at the edge. The impact of the project can be described as follows:

- Resource-efficient deployment will be provided by AI algorithms.
- AI algorithms will be able to exchange data and information with each other.
- Each dyeing process is a batch process with unique definition. AI algorithms will be adapted to different processes.
- Noisy and uncertain data from a machine operating in an industrial environment will be studied.
- The installation of the machines will be easier, faster and guarantee trust.
- Results of these algorithms will be stored in the central database for data analysis on factory basis.
- A typical textile dyeing factory has 30 dyeing machines and control devices. Generally, all machines run simultaneously. The main tank liquid temperature is controlled by using PID, taking about 70% of the duration of the dyeing process.
- During the process, an average of 400 different data are collected. These data are various process values such as analogue input and output values, digital input and output values, alarms, operator interventions, running commands. In a typically slow dyeing process, it suffices to exchange data with PLC at 10 Hz.
- PID parameters will be set automatically during installation of the machine. After installation, the system is planned to continue learning and tune the PID parameter values when necessary.
- Daily production amount is around 30 tons in a 30-dyeing machine factory.

Current AI Shortcomings. Continuous auto configuration of industrial controllers at the edge makes another challenging business use case. This case is introduced by Eliar (an industrial electronics company) and Enforma (a data analytics company). The main challenge is to provide a continuous stream of data to local (i.e. edge) industrial controllers that can then auto-tune their PID (proportional, integral, derivative) controller parameters. This tuning is currently done at the outset by the human operator based on personal know-how. The tuning parameters are later updated at coarse intervals again by a human operator. All this is despite of factory-wide data is collected at a central server at the production facility. While auto-tuning the controller parameters, an important challenge will be to ensure that some supervisory aspects are included so that the edge devices have a more general view and therefore they do not end up configured in local optimums.

Distributed AI Expectations. With successful application of distributed AI algorithms at edge controllers that continuously update themselves, by also accounting for constraints such as insufficient steam sources and changing priorities of goods across neighbouring devices, we expect to have improved results.

The sheer volume of energy, chemicals and textiles involved in the process translates into considerable improvements considering a typical factory with ~30 dyeing machines working, together producing 30 tons of textiles. Heating takes up about 70% of the overall duration during dyeing. Also accounting for the amount of time, dye, other chemicals, water and energy consumed during this process, it becomes clear why the whole industry is in search of getting things "right first time".

Table 1. Consolidation of the high-level requirements of the five MIRAI use cases.

Requirement	UC1	UC2	UC3	UC4	UC5
Support real-time monitoring of edge devices	x	x		x	
Support remote control of edge devices	x			x	
Provide processing/learning capabilities at the edge	x	x	x	x	x
Leverage other edge devices (horizontal scaling)			x		x
Ability to learn even with noisy and missing data			x		x
Ability to handle private data and ensure privacy	x		x	x	
Provide fast response and avoid negative consequences	x	x	x	x	x
Reduce communications to the cloud	x		x	x	
Ensure optimal usage of other (natural) resources	x			x	x

2.6   A First Step Towards a Common Reference Architecture Model

Table 1 presents a first consolidation of the high-level requirements distilled from the MIRAI use cases, as described earlier. We observe, on the one hand, that both providing processing and/or learning capabilities at the edge and providing a fast response to avoid negative consequences are concerns shared by all use cases. On the other hand, each use case requires different functionalities (e.g. horizontal scaling, dealing with noisy and missing data, handling private data) specific to the application domain and context that it targets. Overall, the MIRAI project provides a rich and complementary set of five use cases, each within its own industrial context, covering a broad and diverse range of capabilities necessary to build distributed AI applications. These capabilities form the starting point of the MFBB, i.e. the different components that will enable the realization of distributed AI applications in a resource efficient, fully configurable and composable

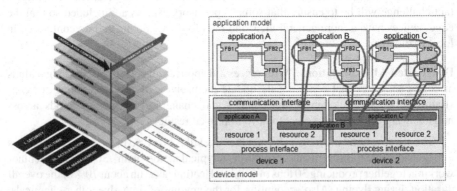

Fig. 1. European Edge Computing Consortium's Reference Architecture Model (EECC RAMEC) (left) and International Electrotechnical Commission's International Standard for Distributed Systems (IEC 61499) Function Blocks (right).

way. In this design, we intend to bring in concepts from the EECC RAMEC[2] and the IEC 61499[3] models (Fig. 1), which address the design and use of function blocks for industrial process, measurement and control systems.

3   Conclusions

This paper presents a first attempt to understand the need for migrating from conventional, cloud-based AI to distributed AI applications, hence enabling an innovative horizontal scaling across edge devices, on top of existing vertical scaling to the cloud. Thanks to the five industrial cases, a common argument has been made as to the shortcomings of the existing paradigms and the need to test out distributed AI methodologies. Through the ITEA3 MIRAI project, we plan to illustrate our points by devising, implementing and validating a framework of distributed AI building blocks, together comprising the MFBB, across a set of industrial use case scenarios.

Acknowledgements. The work in this paper is based on MIRAI, a project labelled by ITEA3 under project no 19034, with funding support from Agência Nacional de Inovação in Portugal, Innoviris in Belgium, and TÜBİTAK in Turkey.

References

1. Kewei, S., Yang, T.A., Wei, W., Davari, S.: A survey of edge computing-based designs for IoT security. Digital Commun. Netw. 195–202 (2020)
2. Talib, M.A., Majzoub, S., Nasir, Q., Jamal, D.: A systematic literature review on hardware implementation of artificial intelligence algorithms. J. Supercomput. **77**(2), 1897–1938 (2020). https://doi.org/10.1007/s11227-020-03325-8
3. Lines, J., Bagnall, A., Caiger-Smith, P., Anderson, S.: Classification of household devices by electricity usage profiles. In: International Conference on Intelligent Data Engineering and Automated Learning (2011)
4. Beckel, C., Sadamori, L., Santini, S.: Automatic socio-economic classification of households using electricity consumption data. In: Proceedings of the Fourth International Conference on Future Energy Systems (2013)
5. Potter, C.W., Archambault, A., Westrick, K.: Building a smarter smart grid through better renewable energy information. In: 2009 IEEE/PES Power Systems Conference and Exposition (2009)
6. Kong, W., Dong, Z.Y., Jia, Y., Hill, D.J., Xu, Y., Zhang, Y.: Short-term residential load forecasting based on LSTM recurrent neural network. IEEE Trans. Smart Grid **10**(1), 841–851 (2017)
7. Bessa, R., Trindade, A., Silva, C.S., Miranda, V.: Probabilistic solar power forecasting in smart grids using distributed information. Int. J. Electr. Power Energy Syst. **72**, 16–23 (2015)
8. Apthorpe, N., Reisman, D., Feamster, N.: A smart home is no castle: privacy vulnerabilities of encrypted IoT traffic. In: Workshop on Data and Algorithmic Transparency (2016)

---

[2] https://ecconsortium.eu/.

[3] https://www.iec61499.de/.

9. Pérez-Díaz, J.A., Amezcua Valdovinos, I., Choo, K.-K.R., Zhu, D.: A flexible SDN-based architecture for identifying and mitigating low-rate DDoS attacks using machine learning. IEEE Access **8**, 155859–155872 (2020)
10. Doshi, R., Apthorpe, N., Feamster, N.: Machine learning DDoS detection for consumer internet of things devices. In: IEEE Security and Privacy Workshops (SPW), pp. 29–35, May 2018
11. Eskandari, M., Janjua, Z.H., Vecchio, M., Antonelli, F.: Passban IDS: an intelligent anomaly-based intrusion detection system for IoT edge devices. IEEE Internet Things J. **7**(8), 6882–6897 (2020)
12. Maurya, S., Choudhary, A.: Deep learning based vulnerable road user detection and collision avoidance (2018)
13. Schleusner, J., Neu, L., Blume, H.: Deep learning based classification of pedestrian vulnerability trained on synthetic datasets. In: 2019 IEEE 9th International Conference on Consumer Electronics (ICCE-Berlin) (2019)
14. Nitinder, M., Kangasharju, J.: Edge-fog cloud: a distributed cloud for internet of things computations. In: 2016 Cloudification of the Internet of Things (CIoT) (2016)
15. Forooghifar, F., Aminifar, A., Atienza, D.: Resource-aware distributed epilepsy monitoring using self-awareness from edge to cloud. IEEE Trans. Biomed. Circuits Syst. **13**(6), 1338–1350 (2019)
16. Liu, Y., Ma, X., Li, Y., Tie, Y., Zhang, Y., Gao, J.: Water pipeline leakage detection based on machine learning and wireless sensor networks. Sensors **19**(23), 5086 (2019)
17. de Souza, C., Kalbusch, A.: Estimation of water consumption in multifamily residential buildings. Acta Scientiarum. Technol. **39**(2), 161–168 (2017)
18. Almeida, R.M., Ramos, N.M., Simões, L.M., de Freitas, V.P.: Energy and water consumption variability in school buildings: review and application of clustering techniques. J. Perform. Constr. Facil. **29**(6), 04014165 (2015)

Distributed Data Compression
for Edge Devices

Kevin Van Vaerenbergh[(✉)] and Tom Tourwé

EluciDATALab Sirris, Boulevard A. Reyerslaan 80, 1030 Brussels, Belgium
kevin.vanvaerenbergh@sirris.be

Abstract. In this paper, we elaborate on the issue of reliable storage
and efficient communication of large quantities of data in the absence
of continuous connectivity. We illustrate how advanced machine learning
techniques can run locally at the edge, in the context of data compression
related to special-purpose vehicles. Two different data compression techniques are compared by calculating general compression metrics, e.g.,
compression rate and root mean-squared error, while also validating the
results using an event detection algorithm. These techniques exploit real-
world usage data captured in the field using the I-HUMS platform provided by our industrial partner ILIAS solutions Inc.

Keywords: IoT · Distributed data analysis · Time series compression

1 Introduction

Ever more industrial assets are being instrumented and connected thanks to significant evolutions in Internet-of-Things (IoT) technology, e.g., smaller sensors
and reliable connectivity. Detailed data on how/when/where an asset is used
can be captured continuously, transferred to a central platform, where it is analysed via advanced data analytics technologies to extract useful insights. This
enables advanced health and usage monitoring applications that help to ensure
availability, reliability and safety of the equipment.

At present, such usage monitoring is mostly done at the level of the individual asset. Many companies however are operating and managing large groups
of assets, and would like to apply advanced data-driven analysis techniques to
extract insights across their entire fleet. Examples are fleets of vehicles operated
at globally-distributed sites, wind turbines arranged within parks, compressors
and pumps in industrial surroundings, etc. In that context, a reliable storage
and efficient communication of large quantities of data is challenging due to the
absence of continuous connectivity [11,14].

Industrial assets can continuously gather data but are not necessarily continuously connected. Some are highly-mobile (e.g. vehicles or aircraft) and sites

This work is supported by the Brussels-capital region - Innoviris.

I. Maglogiannis et al. (Eds.): AIAI 2021 Workshops, IFIP AICT 628, pp. 293–304, 2021.
https://doi.org/10.1007/978-3-030-79157-5_24

where they are deployed can be extremely remote, hence continuous and reliable communication means are not guaranteed. In addition, different connection means are possible (e.g. fast Wi-Fi, sat-com or slower 3/4G), but each technology influences how much data can be transferred, at which speed, at what cost, etc. Finally, data offloading opportunities can be scarce and short and offloading should not interfere with normal operations.

Consequently, data needs to be stored on-asset until it can be off-loaded to a collection point. However, storage comes at a cost and explicitly managing this cost requires carefully considering the amount of data that is retained at asset-level and eventually transferred. To ensure the most relevant data is always retained, data reduction techniques need to be considered. In Sects. 2 and 3, we will detail how we consider two different data compression techniques for special-purpose vehicles in such a distributed context.

1.1 Special-Purpose Vehicle Monitoring

We use vehicle usage data provided by our industrial partner ILIAS Solutions[1]. A fleet of special-purpose vehicles is instrumented by ILIAS' I-HUMS system which captures vehicle usage measurements. It consists of a smart sensor device, a collector antenna and a decentralized data processing server. The device contains several sensors sampling 200 Hz, e.g. 3-axis accelerometer and 3-axis gyroscope, and can connect to a vehicle's

Fig. 1. ILIAS' I-HUMS sensor.

CANbus for extra data collection, sampled 1 Hz. It offloads data via the collector antenna when in the vicinity and transfers it to the server.

The dataset represents 5 months of driving data from one vehicle where three accelerometer-based aggregations are gathered, i.e., minXAcc, minYAcc and minZAcc. These signals represent the minimum value of each accelerometer axis, aggregated 200 Hz 1 Hz.

1.2 Data Compression

Vehicle usage data is gathered at high frequency and to deal with this fine-grained time series data, we employ data compression. Data compression can be lossy or lossless. In contrast to most lossless techniques [13] such as [8,17], a much higher compression rate can be achieved using lossy techniques [15]. Many lossy compression techniques for time series have been researched [5,10,12] with some having trouble on compressing all data types or having a large runtime. Therefore, we investigate intelligent data retention techniques that can be applied on edge devices. The intuition behind data retention methodologies is that all data points are not equally relevant. Many assets have "stable" periods

---

[1] https://www.ilias-solutions.com.

where they are barely active, and periods with higher activity. For instance, a vehicle can be waiting at a traffic light, generating a stable period of mostly irrelevant data. Later on, the vehicle can be driving off-road in mountainous terrain, generating a period with relevant data to better understand/monitor it's behaviour. These methodologies intend to detect the irrelevant periods and retain that data with a lower resolution, e.g. 1 min granularity, while keeping the periods with relevant data at a higher resolution, e.g. 1 s granularity. In this paper, we consider two data retention techniques, data compression using Recurrent Auto-encoders (RAE, Sect. 2) and data compression using Swinging Door Trending (SDT, Sect. 3) and compare them using signal comparison metrics as well as in the context of an event detection algorithm (Sect. 4).

2   Data Compression Using Recurrent Auto-Encoders

The first algorithm we implemented is proposed by [7] and uses a recurrent auto-encoder (RAE) [9] based on an LSTM network [6] for compressing time series signals. The methodology follows three steps, (i) train a model to characterize the data input, i.e. model the stable and active periods, (ii) use the model to detect the stable and active periods in the signal to compress and (iii) compress the stable periods or retain the active periods.

The model used is a recurrent auto-encoder (RAE) (Fig. 2). RAEs are a specific kind of recurrent neural nets (RNN) [16] dedicated to reconstruct an input signal using time-dependent features. It is composed of two long short-term memory nets (LSTM), one encoder and one decoder. The encoder compresses the input signal, which the decoder receives and from which it tries to reconstruct the input signal as closely as possible. Some limitations are given to the decoder in order to avoid a perfect reconstruction of the signal. These limitations ensure that the decoder focuses on the main characteristics of the input signal and discards unnecessary information.

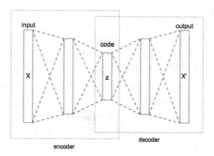

Fig. 2. Basic structure of an auto-encoder where, for this structure, the vertical bars represent the LSTM layers.

The methodology relies on two parameters; standard deviation (STD) threshold, used to segment the signal for training of the RAE and error margin, used to identify the amount of error that the reconstructed signal can have with respect to the original signal.

2.1 Strategy

To train the RAE, we segment the signal given a STD threshold, calculated in an automatic way by bootstrapping a set of segments of distinct sizes from the original signal and averaging their STD. A STD-based threshold is preferable as it represents the evolution of the signal better than e.g., the average. The original segmentation method scans the signal sequentially and defines the periods where the STD threshold is not surpassed. Unfortunately, this approach does not take into account the change in variability of the signal. In some situations, this can lead to a segment that is a combination of a period with high variability, followed by a period of low variability. We added an extra segmentation step to avoid this by first scanning the signal to define the indexes where there is a sudden change in STD over a rolling window. The indexes identified by the first scan, together with the fixed STD thresholds are used to segment the signal properly.

We trained the RAE using the segments defined above offline, using an RAE consisting of two LSTM layers for encoding and decoding, with 32 and 16 as input size for encoding, and the reverse for decoding. The network was trained using 300 epoch, a batch size of 60 and an input size of 32. When the RAE is trained, we can use the model on the edge to compress the signals.

Two different strategies are applied in this paper; (i) we train a separate RAE for each axis, i.e., a x-axis RAE, a y-axis RAE and a z-axis RAE, and (ii) we train a global RAE using the data from all the axes. Since accelerometer data captures the movement of the asset, all three axes capture similar data and therefore can be used combined as a larger training set. We want to validate this assumption by comparing the compression results using both the separate and the combined RAE on all three axis data.

2.2 Separate RAE

For the separate compression, 6 different RAE are trained, 2 RAE's for each signal with varying input sizes, i.e., 16 and 32 RAE for x-axis, y-axis and z-axis acceleration. Each RAE is trained using only the historical data from the appropriate axis. The different signals are then compressed using the RAE that was trained for that specific axis.

Figure 3 shows a segment of the compressed z-axis signal for a certain drive, compare the compressed signals of both RAE trained using only z-axis data. We notice that the 16 size RAE does a better job of tracking the higher peaks of the signal, which in most cases represent the more informative segments.

2.3 Combined RAE

The combined approach compresses the accelerometer signals using the two RAE's that are trained using the historical data from all the axes, one with

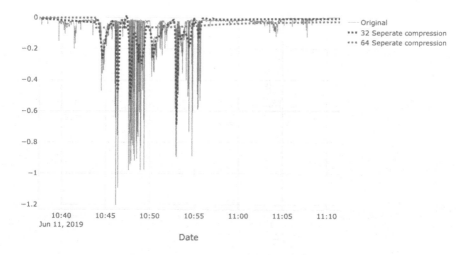

Fig. 3. Comparison of compression results for all the different RAE.

length of 16, the other with length of 32. Since the RAE is trained using all the data, the same RAE is used to compress all the different axes.

Figure 4 presents the comparison between the original z-axis signal for a drive and both compressed signals. The large overshoot just before 10:30 is most notable. We clearly see that the 32 RAE is not reconstructing that part very well. The rest of the signal is properly tracked as with the separate RAE versions.

3   Data Compression Using Swinging Door Trending

The second algorithm we implemented is proposed by [4] and uses Swinging Door Trending (SDT) [1] for intelligent data retention. This algorithm has been successfully used in the wind power ramp event detection for wind turbines [2] and solar ramp detection for solar panels [3].

The swinging door trending technique compresses a sequence of data points by using a simplified linear representation. It is computationally simple, so it can run on low-resource devices without significant overhead. The technique considers an error deviation parameter δy, which determines the error between the original signal and the compressed signal that one is willing to tolerate. The technique passes through the time series data sequentially, starting with the first two points. The first point is retained, a line is drawn between this point and the second point, and a so-called tolerance band is defined by computing the upper and lower bound, based on the deviation parameter. An iterative process is started, where the technique considers the next point in the time series and verifies whether that point falls within the tolerance band. If this is the case, the point does not need to be retained and the next data point is considered. This continues until a point is reached that does not fall within the tolerance band, meaning this point can not be represented by a linear representation between the point last retained and the current point. This last point

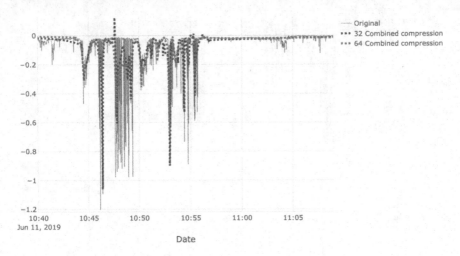

Fig. 4. Comparison of compression results for all the different RAE.

is then also retained, and a new iterative process starts. At each step, the tolerance band is also updated. When a next point is considered, its upper and lower bounds are reconsidered. The upper or lower bounds will be updated if the bounds of the next point fall below or above the previous ones, respectively, i.e. if the upper bound of the new point is lower than the previous upper bound, the upper bound is updated, and vice versa for the lower bound. This ensures that the tolerance band will always become smaller when new points are added, since the more points, the less precise the linear representation will become.

The process is illustrated by the following figures (Fig. 5). In the first step, the technique starts with the first point in the time series, the tolerance band is the whole area after the point. When the second point is considered, a linear interpolation is constructed between these two points and the tolerance band is updated using the deviation parameter δy. When a next point is selected, the new linear representation is constructed between the last point that was retained and the next point, and the new tolerance band is defined. If the next point, i.e. point 4, has the new lower bound lower than the previous lower bound, the tolerance band is not updated (the purple area will not be used as a tolerance band update), similar for the upper bound. As long as there are new points that fall in the tolerance band, they can be represented by the linear representation. Once a new point is considered that falls outside the tolerance band, e.g. point 6, the last point of the linear representation, e.g. point 5, will be retained as the compressed version of points 1 to 5. Starting from point 5 a new linear

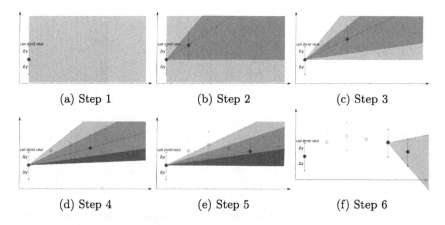

(a) Step 1   (b) Step 2   (c) Step 3

(d) Step 4   (e) Step 5   (f) Step 6

Fig. 5. Process of SDT algorithm.

representation will be constructed with point 6 as the first point to consider. As an end result, the first 5 points will be compressed by a linear representation that is defined by point 1 and point 5, i.e. removing points 2, 3 and 4. A new linear representation will start from point 5.

3.1 Strategy

In this section, we apply the same strategies used in the previous method, (i) considering each of the three accelerometer signals separately and (ii) considering all of the signals combined. For each strategy, we compare the results using three different deviation parameter methods; (i) an automatic definition based on a mean variance bootstrapping method (**ZMEAN**), (ii) an automatic definition based on the value ranges and (**RANGE**) (iii) and fixed deviation parameter for all drives defined by a domain expert (**DEF**).

Separate SDT. The first application of SDT compresses the three signals separately. For each signal and every drive, a deviation parameter is identified using the above mentioned deviation parmeter methods. In this paper, 3 different deviation parameter methods are investigated; (i) an automatic definition based on a mean variance bootstrapping method (**ZMEAN**), (ii) an automatic definition based on the value ranges and (**RANGE**) (iii) and fixed deviation parameter for all drives defined by a domain expert (**DEF**).

Figure 6 compares the resulting compressed signals with respect to the original one for a certain drive. There is clearly a big difference between the different deviation parameter selection methods. The **RANGE** compression follows the original signal best, resulting in a lower compression, while **ZMEAN** and **DEF** compression achieve a higher compression as they discard more datapoints.

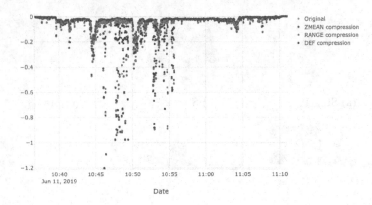

Fig. 6. Comparison on the resulting compression for a subset of the data.

Combined SDT. The combined SDT compresses the signals in a combined fashion where for each drive, all three signals are compressed simultaneously as such that at each timestep, all three signals are compressed or none are compressed. The same methods that were previously mentioned are also investigated using the combined method, namely mean variance bootstrapping, value ranges and fixed deviation parameter definition.

Figure 7 shows the results of the compression of one signal using the three different deviation calculation methods. We noticed that the different methods all compress the signals differently, with the **DEF** method, compression the signal the most and the **RANGE** method compression it the least. The difference between the **RANGE** and the **ZMEAN** method are quite small but still significant is some areas, e.g., between 11:00 and 11:30.

After comparing the SDT and RAE methods internally, we will now compute several compression metrics and do a validation of the compression results of both methods against each other.

4   Validation

To define the performance of both techniques, RAE and SDT, we compare the resulting signals using data compression ratio.

Next to evaluating the compression performance, we should also validate whether the informativeness of the data is retained at a sufficiently high level. The level of informativeness of a dataset is typically linked to the application for which that dataset is used. In what follows, we will consider an event detection approach and validate whether the results of the application are influenced by applying the compression techniques. We apply the approach on the original dataset and on the compressed datasets and compare the results.

First we calculate the performance metrics.

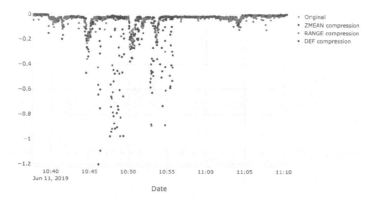

Fig. 7. Comparison on the resulting compression for a subset of the data using the combined SDT approach.

4.1 Compression Ratio

In this section we will compare the achieved compression ratio per technique. The data compression ratio measures the amount of size reduction that is achieved when comparing with the size of the original signal. In Fig. 8, all the compression rates are plotted, with a clear difference between the RAE compression ratios, with on average outperform the SDT ratios, except for the SDT compression using domain knowledge defined deviation parameter. This is due to the fact that this fixed deviation parameter allows a high number of compression error. Another interesting result is the compression ratio of the short RAE models using 32 input size on the x-axis accelerometer data, and the long RAE models using 64 input size. This can be due to the fact that the x-axis accelerometer data is more easy to learn using smaller input segments. For the other axes, all RAE models perform equally indicating that these axes are harder to learn. Since these axes are harder to learn, adding them as extra training data to the combined RAE models, decreases the compression performance substantially on the x-axis. A larger compression rate does not mean the performance is better as the goal of these retention techniques is to compress as much as possible without losing to much informativeness with respect of the original signal.

4.2 Event Detection Validation

To validate the informativeness of the resulting compressed datasets, we apply an event detection algorithm to the original and compressed datasets.

We use a simple event detection approach that defines a threshold for very high/low accelerometer values and flags data points above/below that threshold as events. We also assign a severity to the event, based on the percentage of how much the accelerometer value is exceeding the threshold. Each accelerometer has his own threshold values, X-axis acceleration < -2.5, Y-axis acceleration < -1.8 and Z-axis acceleration < -2.5, and we flag the event based on severity,

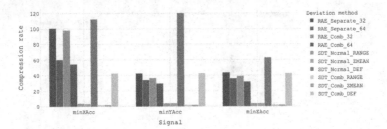

Fig. 8. Comparison of the compression rate of all different methods and parameterisations.

i.e., *WARNING* when value is between 100% and 150%, *INCIDENT* when value is between 150% and 200%, and *HARD INCIDENT* when values is above 200%.

Figure 9 represents the results of the event detection applied on the three compressed signals computed using the separate SDT algorithm (upper figure) and the compressed SDT algorithm (lower figure). We can see that the **ZMEAN** deviation parameter selection produces the best result but it still loses some information as a few *Warning* events are not found and a few *No event* events are predicted as *Warning* events. The other two approached miss-classify more events and therefore "lose" more information after compression. The combined SDT algorithm keeps 100% of the informativeness of the signal after compression for all three different approaches.

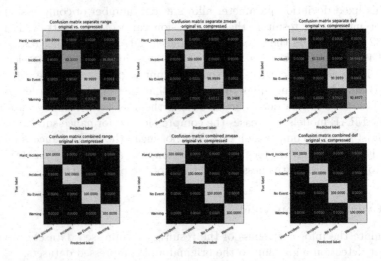

Fig. 9. Results of the event detection for the separate SDT algorithm (upper) and the combined SDT algorithm (lower).

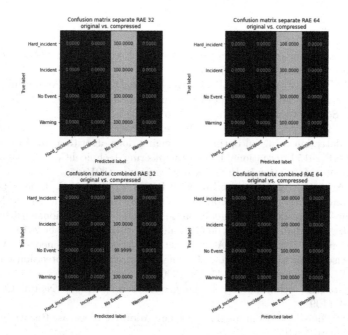

Fig. 10. Results of the event detection for the separate RAE algorithm (upper) and the combined RAE algorithm (lower).

Figure 10 represents the results for the RAE approach using separately trained auto-encoders (upper figures) and combined trained auto-encoders (lower figure). The results are quite poor as most of the signals after compression "lose" a big part of the informativeness. All approaches "loose" the informativeness of the signal as they all classified every event as *No event*.

5   Conclusion

Data retention techniques aim to compress data while trying to retain a high level of informativeness. In this paper, we presented two of such techniques, Swinging Door Trending (SDT) and Recurrent Auto-Encoder (RAE).

We used both techniques to compress accelerometer data captured by a vehicle in two ways, a separate and a combined way.

A technical evaluation showed that the techniques perform differently with respect to the compression rate, with the RAE techniques able to compress up to 100 times the signal. This unfortunately comes with a price as these techniques perform very bad at the validation since they "lose" most of the informativeness of the signals after compression. In that aspect, the SDT compressed signals retain a high level of informativeness after compression with the combined approach still retaining 100% of the informativeness after compression.

References

1. Bristol, E.: Swing door trending: adaptive trend recording. In: ISA National Conference Proceedings, pp. 749–753 (1990)
2. Cui, M., Zhang, J., Florita, A.R., Hodge, B., Ke, D., Sun, Y.: An optimized swinging door algorithm for wind power ramp event detection. In: 2015 IEEE Power Energy Society General Meeting, pp. 1–5 (2015)
3. Cui, M., Zhang, J., Florita, A.R., Hodge, B., Ke, D., Sun, Y.: Solar power ramp events detection using an optimized swinging door algorithm. In: Proceedings of the ASME 2015 International Design Engineering Technical Conferences and Computers and Information in Engineering Conference (2015)
4. David Arias Correa, J., Sandro Roschildt Pinto, A., Montez, C., Leão, E.: Swinging door trending compression algorithm for IoT environments. In: Anais Estendidos do Simpósio Brasileiro de Engenharia de Sistemas Computacionais (SBESC), pp. 143–148. Sociedade Brasileira de Computação - SBC, November 2019
5. Elmeleegy, H., Elmagarmid, A., Cecchet, E., Aref, W., Zwaenepoel, W.: Online piece-wise linear approximation of numerical streams with precision guarantees. Proc. VLDB Endowment 2, 145–156 (2009)
6. Hochreiter, S., Schmidhuber, J.: Long short-term memory. Neural Comput. 9, 1735–80 (1997)
7. Hsu, D.: Time Series Compression Based on Adaptive Piecewise Recurrent Autoencoder, August 2017
8. Huffman, D.A.: A method for the construction of minimum-redundancy codes. Proc. IRE 40(9), 1098–1101 (1952)
9. Kingma, D.P., Welling, M.: Auto-encoding variational Bayes (2013)
10. Lazaridis, I., Mehrotra, S.: Capturing sensor-generated time series with quality guarantees. In: Proceedings 19th International Conference on Data Engineering (Cat. No. 03CH37405), pp. 429–440 (2003)
11. Ma, T., Hempel, M., Peng, D., Sharif, H.: A survey of energy-efficient compression and communication techniques for multimedia in resource constrained systems. IEEE Commun. Surv. Tutorials 15(3), 963–972 (2013)
12. Papaioannou, T.G., Riahi, M., Aberer, K.: Towards online multi-model approximation of time series. In: 2011 IEEE 12th International Conference on Mobile Data Management, vol. 1, pp. 33–38 (2011)
13. Ringwelski, M., Renner, C., Reinhardt, A., Weigel, A., Turau, V.: The Hitchhiker's guide to choosing the compression algorithm for your smart meter data. In: Proceedings of the 2nd IEEE ENERGYCON Conference and Exhibition/ICT for Energy Symposium (ENERGYCON), pp. 998–1003 (2012)
14. Sadler, C.M., Martonosi, M.: Data compression algorithms for energy-constrained devices in delay tolerant networks. In: Proceedings of the 4th International Conference on Embedded Networked Sensor Systems, pp. 265–278 (2006)
15. Salomon, D.: A Concise Introduction to Data Compression. Undergraduate Topics in Computer Science (2008)
16. Sherstinsky, A.: Fundamentals of recurrent neural network (RNN) and long short-term memory (LSTM) network. Physica D 404 (2020)
17. Ziv, J., Lempel, A.: A universal algorithm for sequential data compression. IEEE Trans. Inf. Theory 23(3), 337–343 (1977)

PFilter: Privacy-Aware and Secure Data Filtering at the Edge for Distributed Edge Analytics

Annanda Rath[(✉)], Anna Hristoskova, and Sarah Klein

Software Engineering and Security Department, Sirris, Brussels, Belgium
{annanda.rath,anna.hristoskova,sarah.klein}@sirris.be
http://www.sirris.be/

Abstract. This paper is presenting a conceptual mechanism for lightweight privacy-aware and secure data access control and filtering. This mechanism can be deployed at an edge node in order to assure that all data coming in and going out of it is properly protected and filtered. Goal is to keep private data locally and limit its exposure to outside entities (e.g., Cloud backend, external application or other edge nodes) while preserving the performance and security requirements for edge analytics. The data filtering at the edge node is done in a way that it is not possible for outside entities to identify end-devices and the data associated with them.

Keywords: Privacy filter · Distributed edge analytics · Security · IoT.

1 Introduction

The Internet of Things (IoT) is growing exponentially with connected devices ranging from smart doors to industrial machines and installations. By 2025, it is expected that there will be 41.6 billion connected IoT devices, generating 79.4 zettabytes (ZB) of data[1]. With such amount of data, the current practice of sending data to central platforms (e.g., Cloud) for analysis becomes unsustainable as it does not scale well and represents a single point of failure. Given that, the new paradigm of Edge Computing serves a variety of purposes in the current IoT landscape. This distributed, local computing paradigm can help addressing several issues from latency, bandwidth, connectivity, security and privacy issues that would otherwise make some IoT cases impossible. Data collection, machine learning and AI applications can be distributed at the edge in a federated architecture. Such a solution is robust because tasks can migrate in case of component failures and is scalable since workload can be shared among many computing devices. However, there are also many challenges [2] in federated architectures. One of which is the security of edge analytics as it is no longer a single point

---

[1] https://www.zdnet.com/article/iot-devices-to-generate-79-4zb-of-data-in-2025-says-idc/.

© IFIP International Federation for Information Processing 2021
Published by Springer Nature Switzerland AG 2021
I. Maglogiannis et al. (Eds.): AIAI 2021 Workshops, IFIP AICT 628, pp. 305–310, 2021.
https://doi.org/10.1007/978-3-030-79157-5_25

of concern as in a centralised architecture, but distributed over the federated approach. Privacy-sensitive edge analytics is also a challenging security issue [2], especially, when private data needs to be shared between edge nodes[2] for aggregation, analysis and modelling purposes. Questions arise such as: How to share minimal information without losing its usability? How to control and enforce the use of data in analytics processes, resulting in transparency? This becomes even more challenging in the IoT context since edge nodes tend to have limited computing power and memory where traditional data filtering and minimisation [1] do not fit. Therefore, a lightweight privacy-aware and secure solution is needed. This paper addresses the data security and privacy-preserving issues in the distributed edge computing taking into account the requirements and security constraints in an IoT edge analytics environment. We plan to investigate the following aspects:

1. A lightweight & configurable data filtering mechanism that supports different types of data with different levels of privacy protection requirements.
2. A lightweight access control and a coordinated enforcement mechanism that controls all aspects of data access on the edge node, between edge nodes or between edge nodes and end devices.

This paper is structured as follows. Section 2 highlights the need for privacy-aware and secure data filter and access control mechanism. Section 3 focuses on the description of the industrial cases from different companies within the EUREKA-ITEA3 project MIRAI[3] having similar concerns to what we are envisaging to address. Finally, Sect. 4 provides concluding remarks.

2 The Need of Data Filtering, Access and Usage Control for Data Analytics at the Edge

The key challenge of edge analytics is the hardware constraint. Edge nodes tend to have limited computing footprint. This is why embedding the functionalities of a fully-fledged data analytics mechanism and heavy access control and data filtering process, similar to the ones implemented in the centralised architecture [3], is challenging. This becomes even more challenging in the context of battery-powered IoT edge nodes, that require to run for a prolonged lifespan with minimal intervention. Therefore, a lightweight solution is needed.

2.1 Need of Lightweight Data Filtering and Control on Filtering Process

Edge computing can reduce the number of sensors and actuators connected directly to the Internet. As a result, reducing number of connections to the

---

[2] In this paper, edge node refers to device gateway (or IoT gateway), while end-device refers to IoT devices, such as sensors/actuators.

[3] https://itea3.org/project/mirai.html.

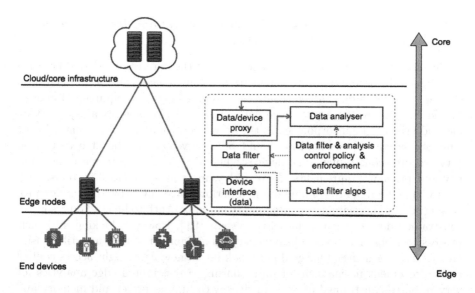

Fig. 1. High level architecture of edge node system components

Internet. This reduces the potential attack vector of security attacks. Local data processing and filtering by an edge node (gateway) can also reduce the amount of sensitive and private information that is sent through a network. Thereby, it addresses privacy needs for the application. However, the data filtering mechanism [1,5–8] that requires heavy processing and computing power is not suitable for resource-constrained edge nodes. There is a need for a lightweight data filtering mechanism that is able to run on devices with very limited computing power and memory without compromising data usability and privacy requirements. Our goal is to investigate a new lightweight data filtering approach that can run on very resource-constrained edge nodes, taking into account the following three factors during its design: (1) minimal processing and less computing, (2) privacy-compliance and zero data leaks, and (3) avoidance of information loss and guaranteed data usability.

In addition, we also envisage to add a security layer on top of the data filtering process at the edge nodes by means of a security control on the data filtering process (see Fig. 1, data filter control policy). This data filter control policy module (see Fig. 1) regulates what and how the data filtering module should process different types of data with different filtering requirements. It also instructs the data filter module which data filter algorithms should be selected. The data filter module outputs the non privacy-sensitive data, to the data analyser where the AI or machine learning is located (see Fig. 1). The data analyser processes and extracts relevant data and outputs to the data proxy (see Fig. 1), which makes the data available to the outside entities (see Fig. 1). The data proxy acts as a secure gateway for the exchange of data between the edge environment and core network (see Fig. 1) and also isolates the edge environment from the core network.

2.2 Need for Data Access and Usage Control and Its Enforcement for Distributed Edge Analytics

In the case of distributed edge analytics, part of the data can be shared between edge nodes. In order to ensure a fine-grained data access control for such data sharing, a reliable data access control and enforcement is required. Moreover, to address privacy concerns in such data-sharing scenarios, a privacy-preserving method needs to be incorporated in the access control and enforcement scheme. This access control mechanism should be lightweight and be able to run on very resource-constrained edge devices while also being able to meet the security and privacy requirements. As of today, most access control systems, such as OAuth, OpenID, are running on high performance devices with complex processing steps. There are many attempts to extend OAuth to be used on resource-constrained devices such as in a IoT system [4,9]. However, looking into their processing steps that involve heavy encryption algorithms, they are still considered as heavy schemes. Our goal is to look into a new lightweight access control and enforcement mechanism for data sharing in distributed edge analytics for very resource-constrained devices, devices with limited power and memory and that require long battery lifespan. We take three following factors into account when designing it: (1) fine-grained and privacy-aware, (2) low computing power and (3) few processing steps.

3 Industrial Cases: Sustainability and Smart City Domain

In this section, we provide a description of actual industrial cases where private data access control and filtering on resource-constrained devices are critical ongoing challenges. These cases are from three companies, Macq, Shayp and 3E[4] within the EUREKA-ITEA3 project MIRAI. They will be used as test cases for our envisaged data filter and access control demonstrator.

3.1 3E Case and Requirements

3E is a Brussels-based company providing consultancy and software solutions for monitoring and improving the performance of sustainable energy installations and for optimising energy consumption. More precisely, 3E SynaptiQ[5] solution enables to manage solar and wind assets, monitor, report and improve their performance, and organise their maintenance. In order to further improve their platform, 3E works on a use case in the domain of distributed renewable energy systems, linked to the following research area: (1) Leveraging the computational power of edge devices in order to reduce latency and (2) tackle both data sharing obstacles and privacy aspects. These research areas relate to the challenges we are addressing in this paper.

---

[4] https://mobility.macq.eu, https://www.shayp.com, https://3e.eu.
[5] https://3e.eu/our-platform.

3.2 Shayp Case and Requirements

Shayp is a Brussels-based company providing solutions for the monitoring and management of water usage and leakages for different types of buildings, ranging from home to large industrial buildings, such as public and business buildings. Shayp collects water consumption information through a connected water metering device installed in those buildings. Water measurements are collected periodically and are sent to the cloud through Sigfox and NB-IoT. From this data, Shayp extracts water consumption analytics and detects potential leakages present in a building. Shayp is currently pursuing several tracks for the further enhancement of their services, among which is privacy-preservation of the data on device (water metering). Shayp aims at securing and filtering data in transit in order to prevent disclosing privacy-sensitive water consumption data. This research links to one of our research goals in this paper.

3.3 Macq Case and Requirements

Macq is a Brussels-based company providing solutions around two main areas: industrial automation and smart mobility. While the former represents the historical market targeted by Macq, smart mobility has become the largest activity domain of the company in the last years and drives many of Macq research activities. Under EUREKA-ITEA3, Macq focuses on the smart mobility where traffic is the main use case. Macq aims at improving the safety of vulnerable road users in the area of railway crossings, school streets and at complex intersections. For this, intelligent street cameras are installed. Macq works towards a solution in the domain of road safety, linked to the different research areas, among which are: (1) efficiency of edge processing without the need to send images to the cloud and (2) private data filtering of images captured by street cameras. These two research cases link to what we are addressing in this paper.

4 Conclusion

This research position paper highlights the potential of data security and privacy-preserving challenges at the edge. We also present some early concepts on how privacy and data filtering at edge nodes should be designed and explain why existing mechanisms do not fit. Our next steps are to extensively work on the above-mentioned concepts and validate them through a demonstrator based on the requirements from the three industrial cases (Macq, 3E and Shayp).

References

1. Abigail, G., Gilad, E., Ron, Sh., Micha, M., Ariel, F.: Data Minimization for GDPR Compliance in Machine Learning Models. IBM Research - Haifa, Haifa University Campus, Haifa, Israel (2020)
2. Shi, W., Cao, J., Zhang, Q., Li, Y., Xu, L.: Edge computing: vision and challenges. IEEE IoT J. **3**(5), 637–646 (2016)

3. Suzan, Al., Nusaybah, A., Muhammad, M.: Survey of centralized and decentralized access control models in cloud computing. Int. J. Adv. Comput. Sci. Appl. **12**(2) (2021)
4. Karim, A., Adnan, M.A.: An OpenID based authentication service mechanisms for internet of things. In: 2019 IEEE 4th International Conference on Computer and Communication Systems (ICCCS), Singapore, pp. 687–692 (2019)
5. Zhang, J., Chen, B., Zhao, Y., Cheng, X., Hu, F.: Data security and privacy-preserving in edge computing paradigm: survey and open issues. IEEE Access **6**, 18209–18237 (2018)
6. Lu, R., Heung, K., Lashkari, A.H., Ghorbani, A.A.: A lightweight privacy-preserving data aggregation scheme for fog computing-enhanced IoT. IEEE Access **5**, 3302–3312 (2017). https://doi.org/10.1109/ACCESS.2017.2677520
7. Tangade, S., Manvi, S.S.: Scalable and privacy-preserving authentication protocol for secure vehicular communications. In: Proceedings of the 2016 IEEE International Conference on Advanced Networks and Telecommunications Systems (ANTS), Bangalore, India, 6 November 2016
8. Chim, T.W., Yiu, S.M., Li, V.O., Hui, L.C., Zhong, J.: PRGA: privacy-preserving recording gateway-assisted authentication of power usage information for smart grid. IEEE Trans. Dependable Secur. Comput. **12**, 85–97 (2015)
9. Mahmood, K., Chaudhry, S.A., Naqvi, H., Shon, T., Ahmad, H.F.: A lightweight message authentication scheme for smart grid communications in power sector. Comput. Electr. Eng. **52**, 114–124 (2016)

Towards a Distributed Learning Architecture for Securing ISP Home Customers

Pedro M. Santos[1,4]([✉]) [iD], Joana Sousa[2,5] [iD], Ricardo Morla[3] [iD], Nuno Martins[2,6], João Tagaio[2,7], João Serra[2], Carlos Silva[2], Mário Sousa[3,4] [iD], Pedro Souto[3,4] [iD], Luís Lino Ferreira[1,4] [iD], João Ferreira[2], and Luís Almeida[3,4] [iD]

[1] Instituto Superior de Engenharia do Porto, Porto, Portugal
{pss,llf}@isep.ipp.pt
[2] NOS Inovação, Lisbon, Portugal
{joana.sousa,nuno.mmartins,joao.tagaio}@parceiros.nos.pt,
{joao.mserra,carlos.a.silva,joao.MFerreira}@nos.pt
[3] Faculdade de Engenharia, Universidade do Porto, Porto, Portugal
{rmorla,msousa,pfs,lda}@fe.up.pt
[4] CISTER Research Center in Real-Time and Embedded Computing Systems, Porto, Portugal
[5] Bold International, Lisbon, Portugal
[6] Caixa Mágica, Lisbon, Portugal
[7] KCSIT, Lisbon, Portugal

Abstract. Networking equipment that connects households to an operator network, such as home gateways and routers, are major victims of cyber-attacks, being exposed to a number of threats, from misappropriation of user accounts by malicious agents to access to personal information and data, threatening users' privacy and security. The exposure surface to threats is even wider when the growing ecosystem of Internet-of-Things devices is considered. Thus, it is beneficial for the operator and customer that a security service is provided to protect this ecosystem. The service should be tailored to the particular needs and Internet usage profile of the customer network. For this purpose, Machine Learning methods can be explored to learn typical behaviours and identify anomalies. In this paper, we present preliminary insights into the architecture and mechanisms of a security service offered by an Internet Service Provider. We focus on Distributed Denial-of-Service kind of attacks and define the system requirements. Finally, we analyse the trade-offs of distributing the service between operator equipment deployed at the customer premises and cloud-hosted servers.

Keywords: Safe home · Cyber-security · Anomaly detection · Distributed systems · Hybrid environment · Machine learning

I. Maglogiannis et al. (Eds.): AIAI 2021 Workshops, IFIP AICT 628, pp. 311–322, 2021.
https://doi.org/10.1007/978-3-030-79157-5_26

1 Introduction

As the number of Internet-of-Things (IoT) devices increases in households, the exposure surface to cyber-attacks grows in proportion. IoT devices are often victims of poor security configurations and subject to zero-day exploits, and then enlisted to carry out Distributed Denial-of-Service (DDoS) attacks on other victims. Internet Service Providers (ISP), in their continuous improvement of the service offered to customers, are keen on extending their security services to protect the client devices from such attacks. To provision the Internet service, the ISP (or simply operator) deploys a set of equipment at the customer premises, called the Customer Premises Equipment (CPE), that typically provides routing to the Internet and local wired and wireless networking. Due to its strategic position, this equipment can play an pivotal role in increasing the security of the IoT ecosystem and of other devices that the customer may have at home.

Traditional rule-based approaches at securing the CPE and the customer network – such as TCP port blocking, IP and TLS certificate blacklisting, and traffic signatures – fail to capture the dynamics of attacks and of legitimate traffic. On the one hand, rules for blacklisting zero-day exploits take some time to be created by the security community and to be deployed at the CPE or at upstream network security devices. On the other hand, the diversity of customer traffic including IoT devices makes it extremely hard and cumbersome to define rules for whitelisting the legitimate traffic at each customer. These limitations call for machine learning (ML) techniques to be deployed on top of traditional approaches. With machine learning, legitimate traffic can be profiled and outliers more easily detected. Outliers may result from legitimate yet infrequent behavior, legitimate failure-related anomalous behavior, or attacks – the latter being of interest to security. Machine learning can also be used to profile malicious traffic, learning to predict attacks that do not reuse blacklisted IPs or certificates.

In this paper we discuss and outline a conceptual architecture for an ISP-supported cyber-security system based on machine learning techniques to provide secure Internet services to customers, particularly to the ecosystem of IoT devices. ML techniques will be explored as a flexible mechanism for studying and modelling the traffic observed by the CPE and the CPE's behaviour itself, e.g., traffic profiling, anomalous traffic detection, number of requests to CPE, number of times CPE is resetting in a certain period of time, among others. The IoT security system will feature a distributed architecture, where software components running at the edge node can be complemented by cloud-hosted components. For example, the ML algorithm can be trained at a cloud server, due to its larger computing capacity, and the edge node may host the trained version of the algorithm (to be updated regularly) to carry out the inference task of identifying potential attacks.

To achieve the conceptual ISP-supported architecture for secure Internet provision to customers' homes, we will follow an agile approach:

- define security models for the attacks of interest and the requirements of the IoT security system (functional, technical, and design);

- design an hybrid architecture (edge and cloud) to host a distributed ML mechanism towards providing security to domestic IoT devices;
- outline the steps of development and testing and concerns associated with the development of such system, e.g., data privacy-related (GRDP);
- understand how can this type of architecture be easily and horizontally explored by other use cases with minor customisation.

The remainder of this document is as follows. We present a review of the related literature in Sect. 2, focusing on DDoS attacks. Our use-case, attack models and requirements elicited are described in Sect. 3. Section 4 presents considerations about the architecture and development of the proposed system. Final remarks are drawn in Sect. 5. This work is being carried out within the Eureka ITEA3 *MIRAI*[1] project.

2   Related Work

A taxonomy of types of attacks can be found in [3] and a review of Machine Learning (ML) solutions for IoT security can be found in [11]. A review of ML techniques specifically applied to anomaly detection is presented in [7]. In the following discussion, we review mostly works proposing Intrusion Detection Systems (IDS) that aim specifically at detecting Distributed Denial-of-Service (DDoS) attacks through ML techniques (and, to a lesser extent, works that aim at undifferentiated detection of abnormal traffic). We observe that much of these efforts rely on supervised learning techniques (leveraging existing public datasets), and that a number of works target networks managed by software-defined networking (SDN) techniques, as the SDN paradigm allows to gather a comprehensive view of the network traffic. Table 1 summarizes the most relevant features from all references.

The authors of [9] propose an intrusion detection system tailored to identify low rate (LR) DDoS attacks in SDN settings. Six ML models are compared (see Table 1), using the Canadian Institute of Cybersecurity (CIC) DoS dataset. A Multi-Layer Perceptron (MLP), a type of neural network, obtained the best accuracy, around 95%. In [10], also four ML techniques are applied to the identification of DDoS attacks, over datasets collected by the authors. Decision trees offered the best detection performance. The work described in [2] also addresses detection of DDoS attacks through multiple ML techniques. The authors explore "IoT-specific network behaviors (e.g., limited number of endpoints and regular time intervals between packets)" to improve accuracy of DDoS detection. The techniques explored are K-nearest neighhours, linear-kernel support vector machine (SVM), decision trees, random forests, and a neural network, over a purposefully-collected dataset. The authors of [12] propose a deep learning approach to DDoS detection, specifically through the use of various types of recurrent neural networks (RNN). It is reported that the error rate is reduced

---

[1] https://itea3.org/project/mirai.html.

Table 1. Review of relevant ML-based techniques for security.

	Title	Focus/Scope	Techniques	Datasets
[9]	A Flexible SDN-Based Architecture for Identifying and Mitigating Low-Rate DDoS Attacks Using Machine Learning	DDoS attack detection in SDN; focus on low-rate attacks	J48, Random Tree, REP Tree, Random Forest, Multi-Layer Perceptron (MLP), Support Vector Machines (SVM)	DDoSSim, GoldenEye, H.U.L.K., R.U.D.Y., Slow Body, Slow Headers, Slowloris, Slow Read
[10]	Machine learning algorithms to detect DDoS attacks in SDN	DDoS attack detection in SDN	MLP, SVM, Decision Tree, Random Forest	Own
[2]	Machine Learning DDoS Detection for Consumer Internet of Things Devices	DDoS attack detection in SDN, focus on IoT devices	K-nearest neighbors "KDTree" algorithm, support vector machine with linear kernel, decision tree and random forest, 4-layer feed-forward NN	Own
[1]	The DDoS attacks detection through machine learning and statistical methods in SDN	DDoS attack detection in SDN; low- and high-volume attacks	Combination of entropy-based method and classification algorithm	UNB-ISCX, CTU-13, ISOT-normal traffic
[12]	DeepDefense: Identifying DDoS Attack via Deep Learning	DDoS attack detection	Various types of neural networks: Convolutional (CNN), Recurrent (RNN), Long Short-Term Memory (LSTM), and Gated Recurrent Unit (GTU)	ISCX2012
[5]	An LSTM-Based Deep Learning Approach for Classifying Malicious Traffic at the Packet Level	Anomaly detection, including but not limited to DDoS attacks	Long Short-Term Memory (LSTM) neural network	USTC-TFC2016, Mirai-RGU, Mirai-CCU
[4]	Unsupervised Deep Learning Model for Early Network Traffic Anomaly Detection	Anomaly detection	Convolutional Neural Network (CNN) and Autoencoder (a type of NN) used in unsupervised mode	ISCX2012, USTC-TFC2016, Mirai-RGU, Mirai-CCU

from 7.517% to 2.103% with respect to conventional machine learning models, specifically Random Forest. In [5], the authors also leverage a Long Short-Term Memory (LSTM) neural network to detect malicious traffic (not exclusively DDoS attacks) at packet-level. The system is evaluated using literature datasets and the authors' own dataset on the MIRAI botnet; an accuracy of 97.22% is reported. Finally, an IDS leveraging an unsupervised technique is proposed in [4]: the authors use a convolutional neural network (CNN) and an unsupervised Auto-Encoder (a type of NN) for network traffic anomaly detection.

There are several AI/ML approaches to perform of anomaly detection and thus thwart DDoS attacks. Neural networks (NN) take the center stage due to their attractive trade-off between computation cost, performance and flexibility (e.g., typically inferior computing cost than SVM; more flexibility than threshold rule-based decision trees), and due to the range of scope-specific architectures (e.g., recurrent NN, LSTM, convolutional NN) that are tailored to particular applications. In spite of this, considerable datasets and computation power are required, which most CPEs have in limited supply. Thus, the importance of exploring hybrid environments (edge and cloud) to implement complex AI algorithms is emerging in order to finally achieve the balance among data, computation and accuracy.

3   Use-Case and Requirements

3.1   Use-Case Description

The proposed IoT security system will ensure coverage of the customers' devices as a flexible protection solution that the customer can configure and adapt to the needs of the household. The system will be integrated directly in home gateways, supported by intelligence in the cloud, and supplemented by mobile applications that ensure services such as household member profiling to adapt browsing protection and parental control as well as privacy management.

3.2   Actors

For convenience, we identify the main actors in the use-case: **Customer**; **Attacker** and **Operator**. The setting is the Customer network, enabled by the Operator equipment and infrastructure. We identify the following relevant infrastructure/equipment/agents:

- **Home Gateway and Router:** equipment deployed by the Operator that: (i) enables the Customer network; and (ii) connects the Customer network to Operator Infrastructure. Typically, both network nodes (gateway and router) are provided by the same physical equipment.
- **Customer-Premises Equipment (CPE):** any type of Operator-provided equipment deployed in the Customer premises, including but not limited to the home gateway and router (e.g., WiFi range extenders). In practice, and unless otherwise noted, the term *CPE* is used to identify the home gateway & router.
- **Customer Network:** network (wireless and wired) enabled by the Operator equipment at the Customer's house to which only Customer devices are connected and that is, ideally, secured against unauthorized associations or attacks.
- **Customer Devices:** the set of devices connected to the Customer network, with particular focus on IoT devices.
- **Attacker Agent (Malware):** an agent (typically software) that can: (i) grant control of a Customer Device to an Attacker; (ii) participate in (D)DoS attacks.
- **Operator Infrastructure:** service and networking infrastructure that connects the Customer network to Internet.
- **IoT Security System (or System):** system aiming to consolidate the security of the Customer network against external threats and attacks.

3.3   Requirements Elicitation

In the context of the setting described in the previous section, we list the requirements of the proposed system.

Functional Requirements

- **Req. #1 - Always-on Monitoring:** The System shall monitor traffic patterns 24/7 to find indicators of security threats and attacks.
- **Req. #2 - Smart and Customized Protection:** The System shall learn the patterns of traffic of applications concerning IoT devices, and use the protection profile that best suits the identified patterns.
- **Req. #3 - Mitigation of Scale Attacks:** The System shall provide mitigation mechanisms against large scale attacks.
- **Req. #4 - Automated Zero-Day Attack Mitigation:** The System shall provide detection and mitigation mechanisms against vulnerabilities of the IoT devices that are unknown *a priori*.
- **Req. #5 - Analysis:** If an attack is ongoing, the System shall provide a detailed report in real-time or near real-time during the attack, and complete resume after it. The System shall provide a global report with information about all installed CPE to have knowledge about how many CPE were exposed to attacks, and which was the attack profile/type.
- **Req. #6 - Metrics:** The System shall provide metrics related to vulnerabilities and attacks that have been identified and thwarted (or not).
- **Req. #7 - Alerts:** The System shall provide the possibility for the Operator and/or Customer to be informed whenever a vulnerability and/or attack is detected.

Design Requirements

- **Req. #1 - Operation in Home Gateways:** The System shall be integrated directly and operate in the Home Gateways.
- **Req. #2 - Edge/cloud architecture:** The System may be complemented by components deployed outside the Home Gateway, namely mechanisms to support the operation of the System deployed in edge and/or cloud platforms.

Technical Requirements

- **Req. #1 - RDK:** The System shall use the operating system RDK at the Home Gateways.

3.4   Attack and Threat Models

To support the functional requirements identified in the previous section, specific attack and threat models need to be defined. By *attack*, we refer to malicious activity that disrupts regular service, targeting customer devices, operator equipment, and/or third-party nodes.

The IoT security system shall provide the following services:

- **Service #1:** detect and mitigate involvement of customer devices in attack attempts (e.g., DoS) to other parties (to other devices in the customer network; to infrastructure of the operator; to external parties);
- **Service #2:** detect and mitigate DoS attacks to the Customer Devices.

Figure 1 represents generically the attack and threat model over the target scenario.

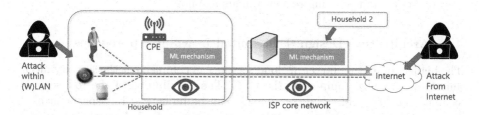

Fig. 1. Attack and threat model to the customer premises.

4   Design Considerations and Development Process

We propose to leverage artificial intelligence and machine learning (AI/ML) and an edge/cloud distributed architecture to implement the IoT security system (or simply system). DoS attacks are best addressed by traffic profiling, as learning the traffic patterns of legitimate customer devices enables the system to identify anomalous behaviours. Profiles are very user-dependent and, as such, an approach based on AI/ML offers the flexibility to extract meaningful characterizing features from a wide variety of traffic profiles. AI/ML techniques typically involve two stages: the learning stage, in which the model is trained, and the inference stage, in which the trained model merely classifies input samples. The two stages need not to be performed in the same physical/logical component, adding to flexibility in the design of the architecture discussed next.

4.1   Development Process

The development of the IoT security system will follow an Agile development (develop, integrate, test, demo, feedback, improve). The ML development lifecycle involves additional steps, such as collecting or identifying datasets to train and test the developed ML models. The following points can already be identified (and are discussed further in subsequent sections):

- **Architecture Design** (Sect. 4.2): we will evaluate existing ML models and how they can be deployed in such distributed edge/cloud computation architecture, taking into consideration: (i) the resource-constrained nature of CPEs vs. higher computing power of cloud nodes; (ii) data availability on either edge and cloud components; and (iii) possibility of using distributed algorithms and/or of the model training and inference stages being performed in different components.
- **Training AI/ML models** (Sect. 4.3): we will produce or identify a dataset of network traffic to build and train ML models in a fashion that complies with the EU Ethics Guidelines for trustworthy AI. The ML model will be refined over multiple iterations to achieve an adequate performance and it will be validated over the distributed architecture.
- **Evaluation and Customer Perception** (Sect. 4.4): When the performance of ML models achieve a good accuracy, the proposed system will be tested in a real-environment using real customers as pilots.

4.2   Architecture Design: Distributed Learning Approaches

The higher computing power of cloud servers can complement the security mechanisms at the edge equipment, the CPE. The distribution of the IoT security system over edge and cloud components can be influenced by aspects such as: (i) adopted ML strategy: some ML approaches may lend themselves better to distributed training than others; (ii) data protection: different strategies may require different exchanges of sensitive data; (iii) required data exchange & bandwidth: moving large (network traffic) datasets between edge and cloud is not ideal. We discuss some of the possible strategies for the distribution of the tools for traffic profiling and anomalous traffic detection.

1. Train and inference at CPE: AI/ML techniques are typically computationally expensive, particularly at the training stage, and CPEs (e.g., home gateway and router) are often limited in computational capacity. To perform training or inference at the resource-constrained CPE, strategies such as trading off classification accuracy for resource usage (e.g., using fixed point instead of floating point variables) can be explored. By keeping all user data at the CPE, there is less exposure of user data while traffic data or profiles are being reported back to cloud, albeit measures are necessary to ensure the protection of locally stored data.

2. Train at Cloud: All traffic between the customer network and the Internet passes through the operator's core network, where the necessary computing power to train the models can be assumed to exist. In this scenario, the model can be trained at the cloud and then either the inference stage is carried out at the cloud server or the trained model can be transferred to the CPE and updated regularly. However, servers at the core network do not observe traffic occurring within the customer network (i.e., device-to-device) unless intentionally mirrored (incurring a penalty in edge-to-cloud traffic). In addition, the observation of customer traffic at the core network may miss information to detect some types of attacks, such as those leveraging covert timing channels.

3. Transfer Learning [13]: The operator may leverage its access to a larger number of households to create generic models that are then fine-tuned to particular customers. This modular training that some ML algorithms can perform allows to ease the training requirements on the CPE. For example, neural networks can be trained by the operator using large datasets from multiple households with similar traffic patterns. At each household, the generic model can be refined by just retraining the last layer of neurons.

4. Federated Learning [6,8]: Federated learning is a variation of the previous approach, aiming at the development of a high-quality centralized model by aggregating updates provided by multiple clients. While some learning takes place at the edge node (CPE), the requirement on the quality of training at the CPE is alleviated, allowing to benefit of techniques for operation in resource-constrained platforms. In turn, and leveraging a transfer learning approach, the high-quality centralized mode can be transferred back to the CPE for inference operation. However, this option requires identifying and developing an ML algorithm that can learn a shared model from local updates. Also, home network-specific aspects captured in the edge updates, such as detection of intrusions originating in the local network, may be eroded when computing the global model.

Table 2 condenses some of the trade-offs to be considered in the final decision. We discuss the expected model quality, required flows between edge and cloud, and the exposure of the user data while in transit between components. On the point of user data exposure, we take as implicit the need to store data securely both at CPE and cloud server; our focus is on identifying whether there is the need to transmit logs or profiles of user behaviours between the edge and cloud components, thus increasing the exposure of that sensitive information. While the first approach is not strictly distributed (*Training/inference at CPE*), it is discussed as a baseline to the remaining. In the second approach (*Train at Cloud*), the operator may choose whether monitoring traffic internal to the customer network is relevant for the service or not; if it is, such option entails transmitting some sensitive customer traffic information to the cloud. Finally, Transfer Learning and Federated Learning offer a similar distributed architecture, with the latter requiring only the transfer of trained updates or models.

4.3 Training AI/ML Models and Ethical Pillars for Trustworthy AI

There are several AI/ML approaches to perform anomaly detection and thus thwart DDoS attacks. The method (or methods) selected for the IoT security system should offer performance that meets the agreed service levels, and be suited to operate over a distributed architecture. From the review performed in Sect. 2, neural networks offer an appealing trade-off between performance and computation cost. Neural networks also benefit of high level of design and

Table 2. Trade-offs to be considered in selecting a distributed architecture.

Approach	Criteria to inform selection			
	Model quality	Edge-cloud flows	Cloud-edge flows	In-transit exposure of user data
Train/inference at CPE	Limited: only CPE resources to train/infer	None	None	Kept solely at CPE
Train at cloud	Limited, if traffic within home network is not considered	Intra-home network traffic data (if desired)	Trained model transferred to edge	In-transit to cloud
Transfer learning	Model training uses traffic data from many customers; edge learning may be limited	Intra-home network traffic data (if desired)	Trained model transferred to edge	In-transit to cloud
Federated learning	Model training uses traffic data from many customers; customer-specific threats may get overlooked	Only training updates sent to cloud	Trained model transfered to edge	Only training updates or models are exchanged

operational flexibility that allows them to be mapped into one of the distributed strategies discussed in the previous subsection.

Developing a system to provide user-tailored security requires the machine learning models to be trained with traffic drawn from actual customer networks. This raises data privacy issues to be addressed within the scope of the General Data Protection Regulation (GDPR). In complement to privacy concerns, the European Commission presented on the April 8th, 2019, the Ethics Guidelines for Trustworthy AI. According to the guidelines, trustworthy AI should be:

1. lawful - respecting all applicable laws and regulations;
2. ethical - respecting ethical principles and values;
3. robust - both from a technical perspective while taking into account its social environment.

Based on these principles, the guidelines provide seven key requirements to use AI assuring its trustworthiness:

1. Human agency and oversight;
2. Technical robustness and safety;
3. Privacy and data governance;
4. Transparency;
5. Diversity, non-discrimination and fairness;
6. Societal and environment well-being;
7. Accountability.

The implementation of the proposed architecture involves the development of AI/ML models and, consequently, collecting data several times throughout the AI/ML development life-cycle. During the implementation, the EU Ethics guidelines will be taken into account in order to assure the transparency and trust, but also to prepare the architecture for a production environment following all

European recommendations. Thus, we will try to adopt Trustworthy AI when developing, deploying or using AI models, and adapt it to our secure IoT framework use case.

4.4 Evaluation and Perception of Security by Customers

When the outcomes of ML models achieve a good accuracy and performance, the proposed architecture will be tested in a real-environment using real customers as pilots. The pilot tests are important not only for getting information about ML models and system performance, but also for gathering feedback from the customers, particularly:

- if they feel safer knowing that the CPE also provides a service to protect their IoT environment;
- if they still have concerns regarding their privacy (not only related to attacks but also data to be processed by the algorithm);
- if they feel that the new service is affecting the quality of Internet service;
- if they would be willing to keep this type of service and, if yes, under which business models (free of charge, subscription, pay-per-use, others...).

5 Conclusion

This work presented the use-case of secure Internet provision to customers that use IoT devices and are served by an Internet Service Provider. The motivation is to develop a security system capable of detecting Denial-of-Service attacks involving the IoT devices. This is a preliminary study in which we defined an attack model and the security system requirements. This work allowed exposing the main design trade-offs that need to be considered when deciding the distribution of the service components between the edge and cloud. Future work involves the service implementation, training and profiling.

Acknowledgements. This work was partially supported by National Funds through FCT/MCTES (Portuguese Foundation for Science and Technology), within the CISTER Research Unit (UIDB/04234/2020), and by the Portuguese National Innovation Agency (ANI) through the Operational Competitiveness Programme and Internationalization (COMPETE 2020) under the PT2020 Partnership Agreement, through the European Regional Development Fund (ERDF), within project(s) grant nr. 69522, POCI-01-0247-FEDER-069522 (MIRAI).

References

1. Dehkordi, A.B., Soltanaghaei, M., Boroujeni, F.Z.: The DDoS attacks detection through machine learning and statistical methods in SDN. J. Supercomput. **77**, 1–33 (2020). https://doi.org/10.1007/s11227-020-03323-w

2. Doshi, R., Apthorpe, N., Feamster, N.: Machine learning DDoS detection for consumer internet of things devices. In: 2018 IEEE Security and Privacy Workshops (SPW), San Francisco, CA, pp. 29–35. IEEE, May 2018. https://doi.org/10.1109/SPW.2018.00013

3. Hassija, V., Chamola, V., Saxena, V., Jain, D., Goyal, P., Sikdar, B.: A survey on IoT security: application areas, security threats, and solution architectures. IEEE Access 7, 82721–82743 (2019). https://doi.org/10.1109/ACCESS.2019.2924045

4. Hwang, R.H., Lin, P.C., Nguyen, V.L.: An unsupervised deep learning model for early network traffic anomaly detection. IEEE Access 8, 13 (2020)

5. Hwang, R.H., Peng, M.C., Nguyen, V.L., Chang, Y.L.: An LSTM-based deep learning approach for classifying malicious traffic at the packet level. Appl. Sci. 9(16), 3414 (2019). https://doi.org/10.3390/app9163414

6. Konečný, J., McMahan, H.B., Yu, F.X., Richtárik, P., Suresh, A.T., Bacon, D.: Federated Learning: Strategies for Improving Communication Efficiency. arXiv:1610.05492 [cs], October 2017

7. Kwon, D., Kim, H., Kim, J., Suh, S.C., Kim, I., Kim, K.J.: A survey of deep learning-based network anomaly detection. Clust. Comput. 22(1), 949–961 (2017). https://doi.org/10.1007/s10586-017-1117-8

8. McMahan, H.B., Moore, E., Ramage, D., Hampson, S., Arcas, B.A.: Communication-Efficient Learning of Deep Networks from Decentralized Data. arXiv:1602.05629 [cs], February 2017

9. Perez-Diaz, J.A., Valdovinos, I.A., Choo, K.K.R., Zhu, D.: A flexible SDN-based architecture for identifying and mitigating low-rate DDoS attacks using machine learning. IEEE Access 8, 155859–155872 (2020). https://doi.org/10.1109/ACCESS.2020.3019330

10. Santos, R., Souza, D., Santo, W., Ribeiro, A., Moreno, E.: Machine learning algorithms to detect DDoS attacks in SDN. Concurr. Comput. Pract. Exp. 32(16), e5402 (2020). https://doi.org/10.1002/cpe.5402

11. Tahsien, S.M., Karimipour, H., Spachos, P.: Machine learning based solutions for security of internet of things (IoT): a survey. J. Netw. Comput. Appl. 161, 102630 (2020). https://doi.org/10.1016/j.jnca.2020.102630

12. Yuan, X., Li, C., Li, X.: DeepDefense: identifying DDoS attack via deep learning. In: 2017 IEEE International Conference on Smart Computing (SMARTCOMP), Hong Kong, China, pp. 1–8. IEEE, May 2017. https://doi.org/10.1109/SMARTCOMP.2017.7946998

13. Zhuang, F., et al.: A comprehensive survey on transfer learning. Proc. IEEE 109(1), 43–76 (2021). https://doi.org/10.1109/JPROC.2020.3004555

Energy Efficiency and Artificial Intelligence Workshop (EEAI 2021)

1st Energy Efficiency and Artificial Intelligence (EEAI) Workshop

Sustainable energy is hands down one of the biggest challenges of our times. As the EU sets its focus to reach its 2030 and 2050 goals, the role of private energy consumers becomes prevalent. The EU and member states are increasingly highlighting the need to complement supply-related measures (e.g. smart/efficient buildings, appliances and meters) with consumption-affecting initiatives (e.g. consumer empowerment, information and education, energy taxes and incentives).

Moreover, rather than only reducing energy consumption, novel approaches are needed that consider solutions for optimal management of local consumption and production due to an increasing number of so-called "prosumers" (consumers who also produce parts of their own energy, e.g. through photo-voltaic installations). This also calls for novel approaches to energy management in communities of prosumers that combine intelligent technologies with community-based incentives and services for a sharing economy.

The EEAI Workshop aims to bring together interdisciplinary approaches that focus on the application of AI-driven solutions for increasing and improving energy efficiency of residential and tertiary buildings and of occupant behaviour. Either applied directly on the building management systems, or aiming towards affecting energy-related occupant behavior to stimulate behavioural change, proposed solutions should enable more energy efficient and sustainable operation of buildings and stimulate energy-efficient consumer behaviour. Of particular interest are human-centered AI approaches that increase trustworthiness with explainable AI models and their results for non-expert users. The workshop also welcomes cross-domain approaches that investigate how to support energy efficiency by addressing both direct and indirect energy-related behaviour.

Organization

Program Chairs

Dimitrios Tzovaras	Information Technologies Institute, Centre for Research and Technology Hellas
Stelios Krinidis	Information Technologies Institute, Centre for Research and Technology Hellas
Jasminko Novak	IACS – Institute for Applied Computer Science, University of Applied Sciences Stralsund

Topics of Interest of EEAI include:

- Activity Tracking
- Recommendation systems
- Human-centered and Explainable AI
- Energy (load, generation) forecasting
- Persuasion Techniques
- Energy related occupant behaviour modelling
- User modeling
- Behavior prediction and analysishumanistic context
- Behavioural change for energy efficiency
- Energy management and services for prosumer communities
- Data visualization and visual analytics techniques
- Gamification
- Non-intrusive Load Monitoring & Disaggregation
- Flexibility estimation
- Building Automation
- Control Optimization

A Recommendation Specific Human Activity Recognition Dataset with Mobile Device's Sensor Data

Alexandros Vrochidis⬤, Vasileios G. Vasilopoulos⬤, Konstantinos Peppas⬤,
Valia Dimaridou, Iordanis Makaratzis, Apostolos C. Tsolakis⬤,
Stelios Krinidis(✉)⬤, and Dimitrios Tzovaras⬤

Information Technologies Institute, Centre for Research and Technology Hellas,
57001 Thessaloniki, Greece
krinidis@iti.gr

Abstract. Human activity recognition is a challenging field that grabbed considerable research attention in the last decade. Two types of models can be used for such predictions, those which use visual data and those which use data from inertial sensors. To improve the classification algorithms in the sensor category, a new dataset has been created, targeting more realistic activities, during which the user may be more prompt to receive and act upon a recommendation. Contrary to previous similar datasets, which were collected with the device in the user's pockets or strapped to their waist, the introduced dataset presents activities during which the user is looking on the screen, and thus most likely interacts with the device. The dataset from an initial sample of 31 participants was gathered using a mobile application that prompted users to do 10 different activities following specific guidelines. Finally, towards evaluating the resulting data, a brief classification benchmarking was performed with two other datasets (i.e., WISDM and Actitracker datasets) by employing a Convolutional Neural Network model. The results acquired demonstrate a promising performance of the model tested, as well as a high quality of the dataset created, which is available online on Zenodo.

Keywords: Mobile inference · Sensor mining · Human activity recognition ·
Deep neural network

1 Introduction

Human Activity Recognition (HAR) is a research topic with applications found in a wide variety of fields. It provides information about someone's activity automatically and unobtrusively, by using sophisticated technologies, such as computer vision and machine learning [1]. In general, depending on the application, the human activities

This work has been co-funded by the European Union and the General Secretariat of Research and Technology, Ministry of Development & Investments, under the project (SIT4Energy - T2EDK-0911) of the Bilateral S&T Cooperation Program Greece – Germany 2017.

© IFIP International Federation for Information Processing 2021
Published by Springer Nature Switzerland AG 2021
I. Maglogiannis et al. (Eds.): AIAI 2021 Workshops, IFIP AICT 628, pp. 327–339, 2021.
https://doi.org/10.1007/978-3-030-79157-5_27

examined can be either simple like jogging or walking, or more complex like peeling a potato. A characteristic example of HAR can be found in the sports field [2], where it can help recognize the sport-related activities over common domestic activities. According to Chen and Shen [3], each individual has its own specific and discriminative movement patterns and should be treated accordingly. Resulting such complexities, an apparent challenge arises, which can be addressed only if there is an adequate amount of data to properly explore the extreme heterogeneity identified. Hence, the need of creating and making available HAR datasets of high quantity and quality becomes apparent.

Quite a lot of such datasets have been collected over the years, not always in the most optimal way. There are datasets for video methods like the 20BN-something-something V2 [4], the VLOG dataset [5], and the EPIC-KITCHENS [6]. This kind of dataset requires camera setups, which introduces a greater risk of violating the privacy of participants, which is one of the reasons that it is more difficult to create this kind of datasets. To tackle this problem, Ryoo et al. [15], proposed a fundamental approach of HAR, that uses low-resolution anonymized videos. In this way, privacy is protected and computing costs are reduced. However, Beyond privacy, there are also additional issues identified and highlighted in the literature. Zhang et al. [12], state what difficulties appeared, on this kind of research, like long-distance and low-quality videos, which are common in these cases. To mitigate such problems, more expensive approaches are used, either in terms of equipment or processing. Pradhan et al. [13] proposed a system based on event-based camera data while facing the very low latency and data sparsity coming from event-based vision sensors. Depth cameras can also be used for classifying human activities. In their research Jalal et al. [14], created a robust HAR model from analyzing continuous sequences of depth map.

On the other hand, sensor-type datasets are not so heavy to manipulate and they do not usually face privacy problems. Some datasets in this category are the Physical Activity Monitoring for Aging People (PAMAP2) [7], which contains 18 different physical activities, the University of Southern California Human Activity Dataset (USC-HAD) [8], which is consisted of low-level daily activities like cleaning the house and the Wearable Human Activity Recognition Folder (WHARF) [9], which includes accelerometer data recordings that are used for the recognition of simple daily life activities with wearable sensing systems. These datasets, used wearable sensors like heart rate monitors, watches, and devices that include IMUs sensors. On the contrary, the Wireless Sensor Data Mining (WISDM) [10] and Actitracker [11] datasets, which are quite extensively being used in the literature and are further analyzed in the next section, are two datasets containing data coming only for mobile devices inertial sensors. Such datasets become more and more important, as mobile devices have become a necessity and are a data-rich environment for various applications.

The dataset presented in the present study belongs to the sensor type of dataset, as it uses triaxial data, coming from inertial sensors of mobile phones. The challenge that the introduce dataset aims to address is that of identifying the optimal timing for delivering a recommendation or a nudge to the user, with the highest probability of acting upon it. Following the notion of micro-moments [16], the ideal moment to deliver a recommendation to the user, with the maximum impact, can be found during or in between other activities, and not when the user is not actively interacting with the mobile device. The ultimate goal is to employ this dataset towards training an activity tracking model that will be able to recognize activities while the mobile screen is activated, meaning that most likely the user is looking at it and interacts with the device.

To create this dataset, an android mobile application was developed and was afterwards circulated to a wide audience throughout Europe. Users were called to perform 10 different activities (i.e., variations of standing, siting, walking, running, lying down, ascending or descending stairs) while they were looking at the mobile screen. Following the authors' re-definition of Micro-moments [16], the activity tracking recognition is only used when the mobile device's screen is turned on because these moments produce the highest probability of the user looking at the device and being alert. Previously used datasets like WISDM [10] and Actitracker [11], were collected through devices that were inside the user's pockets or strapped to a belt in their waist. In this case, for all activities (except the one that mobile is left on a table surface), the dataset is gathered while users look at the phone screen.

To properly assess the created dataset, a benchmarking is also delivered over these three datasets, using a state-of-the-art Convolution Neural Network (CNN), towards evaluating not only the performance of such an approach over the datasets, but also the quality of the dataset itself.

The rest of this paper is organized as follows. In Sect. 2, related work on both the challenge addressed and other related datasets is presented. In Sect. 3, the methodology for creating the dataset is described in detail, followed by brief documentation of the CNN employed for the evaluation, including the relevant metrics in Sect. 4. Then, Sect. 5 presents the evaluation results of the dataset. Finally, Sect. 6 concludes the manuscript, along with future improvements.

2 Related Work

2.1 Human Activity Recognition

Human activity recognition (HAR) is the problem of identifying the specific action of a human, based on sensor data and it is a time-series classification task that is challenging. Actions like these can be, specific movements when someone is indoors or they can also be activities like walking, jogging, and ascending stairs. Sensor data can remotely be recorded and recognition tasks like that seek a profound high-level knowledge of human activities from sensor data. Many of the proposed methods are including deep learning. Wang et al. [17], surveyed the advance of deep learning-based sensor activity recognition. They tried to find which models are the best ones for each activity recognition challenge. Each model is proposed for different activity recognition, depending on its length and type.

Hassan et al. [18], proposed a deep learning method for human activity recognition, that uses smartphone inertial sensors. They first extracted features, using Kernel Principal Component Analysis (KPCA) and Linear Discriminant Analysis (LDA) to make their model robust. Then they trained a Deep Belief Network (DBN) for activity recognition. Comparing their method with Support Vector Machine (SVM) and Artificial Neural Networks (ANN) models, they found that their model has better accuracy in both traditional and non-traditional activities. The overall accuracy of their model was 95.85%.

Two years later, Peppas et al. [19], approached the problem by using Convolutional Neural Networks, proposing a model, which can make real-time physical activity recognition on smart mobile devices. Tri-axial accelerometer data were used, taken from mobile devices of humans when they were in the activities. Then by using a two-layer Convolutional Neural Network (CNN), they achieved 94.18% accuracy on the WISDM dataset, while they reduced storage space by 5–8 times.

HAR can be used for environmental purposes too. In [16], a Google Activity Recognition API was used, for recognizing the user's physical activity, while possible detected activities in this API are in a vehicle, on a bicycle, on foot, still, tilting, and unknown. Researchers used this, for recognizing activities like when someone's device is still and when it is tilting. Tilting is recognized when a device's angle is changed significantly. When someone picks his phone from the table, or when he is sitting and then standing up, the API classifies the activity as tilting. After recognizing the activities, they tried to find some moments, which were redefined as micro-moments, in which energy-related recommendations will be sent to users, to maximize their receptiveness. Their purpose was to create a novel approach to changing energy behavior by using a mobile application for exploiting user attributes of micro-moments.

2.2   Previous HAR Datasets

The Wireless Sensor Data Mining project [10] was developed by Fordham University. Its goal was to explore the research issues related to mining data from mobile device's inertial sensors. An Android-based application was built to collect data from users. Phones that contained tri-axial accelerometers were used to produce data. Their users were 29 volunteers which were asked to do some specific activities while they had their mobile phone in their pocket. These activities were six in total, including jogging, walking, ascending and descending stairs, sitting, and standing.

From raw accelerometer data, 43 features were extracted and they were collected every 50 ms, so for each second, there were 20 samples. After collecting data, some machine learning algorithms were used for evaluating the dataset. Results show that high levels of accuracy can be achieved, for two of the most common activities, which are walking and jogging. For walking the accuracy achieved was 93.6%, by using a logistic regression algorithm and for jogging, the score was 98.3% by using a multilayer perceptron algorithm. High accuracy was also achieved, in other activities. Walking upstairs and walking downstairs were two of the lowest accuracies achieved. In walking upstairs class, the score was 61.5% with multilayer perceptron algorithm and for walking downstairs the accuracy was 55.5% with the J48 algorithm.

Actitracker [11] was a similar project by Fordham University and its difference with WISDM is that this dataset is a real-world one, while the other is a controlled testing dataset. This dataset also consists of tri-axial accelerometer data samples while it is bigger than the previous one. In this project, there were 563 volunteers. In all cases, data were collected in total 20 times for each second.

The activities that were tracked in this dataset were the same as in WISDM. They include walking upstairs and downstairs, standing, sitting, jogging, and walking. The difference here is that these activities take place in an uncontrolled environment. The total number of samples is also much higher due to more volunteers. In this dataset, there were 2.980.765 samples while in WISDM there were 1.098.207.

The main difference with the CHARM dataset is that these datasets, contain data originating from mobile inertial sensors, while the device is either in the user's pocket or mounted on a belt. In the CHARM case, those micro-moments that the user looks at the screen, should be found. This is the reason that a new dataset had to be created with data collected when the user looks at the screen. Moreover, knowing the android model of the device and some demographic information about each user can help in better analysis.

3   CERTH Human Activity Recognition Mobile (CHARM) Dataset

To have a well-formed dataset, a custom android mobile application was created and distributed to various users around Europe. This application was given to each user, alongside some instructions, and each user should give some general demographic information about him. The number of users was restricted to 31 and was distributed remotely due to coronavirus restrictions. After doing this, he should follow the instructions, and he should do activities like walking, running, ascending stairs, etc., while he had his phone on hand. Users could skip an activity in case it was difficult for them to complete. Since there were various mobile devices among the users, the accelerometer calibrations were different and the only common setting was the sampling rate, which contributes to the in the wild nature of the dataset.

Table 1. Information about the activities done by users.

Activity	Number of repetitions	Duration
Sitting on a chair	2 Repetitions	30 s
Sitting on a couch	2 Repetitions	30 s
Standing	2 Repetitions	30 s
Lying up	2 Repetitions	30 s
Lying by side	2 Repetitions	30 s
Device on surface	2 Repetitions	30 s
Walking	2 Repetitions	30 s
Running	2 Repetitions	30 s
Walking upstairs	6 Repetitions	10 s
Walking downstairs	6 Repetitions	10 s

Each activity had a start button, which defines its start and end after 35 s. Walking upstairs and downstairs last 90 s and they are segmented in 15-s intervals, which means that each user has to walk stairs 6 times upwards and 6 downwards. The frequency of the accelerometer data collection is 20 Hz, which means that data were collected every 50 ms. There was a total of 20 samples for each second and after ending, each user was asked if everything went according to the rules, or not. If not, the user should repeat the process. The android application used tri-axial accelerometer data to record each activity. After completing the activities, these data are uploaded to a server, where they can be retrieved afterward. All activities can be seen in Table 1.

Except knowing the device's models of users participated in the CHARM dataset, some demographic information was held, respectively to GDPR law. Most of the users were between the ages 25–50 and between the height of 171–180. 4 participants were less than 25 years old, 21 were between 25–50, and 6 were 51–75, which shows a variety in measurements. As for the height, there were 6 between 150–160 cm, 7 between 161–170 cm, 10 between 171–180 cm, 7 between 181–190 cm, and 1 between 191–200 cm.

The database used is InfluxDB and it is an open-source time-series database. This allows the overall size reduction and easier data handling, while each type of data is stored in separate tables. These tables are the registration, the accelerometer data, and the gyro data. The connection of the mobile application to the database is established through the InfluxDB-java client library. The application requires the SDK28 to run on Android 8.0 or newer versions. Its structure enables the registration of multiple users from the same device. Each user can append measurements to the database, after following specific instructions and confirming the proper completion of the activity. All users could delete personal information from the database and could also delete their measurements, according to GDPR laws. Furthermore, the data of each user is anonymized, so that a user cannot be identified from its data.

Table 2. Number of the CERTH HAR data points per activity.

Activity	Number of data points	Percentage (%)
Sitting on a chair	37.144	12.55
Sitting on a couch	35.344	11.94
Standing	31.190	10.54
Lying up	32.389	10.94
Lying by side	29.984	10.13
Device on surface	30.000	10.13
Walking	27.600	9.32
Running	22.792	7.70
Walking upstairs	24.396	8.24
Walking downstairs	25.188	8.51

Accelerometer data were divided into time windows, in order to exploit the temporal information and periodicity of the signals. Each window had 50 data points and its time duration was 2.5 s. There are 3 vectors $a_{x,y,z}$ in each data point, one for each axis. Then

40 statistical features for each window were created, to encode the global characteristics of the time series. The feature types created were the average (3 features), the standard deviation (3 features), the average absolute difference (3 features), the average resultant acceleration (1 feature), and the binned distribution (30 features). First, each time window of each channel is centered around its average, and then it is being fed to the network. These features are the same as the ones in the WISDM and Actitracker datasets [10] and an analysis of them was conducted in [19].

After completing the dataset retrieval procedure, some preprocessing methods were applied, to clear the dataset from incorrect measurements. Specifically, any measurement with a sampling frequency lower than 98% of the target one, which was 20 Hz, was discarded, along with any null values. The number of data points per activity is presented in Table 2. Some actions have more data points than others because more users completed them and it has to do with how difficult each action was. Some people were not able to run or climb stairs and that's why those actions have fewer data points. Sitting on a chair has most of the data points, while activities like running and walking stairs have the least, due to their difficulty.

4 Experimental Setup

To evaluate the produced dataset, a comparison was made with a state-of-the-art methodology, compared it with the two other datasets identified (i.e., the WISDM and Actitracker datasets).

4.1 Convolutional Neural Network

A convolutional neural network is a hierarchical Feed-Forward Neural Network (FFNN), in which each neuron in one layer is connected to all neurons in the next layer. They are inspired by the biological visual system. Apart from fully connected layers, it consists of convolutional layers. In those layers, the network learns filters that are sliding along the input data and they are applied to its sub-regions. Its architecture is presented in Fig. 1.

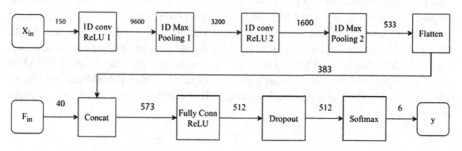

Fig. 1. Representation of the developed CNN architecture.

As explained in detail in [19], CHARM system architecture consists of 7 steps. Firstly, the accelerometer data which are sized 50 × 3 axis, are fed into the first layer with 192 convolutional filters. The kernel1 size is 12, and the stride of the convolution is 1. To its output, applied the ReLU function was applied. After that, a max-pooling layer follows. Its kernel size is 3 × 1 and its stride is 3. This way, feature representation is reduced by 3. Then, another convolutional layer is added, to learn more abstract and hierarchical features. It has 96 convolutional filters and a kernel size of 12. Step convolution is 1 and ReLU function is applied to its output. A final max-pooling layer with kernel size 3 × 1 and a stride of 3 is then used to further reduce the feature representation by 3. The output max-pooling layer is then flattened with the statistical features in 3. The joint vector is given to a fully connected layer that has 512 neurons and the ReLU function is applied to its output. A dropout layer was then added with a rate of 0.5 in order to avoid overfitting. Finally, the output of the layer is passed to a softmax layer, to compute a probability distribution over 10 activity classes. The optimizer used for the training model is a stochastic gradient descent with momentum and a constant learning rate.

4.2 Evaluation Metrics

To evaluate the results of this dataset some of the most common metrics, described in [20] were used to compute the performance of the neural network, with the CHARM dataset given. Firstly, the accuracy metric was calculated, which is the ratio of correct predictions over the total predictions, the precision metric, which represents the rate of correct predictions of a class over the total number of predictions for this class. Also, the recall metric was used, to compute the fraction of correct predictions of a class to the total real data points of it. Finally, using recall and precision, the f1 metric was computed, which is a combination of them and is described among the previously mentioned metrics.

4.3 Evaluation Scenarios

The scenarios used for evaluation were 3 in total, with scenario 1 being the training and testing with the CHARM dataset. In that case, cross-validation was used in order to not have the same data in the training and test split. Scenario 2 included a model trained with the CHARM dataset and tested with the WISDM and Actitracker datasets as input. Cross-validation was also used for computing evaluation metrics. Scenario 3 included two models in total. The first model was trained with the WISDM dataset and tested with the CHARM and the second was trained with the Actitracker dataset and tested with the CHARM dataset. To be able to make comparisons with the other models, CHARM labels were adapted to other dataset's number of labels. The CHARM dataset has 10 labels, while WISDM and Actitracker have 6. This adaptation was necessary, to make comparisons.

5   Results

To test the created dataset (which currently has 31 subjects in total) in real life use cases, we used the CNN model described in Sect. 4.1 and executed the experiments described above. Then the classification quality according to specific metrics, presented in Sect. 4.2

was calculated. Each experiment ran with the previously mentioned CNN in Sect. 4.1. Next, the training parameters used are described. Window size is described as Nw, while epochs are described as e. Optimizer momentum is described as β and learning rate as λ. For all of experiments, the window size had 50 data points. The model was trained for 100 epochs, while optimizer momentum was 0.9 and the learning rate was 0.01. This means that there were Nw = 50, e = 100, β = 0.9 and λ = 0.01. The datasets used for experiments are described in the appropriate Sect. 3.

Firstly, the CNN model was trained on the new dataset, and then, using the appropriate metrics, the model's accuracy, recall, precision, and f1 on the CHARM dataset, were counted. To keep the evaluation user-independent, a 10-fold cross-validation method was implemented and then, one model was trained with an Actitracker dataset and one with WISDM. Then, both of them were tested on the CHARM dataset. The results of CHARM metrics are presented in Table 3.

Table 3. 10-fold cross-validation results for CHARM dataset.

Metric	Average	Std. deviation
Accuracy	69.13%	7.33%
Precision	69.98%	17.81%
Recall	66.64%	18.24%
F1	66.45%	17.69%

Having examined the 10-fold cross-validation results, the confusion matrix of the CHARM dataset was created. In Table 4, the number of predictions for each class is presented and by this, activities that are confused can be seen. First, the average number of predictions for each class is calculated, followed by a percentage, that shows its relationship with the other classes. From this table, it can be seen that both static and dynamic activities are well classified. The activity that has the highest percentage is having the mobile on a surface with 98.8% and it is followed by Lying up with 85.6% and Lying Side reaching 80.5%. There is naturally a common misclassification between sitting on a chair and sitting on a couch. Couch had 33.6% misclassified as a chair, while chair had 27.1% misclassified as a couch. These two were the biggest percentages of misclassification. As for the dynamic activities like walking, running, upstairs, and downstairs, all activities were noticed having accuracy over 60% and the most confused one was upstairs with walking. Surprisingly it is not confused with downstairs. Similar confusion between walking and stairs had been mentioned in [19], however using the WISDM dataset. Walking is also most confused with upstairs and not with running.

After examining the confusion matrix of the CHARM model, comparisons with WISDM and Actitracker datasets were conducted. For scenario 1, the accuracy from cross-validation was 69.13%, while for scenario 2, when testing with the WISDM dataset the accuracy reached 79.73%. When the testing dataset was the Actitracker, the accuracy was 78.30%, which shows that the CHARM model can perform well with other input datasets. For scenario 3 when the training model was the WISDM the accuracy was

Table 4. Confusion matrix of the CHARM dataset.

	Chair	Couch	Standing	Surface	Lying up	Lying side	Walking	Running	Upstairs	Downstairs
Chair	**142.5** (45.4%)	85 (27.1%)	72.9 (23.2%)	2.9 (0.9%)	3 (1.0%)	0.8 (0.3%)	3.3 (1.1%)	0.7 (0.2%)	0.6 (0.2%)	2.5 (0.8%)
Couch	99.7 (33.6%)	**128.3** (43.2%)	33.4 (11.2%)	8.1 (2.7%)	11.4 (3.8%)	4.5 (1.5%)	4.6 (1.5%)	2.2 (0.7%)	1.9 (0.6%)	2.9 (1.0%)
Standing	69.1 (24.7%)	32.5 (11.6%)	**148** (52.9%)	11 (3.9%)	8.4 (3.0%)	0.4 (0.1%)	7.6 (2.7%)	0.1 (0.0%)	0.4 (0.1%)	2.3 (0.8%)
Surface	2.4 (0.9%)	0 (0.0%)	0 (0.0%)	**276.7** (98.8%)	0 (0.0%)	0 (0.0%)	0 (0.0%)	0.4 (0.1%)	0 (0.0%)	0.5 (0.2%)
Lying up	1.2 (0.4%)	13.9 (4.6%)	8.7 (2.9%)	12.5 (4.1%)	**259.5** (85.6%)	4.6 (1.5%)	0.7 (0.2%)	0.2 (0.1%)	0.4 (0.1%)	1.5 (0.5%)
Lying side	11 (3.9%)	19 (6.8%)	0.8 (0.3%)	5.5 (2.0%)	11.5 (4.1%)	**225.2** (80.5%)	2.3 (0.8%)	1.3 (0.5%)	1.1 (0.4%)	2.1 (0.8%)
Walking	2.6 (1.0%)	2.2 (0.9%)	8.7 (3.4%)	11.2 (4.3%)	0 (0.0%)	5 (1.9%)	**168.7** (65.5%)	11 (4.3%)	32.2 (12.5%)	16 (6.2%)
Running	0 (0.0%)	1.7 (0.8%)	0.5 (0.2%)	9.4 (4.4%)	0 (0.0%)	0.2 (0.1%)	17.3 (8.1%)	**128.8** (60.6%)	36.5 (17.2%)	18.3 (8.6%)
Upstairs	1.4 (0.7%)	1.7 (0.9%)	0.7 (0.4%)	6.6 (3.4%)	0 (0.0%)	0.3 (0.2%)	33.5 (17.1%)	8.6 (4.4%)	**125.3** (63.9%)	17.9 (9.1%)
Downstairs	1.6 (0.8%)	1.1 (0.5%)	3.4 (1.7%)	6.4 (3.2%)	0 (0.0%)	0.5 (0.2%)	28.3 (14.1%)	11 (5.5%)	24.2 (12.0%)	**124.9** (62.0%)

46.23% and when it was the Actitracker it was 30.74% which shows that accuracy is increased significantly when using the created dataset for training. This shows that the existing datasets are not accurate enough for our intended use case, so a new dataset such as CHARM is necessary. More detailed results could be seen in Fig. 2. In the left figure, the accuracy of CHARM models is presented in Y-axis, when it has as input the WISDM, Actitracker, and CHARM datasets respectively. In the right figure, scenario 3 is presented.

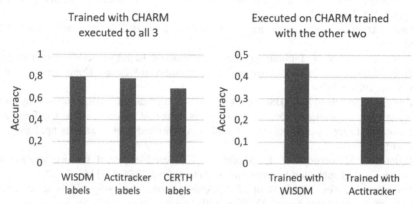

Fig. 2. Evaluation charts presenting CHARM, WISDM and Actitracker datasets.

6   Conclusions

In this paper, a more realistic new dataset has been presented in terms of Human Activity Recognition during activities through which the end-user might be more prompt to receive a recommendation towards a certain action. The presented dataset contains 31 participants and 10 activities, throughout which data from the mobile accelerometer and gyroscope have been collected, including also certain metadata (e.g., android version). After collecting and preprocessing the data, its added value was demonstrated by applying a classification model, based on a state-of-the art CNN model. Based on a benchmarking analysis performed with two other datasets, a 10-fold Cross-validation showed that the explored model works effectively in all three datasets, while the CHARM dataset is of the same high quality with its counterparts. It has also been proved that the model presented can perform well with other input datasets. In future work, the CHARM dataset (openly available in Zenodo [21]) is expected to grow even more, with more users throughout Europe, introducing significant scientific value to the research community.

References

1. Vrigkas, M., Nikou, C., Kakadiaris, I.A.: A review of human activity recognition methods. Front. Robot. AI **2**, 28 (2015)

2. Hsu, Y.L., Yang, S.C., Chang, H.C., Lai, H.C.: Human daily and sport activity recognition using a wearable inertial sensor network. IEEE **6**, 31715–31728 (2018)

3. Chen, Y., Shen, C.: Performance analysis of smartphone-sensor behavior for human activity recognition. IEEE Access **5**, 3095–3110 (2017)

4. Goyal, R., et al.: The "something something" video database for learning and evaluating visual common sense. In: Proceedings of the IEEE International Conference on Computer Vision (ICCV), pp. 5842–5850 (2017)

5. Fouhey, D.F., Kuo, W., Efros, A.A., Malik, J.: From lifestyle vlogs to everyday interactions. In: IEEE/CVF Conference on Computer Vision and Pattern Recognition, Salt Lake City, pp. 4991–5000 (2018)

6. Damen, D., et al.: Scaling egocentric vision: the EPIC-KITCHENS dataset. arXiv:1804.02748 (2018)

7. Reiss, A., Stricker, D.: Introducing a new benchmarked dataset for activity monitoring. In: Proceedings of the 2012 16th International Symposium on Wearable Computers, Newcastle UK, pp. 108–109 (2012)

8. Zhang, M., Sawchuk, A.A.: USC-HAD: a daily activity dataset for ubiquitous activity recognition using wearable sensors. In: Proceedings of the ACM International Conference on Ubiquitous Computing Workshop on Situation, Activity and Goal Awareness, pp. 1036–1043 (2012)

9. Bruno, B., Mastrogiovanni, F., Sgorbissa, A.: Wearable inertial sensors: applications, challenges, and public test benches. Robot. Autom. Mag. IEEE **22**, 116–124 (2015)

10. Kwapisz, J.R., Weiss, G.M., Moore, S.A.: Activity recognition using cell phone accelerometers. SIGKDD Explor. Newsl. **12**, 74–82 (2011)

11. Lockhart, J.W., Weiss, G.M., Xue, J.C., Gallagher, S.T., Grosner, A.B., Pulickal, T.T.: Design considerations for the WISDM smart phone sensor mining architecture. In: Proceedings of the Fifth International Workshop on Knowledge Discovery from Sensor Data, San Diego, CA, USA, 21–24 August, pp. 25–33 (2011)

12. Zhang, S., Wei, Z., Nie, J., Huang, L., Wang, S., Li, Z.: A review on human activity recognition using vision-based method. J. Healthc. Eng. **2017** (2017)

13. Pradhan, B.R., Bethi, Y., Narayanan, S., Chakraborty, A., Thakur, C.S.: n-HAR: a neuromorphic event-based human activity recognition system using memory surfaces. In: IEEE International Symposium on Circuits and Systems, Japan, pp. 1–5 (2019)

14. Jalal, A., Kim, Y.H., Kim, Y.J., Kamal, S., Kim, D.: Robust human activity recognition from depth video using spatiotemporal multi-fused features. Pattern Recogn. **61**, 295–308 (2017)

15. Ryoo, M., Rothrock, B., Fleming, C., Yang, H.J.: Privacy-Preserving human activity recognition from extreme low resolution. In: Proceedings of the AAAI Conference on Artificial Intelligence (2017)

16. Peppas, K., Chouliara, A., Tsolakis, A., Krinidis, S., Tzovaras, D.: Redefining micro-moments for improving energy behaviour: the SIT4Energy approach. In: IEEE SmartWorld, Ubiquitous Intelligence & Computing, Advanced & Trusted Computing, Scalable Computing & Communications, Cloud & Big Data Computing, Internet of People and Smart City Innovation (2019)

17. Wang, J., Yiqiang, C., Shuji, H., Xiaohui, P., Lisha, H.: Deep learning for sensor-based activity recognition: a survey. Pattern Recogn. Lett. **119**, 3–11 (2019)

18. Hassan, M.M., Uddin, M.D.Z., Mohamed, A., Almogren, A.: A robust human activity recognition system using smartphone sensors and deep learning. Futur. Gener. Comput. Syst. **81**, 307–313 (2018)

19. Peppas, K., Tsolakis, A., Krinidis, S., Tzovaras, D.: Real-time physical activity recognition on smart mobile devices using convolutional neural networks. Appl. Sci. **10**(23), 8482 (2020)

20. Sasaki, Y.: The truth of the F-measure. Teach Tutor Master (2007)
21. Vasilopoulos, G.V., et al.: CERTH Human Activity Recognition Mobile (CHARM) dataset. https://doi.org/10.5281/zenodo.4642560

Explainable Needn't Be (Much) Less Accurate: Evaluating an Explainable AI Dashboard for Energy Forecasting

Ana Grimaldo$^{(\boxtimes)}$ and Jasminko Novak

University of Applied Sciences Stralsund, IACS – Institute for Applied Computer Sciences, Stralsund, Germany
`{ana.grimaldo,jasminko.novak}@hochschule-stralsund.de`

Abstract. This paper presents the evaluation results of an improved version of an interactive tool for energy demand and supply forecasting, based on the combination of explainable machine learning with visual analytics. The prototype applies a kNN algorithm to forecast energy demand and supply from historical data (consumption, production, weather) and presents the results in an interactive visual dashboard. The dashboard allows the user to understand how the forecast relates to the input parameters and to analyse different forecast alternatives. It provides small utilities not familiar with AI with an easily understandable, while sufficiently accurate tool for energy forecasting in prosumer scenarios. The evaluation of the forecast accuracy has shown our method to be only 0.26%–1.73% less accurate than more sophisticated, but less explainable machine learning methods. Moreover, the achieved accuracy (MAPE 5.06%) is sufficient for practical needs of the application scenario. The evaluation with potential end-users also provided positive results regarding the usability, understandability and usefulness for the intended application context.

Keywords: Explainable AI · Visual analytics · Energy forecasting · AI benchmarking · Smart Energy Management Dashboard

1 Introduction

The concept of smart grids includes the integration of real-time energy production of renewable sources (e.g. solar power plants) as well as the need for prompt identification of changes in the energy demand [1]. Conventional practices, especially in local or small utilities were focused on heuristic forecasting based on their previous experience or on the application of relatively simple statistical methods to support the operations related to the management of energy supply and demand. However, these practices have become obsolete with the increase of prosumers in the grids as well as the inclusion of additional factors related to renewable energy sources [2]. As a result, utilities are looking for new ways to get accurate forecasts to increase efficiency and productivity.

© IFIP International Federation for Information Processing 2021
Published by Springer Nature Switzerland AG 2021
I. Maglogiannis et al. (Eds.): AIAI 2021 Workshops, IFIP AICT 628, pp. 340–351, 2021.
https://doi.org/10.1007/978-3-030-79157-5_28

To improve their energy-related operations, large utilities have relied on the use of sophisticated forecasting systems; however, these tools usually use complex forecasting methods based on *"black-box"* models which are difficult to understand by people with non-technical knowledge [3, 4]. This is particularly challenging for small utilities that commonly don't have the required technical know-how and AI expertise.

In order to address this situation, several investigations suggested the implementation of explainable machine learning methods to develop forecasting systems. These methods are focused on interpretability and understandability related to promoting users' trust in the obtained results [4]. As a result, the implementation of explainable AI has proven to help users to understand and get access to transparent explanations about the applied algorithms and their obtained results [3, 4]. Common examples of explainable algorithms include rule-based models, decision trees [3] and the kNN [5].

On the other hand, Filz et al. [6] emphasise the role of visual analytics for facilitating the user interaction with massive datasets to understand the data analysis and make informed decisions based on the identification of changes, anomalies and patterns in the data. In this respect, the use of visual tools such as dashboards [7] has demonstrated significant benefits for short-term forecasting in energy grids. According to Miller et al. [8], these benefits can be divided into (i) approaches that focus on finding patterns in energy data and (ii) those focused on energy management. As an example, visualizations help analysts monitor several parameters in the grids to enable them to support their internal planning processes [7, 8].

The first prototype of our approach combining explainable machine learning with visual analytics was previously presented in [9] and provided a proof-of-concept for our application case. In this paper, we present the second, improved version of our solution and the results of its evaluation, in particular regarding the accuracy comparison to other methods. We first give a brief overview of related work in Sect. 2. Section 3 gives an overview of the system design focusing on the main improvements implemented in this version of the prototype. Section 4 presents the results of the accuracy assessment of our approach and a benchmarking evaluation comparing the performance of our method with other machine learning methods. We also present the results from a user-centred evaluation with end-users regarding the usability and understandability of the prototype. Finally, Sect. 5 presents conclusions and pointers for future work.

2 Related Work

In order to support utility analysts to improve their efficiency in their energy-related operations, many investigations have proposed the implementation of systems based on visual analytics methods to support users in the analysis of complex datasets [6, 10], based on machine learning models. As an example, Kandakatla et al. [10] explain the benefits of using visual analytics-based technologies to enable users to understand the outputs derived from the forecasting models. They classify the benefits into the following categories: a) trust in the data and the prediction generation process, b) trust in the model calibration metrics, c) trustworthy communication in cyber-physical systems and d) trust in inferences from black-box predictions. Therefore, applications focused on enhancing users' trust present the major benefits in the process.

Although visualizations simplify the analysis of complex datasets, Markus et al. [11] recommend the implementation of explainable processes to contribute to user trust and facilitate their decision-making. In addition, Guidotti et al. [12] conducted an exhaustive survey on the analysis of explainable black-box models and according to their findings, decision tree, and linear models are considered easily understandable and interpretable for humans. Furthermore, in an attempt to identify explainable algorithms, Dam et al. [13] classified several machine learning methods based on their accuracy and explainability. According to that analysis, the kNN and decision tree-based algorithms are the most explainable. They found that in general the higher the accuracy, the less explainable the algorithm tends to be, and vice-versa. Furthermore, recent research has suggested that explainable algorithms needn't necessarily be less accurate than black-box models [13].

As discussed in [14], the similar-day approach and regression methods are popular approaches for short-term load forecasting due to their simplicity. In a related study, Dong et al. [15] measured the accuracy of a kNN-based algorithm with different datasets related to energy load forecasting to verify the robustness and effectiveness of the model. They presented high accuracy results of the method without sacrificing simplicity. However, in contrast to our work, they didn't evaluate the explainability of their method and didn't use visual elements to specifically support the explainability of the results for the users. In a more general context, Shin [4] conducted an end-user evaluation of several explainability parameters (e.g. trust, performance). According to the results, users like understanding how algorithms work and how the data are analyzed to understand to what extent the results are fair. When the users trust in the results, they tend to believe that content is useful and therefore, user satisfaction increases too. The findings from related work thus support our choice of the kNN method as a suitable candidate for short-term energy demand and supply forecasting in a way that could support understandability and user satisfaction.

3   System Design and Implementation

The first implementation of our solution approach was previously reported in [9], however, for reasons of comprehensibility we present a brief overview in Sects. 3.1 and 3.2. In Sect. 3.3 we then focus on the main functionalities of the improved prototype whose evaluation is presented in Sect. 4.

3.1   Method

Our proposal is based on combining the explainable machine learning method (kNN) with visual analytics methods to implement what we term a Smart Energy Management Dashboard for energy forecasting and analysis. We choose the kNN method as the best candidate with intuitive explainability for users without technical knowledge and AI know-how. The main objective is to support utility analysts to obtain reliable and understandable short-term forecasts of energy demand and supply. The implemented algorithm works with predefined weather input parameters (temperature, wind speed, air pressure and sunshine duration) from a day ahead which are used to identify the most similar days in the historical data. The forecasting results presented to the user are based on calculating the average consumption and production values of the k most similar days identified.

To facilitate the understanding of the forecast, the prototype presents visualizations of the forecasted day, as well as of the k most similar days and the related weather parameters. In this way, the analyst can inspect and compare the visualized information to understand the reasons for the forecasted demand and supply.

3.2 Architecture

The architecture of the Smart Energy Dashboard is presented in Fig. 1. The application uses a MySQL database to store the datasets required for calculating the forecasting results (historical consumption, production and weather conditions) which are also used to create the visualizations. A python script pre-processes and prepares the data in the format needed by the forecasting process. In order to calculate the forecasting results, a modified implementation of the kNN-algorithm developed in python is used to calculate the most similar days regarding the input parameters which are initially preloaded in the tool (average weather conditions). The algorithm is based on comparing the average weather input parameters from a day-ahead weather forecast with historical weather data to obtain the k most similar days. To produce the forecast, the algorithm calculates the average energy supply and demand on the most similar days and this result is presented in the dashboard. The visualizations are created by a web-application (implemented with dash and plotly[1]) that displays the results obtained from the forecasting process. By default, the application presents the forecasting for the next day, however, the user can modify the input parameters to make a customized forecast (e.g. forecasting a "what-if" scenario for a day with more sun hours).

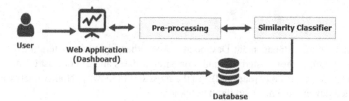

Fig. 1. The architecture of the Smart Energy Management Dashboard.

3.3 Dashboard Design

The prototype includes different visualizations related to the forecasted day as well as the most similar days to support the analysis and understanding of the results. To facilitate the interaction, the dashboard automatically calculates and fills in the input parameters

---

[1] https://dash.plotly.com/.

(Fig. 2a) from a connection with an external weather API. However, the user can change these parameters manually to forecast a customized scenario.

The visualizations include different types of charts such as bar charts, line charts, etc. to inform the forecasting analysis (Fig. 2). However, the user can filter the dates to create customized visualizations to perform a more specific analysis (e.g. selecting two days with the most similar temperature). In addition, Fig. 2c shows the results of the expected consumption of the predicted day as well as the amount of energy consumed on the most similar days. This information is complemented with hourly consumption (Fig. 2d) to perform a more detailed analysis and also to help users to identify the peak consumption time (a typical use case for the analysts).

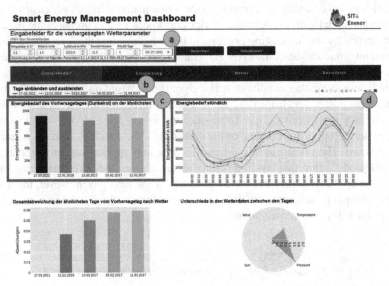

Fig. 2. Smart Energy Management Dashboard: a) Weather input parameters for the forecast b) Filter (toggle) with the forecasted day and most similar dates and c) Forecast of the total energy demand on the forecasted day (dark red) and the most similar days d) Hourly energy demand for the forecasted day and the most similar neighbours.

Additionally, the dashboard includes detailed weather charts (e.g. temperature, sunshine time; see Fig. 3), because they are of paramount importance to understand the forecasted and visualized demand. In this way, the dashboard also contributes to identifying energy-consumption patterns to support the energy planning process.

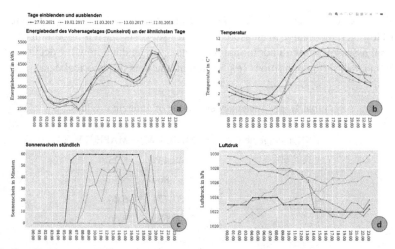

Fig. 3. Detailed weather information in the Smart Energy Management Dashboard: a) Hourly energy demand, b) Temperature, c) Hourly sunshine (in minutes), d) Hourly air pressure.

4 Evaluation

In order to expand the preliminary evaluation reported in [9], we conducted additional tests. The first one focused on an additional accuracy evaluation of the forecasting with respect to different *"k"* values with an improved division of the test and training data. In the second one, we conducted a benchmarking evaluation to compare the performance of our implemented algorithm with other machine learning methods. Finally, a user evaluation was conducted to collect feedback from target users regarding the usefulness and understandability of the prototype.

4.1 Accuracy Evaluation

In order to verify the preliminary accuracy evaluation reported in [9], we improved the method to prepare the datasets to be used in the assessment. In contrast to the first evaluation where the training and test data were obtained by cutting the dataset straight in two halfs, in this evaluation, the data were randomly assigned to the training and testing datasets (keeping the 50%–50% proportion). The data set included one full calendar year of historical data for consumption and production in a small municipality of ca. 13.500 inhabitants (from a utility participating in the project) and weather data from a commercial weather service. The evaluation was based on measuring the accuracy error values of MAE (Mean Absolute Error) and MAPE (Mean Absolute Percentage Error) of the average results of 2 to 10 neighbours. As depicted in Table 1, the best accuracy result with a MAPE of 5.06% was obtained from the average of the 4 most similar neighbours (since the averages from 6 to 10 neighbours did not show any better results, they are not presented in the table).

This is a better result compared to our previous evaluation (MAPE of 5.77% reported in [9]). However, the change in measured accuracy suggests that it is important to conduct additional assessments with additional data sets to understand how the accuracy might change under different conditions (e.g. different amounts of historical data).

Table 1. kNN accuracy evaluation of different k-values.

kNN average neighbours	MAE (kWh)	MAPE(%)
2	2148.434	5.25
3	2263.809	5.56
4	**2057.771**	**5.06**
5	2200.683	5.46

4.2 Benchmarking Evaluation

To assess the relative accuracy of our method with respect to other machine learning methods, we performed a benchmarking evaluation. This consisted of comparing the results of the forecasting based on using our implemented algorithm to the forecast performed with different machine learning methods on the same data. The forecast with the other methods was performed with RapidMiner[2]. As well as in the above evaluation, we measured MAE and MAPE from a dataset from the year 2015 (consumption, production and weather) provided by a local utility. The data were randomly split into training and testing (50%–50%) to be used for each method. The *Gradient Boosted Tree* produced the best results with a MAPE value of 3.3% compared to 5.06% for the *kNN*. However, the accuracy of our method is very close to all methods evaluated, differing only between 0.26%–1.73% (Table 2). Interestingly, the decision tree that is also considered an explainable method [3] performed slightly better than kNN (0.48% better). It would be interesting to perform a more detailed assessment of these two methods regarding their accuracy and explainability trade-off for our application case.

Table 2. Benchmarking comparison with other AI methods.

AI algorithm	MAE (kWh)	MAPE (%)	Accuracy difference (w.r.t. kNN)
kNN	**2057.711**	**5.06**	–
Decision tree	1861.409	4.58	0.48
Deep learning	1967.011	4.80	0.26
Generalized linear model	1893.497	4.61	0.45
Gradient boosted tree	**1378.596**	**3.33**	**1.73**
Random forest tree	1532.055	3.76	1.3
Support vector machine	2104.956	5.24	−0.18

---

[2] https://rapidminer.com/.

4.3   User Evaluation

Finally, we conducted a usability and understandability evaluation with five potential users from a municipal utility in a user workshop. The users were between 21 to 70 years old. Although all participants considered themselves to be highly experienced in the use of computers, all of them reported having no experience in using forecasting tools. Two participants stated a medium level of experience with energy forecasting in general, and three participants stated little experience with that. After the dashboard was introduced and briefly explained, participants answered open questions regarding the current forecasting process and the typical use cases in the company (to verify that the requirements haven't changed from the original analysis [16]). Subsequently, they performed several tasks with the dashboard corresponding to the main use cases (e.g. find out the expected consumption and supply for the next day, identify the peak consumption hours for the next day). During the workshop, participants were asked to *"think-aloud"* to get insights on how they were using the dashboard. At the end, they answered a questionnaire focused on evaluating the usability and understandability of the prototype. The items regarding usefulness i.e. performance expectancy (Table 3) and ease of use (Table 4) were derived from the well-known UTAUT model (unified theory of acceptance and use of technology [17]. The understandability questions were formulated specifically for our case (Table 5). After the questionnaire, we also elicited user feedback in a group discussion. We can summarize the main findings as follows:

Usefulness: All participants stated that the dashboard helps them to make the forecasting process quicker, easier and more effective (Table 3, items 1–3). All participants also considered the dashboard to increase their forecasting productivity (item 5). Four participants considered the dashboard to improve their performance and one was neutral (item 4). All but one participant found the dashboard overall useful for forecasting (item 6; the one exception was neutral). Further, during the interaction with the different charts, they expressed their interest in the analysis of hourly charts. This type of analysis allowed them to solve not only the requested tasks but also additional insights such as the identification of outlier conditions generated mainly by weather changes that could represent important facts for their planning.

Ease of Use: All but one participant found that it was easy to learn to use the dashboard and that the interaction was clear and understandable (item 6–7). Thus, it is surprising that the overall ease of use of the dashboard has been positively assessed by two participants with three being neutral. Feedback from the discussion suggests that this is largely due to different screen sizes used by the participants and that the dashboard should be optimized to better deal with this situation. Most participants interacted with the dashboard on their own computers from their homes (one from the office). As some screens were smaller than others, for some participants it was necessary to increase the zoom in the browser to facilitate the interaction with the charts. The same situation has occurred with some titles and legends in the interface that appeared too small. Also, one user had connection issues during the workshop and it took him a little bit longer to launch the application. Based on these observations we can implement the corresponding improvements in the next version of the prototype.

Table 3. Answers to questionnaire items regarding usefulness: (1) do not agree at all, 2) rather disagree, 3) neutral, 4) rather agree, 5) fully agree.

Statements	1	2	3	4	5
1. I can use the dashboard to make energy demand and supply forecast more quickly	0%	0%	0%	60%	40%
2. Using the dashboard increases my effectiveness in forecasting energy demand and supply	0%	0%	0%	60%	40%
3. Using the dashboard makes it easier to forecast energy demand and forecast	0%	0%	0%	60%	40%
4. Using the dashboard improves my performance in forecasting energy demand and supply	0%	0%	20%	60%	20%
5.Using the dashboard increases my productivity in forecasting energy demand and supply.	0%	0%	0%	40%	60%
6. The dashboard was easy to use	0%	0%	60%	40%	0%

Table 4. Answers to questionnaire items regarding ease of use: (1) do not agree at all, 2) rather disagree, 3) neutral, 4) rather agree, 5) fully agree.

Statements	1	2	3	4	5
7. The interaction with the dashboard is clear and understandable	0%	0%	20%	80%	0%
8. I find it easy to learn how to use the dashboard	0%	0%	20%	80%	0%
9. The dashboard was easy to use	0%	0%	60%	40%	0%

Understandability: The participants were asked to identify the expected forecast for the day ahead. By interacting with the first screen (Fig. 2), they found the expected consumption in the first bar chart (Fig. 2c) and complemented the understanding with the hourly data in the first line chart (Fig. 2d). Three participants explicitly mentioned that "*.. the interaction with the line charts helps to understand better the expected consumption..*". As the results in Table 5 show, the use of visualizations to support the understandability of the forecast has been positively affirmed (one participant was neutral). A "control" question asking specifically about the helpfulness of charts for understandability of the forecast had a slight deviation (one neutral, one negative). This suggests that more investigation should be given to the role of specific charts.

The item about the helpfulness of visualizing the similar days for understanding the forecast was positively affirmed by all. Overall, this suggests that the implemented combination of the kNN forecast with accompanying visualizations to facilitate understandability is a viable approach for our application case. Finally, we identified some insights to further enhance the understandability of the forecast: (i) include additional charts regarding additional weather conditions (e.g. wind speed), (ii) include the numeric value for the total consumption forecast in a visible place on the first screen, for a quick reference immediately after the application has been launched.

Table 5. Answers to questionnaire items regarding understandability: (1) do not agree at all, 2) rather disagree, 3) neutral, 4) rather agree, 5) fully agree.

Statements	1	2	3	4	5
10. Based on the analysis of the visualizations, I can understand the forecast results presented in the dashboard	0%	0%	20%	80%	0%
11. The similar days presented in the dashboard help me to understand how the forecast was calculated	0%	0%	0%	80%	20%
12. The charts in the dashboard help me to understand the forecast of energy demand and supply.	0%	20%	20%	20%	40%
13. Using the dashboard allows me to understand how the expected forecast comes about	0%	20%	20%	60%	0%

5   Conclusions and Future Work

In this paper, we presented the design and evaluation of an explainable AI dashboard for energy forecasting that combines explainable machine learning and visual analytics to enable small utilities to forecast energy demand and supply in an easily understandable way. The presented improved prototype (compared to a previous version [9]), was developed by using open source software (dash, python). This makes the deployment of our solution more accessible, especially for small utilities. The focus on providing an explainable application developed from a user-centred design perspective also facilitates the transition from their traditional forecasting practices to the use of a more sophisticated analytical tool.

The improved evaluation setup has demonstrated a higher accuracy than in the previous test (MAPE 5.06% vs 5.77% presented in [9]). This shows the importance of choosing the appropriate test design with respect to training and test data sets. But it also highlights the potential sensitivity of the method to different data conditions. Therefore, additional evaluations with more extensive and varied datasets should be performed for a final accuracy assessment in future work.

The results of the benchmarking evaluation comparing the accuracy of our method with other machine learning methods confirm the viability of our approach. Although most of the other methods showed a somewhat better accuracy, the difference was very small (0.26–1.73%). Moreover, all but one of the better performing methods are much more complex and difficult to explain to users without profound AI expertise. The decision tree, as the only method with potentially comparable explainability to kNN, has performed with only 0.48% better accuracy than our solution. This suggests that this could be another candidate algorithm to further improve the accuracy while potentially retaining explainability.

However, this is only a hypothesis that should be investigated in future work, in particular, because decision trees can grow quite complex while the kNN mechanism and its results are intuitively easily explained to non-technical users. We consider this intuitive understandability and the simplicity of the kNN implementation to be a major advantage for achieving the goals of our approach: providing an easily implementable and understandable forecasting solution for small utilities with no AI expertise.

This choice is supported by the results of the user-centered evaluation where both the usefulness and the understandability of the implemented forecasting solution have been positively assessed. However, these results need to be taken with caution, since the number of test participants was small (5 participants) and all of them were from one utility. We aim to repeat this evaluation with a larger group of users from different utilities, although for this some organizational and technical challenges need to be solved (e.g. obtaining historical data from different utilities).

The dashboard is currently being tested in a pilot trial with the same participants to gain more insights from everyday use. We will further improve the dashboard design by including the recommendations provided by the users during the evaluation (e.g. increasing the font size to adapt to different screen sizes). The explainability evaluation could also be performed in more detail (e.g. the role of specific visualizations) and with additional metrics, such as interpretability and fidelity [11] in future user studies.

Acknowledgements. The SIT4Energy project has received funding from the German Federal Ministry of Education and Research (BMBF) and the Greek General Secretariat for Research and Technology (GSRT) in the context of the Greek-German Call for Proposals on Bilateral Research and Innovation Cooperation. We thank Stadtwerk Haßfurt for their cooperation and support of this work with input from their practice and experiences as small but innovative utility and to all participants of the workshop.

References

1. Paulescu, M., Brabec, M., Remus, B., Viorel, B.: Structured, physically inspired (gray box) models versus black box modeling for forecasting the output power of photovoltaic plants. Energy **121**, 792–802 (2017)
2. Ahmad, T., Huanxin, C.: Nonlinear autoregressive and random forest approach to forecasting electricity load for utility energy management systems. Sustain. Urban Areas **45**, 460–473 (2019)
3. Linardatos, P., Vasilis, P., Sotiris, K.: Explainable AI: review of machine learning interpretability methods. Entropy **23**, 2021 (2021)
4. Shin, D.: The effects of explainability and causability on perception, trust, and acceptance: Implications for explainable AI. Int. J. Hum. Comput. Stud. **146**, 1–10 (2021)
5. Revina, A., Buza, K., Meister, V.: IT ticket classification: the simpler, the better. IEEE Access **8**, 193380–193395 (2020)
6. Filz, M., Gellrich, S., Herrmann, C., Thiede, S.: Data-driven analysis of product state propagation in manufacturing systems using visual analytics and machine learning. In: 53rd CIRP Conference on Manufacturing Systems (2020)
7. Hock, K.P., McGuiness, D.: Future state visualization in power grid. In: 2018 IEEE International Conference on Environment and Electrical Engineering and 2018 IEEE Industrial and Commercial Power Systems Europe (2018)
8. Miller, C., Nagy, Z., Schlueter, A.: A review of unsupervised statistical learning and visual analytics techniques applied to performance analysis of non-residential buildings. Renew. Sustain. Energy Rev. **81**, 1365–1377 (2018)

9. Grimaldo, A.I., Novak, J.: Combining machine learning with visual analytics for explainable forecasting of energy demand in prosumer scenarios. Proc. Comput. Sci. **175**, 525–532 (2020)

10. Kandakatla, A., Chandan, V., Kundu, S., Chakraborty, I., Cook, K., Dasgupta, A.: Towards trust-augmented visual analytics for data-driven energy modeling. In: 2020 IEEE Workshop on TRust and EXpertise in Visual Analytics (TREX), pp. 16–21 (2020)

11. Markus, A.F., Kors, J.A., Rijnbeek, P.R.: The role of explainability in creating trustworthy artificial intelligence health care: a comprehensive survey of the terminology, design and evaluation strategies. J. Biomed. Inform. **113**, 1–11 (2021)

12. Guidotti, R., Monreale, A., Ruggieri, S., Turini, F., Giannotti, F., Pedreschi, D.: A survey of methods for explaining black box models. ACM Comput. Surv. **5**, 1–42 (2018)

13. Dam, H.K., Tran, T., Ghose, A.: Explainable software analytics. In: ICSE 2018 NIER, Gothenburg, Sweden (2018)

14. Anwar, T., Sharma, B., Chakraborty, K., Sirohia, H.: Introduction to load forecasting. Int. J. Pure Appl. Math. **119**, 1527–1538 (2018)

15. Dong, Y., Ma, X., Fu, T.: Electrical load forecasting: a deep learning approach based on k-nearest neighbours. Appl. Soft Comput. J. **99**(1–15), 106900 (2021)

16. Grimaldo, A.I., Novak, J.: User-centered visual analytics approach for interactive and explainable energy demand analysis in prosumer scenarios. In: Tzovaras, D., Giakoumis, D., Vincze, M., Argyros, A. (eds.) ICVS 2019. LNCS, vol. 11754, pp. 700–710. Springer, Cham (2019). https://doi.org/10.1007/978-3-030-34995-0_64

17. Davis, F.D.: Perceived usefulness, perceived ease of use, and user acceptance of information technology. MIS Q. **13**, 319–340 (1989)

18. Ghalehkhondabi, I., Ardjmand, E., Weckman, G.R., Young, W.A.: An overview of energy demand forecasting methods published in 2005–2015. Energy Syst. **8**(2), 411–447 (2016). https://doi.org/10.1007/s12667-016-0203-y

Improving Energy Efficiency in Tertiary Buildings Through User-Driven Recommendations Delivered on Optimal Micro-moments

Apostolos C. Tsolakis[1]([✉])(iD), George Tsakirakis[2], Vasileios G. Vasilopoulos[1](iD), Konstantinos Peppas[1](iD), Charisios Zafeiris[2], Iordanis Makaratzis[1], Ana Grimaldo[3](iD), Stelios Krinidis[1](iD), Jasminko Novak[3](iD), George Bravos[2], and Dimitrios Tzovaras[1](iD)

[1] Information Technologies Institute, Centre for Research and Technologies Hellas, 57001 Thessaloniki, Greece
tsolakis@iti.gr
[2] Research and Development Department, ITML, 11525 Athens, GR, Greece
gtsa@itml.gr
[3] University of Applied Sciences Stralsund, IACS - Institute for Applied Computer Sciences, Stralsund, Germany
jasminko.novak@hochschule-stralsund.de

Abstract. Sustainable energy is hands down one of the biggest challenges of our times. As the EU sets its focus to reach its 2030 and 2050 goals, the importance of energy efficiency for energy consumers/prosumers becomes prevalent. Over the years, a lot of different approaches have been followed to engage end-users and affect energy-related occupant behaviour towards improving energy efficiency results and long term behaviour changes. This work presents the SIT4Energy user-centered approach for tertiary buildings that delivers an end-to-end solution that takes into consideration a set of tools and models for successfully engaging and affecting the end-user's energy-related behaviour. Starting from appropriate user profiling models for energy-related behaviour models and an explainable recommendation engine, to on the fly human activity tracking and micro-moments detection on mobile devices, a set of recommendations are delivered to the end-users through a mobile device, presenting valuable information with user-tailored context and on the optimal timing. The overall solution is clearly documented, whereas real-life results are presented from the deployment in offices in a university building. From the evaluation performed it is clearly depicted that a positive impact has been achieved both in terms of energy efficiency as well as energy-related behaviour.

This work has been co-funded by the German Federal Ministry of Education and Research, the European Union and the General Secretariat of Research and Technology, Ministry of Development & Investments, under the project (SIT4Energy - T2EDK-0911) of the Bilateral S&T Cooperation Program Greece – Germany 2017. Special thank you to the Harokopio University of Athens for hosting the pilot activities of this study.

I. Maglogiannis et al. (Eds.): AIAI 2021 Workshops, IFIP AICT 628, pp. 352–363, 2021.
https://doi.org/10.1007/978-3-030-79157-5_29

Keywords: Energy efficiency · Recommender systems ·
Micro-moments · Energy-related behaviour

1 Introduction

The impact of building user behaviour on energy consumption is usually not
considered during the design phase or the post-occupancy optimization phase
although changes in human behaviour can increase the efficiency of the energy
used in the building [1]. Lasting changes in behaviour are difficult to achieve,
but new ways to foster energy efficiency have emerged over the past few years.
In fact, following the Fogg's [2] and Oinas-Kukkonen's Frameworks [8], various
ICT-based solutions have been introduced, able to act as persuasion mechanisms for sustainability, health preservation or marketing. New technologies to
measure, store, and display energy information (e.g., smart meters, dashboards,
mobile phone applications) are available and provide data that allow consumers
to make informed choices. While significant investments have already been made
in sensing infrastructures that can provide relevant data, less attention has gone
toward making energy information comprehensible, attractive, and relevant.

In general, studies of the impact of behaviour in public buildings are sparse
or controversial and the impact of user behaviour is difficult to quantify for
methodological reasons [7]. In principal, lighting, thermal and air quality comfort are considered as the three major factors that affect occupants' quality of
living/working in a building environment and also building energy management.
Occupancy status also plays a central role in energy behaviour inside a building
and, as authors in [12,14] support, significant energy savings are possible, by
effectively utilizing occupancy measurements.

However, data by themselves are not enough to accurately capture the state
of a building's performance. The amount of energy consumed depends not only
on the criteria set for the indoor environment and applied technology but also
on the behaviour of occupants. This may create a conflict between strategies
that focus on the reduction of energy consumption and those to maintain a
healthy and comfortable indoor environment. To achieve a balance between comfort and efficiency, synergies between building design, building climate control
and occupant needs have to be established. Developing optimal strategies to control HVAC and lighting systems which also comply with occupant needs require
a) a detailed modelling of the air quality requirements, as well as the respective
thermal and comfort levels that the occupants desire and b) correct estimation
of the current comfort conditions, based on environmental measurements (air
temperature, humidity, illumination etc.) building energy management (BEM)
methodology.

An eco-feedback system was found to lead to significant reductions in energy
consumption [4,9]. This system provides to occupants with information regarding
their historical and current energy consumption. Such knowledge greatly helps
occupants to acknowledge energy saving and waste and to increase awareness of
energy consumption and was found to be a big motivator to encourage energy

efficient practices. A large-scale study of 2000 households has concluded that users respond well to eco-feedback with reported energy savings of 15% [15]. Combining the system with recommendations and tips has been reported to be an effective way to further improve the impact of eco-feedback and provide greater energy savings [3,16]. In fact, tailored information can cause a significant shift in occupant behaviours, as presented in [5] (and the studies therein).

The SIT4energy project[1], addresses the challenge of effective user engagement by delivering an end-to-end solution that not only incorporates state-of-the-art behavioural models and real-time rule-based systems, but also delivers AI-driven lightweight edge computing algorithms that are executed on the user's mobile device. In addition, in contrast to most practices, it introduces the use of redefined micro-moments [10] for effectively identifying the most appropriate timing for delivering user-aware recommendations with enriched incentivisation messages. To evaluate the proposed framework a real-world pilot has been deployed, with some very promising preliminary results in both energy efficiency and user engagement.

The remainder of this paper is structured as follows: Sect. 2 presents the proposed solution in detail, Sect. 3.1 describes the experimental setup and evaluation metrics, whereas Sect. 3 introduces results from the real-life deployment in Athens, Greece. Finally, Sect. 4 concludes this paper and proposes future improvements.

2   The SIT4Energy Solution

The overall architecture of the SIT4Energy framework for tertiary end-users is presented in Fig. 1. Starting from the infrastructure layer, data generated by various sensors, smart meters, or other IoT devices, are pushed to the Service layer, through the Data Retrieval & Profiling tool. After a very simple pre-processing (e.g. outliers removal, filling missing values, etc.) the data are stored in a database. In the same database, an extensive list of recommendations (both generic and personalised, trigger-based) is available. As will be shown in the following paragraphs, beyond a simple tip, the presented framework also introduces an additional incentivisation message that takes into account two key user profiling aspects. By directly accessing all available information stored in the database, a rule-based recommendation engine is able to identify the most appropriate context per user, taking into account not only the current state of the consumption of the building, but also the type of the user and their energy-related behaviour. This enriched recommendation is pushed to the mobile app through an intermediate security layer (i.e. Google Firebase[2]), based on the preferences configured by the user through the app. After receiving the recommendation, the mobile app introduces an AI-driven time-dependent tool for identifying on the fly the

---

[1] https://sit4energy.eu.

[2] https://console.firebase.google.com/.

best timing (in the form of micro-moments) for actually delivering the notification to the user. Each of the individual components, is presented in more detail in the following sections.

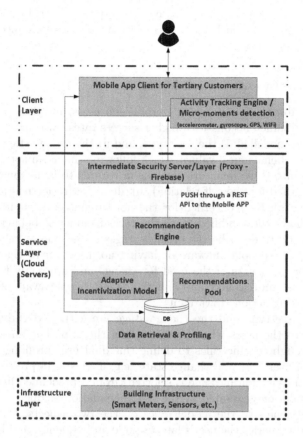

Fig. 1. The SIT4Energy framework architecture for tertiary end-users

2.1 Data Retrieval and Profiling

The SIT4Energy recommender back-end is built on Laravel[3], an open-source PHP web framework using MVC architectural pattern. MVC architecture is used to separate the model which represents the part of the software where the data are stored or created, the view which represents the part that is displayed for the user or sent via a web service and the controller which is the part that changes the view upon request. Although Laravel is designed mainly as an MVC framework, it can be used to create APIs as well. It provides easy to setup user authorization and authentication (OAuth2), along with other modules that are

---

[3] https://laravel.com/.

needed for various operations (such as RESTful web services), using up to a point OOP PHP.

For data retrieval the HomeAssistant[4] tool has been employed for efficiently communicating with both smart meters and sensors deployed within the offices of the tertiary building. Installed locally on a raspberry pi, this module covers a range of measurements, such as temperature, humidity, luminance, occupancy, and energy consumption.

2.2 Adaptive Incentivisation Model

In order to be able to more accurately profile end-users, and thus introduce more user-driven recommendations with higher success rates, two concepts have been introduced and modelled: i) the user type, and ii) the change stage. The former reflects the user behavioural values, which following the norm activation theory, conceptualize into three main orientations in regards to behavioural change: a) egoistic (concerned for the self-relation), b) altruistic (concerned for other people) and c) biospheric (concerned for the non-human, e.g., environment) [13]. The later, follows the modified trans-theoretical model of behavioural change introduced in [6], to describe the distinct stages of behavioural change: a) pre-contemplentation (people unaware or having no intention to change), b) contemplation (people aware of the need for change and are ready to act, but do not do so for certain reasons), and c) action stage (people aware of the need for change and taking actions towards it).

Both the user type and the change stage are extracted through a survey that is given to the users when first installing the app. The answers are then evaluated through specific rules to define this dual user profiling. As a result, for each set of user type and change state (e.g. altruistic in pre-contemplation) a specific incentivisation message is selected (from a predefined list) to support the recommendation generated by the recommendation engine.

The adaptiveness of the model relies on the two aspects. First, the back-end periodically queries the user's latest app login frequency, and based on that alters the users' contemplation state, whereas every two months of app usage, a repetition of the survey is offered to the end-user, which potentially redefines both user type and contemplation state.

2.3 Recommendation Engine

Based on the data collected from the energy meters and smart sensors, the initial recommendation engine implementation is built on a rule-based system with predefined conditions that trigger a recommendation to be sent to the mobile app when these prerequisite conditions are met. In addition, the users must give their consent for receiving recommendations as well as select a preferable timeframe in which they wish to receive the notifications. Both can be defined in the Settings section of the mobile app provided to the user.

---

[4] https://www.home-assistant.io/.

If the rules are only partially satisfied, the engine selects among eligible generic recommendations to be sent to the app, that are still relative to the collected energy consumption type. (i.e. If there is adequate sunlight and light energy consumption then suggest to the user *to switch off the lights*, else if there is only light energy consumption provide a recommendation related to energy saving of type Lights: *"replace light bulbs with led ones to save energy"*). The prioritization of the generic recommendations is based on their overall score collected from the users' feedback.

The precision and validity of the recommendations is further strengthened by combining the user's feedback (for every recommendation sent to the user, a request to rate it is also provided) with comparison of related changes in their energy consumption compared with their historical consumption data.

These rules used in this study are:

1. If no movement is detected in the room for the last 20 min and the lights of the room are switched on, then the user is alerted to turn off the room lights.
2. If outside luminosity is over a predefined threshold and the lights of the room are switched on, then the user is alerted to turn off the room lights.
3. If outside temperature is deemed within a comfortable zone (18–27 °C) and the A/C is switched on, then the user is alerted to turn off the A/C.
4. If inside temperature is over the hot threshold (27 °C), the A/C is switched on and outside temperature is lower than the hot threshold, the user is alerted to turn off the A/C and open the windows to balance the room's temperature with the external conditions.
5. If inside temperature is lower than the cold threshold (18 °C), the air-condition is working and outside temperature is over than this threshold the user is alerted to turn off the A/C and open the windows to balance room's temperature with the external conditions.
6. If inside humidity is above the comfortable threshold (55%) and outside humidity is lower than this threshold, the user is alerted to open the windows to balance room's humidity with the external conditions.
7. If inside humidity is lower than the minimum comfortable threshold (45%) and outside humidity is above this threshold, the user is alerted to open the windows to balance room's humidity with the external conditions.

The recommendation pool, out of which the recommender selects, includes a range of tips that are divided per device type (e.g. lighting, HVAC, office appliances, etc.), customer type (consumer vs prosumer), but also with two added value metrics: the difficulty to apply the recommendation, and the consumption gain, which refers to the importance of the tip towards energy efficiency (higher values lead to higher energy savings). Both these metrics participate in the decision making process.

2.4 Mobile App

The SIT4Energy front-end is a top notch rich HTML5, CSS3 and JavaScript application. It can be wrapped with Apache Cordova, an open source mobile application development framework, enabling programmers to develop a platform-independent application without losing native smartphone functionality such as Geolocation and Notifications. The front-end application has one single responsive code basis and therefore can be easily built for desktop environments as well as various mobile operating systems.

Beyond basic functionalities such as secure login and profile configuration, the users have access to various visualisations, such as consumption graphs, with detail defined by the available level of asset monitoring (e.g. entire office or per device) (Fig. 2). The user is also able to define some target values (daily, monthly, etc.) based on which, if achieved, he/she can gain points and calculate savings (Fig. 3).

Fig. 2. Consumption analysis and energy savings visualisation.

Activity Tracking and Micro-moment Detection Tool. One of the core innovations of the presented framework, that was evaluated in real-life conditions in this study, is the use of a lightweight human activity recognition (HAR) algorithm, fully described in a previous work of the authors [11]. It consists of a novel deep neural network model, which combines feature extraction and convolutional layers, able to recognize in real-time human physical activity based on tri-axial accelerometer data when run on a mobile device.

Based on the results of the HAR model which is executed on the fly, as well as additional information from the mobile device (e.g. the screen is on, home screen enabled, etc.) another decision layer is included for identifying the appropriate micro-moments (as redefined in [10]) for actually delivering incoming recommendations. Hence, an incoming message from the recommendation engine is not directly pushed to the user, but is filtered towards delivering it in the optimal moment during which the user would be more susceptible to a nudge.

Fig. 3. Recommendations with Incentivisation messages and Rewards Representation

By doing so, not only it is possible to increase the percentage of recommendations becoming actual actions, but also increasing overall engagement as the user is more likely to pay attention to the incoming message, than disregarding due to other reasons. As micro-moments can be highly unpredictable and user-specific, such an edge computing tool creates the necessary conditions for customised experience for every user.

3   Experimental Results

3.1   Deployment Setup

The introduced framework was deployed at two working offices (Fig. 4) at the premises of the Informatics and Telematics Faculty of the Harokopio University of Athens. Targeting the academic staff and students of the university the mobile app was distributed to 11 users, providing access to information from the two offices (consumption, temperature, humidity, luminance, and occupancy.

The deployment started on May 2019, when the sensors and meters were installed, and data retrieval has been initiated, for establishing a baseline, as well as to support the implementation of the various tools. A first complete version of the framework was deployed on June-July 2020 for testing purposes, whereas the complete pilot was initiated on September 2020 and will continue until June 2021. Preliminary results extracted, showcase some very interesting and promising aspects.

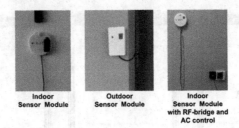

Fig. 4. Sensors deployed at offices in HUA.

3.2   Results

In general, since users have the capability to customise their preferences for receiving recommendations, a different amount of tips is delivered per user, as depicted in Fig. 5.

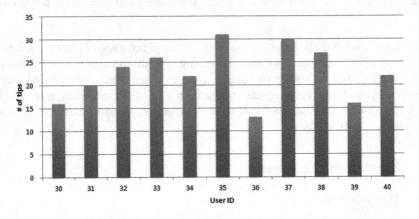

Fig. 5. Amount of tips delivered to the HUA end-users during the deployment.

In terms of energy consumption, and taking into account that from 10th of March to the 4th of May 2020 and from November 2020 to March 2021, Athens was/is under lockdown due to the pandemic, consumption patterns in Q1 and Q4 cannot be taken into account. However, as can been seen in Fig. 6, a slight improvement is observed in the consumption of HVAC units, mainly in Q2, whereas a more evident decrease is observed in the consumption of PCs for both Q2 and Q3 periods.

As external weather conditions may affect these results, a baseline is to be created towards more accurately comparing the two periods. To expand the evaluation, it is also suggested to include the lockdown periods as well, with a proper annotation and a different baseline model.

In terms of users' behaviour evaluation, as the pilot activities are still ongoing, the feedback provided for each recommendation sent is analysed. As can be

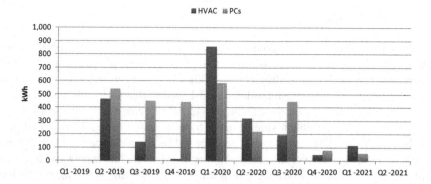

Fig. 6. Energy Consumption at pilot offices in HUA.

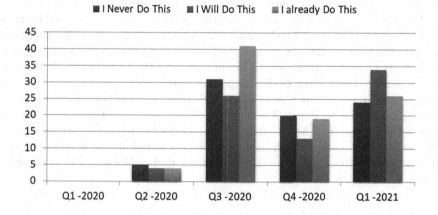

Fig. 7. Users' Feedback on recommendations provided

seen in Fig. 7, during the first three months (Q3) quite a lot of recommendations have been provided to the users with the most being things already performed by them, followed by the ones they never do. The same situation was observed in the fourth trimester as well, but with less recommendations sent to the users. However, in the last trimester included in this study, an interesting change has been observed. The system improved from the previous knowledge and delivered more recommendations that the users are keen to do, and are not already doing. This is quite interesting, as additional actions have been identified and recommended, whereas from all the recommendations delivered, a smaller percentage (compared to the two previous periods) is attributed to actions that the users will not follow. This leads to the assumption that more accurate recommendations were delivered, avoiding things that the users already do or will not do even if recommendations are to be provided. Hence, the system is actively raising awareness, offering to the users more targeted information towards a more energy efficient behaviour.

4   Conclusions

In this paper, the real-life deployment of an end-to-end ICT-based recommender system for tertiary buildings is presented. The framework introduced, covers holistically the challenge addressed, by taking into account real-time data from the building, user behavioural models, asset-based and generic recommendations, fed to a rule based decision making engine for identifying the proper context per user, whereas on the client side, a user friendly mobile app is enriched with a lightweight AI HAR model that supports the identification of the optimal micro-moment, for delivering and engaging the user. The framework has been deployed to real-life infrastructure in a university building, covering two offices, with multiple devices (such as HVAC and PCs) and users (academic staff and students). Preliminary results after six months of deployment have introduced some interesting results, mainly in terms of end-users' behaviour.

In order to be able to assess more accurately energy savings, the need of introducing a more properly defined baseline model is imperative. It is also important to take into account the impact enforced due to the corona virus situation, and evaluate in more detail the periods before and after the intervention. In terms of user behavior, besides the feedback provided upon receiving a notification, the users will fill in once more a survey that will cover both the user type and change stage for the 11 users. Hence, it will be possible to evaluate whether both aspects have been improved or not. Finally, as the number of users is quite limited for the deployment examined, which however seems to deliver the necessary proof-of-concept, to properly validate the framework proposed a larger deployment is required.

References

1. Dunlop, T.: Mind the gap: a social sciences review of energy efficiency. Energy Res. Soc. Sci. **56**, 101216 (2019)
2. Fogg, B.J.: Persuasive technology: using computers to change what we think and do. Ubiquity (5), 2 (2002)
3. Inyim, P., Batouli, M., Reyes, M.P., Carmenate, T., Bobadilla, L., Mostafavi, A.: A smartphone application for personalized and multi-method interventions toward energy saving in buildings. Sustainability **10**(6), 1744 (2018)
4. Jain, R.K., Taylor, J.E., Culligan, P.J.: Investigating the impact eco-feedback information representation has on building occupant energy consumption behavior and savings. Energy Build. **64**, 408–414 (2013)
5. Karlin, B., Zinger, J.F., Ford, R.: The effects of feedback on energy conservation: a meta-analysis. Psychol. Bull. **141**(6), 1205 (2015)
6. Koroleva, K., Melenhorst, M., Novak, J., Herrera Gonzalez, S.L., Fraternali, P., Rizzoli, A.E.: Designing an integrated socio-technical behaviour change system for energy saving. Energy Inf. **2**(1), 1–20 (2019). https://doi.org/10.1186/s42162-019-0088-9
7. Kralikova, R., Andrejiova, M., Wessely, E.: Energy saving techniques and strategies for illumination in industry. Procedia Eng. **100**, 187–195 (2015)

8. Oinas-Kukkonen, H., Harjumaa, M.: Persuasive systems design: key issues, process model and system features 1. In: Routledge Handbook of Policy Design, pp. 87–105. Routledge (2018)
9. Paone, A., Bacher, J.P.: The impact of building occupant behavior on energy efficiency and methods to influence it: a review of the state of the art. Energies **11**(4), 953 (2018)
10. Peppas, K., Chouliara, A., Tsolakis, A., Krinidis, S., Tzovaras, D.: Redefining micro-moments for improving energy behaviour: the sit4energy approach. In: 2019 IEEE SmartWorld, Ubiquitous Intelligence & Computing, Advanced & Trusted Computing, Scalable Computing & Communications, Cloud & Big Data Computing, Internet of People and Smart City Innovation (SmartWorld/SCALCOM/UIC/ATC/CBDCom/IOP/SCI), pp. 1811–1816. IEEE (2019)
11. Peppas, K., Tsolakis, A.C., Krinidis, S., Tzovaras, D.: Real-time physical activity recognition on smart mobile devices using convolutional neural networks. Appl. Sci. **10**(23), 8482 (2020)
12. Squartini, S., Boaro, M., De Angelis, F., Fuselli, D., Piazza, F.: Optimization algorithms for home energy resource scheduling in presence of data uncertainty. In: 2013 Fourth International Conference on Intelligent Control and Information Processing (ICICIP), pp. 323–328. IEEE (2013)
13. Swami, V., Chamorro-Premuzic, T., Snelgar, R., Furnham, A.: Egoistic, altruistic, and biospheric environmental concerns: A path analytic investigation of their determinants. Scand. J. Psychol. **51**(2), 139–145 (2010)
14. Tsolakis, A.C., et al.: Occupancy-based decision support system for building management: from automation to end-user persuasion. Int. J. Energy Res. **43**(6), 2261–2280 (2019)
15. Vassileva, I., Odlare, M., Wallin, F., Dahlquist, E.: The impact of consumers' feedback preferences on domestic electricity consumption. Appl. Energy **93**, 575–582 (2012)
16. Yun, R., et al.: The design and evaluation of intelligent energy dashboard for sustainability in the workplace. In: Marcus, A. (ed.) DUXU 2014. LNCS, vol. 8519, pp. 605–615. Springer, Cham (2014). https://doi.org/10.1007/978-3-319-07635-5_58

Semantic Modeling of Trustworthy IoT Entities in Energy-Efficient Cultural Spaces

Konstantina Zachila[1]([✉])(iD), Konstantinos Kotis[1](iD), Asimina Dimara[1,2](iD),
Stamatia Ladikou[1], and Christos-Nikolaos Anagnostopoulos[1](iD)

[1] Department of Cultural Technology and Communication, Intelligent Systems Lab,
University of the Aegean, Mytilene, Greece
cti20010@ct.aegean.gr, {kotis,sladikou,canag}@aegean.gr
[2] Centre for Research and Technology Hellas, Information Technologies Institute,
Thessaloniki, Greece
adimara@iti.gr

Abstract. In this paper, an ontology related to energy-efficient cultural spaces is presented. Specifically, this research work concerns ongoing efforts towards engineering the Museum Energy-Saving Ontology (MESO) towards meeting the following objectives: a) to represent knowledge related to the trustworthy IoT entities that are deployed in a museum i.e., things (e.g., exhibits, spaces), sensors, actuators, people, data, applications; b) to deal with entities' heterogeneity via semantic interoperability and integration, especially for 'smart' museum applications and generated data; c) to represent knowledge related to saving energy e.g., lights, air-conditioning; d) to represent knowledge related to museum visits and visitors towards enhancing visiting experience while preserving comfort; e) to represent knowledge related to environmental conditions towards protecting and preserving museum artwork via continuous monitoring. The human-centered collaborative, agile and iterative methodology is followed, namely HCOME, towards the development of an evolved, 'live' and modular ontology, while SWRL rules and SPARQL queries are used for its preliminary evaluation.

Keywords: Building energy management system · Museum · Energy-saving · Ontology · IoT

1 Introduction

Nowadays, energy-saving issues have awakened the research community's interest due to the more and more increasing global electricity demand [22]. An excessive use of energy is believed to derive from public and industrial buildings to cover their daily load requirements in the context of the provision of their services [18]. Thus, the necessity of developing energy-efficient buildings could be proved beneficial. Notably, the improvement of buildings' energy efficiency leads to Building

I. Maglogiannis et al. (Eds.): AIAI 2021 Workshops, IFIP AICT 628, pp. 364–376, 2021.
https://doi.org/10.1007/978-3-030-79157-5_30

Energy Management Systems (BEMS) [12]. BEMS objectives include but not limited to: a) the continuous management of energy towards energy consumption optimization (direct contribution); b) the optimization of buildings' visiting conditions towards enhancing visitors experience and comfort (indirect contribution), c) the optimization of buildings' environmental conditions towards the protection and preservation of artifacts (indirect contribution).

The application of BEMS in the context of energy-saving [12] at cultural spaces, and especially at the museums' spaces, is an evolving recent research interest. The protection and preservation of artworks and ancient objects isolated in museums, leads to the necessity of continuous monitoring of the environmental factors and indoor conditions like temperature, humidity and CO_2. This monitoring involves Internet of Things (IoT) entities, which may be considered as an integral part of BEMS, to reduce energy consumption without: a) sacrificing humans' visiting experience and comfort indoor levels, and b) sacrificing artworks' protection and preservation.

In this paper, an ontology for the formal representation of knowledge related to BEMS's trustworthy IoT entities deployed in museums is presented, namely, the Museum Energy-Saving Ontology (MESO). The proposed ontology's aim is to represent trustworthy IoT entities deployed in a cultural space/building such as a museum, along with the representation of knowledge related to BEMS' direct and indirect above mentioned contributions (objectives). MESO is engineered following an agile, human-centered, collaborative and iterative approach to the engineering of modular, evolved and "live" ontologies, namely the Human-centered Collaborative Ontology Engineering Methodology (HCOME) [17]. The objectives of the presented ontology are: a) to represent knowledge related to the trustworthy IoT entities that are deployed in a museum i.e., things (e.g., exhibits, spaces), sensors, actuators, people, data, applications; b) to deal with entities' heterogeneity via semantic interoperability and integration, especially for 'smart' museum applications and generated data; c) to represent knowledge related to saving energy e.g., lights, air-conditioning; d) to represent knowledge related to museum visits and visitors towards enhancing visiting experience while preserving comfort; e) to represent knowledge related to environmental conditions towards protecting and preserving museum artwork via continuous monitoring.

The paper is structured as follows: Sect. 2 presents related work on BEMS semantics and related ontologies. Section 3 presents specific requirements and design issues for the semantic modeling of trustworthy IoT entities in energy-saving museums. Section 4 presents the ongoing work on the engineering of Museum Energy Saving Ontology (MESO) and a preliminary evaluation via SPARQL query answering and SWRL rules reasoning. Finally, Sect. 5 discusses the current and future work on this research line, and concludes the paper.

2   Related Work

An efficient and intelligent energy management of a building has significant advantages. The BEMS is a progressed method for monitoring and controlling the power/energy load requirements of a building. A BEMS is capable of managing the energy balance of a building while monitoring and controlling other essential indoor parameters/conditions such as temperature, humidity, lights, heating and ventilation systems, towards regulating/adjusting comfort levels of the residents/visitors. "Smart" buildings are equipped with sensors, devices and actuators needed for their (automated) deployment and integration of a BEMS. As a result, in order to provide interoperability support for the building automation systems (BAS), while facilitating their seamless collaboration, communication and decision-support level operation, ontologies are of key importance.

Current trends in energy management represent the importance of using ontologies mainly for sensor/actuator and energy-related data. Several energy-based systems have been tested and implemented in various use case scenarios like households and public buildings. Some of the most deployed building- and energy-related ontologies are presented in the following paragraphs[11]:

- KNX IoT Ontology [4]. This ontology represents knowledge about various types of commonly used data points as defined in the KNX specification, like data points for heating, ventilation, and air-conditioning (HVAC), data points for load management, and data points for metering. KNX IoT is a state of the art technology and it supports the communication between various components like miscellaneous equipment. KNX is an open protocol that may support applications like indoor comfort but has a limited support for features like safety and security. The main objective of KNX ontology is to extend the KNX integration into the IoT to facilitate mobile automatic building management while ensuring that all devices can communicate via a shared language. KNX ontology can be easily adopted especially for small scale markets like smart home applications. KNX ontology is accessible from KNX web page [4].
- Smart Appliances REFerence (SAREF) ontology [5]. This ontology serves as a common conceptual model that can support the communication of existing standards, protocols and data-models mainly for smart appliances that use the ETSI TS 103 267: "SmartM2M" Smart Appliances Communication framework [8]. The SAREF's initial data point is each smart device providing specific blocks while allowing recombination and division of various parts of the ontology. The main disadvantage of SAREF is that it does not support all sensors and equipment that usually exist in a building. The SAREF ontology aims to enable interoperability between different solutions, providers, protocols, sensors in the IoT while contributing to the development of a bigger scale market like smart cities. SAREF can be easily adopted for many sectors as health, smart grid, energy management and others by reusing its classes. It is accessible from SAREF's formal web page [5].
- SAREF4ENER ontology [7]. This OWL-DL ontology is tailored to the energy domain and extends SAREF ontology. In order to enable a communication and inner connection of different data models, the Italy- and Germany-based industry association made by EEBus [1] and Energy@Home [2] created the SAREF4ENER ontology. SAREF4ENER is used as a Customer Energy Manager (CEM) for smart grids and smart homes enabling demand

response strategies. SAREF4ENER ontology has two types of classes, i.e., classes reused from other ontologies, like SAREF, and classes introduced in SAREF4ENER. This extension provides the ability to reuse SAREF4ENER classes as an overall ontology schema. The main objective of this ontology is to facilitate smart energy management while adapting users' preferences. One of its main disadvantages is that the data model has no pre-defined classes referring to electricity price. It is accessible from SAREF4ENER formal web page [7].

– SAREF4BLDFG ontology [6]. This ontology is an extension of SAREF tailored in the building domain. Its main modification is the adaptation to the Industry Foundation Classes (IFC) [3] standard for buildings' data and information. As a result, main building information about the building life cycle enables the missing interoperability between various building actors, like architects, and building applications, like construction. SAREF4BLDG is also an OWL-DL ontology that reuses SAREF classes and also has new classes which include IFC devices and other physical objects in building spaces. It is accessible from SAREF4BLDFG's web page [3].

The above list of BEMS-related ontologies is not exhaustive. In this paper, we acknowledge the existence of other related ontologies that due to space limitations, their presentation is not provided. Specifically, we acknowledge the widely-used ontologies of ThinkHome [21], BASont [20], DogOnt [9] and RE-COGNITION ontology [14]. The aforementioned ontologies have been examined, along with the ontologies presented in this paper, to investigate their suitability for reusing them in MESO.

The Semantic Sensor Network (SSN) ontology [10] and the Sensor Observation, Sample and Actuator (SOSA) ontology [13] aim to represent knowledge about entities, relations and activities included in sensing, sampling and actuation in a flexible and coherent way. The SSN/SOSA has been reused in several IoT-related ontologies and is a main/base candidate for reuse in the proposed ontology (MESO) either directly or indirectly (via the reuse of ontologies that already import SSN/SOSA).

The IoT ontology developed in the work of Kotis and Katasonov (2013) [16], supports the automated deployment of IoT entities in heterogeneous IoT environments. It mainly serves as a semantic registry for the registration of devices/systems, as well as for the registration of applications that utilize the services provided by those devices/systems. In further work on this line of research [15], a simple and extensible trust model for representing IoT entities was proposed. This model is integrated in IoT ontologies to ensure the deployment of trustworthy IoT entities. In our work, the representation of trustworthy entities are of particular importance to meet the objectives of MESO ontology, therefor this IoT trust model is reused.

In the related work of Vlachidis (2017) [23], the structure and development of the CrossCult Knowledge Base is described. The authors define the CrossCult Upper-level ontology by using the standard cultural heritage ontology CIDOC-

CRM[1]. In addition, the proposed ontology incorporates a vocabulary for historical related data with a commonly agreed structure and tries to consolidate different cultural heritage data. The CrossCult ontology is reused in the proposed ontology to fulfil the objectives of our work (objective b).

In the work of Martini (2016) [19], the developed ontology represents the knowledge about the emigration phenomena, extracted from the data of the virtual Emigration museum. Based on the ontology of CIDOC-CRM the proposed system tries to automatically translate plain text that includes emigration information into Resource Description Framework scheme (RDF). This work partially fulfils the objectives of our work (objective d).

3   Semantic Modeling of Cultural BEMS

In this paper, the semantic modeling of trustworthy IoT entities in saving-energy museums is proposed, and implemented via the engineering of a new ontology, namely, MESO. This decision is made since related work (ontologies) individually do not fully cover the aim and objectives of our work. Having said that, MESO reuses a number of classes and properties already defined in well-known ontologies such as the SSN/SOSA ontology, the SAREF4BLDG ontology, the Geonames ontology, the CrossCult ontology, and the CIDOC-CRM ontology.

MESO is engineered by a collaborative team of stakeholders (knowledge engineers, domain experts and knowledge workers), following the three distinct engineering phases of the ontology engineering life-cycle proposed in the HCOME methodology, i.e., the Specification, the Conceptualization and the Exploitation phases. Each phase consists of specific processes and tasks that are performed in either the personal space of stakeholders or in a shared space (where they collaboratively discuss, design, implement and evaluate ontological classes and properties related to the domain). The detailed description of the updated HCOME methodology is out of the scope of this paper. However, the main processes and tasks of the methodology are presented in Sect. 3 and 4 of this paper.

The Specification phase is comprised of two processes. In the first process, the aim, objectives and the team of stakeholders are specified. Specifically, regarding the MESO ontology, the aim is to represent the knowledge related to trustworthy IoT entities deployed in energy-saving museums' smart environments, to support the interoperability and integration of entities, data, processes and systems.

The aim and objectives of the proposed ontology were already described in the Introduction Sect. 1.

The ontology engineering (OE) team is comprised of two knowledge workers (users of a BEMS), two knowledge/ontology engineers, and a museum expert (expert in museum studies and in the management of cultural spaces).

In the second process of the Specification phase, the requirements of the ontology are specified and a selective list of domain-specific example queries is shaped to support this process. A representative list is presented below (an one-to-one correspondence between objectives and requirements is considered):

---

[1] http://www.cidoc-crm.org/.

- **Objective (a)** (trustworthy IoT entities' representation and management)
  1. Which exhibits are located in room "UoAMuseumRoomA1"?
  2. How many sensors (all kinds) are hosted by platform "IoTmuseumPlatfromLG"?
- **Objective (b)** (interoperability and integration)
  1. What is the temperature in the rooms that ongoing visits take place (right now)?
  2. For observations that are made for painting "Painting01" of room "UoAMuseumRoomA1" at 09.00 on 15/01/2021, what is its status in terms of its lamp brightness level (energy) and nearby visitors?
- **Objective (c)** (energy saving)
  1. Is there an activation of the light device in "UoAMuseumRoomA2" at 15.30 on 15/11/2020?
  2. Is there an activation of the heating device in "UoAMuseumRoomA1" on 25/11/2020?
- **Objective (d)** (enhancing visiting experience and comfort)
  1. Which rooms have been visited by "visitor01"?
  2. Which exhibit was the most popular in July?
- **Objective (e)** (environmental conditions)
  1. How many temperature measurements have been made in room "UoAMuseumRoomA1" between 09.00 and 17.00 on 07/12/2020?
  2. How many humidity measurements were made in room "UoAMuseumRoomA1" and "UoAMuseumRoomA2" on 30/11/2020 between 18.00 and 20.00, with values greater than 60%?

During the Conceptualization phase, the team formulates scenarios for the use of cultural BEMS based on ontological requirements. A selective representative list of scenarios are listed below:

- **Requirement (a)** (trustworthy IoT entities representation and management):
  - Count all the sculptures of the museum that are related to visits made by trustworthy students (with a trust degree more than 0.8).
  - Name all the trustworthy paintings of the museum created by "Picasso" (paintings that were created by Picasso with a trust degree more than 0.9).
- **Requirement (b)** (interoperability and integration):
  - If there are more than two visitors in room "UoAMuseumRoomA1" close to (nearby) an exhibit, classify this exhibit as an "interesting exhibit in room UoAMuseumRoomA1", turn up the light of this exhibit, and lower the light of the remaining exhibits in the room. This scenario is related to objectives (c) and (d) at the same time.
  - If the temperature of room "UoAMuseumRoomA1" and room "UoAMuseumRoomA2" is less than 18 °C, and there are visits in progress in these rooms, then activate the heating device in the rooms that those visits take place, and deactivate other sources of energy in the remaining rooms of the building. This scenario is related to objectives (c), (d) and (e) at the same time.

- **Requirement (c)** (energy saving):
  - If there are no visitors in room "UoAMuseumRoomA1", then turn the lights off (or all the sources of energy).
  - If the museum's internal and external temperature is between 20 and 30 °C, then keep the heating and cooling devices off.
- **Requirement (d)** (enhancing visiting experience and comfort):
  - When a visitor enters the museum for the first time, send him a message (e.g., SMS or tweet) with the number and types of rooms, the number and collections of exhibits, and the average duration of a visit per room.
  - If a visitor comes out of the museum, then send him a message with the names of the exhibits he liked most based on the observations he made during his/her visit.
- **Requirement (e)** (environmental conditions):
  - If the temperature in room "UoAMuseumRoomA1" is less than 18 °C, then activate the heating device (for visitors' comfort).
  - If the humidity in room A is more than 55%, then activate the humidifier device (for exhibits protection).

The implementation process of the Conceptualization phase is presented in Sect. 4 for presentation reasons.

Last but not least, the Evaluation phase is conducted. A preliminary evaluation of the engineered ontology has been performed by implementing specific scenario-based SWRL rules and running SPARQL queries against the current version of MESO ontology. The ontology along with the example queries are available at Github (https://github.com/KotisK/MESO) for further evaluation from the BEMS community of interest and practice. Alternatively, the ontology and the queries may be downloaded from http://i-lab.aegean.gr/kotis/Ontologies/Meso/.

4   The Museum Energy Saving Ontology (MESO)

MESO is implemented in OWL using Protégé 5.5[2]. Its latest version is publicly available (https://github.com/KotisK/MESO) along with example queries for further evaluation and criticism by the BEMS community (and other related communities) of interest and practice. For the presentation of the ontology's capabilities, specific scenarios have been engineered, as proposed by the HCOME methodology, already described in Sect. 3. The scenario which fully covers the interoperability and integration capabilities of the ontology is highlighted here: *If there are more than two visitors in UoAMuseumRoomA1 close to (nearby) an exhibit, classify this exhibit as an "interesting exhibit in UoAMuseumRoomA1", turn up the light of this exhibit, and lower the light of the remaining exhibits in the room.* This scenario is saving energy of the museum (lower of turn off lights that are not needed) while at the same time enhances user experience (turn up

---

[2] https://protege.stanford.edu/.

lights on a particular exhibit of specific interested nearby visitors to assist in focus).

The main ontological classes and properties of MESO that have been used in the evaluation scenarios and queries are presented in this section. The related namespaces (of the proposed and reused ontologies) along with their prefixes are:

- meso:<http://i-lab.aegean.gr/kotis/Ontologies/Meso/Meso.owl#> (the proposed ontology),
- cross:<http://www.crosscult.eu/UserModel#> (CrossCult ontology),
- sosa:<http://www.w3.org/ns/sosa/> (SOSA ontology),
- saref:<http://saref.etsi.org/saref4bldg/> (SAREF4BLDG ontology),
- geonames:<http://www.geonames.org/ontology#> (Geonames ontology),
- crm:<http://erlangen-crm.org/160714/> (CIDOC-CRM ontology)
- iot:<http://i-lab.aegean.gr/kotis/Ontologies/IoT/IoT-trust-onto.owl#> (IoT-trust ontology).

4.1 Ontology Classes

The main classes that are used in the evaluation scenarios and queries are listed below:

- **meso:MuseumVisit** subclass of cross:Visit, represents the visits of visitors in the museum.
- **meso:ExhibitProximity** subclass of sosa:ObservableProperty, represents the proximity between an exhibit and a visitor.
- **meso:Exhibit** subclass of crm:E22_Man-Made_Object, represents the paintings and sculptures that are hosted in a museum.
- **meso:ExhibitProximityObservation** subclass of sosa:Observation, represents the observations of the proximity between an exhibit and a visitor.
- **meso:InterestingExhibitProximityObservation** subclass of sosa:Observation, represents the interesting exhibits.
- **meso:ObservationToHighLevelEnergy** subclass of sosa:Observation, represents the observations result in turning up the light of an exhibit.
- **meso:SmartLamp** subclass of saref:Lamp, represents the lamps brightening the exhibits.

4.2 Ontology Properties

The main properties of MESO that are used in the evaluation scenarios and queries are listed below:

- **meso:visits** represents the action of a meso:Visitor that visits a meso:MuseumRoom.
- **sosa:madeBySensor** represents the relation between an sosa:Observation and the corresponding sosa:Sensor.

- **sosa:hasFeatureOfInterest** represents the relation between an sosa:Observation and the observed meso:Exhibit.
- **sosa:observedProperty** represents the relation linking an sosa:observation to the observed property e.g., meso:ExhibitProximity.
- **meso:nearByVisitors** subproperty of geonames:nearby, represents the number of visitors (cross:Visitor) close to an meso:Exhibit.
- **meso:brighteningLevel** represents the brightening level (Low, Medium, High) of a meso:SmartLamp that meso:lights an meso:Exhibit.
- **meso:lights** (inverse of meso:isLightedBy) represents the relation linking a meso:SmartLamp to an meso:Exhibit.
- **sosa:resultTime** represents the timestamp of a completed observation.

4.3   SPARQL Queries and SWRL Rules

In order to evaluate the proposed ontology a list of selective representative SPARQL queries answered by MESO is presented below:

- **Which exhibits are located in UoAMuseumRoomA1?**

```
PREFIX geonames:<http://www.geonames.org/ontology#>
PREFIX meso:<http://i-lab.aegean.gr/kotis/Ontologies/Meso/Meso.owl#>
SELECT ?x
WHERE { ?x  geonames:locatedIn  meso:UoAMuseumRoomA1}
```

- **How many sensors (all kinds) are hosted by IoTmuseumPlatformLG?**

```
PREFIX sosa:<http://www.w3.org/ns/sosa/>
PREFIX meso:<http://i-lab.aegean.gr/kotis/Ontologies/Meso/Meso.owl#>
SELECT (COUNT(?x) AS ?numOfSensors)
WHERE {meso:IoTmuseumPlatformLG sosa:hosts ?x}
```

- **Which rooms have been visited by Visitor01?**

```
PREFIX meso:<http://i-lab.aegean.gr/kotis/Ontologies/Meso/Meso.owl#>
SELECT ?x
WHERE {meso:Visitor01 meso:visits ?x}
```

- **What temperature measurements have been made in UoAMuseumRoomA1 between 09.00 and 17.00 on 07/12/2020?**

```
PREFIX xsd:<http://www.w3.org/2001/XMLSchema#>
PREFIX sosa:<http://www.w3.org/ns/sosa/>
PREFIX meso:<http://i-lab.aegean.gr/kotis/Ontologies/Meso/Meso.owl#>
SELECT ?Observations
WHERE {
?Observations sosa:hasFeatureOfInterest meso:UoAMuseumRoomA1.
?Observations sosa:resultTime ?resultTime
FILTER(?resultTime>="2020-12-07T09:00:12Z"^^xsd:dateTime &&
?resultTime<="2020-12-07T17:00:12Z"^^xsd:dateTime).}
```

- **For observations that are made for Painting01 (in UoAMuseumRoomA1) at 09.00 on 15/01/2021, what is its status in terms of its lamp brightness level and nearby visitors?**

```
PREFIX  xsd:<http://www.w3.org/2001/XMLSchema#>
PREFIX  sosa:<http://www.w3.org/ns/sosa/>
PREFIX  meso:<http://i-lab.aegean.gr/kotis/Ontologies/Meso/Meso.owl#>
SELECT  ?observation ?numberofvisitors ?brighteness
WHERE {
?observation  sosa:hasFeatureOfInterest  meso:Painting01 .
?observation  meso:nearByVisitors ?numberofvisitors .
?observation  meso:brighteningLevel ?brighteness .
?observation  sosa:resultTime ?resultTime .
FILTER(?resultTime="2021-01-15T09:00:12Z"^^xsd:dateTime)
}
```

Considering the specific scenario already mentioned, the Semantic Web Rule Language (SWRL) is used to implement rules for the definition of semantically rich axioms related to the specific interoperability/integration scenarios (see Fig. 1).

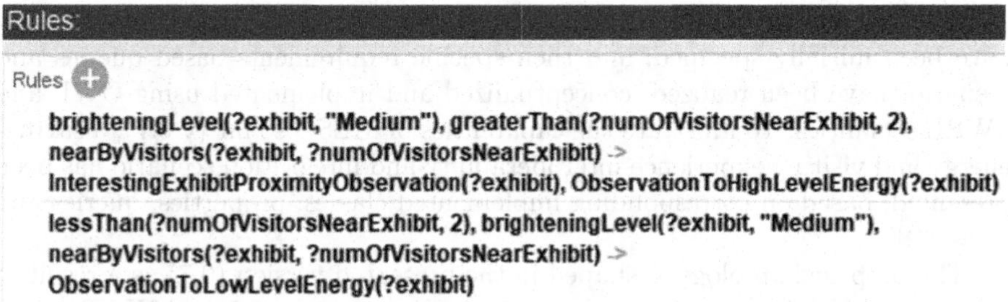

Fig. 1. Scenario-based SWRL rules in MESO (depicted in Protégé 5.5.)

Based on the above SWRL rules and Pellet[3] reasoning engine, the identification (via reasoning i.e., automated classification of instances) of interesting exhibits and energy-related observations (based on sensing visitors' proximity to exhibits and observation of exhibits' lamp brightness level) is realized. The first rule states that if the brightness level of the exhibit lamp is "Medium" and there are more than two visitors near the exhibit, then classify this observation as a) an interesting-exhibit observation and b) an observation to high level energy, meaning that the level of energy (light) for the lamp of the exhibit of this observation must be raised to high. The second rule states that if the brightness level of the exhibit's lamp is "Medium" and less than two visitors are nearby this, then classify this as an observation to low level energy, meaning that the level of energy (light) for the lamp of the exhibit of this observation must be raised to low. The example rules defined in MESO automatically classify (semantically describe) exhibit proximity observations (meso:ExhibitProximityObsrvation) as interesting-exhibit proximity observations (meso:InterestingExhibitProximityObsrvation) and/or observations that must apply a change (decrease or increase) to the level of light (energy) of the observed exhibit (meso:ObservationToHighLevelEnergy or meso:ObservationToLowLevelEnergy). The specific time and location of the observations made are

---

[3] https://www.w3.org/2001/sw/wiki/Pellet.

specified via geonames:locatedIn (for meso:Exhibit) and sosa:resultTime properties (for sosa:Observation).

5   Conclusion and Future Work

This paper presents first steps towards of an ongoing work towards engineering an ontology for the representation of trustworthy IoT entities that harmonically are deployed in an energy-saving museum. MESO ontology represents, in an integrated and interoperable manner, knowledge related to a)trustworthy IoT entities and energy saving; b) enhancing of visiting experience and comfort; c) museum's environmental conditions' monitoring. MESO reuses well-known ontologies such as SOSA, CrossCult, and SAREF4BLDFG. Following the methodological approach of human-centered collaborative and agile ontology engineering, namely HCOME, the aim and objectives of the proposed ontology have been initially specified, and then specific requirements-based queries and scenarios have been realized, conceptualized and implemented using OWL and SWRL semantics. To illustrate the capabilities of MESO so far (v 0.7), a saving-energy and visiting experience interoperability and integration scenario has been presented, based on corresponding implemented classes, properties, queries and rules.

The proposed ontology is shaped in the presented version (0.7) as a result of collaborative engineering (edit, evaluation) using Protege 5.5 and WebProtege, as well as Google docs, e-mails and video-conferencing meetings. During the development of this version, the ontology engineering team has been focused on the implementation of the specific selected scenarios and example queries, as presented in this paper, with an emphasis on the interoperability and integration objectives (considering cases of energy-saving along with visiting and exhibits-related objectives). The limitation of our work, as presented in this paper, is that the selected scenarios and queries do not accentuate integrated knowledge related to the trustworthiness of IoT entities.

Future work will be focused on the completion of MESO, defining additional classes and properties linked to SOSA, CrossCult, SAREF4BLDFG and SAREF4ENRG ontologies, fully covering the ontological objectives and requirements presented in this paper. Furthermore, although the trustworthiness of the museum's IoT entities is represented in the current version of the ontology (via the IoT-trust-onto and the TrustworthinessObject class), this is not adequately demonstrated i.e., by fully reusing our related work on IoT-trust ontology and fuzzyOWL2 semantics. Finally, a complete version of MESO will be evaluated in the context of a real application setting (a "smart" museum setting).

References

1. Eebus. https://www.eebus.org/contact/. Accessed 10 Feb 2021
2. Energy@home. http://www.energy-home.it/SitePages/Home.aspx. Accessed 10 Feb 2021

3. Industry foundation classes. https://www.buildingsmart.org/standards/bsi-standards/industry-foundation-classes/. Accessed 10 Feb 2021
4. Knx ontology. https://www.knx.org/knx-en/for-professionals/benefits/knx-internet-of-things/. Accessed 09 Feb 2021
5. Saref ontology. https://ontology.tno.nl/saref/. Accessed 09 Feb 2021
6. Saref4bldg. https://www.etsi.org/deliver/etsi_ts/103400_103499/10341003/01.01.01_60/ts_10341003v010101p.pdf. Accessed 10 Feb 2021
7. Saref4ener ontology. https://saref.etsi.org/saref4ener/v1.1.2/. Accessed 10 Feb 2021
8. Appliances, S.: Smartm2m; smart appliances; reference ontology and onem2m mapping (2017)
9. Bonino, D., Corno, F.: DogOnt - ontology modeling for intelligent domotic environments. In: Sheth, A., Staab, S., Dean, M., Paolucci, M., Maynard, D., Finin, T., Thirunarayan, K. (eds.) ISWC 2008. LNCS, vol. 5318, pp. 790–803. Springer, Heidelberg (2008). https://doi.org/10.1007/978-3-540-88564-1_51
10. Compton, M., et al.: The SSN ontology of the w3c semantic sensor network incubator group. J. Web Semant. **17**, 25–32 (2012)
11. Cuenca, J., Larrinaga, F., Curry, E.: A unified semantic ontology for energy management applications. In: WSP/WOMoCoE@ ISWC, pp. 86–97 (2017)
12. Doukas, H., Patlitzianas, K.D., Iatropoulos, K., Psarras, J.: Intelligent building energy management system using rule sets. Build. Environ. **42**(10), 3562–3569 (2007)
13. Haller, A., Janowicz, K., Cox, S., Le Phuoc, D., Taylor, K., Lefrançois, M.: Semantic sensor network ontology (2017)
14. Ioannidis, M., Sortsi, S.: Deliverable d3.1-re-cognition common information model and device managers. In: HORIZON GA 815301 (2020). https://re-cognition-project.eu/wp-content/uploads/2020/07/D-3.1_compressed.pdf
15. Kotis, K., Athanasakis, I., Vouros, G.A.: Semantically enabling IoT trust to ensure and secure deployment of IoT entities. Int. J. Internet Things Cyber Assur. **1**(1), 3–21 (2018)
16. Kotis, K., Katasonov, A.: Semantic interoperability on the internet of things: the semantic smart gateway framework. Int. J. Distrib. Syst. Technol. (IJDST) **4**(3), 47–69 (2013)
17. Kotis, K., Papasalouros, A., Vouros, G.A., Pappas, N., Zoumpatianos, K.: Enhancing the collective knowledge for the engineering of ontologies in open and socially constructed learning spaces. J. UCS **17**(12), 1710–1742 (2011)
18. Liu, Y., Chen, H., Zhang, L., Wu, X., Wang, X.J.: Energy consumption prediction and diagnosis of public buildings based on support vector machine learning: a case study in china. J. Clean. Prod. **272**, 122542 (2020)
19. Martini, R.G., Araújo, C., Librelotto, G.R., Henriques, P.R.: A reduced CRM-compatible form ontology for the virtual emigration museum. In: New Advances in Information Systems and Technologies. AISC, vol. 444, pp. 401–410. Springer, Cham (2016). https://doi.org/10.1007/978-3-319-31232-3_38
20. Ploennigs, J., Hensel, B., Dibowski, H., Kabitzsch, K.: BASONT-a modular, adaptive building automation system ontology. In: IECON 2012–38th Annual Conference on IEEE Industrial Electronics Society, pp. 4827–4833. IEEE (2012)
21. Reinisch, C., Kofler, M., Iglesias, F., Kastner, W.: Thinkhome energy efficiency in future smart homes. EURASIP J. Embedd. Syst. **2011**, 1–18 (2011)

22. van Ruijven, B.J., De. Cian, E., Wing, I.S.: Amplification of future energy demand growth due to climate change. Nat. Commun. **10**(1), 1–12 (2019)
23. Vlachidis, A., Bikakis, A., Kyriaki-Manessi, D., Triantafyllou, I., Antoniou, A.: The CrossCult knowledge base: a co-inhabitant of cultural heritage ontology and vocabulary classification. In: Kirikova, M., Nørvåg, K., Papadopoulos, G.A., Gamper, J., Wrembel, R., Darmont, J., Rizzi, S. (eds.) ADBIS 2017. CCIS, vol. 767, pp. 353–362. Springer, Cham (2017). https://doi.org/10.1007/978-3-319-67162-8_35

Short Term Net Imbalance Volume Forecasting Through Machine and Deep Learning: A UK Case Study

Elpiniki Makri[(✉)], Ioannis Koskinas, Apostolos C. Tsolakis[ⓘ],
Dimosthenis Ioannidis[ⓘ], and Dimitrios Tzovaras[ⓘ]

Centre for Research and Technology Hellas, Information Technologies Institute,
6th km Harilaou-Thermis, GR57001 Thessaloniki, Greece
{elpimak,jkosk,tsolakis,djoannid,Dimitrios.Tzovaras}@iti.gr
https://www.iti.gr

Abstract. As energy markets become more and more dynamic, the importance of price forecasting has gained a lot of attention over the last few years. Considering also the introduction of new business models and roles, such as Aggregators and energy flexibility traders, in the constantly evolving energy landscape which follows the general opening of the European electricity markets, the need for anticipating energy price trends and flows holds significant business value. On top of that, the exponential renewable energy sources penetration, adds to the challenges introduced to this dynamic scheme of things. Given their volatile and intermittent nature, supply-demand imbalance can reach critical margins, threatening the overall system stability. In the scope of reducing the power imbalances, a forecast for the imbalance volume will be beneficial either from the perspective of the system operator that could minimise mitigation costs, or the market participants that could target extreme prices for maximising their profit, while effectively managing their risks. The development of a deep learning algorithm for the prediction of the net imbalance volume in the UK market is proposed in this paper in comparison with a common but widely used machine learning approach, namely a gradient boosting trees regression model. The variables which contributed the most on those models were mainly the historical values of net imbalance volume. The deep neural network returns a Root mean squared error (RMSE) and Mean Absolute Error (MAE) equal to 200 and 152 MWh in a range of values between [−1.5, 2.0] GWh, respectively, the gradient boosting trees model has an RMSE and MAE equal to 203 and 154 MWh, in contrast to an ARIMA model that has RMSE and MAE equal to 226 and 173 MWh.

Keywords: Net imbalance volume · Time series forecasting · Long short-term memory · Gradient boosting trees · Machine learning · Energy forecasting · Imbalance forecasting

This paper has been partially funded by the European Union's Horizon 2020 research and innovation programme under Grant Agreement No 773960 (DELTA project).

I. Maglogiannis et al. (Eds.): AIAI 2021 Workshops, IFIP AICT 628, pp. 377–389, 2021.
https://doi.org/10.1007/978-3-030-79157-5_31

1 Introduction

In recent years the attention of energy's community has turned to Renewable Energy Sources (RES) in the direction of clean energy generation and less carbon emissions. However, the incorporation and provision of intermittent energy to the electric grid tends to create grid stability issues or high volatility in the energy prices. Thus, the confrontation of that kind of issues from National Grid Energy System Operator (NGESO) or aggregator's side, demand efficient forecasting tools for mitigation of unexpected net imbalance deviations.

In 2020, information regarding the electricity sector's grid supply for the United Kingdom (UK) came from 55% low-carbon power (including 24.8% from wind, 17.2% nuclear power, 4.4% solar, 1.6% hydroelectricity, 6.5% biomass), 36.1% fossil fuelled power and 8.4% imports. Fuel-based generation and in particular coal-based generation, in contrast to its former domination, nowadays is mainly employed during winter due to pollution and high operational cost [5]. While coal generators have a downward trajectory, renewable power takes the lead and seems to keep constantly growing. By February 2018, UK held the world's sixth place of the largest producers of wind power, with 12,083 MW of onshore capacity and 6,361 MW of offshore capacity, which leads to a total installed capacity of over 18.4 GW. Moreover, solar power consists another RES growing fast in UK (the third-largest solar energy producer in Europe in 2018) [2], providing significant generation during the day, but is considered inadequate in terms of total energy provided.

The role of the Transmission System Operator (TSO) is entrusted with the management and development of the grid transmission as also for maintaining a constant balance between electricity supply from power stations and demand from consumers [8]. Along with TSO, market participants submit their supply for both up-and down-regulation individually. Specifically, the producers urged to be aware of their bids that got approved in the day-ahead market as well the spot price (the amount of electricity the market needs at any moment). During the bids, the participants determine the amount of power and the according value of price it will offered for regulation in each hour of the following day. The market actors that have caused an imbalance in the power market will charged for the balancing reserves that have been activated, in order to restore balance in the power system [9]. Net Imbalance Volume (NIV), which is examined in this paper, represents the volume of balancing actions remaining after the volume of the Buy balancing actions ("Offers"), are netted off against the volume of Sell balancing actions ("Bids"). The NIV as a metric indicates mostly the market participants' response to the modifications in the balancing arrangements, rather than the direct effect caused by the application of those modifications [24].

As dynamic energy markets are relatively new, there are very few findings in the literature regarding imbalance market forecasting, and even more specifically targeting NIV. Imbalance market's Price Forecasting challenge has been addressed from [13,20,27] through probabilistic forecasting models, while [7] denoted the importance of NIV as a highly correlated feature to the price. More specifically in [7], a statistical approach has been followed for the calculation of a transition state probability of NIV over historical data. Traditional time-series algorithms' such as ARIMA were tested in [10] over univariate data, while also conducted autocorrelation and partial autocorrelation analysis in order to explore association between the time periods, to conclude that Feed Forward Networks over multivariate data can achieve higher accuracy because of the problem's complexity. In [3], an encoder-decoder model was designed for a short term probabilistic forecast that was combined with an optimization algorithm for optimal market participation. From the perspective of density forecasting models, [4] endeavoured to predict the imbalances in Austrian energy markets through the exploitation of historical imbalances, the historical load forecast errors, the wind and the solar production. Finally, as the RES can be considered a significant factor for increased or decreased energy reserves during the day, [11], [15] explored the impact of Wind and Solar generation towards the markets' behaviour and price, identifying high correlations between the weather with NIV volatility ratios and prices.

The presented work aims to address the challenge of accurately forecasting NIV in the UK market, by using AI-driven techniques and combining knowledge acquired from historical information within related energy markets, in order to reduce the imbalances of the market as much as possible and introduce an added value service to market stakeholders for optimally participating in dynamic markets and potentially increasing the revenue streams. The remainder of the paper is structured as follows: Sect. 2 introduces the methodology and architecture of the deep learning model designed. Section 3 describes the details of the experimental data set, while Sect. 4 presents the experimental setup and results for the evaluation and validation of the implemented architecture. Finally, Sect. 5 concludes the manuscript with some key points and suggestions for further work in order to expand the research in this area.

2   Methodology

Time series analysis is a statistical technique that deals with time series data, and in particular is considered as the use of a model to predict future values based on previously observed values. In order to determine a forecasting model a representation and further examination of the historical patterns should be beneficial for the analysis. While analysing historical data through time for identifying any trends/patterns, an assumption is made that the existing trend would continue in the future. During the before mentioned exploration the seasonal variation, other cycle variation (i.e. The four stages of the economic cycle, expansion, peak, contraction, and trough) and irregular fluctuations of the series values could be distinguished. End wise, stationarity denotes that the statistical properties of a process generating a time series is stable over time, inevitably its mean, variance and covariance don't have significant changes over time [21].

Forecasts contain ambiguities that will irrevocably lead to forecast errors. In the scope of calculating the extend of forecasting error, Mean Absolute Error (MAE) and Mean Squared Error (MSE) are the metrics serving this objective and are used to evaluate the performance of the model in regression analysis. The Mean absolute error represents the average of the absolute difference between the actual and predicted values. Mean Squared Error represents the average of the squared difference between the original and predicted values. Additionally, another deterministic metric is the square root of Mean Squared error namely the Root Mean Squared Error (RMSE).

Among the numerous methods aimed at achieving accuracy and minimizing losses within time series forecasting, there are several machine learning algorithms that induce high precision and computational efficiency [16]. One important characteristic of NIV forecasting is the structure of the time series of both the input variables and the forecasted output. This transforms the problem of forecasting NIV into a specialized form of regression, thus the predicted outcome matches a numerical or continuous value. Nevertheless, traditional machine learning algorithms are affected relentlessly by the missing values and are governed by the deficiency of recognizing complex pattern. Recurrent Neural Network's (RNN) performance is not significantly affected from missing values, as also RNNs can find complex patterns in the input time series. In addition to standard RNNs, Long Short-Term Memory Networks (LSTM), introduced by Hochreiter & Schmidhuber [23], have been developed to overcome the vanishing gradient problem by improving the gradient flow within the network. This is achieved using a LSTM unit in place of the hidden layer [22].

The cell state into the LSTM cells acts as a highway in order for the gradient to flow better to the earlier states, which in turn allows the model to capture memory that are further back in the past. Information is removed or added to the cell state, carefully regulated by structures called gates. Gates are mainly a pointwise multiplication operation and a sigmoid neural net layer, thus the output values are fluctuated between 0 (all of the information is removed) and 1(all of the information passes through). Three gates constitutes the LSTM, the Forget Gate, the Input Gate and the Output Gate. Forget Gate adjusts the amount of previous data information which will pass through, while the Input Gate decides which values will be updated. Output Gate produces the output that is multiplied by a tanh, in order for the output to be filtered [26]. In this paper we compared the performance of a recurrent neural network (Fig. 1) and a gradient boosting trees (i.e. using the XGBoost implementation [6]) training algorithm for forecasting the NIV value.

The Fig. 1 depicts the architecture of the deep learning neural network which includes 6 LSTM layers. The LSTM model in Keras from Tensorflow[1] framework is defined as a sequence of layers. The first layer in the network defines the 2-dimensional units of the tensors and contains 128 number of neurons. The rest of the layers are stacked by adding them to the sequential process and most specifically the second layer contains 64 units, the third and fourth layer have 128 and 64 respectively and the last two contain 64 and 16 number of units respectively. The activation function used in each layer is the Rectified Linear Units (ReLU) [25], which transforms the output from each unit as the input for

---

[1] https://pypi.org/project/Keras/.

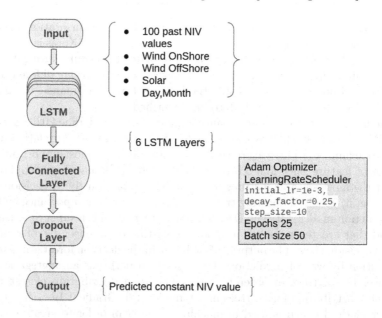

Fig. 1. Recurrent neural network architecture

the next layer. The selection of ReLU is due to simpler mathematical operations, hence less computational complexity, compared to tanh and sigmoid, as also is widely used in cases where vanishing gradient problems need to be avoided and rectified. Subsequently, a Dense layer is added with number of units equal to the number of features (134). In order to avoid overfitting in such a large network and improve performance, some type of regularization and dropout have subjoined to the model. Regularization reduces parameters and simplifies the model by penalizing high-valued regression coefficients and most specific L2 regularization, which is applied on the first layers of the model, adds an L2 penalty equal to the square of the magnitude of coefficient. Ridge regression (L2 regularization) is frequently used when the independent variables are highly correlated (multicollinearity) and the high value of variance causes the deviation of observed values from the actual values. On the attemp of solving this particular issue, a shrinkage parameter lambda is added [18]. L2 regularization decreases the complexity of a model, however it never leads to a coefficient tending to zero rather only minimizes it. On the other hand, the dropout layer randomly sets input units to zero with a frequency of rate at each step during training time. Several values of rates between 10% to 50% have been applied in order to conclude to the value on which the model's performance is optimized. The 20% value for the dropout layer emerged as the most suitable. Finally, the last layer constitutes of a Dense layer with 1 unit and the activation function on this particular layer is linear. As the details about the topology of the network have been clarified, the following step concerns the optimization algorithm and the loss function. The MSE value is selected for the loss function and the Adam optimizer was deemed as the most appropriate. In this implementation instead of a fixed value for learning rate, the LearningRateScheduler of Keras is used which reduces the learning rate according to a pre-defined schedule during training. After the above hyper-parameters have been selected after trying different neural networks and observing at each step the loss function performance, the number of epochs(25) and the batch size(50) are identified.

The historical data are dating since January 2015 until June 2020. Except of the NIV values that are processed, further features and the correlation among them are examined. The feature correlation establish the most important pylon in favor of feature selection. Three different techniques have been employed to extract the most suitable features from the NIV data, namely: i) decision forest regression, ii) gradient boosting trees, and iii) permutation importance on top of the prediction model [14]. The Decision Forest regression is a supervised learning method that creates a regression model consisting of an ensemble of randomly trained decision trees. The outputs of each tree in the decision forest is a Gaussian distribution by way of prediction. The algorithm performs an aggregation over the ensemble of trees in order to find a Gaussian distribution closest to the combined distribution for all trees in the model [17]. Gradient Boosting Trees is another method which is used in machine learning in order to create ensemble models. The algorithm constructs each regression tree step by step. Using the predefined loss function it measures the error in each step and correct it in the next one. The prediction model is an ensemble of the weaker prediction models. In the regression problem, boosting creates a series of trees step-wise, and then using an arbitrary differential loss function, selects the optimal tree [17]. Feature permutation importance measures the predictive value of a feature by evaluating the increase of the prediction error which increases in case of feature's unavailability. The algorithm randomly shuffles the features adding noise, in order to avoid the removal of features and the retraining of the regressor [19].

The scope of the paper lays on the exploration of machine and deep learning techniques for the prediction of the NIV values for the next 30 min based on the preceding values, over a large dataset of five years. Subsequently, the examination of the various factors, which presumably have a catalytic affect on the balancing power volume, was developed. The investigation took place in order to distinguish the variables that can be used as explanatory variables for the balancing power volume when developing the forecasting model. Since the analysis concerns the behavior of the net imbalance volume through the time field, the primary parameters which are placed under the microscope was the date characteristics. The model predicts the target value for the next half hour, thus factors such as price value or power consumption are unknown and cannot be used as inputs to the model. However, the wind power production forecast, both Onshore and Offshore as well as the Solar power production are known when forecasting the balancing power volume, hence are included in the set of features. The past values of the balancing power volume can also be used as a predictor for the balancing power volume.

3   Experimental Dataset

The Balancing Mechanism Reporting Service (BMRS) API of Elexon [1], which constitutes of programming instructions for participants in order to retrieve BRMS data, is suited for users seeking to access historical data or real-time information. The historic values regarding the target data explored in this work are ranged from January 2015 until June 2020, updated every 30 min. Thus, 48 measurements are counted during a day period. In Fig. 2, the NIV time series along the above mentioned period is demonstrated.

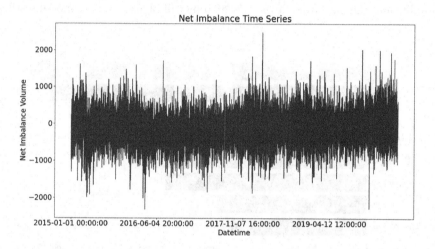

Fig. 2. Net imbalance volume time series

Evidently, NIV time series are non-stationary whereas the mean as well as the standard deviation are not consistent through time. On the assumption of absent of stationarity, differencing technique overtakes this issue. Nevertheless, this paper conducts with non-stationary time series.

Taking into consideration the increasing amount of power that comes from the renewable sources of energy such as wind and sun, uncertain power consumption have lead to imbalances in the power system. Specifically, based on the weather forecast which entails some uncertainty, wind power producers estimate the amount of power that will produce the following day. In addition, there is a bottleneck regarding the fully estimation of the affect of the heating especially in hours where the sun radiation is high compared to previous hours. Thus, the intensity of the sun radiation is unpredictable. Hence, it is implied that those factors should be examined whether affect the imbalancing volume. Wind, both onshore and offshore, and sun measurements during the day are also available through the (BMRS) API of Elexon. Furthermore, analysing the time series in order to locate seasonality, the daily and weekly variation of the balancing power will be processed. Firstly, the day has divided to eight groups of four hours, separating the peculiarity of those hours. Then, the date is distinguished to each day of the week and whether it belongs to a working day, as also it is classified to separated months. Thereafter, mean and differencing value are used as candidate features into the feature selection litigation.

The dataset is divided into two sets, the train set and the test set. The dataset is divided by rows, and in order to ensure that the data that has been used for the model training will not be used for the model testing. The first set, which is 70% of the original dataset will be used to train the model, the second set that represents the remaining 30% of the original dataset will be used to generate the predictions. Thus, the data from 2015 to 2019 will be used for the model training and the data from 2019 to 2020 June will be used for the model testing.

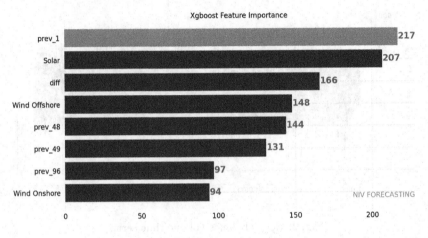

Fig. 3. XgBoost feature importance

Conventionally, feature importance algorithms such as feature permutation importance, random Forest decision tree and gradient boosting trees, which extensively described in Sect. 2, provide a score which implies the importance of each feature for the model. Figure 3 and Fig. 4 depict the outcome of the gradient boosting trees and permutation feature importance algorithms respectively, whereas Fig. 5 presents also feature importance calculation results from the the Random Forest technique.

Comparing the images occurred from feature importance analysis, it's clear that both wind and solar power generation affect the forecasted NIV value. Concerning the NIV historical values (100 past values), it seems that one and two days ago values act on the importance estimator, although the previous value of the forecasted influences the most. Last but not least, the difference calculated on net imbalance volume plays a part on forecasting performance. Although, the date characteristics are not indicated as the most influencing factors, their use in time series analysis is an indisputable benefit.

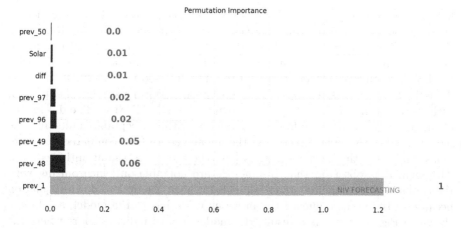

Fig. 4. Permutation importance

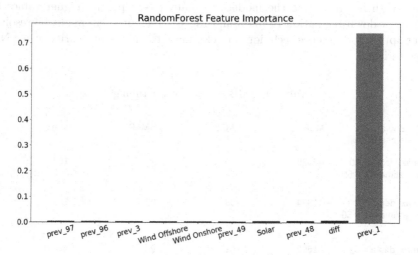

Fig. 5. Random forest importance

4 Results

The Gradient Boosting Tree regression model and the LSTM architecture presented in Sect. 2 are used in the experiment. Training and testing of each model ran independently and the performance of each model was evaluated. The result from the model evaluation are used in order to compare these models and identify the most suitable one for the given forecasting task and dataset. The accuracy of the models has been evaluated by using the Mean Square Error (MSE), Root Mean Squared Error (RMSE), Mean Absolute Error (MAE) and Symmetric Mean Absolute Percentage Error (sMAPE). In addition with the comparing results, the outcome of an Autoregressive integrated moving average (ARIMA), a widely known statistical analysis model that mainly used in time series data, has been added. The Table 1 shows the various parameters which examined in order to conclude on those that produce better results on forecasting. Regarding the capability of the models on forecasting the NIV value for next 30 min, it can be seen from Table 2 that both of the models produce similar results, although the LSTM is slightly better compared to Gradient Boosting Trees on the same dataset. However, it is clear that both models outperform a simplified approach, such as an Autoregressive integrated moving average (ARIMA). The divergence of the actual value and the forecasted value is within acceptable limits and the models predict the right direction of the imbalance. In fact, compared with previous findings with the same metrics [10], the errors are significantly reduced. Although, it is observed that the models are not able on synchronizing with the peaks in the balancing power volumes for both the up-and down-regulation because of the great influence the previous value has to the model, as already shown in Figs. 3, 4, 5. As a result, the models fail to indicate hours where the balancing power volume under the up-or down-regulation will have its peaks. In hours with no regulation the models, in many cases, predict higher values for the up-or down-regulation (Table 3 and Fig. 6). This problem might be resolved after applying difference techniques to eliminate the non-stationarity of the NIV time series.

Table 1. XGBoost parameter tuning

XGBoost Parameter Tuning	MSE	RMSE	SMAPE	MAE
max_depth = 10 n_estimators = 50	46429	215	96	164
max_depth = 5 n_estimators = 50	41394	203	92	154
max_depth = 5 n_estimators = 100	41605	203	93	154
max_depth = 5 n_estimators =200	42241	205	93	155

Table 2. Comparative error metrics

Models	MSE	RMSE	MAE	SMAPE
LSTM	40292	200	152	92
XGBoost	41394	203	154	92
ARIMA	51240	226	173	91

Table 3. Error metrics for deep learning model in ranges

Range (MWh)	MSE	RMSE	MAE
0 - 300	27079	164	127
300 - 500	58616	242	193
500 - 2000	147818	384	313

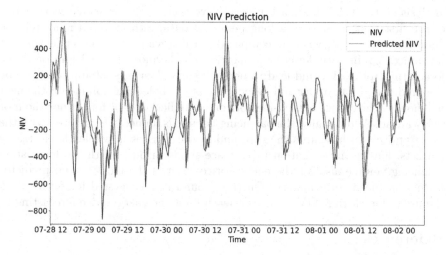

Fig. 6. Actual and forecasted NIV values from LSTM model

5   Conclusion and Future Work

The aim of this paper was to examine the set of variables which affect the NIV
forecasting and design, evaluate and validate the performance of a Deep learning
algorithm for predicting short-term future values. NIV describes the necessary
energy required to be sold or purchased from the System Operator (SO) towards
maintaining the energy system in balance. An accurate forecast can significantly
reduce balancing costs, as well as define the necessary preventive mechanisms
and early corrective actions to avoid high NIV values. On the other hand, market
participants could more efficiently place their bids in the dynamic markets, like
the balancing markets, minimizing their risk while maximising their revenues.

From the side of development this paper proposes the implementation of
deep learning algorithms which results in slightly better performance than a
machine learning counterpart, with the prospect of updating the networks regularly, since the deeper the recurrent network the more data needed in order
to preserve lower values in error metrics. The challenges that emerged during
the analysis are divided in two main categories. The first one was the missing

values in the dataset as well as the general lack of data to create a highly reliable reference model due to young market conditions. The second one is related to the development of a flexible methodology that can surpass the various parameters which directly affect the market (e.g. unusual market condition such as the incident on September 15,2020, which The UK's electricity system price spiked to over £ 500/MWh in response to low levels of wind generation [12]).

Despite the fact that the results of the NIV forecasting presented for the next 30 min are not optimal -RMSE is equals to 200 MWh- the 63% of the NIV values in dataset have as absolute value less than 300 MWh, which in that case the RMSE is 164. This paper can be the basis for further work and analysis on the balancing market area. Nevertheless, the presented work is one of the first that cover such a long period of data, introducing a more reliable data-driven analysis, whereas compared with previous research endeavours it introduces significantly lower error metrics. Furthermore, the redefinition of the forecasting approach could lead to better results. A suggested approach can be the prediction of an upper and lower value of the balancing volume for the next half hour or the change of the time horizon of prediction to be for the next hour or a day ahead. Additionally, the balancing volume is immediately related with the energy price which regards the spot and forward prices in wholesale electricity markets. Further investigation takes place simultaneously with the forecasting balancing volume also for the energy price, as it is the most crucial predictor factor that needs to examined. On this ground it is suggested for future work the use of forecasting NIV value as a feature for the energy price forecasting.

References

1. Elexon. https://www.elexon.co.uk/. Accessed 12 Mar 2021
2. Besta, S.: Europe's top five solar power producing countries. NS Energy (2019)
3. Bottieau, J., Hubert, L., De Greve, Z., Vallee, F., Toubeau, J.F.: Very-short-term probabilistic forecasting for a risk-aware participation in the single price imbalance settlement. IEEE Trans. Power Syst. **35**, 1218–1230 (2020). https://doi.org/10.1109/TPWRS.2019.2940756
4. Bunn, D.W., Gianfreda, A., Kermer, S.: A trading-based evaluation of density forecasts in a real-time electricity market. Energies **11**(10) (2018). https://doi.org/10.3390/en11102658. https://www.mdpi.com/1996-1073/11/10/2658
5. Department for Business, E.I.S.: UK energy in brief 2020 pp. 31–35 (2020). https://www.gov.uk/government/statistics/uk-energy-in-brief-2020
6. Chen, T., Guestrin, C.: Xgboost: a scalable tree boosting system. In: Proceedings of the 22nd ACM SIGKDD International Conference on Knowledge Discovery and Data Mining, pp. 785–794 (2016)
7. Dumas, J., Boukas, I., de Villena, M.M., Mathieu, S., Cornélusse, B.: Probabilistic forecasting of imbalance prices in the Belgian context. In: 2019 16th International Conference on the European Energy Market (EEM), pp. 1–7 (2019). https://doi.org/10.1109/EEM.2019.8916375
8. Eduardo A., Martínez Ceseña, P.M.: Smart distribution networks, demand side response, and community energy systems: field trial experiences and smart grid modeling advances in the United Kingdom, pp. 275–311 (2018). https://doi.org/10.1016/B978-0-12-803128-5.00008-8

9. Ferreira, P.P.: Volume and price in the nordic balancing power market, pp. 18–21, 29–34 (2016). https://core.ac.uk/download/pdf/154676684.pdf
10. Garcia, M.P., Kirschen, D.S.: Forecasting system imbalance volumes in competitive electricity markets. IEEE Trans. Power Syst. **21**(1), 240–248 (2006)
11. Green, R., Vasilakos, N.: Market behaviour with large amounts of intermittent generation. Energy Policy **38**, 3211–3220 (2010). https://doi.org/10.1016/j.enpol.2009.07.038
12. Grundy, A.: UK electricity system price spikes to over 500/mwh due to low wind. Current (2020)
13. Hong, T., Pinson, P., Fan, S.: Global energy forecasting competition 2012. Int. J. Forecast. **30**(2), 357–363 (2014). https://doi.org/10.1016/j.ijforecast.2013.07.001. https://www.sciencedirect.com/science/article/pii/S0169207013000745
14. Huang, N., Lu, G., Xu, D.: A permutation importance-based feature selection method for short-term electricity load forecasting using random forest. Energies **9**(10), 767 (2016)
15. Ketterer, J.: The impact of wind power generation on the electricity price in Germany. Energy Economics **44** (2014). https://doi.org/10.1016/j.eneco.2014.04.003
16. Lago, J., De Ridder, F., De Schutter, B.: Forecasting spot electricity prices: deep learning approaches and empirical comparison of traditional algorithms. Appl. Energy **221**, 386–405 (2018)
17. Nagpal, A.: Decision tree ensembles- bagging and boosting. Towards Data Science (2017). https://towardsdatascience.com/decision-tree-ensembles-bagging-and-boosting-266a8ba60fd9
18. Nagpal, A.: L1 and l2 regularization methods. Towards Data Science (2017)
19. Huang, N., Guobo Lu, D.X.: A permutation importance-based feature selection method for short-term electricity load forecasting using random forest. Energies (2016). https://doi.org/10.3390/en9100767
20. Nowotarski, J., Weron, R.: Recent advances in electricity price forecasting: a review of probabilistic forecasting. Renewable and Sustain. Energy Rev. **81**, 1548–1568 (2018). https://doi.org/10.1016/j.rser.2017.05.234. https://www.sciencedirect.com/science/article/pii/S1364032117308808
21. Palachy, S.: Stationarity in time series analysis. Towards Data Science (2019). https://towardsdatascience.com/stationarity-in-time-series-analysis-90c94f27322
22. Pra, M.D.: Time series forecasting with deep learning and attention mechanism. Towards Data Science (2020). https://towardsdatascience.com/time-series-forecasting-with-deep-learning-and-attention-mechanism-2d001fc871fc
23. Sepp Hochreiter, J.S.: Long short-term memory **9** (1997). https://doi.org/10.1162/neco.1997.9.8.1735
24. Shah, A.G.A.: Analysis of the first phase of the electricity balancing significant code review. The Office of Gas and Electricity Markets (Ofgem), p. 16 (2018)
25. Sharma, S.: Activation functions in neural networks. Towards Data Science (2017)
26. Steven Elsworth, S.G.: Time series forecasting using LSTM networks: A symbolic approach (2020)
27. Zhang, Y., Wang, J., Wang, X.: Review on probabilistic forecasting of wind power generation. Renewable and Sustainable Energy Rev. **32**, 255–270 (2014). https://doi.org/10.1016/j.rser.2014.01.033. https://www.sciencedirect.com/science/article/pii/S1364032114000446

10th Mining Humanistic Data Workshop (MHDW 2021)

MHDW 2021 Workshop

The abundance of available data, which is retrieved from or is related to the areas of humanities and the human condition, challenges the research community in processing and analyzing it. The aim is two-fold: on the one hand, to extract knowledge that will help to understand human behavior, creativity, ways of thinking, reasoning, learning, decision making, socializing, and even biological processes, and on the other hand, to exploit the extracted knowledge by incorporating it into intelligent systems that will support humans in their everyday activities.

The nature of humanistic data can be multimodal, semantically heterogeneous, dynamic, and time- and space-dependent, as well as highly complicated. Translating humanistic information, e.g., behavior, state of mind, artistic creation, linguistic utterance, learning, and genomic information, into numerical or categorical low-level data is considered a significant challenge on its own. New techniques, appropriate to deal with this type of data, need to be proposed whereas existing ones must be adapted to its special characteristics.

The Mining Humanistic Data Workshop (MHDW) aims to bring together inter-disciplinary approaches that focus on the application of both existing and innovative data matching, fusion, and mining techniques, as well as knowledge discovery and management techniques (like decision rules, decision trees, association rules, ontologies and alignments, clustering, filtering, learning, classifier systems, neural networks, support vector machines, preprocessing, post processing, feature selection, and visualization), to data derived from all areas of humanistic sciences, e.g. linguistic, historical, behavioral, psychological, artistic, musical, educational, social, etc. in ubiquitous computing as well as bioinformatics.

Ubiquitous computing applications (such as pervasive computing, mobile computing, ambient intelligence, etc.) collect large volumes of usually heterogeneous data to improve adaptation, learning, and, in a general context, awareness. Data matching, fusion, and mining techniques are necessary to ensure human-centered application functionality.

An important aspect of humanistic centers consists of managing, processing and computationally analyzing Biological and Biomedical data. Hence, one of the aims of this MHDW 2021 was to attract researchers that are interested in designing, developing, and applying efficient data and text mining techniques for discovering the underlying knowledge existing in biomedical data, such as sequences, gene expressions, and pathways.

Topics of interest at MHDW 2021 included, but were not limited to, the following:

- Humanistic data collection and interpretation
- Data pre-processing
- Feature selection methodologies
- Supervised or unsupervised learning of humanistic knowledge
- Clustering/classification techniques
- Fuzzy modeling
- Heterogeneous data fusion

- Knowledge representation and reasoning
- Linguistic data mining
- Educational data mining
- Music information retrieval
- Data-driven profiling/personalization
- User modeling
- Behavior prediction
- Recommender systems
- Web sentiment analysis
- Social data mining
- Data visualization techniques
- Integration of data mining results into real-world applications with humanistic context
- Ontologies, ontology matching, and alignment
- Mining humanistic data in the cloud
- Game data mining
- Virtual-world data mining
- Speech and audio data processing
- Data mining techniques for knowledge discovery
- Biomedical data mining
- Bioinformatics
- Content creation, annotation, and modeling for semantic and social web
- Computational intelligence for media adaptation and personalization
- Semantics-driven indexing and retrieval of multimedia contents
- Semantic context modeling and extraction
- Context-aware applications
- Social web economics and business
- Privacy/security issues in social and personalized applications
- Privacy preserving data mining and Social networks
- Social data analytics

Organization

Program Chairs

Andreas Kanavos   Ionian University, Greece
Christos Makris   University of Patras, Greece
Phivos Mylonas   Ionian University, Greece

Steering Committee Members

Ioannis Karydis   Ionian University, Greece
Katia-Lida Kermanidis   Ionian University, Greece
Spyros Sioutas   University of Patras, Greece

Community Detection Algorithms for Cultural and Natural Heritage Data in Social Networks

Andreas Kanavos[1,2(✉)], Maria Trigka[2], Elias Dritsas[2], Gerasimos Vonitsanos[2], and Phivos Mylonas[3,4]

[1] Department of Regional Development, Ionian University, Lefkada, Greece
akanavos@ionio.gr
[2] Computer Engineering and Informatics Department, University of Patras, Patras, Greece
{trigka,dritsase,mvonitsanos}@ceid.upatras.gr
[3] Department of Informatics, Ionian University, Corfu, Greece
fmylonas@ionio.gr
[4] Institute of Entrepreneurship Development, Larissa, Greece

Abstract. In social network analysis, it is crucial to discover a community through the retrospective decomposition of a large social graph into easily interpretable subgraphs. Four major community discovery algorithms, namely the Breadth-First Search, the Louvain, the MaxToMin, and the Propinquity Dynamics, are implemented. Their correctness was functionally evaluated in the four most widely used graphs with vastly different characteristics and a dataset retrieved from Twitter regarding cultural and natural heritage data because this platform reflects public perception about historical events through means such as advanced storytelling in users timelines. The primary finding was that the Propinquity Dynamics algorithm outperforms the other algorithms in terms of NMI for most graphs. In contrast, this algorithm with the Louvain performs almost the same regarding modularity.

Keywords: Community detection · Cultural and natural heritage management · Graph mining · Modularity · NMI · Social networks

1 Introduction

To extract essential knowledge, researchers are led to process and analyze the excessively growing abundance of data [36]. The management of cultural information related to cultural and natural resources has become a crucial driver of the industry. The demand for collections of services that include guided visits to historical monuments, is continuously high worldwide in physical and digital markets. Today, the digital world plays a vital role in promoting cultural and natural content. Through its continuous expansion, the contribution to the preservation of the cultural and natural heritage and the discovery of new elements is achieved.

I. Maglogiannis et al. (Eds.): AIAI 2021 Workshops, IFIP AICT 628, pp. 395–406, 2021.
https://doi.org/10.1007/978-3-030-79157-5_32

In general, the term network can refer to any interconnected group or system that interacts in a complex way to serve a purpose. The needs of modern society and the development of technology, have contributed to creating various types of networks. The main categories of networks are business networks, financial networks, hotel networks, and social networks. Besides, the widespread use of web applications is responsible for creating even more social networks [29]. The particular interest of this study is networking, originating from Social Media. In social networks, there are differences between the entities and the types of relationships that are created. Nevertheless, we can gain insights into several social phenomena. Also, extracted knowledge such as detecting communities, can be used supportively in several other tasks.

The last decade, social networks are an integral part of individuals in every aspect of daily life. Through these networks, users share data, such as images, videos, music, movies, experiences, beliefs, and interests. Moreover, they have the opportunity to exchange views and be informed about issues that concern them. As the number of social networks and their users' increases, scientists in turn struggle to provide users with high-quality services. Users grouping can help to highlight interaction patterns and identify common attributes amongst individuals in real-world activities.

Social networks are usually made up of people who communicate with each other and belong to connected communities. The identification of these communities constitutes an elementary task in social network analysis. As the nature of these networks is complex and dynamic, communities are not easily identified. This is an open and often challenging issue and can be considered an optimization problem. The aim is to identify sets of nodes with more interconnections and simultaneously fewer intra-links with other nodes. Since community detection is usually categorized as an NP-Hard problem, these evolutionary algorithms have attracted massive attention in this field in recent years.

Studies indicate that in social networks, the distribution of the clustering coefficient follows the power law, and it decreases when the degree of nodes increases. The clustering coefficient is an essential factor in a graph that measures the tendency of the nodes to cluster together. This characteristic implies that nodes in social networks tend to form sub-graphs. In other words, social networks are formed by connected communities. Discovering these communities is essential in order to understand the structure of the network. Therefore, a lot of research has been conducted to render them efficient. Generally, a community is defined as a group of nodes with more links between themselves and fewer external links to other nodes.

In this paper, we aim to identify the types of relations between Twitter network users while also detect communities in data related to DIMOLEON project. Initially, four major community discovery algorithms, namely the Breadth-First Search, the Louvain, the MaxToMin, and the Propinquity Dynamics are evaluated in four most widely used graphs with vastly different characteristics in terms of two popular metrics, namely the Normalized Mutual Information (NMI) and Modularity. In following, a dataset retrieved from Twitter regarding cultural and natural heritage data was employed, where users evaluate the extracted communities from each algorithm. One major contribution of this work is the employment of Twitter derived content, as well as the proposal of a methodology that identifies users with similar behavior and features in terms of the platform towards its efficient utilization.

The rest of the paper is organized as follows. In Sect. 2 the main research in this area is reviewed. In Sect. 3, some preliminaries regarding metrics are introduced whereas in Sect. 4, the algorithms are described in detail. Implementation details are presented in Sect. 5 and evaluation with results are discussed in Sect. 6. Finally Sect. 7 concludes the paper.

2 Related Work

Social networks analysis is strongly related to graph clustering algorithms, and web searching algorithms; for a complete review of this area, one should consult [9,10,21,23]. A group of network nodes, where the links between the nodes are dense, is defined as a community [37]. It refers to groups of nodes in a network or graph with common properties in system operations. The field is related to the HITS algorithm [20], as well as the link analysis in the web with cornerstone the analysis of the significance of web pages in Google using the PageRank citation metric [28], and other numerous variants proposed in [22]. In HITS, two metrics are used: a web page as an information authority and a hub. In PageRank, a metric based on the level of the importance of the incoming links is employed.

Various algorithms have been introduced in the literature on community detection, [10,29,31,32]. HITS can be used to compute communities if used to explore non-principal eigenvectors. In bibliography, we come across the problem related with communities regarding graph partitioning. The proposed algorithms are mainly related to spectral distribution approaches that achieve the partition of objects through the eigenvectors of the matrices [27,35]. The technique of spectral partitioning was proposed in [8,33]. In [34], the utilization of hierarchical clustering for graph partitioning is brought forward.

An important method by which the initiative for further research was made was advocated in [11], where modularity was introduced along with a divisive method for the problem of community detection. Besides, some works [1,25,26] suggest an algorithm that selects the partition that will maximize modularity using it as a measure of partition quality. The modularity-based criterion is an important way of identifying community structures in networks, as the quality of identified communities is quantified. The criterion for determining the partition of communities is the dense internal connections within the communities and the few connections between them. Researchers have considered algorithms with different approaches based on the concept of modularity. In complex networks, some of these algorithms show low performance while regarding other algorithms, prior knowledge of the network is required [3,12,14,30].

Also, in [13–15], the concept of influence from the side of users to the side of networks is expanded and personality has been utilized as the key characteristic for identifying influential networks. The result is to create this type of communities in Twitter graphs using a modularity-based community detection algorithm, taking into account users' personalities. Additionally, the edges of the graph based on the user personality, are eliminated by the insertion of a pre-processing step. Moreover in [17–19], the behavior of users on an emotional level is enhanced by introducing a new methodology that effectively aids in community detection.

Similarly, there are several ways to assess the clustering quality, namely community coherence [24]. However, most of the existing coherence metrics are either prohibitively expensive, such as the maximum distance between vertices, or are prone to outliers, such as the diameter-based metrics [6,7]. In [5,16] are described implementations of established community discovery algorithms, namely the CNM over Neo4j, the Walktrap, the Louvain, and the Edge Betweeness or Newman-Girvan. To evaluate these algorithms efficiently, we rely mainly on how the graph partitioning obtained by such an algorithm translates into the functional Twitter domain and not on other structural criteria.

3   Preliminaries

In this section, some details regarding the structure of the community along with the metrics of centrality and modularity will be introduced.

3.1   Community Structure

Typically, a network is considered as an undirected graph $G = (V, E)$, where $V = \{v_i | i \in [1, 2, \ldots, N]\}$ is the set of vertices and $E = \{e_{ij} | i, j \in [1, 2, \ldots, N]\}$ is the set of edges. Let us assume that $deg(v)$ is the degree of v in the graph G.

3.2   Basic Metrics

Centrality. One indicator that is widely used for network data is centrality measures. They reflect the prominence of a unit in different substantive settings, such as status, visibility, structural power, or prestige [4]. These measures can be distinguished in the following:

1. The *Degree Centrality* of a node v indicates the number of nodes, which are directly linked to this node. It is defined as

$$C_D(v) = deg(v) \tag{1}$$

2. The *Closeness Centrality* is related to the closeness of a vertex v and indicates how close a node is to all other nodes in the network. It is defined as

$$C_C(u) = \sum_{v \in V} d(u, v) \tag{2}$$

where $d(u, v)$ is the number of edges in a shortest path connecting the vertices u and v, known as geodesic distance.

3. The *Betweenness Centrality* indicates how much a vertex is in-between others. This metric is computed as the number of shortest paths between any couple of nodes in the graph containing target node v. It is defined as

$$C_{\mathrm{B}}(v) = \sum_{y \neq z \in N} \frac{p_{st}(v)}{p_{st}} \tag{3}$$

where $p_{st}(v)$ denotes the number of shortest paths between s and t containing v, and p_{st} denotes the number of all shortest paths between s and t in the network.

Modularity. It is a measure that captures the structure of the network and is used to evaluate the strength of a network division into communities [40]. In general, it is defined as

$$Q(V) = \frac{1}{2M} \sum_{v_i, v_j \in V} \left(A_{i,j} - \frac{deg(v_i)deg(v_j)}{2M} \right) \delta_{c_i, c_j}, \tag{4}$$

where $M = \frac{1}{2} \sum_i deg(v_i)$ and $\boldsymbol{A} = [A_{ij}] \in \mathbb{N}^{N \times N}$ is the adjacency matrix of given graph having values equal to 0 and 1; $A_{ij} = 1$ when two nodes are connected with an edge with $e_{ij} \in E$. Additionally, $\frac{deg(v_i)deg(v_j)}{2M}$ captures the expected number of edges between nodes v_i and v_j when edges are randomly distributed. If $c_i = c_j$ then $\delta_{c_i, c_j} = 1$, or if $c_i \neq c_j$ then $\delta_{c_i, c_j} = 0$, where c_i denotes that v_i belongs to the community c. The higher values of modularity indicate better quality of community detection.

It should be noted that although Louvain algorithm is based on the modularity optimization for detecting communities in networks, a limitation of this type of methods is their inability to detect small communities.

4   Community Detection Algorithms

In this section, the community detection algorithms considered in the experimental evaluation, are properly analyzed.

4.1   Louvain Algorithm

This algorithm constitutes a greedy approach of modularity maximization. As mentioned above, the strength by which a network is divided into communities is measured through modularity. Connections between nodes within communities on social networks with high modularity are dense, while between nodes of different communities are sparse.

The algorithm starts by assigning each node to a separate community and evolves with the movement of nodes to neighbouring communities to improve modularity. Precisely, it consists of two phases, the *Modularity Optimization* and the *Folding*. In the first phase, the first step assumes that on the original graph G, each node $v \in V$ is assigned to a separate community, whereas in the second step, each node v is placed in the community where the network modularity is maximized; this step is repeated until there are no moves. In following, in the second phase, the algorithm checks whether the new modularity is higher than the previous one and if so, the graph G is replaced by the one formed between the communities and returns to second-last step, otherwise it terminates.

During the folding phase, a new graph G' is created, where each node of this new graph represents a community of G. Each pair of nodes $v'_i, v'_j \in G'$ are linked if the corresponding communities of G have edges between them. The weight of the edge (v'_i, v'_j) is equal to the sum of the weights between communities. In addition, the sum of the inner edges of the communities of G is represented by a self-loop edge at node v' of G'.

Finally, as this method generates a hierarchical structure of communities, it has complexity equal to $O(Nlog_2N)$, where N is the number of nodes in the network.

4.2   Propinquity Dynamics

The term propinquity comes from sociology and refers to the physical or psychological proximity among individuals. In community detection, this specific term captures the probability of two nodes to be involved in a coherent community. The Propinquity Dynamics (PD) algorithm does not require prior knowledge of the communities' structure and obtains the propinquity information from the topology of the graph from a self-organized dynamic process [39].

Through several rounds of mutual reinforcement between the topology and propinquity, the community structures are naturally emerged. To achieve the highest efficiency, the propinquity is calculated in an incremental way. Nodes that belong to more than one communities (e.g., there are overlaps) can be determined by post-processing.

The PD algorithm can efficiently discover communities from very large scale graph data with complexity equal to $O(k|V|)$ in sparse graphs, where V and k are the number of graph nodes and the iteration count, respectively. Another advantage of the algorithm is that it emphasizes on scaling without loss of community quality.

Coherent Neighborhood Propinquity: Given that the diameter in a coherent graph is not greater than 2, the propinquity considers only the local 2-hop neighborhood, assuming the resulting communities are cohesive. Based on this, the number of common neighbours of a node pair is an important criterion for defining their neighborhood. Therefore, the total connectivity of the local neighborhood must be taken into account for the evaluation of the neighborhood.

Propinquity Calculation: The propinquity calculation can be implemented by finding for each pair of nodes the intersection of their neighbours and then counting the edges that connect the common neighbours. The complexity of this calculation is approximately $O((|V| + |E|)|E|)$, where E is the number of edges.

4.3   MaxToMin Algorithm

PD creates a graph topology with many communities, whereas the Breadth-First Search (BFS) identifies communities with the limitation that there may exist nodes that do not belong exclusively to one community. To address the above weaknesses, the algorithm MaxToMin has been proposed.

Initially, MaxToMin randomly starts from the node that is connected to the "strongest" edge (where the neighborhood size is considered as the corresponding weight) in the graph, i.e. the edge having the highest weight. MaxToMin will then try to access the nodes with the strongest edges that are neighbours of that node and attach them in the same community.

The algorithm moves from strong to less strong edges, without being able to move from a weak connection to a sounder one. An iteration of the algorithm achieves the finding of a community, and terminates when no other weak edges associated with the accessed are considered. In case a node can be accessed by its L independent executions of the algorithm, then this node is assigned to the corresponding L communities and is considered as an overlap to these communities.

5   Implementation

Our aim is to evaluate the performance of the Breadth-First Search, the Louvain, the MaxToMin and the Propinquity Dynamics algorithms in terms of Normalized Mutual Information (NMI) and Modularity. NMI is considered a normalization of the Mutual Information (MI) score; it takes values from 0, which refers to no mutual information, to 1, which denotes perfect correlation. Connections between nodes within communities with high modularity are dense, while on the other hand, connections between nodes of different communities are sparse.

5.1   Graphs

Initially, we chose four most widely used graphs in order to utilize our experimental evaluation, namely Zachary Karate Club, Dolphin Network, Polbooks and American College Football [2,38]. A synopsis of these networks is presented in Table 1 in ascending order, according to their number of vertices.

Initially, Zachary Karate Club dataset is considered a social network of friendships between 34 members of a karate club at a US university in the 1970s. A conflict between president and instructor led to a partition of the club into two organizations of nearly equal size. Furthermore, Dolphin Network is an undirected social network of frequent relationships between 62 dolphins in a community living off Doubtful Sound in New Zealand. The Polbooks dataset consists of a directed network of hyperlinks between weblogs on US politics, recorded in 2005. This network is divided according to blog political orientation, that is either conservative or liberal. Finally, American College Football dataset is considered a network of American football games between division colleges during the regular season fall of 2000; it has 115 teams separated into 12 divisions, where each division consists of 8 to 12 teams.

Table 1. Graphs synopsis

Name	Description	Vertices	Edges
Karate	Zachary's karate club	34	78
Dolphins	Dolphin social network	62	159
Polbooks	Books about US Politics	105	441
Football	American college football	115	613

5.2 Twitter Dataset

An approach based on specific topics was used for collecting tweets via a keyword search query for the generation of our test dataset. Keywords that are relevant to cultural and natural heritage in the domain of Greece and in conjunction to DIMOLEON project were downloaded. These keywords are related to different heritages, specific tourist destinations and activities. The filtered dataset resulted in 5,000 tweets from 01/02/2021 to 28/02/2021 as we have only kept tweets posted in English language.

6   Evaluation

In this section, the performance of the four community detection algorithms in terms of the four graphs and the retrieved dataset from Twitter, were evaluated.

6.1 Graphs

Table 2 presents the results of the performance of MaxToMin and Breadth-First Search in terms of NMI metric, the number of iterations, and vertices without community for the four different graphs. MaxToMin algorithm outperforms Breadth-First algorithm regarding the NMI in all graphs while the number of iterations is relatively low. Also, there are no vertices that do not belong to any community regarding the Karate and Dolphins graphs.

Table 2. Normalized mutual information for MaxToMin and Breadth-First Search algorithms

Graph	MaxToMin			Breadth-First Search		
	NMI	Iterations	Vertices without community	NMI	Iterations	Vertices without community
Karate	0.9240	1	0	0.3098	3	22
Dolphins	0.5989	1	0	0.4687	22	2
Polbooks	0.5778	4	15	0.4947	4	15
Football	0.9268	4	2	0.9099	4	8

The results of the other two algorithms in terms of NMI and Modularity metrics are depicted in Table 3. PD algorithm has higher values of NMI, and in some graphs, the difference is over 20%; specifically, in Dolphins graph, the difference is higher than 30%. The two algorithms achieve almost the same performance regarding modularity, except the Karate graph where Louvain outperforms PD by almost 3%.

Table 3. Normalized mutual information and modularity for Louvain and propinquity dynamics algorithms

	Normalized mutual information		Modularity	
Graph	Louvain	Propinquity dynamics	Louvain	Propinquity dynamics
Karate	0.6994	0.9240	0.4020	0.3714
Dolphins	0.6324	0.9428	0.5171	0.5143
Polbooks	0.5537	0.6383	0.5220	0.5124
Football	0.9111	0.9268	0.5811	0.6010

6.2   User Evaluation

For user evaluation of the downloaded Twitter dataset, we organized an online survey and asked students associated with the University of Patras to evaluate the extracted communities from each algorithm.

Users were presented with the communities wherein each community, the corresponding user with their tweets, was considered. After browsing through the dataset, users were asked to choose whether each community contains users with similar features. According to their personal beliefs, we examine three options: dense community, sparse community, and in-between.

The results are presented in the following Table 4 where users evaluate the communities discovered from the four algorithms, and the percentages of communities are depicted. As in previous experiments utilized for the four graphs, Louvain and Propinquity Dynamics have the highest number of dense communities. All four algorithms perform almost the same regarding the number of sparse communities. We have to consider that more features can further improve the performance of the algorithms, e.g., Twitter metrics, like the number of followers and the number of tweets per user.

It is worth mentioning the fact that the majority of hashtags regarding this dataset consists of terms like #Acropolis, #Ancientathens, #Ancientgreece, #Epidaurus, #HerodesAtticus, #Knossos, #Mycenae, #Parthenon, #Thermopylae as well as #Vergina.

Table 4. Percentages of Communities with similar Nodes

Algorithm	Dense	Sparse	In-between
Breadth-First Search	22	23	55
Louvain	32	23	45
MaxToMin	27	22	51
Propinquity dynamics	33	20	47

7   Conclusions and Future Work

In this paper, we aim to understand the community detection problem in terms of cultural and natural heritage data. More to the point, four major community discovery algorithms, namely the Breadth-First Search, the Louvain, the Max-ToMin, and the Propinquity Dynamics are evaluated in several popular graphs having different characteristics in terms of two well-known metrics, namely the Normalized Mutual Information (NMI) and Modularity. Furthermore, a dataset retrieved from Twitter regarding cultural heritage data was taken into consideration. In following, users evaluated the extracted communities from each algorithm by rating the density of each community. A methodology, tailored to the prerequisites of the digital culture domain and generic for summarizing the plethora of cultural items, is proposed as it supports sufficient multi-modal clustering and semantic annotations for such cultural items.

As future work, it is in our keen interest to investigate the scalability problems that are considered when dealing with more extensive graphs. Withal, we aim to conduct an additional series of experiments using other subjects in order to identify the parameters that influence the outcomes of the algorithms at a more refined granularity level. The dimension of time in social network analysis can gain potential due to the dynamic nature of these networks; that is, the communities evolution over time should be measured in terms of functionality and size. Ultimately, the incorporation of advanced data structures that could offer more efficient solutions can be considered a future aspect to be tackled within the current DIMOLEON project research activities.

Acknowledgement. This research has been co-financed by the European Union and Greek national funds through the Competitiveness, Entrepreneurship and Innovation Operational Programme, under the Call "Research - Create - Innovate", project title: "Using Digital Tools and Applications for Outdoor Alternative Tourism Operators - DIMOLEON", project code: T2EDK-03168, MIS code: 5069920.

References

1. Blondel, V.D., Guillaume, J.L., Lambiotte, R., Lefebvre, E.: Fast unfolding of communities in large networks. J. Stat. Mech. Theory Exper. **2008**(10), P10008 (2008)

2. Chen, Y., Zhao, P., Li, P., Zhang, K., Zhang, J.: Finding communities by their centers. Sci. Rep. **6**(1), 1–8 (2016)
3. Clauset, A., Newman, M.E.J., Moore, C.: Finding community structure in very large networks. Phys. Rev. E **70**(6), 066111 (2004)
4. Das, K., Samanta, S., Pal, M.: Study on centrality measures in social networks: a survey. Soc. Netw. Analy. Min. **8**(1), 13 (2018)
5. Drakopoulos, G., Gourgaris, P., Kanavos, A.: Graph communities in Neo4j. Evolving Syst. **11**(3), 397–407 (2020)
6. Drakopoulos, G., Kanavos, A., Makris, C., Megalooikonomou, V.: On converting community detection algorithms for fuzzy graphs in Neo4j. In: International Workshop on Combinations of Intelligent Methods and Applications (2015)
7. Drakopoulos, G., Kanavos, A., Makris, C., Megalooikonomou, V.: Comparing algorithmic principles for fuzzy graph communities over Neo4j. In: Hatzilygeroudis, I., Palade, V., Prentzas, J. (eds.) Advances in Combining Intelligent Methods. ISRL, vol. 116, pp. 47–73. Springer, Cham (2017). https://doi.org/10.1007/978-3-319-46200-4_3
8. Fiedler, M.: Algebraic connectivity of graphs. Czechoslovak Math. J. **23**(2), 298–305 (1973)
9. Flake, G.W., Lawrence, S., Giles, C.L.: Efficient identification of web communities. In: 6th ACM SIGKDD International Conference on Knowledge Discovery and Data Mining, pp. 150–160 (2000)
10. Fortunato, S.: Community detection in graphs. Phys. Rep. **486**(3–5), 75–174 (2010)
11. Girvan, M., Newman, M.E.J.: Community structure in social and biological networks. Proc. Natl. Acad. Sci. **99**(12), 7821–7826 (2002)
12. Jia, G., et al.: Community detection in social and biological networks using differential evolution. In: Hamadi, Y., Schoenauer, M. (eds.) LION 2012. LNCS, pp. 71–85. Springer, Heidelberg (2012). https://doi.org/10.1007/978-3-642-34413-8_6
13. Kafeza, E., Kanavos, A., Makris, C., Chiu, D.K.W.: Identifying personality-based communities in social networks. Adv. Conceptual Model. **8697**, 7–13 (2013)
14. Kafeza, E., Kanavos, A., Makris, C., Pispirigos, G., Vikatos, P.: T-PCCE: twitter personality based communicative communities extraction system for big data. IEEE Trans. Knowl. Data Eng. **32**(8), 1625–1638 (2020)
15. Kafeza, E., Kanavos, A., Makris, C., Vikatos, P.: T-PICE: twitter personality based influential communities extraction system. In: IEEE International Congress on Big Data, pp. 212–219 (2014)
16. Kanavos, A., Drakopoulos, G., Tsakalidis, A.K.: Graph community discovery algorithms in neo4j with a regularization-based evaluation metric. In: 13th International Conference on Web Information Systems and Technologies (WEBIST), pp. 403–410 (2017)
17. Kanavos, A., Perikos, I.: Towards detecting emotional communities in twitter. In: 9th IEEE International Conference on Research Challenges in Information Science (RCIS), pp. 524–525 (2015)
18. Kanavos, A., Perikos, I., Hatzilygeroudis, I., Tsakalidis, A.K.: Integrating user's emotional behavior for community detection in social networks. In: 12th International Conference on Web Information Systems and Technologies (WEBIST), pp. 355–362 (2016)
19. Kanavos, A., Perikos, I., Hatzilygeroudis, I., Tsakalidis, A.K.: Emotional community detection in social networks. Comput. Electr. Eng. **65**, 449–460 (2018)
20. Kleinberg, J.M.: Authoritative sources in a hyperlinked environment. J. ACM **46**(5), 604–632 (1999)

21. Lancichinetti, A., Fortunato, S.: Community detection algorithms: a comparative analysis. Phys. Rev. E **80**(5), 049902 (2009)
22. Langville, A.N., Meyer, C.D.: Google's PageRank and Beyond: The Science of Search Engine Rankings. Princeton University Press, Princeton (2006)
23. Leskovec, J., Lang, K.J., Mahoney, M.W.: Empirical comparison of algorithms for network community detection. In: 19th International Conference on World Wide Web (WWW), pp. 631–640 (2010)
24. Mylonas, P., Wallace, M., Kollias, S.: Using k-nearest neighbor and feature selection as an improvement to hierarchical clustering. In: Vouros, G.A., Panayiotopoulos, T. (eds.) SETN 2004. LNCS (LNAI), vol. 3025, pp. 191–200. Springer, Heidelberg (2004). https://doi.org/10.1007/978-3-540-24674-9_21
25. Newman, M.E.J.: Fast algorithm for detecting community structure in networks. Phys. Rev. E **69**(6), 066133 (2004)
26. Newman, M.E.J.: Modularity and community structure in networks. Proc. Natl. Acad. Sci. **103**(23), 8577–8582 (2006)
27. Ng, A.Y., Jordan, M.I., Weiss, Y.: On spectral clustering: Analysis and an algorithm. In: Advances in Neural Information Processing Systems (NIPS), pp. 849–856 (2001)
28. Page, L., Brin, S., Motwani, R., Winograd, T.: The pagerank citation ranking: Bringing order to the web. Technical report (1999)
29. Papadopoulos, S., Kompatsiaris, Y., Vakali, A., Spyridonos, P.: Community detection in social media. Data Min. Knowl. Discov. **24**(3), 515–554 (2012)
30. Pizzuti, C.: GA-Net: a genetic algorithm for community detection in social networks. In: Rudolph, G., Jansen, T., Beume, N., Lucas, S., Poloni, C. (eds.) PPSN 2008. LNCS, vol. 5199, pp. 1081–1090. Springer, Heidelberg (2008). https://doi.org/10.1007/978-3-540-87700-4_107
31. Plantié, M., Crampes, M.: Survey on social community detection. In: Social Media Retrieval, pp. 65–85. Computer Communications and Networks (2013)
32. Porter, M.A., Onnela, J., Mucha, P.J.: Communities in networks. CoRR (2009)
33. Pothen, A., Simon, H.D., Liu, K.P.P.: Partitioning sparse matrices with eigenvectors of graphs. SIAM J. Matrix Anal. Appl. **11**(3), 430–452 (1990)
34. Scott, J.: Social network analysis. Sociology **22**(1), 109–127 (1988)
35. Shi, J., Malik, J.: Normalized cuts and image segmentation. IEEE Trans. Pattern Anal. Mach. Intell. (TPAMI) **22**(8), 888–905 (2000)
36. Vallet, D., Fernández, M., Castells, P., Mylonas, P., Avrithis, Y.: A contextual personalization approach based on ontological knowledge. In: 2nd International Workshop on Contexts and Ontologies: Theory, Practice and Applications (C&O-2006) Collocated with the 17th European Conference on Artificial Intelligence (ECAI-2006), vol. 210 (2006)
37. Yang, B., Liu, D., Liu, J.: Discovering communities from social networks: methodologies and applications. In: Handbook of Social Network Technologies and Applications, pp. 331–346 (2010)
38. Yin, C., Zhu, S., Chen, H., Zhang, B., David, B.: A method for community detection of complex networks based on hierarchical clustering. Int. J. Distrib. Sens. Netw. **11**, 849140:1–849140:9 (2015)
39. Zhang, Y., Wang, J., Wang, Y., Zhou, L.: Parallel community detection on large networks with propinquity dynamics. In: 15th ACM SIGKDD International Conference on Knowledge Discovery and Data Mining (KDD), pp. 997–1006 (2009)
40. Zhu, J., Chen, B., Zeng, Y.: Community detection based on modularity and k-plexes. Inf. Sci. **513**, 127–142 (2020)

Forecasting Air Flight Delays and Enabling Smart Airport Services in Apache Spark

Gerasimos Vonitsanos[1], Theodor Panagiotakopoulos[2,3],
Andreas Kanavos[1,2(✉)], and Athanasios Tsakalidis[1]

[1] Computer Engineering and Informatics Department, University of Patras,
Patras, Greece
{mvonitsanos,kanavos,tsak}@ceid.upatras.gr
[2] School of Technology and Science, Hellenic Open University, Patras, Greece
panagiotakopoulos@eap.gr
[3] Business School, University of Nicosia, Nicosia, Cyprus

Abstract. In light of the rapidly growing passenger and flight volumes,
airports seek for sustainable solutions to improve passengers' experience
and comfort, while maximizing their profits. A major technological solution towards improving service quality and management processes in airports comprises Internet of Things (IoT) systems that realize the concept
of smart airports and offer interconnection potential with other public
infrastructures and utilities of smart cities. In order to deliver smart
airport services, real-time flight delay data and forecasts are a critical
source of information. This paper introduces an essential methodology
using machine learning techniques on Apache Spark, a cloud computing
framework, with Apache MLlib, a machine learning library to develop
and implement prediction models for air flight delays that could be integrated with information systems in order to provide up-to-date analytics.
The experimental results have been implemented with various algorithms
in terms of classification as well as regression, thus manifesting the potential of the proposed framework.

Keywords: Air flight delays forecasting · Apache spark · Classification ·
Machine learning · Regression · Smart airports · Smart cities

1 Introduction

Airports have evolved from state-owned enterprises to facilities controlled and
managed by private companies with complex business models that offer a variety of services to passengers and stakeholders [9]. This transition, driven by
liberalization in the air transport market and privatization, favored new business opportunities and an increasingly competitive environment wherein airports
compete to retain and attract new airlines and passengers [18]. In this context,

I. Maglogiannis et al. (Eds.): AIAI 2021 Workshops, IFIP AICT 628, pp. 407–417, 2021.
https://doi.org/10.1007/978-3-030-79157-5_33

airport service quality consists a significant performance indicator for airport management and operation, and plays fundamental role for increasing passengers' satisfaction and achieving competitive advantage [16].

At the same time, the aviation industry is developing very fast; passenger volumes are growing rapidly, flight volumes and airports seek for sustainable solutions to ameliorate passengers' experience and comfort, while maximizing their profits. To this end, airports have already started to invest significant amounts of money on IT systems, which according to SITA (Société Internationale de Telecommunications Aeronautiques, a tech provider owned by airlines) reached 11.8 billion dollars in 2019[1]. A major technological solution towards improving service quality and management processes in airports comprises Internet of Things (IoT) systems, which bring a plethora of advantages such as enhanced passengers' convenience, sounder security, increased operational efficiency and optimized resource management [31].

Smart airports rely on internal and external streams of data for smart service delivery. Among external data streams, real-time flight delay data and forecasts are a critical source of information which can be inferred from historical records or IoT based systems [4]. Smart airport systems can utilize flight delay data to improve the passenger experience by tailoring and/or adjusting airport services. For instance, flight delay data can be used to estimate incoming and outgoing passengers for realizing a smart cleaning service with the aim of keeping restroom cleanliness above predefined levels to improve passenger satisfaction [22]. In [3], air flight delay information is used by a smart airport mobile application to notify passengers upon reaching the boarding gate. Furthermore, the Incheon International Airport has employed real-time monitoring of flight delay times to improve on-time performance and passenger convenience[2].

Several other services that could be triggered based on flight delays' status have been reported in the literature, such as sending alerts to hotels, car rental and taxi services. In addition, in a view of airports as "transient smart cities" and considering them as integral part of smart cities [34], smart airports could be interconnected with other public spaces and utilities like public transportation to offer tailored services to passengers that have suffered from flight delays. Evidently, information on flight delays is important for developing efficient monitoring and decision making systems to deliver smart airport services for passengers' satisfaction improvement.

In general, flight delays are a very challenging issue massively affecting all major stakeholders in the entire air transport system and have a negative impact on airports in terms of efficiency, reputation and ultimately revenues [4]. Some remarkable rationale for commercially planned flights that are delayed are unfavorable climate conditions, air traffic congestion, late coming aircraft to be utilized for the flight from previous flight, as well as security and maintenance issues [5,7]. The desire to maximize aircraft utilization decreases the time buffer between arrivals and departures and as a result, it expands the probability of delay propagation [1].

---

[1] https://www.sita.aero/globalassets/docs/surveys--reports/it-insights-2019.pdf.

[2] https://www.airport.kr/co_file/ko/file01/SR_2018_eng.pdf.

The problem of detecting delays in aviation can be treated either as a classification or as a regression problem. The classification problem focuses on training an efficient model that is able to correctly classify a flight in the respective class. Each class in the classification problem represents the interval in which the delay varies in time units. In the other case, regarding the regression problem, in order to predict the delay of a flight, an attempt is made to train an efficient model that can predict how long a flight will be delayed to reach its destination, if it is delayed in units of time.

In this paper, a novel approach utilizing machine learning techniques on the Apache Spark computing system, in collaboration with Apache MLlib machine learning library, is presented. The prediction models are developed and implemented for air flight data, which can be considered a very challenging but useful dataset. This work aims to develop a precise multivariate prediction model, which can be incorporated with information systems in order to offer up-to-date analytics. The proposed strategy can be effectively adjusted for providing profitable information for all the countries and continents as well as for different airline companies because of the distinctive characteristics of the analytics platform, which provides robustness and scalability.

The remainder of the paper is structured as follows. Section 2 introduces the corresponding related work while Sect. 3 presents the recommended schema as well as the machine learning algorithms, which were used in the system. Section 4 focuses on the dataset used as well as the pre-processing steps. Furthermore, Sect. 5 presents the experiments and their evaluation as well as. Ultimately, Sect. 6 introduces the conclusions and draws directions for future work.

2 Related Work

The analysis of large volumes of data with the use of cloud computing frameworks has been extensively studied in numerous works showing the potential of this topic [6,19,20,26]. Many studies have been utilized in the past regarding airline planning problems using machine learning or deep learning along with Big Data frameworks. Nevertheless, few of them have been employed on the features of carrier delays and the forecasting of the statistics of these delays.

A similar study is presented in [12], where flight data of US domestic flights operated by American Airlines, reporting the top 5 busiest airports of US and forecasting potential flight arrival delay with the use of machine learning and data mining approaches, is here introduced. The Gradient Boosting classifier, after some tuning in hyper-parameters, achieves a maximum accuracy of 85.73%. Authors in [21] tried to identify the parameters that enabled effective estimation of delay and in following applied Bayesian model, decision tree, hybrid classification methods and random forest in order to approximate the occurrences and delay magnitude in a network. These methodologies were implemented on a dataset with US flights as well as on a processed one regarding a big Iranian airline network. The experimental results depicted that the parameters inducing potential delays in US flights were departure time, visibility as well as wind, whereas those inducing delays in the Iranian flights constitute aircraft type and fleet age.

In a similar study, delays in terms of air transportation system were predicted using supervised machine learning and concretely, a detailed examination of the performance of individual airlines and airports in order to achieve a well-assessed decision, is proposed. The analysis and the development of the utilized model offer important decision-making strategies that are vital for different roles present in the aviation industry [29]. Authors in [14] claimed to address the concrete problem of feature selection, prevalent in most machine learning researches in air traffic management, as they proposed an optimal feature selection process for improving the forecasting performance of the machine learning model.

Authors in Lu [24] introduced both Bayesian network and decision tree algorithms to model flight delays and claimed that the precise forecasting of this kind of delays was exceptionally difficult. Also, the performance of decision tree, Naive Bayes as well as neural network models in predicting delays on the basis of huge datasets is compared in [25]. A similar work based on the investigation of the effects of airports on flight delays was proposed in [10] where graph theory for analyzing directed weighted graphs, which represent the delays propagation across the National Airspace System of America, was utilized. Experimental evaluation depicted that New York area had a major impact for 15% of injected and for 9% of propagated delays in the National Airspace System.

Forecasting air traffic delays with the use of random forests and regression models was implemented in [32], where authors utilized their approaches with use of the 100 most frequently delayed posts in the National Airspace System. The average test error over this number of posts was 19% while the average median test error was 21 min. Another work is related to flight delays prediction on the basis of certain data patterns employed from previously obtained flight information [28]. OneR algorithm outperformed the other classification models with an estimation accuracy of 64.08%. Authors in [30] aim at evaluating the dimension of air traffic delay propagation using a queuing network model consisting of the OEP-35 airports in the US and acknowledging that the goal of this approach is to replicate the existing behaviors and trends.

Furthermore, a statistical model for exploring the impacts of different factors, like congestion, day time as well as weather conditions on flight delays is proposed in [17]. Within the same concept lies the work in [33], where the essential reasons for delays were examined by considering important parameters, like seasonality, the station type and weather conditions. A prediction model for the delay of an arrival flight because of weather conditions has been implemented in [8].

A probabilistic function for classifying the delays of the subsequent flights with the use of a transition matrix, was proposed in [11]. The conditional probability of flight cancellation in the presence of a flight delay from preceding ones, after the examination of cancellations, was determined. Moreover, arrival and departure delays were effectively forecasted with the utilization of a proposed model based on ensemble fuzzy Support Vector Machine with a weighted margin [13]. The experimental evaluation, based on the distinctness of five classes of delays, showed the high prediction accuracy of the fuzzy implementation as compared to the traditional Support Vector Machine.

3 Methodology

3.1 Proposed Schema

The problem of forecasting delays in aviation area can be treated either as a classification or as a regression one. Regarding classification, this method focuses on training an efficient model that can correctly classify a flight in the respective class. Each class represents the interval in which the delay varies in time units, e.g. 0 to 15 min, 16 to 30 min, and so on. On the other hand, when dealing with regression, the aim is to predict the exact delay of a flight. So, the challenge is to develop and train an efficient model that can forecast the time units that a flight will be delayed in order to reach its destination, if delayed.

In the present work, our proposed system can forecast two different types of flight delay problems; the binary classification problem with one class representing all the flights with no delay and the other class representing all flights with a delay or even a cancellation. As the second problem we consider the regression one where machine learning models are trained in order to predict the flight delay, if any, in minutes.

3.2 Machine Learning Algorithms

In this work, we utilized four algorithms in terms of the classification problem and three algorithms regarding the regression problem. The four algorithms utilized are Multilayer Percepton, Naive Bayes, Random Forest and Support Vector Machine for classification model, whereas Isotonic Regression, Linear Regression and Random Forest Regression for the training of the flight delay prediction model.

3.2.1 Multilayer Percepton

The multilayer perceptron is an artificial neural network model that maps a collection of input vectors to a collection of known classes. It includes a number of layers, where each one consists of nodes with a particular weight, which are completely connected to the nodes of the next level. The back-propagation method alternates the connection weights of each node to the nodes of the latter layer with the aim of minimizing the output error and can be used in order for the multilayer perceptron, given a concrete dataset, to be trained.

3.2.2 Naive Bayes

Naive Bayes is a simple but popular classification algorithm based on Bayes' theorem. Each instance can be considered as a feature vector and each feature value is independent of any other feature value. One primary advantage is that this algorithm can be effectively trained, as only a single pass of the training data is needed. At first, for a concrete class, the conditional probability distribution of every feature is computed, and in following, Naive Bayes is applied to predict the class of this specific instance.

3.2.3   Random Forest

Random forest comprises of a set of decision trees and so can be considered as a generalization of the decision tree classifier. The classification of a new input takes place by inserting it in each tree of the forest and ends in the "vote" of an output class. In following, the class with the most number of votes constitutes the output class of the random forest. For the construction of each tree, a number of instances from the input data will be sampled and then, a subset of the features of that specific selection are taken into consideration in order for the tree size to be increased; the number of instances is equal to the number of trees of the corresponding forest.

3.2.4   Support Vector Machine

Support Vector Machine (SVM) makes up a linear model for both classification and regression problems. Furthermore, SVM can resolve linear as well as non-linear problems and works efficiently for numerous practical problems. The aim of this algorithm is to form the most effective decision boundary that can segregate n-dimensional space into classes in a way that any novel data point can be easily placed on the correct category within the future. This decision boundary is entitled hyperplane.

3.2.5   Isotonic Regression

Isotonic regression is a free-form linear model that can predict sequences of observations. An isotonic function must not be non-decreasing because it is a monotonic function, meaning a function that preserves or reverses a given order. A benefit is that it is not compelled by any functional frame, like the linearity forced by linear regression, as long as the function is monotonically increasing.

3.2.6   Linear Regression

Linear regression is a model that aims to map the relationship amongst two factors by fitting a linear equation to distinguished data. Specifically, the first factor is an explanatory variable, whereas the second factor is a dependent one.

4   Implementation

The proposed model does not take into consideration certain features such as the flight delay either for arrival or departure, which must be known in advance. So, the absence of these features drives this model to lower performance. Another problem that was identified and probably affects the performance of the model, refers to the data imbalance where the majority of the instances concerns flights that are considered as delayed. This issue was addressed by selecting an appropriate number of instances of the specific class as Apache MLlib does not have oversampling methods. The removal of several observations, however, led to the loss of information and therefore to insufficient training.

The separation of the dataset to training and test set has been implemented with the use of cross validation procedure. The 70% of the instances are used as the training set and the rest 30% as the testing set.

4.1 Dataset

The dataset used in our experiments is derived from Bureau of Transportation Statistics[3]. The input data are presented in Table 1. We have retrieved flight data from this dataset for the American Airlines in the form of csv files. The data commence from year 1987; one can choose the desired year and month and in following select the appropriate features. Each line of the dataset is related to a specific flight. In our paper, the flight data were downloaded for 3 specific years, namely 2017 to 2019.

Table 1. Input data for all the models

Features	Description
DayofMonth	The month's day of the flight
DayOfWeek	The week's day of the flight
Month	The month of the flight
IATACodeReportingAirline	Code specified by IATA and used to identify a unique airline (carrier)
OriginAirportID	Number for identifying a certain origin airport
DestAirportID	Number for identifying a certain destination airport
Distance	Distance between airports (miles)
SameOriginFlightsCount	The number of flights departing on the same date from the same airport with the corresponding flight
AverageAirlineDelay	The average flight delay for a carrier and is calculated from the field ArrDelay (which implies the difference in minutes between scheduled and actual arrival time) and IATACodeReportingAirline
AverageOriginDelay	The average airport delay for a flight departure and is calculated in a similar way to the AverageAirlineDelay, that is from the field DepDelay (which implies the difference in minutes between scheduled and actual departure time) and OriginAirportID
Classification: Cancelled	Predict if there is delay or cancellation
Regression: ArrDelay	Predict the delay of a flight, if any, in minutes

---

[3] https://www.transtats.bts.gov/Fields.asp?gnoyr_VQ=FGJ.

4.2 Data Pre-processing

The effective implementation of prediction models can be achieved with the use of two primary and important issues, namely the data quality and data representativity. Furthermore, the data pre-processing step regularly impacts the generalization ability of a machine learning algorithm [15,23].

In the current dataset, when a flight delay of more than 15 min is considered, then this flight belongs to the class of *Cancelled*, otherwise it falls under the category of *non-Cancelled*. Regarding the number of instances, as the classified of *Cancelled* is almost 80%, we randomly select a number of instances of this class equal to the number of instances of the class *non-Cancelled* (that is about 20% of the whole dataset).

4.3 Cloud Computing Infrastructure

The proposed algorithmic framework has been implemented with the utilization of Apache Spark cloud infrastructure. The cluster used for our experiments includes 4 computing nodes, i.e. VMs, where each of them has four 2.5 GHz CPU processors, 11 GB of memory and 45 GB hard disk. One of the VMs is considered the master node and the other three VMs are used as the slave nodes.

5 Evaluation

The results of our paper are depicted in Tables 2 and 3. The metrics of Precision, Recall, and F-Measure evaluate the performance of each classifier for the classification problem. Also, the Mean Square Error (MSE) and the Root Mean Square Error (RMSE) are presented regarding the regression problem. The Mean Absolute Error is defined as the average of the absolute difference between the predictions and the actual data values, while the Root Mean Square Error amplifies the contributions of the absolute errors between these two values.

Concerning the classification in Table 2, the higher value of the F-Measure is achieved in Random Forest and was equal to 63.75%. The other three classifiers, i.e. Multilayer Percepton, Naive Bayes and Support Vector Machine, perform almost the same as they achieve values equal to 54%. The performance can be further improved either by using oversampling methods or by taking into consideration additional features so as to enhance the input of the classifiers.

Table 2. Classification results

Algorithm	Precision	Recall	F-Measure
Multilayer percepton	54.37	53.40	54.35
Naive Bayes	55.54	53.77	54.11
Random forest	63.79	63.65	63.75
Support vector machine	54.13	53.95	53.95

Concerning the regression problem in Table 3, the Random Forest classifier performed better as in classification with MSE value equal to 993.75 and RMSE equal to 33.86 min. The second best performance is achieved by Linear Regression while Isotonic Regression has the worst results. Let us consider that RMSE metric depicts the delay minutes of arrival of the corresponding flight. Results show that our proposed methodology can predict within a reasonable amount of time how long a flight will be delayed to reach its destination, in units of time.

Table 3. Regression results

Algorithm	MSE	RMSE (minutes)
Isotonic regression	17333.55	133.15
Linear regression	2242.43	48.65
Random forest	993.75	33.86

6   Conclusions and Future Work

In our paper, we tried to identify key aspects regarding the performance of numerous classification and regression algorithms in a distributed environment for the problem of forecasting air flight delays. Two problems were considered as we initially studied the existence, if any, in flight delays and in following, our aim was to predict the exact flight delay. The Random Forest classifier outperformed all the other classification methods and achieved reasonable results. The experiments were conducted with the use of some popular metrics for both the classification and regression problem.

As future works, one can consider the application of unique and more advanced pre-processing approaches, as well as sampling algorithms and hybrid machine learning models in order to achieve better classification and regression results [2]. Moreover, the specified level of smart technology adjustment in airport operations related to the investment return can be effectively identified. In conclusion, more attention for providing practise related knowledge on how to model smart airport aspects, specifically in emerging and rising economies as well as tourism sector focused countries, is required; such infrastructure advancements result in the impact of associated industries [27, 35].

Acknowledgement. Supported by the Erasmus+ KA2 under the project DEVOPS, "DevOps competences for Smart Cities" (Project No.: 601015-EPP-1-2018-1-EL-EPPKA2-SSA Erasmus+ Program, KA2: Cooperation for innovation and the exchange of good practices-Sector Skills Alliances, started in 2019, January 1).

References

1. AhmadBeygi, S., Cohn, A., Guan, Y., Belobaba, P.: Analysis of the potential for delay propagation in passenger airline networks. J. Air Transp. Manage. **14**(5), 221–236 (2008)
2. Alexopoulos, A., Drakopoulos, G., Kanavos, A., Sioutas, S., Vonitsanos, G.: Parametric evaluation of collaborative filtering over apache spark. In: 5th South-East Europe Design Automation, Computer Engineering, Computer Networks and Social Media Conference (SEEDA-CECNSM), pp. 1–8 (2020)
3. Alghadeir, A., Al-Sakran, H.: Smart airport architecture using Internet of Things. Int. J. Innov. Res. Comput. Sci. Technol. **4**, 148–155 (2016)
4. Aljubairy, A., Zhang, W.E., Shemshadi, A., Mahmood, A., Sheng, Q.Z.: A system for effectively predicting flight delays based on IoT data. Computing **102**(9), 2025–2048 (2020)
5. Allan, S.S., Beesley, J.A., Evans, J.E., Gaddy, S.G.: Analysis of delay causality at Newark international airport. In: 4th USA/Europe Air Traffic Management R&D Seminar, pp. 1–11 (2001)
6. Baltas, A., Kanavos, A., Tsakalidis, A.K.: An apache spark implementation for sentiment analysis on twitter data. In: Sellis, T., Oikonomou, K. (eds.) ALGO-CLOUD 2016. LNCS, vol. 10230, pp. 15–25. Springer, Cham (2017). https://doi.org/10.1007/978-3-319-57045-7_2
7. Barnhart, C., Smith, B.: Quantitative Problem Solving Methods in the Airline Industry, vol. 169, (2012)
8. Belcastro, L., Marozzo, F., Talia, D., Trunfio, P.: Using scalable data mining for predicting flight delays. ACM Trans. Intell. Syst. Technol. **8**(1), 5:1–5:20 (2016)
9. Bezerra, G.C.L., Gomes, C.F.: Performance measurement in airport settings: a systematic literature review. benchmarking: An Int. J. **23**(4), 1027–1050 (2016)
10. Bolaños, M.E., Murphy, D.: How much delay does New York inject into the national airspace system? a graph theory analysis. In: Aviation Technology, Integration and Operations Conference, p. 4221 (2013)
11. Boswell, S.B., Evans, J.E.: Analysis of Downstream Impacts of Air Traffic Delay. Lincoln Laboratory, Massachusetts Institute of Technology (1997)
12. Chakrabarty, N.: A data mining approach to flight arrival delay prediction for American airlines. In: 9th Annual Information Technology, Electromechanical Engineering and Microelectronics Conference (IEMECON), pp. 102–107 (2019)
13. Chen, H., Wang, J., Yan, X.: A fuzzy support vector machine with weighted margin for flight delay early warning. In: 15th International Conference on Fuzzy Systems and Knowledge Discovery (FSKD), pp. 331–335 (2008)
14. Chen, J., Li, M.: Chained predictions of flight delay using machine learning. In: AIAA Scitech 2019 forum, p. 1661 (2019)
15. García, S., Luengo, J., Herrera, F.: Data Preprocessing in Data Mining, Intelligent Systems Reference Library, vol. 72. Springer, Heidelberg (2015)
16. Hong, S.J., Choi, D., Chae, J.: Exploring different airport users' service quality satisfaction between service providers and air travelers. J. Retail. Consum. Serv. **52** (2020)
17. Hsiao, C.Y., Hansen, M.: Econometric analysis of U.S. airline flight delays with time-of-day effects. transportation research record: J. Transp. Res. Board **1951**(1), 104–112 (2006)
18. Jimenez, E., Claro, J., de Sousa, J.P.: The airport business in a competitive environment. Procedia - Soc. Behav. Sci. **111**, 947–954 (2014)

19. Kanavos, A., Nodarakis, N., Sioutas, S., Tsakalidis, A., Tsolis, D., Tzimas, G.: Large scale implementations for twitter sentiment classification. Algorithms **10**(1), 33 (2017)
20. Kanavos, A., Perikos, I., Hatzilygeroudis, I., Tsakalidis, A.: Emotional community detection in social networks. Comput. Electr. Eng. **65**, 449–460 (2018)
21. Khaksar, H., Sheikholeslami, A.: Airline delay prediction by machine learning algorithms. Sci. Iranica **26**(5), 2689–2702 (2019)
22. Knoch, S., Staudt, P., Puzzolante, B., Maggi, A.: A smart digital platform for airport services improving passenger satisfaction. In: 22nd IEEE Conference on Business Informatics (CBI), pp. 250–259 (2020)
23. Kotsiantis, S.B., Kanellopoulos, D.N., Pintelas, P.E.: Data preprocessing for supervised leaning. Int. J. Comput. Sci. **1**(2), 111–117 (2006)
24. Lu, Z.: Alarming large scale of flight delays: an application of machine learning. Mach. Learn. 239–250 (2010)
25. Lu, Z., Wang, J., Zheng, G.: A new method to alarm large scale of flights delay based on machine learning. In: International Symposium on Knowledge Acquisition and Modeling (KAM), pp. 589–592 (2008)
26. Meng, X., et al.: Mllib: machine learning in apache spark. J. Mach. Learn. Res. **17**, 34:1–34:7 (2016)
27. Ntaliakouras, N., Vonitsanos, G., Kanavos, A., Dritsas, E.: An apache spark methodology for forecasting tourism demand in Greece. In: 10th International Conference on Information, Intelligence, Systems and Applications (IISA), pp. 1–5 (2019)
28. Oza, S., Sharma, S., Sangoi, H., Raut, R., Kotak, V.C.: Flight delay prediction system using weighted multiple linear regression. Int. J. Eng. Comput. Sci. **4**(4), 11668–11677 (2015)
29. Prabakaran, N., Kannadasan, R.: Airline delay predictions using supervised machine learning. Int. J. Pure Appl. Math. **119**(7), 329–337 (2018)
30. Pyrgiotis, N., Malone, K.M., Odoni, A.: Modelling delay propagation within an airport network. Transp. Res. Part C: Emerg. Technol. **27**, 60–75 (2013)
31. Rajapaksha, A., Jayasuriya, N.: Smart airport: a review on future of the airport operation. Glob. J. Manage. Bus. Res. **20**(3) (2020)
32. Rebollo, J.J., Balakrishnan, H.: Characterization and prediction of air traffic delays. Transp. Res. Part C: Emerg. Technol. **44**, 231–241 (2014)
33. Rupp, N.G.: Investigating the causes of flight delays. Tech. rep (2007)
34. Streitz, N.: Reconciling humans and technology: the role of ambient intelligence. In: Braun, A., Wichert, R., Maña, A. (eds.) AmI 2017. LNCS, vol. 10217, pp. 1–16. Springer, Cham (2017). https://doi.org/10.1007/978-3-319-56997-0_1
35. Vonitsanos, G., Kanavos, A., Mylonas, P., Sioutas, S.: A nosql database approach for modeling heterogeneous and semi-structured information. In: 9th International Conference on Information, Intelligence, Systems and Applications (IISA), pp. 1–8 (2018)

Movie Recommendation System Based on Character Graph Embeddings

Agisilaos Kounelis[✉], Pantelis Vikatos, and Christos Makris

Computer Engineering and Informatics Department University of Patras,
26504 Patras, Greece
{agis,vikatos,makri}@ceid.upatras.gr

Abstract. This paper presents a novel approach for recommending movies based on weighted Character Graphs. This approach proposes a dedicated crawler that gathers movie screenplays and a methodology of character graphs generation that contains all the necessary information needed for the representation of movie plots. A representative vector is extracted for each graph and used along with user ratings, as an input for a gradient boosting algorithm to predict movie ratings. The proposed method is tested on a publicly available MovieLens dataset and it was experimentally shown that it outperforms the fundamental collaborative filtering recommendation algorithms.

Keywords: Recommendation systems · Character graphs · Graph embeddings

1 Introduction

Creating recommendations able to be useful to humans has long been a challenge for researchers in the fields of information retrieval and AI. Broadly speaking, there are existing kinds of research efforts and platforms related to recommendations in topics such as books [18], movies [7], music [19] and university courses [15]. Recommendations Systems (RS) cover the needs of well-known online platforms i.e. Netflix, Amazon, Booking. The topic of movie recommendations gained the interest of research teams especially during the Netflix Prize competition and the award of $1M Grand Prize to team BellKor's Pragmatic Chaos.

Regarding movie suggestions, a plethora of research efforts [22] target a given number of rated user preferences or use the context and metadata of the movie to provide recommendations and predict the movie ratings. However, there are many different factors [21] which have an impact on a user's movie preference. Features such as film category, quality of the director or participation of specific actors can be determinants for selection and high rating. Online platforms such as the well-known IMDB[1] provide the basic descriptive information about each

---

[1] IMDb: https://www.imdb.com/.

© IFIP International Federation for Information Processing 2021
Published by Springer Nature Switzerland AG 2021
I. Maglogiannis et al. (Eds.): AIAI 2021 Workshops, IFIP AICT 628, pp. 418–430, 2021.
https://doi.org/10.1007/978-3-030-79157-5_34

movie such as category, actors, writers and a short description. However additional features like the alternation of scenes, the plethora of characters throughout the same scenes, the frequency of monologues or common appearances of the film's heroes are missing. The research effort of Lee & Jung [11] shows that common stories of movies are strongly correlated with the efficiency of the recommendations. More specifically, they propose an innovative recommendation system using an effective and dynamic co-occurrence signed network representing the friendships between characters. This research inspires us to focus on movie plots as the factor that develops the user's movie needs.

In our paper, we represent movie plot as a weighted Character Graph (CG) whose nodes and edges correspond to the characters and the co-occurrence of characters in the same scenes respectively. An essential step in our approach constitutes the gathering of screenplays and the extraction of the characters. The identification and separation of the scenes in the screenplay relies on the well-defined structure of the script. The generated character graph contains all the necessary information needed for the depiction of the movie plot. However, for each character graph, a graph embedding is generated i.e. a single vector; which is more convenient for feeding a Machine Learning Algorithm. Our main challenge is to extract the representative vector (centroid) of each user that declares the mixture of plots that consumes and reflects his/her profile. We use the representative vector and the embedding of a candidate movie as an input for a gradient boosting algorithm to predict the movie rating. The evaluation of the recommendation system follows the common standards of the most published efforts in recommendation algorithms, using a public dataset and comparing the proposed method with the fundamental ones. We declare that after publication both the dataset and the source will be provided for re-generation of the results of the paper.

The significance of our contribution can be summarized as follows:

- Implement a dedicated crawler for gathering movie screenplays.
- Describe an efficient procedure to generate a movie character graph.
- Extract the movie embeddings and calculate the user representative vectors.
- Introduce a recommendation system architecture based on independent sub-modules.
- Train and evaluate a gradient boosting machine learning algorithm for rating prediction.

The rest of the paper is structured as follows. Section 2 overviews related work. We motivate our research from current challenges regarding related studies. In Sect. 3, we provide an overview of the methodology that we propose which is separated in sub-modules. Section 4 overviews details of the implementation of the system and Sect. 5 presents a reference to our experimental results and the discussion of our work. Finally, in Sect. 6, we declare the strengths and limitations of our approach as well as an outlook on future work.

2   Related Work

We present the related work in three fields. The first refers to topics of character graphs. The second provides studies related to graph embeddings. The third includes literature of recommendation systems and methodologies.

Study [14] presents a first approach in the field of character graphs, mapping out texts according to geography, social connections and other variables. A study to extract social networks from nineteenth-century British novels and serials is presented in research [4], in which the networks have been constructed by dialogue interactions. A similar study is presented in effort [2], related to social event detection and social network extraction from a literary text and particularly the book Alice in Wonderland. An expansion to movie screenplay, as a source of unstructured literary, is presented in studies [1,2,5,27]. In effort [27] the extraction of the social network by parsing the screenplay is proposed in order to investigate communities, hidden semantic information and automate story segmentation. Another study [5] is focused on character interaction and networks between characters from plays and movies. In research effort [1] it is presented a formalization of the task of parsing movie screenplays as well as the extraction of the social network of all characters having a dialogue with each other in a scene.

Study [13] provides the well known word2vec technique. It is arguably the most famous face of the neural network natural language processing revolution, taking as input a text corpus and returning a set of vectors as the output. The contribution in study [10] is a generalization of the word2vec method representing entire documents as vectors known as doc2vec. graph2vec [17] proceeds the method of doc2vec to the next stage, representing a graph as a vector facilitating comparisons between graphs.

The most common technique used by recommendation systems is Collaborative Filtering (CF) [22]. CF systems aggregate user interactions, discover similar users based on preferences and rank items group-wise. Matrix factorization [8] constitutes a well-known technique for collaborative filtering, providing dimensionality reduction of the sparse user-item matrix. Content-based systems recommend items based on similarity to content information. Recent research attempts of Suglia et al. [23] and Musto et al. [16] describe the use of embeddings for comparison, generating a representation for each user by averaging the description embeddings of the items that the user has interacted with.

3   Model

We depict the overall model architecture in Fig. 1. The proposed model introduces the concept of a movie plot to create recommendations. The fundamental step in the methodology is the automated plot extraction from the film screenplay and the representation in a form that will be ready for use by machine learning algorithms. Given the existence of the script and the characters of the film from heterogeneous sources, we represent the plot as a weighted undirected

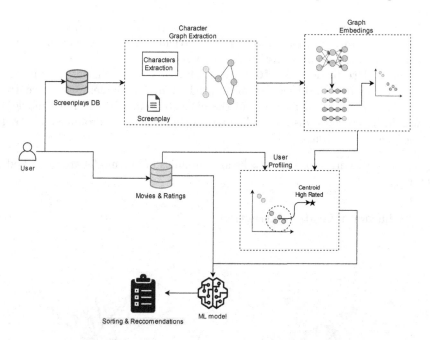

Fig. 1. Model architecture

graph which is called Character Graph (CG). Graph's nodes and edges correspond to the characters and the co-occurrence of the character pairs in the same
scene respectively. An embedding is generated for each character graph though
a Graph to Vector approach. The set of graph embeddings, movie ratings and
a user's representative centroids of their highest rated movies constitute user
profiling. A trained model uses the combination of the centroid embedding and
the embedding of a movie target to predict the rating. The ordered list of the
candidate's targets forms the recommendations for our system.

A summary of the independent tasks that our methodology consists of is
given below:

– **Character Graphs Construction**. The prerequisite export of the characters is generated by utilizing external sources that list information about the
film characters. The screenplay is modeled as an undirected graph G, where
nodes and edges are characters and co-occurrence in scenes respectively. Each
edge includes a weight that represents the frequency of the co-occurrence of
the two characters in the same scenes.
– **Generation of Graph Embeddings**. This task is dedicated to the transformation of a character graph into a single vector. Using the graph2vec
methodology, graph embeddings are learned in an unsupervised manner given
a dimension size.

- **User Profiling.** The user profiling contains the set of the movie vectors as well as the rating of each movie for a particular user. The mixture of most preferable movie plots constitutes a user signature.
- **Rating Prediction & Recommendations.** An efficient classification model is trained and used for rating prediction. The model uses the centroid of a user's top rated movies and the extracted embedding of the movie for which the prediction is made. The recommendations are produced by sorting the predicted ratings.

In the following subsection tasks and modules of our model are described in detail.

3.1   Character Graph Extraction

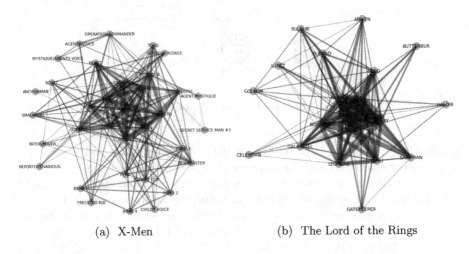

(a) X-Men   (b) The Lord of the Rings

Fig. 2. Social networks of co-occurrence characters in screenplay scenes

We consider that this process consists of four main steps: 1) the identification of scenes; 2) the identification of characters; 3) the quantification of their interactions; 4) the extraction of the proper graph.

Due to the structure of screenplays, scenes can be easily separated. Afterwards, there are several direct and indirect methods for identification of characters in a text [3,12,26]. Authors in [9] mention that there are various ways to eliminate possible errors related characters recognition. Those methods include removing: infrequent names, characters that appear not frequent enough, a character if he appears three times or fewer, or a character when he amounts to 1% or less of all occurrences. We collect the top-10 characters per movie keeping only the most significant characters. We declare that the characters that interact with each other should have at least one co-occurrence in the same scene. Every co-occurrence detected in a scene increases the weight of the edge that connects the corresponding pair of characters. Each link contains a weight related to the frequency of the co-occurrence in the whole screenplay. In Fig. 2 samples of movie character graphs are depicted. The Graph Extraction algorithm is described in Algorithm 1.

Algorithm 1: GetGraph (*Screenplay, Characters*)

---

   input : *Screenplay*: The Screenplay of the Movie in text format
               Characters: The list of the Movie's Characters
   output: $G = (V, E)$: The Character Network Graph of *Screenplay*
   $V = C$, $E = \varnothing$
   Scenes = {text sections between *EXT* and *INT* tags of *Screenplay*}
   begin
       foreach *Scene* ∈ *Scenes* **do**
           SceneCharacters = *FindCharacters(Scene)*
           Cooccurrences = {$(a, b) \mid a, b \in$ *SceneCharacters* and $a \neq b$}
           foreach $(a, b) \in$ *Cooccurrences* **do**
               if $(a, b) \notin E$ **then**
                   $E \leftarrow E \cup (a, b)$
               $(a, b).weight \leftarrow (a, b).weight + 1$
       return $G = (V, E)$

3.2 Generation of Graph Embeddings

The main objective of this module is the transformation of the character graphs to a form that applies to machine learning approaches. Vector representations of data range from feature vectors, via automatically constructed graph kernels, to learned representations, either computed by dedicated embedding algorithms or implicitly computed by learning architectures, like graph neural networks. The performance of machine learning methods crucially depends on the quality of the vector representations. We introduce the methodology of graph2vec as implemented in [20]. In graph2vec, Graph Embeddings are learned in an unsupervised manner given a dimension size. The purpose of graph2vec technique is to transform a graph to a vector. In this way, the similarity percentage of two graphs is the same as the similarity percentage of their two corresponding vectors. This is a way to approximate the graph isomorphism (GI) problem [6] for the Character Graphs.

3.3 User Profiling

An active user in online movie platforms e.g. IMDb; has the option to rate a movie based on his/her own criteria. We consider that one important factor which influences the rating is the plot of the movie. Thus, we formulate a user profile based on the high rated movies and the graph embeddings extracted from the screenplays. We extract as user signature, the centroid of the graph embeddings of user's highest rated movies.

3.4 Rating Prediction and Recommendations

The methodology provides recommendations using rating estimations for each movie that a particular user has not rated. We trained and used the XGBoost classifier since it was the one achieving the best score compared with other classifiers. The model makes use of the user's centroid vector as well as the embedding of the target movie. The Rating Prediction algorithm is described in Algorithm 2, taking advantage of the *GetGraph* function described above.

Algorithm 2: GetPredictions (*Screenplays, Ratings*)

input : *Screenplays*: The Screenplays of the Movies in text format
            Ratings: The ratings of users in $(user, movie, rating)$ format
output: *Predictions*: The missing ratings predictions in
            $(user, movie, rating)$ format
$Graphs = \varnothing, Centroids = \varnothing, Predictions = \varnothing$
begin
     foreach $Screenplay \in Screenplays$ **do**
         $Graph = GetGraph(Screenplay)$
         $Graphs \leftarrow Graphs \cup Graph$
     $Embeddings = Graph2Vec(Graphs)$
     foreach $User \in Ratings$ **do**
         $UserCentroid = FindCentroid(User, Embeddings, Ratings)$
         $Centroids \leftarrow Centroids \cup (User, UserCentroid)$
     $Predictions = XGB(Centroids, Embeddings, Ratings)$
     return $Predictions$

---

4 Implementation

A multi-threaded IMSDb crawler using Python was implemented and a set of 1061 movie screenplays was gathered from The Internet Movie Script Database (IMSDb)[2]. Studies [1,24] mention that scenes are bounded by $INT.$ and $EXT.$ tags, as shown in Fig. 3. Regarding scenes separation and characters recognition, the HTML-formatted screenplays that these tags occur were only retained. The name of each movie was the same as the name of the script, with the only exception being movies whose title starts with "The" or "A". Such an example is "The Theory of Everything" whose script name is "Theory of Everything, The". We handled such cases using the proper movie names for collecting the characters. We collected movie's characters using data from The Movie Database (TMDb) API[3], which guarantees data consistency API. For each movie the top-10 characters along with their TMDb id were stored.

---

[2] IMSDb: https://imsdb.com/.
[3] TMDb: https://www.themoviedb.org/.

Fig. 3. Screenplay structure

The graph representations were generated using the NetworkX[4]. The automatic extraction of necessary entities using was occurred by the Named-entity recognition (NER) open-source library, spaCy[5]. We used fuzzywuzzy[6] to match names using the Levenshtein Distance from the collected movie characters, with a minimum threshold of 80%. The weight of the edge that connects two actors were increased representing the co-occurrence. Each isolated node was removed from the graph. That practically means that our technique was unable to identify a co-occurrence of him/her with another character in the entire screenplay.

Regarding to the type of the graph, the graph2vec approach of the generation of graph embeddings, uses graphs with node weights. The generated character graph contains only edge weight. Thus, we created a label for each node using the Normalized Degree Centrality $(C_D(u) = \frac{degree(u)}{\sum_{e \in E} weight(e)})$ rounded to one decimal place. Intuitively, each label represents the percentage of participation of the corresponding character in the movie network. After parameter tuning, we concluded to setting the dimensionality of the embeddings to 70, the number of Weisfeiler-Lehman iterations to 2 and the minimal count of graph feature occurrences to 1. We used the XGBoost classifier[7] for machine learning purposes.

5   Evaluation and Results

The number of screenplays downloaded from IMSDb was 1061. The extracted characters from the plots were found from TMDB API for 1029 movies. Characters were recognized using our method in 986 movies and the same number of graphs was generated. The MovieLens 1M Dataset[8], containing 6040 users

[4] NetworkX: https://networkx.github.io.

[5] spaCy: https://spacy.io/.

[6] fuzzywuzzy: https://pypi.org/project/fuzzywuzzy/.

[7] XGBoost: https://pypi.python.org/pypi/xgboost.

[8] MovieLens: https://grouplens.org/datasets/movielens/1m/.

and 3952 movies, was used in an attempt to test our recommendation system. 311658 ratings were found for 969 of the downloaded screenplays. At first, for each user, a centroid was extracted from the embeddings of his highest rated movies (more than 4 out of 5).

Table 1. Number of movies in preprocessing steps

Procedure	#movies
Crawling IMSDB	1061
Merging TMDB	1029
Creating character graphs	986
Merging movielens	969

The machine learning model was trained and tested using K-Fold Cross-Validation (K = 10). We evaluated the classifier in the performance metrics of precision, recall and F-measure (F1 score) which is the harmonic mean of precision and recall. Figure 4 presents the performance of F-measure XGB in comparison to the increasing number of training samples. We used as input for training and evaluation a percentage of the available dataset. The F-measure reaches the highest value, 0.8, using 90% of the available dataset. The lowest value of F-measure is 0.6 using 10% of the dataset. The performance seems to have a linear correlation with training samples until 60% but it continues at a high peak of 70%.

Table 2. Evaluation metrics of gradient boosting algorithm (XGB)

Trainset (%)	Precision	Recall	F1
10	0.63	0.61	0.6
20	0.65	0.63	0.62
30	0.66	0.64	0.63
40	0.67	0.65	0.65
50	0.69	0.67	0.66
60	0.7	0.68	0.68
70	0.77	0.76	0.75
80	0.79	0.78	0.78
90	0.81	0.8	0.8

The remaining part of the dataset constitutes the evaluation set in the following procedure of recommendations.

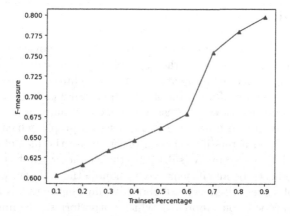

Fig. 4. Performance of XGB model

Our method is evaluated using the average Normalized Discounted Cumulative Gain (nDCG) of the users. We simulate 10 times the production of evaluation results and the score is calculated as the average of nDCG measurements.

The Discounted Cumulative Gain functions used are $DCG_p^1 = \sum_{i=1}^{p} \frac{rel_i}{2^i}$ and $DCG_p^2 = \sum_{i=1}^{p} \frac{rel_i}{\sqrt{i}}$ as presented in [25].

Our method outperforms other fundamental approaches, such as kNN (user-based nearest neighbor approach) and SVD (matrix factorization approach). Figure 5 presents the nDCG measurement in each train set percentage. Our method, Graph Embeddings, reaches the highest nDCG value, 0.98, increasing 0.03% the performance from methods kNN and SVD. We add the random selection and we produce the nDCG score shuffling the movie scores on a user level. It's clear that our ranking function converges to a different limit and distinguishes well from the other ranking functions.

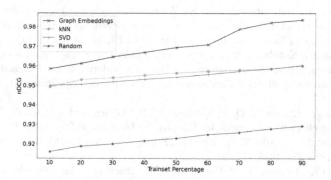

Fig. 5. A comparison based on nDCG between the proposed and other popular methods

6   Conclusions

In this paper, we present an innovative methodology for movie recommendations based on the automated movie character graph and a dedicated machine learning model for rating prediction. We focus on a model architecture initiating from the gather of the necessary information of screenplays and ending to movies rating prediction, which constitutes the basic component of our work.

We propose a way to use movie social network graphs which represent the co-occurrence of characters in scenes in order to use the plot of the movies in our recommendation system. We substitute the character graphs to their embeddings which seems to be an efficient way to handle them. Then, we evaluate the performance of some well-known collaborative filtering methods and compared their performance with our approach, which outperforms. The limitation of this approach is usually associated with the lack of publicly available screenplays. Also, some scripts follow their format, something that prevents the recognition of co-occurrences because our proposed method needs the declaration of the boundaries of the scene. Besides, our method relies on the specification of the cast from external sources. According to experimental results, our novel methodology ultimately aims to provide a good basis for future works that want to establish a possibly iterative procedure through which they can continually train and improve on the results and generalization ability of an existing predictor.

As future work, we are interested in extending our methodology beyond movies (e.g., books, series) and recognize the factors that influence the outcomes of our algorithm at a finer granularity level. Furthermore, our current interests are directed on utilizing cloud computing technologies in our method and the study of scalability issues that will help in reducing the computational time needed.

References

1. Agarwal, A., Balasubramanian, S., Zheng, J., Dash, S.: Parsing screenplays for extracting social networks from movies. In: Proceedings of the 3rd Workshop on Computational Linguistics for Literature (CLFL), pp. 50–58 (2014)
2. Agarwal, A., Kotalwar, A., Rambow, O.: Automatic extraction of social networks from literary text: a case study on alice in wonderland. In: Proceedings of the Sixth International Joint Conference on Natural Language Processing, pp. 1202–1208 (2013)
3. Bonato, A., D'Angelo, D.R., Elenberg, E.R., Gleich, D.F., Hou, Y.: Mining and modeling character networks. In: Bonato, A., Graham, F.C., Pralat, P. (eds.) WAW 2016. LNCS, vol. 10088, pp. 100–114. Springer, Cham (2016). https://doi.org/10.1007/978-3-319-49787-7_9
4. Elson, D.K., Dames, N., McKeown, K.R.: Extracting social networks from literary fiction. In: Proceedings of the 48th Annual Meeting of the Association for Computational Linguistics, pp. 138–147. Association for Computational Linguistics (2010)
5. Gil, S., Kuenzel, L., Caroline, S.: Extraction and analysis of character interaction networks from plays and movies. Retrieved June 15, 2016 (2011)

6. Grohe, M.: word2vec, node2vec, graph2vec, x2vec: towards a theory of vector embeddings of structured data. In: Proceedings of the 39th ACM SIGMOD-SIGACT-SIGAI Symposium on Principles of Database Systems, pp. 1–16 (2020)

7. Harper, F.M., Konstan, J.A.: The movielens datasets: history and context. ACM Trans. Interact. Intell. Syst. (TIIS) **5**(4), 1–19 (2015)

8. Koren, Y., Bell, R., Volinsky, C.: Matrix factorization techniques for recommender systems. Computer **42**(8), 30–37 (2009)

9. Labatut, V., Bost, X.: Extraction and analysis of fictional character networks: a survey. ACM Comput. Surv. (CSUR) **52**(5), 1–40 (2019)

10. Le, Q., Mikolov, T.: Distributed representations of sentences and documents. In: International Conference on Machine Learning, pp. 1188–1196 (2014)

11. Lee, O.J., Jung, J.J.: Modeling affective character network for story analytics. Future Gener. Comput. Syst. **92**, 458–478 (2019)

12. Makris, C., Vikatos, P.: Community detection of screenplay characters. In: Iliadis, L., Maglogiannis, I. (eds.) AIAI 2016. IAICT, vol. 475, pp. 463–470. Springer, Cham (2016). https://doi.org/10.1007/978-3-319-44944-9_40

13. Mikolov, T., Chen, K., Corrado, G., Dean, J.: Efficient estimation of word representations in vector space. arXiv preprint arXiv:1301.3781 (2013)

14. Moretti, F.: Graphs, maps, trees: abstract models for a literary history. Verso (2005)

15. Morsy, S., Karypis, G.: Will this course increase or decrease your gpa? towards grade-aware course recommendation. arXiv preprint arXiv:1904.11798 (2019)

16. Musto, C., Semeraro, G., de Gemmis, M., Lops, P.: Learning word embeddings from wikipedia for content-based recommender systems. In: Ferro, N., et al. (eds.) ECIR 2016. LNCS, vol. 9626, pp. 729–734. Springer, Cham (2016). https://doi.org/10.1007/978-3-319-30671-1_60

17. Narayanan, A., Chandramohan, M., Venkatesan, R., Chen, L., Liu, Y., Jaiswal, S.: graph2vec: Learning distributed representations of graphs. arXiv preprint arXiv:1707.05005 (2017)

18. Núñez-Valdéz, E.R., Lovelle, J.M.C., Martínez, O.S., García-Díaz, V., De. Pablos, P.O., Marín, C.E.M.: Implicit feedback techniques on recommender systems applied to electronic books. Comput. Hum. Behav. **28**(4), 1186–1193 (2012)

19. Van den Oord, A., Dieleman, S., Schrauwen, B.: Deep content-based music recommendation. In: Advances in Neural Information Processing Systems, pp. 2643–2651 (2013)

20. Rozemberczki, B., Kiss, O., Sarkar, R.: An api oriented open-source python framework for unsupervised learning on graphs (2020)

21. Su, J.: Content based recommendation system, 5 Jan 2016. uS Patent 9,230,212

22. Su, X., Khoshgoftaar, T.M.: A survey of collaborative filtering techniques. Advances in Artificial Intelligence, vol. 2009 (2009)

23. Suglia, A., Greco, C., Musto, C., De Gemmis, M., Lops, P., Semeraro, G.: A deep architecture for content-based recommendations exploiting recurrent neural networks. In: Proceedings of the 25th Conference on User Modeling, Adaptation and Personalization, pp. 202–211 (2017)

24. Turetsky, R., Dimitrova, N.: Screenplay alignment for closed-system speaker identification and analysis of feature films. In: 2004 IEEE International Conference on Multimedia and Expo (ICME) (IEEE Cat. No. 04TH8763), vol. 3, pp. 1659–1662. IEEE (2004)

25. Wang, Y., Wang, L., Li, Y., He, D., Liu, T.Y., Chen, W.: A theoretical analysis of NDCG type ranking measures (2013)

26. Weng, C.Y., Chu, W.T., Wu, J.L.: Movie analysis based on roles' social network. In: 2007 IEEE International Conference on Multimedia and Expo, pp. 1403–1406. IEEE (2007)
27. Weng, C.Y., Chu, W.T., Wu, J.L.: Rolenet: movie analysis from the perspective of social networks. IEEE Trans. Multimedia **11**(2), 256–271 (2009)

Privacy-Preserving Text Labelling Through Crowdsourcing

Giannis Haralabopoulos[1]([⊠])[iD], Mercedes Torres Torres[1],
Ioannis Anagnostopoulos[2], and Derek McAuley[1]

[1] University of Nottingham, Nottingham, UK
{Giannis.Haralabopoulos,Mercedes.Torres,Derek.McAuley}@nottingham.ac.uk
[2] University of Thessaly, Lamia, Greece
janag@dib.uth.gr

Abstract. The extensive use of online social media has highlighted the importance of privacy in the digital space. As more scientists analyse the data created in these platforms, privacy concerns have extended to data usage within the academia. Although text analysis is a well documented topic in academic literature with a multitude of applications, ensuring privacy of user-generated content has been overlooked. In an effort to reduce the exposure of online users' information, we propose a privacy-preserving text labelling method for varying applications, based in crowdsourcing. We transform text with different levels of privacy and analyse the effectiveness of the transformation with regards to label correlation. To demonstrate the adaptive nature of our approach we also employ a TF/IDF filtering transformation. Our results suggest that total privacy can be implemented in labelling, retaining the annotational diversity and subjectivity of traditional labelling. The privacy-preserving labelling, with the use of NRC lexicon, demonstrates an average 0.11 Mean Spearman's Rho correlation, boosted to 0.124 with TF/IDF filtering.

Keywords: Privacy · Crowdsourcing · Labelling · Natural language processing

1 Introduction

Sentiment analysis is a human-centred task, where emotions are uncovered from information. Modern methods can work with almost any type of emotion-evoking information such as multimedia content or images. Modern emotion models rely on simple textual information found in OSNs (Online Social Networks) or online review sources.

Text collections are labelled and analysed to create emotion detection and prediction algorithms [6]. Labelling can happen at paragraph, sentence, or term group level. In lexicon-based supervised learning, words are matched to an emotion using a predefined lexicon (sentiment lexicon) often created through crowdsourcing. Crowdsourcing enables researchers to reach a wide range of non expert individual contributors, using various platforms.

© IFIP International Federation for Information Processing 2021
Published by Springer Nature Switzerland AG 2021
I. Maglogiannis et al. (Eds.): AIAI 2021 Workshops, IFIP AICT 628, pp. 431–445, 2021.
https://doi.org/10.1007/978-3-030-79157-5_35

The quality of a lexicon-based learning method depends on multiple factors such as the lexicon, the number of labels, and the model. When dealing with OSNs, the group of words that requires labelling is an OSN submission as a whole. A commonly used practice, that overlooks user privacy, is when the OSN submissions are provided unaltered to crowdsourcing contributors, which makes the creator of the submission potentially traceable. Data submitted in Social Networks is owned by the Social Network itself and is considered open data for any interested individual. This should not reduce our share of responsibility to ethically handle that data. We consider online data as personal data and therefore our study aims to minimise data exposure.

We propose a method for masking text elements based on specific text properties, emotions in our case. This introduces a layer of privacy between the social media users, whose submissions are used in a crowdsourcing task, and the crowd contributors that annotate these submissions. We assess the feasibility of privacy-preserving labelling based on individual term lexicons. Although lexicon-based methods and individual term labelling are governed by a certain level of decontexualisation and their meaning might be miss-interpreted, they are the simplest ingredient of supervised sentiment analysis.

As mentioned, the transformations we propose are based on textual properties. In sentiment analysis, these properties are the emotions conveyed through text. We demonstrate the effectiveness of masking in emotion labelling. In our study each term corresponds to a range of emotions. We experiment with four different text transformations of varying levels of privacy. We explore the results of these transformations with regards to the emotional diversity contributed and suggest an aggregation of individual term emotions as a validator for sentence labels. The results are compared to usual text annotation, to outline the similarities or differences of subjective privacy-aware labelling versus traditional labelling.

1.1 Motivation and Contributions

As mentioned, Online data is considered open data. If a user publicly submits an item (post, photo, video) to a public domain, the consensus is that everyone can use that data freely. We argue that since users do not explicitly agree for their content distribution, such usage is unethical. Furthermore, as researchers we usually have to expose public data to third parties. This exposure is harmful for both the content creator and the third party. Our study is based on the notion that there should be a layer of privacy in-between OSN users and third parties. For example, Psychology researchers usually have to expose themselves to mentally harmful text data in order to perform a task. Our method can maintain a certain level of information and at the same time provide an alternate visualisation of the data.

We aim to create a method that can produce usable labels for automated tasks. With our data transformation method we protect both the individual content creators and third parties exposed to the content. Our proposed transformation method is an initial implementation of privacy-preserving text analysis. Furthermore, to evaluate sentence labelling 'without prior knowledge or gold standards, we propose a naive aggregation of the per term emotion. Finally, we demonstrate the flexibility of our transformation method by employing a Term Frequency/Inverse Document Frequency (TF/IDF) term weighing.

2   Related Work

Since our text transformation method is quite novel and no similar study exists, we will focus on the most significant crowdsourcing studies that address any form of privacy concern. OSNs privacy has been extensively studied since the early 2000 s, but privacy of OSN users with regards to the analysis of their social media submissions is relatively unexplored. Researchers have assessed user vulnerabilities in social media and their actions and those of their social circle [5], noting that users' privacy may be easily infringed [15] even when scientists and developers use data for fair purposes, such as creating personalized experiences. In [22], the authors propose the segregation of privacy concerns to sets of varying privacy priority.

The privacy paradox, as introduced by Banrnes [1], and its applicability to OSN users is the subject of [3]. The study highlights the correlation of online privacy attitudes with personal privacy attitudes, and concludes that online privacy should no longer be considered as paradoxical to real life privacy. Smart living has brought interconnected devices to our daily lives, along with the need for privacy in the IoT space. At a hardware level, [2] introduces a privacy-enhanced participatory query infrastructure for devices and users.

Privacy-enhancing technologies for analysing personal data are also proposed in [21], which focus on Mobile Crowdsourcing Networks. Spatial crowdsourcing is studied in [14] where authors employ an encryption of coordinates to preserve location privacy in geometry based tasks. Contributors are also engaged to assess privacy, especially in computer vision: in [12] crowd-workers compare blurring, pixelisation, and masking video effects with regards to privacy, and privacy intrusiveness of HDR imaging is studied in [13] with crowdsourced evaluation. Authors of [20] experiment on privacy-preserving action recognition. Crowd sourced OSN data published "as is" poses privacy threats for the participating individuals. The authors of [19] propose a privacy-preserving framework for real-time crowd sourced spatio-temporal data. Databox explores privacy-aware digital life [17] and acts as a personal locally-stored data repository to empower users to manage their personal data.

Privacy and crowdsourcing are the governing themes of our study, while the IoT space is a fitting area of application. With the data-box architecture and data anonymisation in mind [17], we propose a text masking method for the analysis of social media submissions. Our method transforms text to vectors and/or images, challenging the perception of participating workers.

3   Proposed Methodology

Our proposed process of text transformation, Fig. 1, can be summarised as follows. Given a preprocessed cleaned text corpus, we define the text properties of

434   G. Haralabopoulos et al.

interest. We then use a per term annotation of the desired properties to transform each term, and in turn each sentence, to a privacy-preserving format. The transformed sentence is then labelled via crowdsourcing. In cases where per-term annotation labels do not exist, they can easily be crowdsourced as single terms, with no privacy concerns.

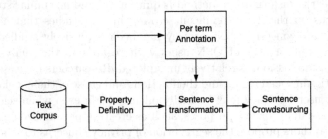

Fig. 1. The process of text transformation

3.1 Lexicon

The sentiment of text can be defined through human labelling. In OSNs, text collections are usually comprised of submissions made from users. The original submission is shown to annotators, who classify the submission according to its sentiment(s). Although public posts in OSNs are considered as public domain, OSN users do not provide an explicit consent for the use of their data in a labelling task, while annotators can easily trace the original author via simple search engine queries. In our study we deal with the transformation of OSN submissions and introduce a privacy layer in-between the crowd and the OSN user.

We propose a privacy-preserving transformation, where words are replaced by their properties. In sentiment analysis applications, the property of interest is emotion. In our study, each word is represented by the emotion it conveys. The Pure Emotion Lexicon (PEL) [7,11] contains a beyond polarity emotion vector, instead of a single emotion (MPQA, WordNet). The emotional vectors are normalised emotion classification results for each term and correspond to the eight basic emotions, as defined by Plutchik [18].

For instance, the word "normal" received the following annotations in PEL: 0 for anticipation, 0 for sadness, 3 for joy, 0 for disgust, 4 for trust, 0 for anger, 0 for fear and 0 for surprise. Its emotional vector is: [0, 3, 4, 0, 0, 0, 0, 0] and its normalised vector is: [0, 0.75, 1, 0, 0, 0, 0, 0]. We also employ a second lexicon, NRC [16]. NRC is also converted to the same normalised vector format of the eight basic emotions. In total, PEL[1] contains 9736 stems from 17739 terms, while NRC[2] included 3860 stems based on 4463 terms. The emotional distribution within each lexicon can be seen in Fig. 2. PEL is dominated by joy annotations, while NRC has a high number of fear annotations.

---

[1] https://github.com/GiannisHaralabopoulos/Lexicon.
[2] http://www.saifmohammad.com/WebPages/NRC-Emotion-Lexicon.htm.

3.2   Privacy

The mathematics formalization of the privacy filter can be described as following. Let d be a text collection with n number of words w.

$$d = [w_1, w_2, ..., w_n] \tag{1}$$

A word w_i is a vector of 8 elements, representing the properties of each word, $e \in [0, 1]$:

$$w_i = [e_1, e_2, ..., e_8] \tag{2}$$

Assuming element e can only have two decimals (i.e. e can have one out of 101 possible values), the number of possible vector permutations for a word w is 101^8.

A document d with n number of words has:

$$(101^8)^n \tag{3}$$

possible permutations. The number of possible three words sentences is more than 10^{48}. In comparison, a 256-bit encryption method has roughly 10^{77} different keys.

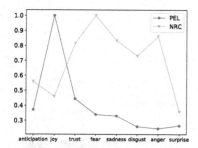

Fig. 2. Distribution of emotions in lexicons

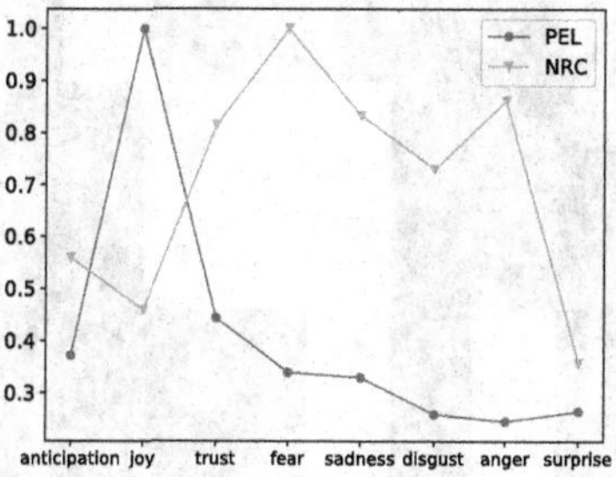

Fig. 3. Distribution of permutations in lexicon

Currently, there are 1502 different emotion vector permutations in the PEL lexicon, distributed as shown in Fig. 3.

Given that the emotional vectors are unknown, the permutations for a document d with n number of words from PEL lexicon is:

$$(1502)^n \tag{4}$$

The number of possible three word sentences is almost 10^{10}.

As the number of possible word permutations increases, the identification of the post (and/or the user that submitted it) becomes more and more complex. So that with only three words in a sentence, the number of possible three words sentences is enough to guarantee a high level of privacy. This is without taking into account the image transformation variability, e.g. colour hues, which will be presented in the following subsection.

Table 1. List of vectors transformation

Ant	Joy	Tru	Fear	Sad	Dis	Ang	Sur
0	0	0	0	0	0	0	0
0	0	0	0	0	0	0.25	0
0	0	0	0.33	0.33	0.33	0	0
0	0.15	0	0.85	0	0	0	0

3.3 Transformation

The challenge is to create a representation of text, based on word-property association (emotions in our case) vectors, that will retain labelling performance and annotation diversity. To that end we propose two document transformations that preserve privacy. The proposed text transformations are: List of Vectors (LoV) and Image Vectors (IV).

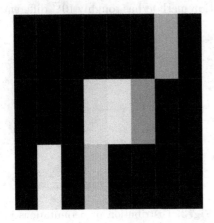

Fig. 4. Image vector transformation

Fig. 5. Anger hue range based on vector value

LoV and IoV transformations rely on the vector representation of each word, Eq. 2. Let us use the sentence *"They have corruption issues"* to demonstrate the transformation for each method. By using the sentiment vectors we can create an ordered list of representation vectors for LoV, Table 1, where normalized row values correspond to the eight basic emotions (anticipation, joy, trust, fear, sadness, disgust, anger, surprise).

Image Vector Transformation (IV) uses the non zero rows of the LoV transformation to create an image representation of the sentence, Fig. 4. Words without at least one emotional annotation, (i.e. "the"), are not drawn. Each vector value is transformed into a certain RGB colour with variable hue. The hue is exponentially analogous to the value it represents, the full hue range for anger can be seen in Fig. 5.

The aforementioned example deals with a part of a sentence. Given a document, the analysed parts/sentences can be aggregated, e.g. based on emotional valence, to provide the overall document sentiment. We compare two simple aggregations methods, that can be used to estimate the sentence sentiment based on all the per-term sentiments. These aggregations are: the averaged sum of normalised emotion values per term in a single sentence and the difference of that averaged sum to the mean lexicon emotion.

Table 2. Privacy levels

No privacy	**Text**
Low privacy	**Shuffled**
Medium privacy	**List of Vectors (LoV)**
High privacy	**Image Vectors (IV)**

Four crowdsourcing tasks per lexicon are performed. In each task, annotators are presented with only one transformation. E.g. The third task presents LoV tables to annotators, and the annotators must decide on the dominant emotion based on matrices similar to Table 1 with no knowledge of the underlying terms.

4 Experiments

We consider 4 privacy levels in correspondence with the text transformations described above, Table 2. Given an online text submission, the complexity of identifying the user -that submitted the information - increases with each privacy level. We created 4 crowdsourcing tasks per lexicon to analyze the labelling performance of the crowd in diverse privacy settings.

The crowdsourcing tasks were hosted in FigureEight[3] crowdsourcing platform. We selected contributors with higher than B.Sc. education, with native English language skills and the highest level of task completion in the platform. We assess the quality of each participant in our tasks with a subjective quality assurance method that injects objective sentences into the subjective corpus [9]. We also apply a spamming filter at 30% single annotation percentage on all sentence annotations except LoV transformation for "book" and "osn" sources, where 40% and 45% thresholds were applied to retain a sample of statistical significance.

Each sentence in each of the tasks received exactly 10 annotations. Contributors were able to only contribute in one of the tasks, and were excluded from the other three tasks. The use of external crowdsourcing eliminates biases that exist in an internal crowdsourcing task [10]. We ask contributors a simple question "What is the dominant emotion/colour?". Participants in Text had the full

---

[3] https://www.figure-eight.com/.

text presented to them, while in all other tasks participants could only view the corresponding transformation and not the initial text. In all tasks except IoV transformation task, the available answers are the eight basic emotions as defined by Plutchik [18]. In the IoV transformation task, the available answers are eight colours, based in the circumplex of emotions [18].

Each set consists of 100 sentences with terms contained in both PEL and NRC lexicons. The sentences were obtained from three sources, a book[4] a news site[5], crawled from Reddit[6] and Twitter[7]. These sources will provide diversity in both formality, sentence size and vocabulary.

As the labels and term annotations are provided via crowdsourcing by anonymous contributors and the task is purely subjective, we only assess contributors based on objective annotations of randomly injected terms [9]. The results are analysed in the triad of Distribution, Difference and Dominance.

Each of the four privacy levels requires different thought process during labelling. *No* and *Low Privacy* levels provide contributors with text and no other emotional information, with *Low Privacy* shuffling the words randomly. *Medium privacy* provides numeric values that correspond to the emotional significance of each term, while *High privacy* level only provides a palette of colours where the emotional significance is represented by hue.

As mentioned, emotional labelling is mainly subjective. Thus, we will use *No Privacy* labels as baseline for comparison with the other Privacy levels. However, *No Privacy* labels should not be interpreted as the correct labels nor as the gold standard. We will present two sets of results, based on the lexicons used to create the transformations, PEL or NRC.

4.1 PEL

LoV and IV are created by using lexicon annotation distributions, therefore PEL acts as the transformation agent of a sentence and the resulting annotations follow the PEL distribution, Fig. 2. Labels obtained through IV provided an annotation distribution closer to Text than LoV in 19 out of 24 occasions, and in fewer cases outperformed Shuffled.

Simirarly, the annotational difference follows joy annotations of the PEL lexicon, reflected in both LoV and IV transformations. Sentence annotations via Shuffled method present a slight variation in four out of eight emotions. While, sentences from *osn* source have significant positive 'joy' and negative 'trust' differences due to LoV and IV transformations.

The strength of the dominant emotion for each sentence label, as defined by the majority strength of the annotations, is portrayed in Figs. 6. The Text and Shuffled transformation have a low dominant emotion agreement, which indicates diversity of opinions, the subjective nature of the annotation task. LoV

---

[4] https://www.gutenberg.org/ebooks/135.

[5] https://open-platform.theguardian.com/.

[6] https://www.reddit.com/.

[7] https://twitter.com/.

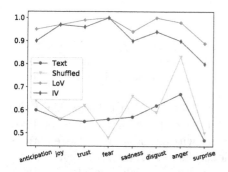

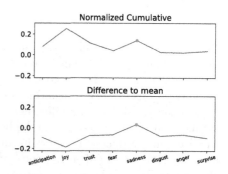

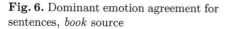

Fig. 6. Dominant emotion agreement for sentences, *book* source

Fig. 7. Per term aggregation based on PEL and Difference to mean PEL aggregation for **sadness** sentences via *IV*

and IV transformations have high dominant emotional agreement, probably due to differences in the presentation of the task.

Dominant emotion is characterised by low Text and high LoV and IV agreement regardless of source, while Shuffled sentence agreement varies across sources. Sentences from *book* are a good example of that, Fig. 6. Sentences from *news* source have similarly low Text and high LoV agreement, but Shuffled and IV transformations agreements fall within the area of 65% to 90%. Regardless of the source, LoV presents the highest level of agreement followed by IV.

When we aggregate the per term emotion vectors of a sentence, joy is prominent. However, when we calculate the difference of the normalised cumulative sentence emotion to the normalised mean lexicon emotion (diff-aggregation), we can uncover the prominent sentence emotion with high enough certainty, Fig. 7. A correlation of the diff-aggregation and the actual sentence annotation is evident in most transformations and sources.

Table 3. Sentence annotation *(column 1)* and top three IV term aggregation scores for PEL lexicon, *osn* source

Ant.	Joy	Trust	Fear	Sadness	Disgust	Anger	Surprise
Joy: 0.94	**Joy: 1.89**	Joy: 0.37	Joy: 0.18	Ant: 0.17	Joy: 0.29	Tru: 0.05	**Sur: 0.32**
Ant: 0.62	Ant: 0.58	**Tru: 0.36**	Ant: 0.13	Joy: 0.14	**Dis: 0.12**	Joy: 0.04	Joy: 0.22
Tru: 0.51	Tru: 0.5	Dis: 0.12	**Fear: 0.13**	Tru: 0.11	Tru: 0.12	Ant: 0.03	Tru: 0.19

Table 3 presents the simple aggregation of terms in relation to the emotion annotation of the sentence for *osn*. The simple aggregation of terms presents high joy annotations, especially in LoV and IV transformations, Table 3. The diff-aggregation corresponds to the Text sentence annotation in 96% of IV transformations. A strong indication of term to sentence relationship, as mentioned in [4].

4.2 NRC

The distribution of sentence annotations for *news* source with NRC transformation is significantly different compared to PEL. 'Joy' was the least annotated emotion in *news* for IV transformation, which is in line with the low number of joy annotations in Text transformation.

The mean annotational difference of LoV and IV to Text is lower than PEL. 'Sadness' in *news* source has the highest difference to the annotations of Text. There is a clear reduction in emotional diversity, with one or -at most- two emotions receiving high number of annotations, while the rest of the emotions are negatively affected. In PEL 'joy' was a key factor in transformation, whereas NRC emotions that positively influence annotations are 'anticipation', 'trust' and 'joy'.

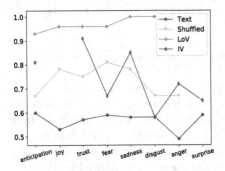

Fig. 8. Dominant emotion agreement for sentences, *news* source

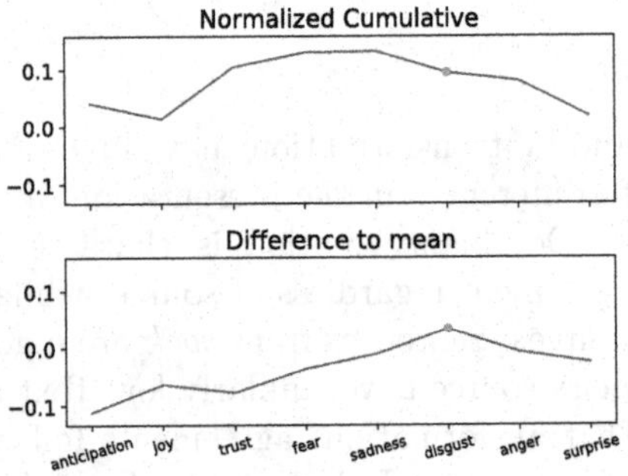

Fig. 9. Per term aggregation based on NRC and Difference to mean NRC aggregation for sentences annotated with **disgust** via *IV*

The annotational agreement for sentences from *book* sources is similar to PEL transformed sentences. The emotion agreement in *news* suggests a greater diversity of opinions, Fig. 8.

Table 4. Sentence annotation *(column 1)* and top three IV term aggregation scores for NRC lexicon, *osn* source

Ant.	Joy	Trust	Fear	Sadness	Disgust	Anger	Surprise
Ant: 0.52	**Joy: 0.15**	**Tru: 0.6**	Tru: 0.22	**Sad: 0.23**	Tru: 0.11	Fear: 0.14	**Sur: 0.08**
Joy: 0.3	Tru: 0.11	Ang: 0.25	**Fear: 0.18**	Ant: 0.15	Joy: 0.05	Tru: 0.11	Joy: 0.07
Tru: 0.27	Ant: 0.06	Ant: 0.23	Ang: 0.12	Fear: 0.12	Ant: 0.04	**Ang: 0.11**	Tru: 0.07

Throughout the transformations, the high number of 'trust' annotations in NRC, results in high aggregations for the majority of sentence labels, Table 4. Five out of eight emotions for *osn* source with IV transformation, based on NRC simple emotion aggregation, are highly correlated with the sentence annotation.

Diff-aggregation can also be used to determine the most appropriate emotion in more than 93% of the cases, Figs. 9.

Table 5. Mean Spearman's Rho per source and method, compared to Text annotations (Shuffled is independent of lexicon)

Source	Book			News			Osn		
Method	Shuffled	LoV	IV	Shuffled	LoV	IV	Shuffled	LoV	IV
PEL	0.2645	0.0678	0.0615	0.1788	−0.0001	0.0069	0.1677	0.0611	0.0567
NRC		0.2065	0.1522		0.0921	0.0988		0.1365	0.0905

4.3   Correlation to Traditional Labelling

Spearman's Rho correlation of Text annotations against all of our proposed transformations is low when PEL is used as the transformation agent, but greatly improves when we replace PEL with NRC lexicon, Table 5. Shuffled was included as a simple privacy measure, but also demonstrates the highest correlation to Text annotations, despite the fact the Shuffled transformation could exhibit sentiment loss due to rearrangement of terms. The use of a higher quality lexicon improves the correlation, i.e. improving the transformation agent improves the quality of the labelling process.

5   TF-IDF Weighing

Table 6. LoV transformation before TF-IDF (after TF-IDF)

Ant	Joy	Tru	Fear	Sad	Dis	Ang	Sur
0	0	0	0	0	1 (.48)	0	0
0	0	0	0	.06 (.32)	0	0	0
0	.33 (.21)	0	0	0	0	.33 (.21)	0

To demonstrate the flexibility of our approach, we combine emotion embeddings and a more traditional Term Frequency - Inverse Document Frequency (TF-IDF) calculation. For each term in the corpus we calculate its maximum TF-IDF value, ranging from 0 to 1. This value is then multiplied to the whole emotional vector. For example: the sentence "the insult is not to him but to the law" has an initial LoV transformation as shown in Table 6. After TF-IDF is applied, it has an LoV transformation as shown in parenthesis of Table 6. Similarly, the IV transformation is affected by the TF-IDF weighting. Since each colour is proportionally vibrant to the emotion score, a high TF-IDF enriches colours while a low TF-IDF makes them more subtle. For example "the insult is not to him but to the law" would be transformed as seen in Fig. 10. Since none of the terms has a emotion score close to 1, no cell is particularly vibrant in Fig. 10b.

We apply the TF-IDF term weighting in the same set of sentence as before. The exact same tasks are performed in the Amazon Mechanical Turk[8] crowd-sourcing platform. Unfortunately, figure eight platform is no longer accessible to researchers. Hence the difference between the shuffled values of Table 5 and Table 7. The TF-IDF approach demonstrates the flexibility of privacy aware crowdsourcing. Furthermore, the mean shuffled correlation is improved by at least 82% (*book* source) and up to 152% (*news* source).

When the PEL lexicon is used as the transformation agent and in *book* and *news* sources, the IV transformation improves the correlation with Text. This indicates that the visual representation could better convey the emotional information when compared to a list of numerical values. Similarly to the previous experiments, the NRC functions as a better transformation agent and all the correlations are better than those of PEL. The most probable explanation for the low correlation values in *osn* is the frequent absence of context from online submissions, which is in turn transferred to the transformations.

5.1 Implications

Based on our results, there exists a positive correlation of the actual labels and the IV/LoV labels. This correlation is lexicon dependent; PEL lexicon is affected by spam, while NRC lexicon miss-represents a range of emotions. Both the method and the lexicon resource can be further improved. The transformation method is positively affected by a TF/IDF term weighting and correlation is improved by 21.2% on average with NRC and 75% with PEL. TF/IDF is only one type of term weighing that can be applied. Other methods can be used to

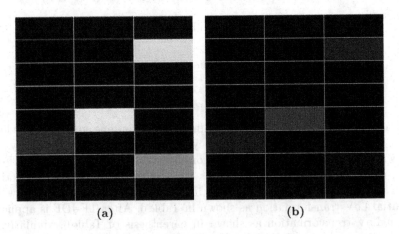

Fig. 10. IV transformation before(a) and after(b) TF-IDF

[8] https://www.mturk.com/.

perform similarity measurements across the dataset or even further enrich the initial term lexicon.

Table 7. Mean Spearman's Rho per source and method, compared to Text annotations (Shuffled is independent of lexicon) with TF-IDF

Source	Book			News			Osn		
Method	Shuffled	LoV	IV	Shuffled	LoV	IV	Shuffled	LoV	IV
PEL	0.4815	0.141	0.1535	0.3848	0.0304	0.1005	0.3609	0.0568	0.0147
NRC		0.2407	0.1548		0.1486	0.1311		0.1618	0.0875

The proposed method is designed to work with any type of information. For example, if researchers are interested in classifying a corpus based on abuse terms, or in a corporate environment where a mental health term lexicon can be used to transform email correspondence to decontextualised and privacy-preserving images. We hope that this study leads to further research in the field of privacy content preservation in crowdsourcing. Up till now, the field is focused in preserving spatial privacy, but our study highlights the feasibility of textual content privacy-preservation as well.

6   Conclusions

We presented a novel approach to privacy-aware labelling that retains subjectivity and is performed through crowdsourcing. The key outcome of our study is: the trade-off between privacy and an as-is presentation is interconnected to the trade-off of agreement and diversity. Text transformations that ensures privacy acts as a curb to contribution diversity, a much needed quality in subjective crowdsourcing tasks [9]. Although manual labelling is not state of the art for NLP machine learning tasks, labelling of sentences and text is widely used in computer applications [6,8].

We demonstrated how simple NLP methods, such as TF-IDF weighing, can be used to further improve the correlation results of the LoV and IV transformations. We also presented two naive per term emotion aggregation, capable of acting as a time-effective methods to validate labels. The evaluation of the results is performed via a direct comparison of the privacy aware annotations to non private annotations. We refrain from evaluating the labels in a downstream task, as such an evaluation would add a range of new variables to the experiment.

The lexicons we used contain a low number of emotional permutations and high level of certain emotion annotations, 'joy' for PEL and 'trust' for NRC. Sentences were split based on punctuation, but different splitting methods (e.g. syntactic) should be studied in order to determine the most appropriate approach to privacy-preservation. In addition, the transformation of negation, in a similar text to image scenario, has to be considered. Finally, scaling factor for hues and vibrancy is exponential in our experiment, but different scaling functions can be used to better convey the transformed emotion.

Our proposed text transformation can be applied not only in sentiment analysis tasks. Psychology researchers are often put up against disturbing reports that affect their well-being. A text transformation method can be applied to perform tasks that do not require meticulous study, e.g. a classification of texts based on abuse type. The transition from the traditional text annotation to a more objective visual representation poses challenges to annotators and requesters. Annotators have to adjust their skills to a visual representations, while requesters need to carefully design the transformations in order to preserve the subjectivity of annotations. Emotion transformation is just one of the possible text to property associations that can be used to analyse text. LoV and most importantly IV mask text in a way that provides privacy to the creator and usability to researchers.

References

1. Barnes, S.B.: A privacy paradox: social networking in the united states. First Monday, vol. 11, no. 9 (2006)
2. De Cristofaro, E., Soriente, C.: Short paper: pepsi–privacy-enhanced participatory sensing infrastructure. In: Proceedings of the Fourth ACM Conference on Wireless Network Security, pp. 23–28. ACM (2011)
3. Dienlin, T., Trepte, S.: Is the privacy paradox a relic of the past? an in-depth analysis of privacy attitudes and privacy behaviors. Eur. J. Soc. Psychol. **45**(3), 285–297 (2015)
4. Giatsoglou, M., Vozalis, M.G., Diamantaras, K., Vakali, A., Sarigiannidis, G., Chatzisavvas, K.C.: Sentiment analysis leveraging emotions and word embeddings. Expert Syst. Appl. **69**, 214–224 (2017)
5. Gundecha, P., Liu, H.: Mining social media: a brief introduction. In: New Directions in Informatics, Optimization, Logistics, and Production, pp. 1–17. Informs (2012)
6. Haralabopoulos, G., Anagnostopoulos, I., McAuley, D.: Ensemble deep learning for multilabel binary classification of user-generated content. Algorithms **13**(4), 83 (2020)
7. Haralabopoulos, G., Simperl, E.: Crowdsourcing for beyond polarity sentiment analysis a pure emotion lexicon. arXiv preprint arXiv:1710.04203 (2017)
8. Haralabopoulos, G., Torres, M.T., Anagnostopoulos, I., McAuley, D.: Text data augmentations: permutation, antonyms and negation. Expert Syst. Appl. **177**, 114769 (2021)
9. Haralabopoulos, G., Tsikandilakis, M., Torres Torres, M., McAuley, D.: Objective assessment of subjective tasks in crowdsourcing applications. In: Proceedings of the LREC 2020 Workshop on "Citizen Linguistics in Language Resource Development", pp. 15–25. European Language Resources Association, Marseille, France, May 2020. https://www.aclweb.org/anthology/2020.cllrd-1.3
10. Haralabopoulos, G., Wagner, C., McAuley, D., Anagnostopoulos, I.: Paid crowdsourcing, low income contributors, and subjectivity. In: MacIntyre, J., Maglogiannis, I., Iliadis, L., Pimenidis, E. (eds.) AIAI 2019. IAICT, vol. 560, pp. 225–231. Springer, Cham (2019). https://doi.org/10.1007/978-3-030-19909-8_20

11. Haralabopoulos, G., Wagner, C., McAuley, D., Simperl, E.: A multivalued emotion lexicon created and evaluated by the crowd. In: 2018 Fifth International Conference on Social Networks Analysis, Management and Security (SNAMS), pp. 355–362. IEEE (2018)
12. Korshunov, P., Cai, S., Ebrahimi, T.: Crowdsourcing approach for evaluation of privacy filters in video surveillance. In: Proceedings of the ACM Multimedia 2012 Workshop on Crowdsourcing for Multimedia, pp. 35–40. ACM (2012)
13. Korshunov, P., Nemoto, H., Skodras, A., Ebrahimi, T.: Crowdsourcing-based evaluation of privacy in HDR images. In: Optics, Photonics, and Digital Technologies for Multimedia Applications III, vol. 9138, p. 913802. International Society for Optics and Photonics (2014)
14. Li, Y., Yi, G., Shin, B.-S.: Spatial task management method for location privacy aware crowdsourcing. Cluster Comput. **22**(1), 1797–1803 (2017). https://doi.org/10.1007/s10586-017-1598-5
15. Mitrou, L., Kandias, M., Stavrou, V., Gritzalis, D.: Social media profiling: a panopticon or omniopticon tool? In: Proceedings of the 6th Conference of the Surveillance Studies Network. Barcelona, Spain (2014)
16. Mohammad, S.M., Turney, P.D.: Emotions evoked by common words and phrases: using mechanical turk to create an emotion lexicon, pp. 26–34. Association for Computational Linguistics (2010)
17. Mortier, R., et al.: Personal data management with the databox: what's inside the box? In: Proceedings of the 2016 ACM Workshop on Cloud-Assisted Networking, pp. 49–54. ACM (2016)
18. Plutchik, R.: A general psychoevolutionary theory of emotion. Theor. Emotion **1**(3–31), 4 (1980)
19. Wang, Q., Zhang, Y., Lu, X., Wang, Z., Qin, Z., Ren, K.: Real-time and spatio-temporal crowd-sourced social network data publishing with differential privacy. IEEE Trans. Dependable Secure Comput. **15**(4), 591–606 (2016)
20. Wu, Z., Wang, Z., Wang, Z., Jin, H.: Towards privacy-preserving visual recognition via adversarial training: A pilot study. arXiv preprint arXiv:1807.08379 (2018)
21. Yang, K., Zhang, K., Ren, J., Shen, X.: Security and privacy in mobile crowdsourcing networks: challenges and opportunities. IEEE Commun. Mag. **53**(8), 75–81 (2015)
22. Zheng, X., Luo, G., Cai, Z.: A fair mechanism for private data publication in online social networks. IEEE Trans. Netw. Sci. Eng. **7**(2), 880–891 (2018)

Recognition of Epidemic Cases in Social Web texts

Eleftherios Alexiou, Apostolos Antonakakis[✉], Nemanja Jevtic,
Georgios Sideras, Eftichia Farmaki, Sofronia Foutsitzi,
and Katia-Lida Kermanidis

Department of Informatics, Ionian University, 7 Tsirigoti Square, Corfu, Greece
{p17alex,p17anto2,p17pevt,p17side,p17farm,p17fout,kerman}@ionio.gr

Abstract. Since December 2019, Covid-19 has been spreading rapidly across the world. Unsurprisingly, conversation in social networks about Covid-19 is increasing as well. The aim of this study is to identify tentative Covid-19 infection cases through social networks and, specifically, on Twitter, using machine learning techniques. Tweets were collected using the data set "Covid-19 Twitter", between November 1, 2020 and December 30, 2020, and manually marked by the authors of this study as positive (describing a tentative Covid-19 infection case) or negative (pertaining to any other Covid-19 related issue) cases of Covid-19, creating a smaller but more focused dataset. This study was conducted in three phases: a. data collection and data cleaning, b. processing and analysis of tweets by machine learning techniques, and c. evaluation and qualitative/quantitative analysis of the achieved results. The implementation was based on Gradient Boosting Decision Trees, Support Vector Machines (SVM) and Deep Learning algorithms.

Keywords: Covid · Machine learning · Twitter · Natural language processing

1 Introduction

Social media is a way to connect people around the world with extreme ease. As a result, users share a lot of information about their social life, transforming social channels into a powerful data collection tool for scientific purposes. During the current state of the Covid-19 pandemic global spreading, the processing of textual information shared on social media can help us identify tentative infection cases. This knowledge can help authorities to timely analyse activities and plan optimal solutions for addressing the virus outbreak.

Bearing this in mind, this study aims to use collected data from the social media platform Twitter [3], based on basic keywords related to the current pandemic outbreak of the virus SARS-CoV-2, and automatically identify positive (describing a tentative infection case) from negative (pertaining to any other

© IFIP International Federation for Information Processing 2021
Published by Springer Nature Switzerland AG 2021
I. Maglogiannis et al. (Eds.): AIAI 2021 Workshops, IFIP AICT 628, pp. 446–454, 2021.
https://doi.org/10.1007/978-3-030-79157-5_36

Covid-related issue) tweets. The automatic identification was achieved with machine learning algorithms such as Gradient Boosting Decision Trees, Support Vector Machines (SVM) and Deep Learning, using RapidMiner Studio[1], the machine learning workbench. In order to implement this framework, data was firstly collected from GitHub repositories and filtered through new keywords, creating a new dataset, more focused towards the needs of this study. The new dataset was then annotated, whether each tweet was referencing a probabilistic case or not. Finally, RapidMiner was used as a machine learning interface for Gradient Boosting Decision Tree, Support Vector Machines (SVM) and Deep Learning algorithms.

The remainder of this paper is organized as follows: Sect. 2 describes the related work that helped define the purpose of this study. Section 3 presents the selection and the usage of the data. Section 4 explains the methods, the algorithms and the evaluation metrics employed, Sect. 5 displays and explains the results that were achieved. Finally, Sect. 6 concludes the work, and suggests directions for future research.

2   Related Work

This section covers the literature review which is related to Twitter, NLP (Natural Language Processing) and machine learning methods for text mining. Most of the studies collect data in the English language [10], however, there are approaches based on multilingual data sets [3,18]. Data sets are filtered with keywords which pertain to Covid-19 ("covid-19", "coronavirus" "epidemic", "pandemic", "fever") [3], and are collected from Twitter [10,12,16] and other social networks, like weibo [17]. Wakamiya et al. [19] chose to manually write a large amount of twitter-like messages in multiple languages, labelling them for more than one disease. Sick Posts are defined as posts that report any symptoms or diagnoses that are likely to be related to COVID-19, based on published research [17]. For data analysis, machine learning techniques have been used to classify whether a text is related to the pandemic. Linear Regression, Naive Bayes Classification, Logistic Regression, k-nearest neighbours are some of the methods that studies have used to identify posts on social media which describe a virus infection case [16].

The focus of this paper is on identifying positive test cases by user announcements on social media by creating a new dataset based on an already existing one [3]. This dataset, albeit smaller, is less generic and more suited for the purposes of this study.

3   Data

In the next sub-sections, the methodology for data collection and annotation is presented.

---

[1] https://rapidminer.com/products/studio/.

3.1 Data Collection

Initially, the data in the present work is gathered from "Covid-19 Twitter" [3], which is available on the COVID-19-TweetIDs GitHub repository. This dataset is using Twitter's search API and Tweepy to collect real time multilingual tweets published from verified users that mention specific keywords. These tweets are compartmentalized in file names that follow the same structure (year-month-day-hour). Afterwards, Hydrator[2] was used, a tool for hydrating tweet IDs, as in collecting and storing data and metadata of each tweet. A Python script, implemented by the authors of this paper was used in order to filter out languages other than English, and to filter the tweets through new keywords, chosen for the purpose of creating the new dataset. Table 1 shows the keywords used.

Table 1. Keywords used to filter the existing dataset.

Positive	Tested	Self-isolation	Dry cough
I have covid	Symptoms	Has covid	Covid test

3.2 Data Annotation

The dataset was annotated by the authors, with 2 annotators on each tweet and in constant communication. Tweets that describe tentative Covid-19 infection cases related to the author himself or to his surroundings (family, friends, colleagues or even famous people) were labeled as **True**, and every tweet that is Covid-19 related, but does not describe a tentative infection as **False**. This resulted in a dataset of nearly 4000 entries.

Some examples of the annotation follow:

- Weekly covid tests are a drag but it brings a piece of mind: **False**
- Positive of covid: seeing more kids walking home after school with a parent: **False**
- Nothing will traumatize you like receiving a text informing you that, one of the learners in your child's class was tested positive of covid-19!! text i received from my daughter's teacher yesterday: **True**

3.3 Data Transformation

Afterwards, the dataset was imported into RapidMiner. Before actually applying any classification algorithm, we applied a few operators available in the Text Processing extension of RapidMiner on our dataset:

- **Tokenization:** The process of splitting a text into a sequence of tokens, spanning a word each.

---

[2] https://github.com/DocNow/hydrator.

- **Stemming:** The process of combining all words of the same root into one. For the purposes of this study, we used the Porter Stemmer [14] for English words, an algorithm that applies an iterative and rule-based replacement of word suffixes.
- **Filter Stopwords:** Removes english stopwords, words that don't convey important information, such as articles, from the dataset.
- **TF-IDF:** A weight factor for each of the tokens based on the term frequency, offset by the number of tweets that contain the word.
- **Pruning**: Removes tokens that appear only once in the entire dataset.

The result was a dataset of 3947 attributes, word roots with a weight variable representing their importance in the overall context, some of which are language usage conventions of the Twitter community (hashtags, abbreviations or emojis), or even spelling mistakes. The machine learning algorithms that were used did a adequate job of ruling those out.

4 Methods

4.1 Algorithms

RapidMiner gives a handful of machine learning services and tools to work with. After the pre-processing of the data, several algorithms were experimented with for automatic classification. More specifically, RapidMiner's stock implementations of Gradient Boosted Decision Trees, Support Vector Machines and Deep Learning classifiers were employed. A short briefing follows on each of them in the next sub-sections.

Gradient Boosted Decision Trees (GBDT) [4], is a well known algorithm used in machine learning, which plays a vital role in multi-class classification [11], click prediction [15], and the ability to rank its learnings [2]. It starts with an ensemble of weak trees, gradually increasing their estimation accuracy through Boosting [9]. While boosting trees increases their accuracy, it also decreases speed and human interpretability. The gradient boosting method generalizes tree boosting to minimize these issues. RapidMiner's implementation of GBDT is based on the H2O framework. Contrary to the original implementation of H2O, which uses a distributed cluster of nodes representing trees [13], RapidMiner creates a 1-node cluster, supporting parallelism through threads [6].

Support Vector Machines (SVM). Algorithms like support vector machines can be used for both regression and classification. Classification is derived from the statistical learning theory [1]. To give an illustration, a set of already trained examples are marked in two categories and then the SVM assigns new input into one category based on his algorithm thus making it a non-probabilistic binary linear classifier. In other words, it maps the training examples to points in the threshold space between the two categories, in order to maximize the gap between them. When new examples are imported, they are placed onto the same space, and then they are categorized into one category based on the side of the gap on which they fall. In addition to this, the SVM algorithm can also perform a non-linear classification with the help of kernel functions. Then again, the mapping is happening implicitly into high-dimensional feature spaces. Rapid-Miner's implementation of SVM is based on the internal Java implementation mySVM [8].

Deep Learning (DL) is not one single algorithm, but a family of different machine learning algorithms based on neural networks. Its differentiating attribute is the fact that there are many layers involved, each responsible for learning one piece of the model knowledge. The learning method can be either supervised, semi-supervised or unsupervised. Getting into the specifics, a deep neural network always consists of the following components: neurons, synapses, weights, biases and functions. They try to mimic a human brain and that's where the name comes from. Ultimately, the DNNs are feedforward networks, where data flows from the first layer or the input layer to multiple hidden layers connected with each other, as a map with different weights on each connection. The weights are initialized with uniform random values, but these are updated during the training process until the network achieves optimal performance. More specifically, if the network does not recognize the pattern to be learned correctly, the weights are adjusted using back propagation, and the input is fed again into the network, defining a new learning epoch [9]. RapidMiner's implementation of Deep Learning is based on the H2O framework. It creates a 1-node cluster and supports parallelism through threads [5].

4.2 Performance Metrics

Three metrics were used to evaluate the algorithms: accuracy, precision and recall. Firstly, the results are loaded on a 2×2 confusion matrix with the following measures [7]:

- **True Positives:** Correctly identified positive examples.
- **False Positives:** Incorrectly identified positive examples.
- **True Negatives:** Correctly identified negative examples.
- **False Negatives:** Incorrectly identified negative examples.

Then, the metrics are calculated:

- **Accuracy:**
$$\frac{TP + TN}{TP + FP + FN + TN}$$

- **Precision:**
$$\frac{TP}{TP + FP}$$

- **Recall:**
$$\frac{TP}{TP + FN}$$

4.3   Optimal Parameters

Table 2 presents the optimal parameters found.

Table 2. The optimal parameters of each algorithm

Support Vector Machines	Kernel type	Dot
	C	0
Gradient Boosted Trees	Number of Trees	50
	Maximal Depth	8
	Learning Rate	0.01
Deep Learning	Activation	Tanh
	Hidden Layers	2
	HL 1 Size	200
	HL 2 Size	100
	Epochs	50

In RapidMiner, the kernel type Dot in SVMs is the equivalent of Linear [8], and the activation Tanh in DL the equivalent of a shifted and scaled Sigmoid [5]. In addition, in RapidMiner, the output layer of DL uses Softmax activation by default.

5   Results

As seen in Table 3, the Gradient Boosted Decision Trees algorithm has better accuracy and better recall, meaning that it identified the most True labels, but it identified as True many False labels in comparison to Deep Learning. Deep Learning follows with a better Precision but a worse Accuracy, which means that it was more selective in its True identification.

Table 3. Effectiveness of the algorithms

Operator	Accuracy	Precision	Recall
Gradient Boosted Trees	80.93%	75.81%	85.10%
Support Vector Machines	75.58%	74.16%	70.60%
Deep Learning	78.50%	77.07%	74.91%

In RapidMiner, the Result Analysis of SVMs outputs the weight towards a True and a False identification, while the GBDT and DL equivalent outputs only the Importance Factor, i.e. the overall weight without an orientation towards True or False identification. The Weight and Importance Factors follow in Table 4.

Table 4. Weight and Importance Factors

SVM		GBDT	DL
Positive	**Negative**	**Importance Factor**	
posit	neg	posit	posit
ha	get	test	covid
i	symptom	covid	test
player	free	fals	i
mom	line	symptom	neg
week	vaccin	i	ha

The greyed out words are words used to filter the
dataset

The keyword symptom is a negative weight factor meaning that when someone mentions symptoms he has, it is usually in the context of getting tested
because of it, or expressing relief when he gets tested negative. This is also
supported by the fact that the keyword "test" exists in both algorithms' most
important factors, but it doesn't appear as a positive or a negative factor. The
keywords "player" and "mom" are positive weight factors, because when someone refers to family members or athletes in a "Covid-19" context, it is usually
to announce that they tested positive.

6   Conclusions and Future Work

In this study, a novel approach is described for automatically identifying tweet
text that describes a tentative Covid-19 infection. The models and algorithms
used here can be found in most of the related work. Our contribution lies mainly
in the labelling of the already existing dataset, resulting in a new dataset, and
in making the basic implementation of a classification model for monitoring the
self-reporting in the pandemic, as well as analysing the results' weight factors.
Furthermore, if data is gathered from different social media sources (e.g. Facebook, Instagram, LinkedIn) and more generic keywords are used, more accurate
classification may be achieved, especially by Deep Learning and Neural Networks
in general, and medical intervention as well as government regulations can be
performed on time.

Future work may include the revaluation of used algorithms, as well an
expanded dataset. Use of the model presented could also be used to examine
the correlation of self-reporting on social media in an area and the area wide
positive cases. Integration in an external monitoring, visualisation and geospatial
analysis application should also be considered.

References

1. Boser, B.E., Guyon, I.M., Vapnik, V.N.: A training algorithm for optimal margin classifiers. In: Proceedings of the Fifth Annual Workshop on Computational Learning Theory, pp. 144–152. Association for Computing Machinery (1992). https://doi.org/10.1145/130385.130401

2. Burges, C.J.: From ranknet to lambdarank to lambdamart: An overview. Technical report MSR-TR-2010-82 (2010). https://www.microsoft.com/en-us/research/publication/from-ranknet-to-lambdarank-to-lambdamart-an-overview/

3. Chen, E., Lerman, K., Ferrara, E.: Tracking social media discourse about the COVID-19 pandemic: development of a public coronavirus twitter data set. JMIR Public Health Surveill. **6**(2), e19273 (2020). https://doi.org/10.2196/19273

4. Friedman, J.H.: Greedy function approximation: a gradient boosting machine. Ann. Stat. **9**(5) (2001). https://doi.org/10.1214/aos/1013203451

5. GmbH, R.: Deep Learning. https://docs.rapidminer.com/latest/studio/operators/modeling/predictive/neuralnets/deeplearning.html

6. GmbH, R.: Gradient Boosted Trees. https://docs.rapidminer.com/latest/studio/operators/modeling/predictive/trees/gradientboostedtrees.html

7. GmbH, R.: Performance (Binominal Classification). https://docs.rapidminer.com/latest/studio/operators/validation/performance/predictive/performancebinominalclassification.html

8. GmbH, R.: Support Vector Machine. https://docs.rapidminer.com/latest/studio/operators/modeling/predictive/supportvectormachines/supportvectormachine.html

9. Hastie, T., Tibshirani, R., Friedman, J.: The Elements of Statistical Learning: Data Mining, Inference, and Prediction, pp. 337–380, 2nd Edn. Springer, New York (2021). https://doi.org/10.1007/978-0-387-21606-5

10. Kabir, M.Y., Madria, S.: Coronavis: a real-time covid-19 tweets data analyzer and data repository (2020). preprint https://arxiv.org/abs/2004.13932

11. Li, P.: Robust logitboost and adaptive base class (abc) logitboost. In: Proceedings of the Twenty-Sixth Conference on Uncertainty in Artificial Intelligence, UAI'10, Arlington, Virginia, USA, pp. 302–311. AUAI Press (2010)

12. Mackey, T., et al.: Machine learning to detect self-reporting of symptoms, testing access, and recovery associated with COVID-19 on Twitter: retrospective big data infoveillance study. JMIR Public Health Surveill. **6**(2), e19509 (2020). https://doi.org/10.2196/19509

13. Malohlava, M., Candel, A.: Gradient Boosting Machine with H2O (2021). https://www.h2o.ai/resources/booklet/gradient-boosting-machine-with-h2o/

14. Porter, M.: An algorithm for suffix stripping. Program **14**(3), 130–137 (1980). https://doi.org/10.1108/eb046814

15. Richardson, M., Dominowska, E., Ragno, R.: Predicting clicks: estimating the click-through rate for new ads. In: Proceedings of the 16th International World Wide Web Conference (WWW-2007), January 2007. https://www.microsoft.com/en-us/research/publication/predicting-clicks-estimating-the-click-through-rate-for-new-ads/

16. Samuel, J., Ali, G.G.M.N., Rahman, M.M., Esawi, E., Samuel, Y.: COVID-19 public sentiment insights and machine learning for tweets classification. SSRN Electron. J. (2020). https://doi.org/10.2139/ssrn.3584990

17. Shen, C., Chen, A., Luo, C., Zhang, J., Feng, B., Liao, W.: Using reports of symptoms and diagnoses on social media to predict COVID-19 case counts in mainland China: observational infoveillance study. J. Med. Internet Res. **22**(5), e19421 (2020). https://doi.org/10.2196/19421

18. Singh, L., et al.: A first look at COVID-19 information and misinformation sharing on Twitter (2020). preprint https://arxiv.org/abs/2003.13907

19. Wakamiya, S., Morita, M., Kano, Y., Ohkuma, T., Aramaki, E.: Overview of the NTCIR-13: Medweb task. In: Proceedings of the 13th NTCIR Conference on Evaluation of Information Access Technologies (2017)

Active Bagging Ensemble Selection

Vangjel Kazllarof and Sotiris Kotsiantis[(✉)]

University of Patras, 26504 Rio Achaia, Greece
sotos@math.upatras.gr

Abstract. As technology progresses with more and more data collected, the need of finding the appropriate label for them increases. However, many times the labeling process is a very difficult or/and expensive task and in most cases a help of an expert or expensive equipment is needed. For this reason the need of labeling only the most appropriate instances rises. Active Learning techniques can accomplish this by querying only those instances that a trained model finds the greatest amount of information and providing them to a human expert in order to label them. Combining these techniques with a fast ensemble classifier, a very performant in terms of classification accuracy schema can emerge where a trained model in a small amount of labeled instances can grow by adding only the most informative instances from a much greater pool of unlabeled instances. In this paper, we will propose such a schema using Bagging Ensemble Selection that uses REPTree as base classifier under Active Learning techniques and we will compare it to four well-known ensemble classifiers under the same techniques on 61 real world datasets.

Keywords: Active learning · Ensemble classifiers · Algorithms

1 Introduction

Nowadays large amount of data are collected from various sources. However, not all of this data comes with a classified label because it might be quite difficult, time consuming [1] or/and expensive [2] to find it. Many times the labeling process is bounded by a budget plan allowing only a small amount of the unlabeled data for annotating. For these reasons creating accurate models with the use of as least as possible data becomes essential. This rises the need of finding a way to discard the data that provide no useful information and find the label for only the ones that will improve the initial model. A field in Machine Learning called Weakly Supervised Learning has emerged that tackles the problems described above, with Active Learning (AL) [3] playing a leading role in the field. The AL process is utilized by performing queries to the unlabeled data in order to find those instances that provide the most amount of information. Essential fact to create accurate models under AL schema is the use of robust and accurate ensemble classifiers with fast and accurate base classifiers.

In this work we will propose an AL schema with the use of Bagging Ensemble Selection (BES) that uses Reduced Error Pruning Tree (REPTree) [4] as base classifier

© IFIP International Federation for Information Processing 2021
Published by Springer Nature Switzerland AG 2021
I. Maglogiannis et al. (Eds.): AIAI 2021 Workshops, IFIP AICT 628, pp. 455–465, 2021.
https://doi.org/10.1007/978-3-030-79157-5_37

and we will compare it with other well-known ensemble classifiers under the same AL schema proving that the proposed one can outperform the rest in terms of classification accuracy, especially when the portion of initial labeled data is very small compared to the unlabeled one.

In the following section a brief introduction of the AL theory and the BES with the use of REPTree as base classifier will be presented along with the related work. In Sect. 3, we will demonstrate the proposed algorithm. The experimental procedure and the results of our experiments will be described in Sect. 4 following with the conclusions and the future work in Sect. 5.

2   Related Work

To begin with, a number of techniques in querying unlabeled instances have been developed and they are called Scenarios. Membership Query Synthesis [5] is one of them in which the model generates instances de novo and then queries them. Another is the Stream Based Selective Sampling [6] in which unlabeled instances come one-by-one from an input stream and the model decides whether will be queried or discarded. The last one is Pool Based [7] scenario, probably the most popular one, in which assumes that there is a small pool of labeled instances (L) and a much larger pool of unlabeled ones (U). The model rates all the instances of U and selects those with the greatest value to query.

For measuring the informativeness of the unlabeled instances, several Query Strategies (QS) have been developed [3]. Uncertainty Sampling [7] is one of the most known strategies in which the model rates the instances based on the uncertainty level. The selected instances for querying are the one that the model is most uncertain.

AL methods with the use of ensemble classifiers have been widely used in both experimental and real life problems. In Gesture Recognition area, algorithms that use AL with the use of a number of ensemble methods and Random Forest have been proposed in [8] and [9] respectively. In both works a good classification accuracy has been achieved by using only a small subset of the whole dataset. Continuing in the Image Recognition field, an ensemble of Convolutional Neural Networks has been proposed in [10] under an AL schema for the uncertainty estimation of unlabeled data. It was compared against Monte Carlo Dropout and geometric approaches showing that the proposed algorithm outperformed its rivals in classification image datasets used in the literature and in real-world images for diabetic retinopathy detection. A study on the Data Stream Mining have been demonstrated in [11] where Active Online Ensembles is proposed in which accurate models are built with the use small-sized ensembles. In the study online Bagging and online Boosting that use Hoeffding tree and k-Nearest Neighbors as base classifiers have been extended with an AL component and showed great results in classification accuracy with much smaller ensemble size against traditional online Bagging and online Boosting contributing in the training performance as well.

Moreover, algorithms that combine AL and ensemble trees have been proposed in [12] and [13] in which Rotation Forest and Logitboost with the use of M5P as base classifier have been exploited respectively, showing good results in classification accuracy against other simple and ensemble classifiers under the same AL schemas on real-world datasets. Similar approach is implemented in the current work, adding BES with the use of REPTree base classifier in the pool of accurate ensembles under AL schema.

3   Active Learning BESTrees

3.1   Bagging Ensemble Selection

For the ensemble strategy, an extension of Ensemble Selection (ES) [14] that uses a library of base learners to construct the ensemble one is chosen in this work. It uses a construction strategy in order to extract a well performing subset of models that are trained with the base learners. Forward step-wise selection strategy was proposed in [14] that started with an empty ensemble and it was gradually populated by the models that maximize the ensemble's performance on a hillclimb set, until all models are examined.

Although ES has shown great advantages compared to other ensemble strategies, many times it has suffered from overfitting on the hillclimb set, hitting the performance of the model on the test set. To overcome this, BES [15] was proposed that in its simplest implementation, ES is treated as a base classifier for bagging.

Moreover, an extension of BES, named BES-out-of-bag (BES-OOB), was proposed in [15] that uses all of the bootstrap sample in order to generate the models and the respective out-of-bag (OOB) instances as the hillclimb set. Then, base classifiers were trained in the bootstrap sample and ensemble selection was applied to them according to their performance in the OOB sample.

The implementation of BES-OOB method with the use of REPTree (BESTrees) as base classifier was compared with other ensemble strategies in [16] showing better results against Stochastic Gradient Boosting and Bagging and being comparable against an ensemble that combines both Bagging and Stochastic Gradient Boosting.

Although BES has shown great performance, it has not been widely used in the literature. BESTrees was found to be used for Sentiment Classification in [17] resulting, however, worse results than Random Forest, on a dataset produced by tweets. More promising results was shown on a lightweight extension of BESTrees in [18] where BES classification was used for Activity Recognition on a smart home system using mobile phones and iBeacons. It was compared against other existing lightweight algorithms outperforming them in both classification accuracy and efficiency in terms of hardware resources.

3.2   Proposed Algorithm

First of all, the Labeled Ratio (R) is defined as the percentage of the size of L compared to the sum of the sizes of L and U and it is described by the following formula:

$$R = \frac{Size(L)}{Size(L) + Size(U)} * 100 \tag{1}$$

Starting now with L sized with a small R, the AL procedure creates an initial model and then uses it to rate the instances of U, given the selected QS. After finding the most informative instances, the next step is to provide them to a Human Expert (HE) one-by-one or in batches of fixed or dynamic size, depending of the size of the initial L. The HE is an ideal labeler in this work that always annotates correctly the provided instances. Then, the new labeled instances are removed from U and added to L, ending an AL circle [3].

In the next step, the new formatted L is trained again and this procedure goes on until the stopping criterion is met. For the stopping criterion we used the max iterations method by stopping the whole process after 15 iterations. The output of the algorithm is the trained model on L formatted in the last iteration of the algorithm. This model then is used to predict the test set.

The chosen ensemble classifier is the BESTrees as described above and under AL schema the Active Learning BESTrees (ALBESTrees) emerges and it is described in the following algorithm:

```
Algorithm ALBESTrees:
    HE: Human Expert (Oracle);
    CL: Classifier (BESTrees);
    MI: Max Iterations (15);
    QS: Query Strategy (Uncertainty Sampling);
    I:  Current Iteration (0);
    L:  Initial Labeled Set;
    U:  Initial Unlabeled Set;
    R:  Labeled Ratio;
    T:  Test Set;
    B:  Batch Size (Ceil((Size(L)+Size(U)) * R / MI));
    TR: Top Rated Instances;
    Begin:
       Train CL in L;
       While I < MI:
          Assign uncertainty values to U using QS(CL);
          Add B top rated instances in TR;
          Remove TR from U;
          Ask HE for labeling instances in TR;
          Merge TR in L;
          Empty TR;
          Retrain CL in new L;
          Assign I+1 in I;
       End
       Predict labels of T using last trained CL;
    End
End
```

For each iteration we used the batch mode sampling (B) where the top rated instances are selected in batches from the U set. The size of the batches is different for each dataset and it is calculated with the following equation:

$$B = \left\lceil \frac{(Size(L) + Size(U))}{MaxIterations} \right\rceil \qquad (2)$$

This way, we eliminate the size dependency of the datasets compared to the iterations. This way, the size of L in the last iteration will be always doubled from starting the size of the procedure.

4 Experiments and Results

4.1 Datasets

For our experiments we selected 61 real-world datasets from UCI repository [19]. The datasets consist of 27 binary and 34 multiclass classification problems. They have a great variety of sizes with the smallest one to have only 208 (sonar) instances while the largest 67557 instances (connect-4). The number of classes vary from 2 classes for binary datasets to a maximum of 28 classes for multiclass (abalone). As for the number attributes, all datasets have a range of 2 (banana) to 90 (movement_libras) different attributes where many of them are constructed form only numerical or categorical types while other from both.

For the imbalance factor, the binary datasets are almost all balanced with only one exception (coil200) being quite imbalance with almost 6% of instances classified in the minority class. On the other hand, many multiclass datasets have a great imbalance factor with the instances classified to the minority class less than 5%.

4.2 Experimental Procedure

The AL schema starts with Pool Based scenario with the use of a small L and big U as starting sets. For R we selected four different values to experiment with and these are 5%, 10%, 15% and 20% in order to examine the behavior of the algorithm in both small and big initial L. The model in the last iteration is trained to an L doubled in size being 10%, 20%, 30% and 40% of the whole dataset for each R value respectively.

In order to rate the instances in the U set, we used Uncertainty Sampling (UncSamp) with three different methods in order to measure the uncertainty. The first is Entropy in which the top rated instances are the one that increase the entropy of the model, the second is Least Confidence that rates the instances in favor of the one that the model has the least confidence and the last one is Smallest Margin that aims to select the instances that have the smallest margin between the two most probable classes that the model decides. To compare with, we also run the experiments with Random Sampling that selects the instances from U in a random manner.

For rivals we selected 3 well-known ensemble techniques with the use of 3 different tree classifiers as base classifier. The first one is Bagging technique with base classifiers the REPTree, that is used in the proposed algorithm as well, and J48 that is a Java implementation of the C4.5 decision tree. The next two ensemble techniques belong to the Boosting family and these are LogitBoost [20] and AdaBoostM1 [21] with the use of Decision Stump as base classifier.

In the training process we used 3-fold validation that separates the train set in three folds and uses 2/3 for training and the rest 1/3 for testing, repeating the process three times until all folds are tested. The classification accuracy of the model is the average of results of each testing phase.

It is worth mentioning that every experiment ran 3 times for every dataset, QS, R and classifier and the final result is the average of the results of each experiment. For software we used WEKA [4] with the use of JCLAL [22] framework for the AL setup and for each classifier we used the default parameters provided by the software.

4.3   Results

In Table 1 and Table 2 we demonstrate the results of the classification accuracy of each algorithm for both binary and multiclass datasets respectively annotating with bold text the best classification accuracy for each dataset. Due to lack of space, we only included the results of classification accuracy for R = 5% using the Uncertainty Sampling with Entropy method against the rest of the selected ensemble methods. The rest of the results can be found in the link: http://ml.math.upatras.gr/wp-content/uploads/2021/03/Active-BES-Results.zip.

Table 1. Classification accuracy of the ALBESTrees against the selected ensemble methods for binary datasets under UncSamp(Entropy) strategy for R = 5%

Dataset	BES (REPTree)	Bagging (REPTree)	Bagging (J48)	Logitboost (Decision St.)	Adaboost (Decision St.)
banana	70.81	82.10	83.35	**84.48**	59.25
bands	**56.90**	44.74	47.21	49.32	55.14
chess	91.94	93.19	**95.78**	90.00	84.38
coil2000	**94.03**	93.96	93.49	92.30	**94.03**
credit-a	**85.94**	71.40	81.06	72.75	84.88
credit-g	**71.57**	70.13	69.53	68.53	70.63
german	**71.57**	70.10	68.73	68.37	70.47
heart-statlog	**72.59**	55.56	60.25	69.14	70.49
housevotes	**96.98**	95.25	94.67	91.82	94.82
ionosphere	**87.84**	56.89	62.20	69.92	74.45
kr-vs-kp	92.09	94.50	**95.58**	90.39	86.57
magic	**85.59**	83.26	82.88	81.73	77.14
mammographic	**83.41**	70.68	79.52	74.66	79.92
monk-2	**98.07**	97.22	97.22	90.48	95.76
mushroom	**99.94**	99.74	99.36	99.41	97.58
phoneme	**83.78**	79.16	80.47	78.26	72.25
pima	**73.39**	67.97	69.01	69.84	70.66
ring	**95.58**	85.67	87.62	82.30	49.51
sonar	**62.85**	45.53	52.57	59.48	60.73

(continued)

Table 1. (*continued*)

Dataset	BES (REPTree)	Bagging (REPTree)	Bagging (J48)	Logitboost (Decision St.)	Adaboost (Decision St.)
spambase	**92.94**	88.80	89.66	85.08	83.76
spectfheart	**76.78**	43.07	49.44	59.70	69.91
tic-tac-toe	71.40	67.88	67.40	**75.01**	69.07
titanic	71.20	77.65	**78.27**	77.15	77.66
twonorm	**95.82**	84.77	86.36	85.82	84.81
vote	90.50	78.08	88.35	91.56	**92.72**
wdbc	**94.43**	85.18	85.76	89.87	94.38
wisconsin	**96.88**	89.95	92.97	92.02	92.97

Table 2. Classification accuracy of the ALBESTrees against the selected ensemble methods for multiclass datasets under UncSamp(Entropy) strategy for R = 5%

Dataset	BES (REPTree)	Bagging (REPTree)	Bagging (J48)	Logitboost (Decision St.)	Adaboost (Decision St.)
abalone	**24.91**	21.88	19.94	18.73	16.73
anneal	**90.05**	84.11	85.15	89.03	77.02
audiology	29.80	33.04	**49.10**	38.91	33.90
balance-scale	73.92	62.61	71.84	**74.96**	49.81
balance	74.93	69.17	66.98	**76.28**	55.90
car	**83.82**	74.19	78.34	80.56	70.79
cleveland	**56.57**	53.87	53.87	51.70	53.98
connect-4	69.41	71.71	**72.67**	70.24	65.83
dermatology	**93.48**	75.69	86.31	76.17	48.70
ecoli	**74.80**	68.35	68.15	63.99	62.00
flare	69.23	**70.04**	68.73	68.49	53.47
kr-vs-kp	**36.34**	27.27	33.56	35.84	10.04
led7digit	**54.73**	41.59	47.00	48.78	14.94
letter	**80.84**	62.47	68.15	71.02	6.91
marketing	**31.53**	28.56	26.59	25.89	18.64
movement_libras	**35.74**	20.74	24.35	27.24	10.93
newthyroid	**81.41**	81.11	78.79	80.70	81.26

(*continued*)

Table 2. (*continued*)

Dataset	BES (REPTree)	Bagging (REPTree)	Bagging (J48)	Logitboost (Decision St.)	Adaboost (Decision St.)
nursery	88.79	89.17	**90.74**	90.41	64.54
optdigits	**91.48**	79.94	81.60	78.35	18.74
page-blocks	**96.91**	95.74	96.06	95.04	92.60
penbased	**96.31**	89.92	91.95	89.72	20.52
primary-tumor	25.86	25.17	24.39	**28.81**	25.86
satimage	**86.23**	80.95	81.66	73.37	33.63
segment	**93.67**	88.66	89.25	85.34	28.51
shuttle	**99.96**	99.90	**99.96**	99.83	84.23
soybean	**64.13**	20.45	43.88	60.24	13.47
texture	**92.28**	81.48	84.93	83.45	16.08
thyroid	99.11	99.30	**99.36**	96.62	96.87
vehicle	**62.37**	48.35	52.44	56.34	26.04
vowel	**43.30**	10.91	39.66	35.93	14.14
waveform-5000	**82.03**	75.11	75.00	70.28	55.37
winequality-red	**49.86**	45.03	46.32	40.70	42.21
winequality-white	**50.52**	46.86	47.39	40.94	31.19
yeast	**49.10**	45.15	47.15	41.40	21.29

Moreover, we calculated the total winnings of each algorithm in terms of classification accuracy for every initial R and every query strategy method for both binary and multiclass datasets. The proposed algorithm outperformed its rivals in all of the uncertainty sampling metrics and initial labeled ratios with a total of 574 winnings followed by Bagging(J48) with 127 winnings. It is worth mentioning that most winnings of the proposed algorithm are accomplished for R = 5% proving that it is a better choice when there are very few labeled instances compared to the unlabeled one.

For the statistical analysis of the performance of the algorithms, we used non-parametrical Friedman tests that examines if the null hypothesis of the similarity of the algorithms that it compares holds [23]. In Fig. 1, we demonstrate these results comparing all algorithms with the use of Uncertainty Sampling and Random Sampling query strategies using violin plot.

From the results it is shown that the proposed algorithm has the best ranking in all cases compared to its rivals. Moreover, Uncertainty Sampling shows better rankings compared to Random Sampling proving that AL techniques can be very beneficial in order to choose the most appropriate instances.

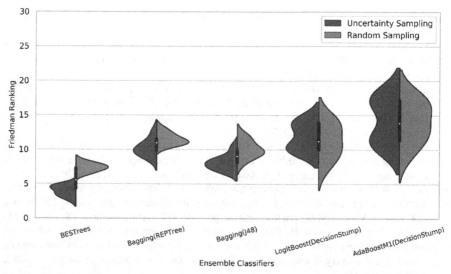

Fig. 1. Violin plot presenting the distribution of Friedman ranking of the ensemble classifiers comparing the selected query strategy against random sampling

5 Conclusions and Future Work

In this work we proposed BES with the use of REPTree as base classifier under AL schema. We compared it with other well-known ensemble methods on both binary and multiclass classification datasets under the same AL schema. From the results it is shown that the proposed algorithm outperforms its rivals with statistical significance according to non-parametrical Friedman tests, making it a great candidate for problems where acquiring labels of unlabeled data is constrained by a budget plan.

For future work, we will compare the proposed algorithm with other state-of-the-art ensemble algorithms like Random Forest, Rotation Forest and Neural Networks Ensembles in both classification accuracy and training efficiency. Moreover, we will experiment with Noisy Oracles where HE has an error ratio on its annotations, in order to simulate more real life scenarios [24].

References

1. Zhu, X., Lafferty, J., Ghahramani, Z.: Combining active learning and semi-supervised learning using gaussian fields and harmonic functions. In: ICML 2003 Workshop on the Continuum from Labeled to Unlabeled Data in Machine Learning and Data Mining, pp. 58–65 (2003)
2. Settles, B., Craven, M., Friedl, L.: Active learning with real annotation costs. In: Proceedings of the NIPS Workshop on Cost-Sensitive Learning, pp. 1–10 (2008)
3. Settles, B.: Active learning. Synth. Lect. Artif. Intell. Mach. Learn. **18**, 1–111 (2012). https://doi.org/10.2200/S00429ED1V01Y201207AIM018
4. Hall, M., Frank, E., Holmes, G., Pfahringer, B., Reutemann, P., Witten, I.H.: The WEKA Data Mining Software: An Update. SIGKDD Explor 11 (2009)
5. Angluin, D.: Queries and concept learning. Mach. Learn. **2**, 319–342 (1987)

6. Cohn, D., Ladner, R., Waibel, A.: Improving generalization with active learning. Mach. Learn. **15**, 201–221 (1994)

7. Lewis, D.D., Gale, W.A.: A sequential algorithm for training text classifiers. In: Proceedings of the ACM SIGIR Conference on Research and Development in Information Retrieval, pp. 3–12. ACM/Springer (1994)

8. Schumacher, J., Sakic, D., Grumpe, A., Fink, G.A., Wöhler, C.: Active learning of ensemble classifiers for gesture recognition. In: Pinz, A., Pock, T., Bischof, H., Leberl, F. (eds.) DAGM/OAGM 2012. LNCS, vol. 7476, pp. 498–507. Springer, Heidelberg (2012). https://doi.org/10.1007/978-3-642-32717-9_50

9. Kazllarof, V., Kotsiantis, S., Karlos, S., Xenos, M.: Automated hand gesture recognition exploiting active learning methods. In: PCI 2017: Proceedings of the 21st Pan-Hellenic Conference on Informatics, pp. 1–6. Association for Computing Machinery (2017)

10. Beluch, W.H., Genewein, T., Nürnberger, A., Köhler, J.M.: The power of ensembles for active learning in image classification. In: Proceedings of the IEEE Computer Society Conference on Computer Vision and Pattern Recognition, pp. 9368–9377. IEEE Computer Society (2018)

11. Alabdulrahman, R., Viktor, H., Paquet, E.: An active learning approach for ensemble-based data stream mining. In: IC3K 2016 - Proceedings of the 8th International Joint Conference on Knowledge Discovery, Knowledge Engineering and Knowledge Management, pp. 275–282. SciTePress (2016)

12. Kazllarof, V., Karlos, S., Kotsiantis, S.: Active learning Rotation Forest for multiclass classification. Comput. Intell. **35**, 891–918 (2019). https://doi.org/10.1111/coin.12217

13. Kazllarof, V., Karlos, S., Kotsiantis, S.: Investigation of combining logitboost (M5P) under active learning classification tasks. Informatics. **7**, 50 (2020). https://doi.org/10.3390/informatics7040050

14. Caruana, R., Niculescu-Mizil, A., Crew, G., Ksikes, A.: Ensemble selection from libraries of models. In: Proceedings of the 21st International Conference on Machine Learning, pp. 137–144 (2004)

15. Sun, Q., Pfahringer, B.: Bagging ensemble selection. In: Wang, D., Reynolds, M. (eds.) AI 2011. LNCS (LNAI), vol. 7106, pp. 251–260. Springer, Heidelberg (2011). https://doi.org/10.1007/978-3-642-25832-9_26

16. Sun, Q., Pfahringer, B.: Bagging ensemble selection for regression. In: Thielscher, M., Zhang, D. (eds.) AI 2012. LNCS (LNAI), vol. 7691, pp. 695–706. Springer, Heidelberg (2012). https://doi.org/10.1007/978-3-642-35101-3_59

17. Moreira, S., Filgueiras, J., Martins, B., Couto, F., Silva, M.J.: REACTION: a naive machine learning approach for sentiment classification. In: Second Joint Conference on Lexical and Computational Semantics (*SEM), Volume 2: Proceedings of the Seventh International Workshop on Semantic Evaluation (SemEval 2013), pp. 490–494, Atlanta. Association for Computational Linguistics (2013)

18. Alam, M.A.U., Pathak, N., Roy, N.: Mobeacon: an iBeacon-assisted smartphone-based real time activity recognition framework. In: Proceedings of the 12th EAI International Conference on Mobile and Ubiquitous Systems: Computing, Networking and Services, pp. 130–139. Institute for Computer Sciences, Social Informatics and Telecommunications Engineering (ICST) (2015)

19. Dua, D., Graff, C.: UCI Machine Learning Repository. http://archive.ics.uci.edu/ml

20. Friedman, J., Hastie, T., Tibshirani, R.: Additive logistic regression: a statistical view of boosting. Ann. Stat. **28**, 337–407 (2000). https://doi.org/10.1214/aos/1016218223

21. Freund, Y., Schapire, R.E.: Experiments with a new boosting algorithm. In: Proceedings of the Thirteenth International Conference on International Conference Machine Learning, pp. 148–156 (1996)

22. Reyes, O., Pérez, E., Fardoun, H.M., Ventura, S.: JCLAL: a java framework for active learning. J. Mach. Learn. Res. **17**, 1–5 (2016). https://doi.org/10.5555/2946645.3007048

23. Eisinga, R., Heskes, T., Pelzer, B., Te. Grotenhuis, M.: Exact p-values for pairwise comparison of Friedman rank sums, with application to comparing classifiers. BMC Bioinform. **18**, 68 (2017). https://doi.org/10.1186/s12859-017-1486-2
24. Gupta, G., Sahu, A.K., Lin, W.Y.: Noisy Batch Active Learning with Deterministic Annealing (2019)

Applying Machine Learning to Predict Whether Learners Will Start a MOOC After Initial Registration

Theodor Panagiotakopoulos[1,2($\boxtimes$)], Sotiris Kotsiantis[3], Spiros Borotis[1],
Fotis Lazarinis[1], and Achilles Kameas[1]

[1] School of Science and Technology, Hellenic Open University, Patras, Greece
{panagiotakopoulos,kameas}@eap.gr, borotis@daissy.eap.gr,
fotis.lazarinis@ac.eap.gr
[2] Business School, University of Nicosia, Nicosia, Cyprus
[3] Department of Mathematics, University of Patras, Patras, Greece
kotsiantis@upatras.gr

Abstract. Online learning has developed rapidly in the past decade, leading to increased scientific interest in e-learning environments. Specifically, Massive Open Online Courses (MOOCs) attract a large number of people with respective enrollments meeting an exponential growth during the COVID-19 pandemic. However, only a small number of enrolled learners successfully complete their studies creating an interest in early prediction of dropout. This paper presents the findings of a study conducted during a MOOC for smart city professionals, in which we analyzed demographic and personal information on their own and in tandem with a small set of interaction data between learners and the MOOC, in order to identify factors influencing the decision of starting the MOOC or not. We also applied different models for predicting whether a person previously registered to a MOOC will eventually start it or not, as well as for identifying the most informative attributes for the prediction process. Results show that prediction reached 85% accuracy based only on the number of the first days' logins in the MOOC and few demographic data such as current job role or occupation and number of study hours that the learner estimates he/she can devote on a weekly basis. This information can be exploited by MOOC providers to implement learner engagement strategies in a timely fashion.

Keywords: Dropout prediction · MOOC · Machine learning · Smart cities

1 Introduction

The recent popularity of Massive Open Online Courses (MOOCs), with their huge number of enrolled learners—out of which only a fraction completes their studies successfully [1]—has led to increased interest in dropout prediction. Knowing which learners are likely to quit a MOOC helps distance learning institutions and MOOC providers to

I. Maglogiannis et al. (Eds.): AIAI 2021 Workshops, IFIP AICT 628, pp. 466–475, 2021.
https://doi.org/10.1007/978-3-030-79157-5_38

develop intervention strategies and remedial actions so as to provide personalized support [2]. According to the Coursera 2020 Impact Report [3], more than 80% of the learners report career benefits six months after completing a course on the platform. Given the fact that MOOCs are typically free of charge, people select courses to attend many times without being ready to commit to learning, or even disposing the required study skills. Therefore, MOOCs face increased drop-out rates compared to other learning modalities, an outcome that affects the business models of MOOC providers, their suppliers, and even the learners themselves. In this regard, it is essential for MOOC providers to understand early enough their audiences – ideally from the phase of registration in a course.

Educational Data Mining (EDM) is a proper tool for effectively analyzing learners' behavior and predicting their performance. In this research, we explore the potential of demographic information in tandem with minimal interaction data between learners and MOOCs to identify factors of influence and predict whether a person previously registered in a MOOC will eventually start it or not. Moreover, we examine if such a prediction could be done in a timely manner giving the opportunity to implement early interventions.

The rest of the paper is organized as follows: Sect. 2 reviews recent studies concerning the implementation of machine learning techniques for detecting high-risk students in terms of course completion and performance. Section 3 describes the data collection process, provides a description of the dataset and illustrates the results of data mining and statistical methods. In Sect. 4, we present the classification experiments that were conducted and the results obtained. Finally, the paper concludes by summarizing the main findings of the study and considering some thoughts for future research.

2 Related Work

There are few empirical studies of the relationship between MOOC learners' demographics and completion rates. Guo and Reinecke [4] studied four Open edX MOOCs with data from 140,546 students and found that age was positively correlated with the volume of coverage, which in turn was positively correlated with final grade. On the other hand, Cisel [5] found that employment status had an influence on performance. Unemployed learners achieved higher grades than working students. Morris et al. [6] also found that learners who are older, not working, as well as those with prior online experiences and with prior educational attainment are more likely to complete their course.

Brooks et al. [7] explored the predictive power of learner demographics compared to interaction trace data generated by students in two MOOCs in terms of student success. The authors showed that demographic information offers minimal predictive power in relation to interaction data. Interaction trace data helped models very early in the course. Kizilcec et al. [8] divided students into few stereotypes using a clustering algorithm. The authors used for clustering different data such as students' demographic data, behavior data, geographic and students' course enrollment data. Through their analysis, the authors presented a framework for the conversation about MOOC engagement.

Hone & Said [9] reported a survey study of 379 participants enrolled in a MOOC at university in Cairo. The authors reported that 32.2% out of the participants completed the entire course. The authors stated no significant differences in completion rates by gender and level of study (undergraduate or postgraduate). Qiu et al. [10] proposed a framework to predict learners at risk of not completing the MOOC. This framework used feature selection methods and logistic regression. The presented method searched for the most influential features for training and recurrently tested the predictive power of the model to improve its accuracy. The clickstream data was found as useful. Rizvi et al. [11] compared the influence of demographic characteristics on online learning outcomes using a sample of UK based learners across four Open University online courses. The authors found that region, neighborhood poverty level as well as prior education to have strong influence on overall learning outcomes. However, such influence varied as the course progressed.

The review shows that a number of attempts have been made to predict the completion rates based on demographics, interaction and previous e-learning experiences. The results show that prediction is challenging, especially when relying only on demographics. That is why we employed login data during the first days of the e-course in addition to demographics.

3   Data

Our study was performed in the context of the Erasmus + Sector Skills Alliance project "DevOps: Competences for Smart Cities"[1]. DevOps focuses on equipping current and prospective professionals in municipalities and regional authorities with appropriate competences to support the emerging smart city concept, needs and requirements [12]. Registrations in the DevOps MOOC[2,3] lasted from September 15 to October 15, 2020, while the MOOC started on October 19, 2020. It lasted approximately 3 months and it was structured on a weekly format delivering 1 or 2 training modules (i.e. competences) per week. Each training module – available in English - comprised 2 to 5 learning units, each of which included an automatically graded assessment test. The content delivered to the learners was designed so as to address the European Qualifications Framework level 5, as this is the required level of autonomy and responsibility for smart city professionals. The registration form included a questionnaire asking applicants to provide personal and demographic data notifying them that all data would be acquired and used according to the General Data Protection Regulation Data protection (EU) 2016/679 and the Regulation (EU) No. 2018/1725 to evaluate the quality of the DevOps MOOC. All applicants were requested to provide their consent to store and use this data; otherwise they could skip this questionnaire and proceed with registration only providing their full name and email.

Personal and demographic information included sex, age, nationality, country of residence, mother tongue, education level, current employment status, current job role or occupation, years of experience in the role/occupation, average amount of daily working hours, level of technical English language skills, current digital proficiency, number of under aged children, available amount of study hours on a weekly basis and prior MOOC

---

[1] https://devops.uth.gr/dev/.

[2] https://devops.uth.gr/dev/about-the-mooc/.

[3] https://smartdevopsmooc.eu/moodle/pages/login.php.

attendance. A total of 961 people applied for the DevOps MOOC, the vast majority of which were from the EU, where the MOOC was promoted. 944 of them provided sociographic information which, after being anonymized, consisted the initial set of attributes along with the number of the first two days logins in the MOOC. Registered learners who did not submit any of the first week's assessment tests (the first training module included 5 assessment tests) are considered as "Not Starting the MOOC" class, while the remaining learners are considered as "Starting the MOOC" class. Figures 1–5 show the impact of various types of demographic and personal information on starting the MOOC or not.

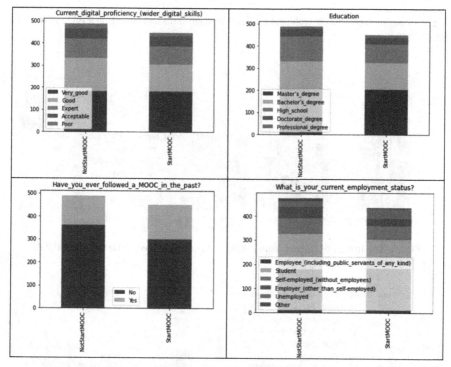

Fig. 1. The impact of some registration information in starting the MOOC.

Figure 1 shows the distribution between those who actually started the MOOC and those who did not start it in relation to their level of education, their employment status and their digital skills and their past e-learning experiences. Approximately 46% started the MOOC. Based on the diagrams of Fig. 1, there are no noticeable differences among the two groups, which corroborates with the findings of the literature review.

Figures 2, 3, 4 and 5 present the data of only those who have not started the MOOC with respect to language competence, digital skills, education level and previous e-learning experiences. Again, it is difficult to draw definite conclusions as the data indicate a balanced distribution among the different groups and among the different skill levels within each group. From Fig. 4, it could be argued that those who have not previously

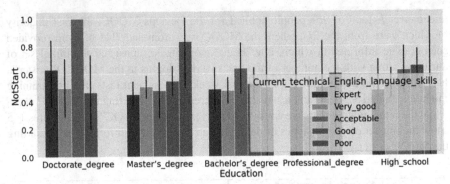

Fig. 2. The impact of current technical English language skills and education level in starting the MOOC

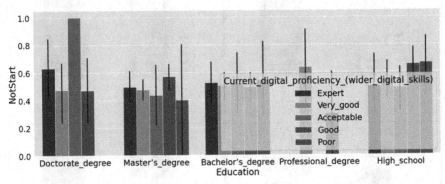

Fig. 3. The impact of current digital skills and education level in starting the MOOC

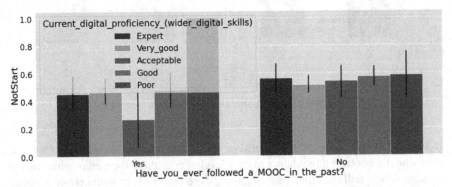

Fig. 4. The impact of current digital skills and the previous experience in MOOCs in starting the MOOC

attended a MOOC have a higher chance of not starting the MOOC. Those with poor digital skills who have already attended a MOOC have a high probability of not starting the MOOC, although this observation needs more thorough analysis and more data to

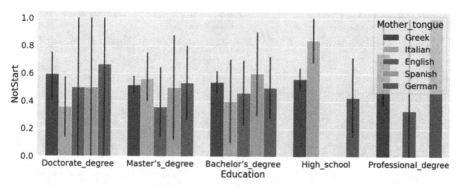

Fig. 5. The impact of mother language and education level in starting the MOOC

verify it. In general, these data should be combined with user logins to understand early in the training period who has a higher probability of not starting the MOOC and to provide more tailored assistance.

An examination of repeated patterns in the learners' data was also performed using association rules [13]. First and foremost, all learners that logged in to the MOOC at least 16 times and declared initially that are able to devote on average at least 5 h per week for their learning, started the MOOC. Second, the learners that logged in to the MOOC less than two times the first (learning) week, did not eventually start the MOOC on a degree of 97%. Third, the learners that logged in to the MOOC less than fifteen times, and their current occupational status was declared as 'employee' (including public servants) or student or unemployed, and could devote between two and twelve hours per week for their learning, started the MOOC. These three rules strengthen the importance of monitoring learners' login activity in the e-course so as to identify whether they shall eventually start their training. Complementary to that, they underline the - even limited - significance of the employment status and the available time for learning as characteristics of the target group that accumulates increased chances to start the MOOC.

4 Prediction Models and Experiments

As we have already said, it is important to recognize the learners that will most probably not start the MOOC at an early stage, in order to implement timely interventions. Thus, the attributes that were collected during registration (i.e. personal and demographic information), as well as those collected during the initial offer period of the MOOC (i.e. first two days logins in the MOOC) were used to identify learners that would potentially not start the MOOC using six different prediction models: Cart decision tree [14], Random forest [15], Multi-layer Perceptron (MLP) classifier [16], Adaboost Classifier [17], Naive Bayes algorithm and Logistic regression [18]. In order to calculate the classifiers' accuracy, stratified ten cross validation was used. Figure 6 depicts the learning curves of the examined learning algorithms.

From the learning curve analysis, we can observe that we can take accurate results using only 100 instances as training set. This rather small number of instances enables MOOC providers with predicting results with even decreased number or resources

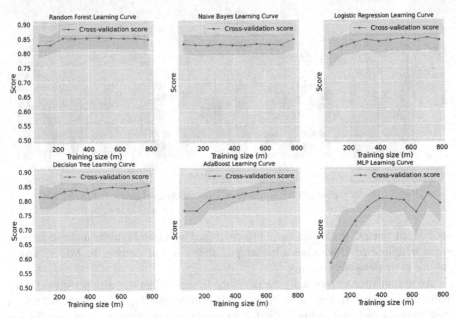

Fig. 6. Classifiers' learning curves

invested for this effort. It must be mentioned that the four examined classifiers pro-duce similar results. There is not one learning algorithm that produces statistically better results than the rest examined methods. However, Random Forest seems to produce slightly better results using less training data.

We then used the Random Forest algorithm for feature importance (see Fig. 7) implemented in scikit-learn [19]. Permutation feature importance is a technique for calculating relative importance scores that is independent of the model used. First, a model is fit on the dataset, such as a model that does not support native feature importance scores. Then the model is used to make predictions on a dataset, although the values of a feature (column) in the dataset are scrambled. This is repeated for each feature in the dataset. Then this whole process is repeated 10 times. The result is a mean importance score for each input feature (and distribution of scores given the repeats), as shown in Fig. 8.

Using ideas from coalitional game theory, the SHAP method [20] computes the Shapley value of a feature, which is the average of the marginal contributions of that feature to all predictions across all permutations of selected features (Fig. 9).

The most informative attributes according to the examined feature importance strate-gies are user total logins, current job role or occupation and number of hours learners can devote on average per week for learning. The two out of the three features are known before the MOOC starts, enabling MOOC providers to act early enough. Using only the three most informative attributes, the examined learning algorithms lose only about 1% of their accuracy produced with the whole feature space.

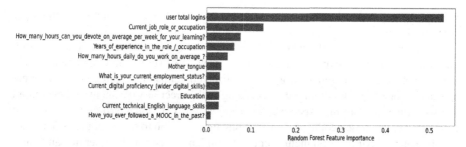

Fig. 7. Random forest feature importance

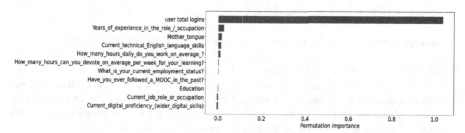

Fig. 8. Permutation feature importance

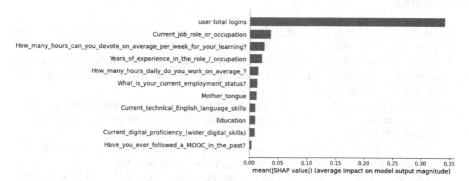

Fig. 9. Mean Shape value

5   Conclusions and Future Work

This paper presented a study concerning the identification of factors affecting the decision of starting the MOOC or not of people who have registered in it. Taking into account learners' logins in the first two days of the MOOC, we employed data mining techniques that revealed interesting patterns linking the actual number of logins on the start of the "MOOC journey" of the learners with characteristics related to their profile. It was shown that the learning algorithms can predict if a learner will start the MOOC after the initial registration. The accuracy reaches 85% based only on the number of the first days' logins in the MOOC and some demographic data such as the current job role or occupation as well as the number of hours that the learner estimates that can devote on average per week for learning.

Being able to know and predict early on the training cycle those more likely to drop out of the course is quite important for MOOC providers to create and implement timely learner engagement strategies. More personalized content and support could be offered, especially for people that relate their learning with career advancement and decreased available time for learning respectively; micro-learning [21] and micro-credentials could be employed for those people as well, opening up education to more people as they support by nature flexibility and inclusiveness. Complementary list of runner up candidates could be exploited, so as to replace those who are likely to drop out; alternative registration policies could be coined; and personalized learning paths could be offered addressing different learning behaviors.

Acknowledgement Supported by the Erasmus+ KA2 under the project DEVOPS, "DevOps competences for Smart Cities" (Project No.: 601015-EPP-1–2018-1-EL-EPPKA2-SSA Erasmus+ Program, KA2: Cooperation for innovation and the exchange of good practices-Sector Skills Alliances).The European Commission's support for the production of this publication does not constitute an endorsement of the contents, which reflect the views only of the authors, and the Commission cannot be held responsible for any use which may be made of the information contained therein.

Co-funded by the
Erasmus+ Programme
of the European Union

References

1. Onah, D.F., Sinclair, J., Boyatt, R.: Dropout rates of massive open online courses: behavioural patterns. In: EDULEARN14 Proceedings, pp. 5825–5834 (2014)
2. Assami, S., Daoudi, N., Ajhoun, R.: Personalization criteria for enhancing learner engagement in MOOC platforms. In: 2018 IEEE Global Engineering Education Conference (EDUCON), pp. 1265–1272. IEEE (2018)
3. Coursera. Coursera 2020 Impact Report. Serving the world through learning. https://about.coursera.org/press/wp-content/uploads/2020/09/Coursera-Impact-Report-2020.pdf. Accessed Mar 2021
4. Guo, P.J., Reinecke, K.: Demographic differences in how students navigate through MOOCS. In: 1st ACM Conference on Learning@scale, pp. 21–30. ACM (2014)
5. Cisel, M.: Analysing completion rates in the First French xMOOC. In: EMOOCs 2014: European MOOCs Stakeholders Summit. Proceedings. Research Track, pp. 26–32 (2014)
6. Morris, N.P., Swinnerton, B.J.D., Hotchkiss, S.: Can demographic information predict MOOC learner outcomes? In: Experience Track: Proceedings of the European MOOC Stakeholder. eMOOCs Conference, Mons, Belgium (2015)
7. Brooks, C., Thompson, C., Teasley, S.: Who you are or what you do: comparing the predictive power of demographics vs. activity patterns in massive open online courses (MOOCs). In: 2nd ACM Conference on Learning@ Scale, pp. 245–248. ACM (2015)
8. Kizilcec, R.F., Piech, C., Schneider, E.: Deconstructing disengagement: analyzing learner subpopulations in massive open online courses. In: Proceedings of the Third International Conference on Learning Analytics and Knowledge, pp. 170–179. ACM (2013)
9. Hone, K.S., El. Said, G.R.: Exploring the factors affecting MOOC retention: a survey study. Comput. Educ. **98**, 157–168 (2016)
10. Qiu, L., Liu, Y., Liu, Y.: An integrated framework with feature selection for dropout prediction in massive open online courses. IEEE Access **6**, 71474–71484 (2018)

11. Rizvi, S., Rienties, B., Khoja, S.A.: The role of demographics in online learning; a decision tree based approach. Comput. Educ. **137**, 32–47 (2019)
12. Iatrellis, O., Panagiotakopoulos, T., Gerogiannis, V.C., Fitsilis, P., Kameas, A.: Cloud computing and semantic web technologies for ubiquitous management of smart cities-related competences. Educ. Inf. Technol. **26**(2), 2143–2164 (2020). https://doi.org/10.1007/s10639-020-10351-9
13. Abdullah, Z., Herawan, T., Ahmad, N., Deris, M.M.: Mining significant association rules from educational data using critical relative support approach. Procedia-Soc. Behav. Sci. **28**, 97–101 (2011)
14. Breiman, L., Friedman, J., Olshen, R., Stone, C.: Classification and Regression Trees. Wadsworth, Belmont (1984)
15. Breiman, L.: Random forests. Mach. Learn. **45**(1), 5–32 (2001)
16. Rumelhart, D.E., Hinton, G.E., Williams, R.J.: Learning representations by back-propagating errors. Nature **323**(6088), 533–536 (1986)
17. Freund, Y., Schapire, R.E.: A decision-theoretic generalization of on-line learning and an application to boosting. J. Comput. Syst. Sci. **55**(1), 119–139 (1997)
18. Ng, A.Y., Jordan, M.I.: On discriminative vs. generative classifiers: a comparison of logistic regression and naive bayes. Adv. Neural Inf. Process. Syst. **2**, 841–848 (2002)
19. Pedregosa, F., et al.: Scikit-learn: machine learning in Python. J. Mach. Learn. Res. **12**, 2825–2830 (2011)
20. Lundberg, S., Lee, S.I.: A unified approach to interpreting model predictions. arXiv preprint arXiv:1705.07874 (2017)
21. Emerson, L.C., Berge, Z.L.: Microlearning: Knowledge management applications and competency-based training in the workplace. Knowl. Manage. E-Learn. **10**(2), 125–132 (2018)

Self-supervised Approach for Urban Tree Recognition on Aerial Images

Lakshmi Babu Saheer[✉] and Mohamed Shahawy

Anglia Ruskin University, Cambridge, UK
lakshmi.babu-saheer@aru.ac.uk, mohamed.shahawy@student.aru.ac.uk

Abstract. In the light of Artificial Intelligence aiding modern society in tackling climate change, this research looks at how to detect vegetation from aerial view images using deep learning models. This task is part of a proposed larger framework to build an eco-system to monitor air quality and the related factors like weather, transport, and vegetation, as the number of trees for any urban city in the world. The challenge involves building or adapting the tree recognition models to a new city with minimum or no labeled data. This paper explores self-supervised approaches to this problem and comes up with a system with 0.89 mean average precision on the Google Earth images for Cambridge city.

1 Introduction

Artificial Intelligence (AI) researchers around the world are gathering to find solutions to various problems affecting climate change. One of the domains that has gathered a lot of attention in the recent years is the urban city planning. Big data available in this domain including traffic and air quality monitoring systems can directly help us plan our cities and traffic routes or even come up with policies and regulations to keep our carbon footprint under control. In fact, one of the major factors affecting the air quality and concentration of pollutants in atmosphere is the vegetation [5].

Various impact of tree plantations around urban cities including highway borders have been investigated as an effort to improve urban air quality [1, 6,9]. Researchers have studied the influence of vegetation on both particulate and gaseous pollutants. Detailed reports have been generated by experts in the field to aid authorities in urban green space development [4,5]. Recent efforts in sustainable urban transportation planning has also influenced the vegetation planted around the cities and highways [4].

Building on our initial studies [3], this research aims to automatically detect the distribution of vegetation around urban cities in order to understand its influence on the measured pollutant concentration. Understanding vegetation distribution around urban cities can help urban planners to build sustainable green spaces around the cities. The vegetation itself may be a tricky factor to monitor. Some of the local authorities such as UK city councils have tried to maintain record of tree plantations [16]. But there are limited incomplete

© IFIP International Federation for Information Processing 2021
Published by Springer Nature Switzerland AG 2021
I. Maglogiannis et al. (Eds.): AIAI 2021 Workshops, IFIP AICT 628, pp. 476–486, 2021.
https://doi.org/10.1007/978-3-030-79157-5_39

records of vegetation around the city. It would be easier to automatically detect this information from remote sensing or satellite images. Remote sensing using LIDAR and drones would be expensive and not easy to scale.

Google Earth images are a good source of high resolution aerial view images collected from reliable sources and are regularly updated. The main challenge with these images are that there is no labelled data available to train tree recognition models. Unsupervised or semi-supervised or self-supervised modelling techniques may need to be explored for detecting the vegetation from these images. To this end, the research presented in this paper looks at detecting and understanding vegetation as number of trees in and around an urban area from Google Earth images. Detecting the trees from aerial view is traditionally performed as tree crown delineation which could determine the individual trees from their crowns in high resolution remote sensing data which can determine the count, density, and even health and species of the trees. The approach used in this work is "tree recognition", also referred to as "tree crown recognition" is locating the bounding boxes with trees in a RGB image. The tree crown recognition could be modelled using deep learning algorithms on aerial view images to find the count of the trees and may even be extended to tree species classification. This paper presents different approaches undertaken to generate a decently performing tree crown recognition model from unlabelled aerial images of Cambridge city. The city of Cambridge has been chosen for this pilot study as it has publicly available pollutant concentration data (being monitored by local authorities) to work towards the proposed air quality monitoring framework.

This paper is organized as follows. Section 2 will discuss the details of earlier work in the domain of tree crown recognition. The details of the data set followed by data analysis and pre-processing will be presented in Sect. 3. Section 4 will discuss different approaches undertaken in this research along with the results.

2   Related Work

In the past years, forestry survey, health and volume monitoring have all been automated with the use of high resolution spatial images obtained through remote sensing [10,23]. Standard image processing and computer vision techniques have been rendered useful in performing spatial filtering of these images. Tree crowns were detected from aerial images using image segmentation and other advanced image processing techniques [12,14,15]. Gomes and Malliard [10] discussed and compared image segmentation approaches like Local Maxima Filtering, Template Matching, Valley Following or Water Shed or Region Growing segmentation, Marked Point Process (MPP) and hybrid methods as combinations of above techniques for detecting tree crowns in a high resolution image. The authors presented hybrid approaches by integrating geometrical-optical modeling (GOM), marked point processes (MPP), and template matching (TM) to detect individual tree crowns. This resulted in an average performance rate of 82% for tree detection in an urban environment and above 90% for tree counting in orchards.

Wu et al. [23] used an UAV-based LiDAR data collected to estimate the canopy cover of a pure ginkgo planted forest in China. Different image segmentation and mathematical modeling (canopy height model) techniques like point cloud segmentation (PCS), individual tree crown segmentation (ITCS), water shed, and polynomial fitting were compared. It was concluded that, the PCS algorithm had the highest accuracy (F = 0.83), followed by the ITCS (F = 0.82) and watershed (F = 0.79) algorithms; the polynomial fitting algorithm had the lowest accuracy (F = 0.77).

Recently, deep learning has become a popular technique for vegetation detection [2,11]. Convolutional Neural Network (CNN) have been widely used in image recognition and object detection due to its power in detecting useful image features and ability to represent semantic data in terms of image features. Guirado et al. [11] compared ResNet based CNN models with the state-of-the-art object based image analysis (OBIA) on high resolution Google earth images. It was concluded that CNNs achieved 12% improvement in precision and 30% in recall for the shrub detection task along with accelerating the detection process due to the ability to reuse models and further improve OBIA methods. CNNs have been proven useful in both classification of high resolution multi-band imagery [24] and also in scene classification which tags the aerial RGB images [13]. These aforementioned tasks deal with large amounts of manually labeled images (e.g. the Brazilian Coffee Scenes dataset contains 50,000 images and UC-Merced dataset contains 2100 images) and attained classification accuracy greater than 95% [8,13]. CNNs or any similar deep learning models demand large amount of labelled training data. Insufficient training data can usually be covered by semi-supervised or self-supervised model training methodology. A self supervised model could be trained starting from an unsupervised model and improved using small sets of hand-corrected labels with multiple training iterations for tree crown delineation and detection [22]. In [22], authors investigated couple of ResNet architectures to achieve a recall rate of 14% at intersection over union score of 0.5 for tree crown detection. Weinstein et al. [22] also highlight that unsupervised tree detection algorithms have been shown to be more effective at very high point densities [19].

These techniques and approaches presented above would work well in a structured homogeneous dense tree region like a planted forest or an orchard. The trees are in these cases of the same species. The imagery is usually high resolution multi-spectral band images and gives depth information like a 3-D view. Our research aims to find trees from the low spectral resolution (RGB) aerial view images of urban cities which may have sparse heterogeneous tree plantations. There is no single (or a set of) species of trees that could be focused on to be modeled effectively with labelled data from other sources. The self-supervised method in [22] initialises the model using LiDAR data and iterates on noisy labels which are hand corrected to improve the model. It is claimed in [22] that a minimum of 2000 hand labelled tree images are needed to achieve a decent performance with a precision of 0.61 and recall of 0.69. This limits the scaling capability of this technique as 2000 images are still a large number of images to label by hand. Moreover, the aim of this research is to understand the correlation of air quality to vegetation which may not require a very accurate count of trees. Mainly due to the fact that it looks at only very small area around an established air quality monitoring station and the aim is to look for a relative correlation of trees with pollutants. This argument is deduced from our earlier study [3] which used a list of London trees as accounted by the council authorities which was a noisy data set and did not have a very accurate account of the trees.

3   Setting the Scene

This research looks at approaches to recognize the number of trees from aerial view images in a scenario where very little or no labelled data is available. Self-supervised and semi-supervised approaches of modeling including transfer learning are investigated on Google Earth images. The research started by looking at existing projects for urban tree detection. Pasadena urban trees dataset and model (RegisTree [20]) proved to be very useful resources and a good starting point for this task. Similarly, there is also a tree crown recognition model named DeepForest [21] which could be used for building the self-supervised model. This model was generated using synthetic image data. These two resources could potentially be used to experiment with ways to generate a tree crown recognition model without the tedious effort of hand-labelling large amounts of aerial images.

RegisTree is a project revolving around cataloging public objects, relied on the collection of aerial and street-level images in certain cities to train a classification model [20]. The Pasadena Urban dataset [22] is made up of about 80,000 trees tagged with species labels and geographic locations, along with a comprehensive set of aerial, street view, and map images downloaded from Google Maps (>100,000 images). The research used multi-view geometry and mapped data to obtain multi-view visual detection and recognition. The multi-view recognition of 3D objects provided significant empirical gains over the customary single view approach: mean average precision increases from 42% to 71% for tree detection, and tree species recognition accuracy improved from 70% to 80%.

DeepForest [21], uses the deep learning technique to detect individual trees in high resolution RGB imagery which required a large amount of training data. DeepForest used LiDAR synthesized tree crown data to overcome this limitation. The model was pre-trained on over 30 million algorithmically generated crowns from 22 forests and fine-tuned using 10,000 hand-labeled crowns from 6 diverse forests. The model itself could be deemed as a baseline for any tree crown recognition model analogous to the VGGNet or ResNet models for image recognition. DeepForest is an open source Python package released with one pre-build model trained on data from the National Ecological Observatory Network (NEON) using a semi-supervised approach from Weinstein et al. [22]. The aim here is leverage the RegisTree dataset and DeepForest model to come up with techniques to detect tree crowns in Google Earth images of Cambridge city.

Transfer Learning [18] refers to the technique which leverages existing pre-build models to perform new tasks in different domains. The models could act as a feature extractor or sometimes just fine-tuned to perform the same task on a different data set. This technique has been used in the area of remote sensing for tasks like determining a specific plant species [7]. The pre-built neural network model from DeepForest can be used to learn new tree features and image backgrounds by leveraging information from the existing model weights based on data from a diverse set of forests. This "transfer learning" technique can be used to train new models with very limited amounts of labelled data in contrast to tens of thousands of labelled data required to train a network from scratch. Here, the weights could be just fine-tuned with a very limited amount of labelled data of the order of hundreds of images.

3.1 Data Mining

Collecting a dataset for the purpose of tree recognition is not an easy task. With the scarcity of publicly available formatted dataset and the dependency on specific geographically bounded locations, a more flexible source of data was required. As mentioned earlier, RegisTree project is one such source. Although the model generated by the group is proprietary, the dataset is available upon request. The only downside to an otherwise perfect source of data is the lack of labels or bounding boxes for the samples within the dataset. RegisTree thus provides a good unlabelled set of training data. With no alternative solution for a flexible and scale-able source of data or tree crown recognition model, Google Earth images are considered. According to official sources from Google, the Google Earth images could be combination of Satellite and Aerial (Airplane) images depending upon the availability of data in the area. It can be seen from Cambridge and Camden images that these are aerial (RGB) images. The exact value for the spatial resolution of this particular set could not be located but seems to be good enough in visually locating trees. An end-to-end pipeline is developed using these data sets, consisting of data-collection, pre-processing, and image-recognition.

Using Google Maps API, a convolution approach was used to collect images of a bounded geographical square region; given that each image (at zoom level 20) represented a 70 m^2 area, the *sliding window* had to be offset by 70 m across until the horizontal boundary is reached. Since Google Maps API requires the anchor point (top left corner of the image) to be given as a pair of coordinates (longitude and latitude), the offset amount has to be in terms of geographical coordinates. If earth was a plane, then the point that is r meters away at a bearing of a degrees east of north is displaced by $r*cos(a)$ in the north direction and $r*sin(a)$ in the east direction. But since Earth's surface takes a curved ellipsoid shape, the longitude offset amount had to be a function of the latitude. This algorithm was applied to collect aerial images of the Camden borough in London, and the much larger Cambridge city, totaling up to approximately 500,000 images. Figures 1 and 2 show a few urban images downloaded using the Google APIs. It can be seen that unlike the typical forest regions with just vegetation, urban images have multiple objects and not just trees. It might be even tricky to differentiate between bushes and trees.

3.2 Data Pre-processing

Since the image dataset can be rendered and visualised, it was noticed that the satellite images collected through Google APIs were slightly different in image quality compared to the RegisTree dataset. Hence, the next step in the pipeline is to normalize the images in terms of saturation, brightness, and contrast to have an identical profile prior to the recognition phase. The perceived brightness, contrast, and saturation was calculated for the images in the entire dataset and was used to normalize the Google images so that all images could have an unified image quality. Each of the three aforementioned image properties are normalised using the predefined constant threshold shown below. $(perceived_{threshold} - perceived_{stat})/perceived_{threshold}$. The effects of this normalisation is shown in Fig. 1 where the trees are more visible.

4   Tree Crown Recognition Models

Tree crown recognition based on the RegisTree dataset and DeepForest models were tried using multiple deep learning architectures. The current section discusses the details and performance of these models.

4.1   YOLO Model Training

There are default object recognition models like YOLOv3 [17] available to train with a minimal set of train images. The model uses ground truth bounding box as prior to train and predict the multi-label classes. In order to use this set of multi-class labels, the system uses a group of logistic classifiers rather than a softmax classifier. It is based on the DarkNet53 model as 53 convolutional layers acting as feature extractors [17].

The first attempt at developing a solution for trees recognition was using this popular YOLOv3 model and training it on a subset of the collected (RegisTree) dataset. The glaring issue with that approach, however, is the lack of labeled data as bounding boxes. The RegisTree dataset does not provide bounding boxes to represent the tree crown from these aerial images. The whole image is labelled as having trees or with a specific species of the trees. If the bounding boxes were to cover the entire image, the training process would be thrown off as there are multiple objects per image. It might have still worked on a homogeneous tree plantation like an orchard or forest region. But, the target here is an urban city with lots of varying objects rather than just trees. Labelled data refers to having bounding boxes enclosing each tree crown, and large amount of manual labeling was not feasible. Hence, alternative approaches are explored.

4.2   DeepForest Model

Even though the data for the target region was successfully collected and pre-processed, there was still a persisting issue: the lack of labels (as bounding boxes). It became apparent that a pre-trained model was needed that could be minimally tuned to fit the newly collected and pre-processed dataset. YOLOv3 was a generic object recognition system which can be tailored to any type of object recognition problem and not particularly aligned with tree recognition. It is useful to have pre-trained model for tree crown recognition. This brings us to the

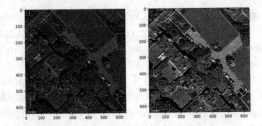

Fig. 1. Effects of normalising the image - before and after normalisation

Fig. 2. Prior to normalisation (detected trees in red bounding boxes) (Color figure online)

open source Python package, DeepForest. The DeepForest model is able to predict the bounding boxes of tree crowns on images as its output. The model itself uses the semi-supervised approach of initial model training with synthesized images which are further optimised by retraining with hand-labelled data.

The raw RGB images downloaded using Google APIs could directly be tested with these models. But, the model did not recognize much trees from the original Google images. A closer look at DeepForest model workflow reveals a RGB normalisation step. It would be useful to perform a similar normalisation on the Google images to match the functionality. Once a similar normalisation (as explained in Sect. 3.2) was tried, the tree recognition considerably improved. Figure 1 shows many more bounding boxes than from the original image. But, it can be seen from these images that still a lot of tree crowns are missed by the model. Prior to any further fine-tuning of the model, based on the newly collected and pre-processed dataset, the model was used to predict the collected images of the Camden borough. The resulting predictions had an average confidence score of just 31.2%. The next step to improve such a model is to fine tune the model using transfer learning techniques.

4.3   Transfer Learning

Transfer learning is a technique of fine-tuning a pre-trained model which can result in decently performing models for tasks with limited data [18]. The pre-trained model itself should be trained with a large amount of data and should be able to generalise well for the task. The pre-built model weights may be returned or fine tuned for only desired layers that need to be optimised. This technique of freezing certain layers and fine-tuning others has become a popular technique to generate new models with short training times.

CNNs with their convolutional layers have been very popular in acting as feature extractors for image datasets. This results in pre-trained CNN models being fine tuned (usually only the final softmax or prediction layers) with a small set of data to adapt to a particular image recognition task. There are multiple options for obtaining a pre-built model. Sometimes, there is a large dataset (similar to ImageNet) available and researchers use it to generate their own customised pre-built models before fine tuning with the small dataset for the task at hand. Sometimes, researchers share a model (like VGG16 or ResNet) that was build with huge amount of data which can be reused as a starting point and optimised for other similar tasks.

For the task at hand, which is tree crown recognition, DeepForest model could act as the pre-built model as it is trained for performing exactly same task on a different dataset. It was noted that without any fine-tuning, the model did not perform very well. But, there is no labelled data available to perform this fine tuning. There are some noisy data labels being generated by this initial model which can be used to fine tune the pre-built model. Hence, a semi-supervised approach was used to fine-tune the base model further. The labelled data was taken from the previously predicted results using the same DeepForest model. Although the average confidence score was low, a portion of the dataset (approximately 1,500 images) scored over 70% for confidence measure. This data was filtered out and used as the retraining data. Unlike the earlier efforts [22] of hand correcting or hand labelling the data before using it for retraining, our approach did not make any efforts to correct these data predictions or labels. The hypothesis behind such an approach is that recognition with a higher confidence should automatically result in cleaner labels.

5   Results and Discussions

Table 1. Results comparing model retraining on the unseen test set (Cambridge).

Model	Performance
DeepForest model before retraining	0.28 mAP
Self supervised learning on DeepForest model	0.89 mAP
Comparable baseline with hand corrected labels [22]	0.61 mAP

The DeepForest model was retrained on the filtered data by freezing the backbone layers and fine-tuning the other remaining layers of the network. This considerably improved the model performance. After retraining, the model performance was tested on the collected Cambridge dataset, where 150 unseen test images were manually labeled for performance measurement purposes. The

Fig. 3. Positive results with self supervised model (trees in red bounding boxes) (Color figure online)

Fig. 4. Errors with self supervised model (trees in red bounding boxes) (Color figure online)

resulting mean average precision (mAP) obtained was 0.89 (refer Table 1). It should be noted that this test data is from a different city (Cambridge) and not the one used for fine-tuning the model (Camden, London). This further proves that the approach could be scaled to new urban regions. This can be considered a huge leap over the untrained model (0.28 mAP). Also outperforms pre-existing results in literature on other datasets like the semi-supervised approach using hand labeled data with a maximum performance of 0.61 precision at an intersection over union threshold of 0.5 [22]. Furthermore, our research only hand-labelled images to test the performance of the model and not for training.

Looking at some of the images prior to pre-processing (Fig. 2), most of the trees were not detected. It can be observed that the self-supervised model with normalised images results in very good recognition of tree crowns as seen in Fig. 3). It can also be observed that there are a few images with missed detections as in Fig. 4. These are mainly due to blurred tree cones which is the main feature that the DeepForest model identifies. Even in these images, the model does not give false positives on bushes or grass. Given the performance seems acceptable for the general framework of modeling air quality in urban region, this optimisation is left as a future work. The next step in this research is to map these tree detection as the vegetation count for mapping the different factors for air quality in urban cities. The models will also be tested in some more new cities to ensure that the approach really scales and can be generalised to any urban region.

6 Conclusion

Deep learning especially, CNNs have made their mark in different image recognition tasks. Remote sensing or RGB aerial view imagery can provide data that can be used to detect the vegetation or tree crowns in a region. This research looked at transfer learning approach on a pre-built aerial view image data model to recognize tree crowns from Google Earth images. The data pre-processing, especially image normalisation resulted to be a very important step in improving the accuracy of the model detection. With over 500,000 images from Google, the system was optimized using the images classified (for Camden, London) with 70% confidence and a final performance of around 0.89 for precision was obtained on an unseen test dataset from another location (Cambridge). With only couple of hundreds of hand labelled evaluation data for estimating performance, the model can be concluded as a very good trade-off for a self-supervised model.

References

1. Al-Dabbous, A.N., Kumar, P.: The influence of roadside vegetation barriers on airborne nanoparticles and pedestrians exposure under varying wind conditions. Atmos. Environ. **90**, 113–124 (2014). https://doi.org/10.1016/j.atmosenv.2014.03.040

2. Ayrey, E., Hayes, D.: The use of three-dimensional convolutional neural networks to interpret LiDAR for forest inventory. Remote Sens. **10**(4), 649 (2018). https://doi.org/10.3390/rs10040649

3. Babu Saheer, L., Shahawy, M., Zarrin, J.: Mining and analysis of air quality data to aid climate change. In: Maglogiannis, I., Iliadis, L., Pimenidis, E. (eds.) AIAI 2020. IAICT, vol. 585, pp. 232–243. Springer, Cham (2020). https://doi.org/10.1007/978-3-030-49190-1_21

4. Baldauf, R., et al.: Integrating vegetation and green infrastructure into sustainable transportation planning. Transp. News **288**(5), 14–18 (2013)

5. Bealey, W., et al.: Estimating the reduction of urban pm10 concentrations by trees within an environmental information system for planners. J. Environ. Manag. **85**(1), 44–58 (2007). https://doi.org/10.1016/j.jenvman.2006.07.007

6. Benjamin, M.T., Winer, A.M.: Estimating the ozone-forming potential of urban trees and shrubs. Atmos. Environ. **32**(1), 53–68 (1998). https://doi.org/10.1016/S1352-2310(97)00176-3

7. Bonet, I., Caraffini, F., Peña, A., Puerta, A., Gongora, M.: Oil palm detection via deep transfer learning. In: 2020 IEEE Congress on Evolutionary Computation (CEC), pp. 1–8 (2020). https://doi.org/10.1109/CEC48606.2020.9185838

8. Castelluccio, M., Poggi, G., Sansone, C., Verdoliva, L.: Land use classification in remote sensing images by convolutional neural networks. CoRR abs/1508.00092 (2015). arXiv:1508.00092

9. Fares, S., et al.: Particle deposition in a peri-urban mediterranean forest. Environ. Pollut. **218**, 1278–1286 (2016). https://doi.org/10.1016/j.envpol.2016.08.086

10. Gomes, M.F., Maillard, P.: Detection of tree crowns in very high spatial resolution images. In: Marghany, M. (ed.) Environmental Applications of Remote Sensing, chap. 2. IntechOpen, Rijeka (2016). https://doi.org/10.5772/62122

11. Guirado, E., Tabik, S., Alcaraz-Segura, D., Cabello, J., Herrera, F.: Deep-learning versus OBIA for scattered shrub detection with Google Earth imagery: Ziziphus lotus as case study. Remote Sens. **9**(12), 1220 (2017). https://doi.org/10.3390/rs9121220

12. Hay, G.J., Castilla, G.: Geographic object-based image analysis (GEOBIA): a new name for a new discipline. In: Blaschke, T., Lang, S., Hay, G.J. (eds.) Object-Based Image Analysis. Lecture Notes in Geoinformation and Cartography. Springer, Heidelberg (2008). https://doi.org/10.1007/978-3-540-77058-9_4

13. Hu, F., Xia, G.S., Hu, J., Zhang, L.: Transferring deep convolutional neural networks for the scene classification of high-resolution remote sensing imagery. Remote Sens. **7**(11), 14680–14707 (2015). https://doi.org/10.3390/rs71114680

14. Ke, Y., Quackenbush, L.J.: A review of methods for automatic individual tree-crown detection and delineation from passive remote sensing. Int. J. Remote Sens. **32**(17), 4725–4747 (2011). https://doi.org/10.1080/01431161.2010.494184

15. Larsen, M., Eriksson, M., Descombes, X., Perrin, G., Brandtberg, T., Gougeon, F.A.: Comparison of six individual tree crown detection algorithms evaluated under varying forest conditions. Int. J. Remote Sens. **32**(20), 5827–5852 (2011). https://doi.org/10.1080/01431161.2010.507790

16. London Local Authority Maintained Trees: Londontrees (2019). https://data.london.gov.uk/dataset/local-authority-maintained-trees

17. Redmon, J., Farhadi, A.: Yolov3: an incremental improvement (2018)

18. Shin, H., et al.: Deep convolutional neural networks for computer-aided detection: CNN architectures, dataset characteristics and transfer learning. IEEE Trans. Med. Imaging **35**(5), 1285–1298 (2016). https://doi.org/10.1109/TMI.2016.2528162

19. Wallace, L., Lucieer, A., Watson, C.: Evaluating tree detection and segmentation routines on very high resolution UAV LiDAR data. IEEE Trans. Geosci. Remote Sens. **52**, 7619–7628 (2014). https://doi.org/10.3390/rs10040649

20. Wegner, J.D., Branson, S., Hall, D., Schindler, K., Perona, P.: Cataloging public objects using aerial and street-level images - urban trees. In: Proceedings of the IEEE Conference on Computer Vision and Pattern Recognition (CVPR) (2016)

21. Weinstein, B.G., Marconi, S., Aubry-Kientz, M., Vincent, G., Senyondo, H., White, E.: DeepForest: a python package for RGB deep learning tree crown delineation. bioRxiv (2020). https://doi.org/10.1101/2020.07.07.191551

22. Weinstein, B.G., Marconi, S., Bohlman, S., Zare, A., White, E.: Individual tree-crown detection in RGB imagery using semi-supervised deep learning neural networks. Remote Sens. **11**(11), 1309 (2019). https://doi.org/10.3390/rs11111309

23. Wu, X., Shen, X., Cao, L., Wang, G., Cao, F.: Assessment of individual tree detection and canopy cover estimation using unmanned aerial vehicle based light detection and ranging (UAV-LiDAR) data in planted forests. Remote Sens. **11**(8), 908 (2019). https://doi.org/10.3390/rs11080908

24. Zhao, W., Du, S., Emery, W.J.: Object-based convolutional neural network for high-resolution imagery classification. IEEE J. Sel. Top. Appl. Earth Obs. Remote Sens. **10**(7), 3386–3396 (2017). https://doi.org/10.1109/JSTARS.2017.2680324

Visitor Behavior Analysis for an Ancient Greek Technology Exhibition

Dimitrios Kosmopoulos[✉] and Kali Tzortzi

University of Patras, 26500 Rio, Greece
{dkosmo,ktzortzi}@upatras.gr

Abstract. The paper reports the findings from research aimed at the analysis of visitor behavior in the Herakleidon Museum in Athens - Greece, which hosts an ancient Greek technology exhibition. Based on behavioral data gathered by direct observation, we aim to implement services to assist museum curators and enhance the visitors' experience. We describe the data collection, analysis and prediction of the visitors' preferences concerning the exhibits of the museum given their past preferences.

Keywords: Museum · Visitor experience · Recommendation systems

1 Introduction

Museums are among the most important institutions for the preservation and the dissemination of the global cultural heritage. They are places of education and enjoyment, as well as drivers of tourism and economic development. A key objective in the design of museums and exhibitions is to produce a deeper engagement with the displays and create experiences that are meaningful to visitors. A quantification on measuring the success of addressing this objective would be very useful, however the information collected by curators for measuring an exhibition's impact is mostly qualitative.

The prediction of visitors' interest can be such a quantitative measure and can be associated to recommender systems. These are systems that offer "relevant" suggestions to users of electronic services such as video on demand, song playlists, electronic market places etc. They are based on some popular machine learning algorithms that essentially check the similarity of the users (collaborative filtering), or the similarity among the available items (content-based filtering), or combinations of both.

The recommender systems are often employed as part of the guidance experience in museums or other places of cultural interest. Those are learning spaces that typically offer a large amount of information, including the objects on display, as well as the additional interpretative material.

Visitors with limited time or no prior experience visiting a particular museum, or museums in general, may become overwhelmed by the wealth of information,

© IFIP International Federation for Information Processing 2021
Published by Springer Nature Switzerland AG 2021
I. Maglogiannis et al. (Eds.): AIAI 2021 Workshops, IFIP AICT 628, pp. 487–495, 2021.
https://doi.org/10.1007/978-3-030-79157-5_40

which in turn may offer an experience which is far below their expectations. Furthermore, curators need to measure in a reliable and objective manner the impact of exhibitions. It is important that they have knowledge of the attraction power of exhibits, and if the supplementary material makes them more attractive; this is an essential part of a constant feedback loop that may lead to exhibition optimization [8].

In this paper we present a part of a larger case study, which aims to develop a guide application, which among others includes a tool for the curator to monitor exhibit popularity and an exhibit - recommendation system. Our contribution includes the collection of a museum-specific dataset. Furthermore, we examine the feasibility of predicting the preferences of visitors using some mainstream methods in order to exploit this knowledge to evaluate the impact of the exhibition. This can also be used to implement electronic recommendation services for the visitors. It is to be installed in the Herakleidon Museum (herakleidon.org) in Athens - Greece, which hosts an exhibition of Ancient Greek technology.

The paper is organized as follows. In Sect. 2 we present the related work on museum visitor behavior tracking and museum recommenders; in Sect. 3 we describe the data collection and visitor analysis that we applied; in Sect. 4 we discuss the experimental results on visitor preferences prediction using collaborative filtering; finally Sect. 5 concludes by identifying further research directions for visitor behaviour analysis.

2   Related Work

With the goal of understanding how people move, explore and use space and display, we carried out a study of visitor behavior, in particular their patterns of moving and viewing. 'Timing and Tracking' studies, which record traces of visitor movement and activity, were initiated in the early twentieth century, marked by key milestones in the work of Robinson (1928) [13] and Melton (1935) [9]. Since then, they have become a key element in feedback studies on museum performance. These studies commonly aim at improving design (reviewed in [3,19]), assessing the educational effectiveness of exhibitions (for example, [14]), understanding the characteristics that make exhibits attractive –or unattractive– to visitors [10], identifying styles of moving through gallery space, often described using metaphors, such as ant, butterfly, fish, and grasshopper, as in the case of the study of a natural history museum by Veron and Levasseur (1983) [17], and investigating how far the morphology of movement and encounter in the museum settings is shaped by spatial layout (see, for example, review of syntactic studies of museums in [16]). Timing and tracking and observation studies are also among the standard research methods for understanding interaction patterns and usability issues in the field of HCI [4].

Considering the general recommendation problem, the *filtering methods* can be largely classified into the following: *Demographic filtering - DF* makes the assumption that individuals with certain common personal attributes (sex, age, country, etc.), which are captured during the registration process will also have common interests, e.g., [12]. *Content-based filtering - CBF* makes recommendations based on the semantics of the artifacts. The matching can be based on explicitly asking the users' preferences upon registration to map them to ontology concepts, or by implicit matching via a questionnaire, where representative artifacts have to be rated [18]. It can also be based on previous preferences by the users during the visit. The similarity can be based on (a) the ontology-based semantic attributes (b) the computational analysis of the supplementary text to extract meaning (c) from audio-visual analysis of related digital material. CBF will benefit from the standardization of the metadata for museum artifacts [20]. *Collaborative Filtering - CF* is based on the ratings provided by users of similar profile. The ratings can be acquired explicitly by direct asking or implicitly, acquired (e.g., access, time spent). *Hybrid filtering - HF* uses combinations between the aforementioned filtering techniques to achieve optimal performance to exploit merits of each one of them. For further details on the application of recommender systems in museums the reader can refer to related survey papers such as [1,8].

The advent of deep learning has revolutionized several fields, among them the recommendation systems. A taxonomy can be found in [21]. Unfortunately our dataset is currently small, due to manual collection and cannot utilize such models.

Our work is related to [2], where a real-world dataset of visitor pathways was collected at Melbourne Museum (Melbourne, Australia). It suggests that utilising walking and semantic distances between exhibits enables more accurate predictions of a visitor's viewing times of unseen exhibits than using distances derived from observed exhibit viewing times. The time tracking was referring to exhibit areas, while in our approach we measured individual exhibits.

Fig. 1. A view of the "Hero" Warrior of the Mycenaean Period' gallery, showing the combination of reconstructed objects and rich interpretive material.

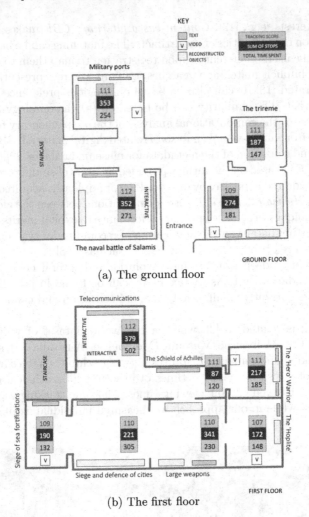

(a) The ground floor

(b) The first floor

Fig. 2. Basic observation data on the ground and the first floor of the Herakleidon Museum

3   Exhibition Features and Data Collection

Our study focused on the exhibition 'Technology of War in Ancient Greece' (2018–2020), created by the Herakleidon Museum in collaboration with the Association for the Study of Ancient Greek and Byzantine Technology (see Fig. 1). The exhibition was arranged on the two floors of the main building of the Museum (Apostolou Pavlou), and organized in terms of themes, such as 'The trireme', 'The Naval Battle of Salamis' on the ground floor and 'The "Hero" Warrior of the Mycenean Period' and "Siege of a city" (Fig. 1). The display of each room was self-contained and the presentation of objects (mainly reconstructions) was accompanied by rich interpretative material, ranging from informative texts, videos and models to interactive exhibits. Overall, the spatial layout of the display was structured, and choice of route was offered at a localized level.

The field study was carried out in July–August 2019. The visitors were tracked manually during their visit. The approximate time of observation of each of the exhibits was measured as a quantification metric of their interest. The measurements has a resolution if 0.25 min.

The visitors were aged between 18 and 65+, and men and women were equally represented in the sample. It should also be noted that the behavioral data gathered by direct observation was combined with questionnaire scores. More details on the demographic data that we collected can be found in [15].

In our study, visitor behavior, was analysed using some established techniques. First, the arrangement of the display was recorded on the building layout as the basis for designing the observation record sheet for mapping visitors' movement and interactions with the displays. Traces of the paths of 112 visitors, who were randomly selected, spreaded across time periods, and had consented to take part in the research, were recorded unobtrusively for their whole visit to the gallery spaces – that is, from the moment they entered the exhibition to the moment of exit. When the visitor stopped to look at a work, read a text, or watch a video, a stopping point was recorded on the plan of the exhibition by the observer. Other symbols were used to clarify where a visitor stopped for longer periods of time. The traces were used to measure a series of space use variables, such as the tracking score of a space, which is the percentage of visitors visiting each space. Furthermore, based on the tracking data, it was possible to obtain a picture of the average rate and distribution of stops made in each space (sum of stops). These are taken to indicate visitors' preference for particular displays and exhibits. The total time they spent in the exhibition (time spent) was also recorded, and we used both to characterize individual visitors and to represent the attraction power of particular displays. The depictions of our visitor measurements are presented in Fig. 2.

The analysis of the behavior data gathered by direct observation enabled us on the one hand to understand whether visitors moved selectively or tended to exhaust all spaces, and to obtain an impression of their preference for particular displays and a range of degrees of interaction with the exhibits; on the other hand, they were used to characterize individual visitors. It was found, for example, that almost a quarter of people observed were individual visitors and half of them were part of a group of two people visiting together. A key feature of the pattern of visitor behavior was the homogeneity of movement: there was little difference in gallery spaces in terms of tracking score, as expected from the relative uniform layout of the museum. In terms of viewing patterns, it was of particular interest that the highest number of stops were found in the last space of the narrative sequence, that is, space 11, on the second level, dedicated to "Telecommunications". Significantly, timing data confirmed this in that the mean time spent in this gallery is the highest in the sample (twice as high as the average time of stay in each gallery). So stopping patterns are likely to be due to the attraction of exhibits (for instance, in space 11 objects for handling invite the active involvement of the visitor), unaided by their strategic location. Finally, visitors stayed an average of 28 min, though many (40%) stayed longer than this (up to a maximum of 80 min).

4   Interest Prediction

We predicted the interest of the visitors on the basis of their previous observations. To this end used some standard collaborative filtering methods. The methods are briefly described in the following section and the respective results are given in Table 1.

To evaluate the methods we have measured the mean absolute error and the root mean square error of the predictions for the time spent viewing an exhibit. We have done a ten-fold cross validation involving all users and items in each fold. The time was measured in logarithmic scale as some visitors may spend disproportionate amount of time in some exhibits. This is compatible to the approach described in [2].

In our first collaborative filtering approach we used a standard k-NN method for the users (user-based) and the museum exhibits (item-based) for various neighborhood sizes k.

Then we tested factorization methods starting from a basic matrix factorization. It works by decomposing the user-item interaction matrix into the product of two rectangular matrices of lower dimensionality, a low-rank user matrix and a low-rank item matrix [7]. The amount of factors to use is a method hyperparameter.

We then tested the regularized singular value decomposition of data with missing values, K-means, postprocessing SVD with KNN according to [11]. It extends the set of predictors with the following methods: addition of biases to the regularized SVD, post-processing SVD with kernel ridge regression, using a separate linear model for each item, and using methods similar to the regularized SVD, but with fewer parameters. We finally evaluated the SVD++ method [6]. It merges a latent factor model that captures users and items with a neighborhood model.

As baseline we made predictions using only the items' scores, i.e., without any personalization. It gave MAE = 0.540 and RMSE = 0.658. It appears that all collaborative filtering-based methods can do better, if we select the hyperparameters appropriately.

Surprisingly, the simple item-based k-NN method gave the best results in comparison to the rest and more elaborate of the methods both in terms of mean absolute error and root mean square error. The user-based k-NN follows, but requires significantly more neighbors, which affects efficiency accordingly.

Table 1. Results for recommendation algorithms prediction. MAE stands for mean absolute error, while the RMSE stands for root mean squared error.

Algorithm	MAE	RMSE
User-KNN, k = 1	0.594	0.739
User-KNN, k = 5	0.577	0.732
User-KNN, k = 10	0.530	0.660
User-KNN, k = 20	0.495	0.623
User-KNN, k = 30	0.484	0.608
User-KNN, k = 40	0.481	0.603
User-KNN, k = 50	0.480	0.602
User-KNN, k = 60	0.477	0.598
User-KNN, k = 70	0.478	0.599
Item-KNN, k = 1	0.540	0.680
Item-KNN, k = 3	0.500	0.631
Item-KNN, k = 5	0.478	0.601
Item-KNN, k = 7	0.475	0.597
Item-KNN, k = 8	**0.474**	**0.595**
Item-KNN, k = 9	0.475	0.595
Item-KNN, k = 10	0.479	0.601
Basic matrix factorization, 1 factor	0.488	0.610
Basic matrix factorization, 2 factors	0.501	0.636
Basic matrix factorization, 3 factors	0.507	0.650
Basic matrix factorization, 5 factors	0.559	0.715
Basic matrix factorization, 7 factors	0.587	0.748
Singular value decomposition, 1 factor	0.489	0.630
Singular value decomposition, 2 factors	0.502	0.640
Singular value decomposition, 3 factors	0.527	0.677
Singular value decomposition, 5 factors	0.555	0.704
Singular value decomposition, 7 factors	0.551	0.690
SVD++, 1 factor	0.503	0.645
SVD++, 2 factors	0.511	0.649
SVD++, 3 factors	0.547	0.696
SVD++, 5 factors	0.580	0.738
SVD++, 7 factors	0.594	0.743
Item - based (baseline)	0.540	0.658

Furthermore, regarding the factorization methods, they seem to perform better with a single factor and their performance deteriorates with two or more factors. This is an indication that the personalization factors (factors 2, 3, 4 etc.) are rather weak and lead to overfitting; the available data support models that appear to be closer to the baseline method [5]. We expect this behavior to change significantly in favor of the factorization methods by collecting more data, i.e., more visitors are expected to contribute more knowledge to those latent factors.

5   Conclusions

We have presented our work on the behavior analysis of museum visitors using a custom collected dataset in the Herakleidon Museum, in an Ancient Greek technology exhibition. We have demonstrated the feasibility of predicting the visitors' preferences given past preferences using collaborative filtering. The exhibits' overall popularity may result from summing up the predicted interests of all user groups. We showed that in this application there is some added value compared to the baseline approach that uses only the items' popularity.

In the future we plan to collect more data, manually and automatically using the mobile devices of the visitors. That will enable a better estimate of the exhibition impact and the use of more elaborate deep learning methods for preference predictions. Furthermore, we plan to apply some content-based or hybrid methods given the textual analysis of the descriptions for each exhibit (i.e., via topic modeling).

Acknowledgement. This work was supported by the $T1E\Delta K$-00502 Muse-Learn project, which is implemented within the framework of "Competitiveness, Entrepreneurship and Innovation" (EPAnEK) Operational Programme 2014–2020, funded by the EU and national funds (www.muselearn.gr).

References

1. Ardissono, L., Kuflik, T., Petrelli, D.: Personalization in cultural heritage: the road travelled and the one ahead. User Model. User-Adapt. Interact. **22**(1), 73–99 (2012)
2. Bohnert, F., Zukerman, I.: Personalised viewing-time prediction in museums. User Model. User-Adapt. Interact. **24**(4), 263–314 (2013). https://doi.org/10.1007/s11257-013-9141-8
3. Bollo, A.: Analysis of visitor behaviour inside the museum: an empirical study. In: International Conference on Arts and Cultural Management, HEC Montreal (2005)
4. Hornecker, E., Ciolfi, L.: Human-Computer Interactions in Museums. Morgan & Claypool, San Rafael (2019)
5. Jannach, D., Lerche, L., Gedikli, F., Bonnin, G.: What recommenders recommend – an analysis of accuracy, popularity, and sales diversity effects. In: Carberry, S., Weibelzahl, S., Micarelli, A., Semeraro, G. (eds.) UMAP 2013. LNCS, vol. 7899, pp. 25–37. Springer, Heidelberg (2013). https://doi.org/10.1007/978-3-642-38844-6_3
6. Koren, Y.: Factorization meets the neighborhood: a multifaceted collaborative filtering model. In: Proceedings of the 14th ACM SIGKDD International Conference on Knowledge Discovery and Data Mining, KDD 2008, pp. 426–434. Association for Computing Machinery, New York (2008)

7. Koren, Y., Bell, R., Volinsky, C.: Matrix factorization techniques for recommender systems. Computer **42**(8), 30–37 (2009)
8. Kosmopoulos, D., Styliaras, G.D.: A survey on developing personalized content services in museums. Pervasive Mob. Comput. **47**, 54–77 (2018)
9. Melton, A.: Problems of Installation in Museums of Art, vol. 14. Washington DC (1935)
10. Monti, F., Keene, S.: Museums and Silent Objects: Designing Effective Exhibitions. Ashgate, Farnham (2013)
11. Paterek, A.: Improving regularized singular value decomposition for collaborative filtering (2007)
12. Petrelli, D., Not, E.: User-centred design of flexible hypermedia for a mobile guide: reflections on the hyperaudio experience. User Model. User-Adapt. Interact. **15**(3–4), 303–338 (2005)
13. Robinson, E.S.: The Behavior of the Museum Visitor. American Association of Museums, Washington, DC (1928)
14. Serrell, B.: Paying Attention: Visitors and Museum Exhibitions. American Association of Museums, Washington DC (1998)
15. Styliaras, G., et al.: The MuseLearn platform: personalized content for museum visitors assisted by vision-based recognition and 3D pose estimation of exhibits. In: Maglogiannis, I., Iliadis, L., Pimenidis, E. (eds.) AIAI 2020. IAICT, vol. 583, pp. 439–451. Springer, Cham (2020). https://doi.org/10.1007/978-3-030-49161-1_37
16. Tzortzi, K.: Museum Space: Where Architecture Meets Museology. Routledge, London (2015)
17. Veron, E., Levasseur, M.: Ethnographie de l'Exposition. Bibliothque publique d'Information, Centre Georges Pompidou, Paris (1983)
18. Wang, Y., Wang, S., Stash, N., Aroyo, L., Schreiber, G.: Enhancing content-based recommendation with the task model of classification. In: Cimiano, P., Pinto, H.S. (eds.) EKAW 2010. LNCS (LNAI), vol. 6317, pp. 431–440. Springer, Heidelberg (2010). https://doi.org/10.1007/978-3-642-16438-5_33
19. Yalowitz, S.S., Bronnenkant, K.: Timing and tracking: unlocking visitor behavior. Visit. Stud. **12**(1), 49–64 (2009)
20. Yu, C.H., Hunter, J.: Documenting and sharing comparative analyses of 3D digital museum artifacts through semantic web annotations. J. Comput. Cult. Herit. **6**(4), 18:1–18:20 (2013)
21. Zhang, S., Yao, L., Sun, A., Tay, Y.: Deep learning based recommender system. ACM Comput. Surv. **52**(1), 1–38 (2019)

Author Index

Printed in the United States
by Baker & Taylor Publisher Services